Princess Jellyfish 01
Akiko Higashimura

O Ie.
Bitch

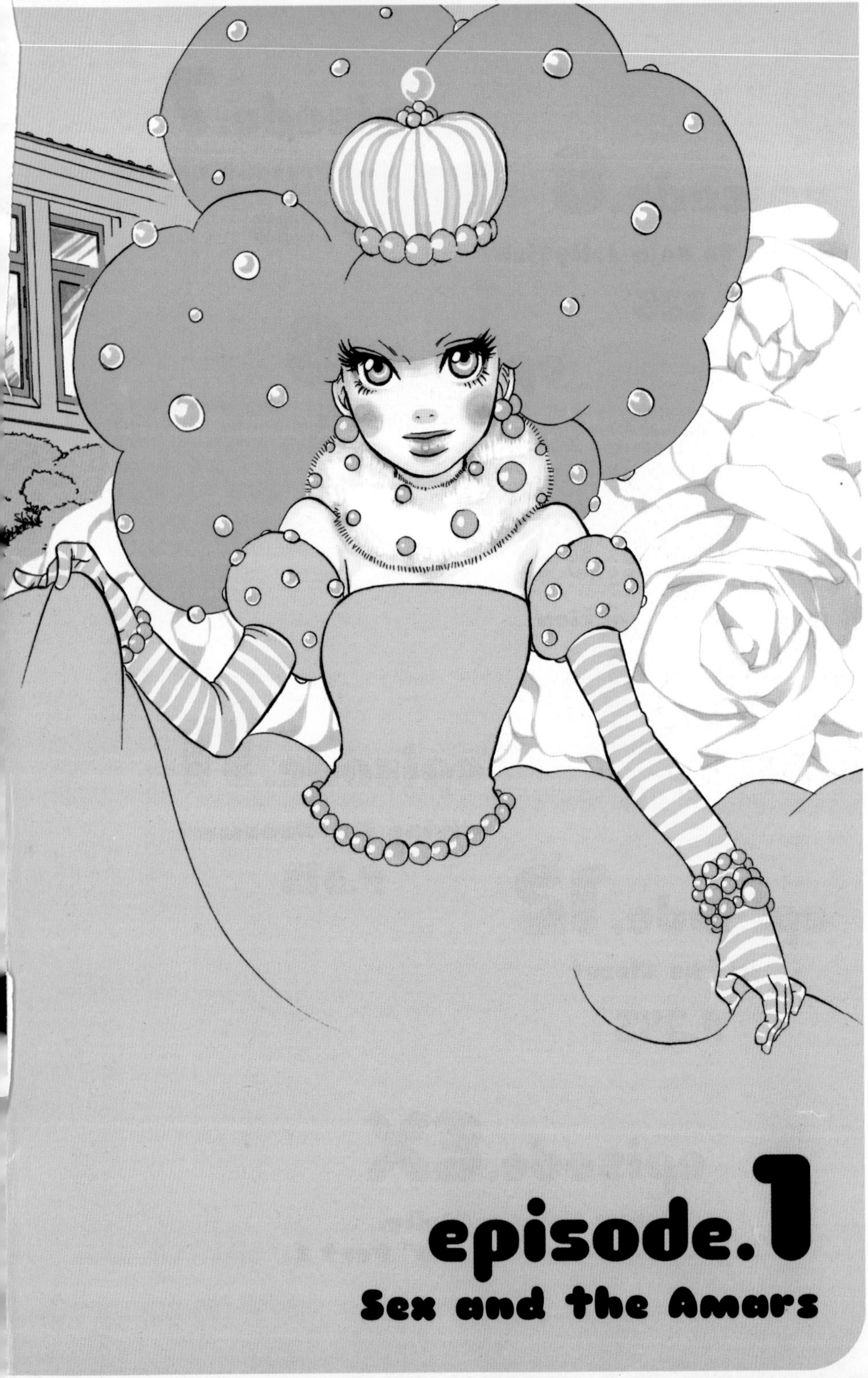

episode.1
Sex and the Amars

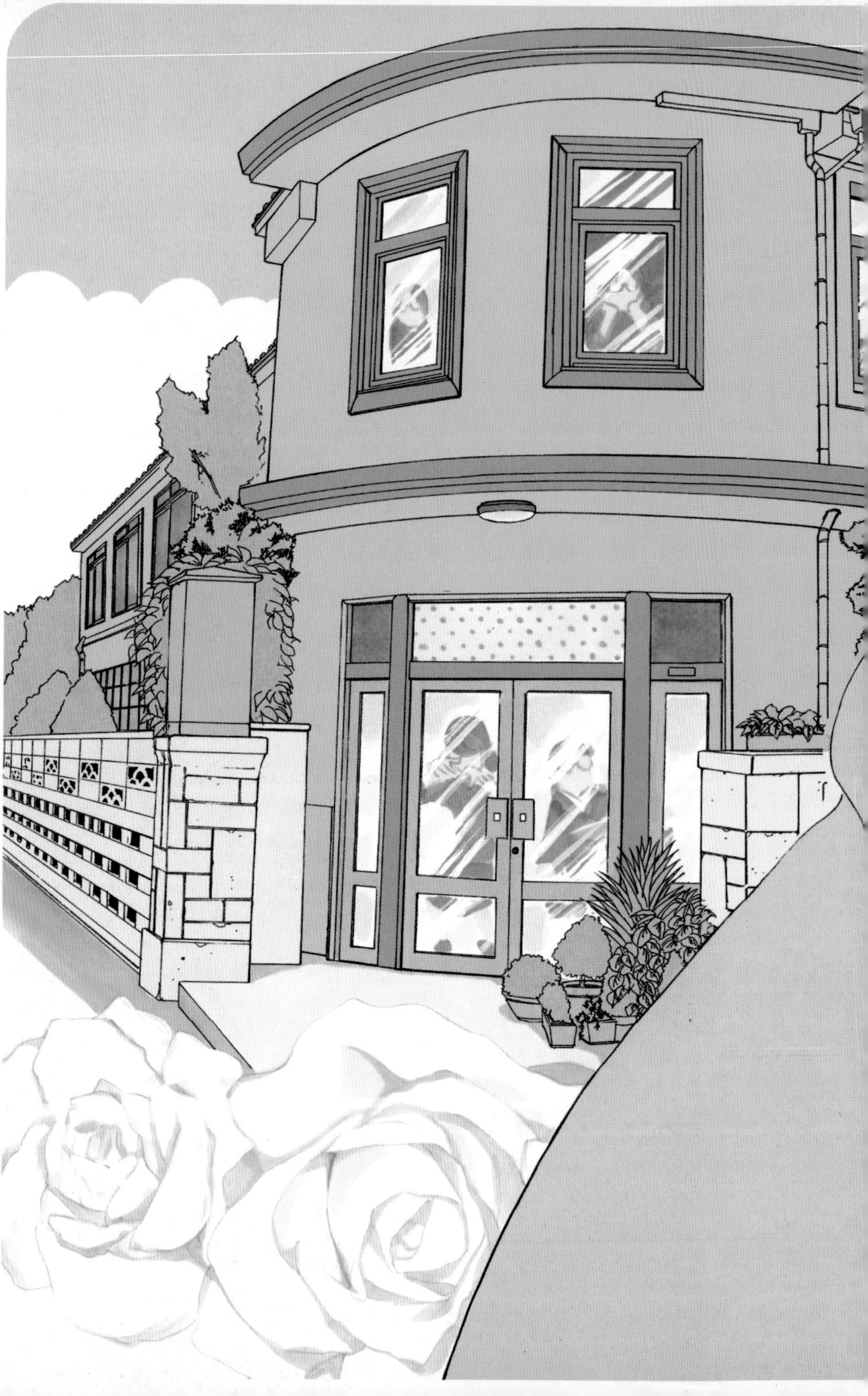

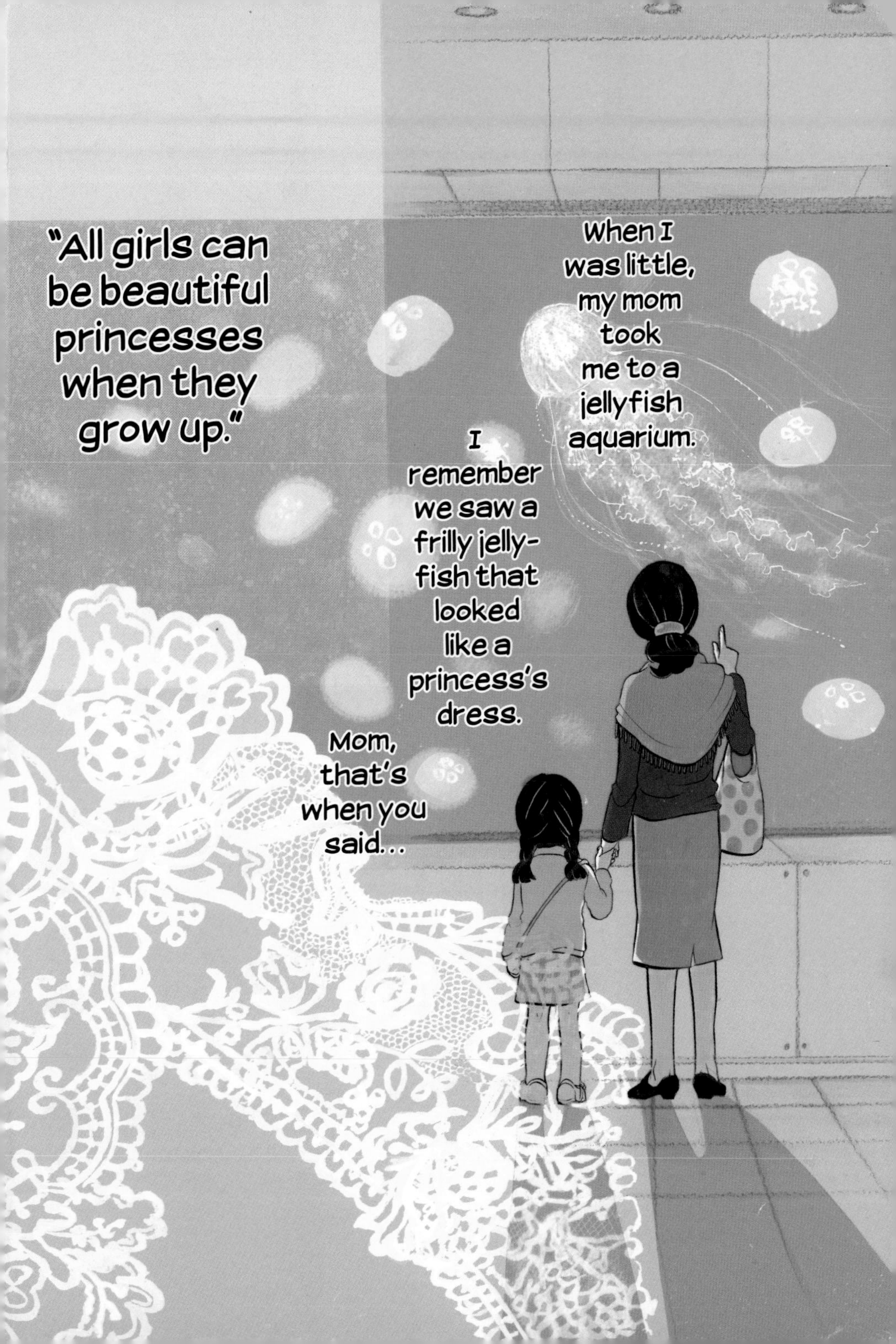
When I was little, my mom took me to a jellyfish aquarium.
I remember we saw a frilly jelly-fish that looked like a princess's dress.
Mom, that's when you said...
"All girls can be beautiful princesses when they grow up."

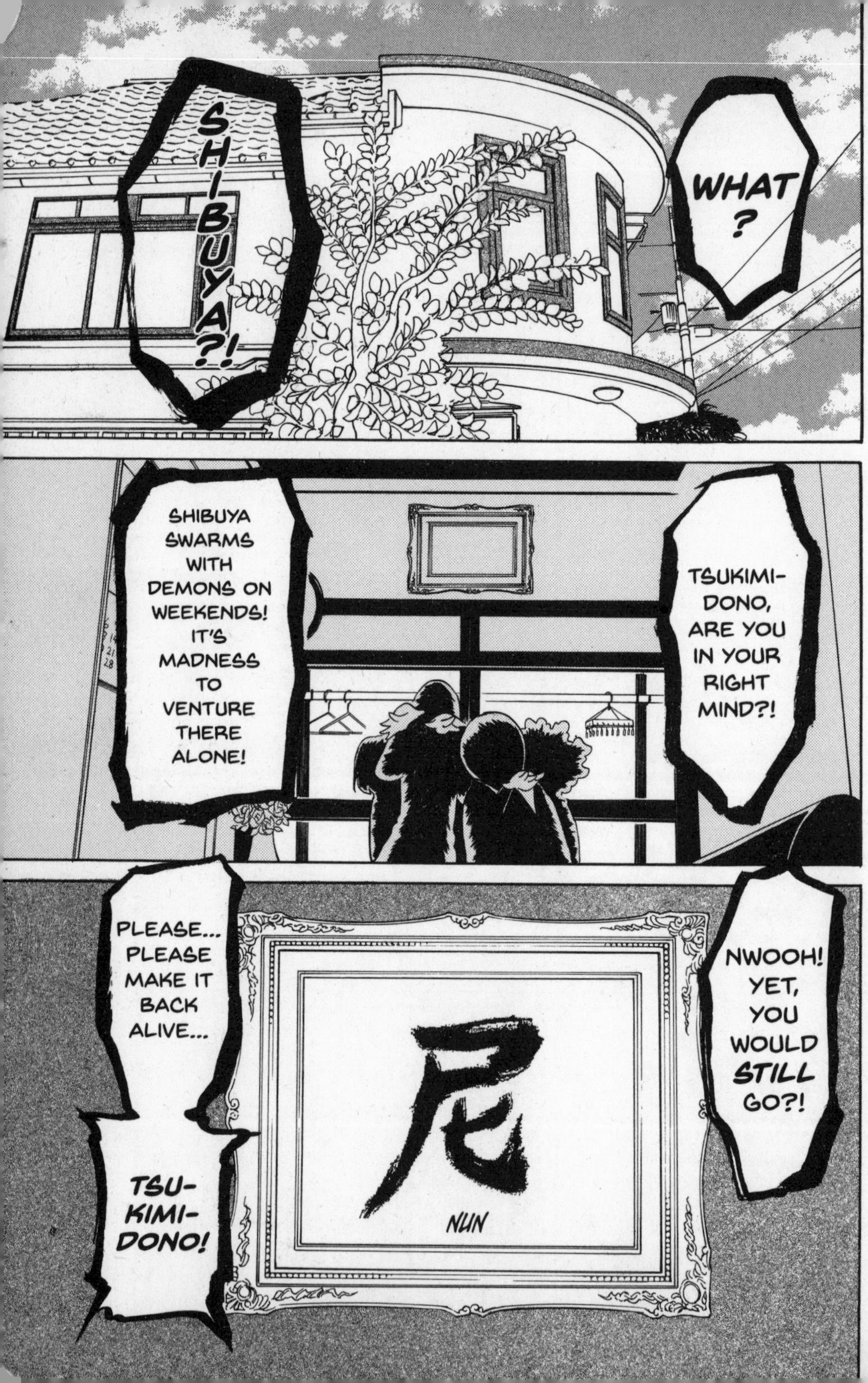
WHAT?
SHIBUYA?!
TSUKIMI-DONO, ARE YOU IN YOUR RIGHT MIND?!
SHIBUYA SWARMS WITH DEMONS ON WEEKENDS! IT'S MADNESS TO VENTURE THERE ALONE!
NWOOH! YET, YOU WOULD STILL GO?!
尼
NUN
PLEASE... PLEASE MAKE IT BACK ALIVE...
TSU-KIMI-DONO!

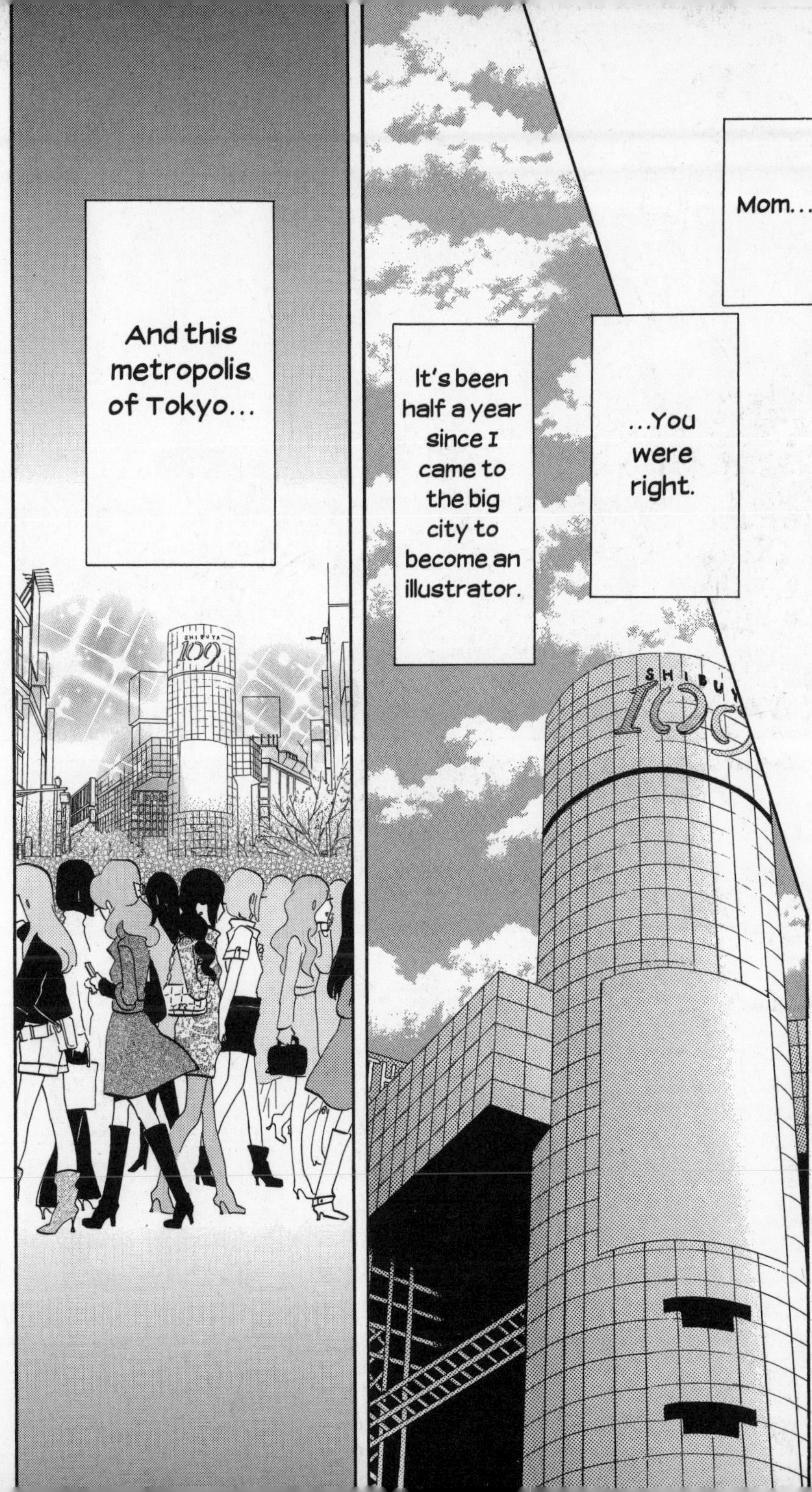
Mom...
...You were right.
It's been half a year since I came to the big city to become an illustrator.
And this metropolis of Tokyo...

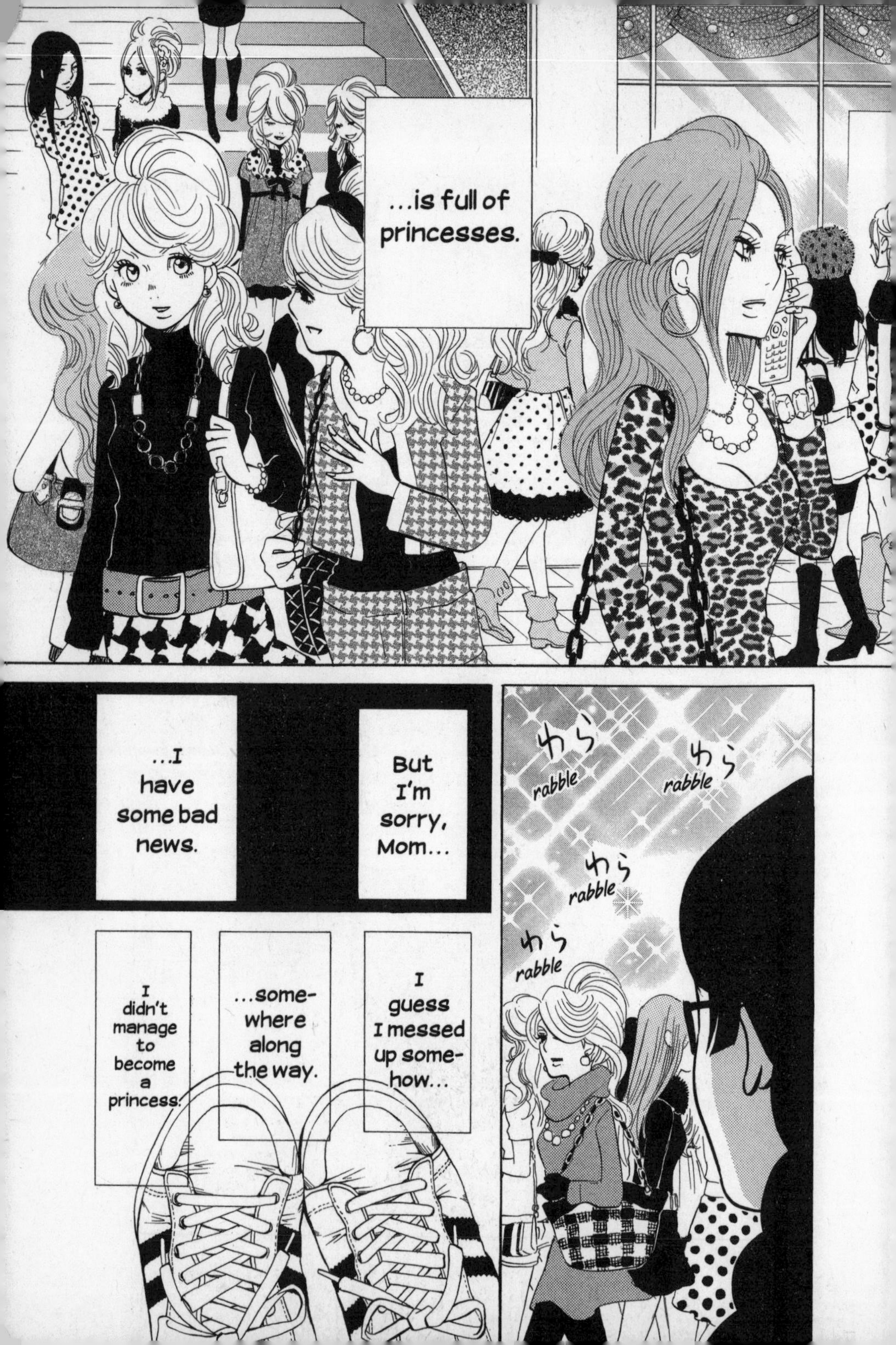
...is full of princesses.
わら rabble
わら rabble
わら rabble
わら rabble
But I'm sorry, Mom...
...I have some bad news.
I guess I messed up some-how...
...some-where along the way.
I didn't manage to become a princess.

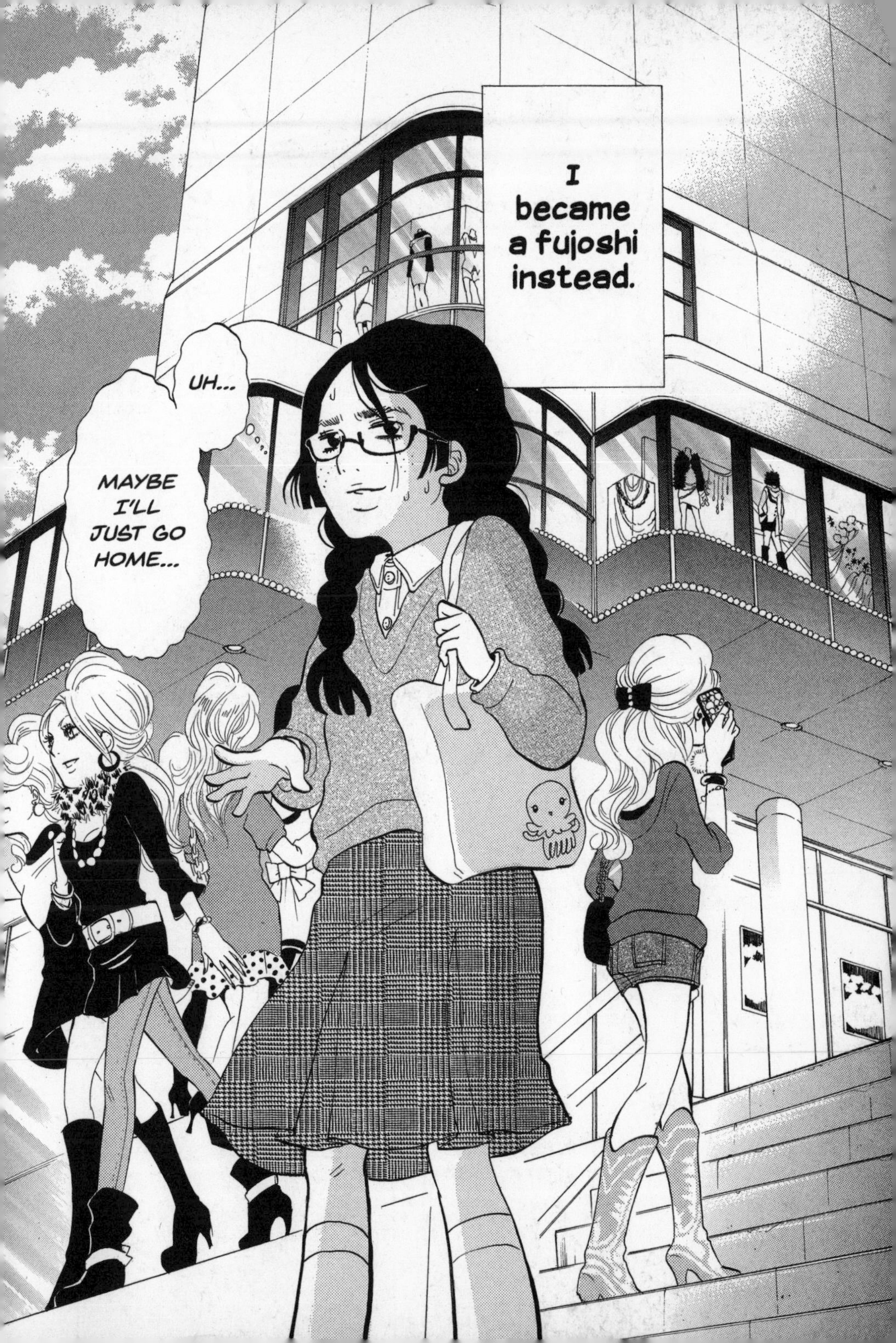
I became a fujoshi instead.
UH...
MAYBE I'LL JUST GO HOME...

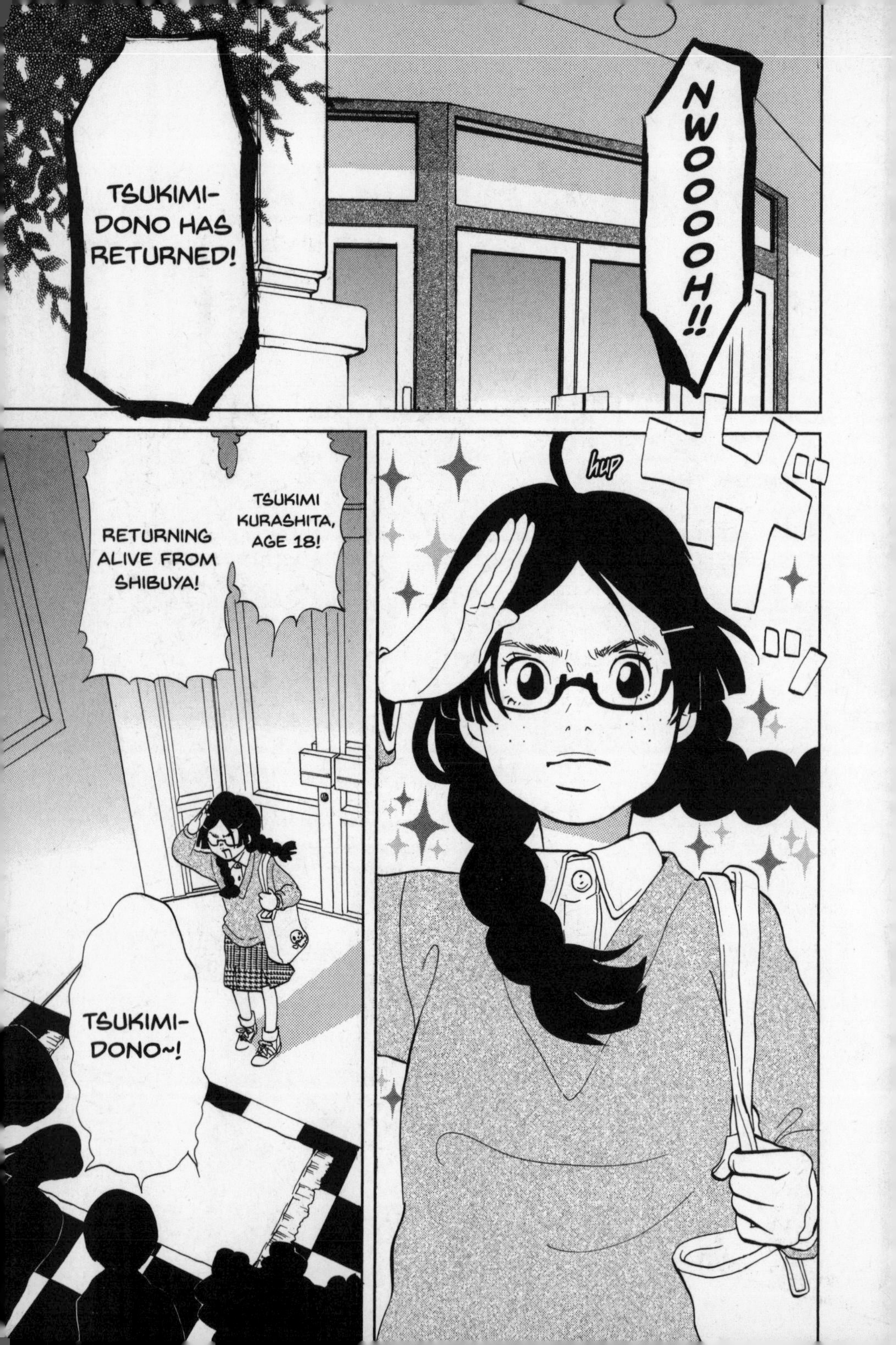
NWOOOOOH!!
TSUKIMI-DONO HAS RETURNED!
hup
TSUKIMI KURASHITA, AGE 18!
RETURNING ALIVE FROM SHIBUYA!
TSUKIMI-DONO~!

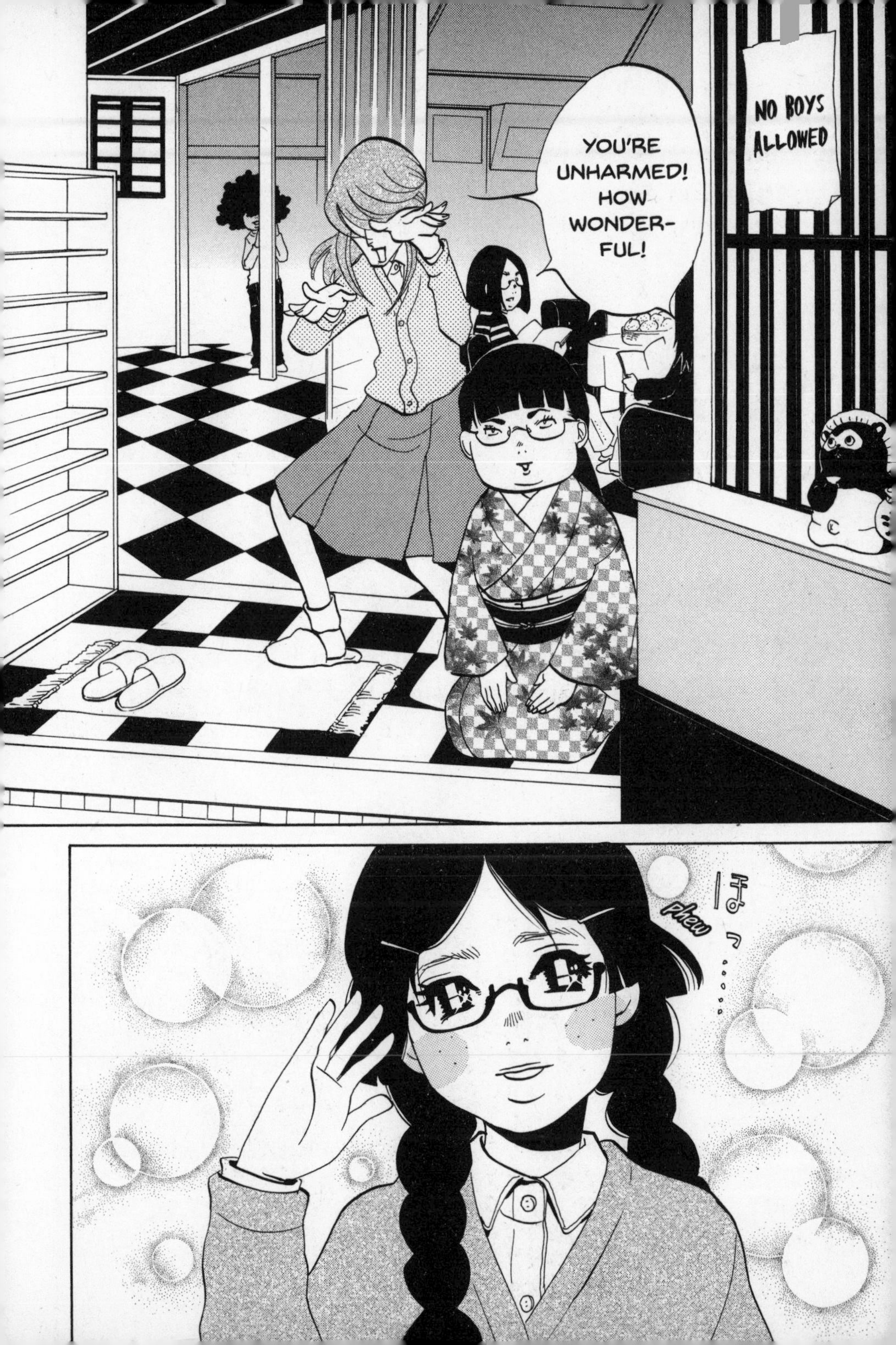
NO BOYS ALLOWED
YOU'RE UNHARMED! HOW WONDER-FUL!
ほっ
phew

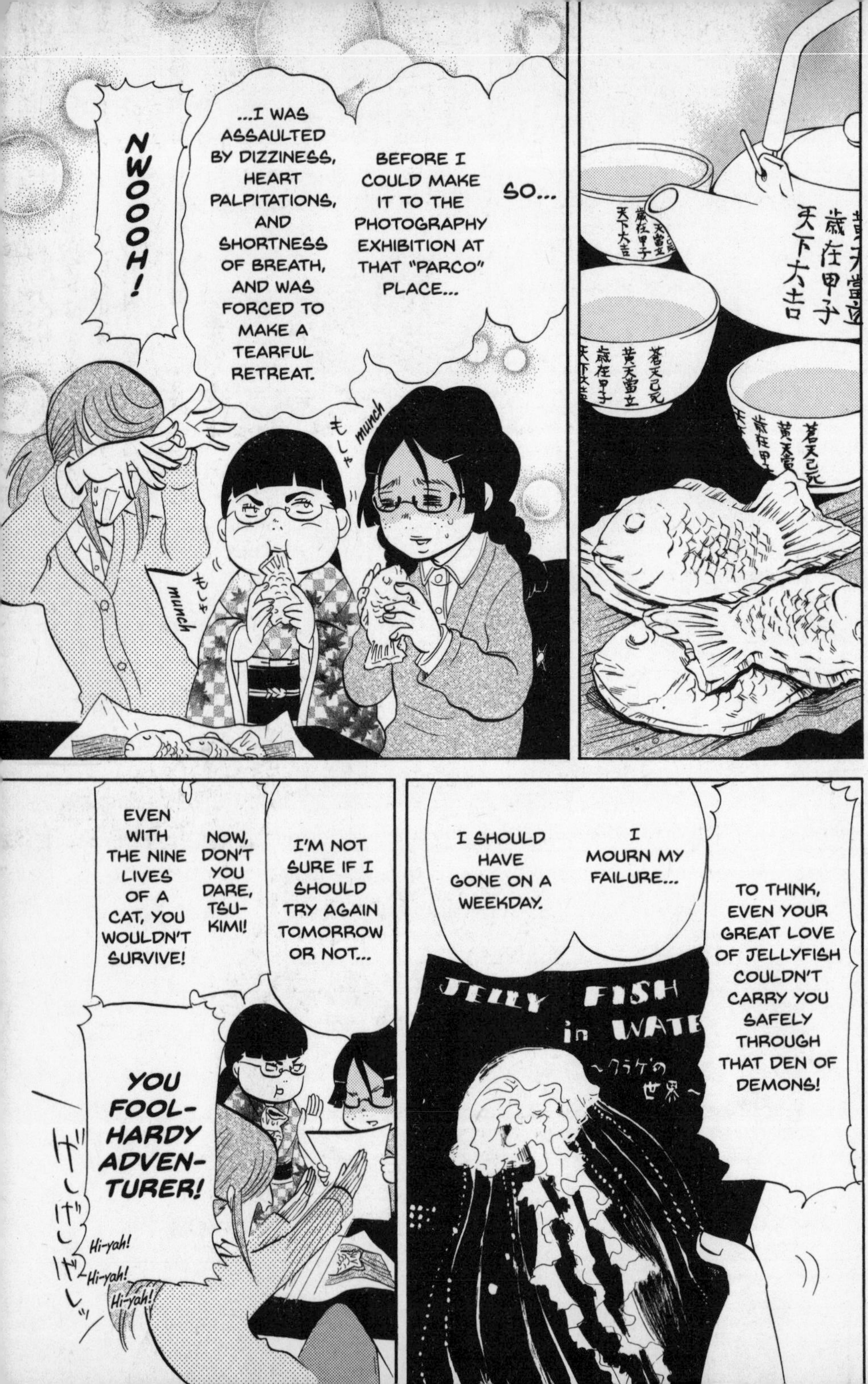
蒼天已死
黄天當立
歳在甲子
天下大吉
SO...
BEFORE I COULD MAKE IT TO THE PHOTOGRAPHY EXHIBITION AT THAT "PARCO" PLACE...
...I WAS ASSAULTED BY DIZZINESS, HEART PALPITATIONS, AND SHORTNESS OF BREATH, AND WAS FORCED TO MAKE A TEARFUL RETREAT.
NWOOOOH!
もしゃ munch
もしゃ munch
I MOURN MY FAILURE...
I SHOULD HAVE GONE ON A WEEKDAY.
TO THINK, EVEN YOUR GREAT LOVE OF JELLYFISH COULDN'T CARRY YOU SAFELY THROUGH THAT DEN OF DEMONS!
JELLY FISH in WATE
～クラゲの世界～
I'M NOT SURE IF I SHOULD TRY AGAIN TOMORROW OR NOT...
NOW, DON'T YOU DARE, TSUKIMI!
EVEN WITH THE NINE LIVES OF A CAT, YOU WOULDN'T SURVIVE!
YOU FOOL-HARDY ADVEN-TURER!
げしげしげしッ
Hi-yah! Hi-yah! Hi-yah!

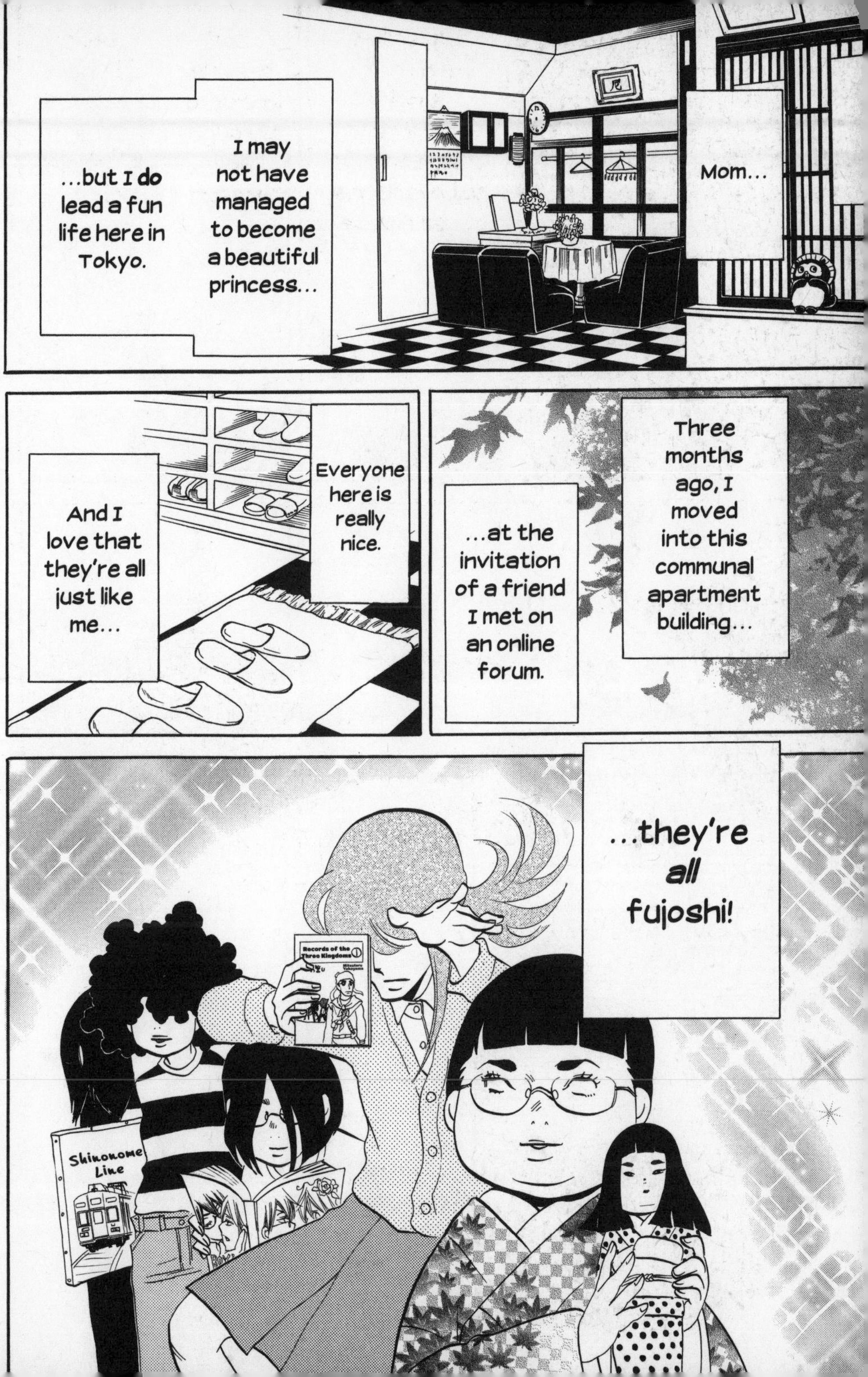
Mom...
I may not have managed to become a beautiful princess...
...but I **do** lead a fun life here in Tokyo.
Three months ago, I moved into this communal apartment building...
...at the invitation of a friend I met on an online forum.
Everyone here is really nice.
And I love that they're all just like me...
...they're *all* fujoshi!
Records of the Three Kingdoms
Mitsuteru Yokoyama
Shinonome Line

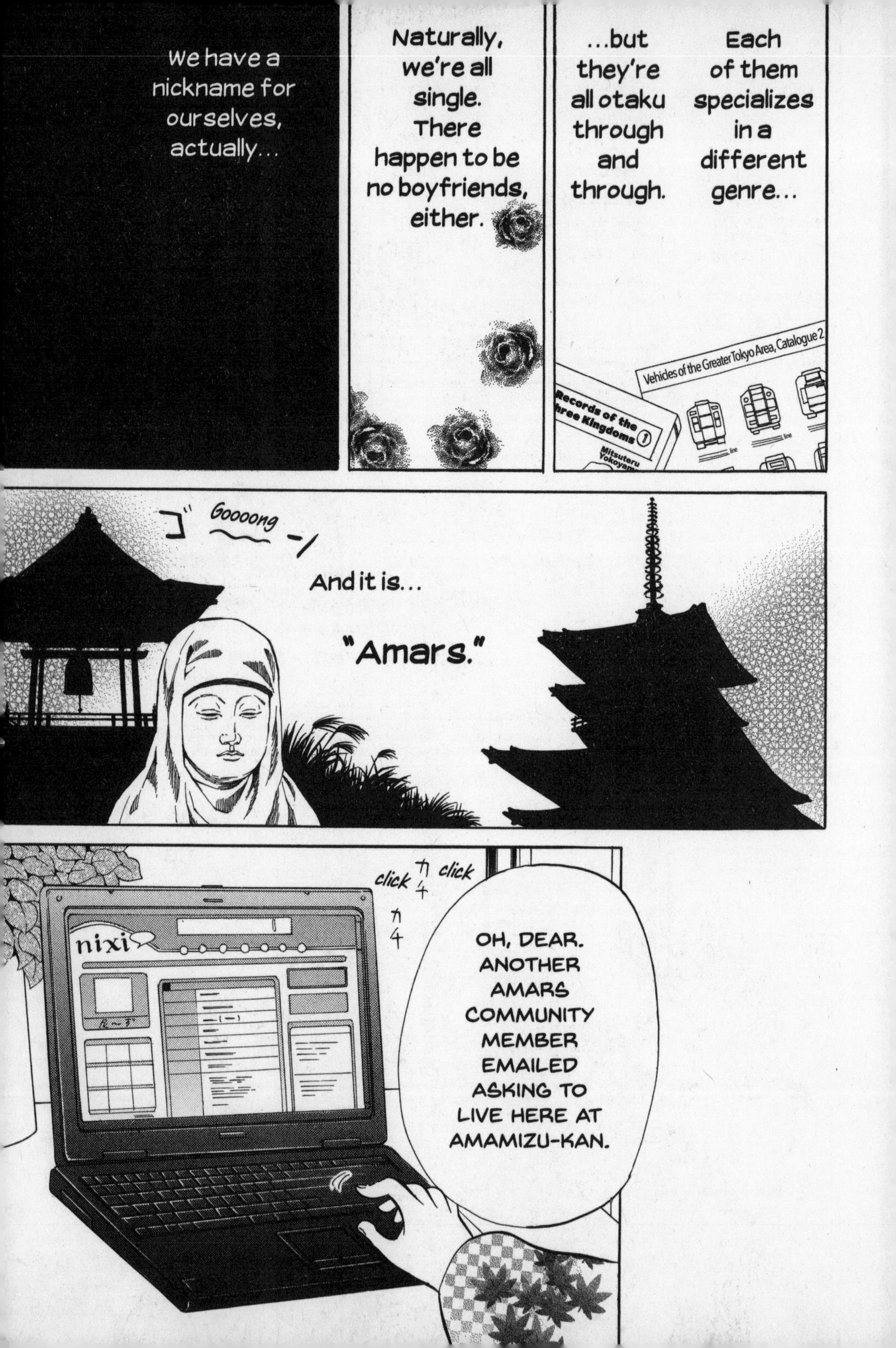
Each of them specializes in a different genre...
...but they're all otaku through and through.
Vehicles of the Greater Tokyo Area, Catalogue 2
Records of the
hree Kingdoms 1
Mitsuteru
Yokoyam
Naturally, we're all single. There happen to be no boyfriends, either.
We have a nickname for ourselves, actually...
Goooong
And it is...
"Amars."
click
click
nixi
OH, DEAR. ANOTHER AMARS COMMUNITY MEMBER EMAILED ASKING TO LIVE HERE AT AMAMIZU-KAN.

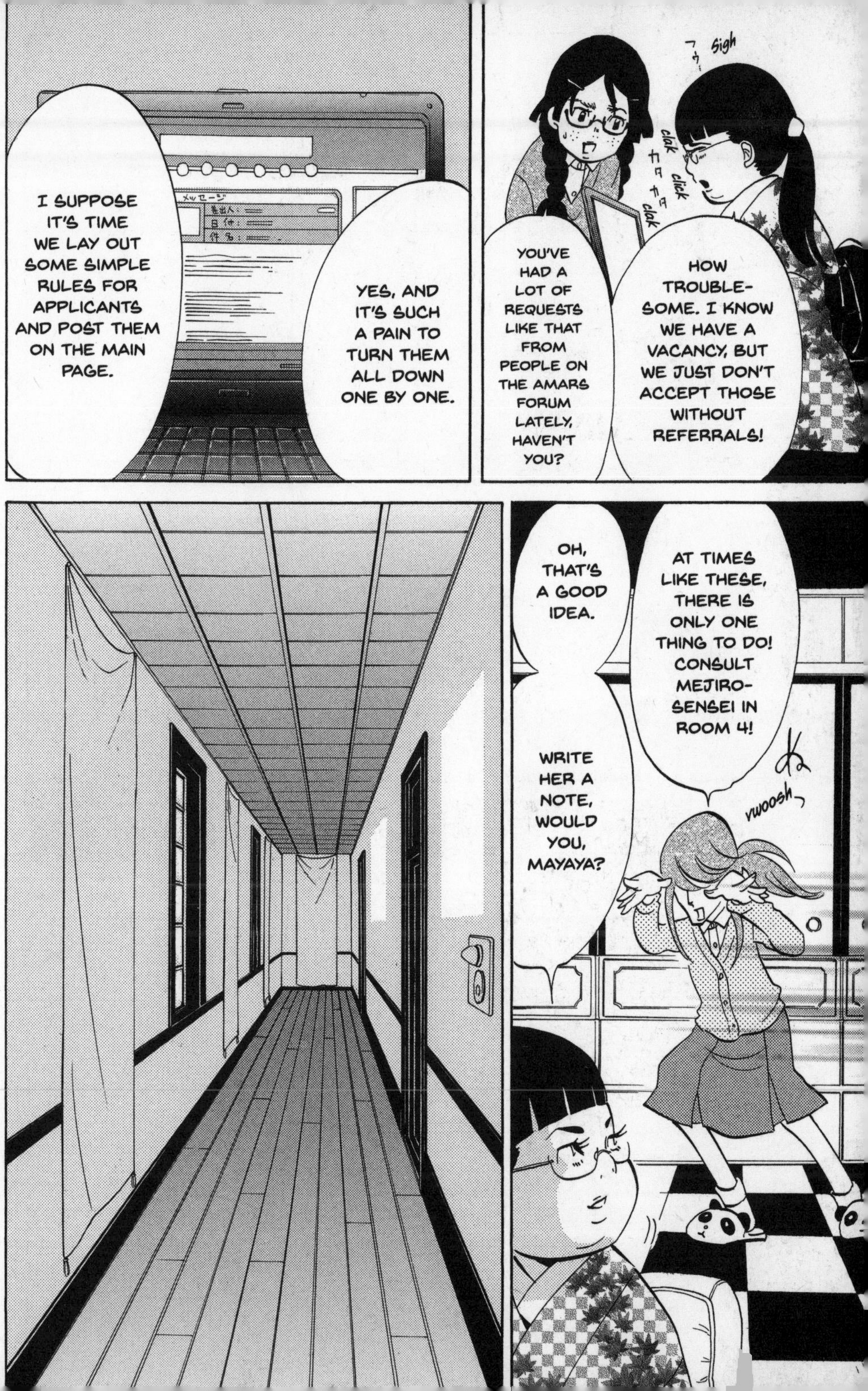
Sigh
clak click clak
HOW TROUBLESOME. I KNOW WE HAVE A VACANCY, BUT WE JUST DON'T ACCEPT THOSE WITHOUT REFERRALS!
YOU'VE HAD A LOT OF REQUESTS LIKE THAT FROM PEOPLE ON THE AMARS FORUM LATELY, HAVEN'T YOU?
YES, AND IT'S SUCH A PAIN TO TURN THEM ALL DOWN ONE BY ONE.
I SUPPOSE IT'S TIME WE LAY OUT SOME SIMPLE RULES FOR APPLICANTS AND POST THEM ON THE MAIN PAGE.
AT TIMES LIKE THESE, THERE IS ONLY ONE THING TO DO! CONSULT MEJIRO-SENSEI IN ROOM 4!
vwoosh
OH, THAT'S A GOOD IDEA.
WRITE HER A NOTE, WOULD YOU, MAYAYA?

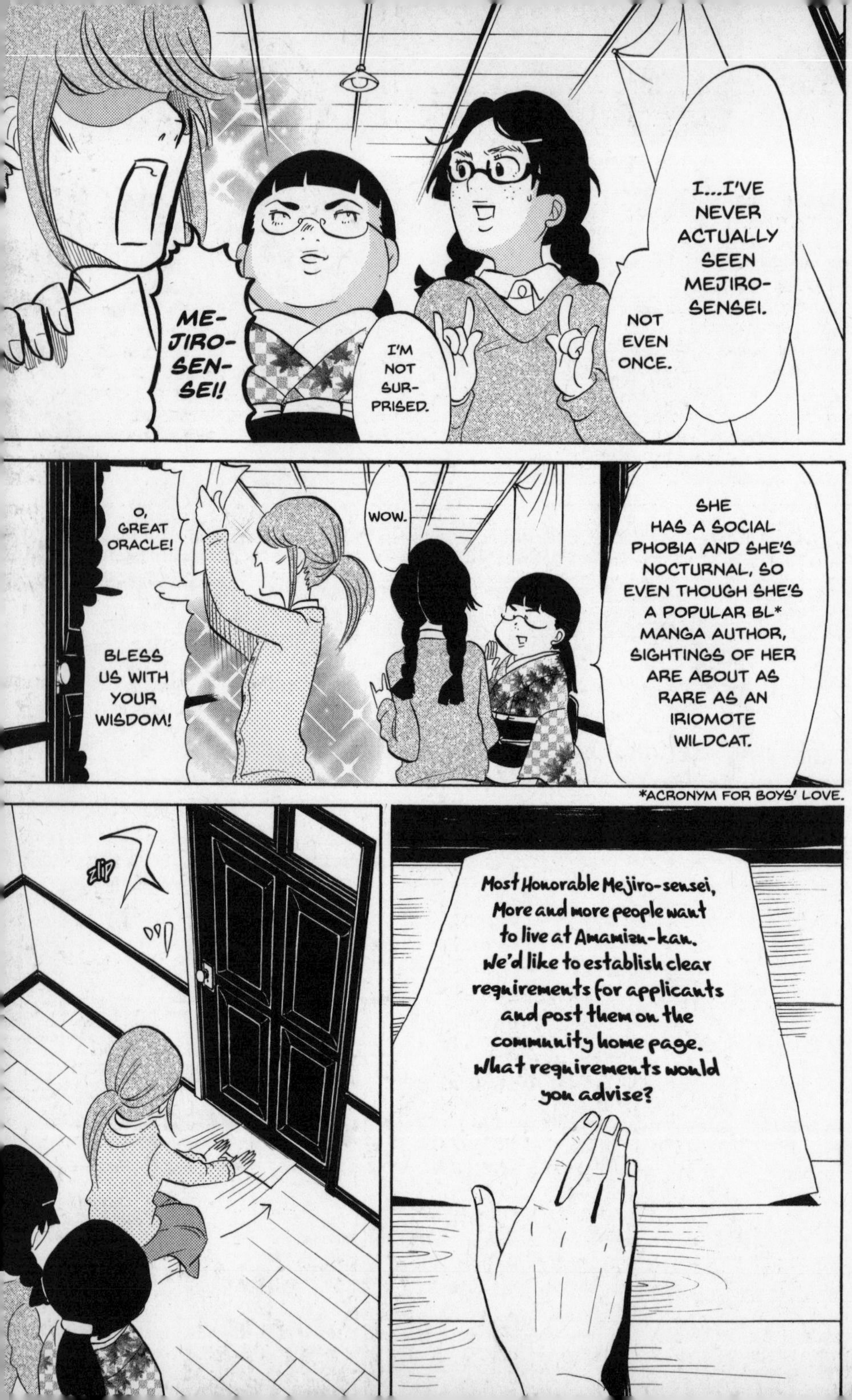
I...I'VE NEVER ACTUALLY SEEN MEJIRO-SENSEI.
NOT EVEN ONCE.
I'M NOT SUR-PRISED.
ME-JIRO-SEN-SEI!
SHE HAS A SOCIAL PHOBIA AND SHE'S NOCTURNAL, SO EVEN THOUGH SHE'S A POPULAR BL* MANGA AUTHOR, SIGHTINGS OF HER ARE ABOUT AS RARE AS AN IRIOMOTE WILDCAT.
WOW.
O, GREAT ORACLE!
BLESS US WITH YOUR WISDOM!
*ACRONYM FOR BOYS' LOVE.
Most Honorable Mejiro-sensei, More and more people want to live at Amamizu-kan. We'd like to establish clear requirements for applicants and post them on the community home page. What requirements would you advise?
zip

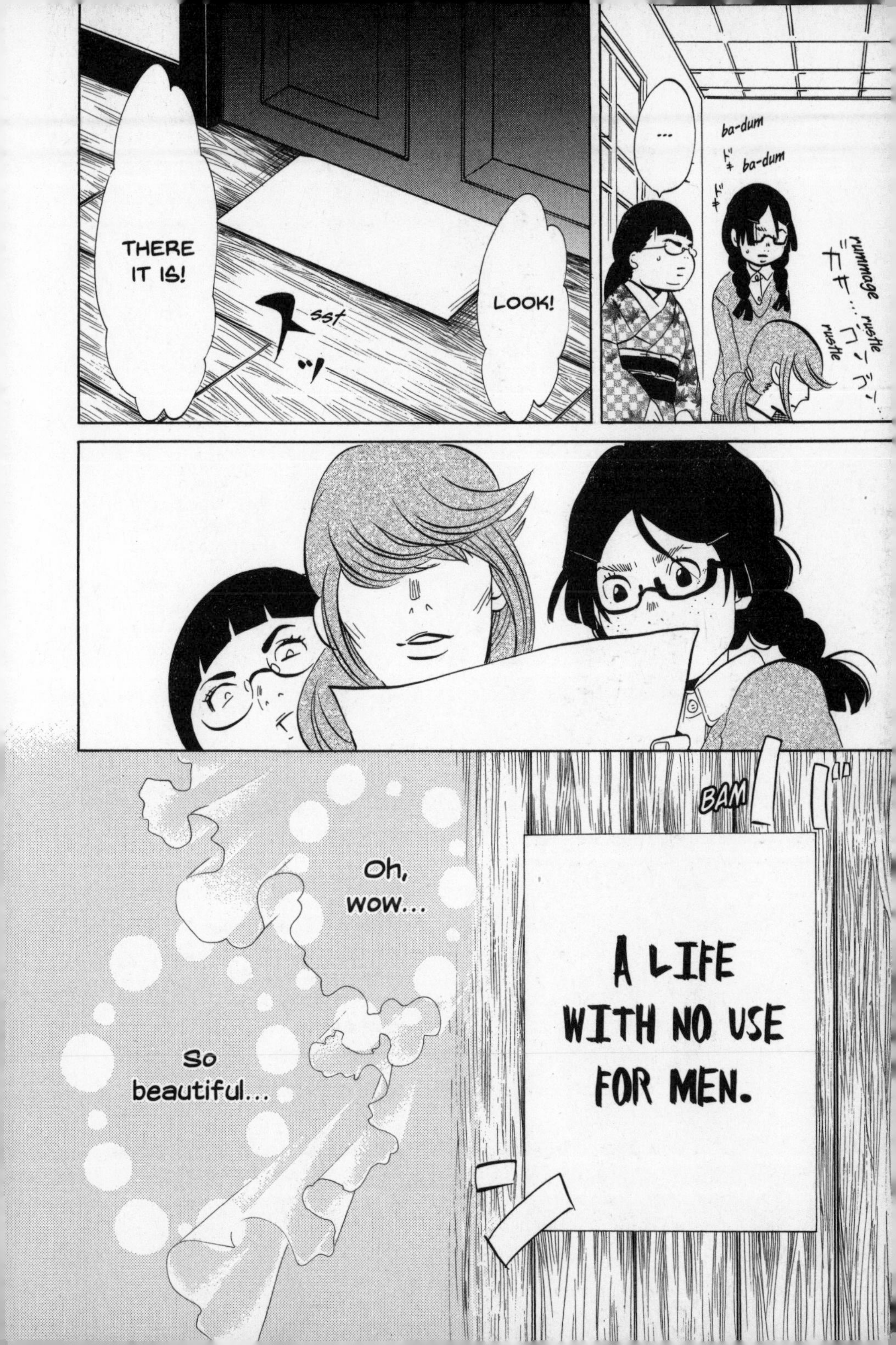
...
ba-dum
ba-dum
rummage... rustle
rustle
LOOK!
sst
THERE IT IS!
BAM
A LIFE WITH NO USE FOR MEN.
Oh, wow...
So beautiful...

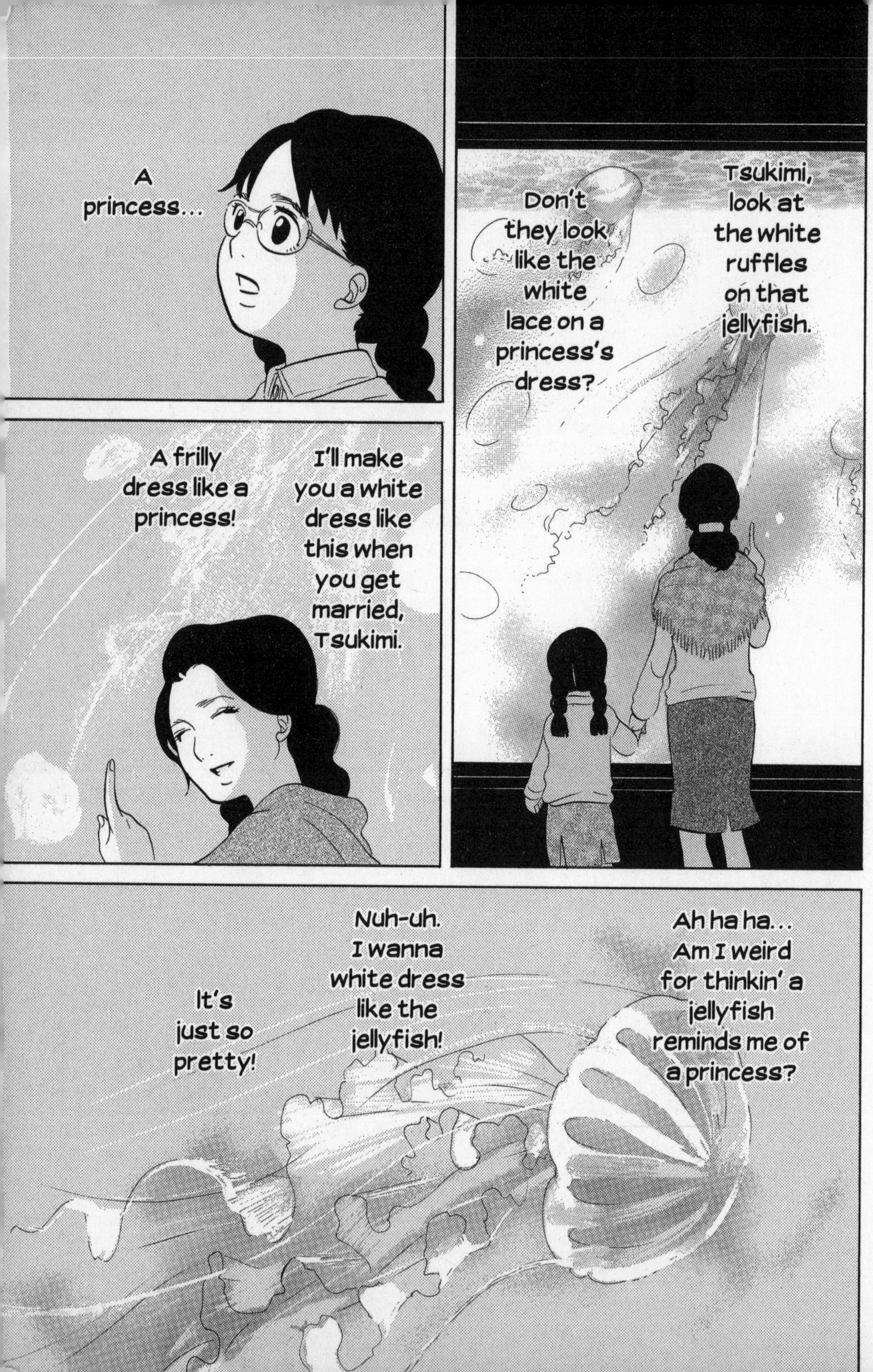
Tsukimi, look at the white ruffles on that jellyfish.
Don't they look like the white lace on a princess's dress?
A princess...
I'll make you a white dress like this when you get married, Tsukimi.
A frilly dress like a princess!
Ah ha ha... Am I weird for thinkin' a jellyfish reminds me of a princess?
Nuh-uh. I wanna white dress like the jellyfish!
It's just so pretty!

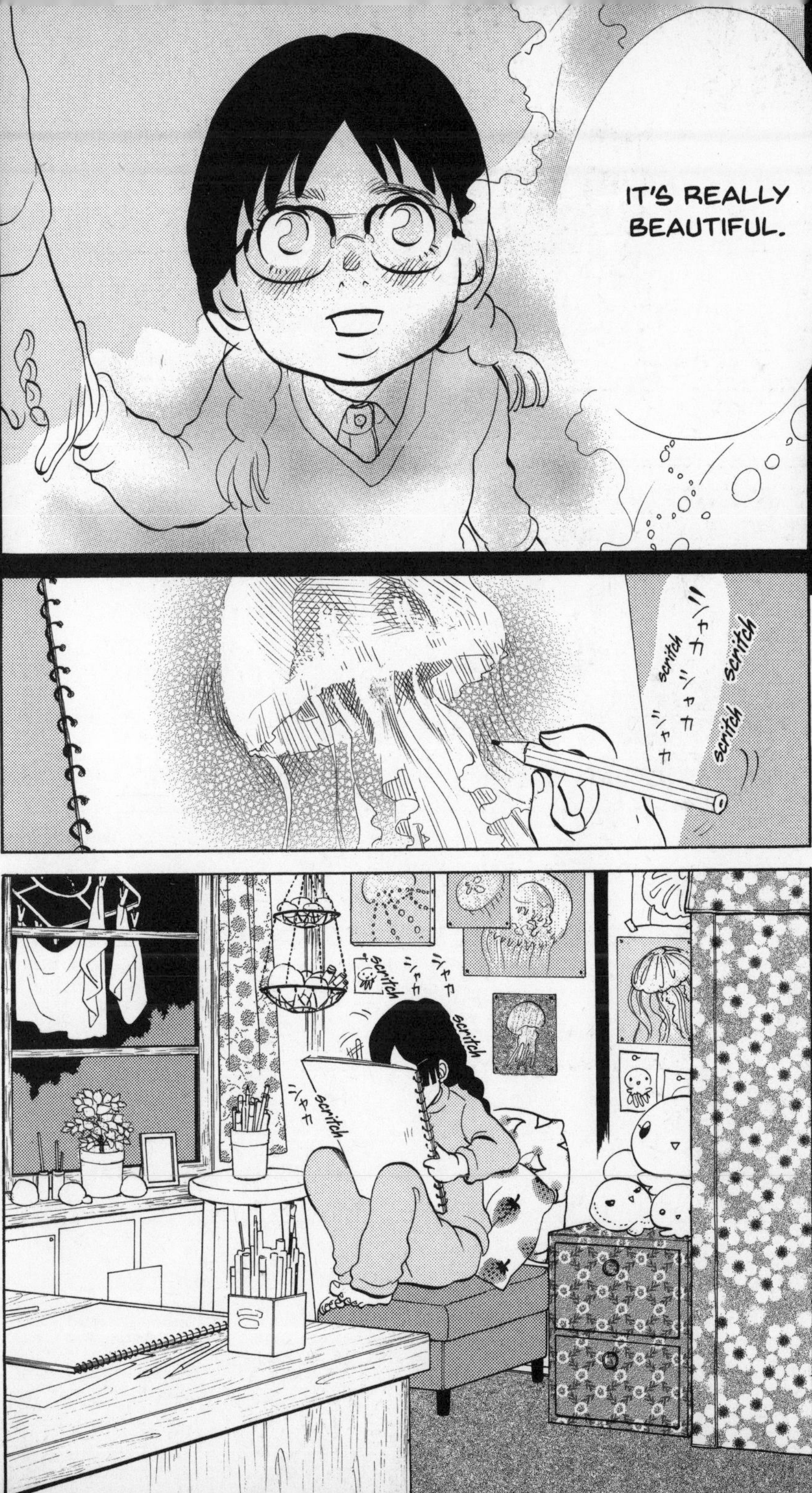
IT'S REALLY BEAUTIFUL.
scritch
scritch
シャカ
シャカ
シャカ
scritch
シャカ
シャカ
scritch
scritch
シャカ
scritch

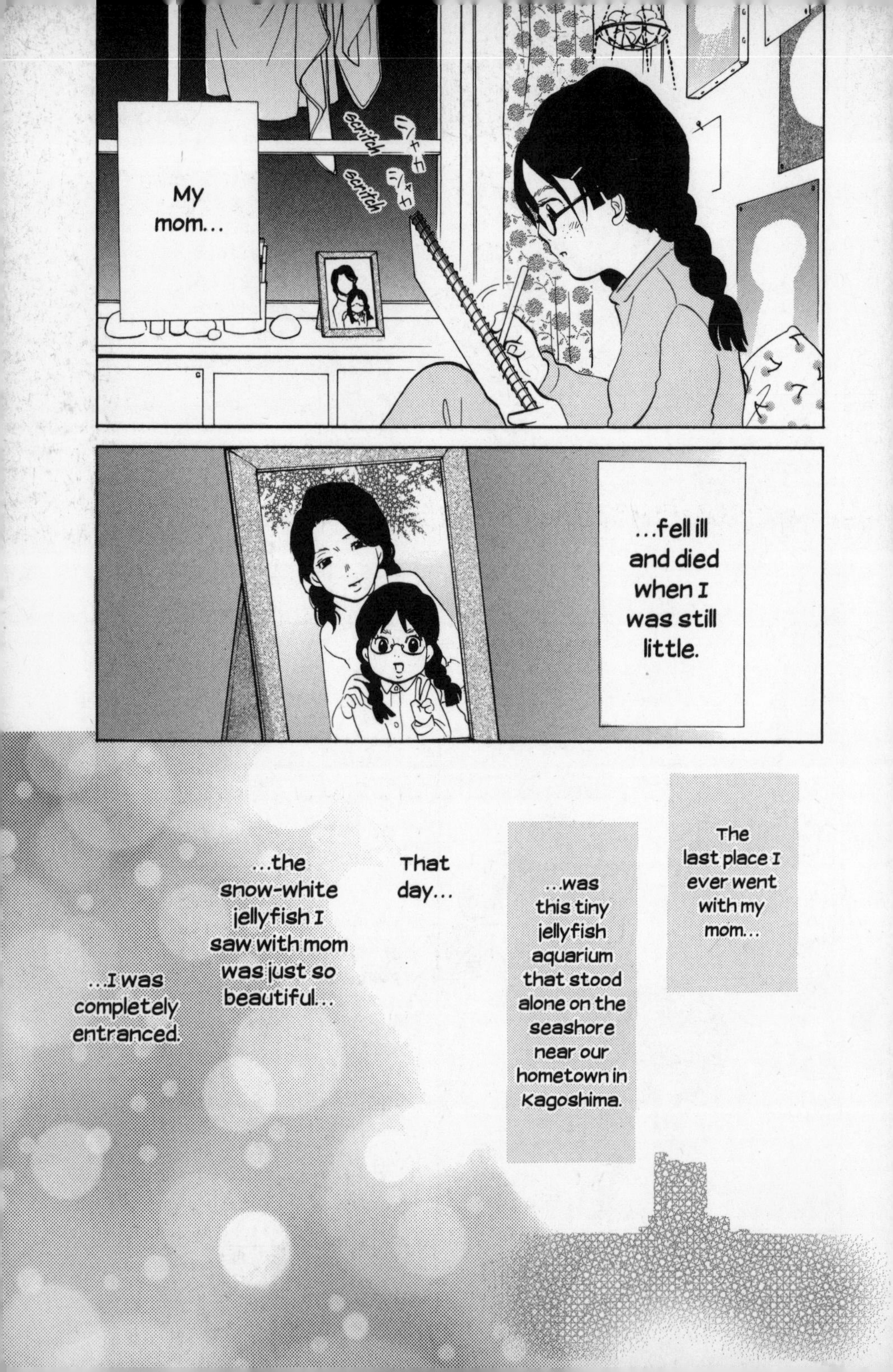
My mom…
scritch
scritch
…fell ill and died when I was still little.
The last place I ever went with my mom…
…was this tiny jellyfish aquarium that stood alone on the seashore near our hometown in Kagoshima.
That day…
…the snow-white jellyfish I saw with mom was just so beautiful…
…I was completely entranced.

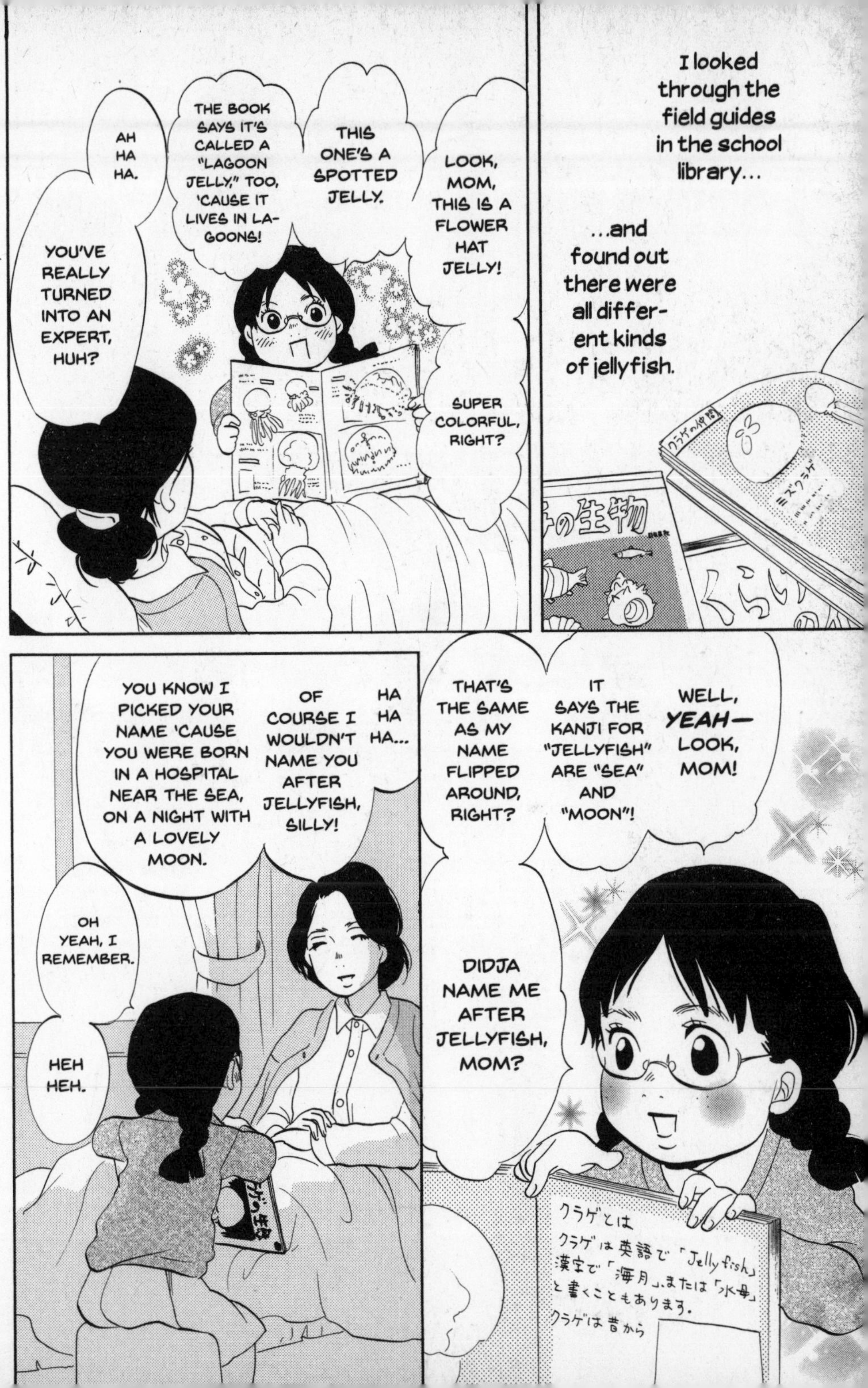
I looked through the field guides in the school library...
...and found out there were all different kinds of jellyfish.
クラゲの仲間
ミズクラゲ
LOOK, MOM, THIS IS A FLOWER HAT JELLY!
SUPER COLORFUL, RIGHT?
THIS ONE'S A SPOTTED JELLY.
THE BOOK SAYS IT'S CALLED A "LAGOON JELLY," TOO, 'CAUSE IT LIVES IN LAGOONS!
AH HA HA.
YOU'VE REALLY TURNED INTO AN EXPERT, HUH?
WELL, **YEAH**— LOOK, MOM!
IT SAYS THE KANJI FOR "JELLYFISH" ARE "SEA" AND "MOON"!
THAT'S THE SAME AS MY NAME FLIPPED AROUND, RIGHT?
DIDJA NAME ME AFTER JELLYFISH, MOM?
クラゲとは
クラゲは英語で「Jellyfish」
漢字で「海月」、または「水母」
と書くこともあります。
クラゲは昔から
HA HA HA...
OF COURSE I WOULDN'T NAME YOU AFTER JELLYFISH, SILLY!
YOU KNOW I PICKED YOUR NAME 'CAUSE YOU WERE BORN IN A HOSPITAL NEAR THE SEA, ON A NIGHT WITH A LOVELY MOON.
OH YEAH, I REMEMBER.
HEH HEH.

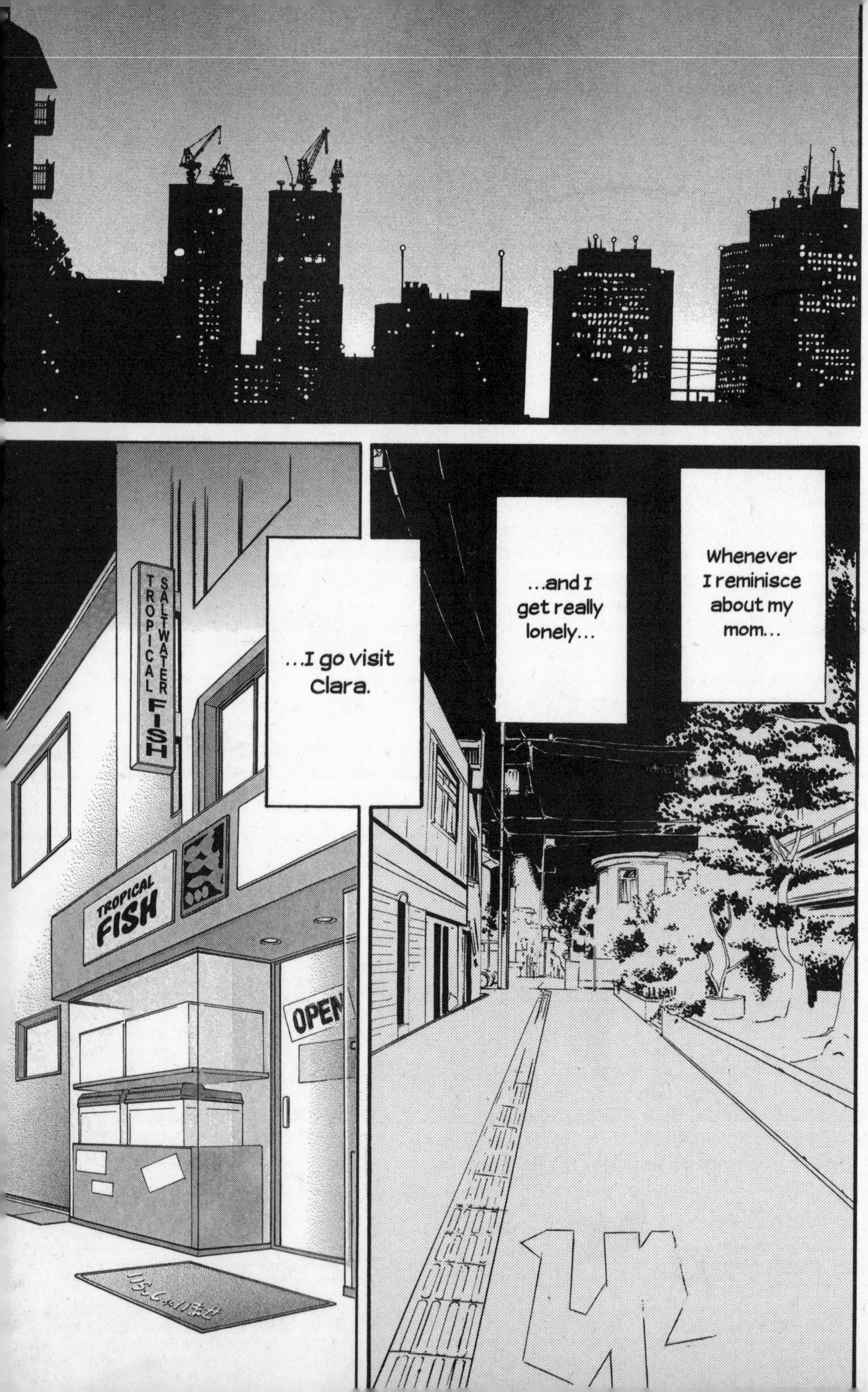
Whenever I reminisce about my mom...
...and I get really lonely...
...I go visit Clara.
TROPICAL SALTWATER FISH
TROPICAL FISH
OPEN
いらっしゃいませ

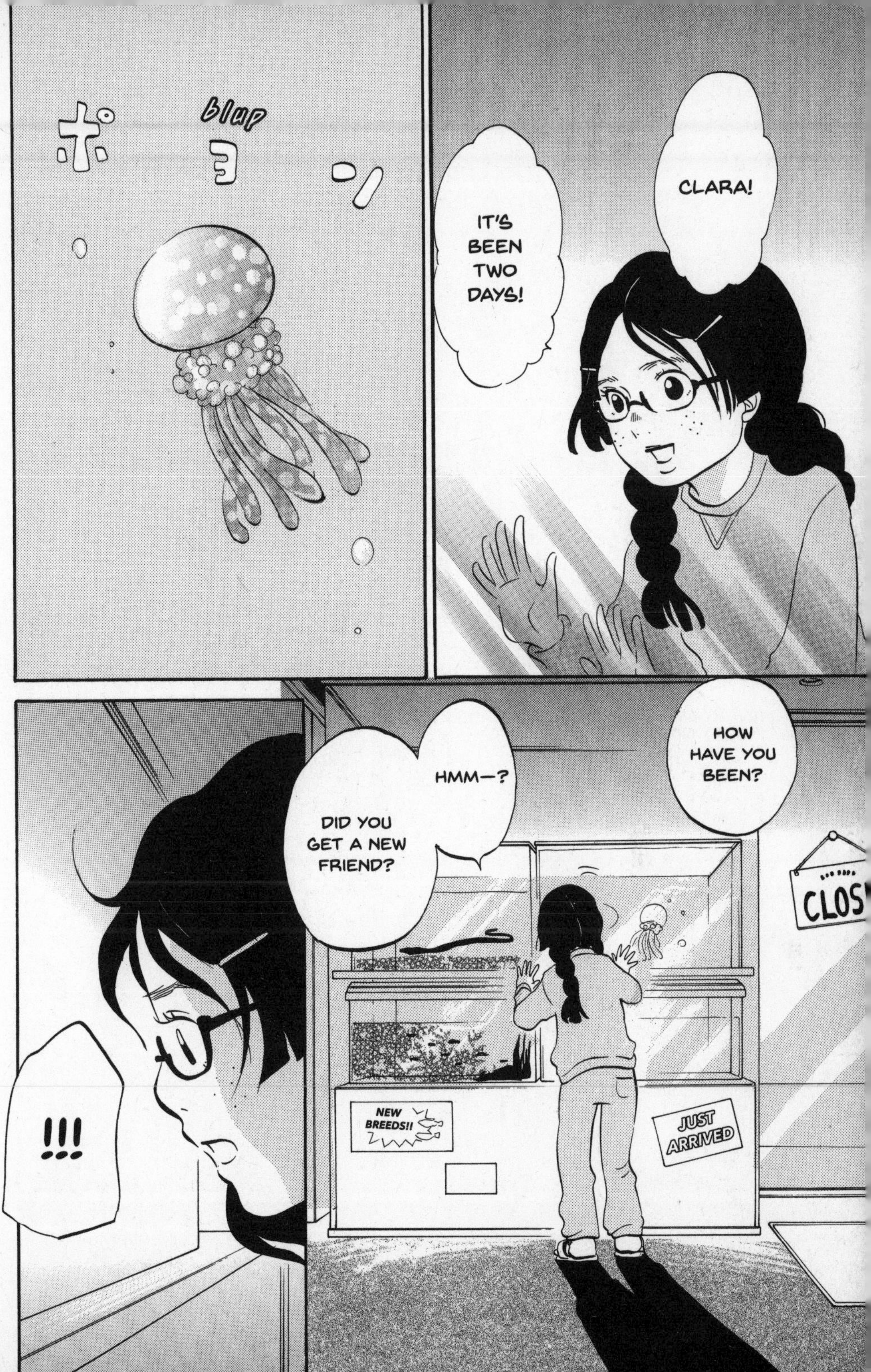
CLARA!
IT'S BEEN TWO DAYS!
ポヨン
blup
HOW HAVE YOU BEEN?
HMM—?
DID YOU GET A NEW FRIEND?
CLOS
JUST ARRIVED
NEW BREEDS!!
!!!

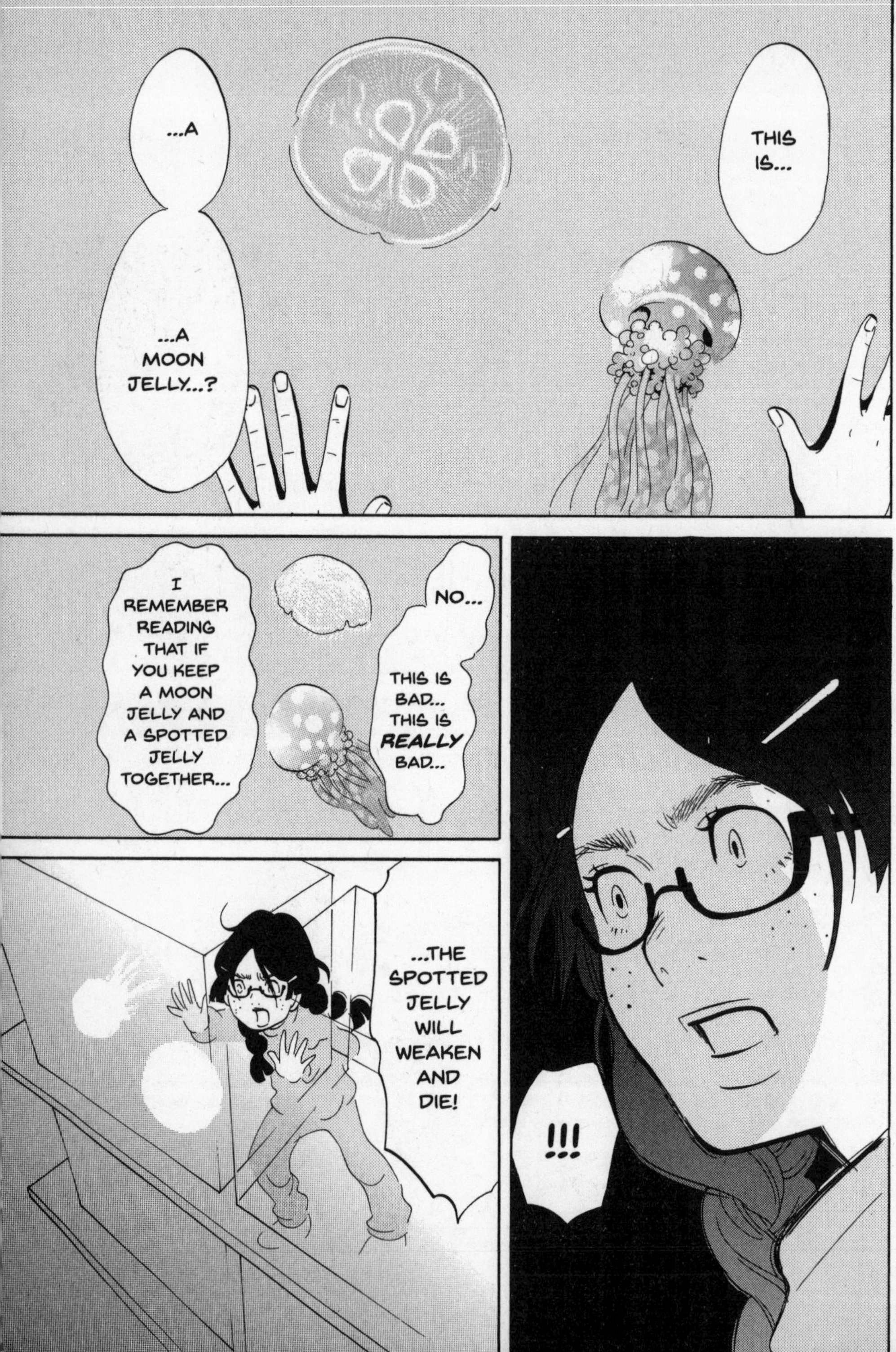
THIS IS...
...A
...A MOON JELLY...?
!!!
NO...
THIS IS BAD... THIS IS *REALLY* BAD...
I REMEMBER READING THAT IF YOU KEEP A MOON JELLY AND A SPOTTED JELLY TOGETHER...
...THE SPOTTED JELLY WILL WEAKEN AND DIE!

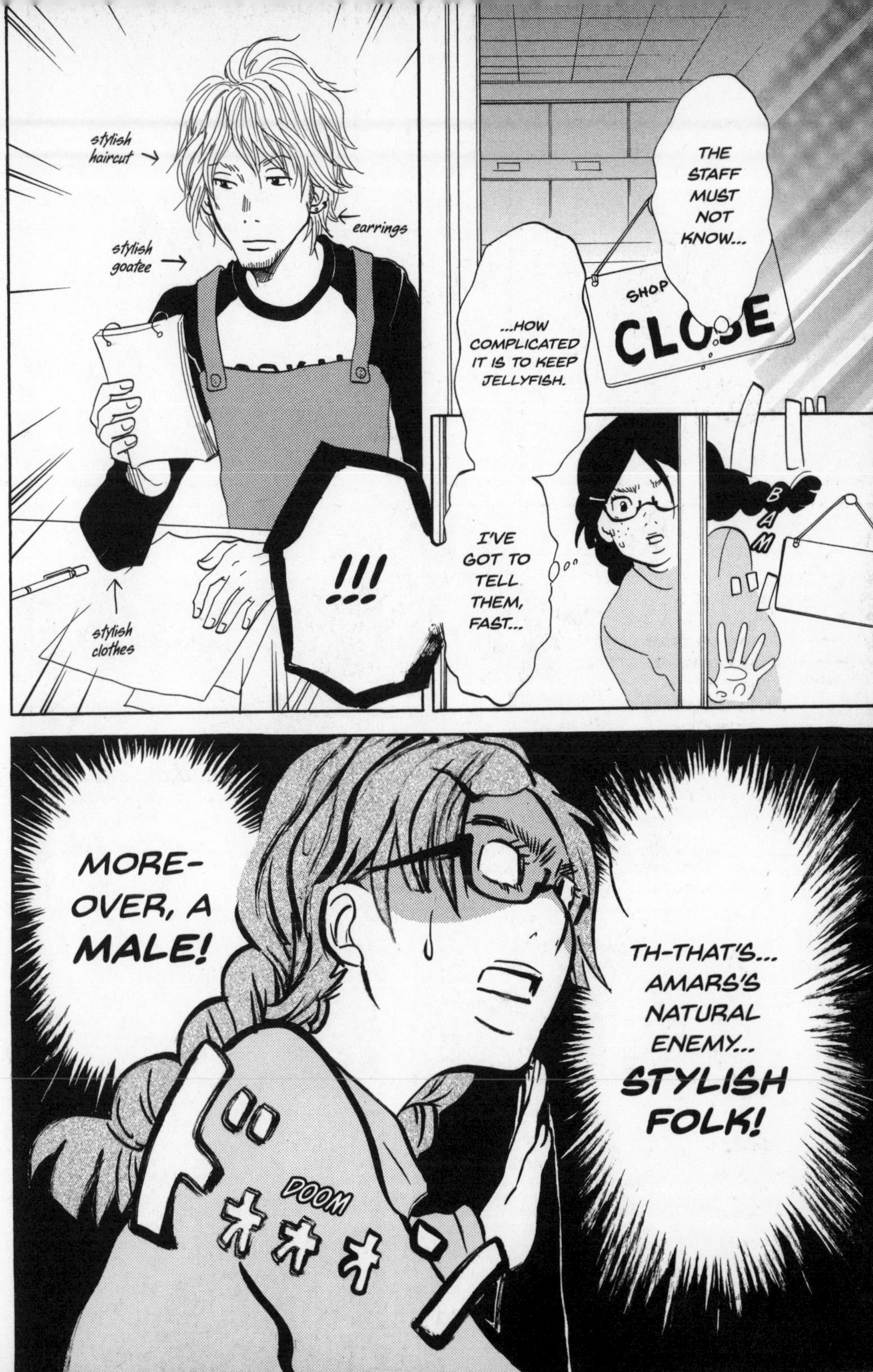
THE STAFF MUST NOT KNOW...
...HOW COMPLICATED IT IS TO KEEP JELLYFISH.
SHOP CLOSE
BAM
I'VE GOT TO TELL THEM, FAST...
!!!
stylish haircut
earrings
stylish goatee
stylish clothes
TH-THAT'S... AMARS'S NATURAL ENEMY... STYLISH FOLK!
MORE-OVER, A MALE!
DOOM

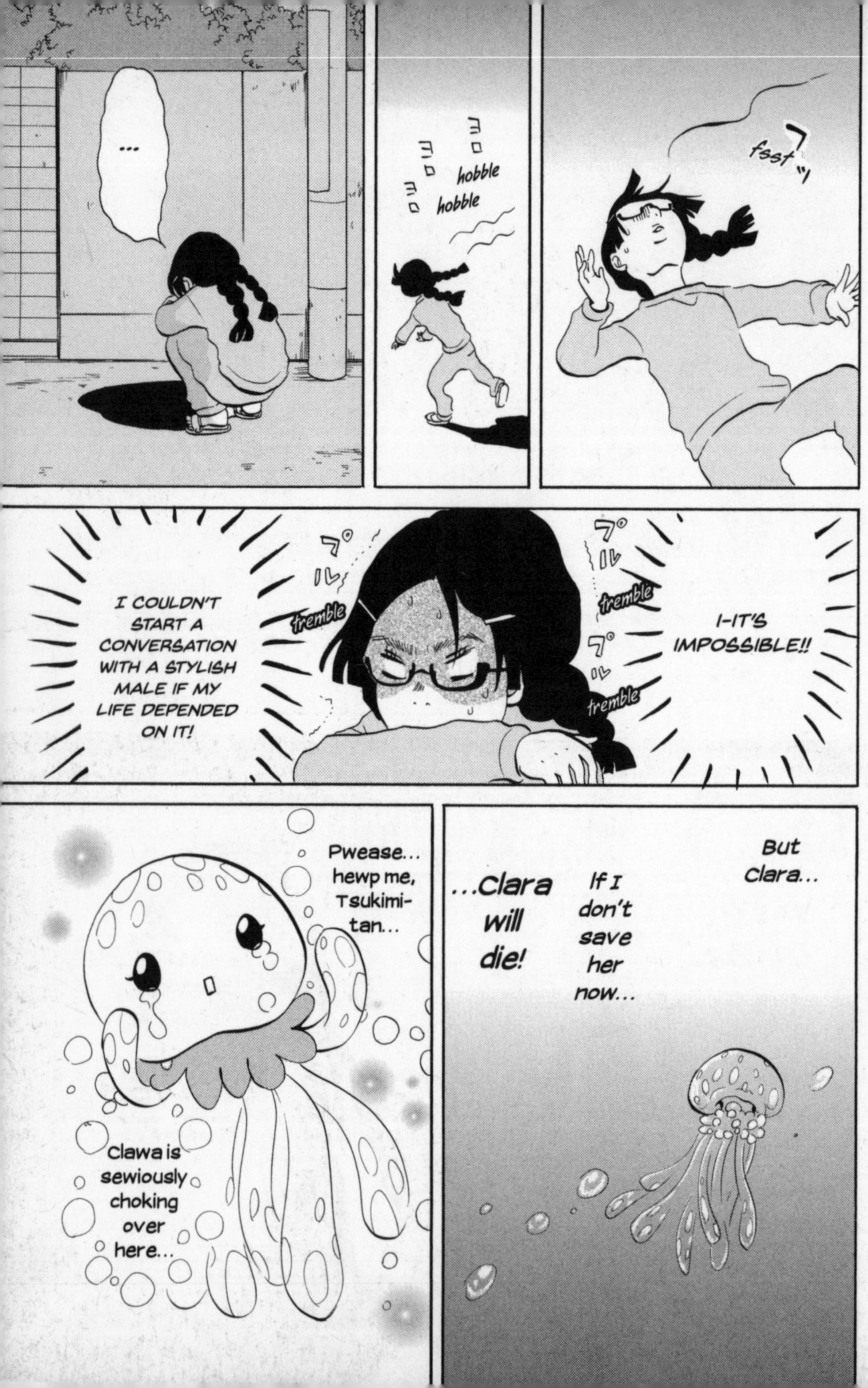

fsst
ヨロ ヨロ ヨロ
hobble hobble
...
プル
tremble
I-IT'S IMPOSSIBLE!!
プル
tremble
プル
tremble
I COULDN'T START A CONVERSATION WITH A STYLISH MALE IF MY LIFE DEPENDED ON IT!
But Clara...
If I don't save her now...
...Clara will die!
Pwease... hewp me, Tsukimi-tan...
Clawa is sewiously choking over here...

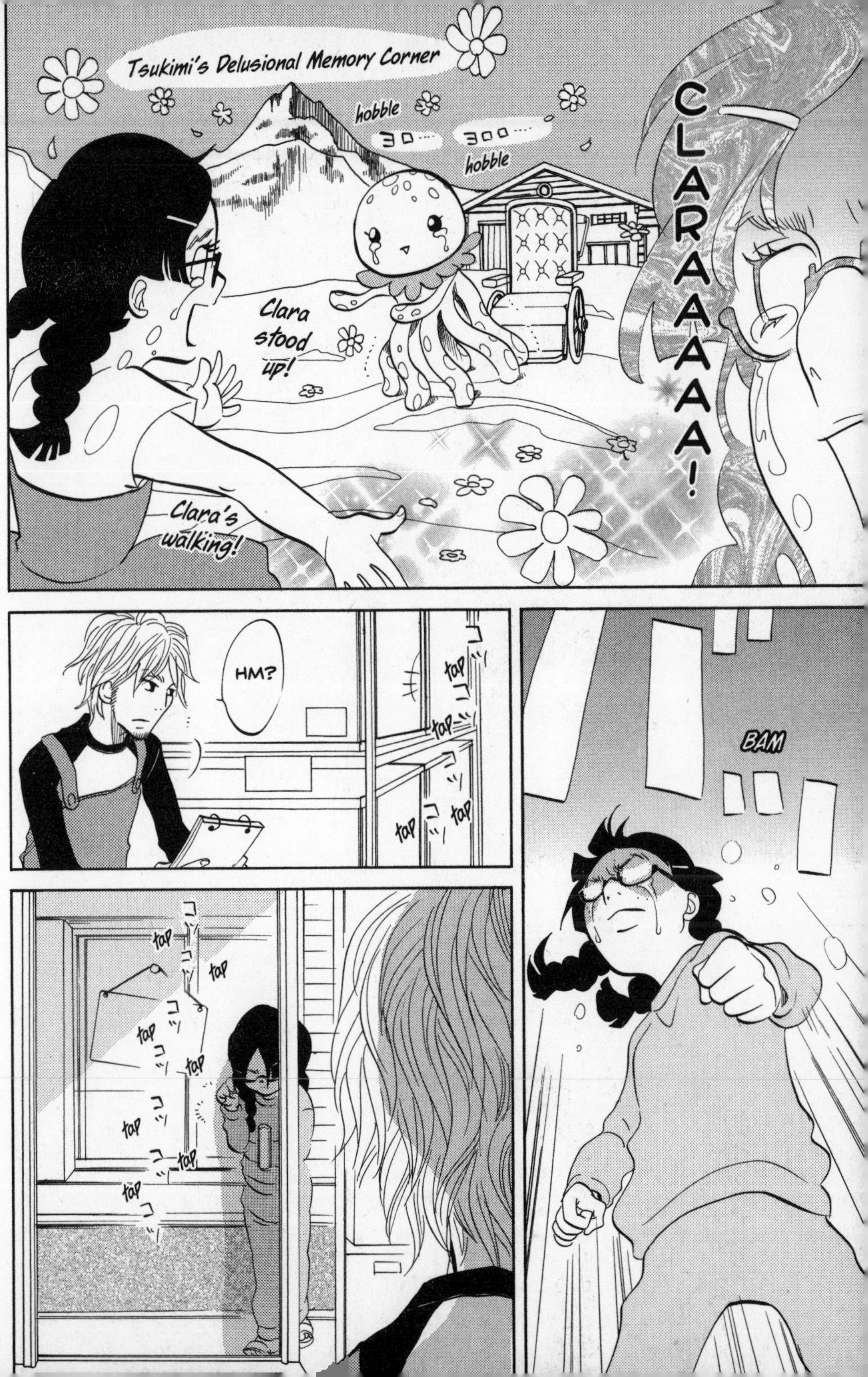
CLARAAAAAA!
Tsukimi's Delusional Memory Corner
hobble
ヨロ…
ヨロロ…
hobble
Clara stood up!
Clara's walking!
BAM
HM?
tap
tap
tap
tap
tap
tap
tap
tap
tap
tap
tap
tap

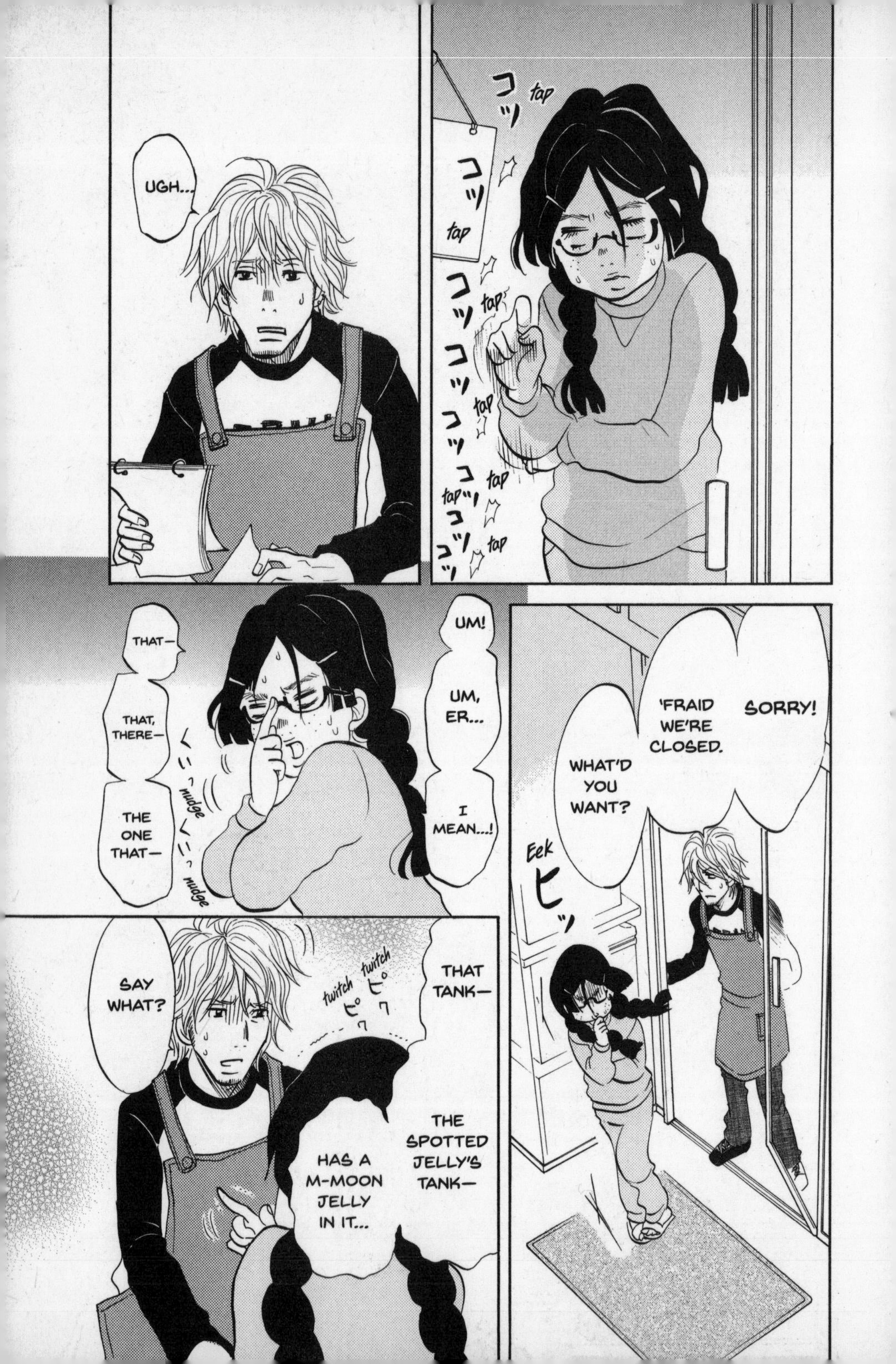
コッ tap
コッ tap
コッ tap
コッ tap
コッ tap
コッ tap
コッ tap
UGH...
SORRY!
'FRAID WE'RE CLOSED.
WHAT'D YOU WANT?
Eek ヒッ
UM!
UM, ER...
I MEAN...!
くい mudge
くい mudge
THAT—
THAT, THERE—
THE ONE THAT—
THAT TANK—
THE SPOTTED JELLY'S TANK—
HAS A M-MOON JELLY IN IT...
ピク twitch
ピク twitch
SAY WHAT?

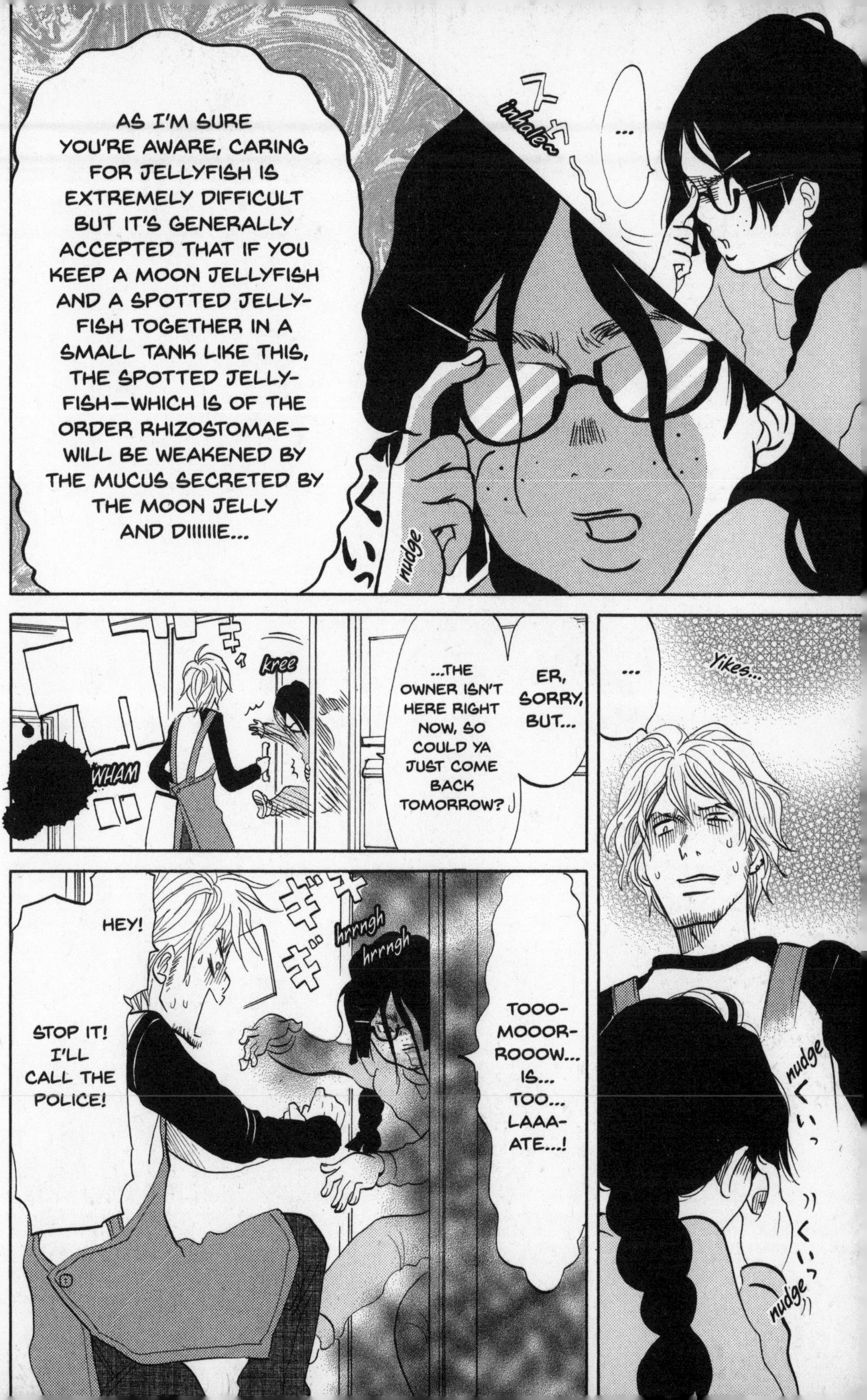

inhale~
...
AS I'M SURE YOU'RE AWARE, CARING FOR JELLYFISH IS EXTREMELY DIFFICULT BUT IT'S GENERALLY ACCEPTED THAT IF YOU KEEP A MOON JELLYFISH AND A SPOTTED JELLY-FISH TOGETHER IN A SMALL TANK LIKE THIS, THE SPOTTED JELLY-FISH—WHICH IS OF THE ORDER RHIZOSTOMAE—WILL BE WEAKENED BY THE MUCUS SECRETED BY THE MOON JELLY AND DIIIIIIE...
nudge
...
Yikes...
nudge
nudge
ER, SORRY, BUT...
...THE OWNER ISN'T HERE RIGHT NOW, SO COULD YA JUST COME BACK TOMORROW?
kree
WHAM
TOOO-MOOOR-ROOOW... IS... TOO... LAAA-ATE...!
hrrngh
hrrngh
HEY!
STOP IT! I'LL CALL THE POLICE!

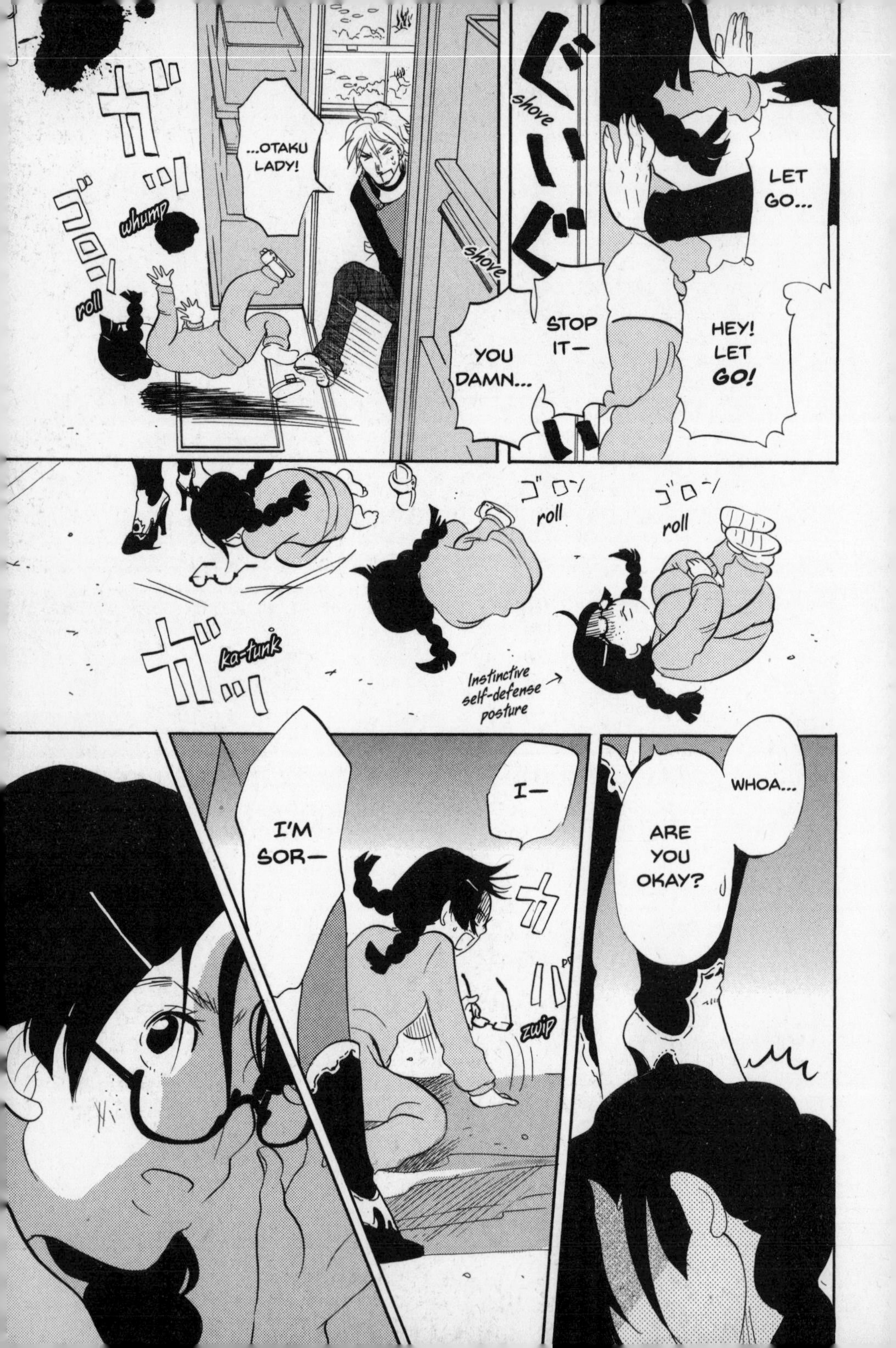

LET GO...
HEY! LET GO!
shove
shove
STOP IT—
YOU DAMN...
...OTAKU LADY!
whump
roll
ゴロン
roll
ゴロン
roll
ka-tunk
Instinctive self-defense posture
WHOA...
ARE YOU OKAY?
I—
I'M SOR—
zwip

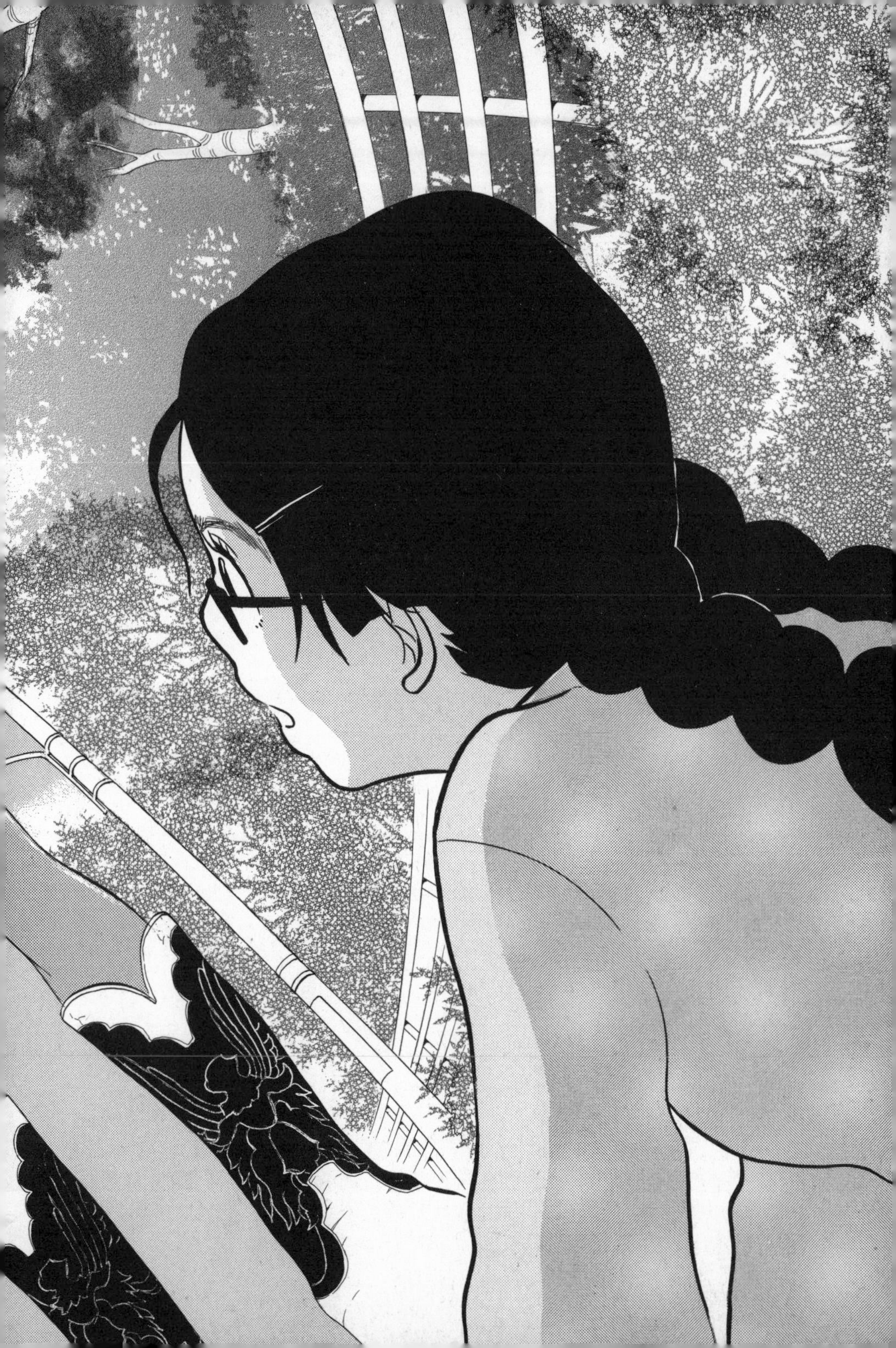

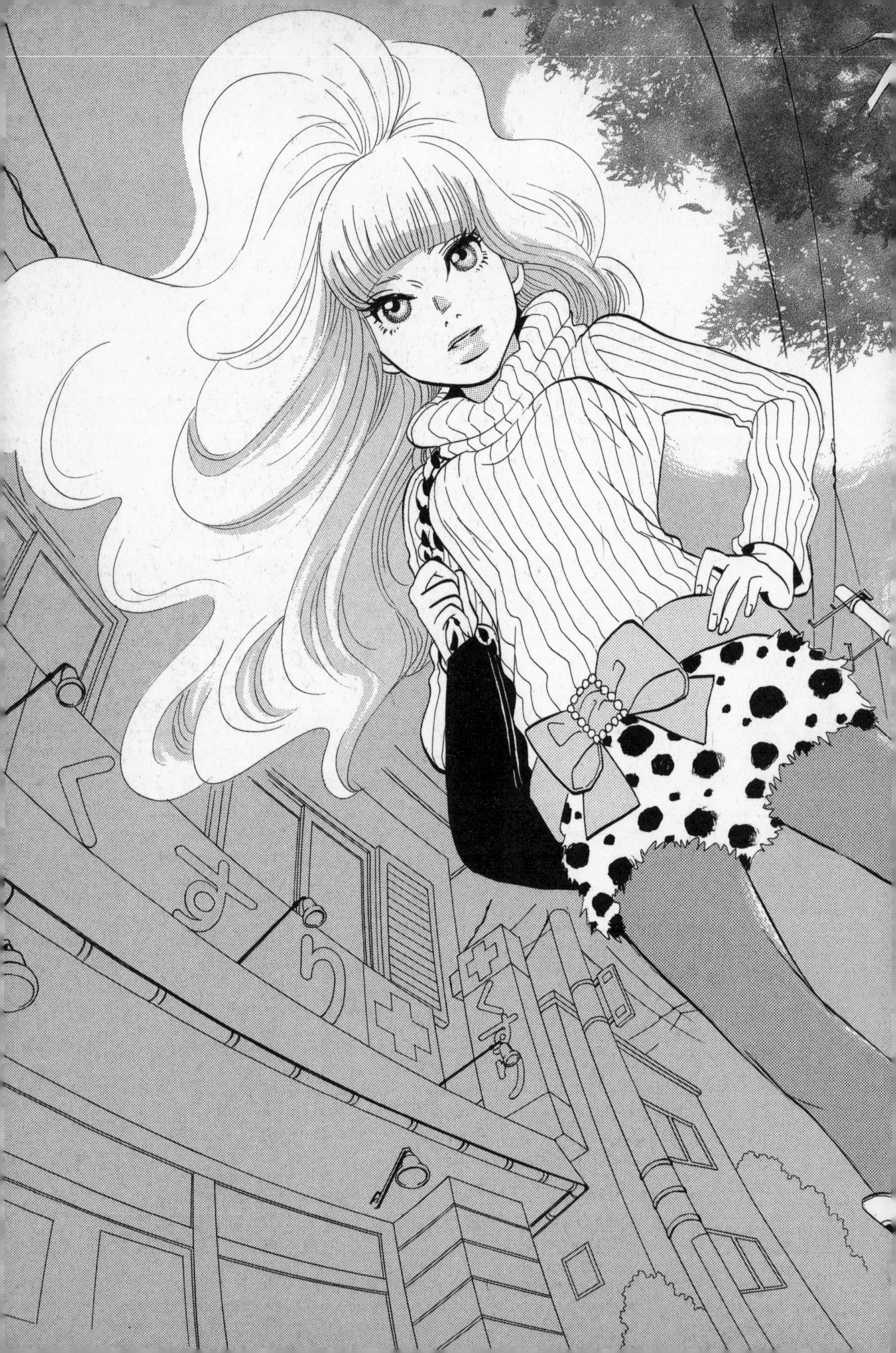

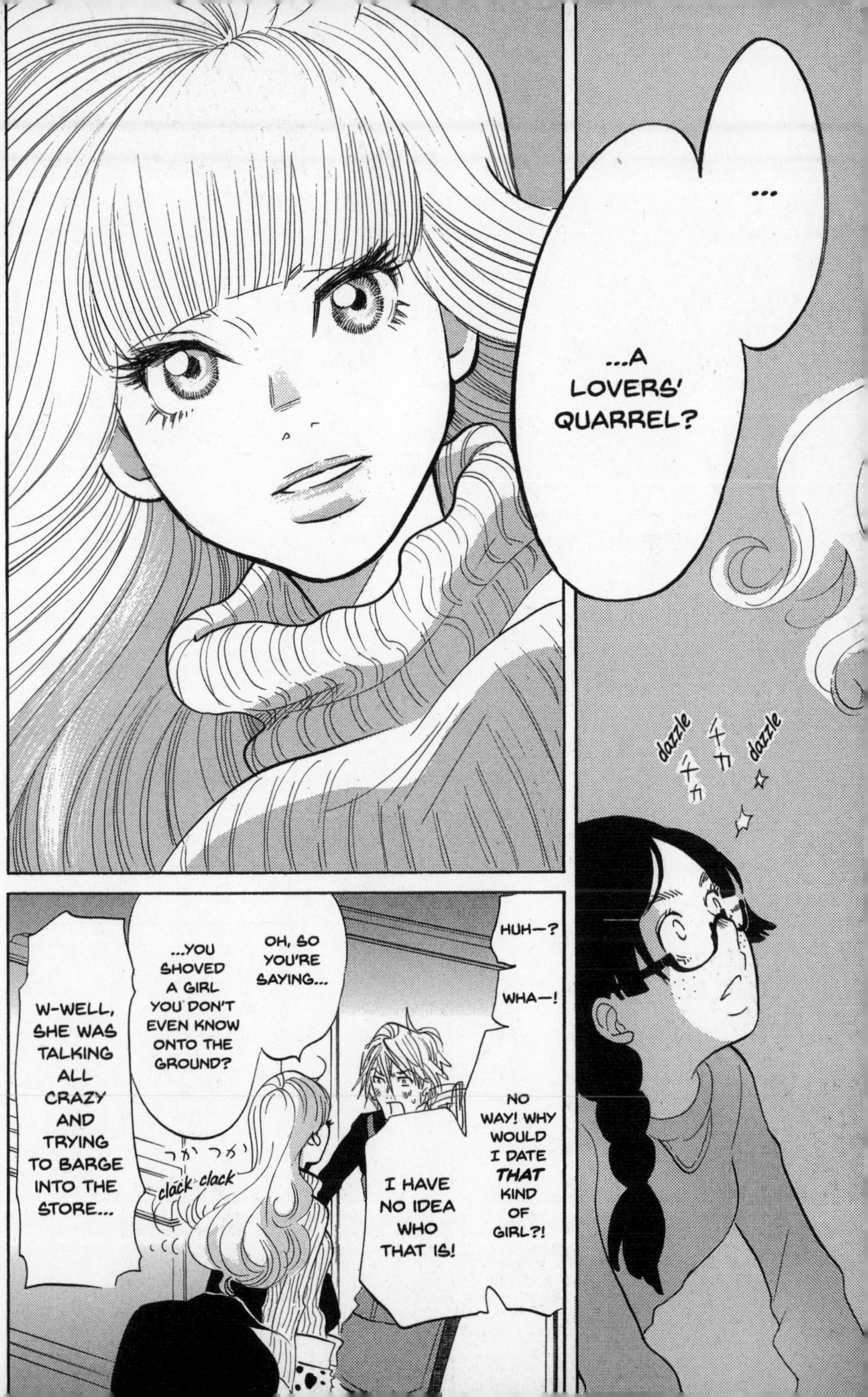
...
...A LOVERS' QUARREL?
dazzle
チカ チカ
dazzle
HUH—?
WHA—!
NO WAY! WHY WOULD I DATE *THAT* KIND OF GIRL?!
I HAVE NO IDEA WHO THAT IS!
OH, SO YOU'RE SAYING...
...YOU SHOVED A GIRL YOU DON'T EVEN KNOW ONTO THE GROUND?
つか つか
clack clack
W-WELL, SHE WAS TALKING ALL CRAZY AND TRYING TO BARGE INTO THE STORE...

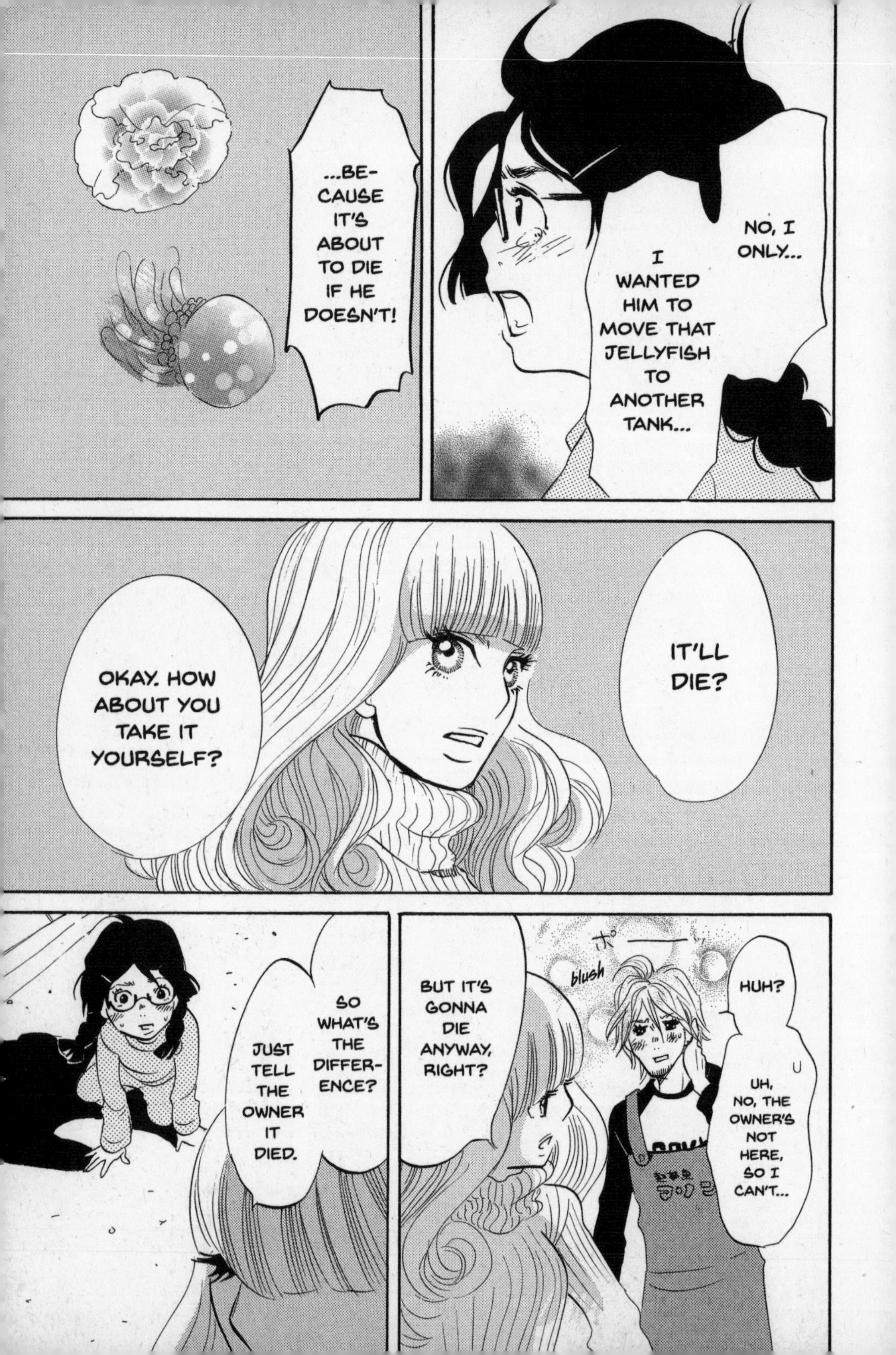
NO, I ONLY...
I WANTED HIM TO MOVE THAT JELLYFISH TO ANOTHER TANK...
...BE-CAUSE IT'S ABOUT TO DIE IF HE DOESN'T!
IT'LL DIE?
OKAY. HOW ABOUT YOU TAKE IT YOURSELF?
HUH?
ポーッ
blush
UH, NO, THE OWNER'S NOT HERE, SO I CAN'T...
BUT IT'S GONNA DIE ANYWAY, RIGHT?
SO WHAT'S THE DIFFER-ENCE?
JUST TELL THE OWNER IT DIED.

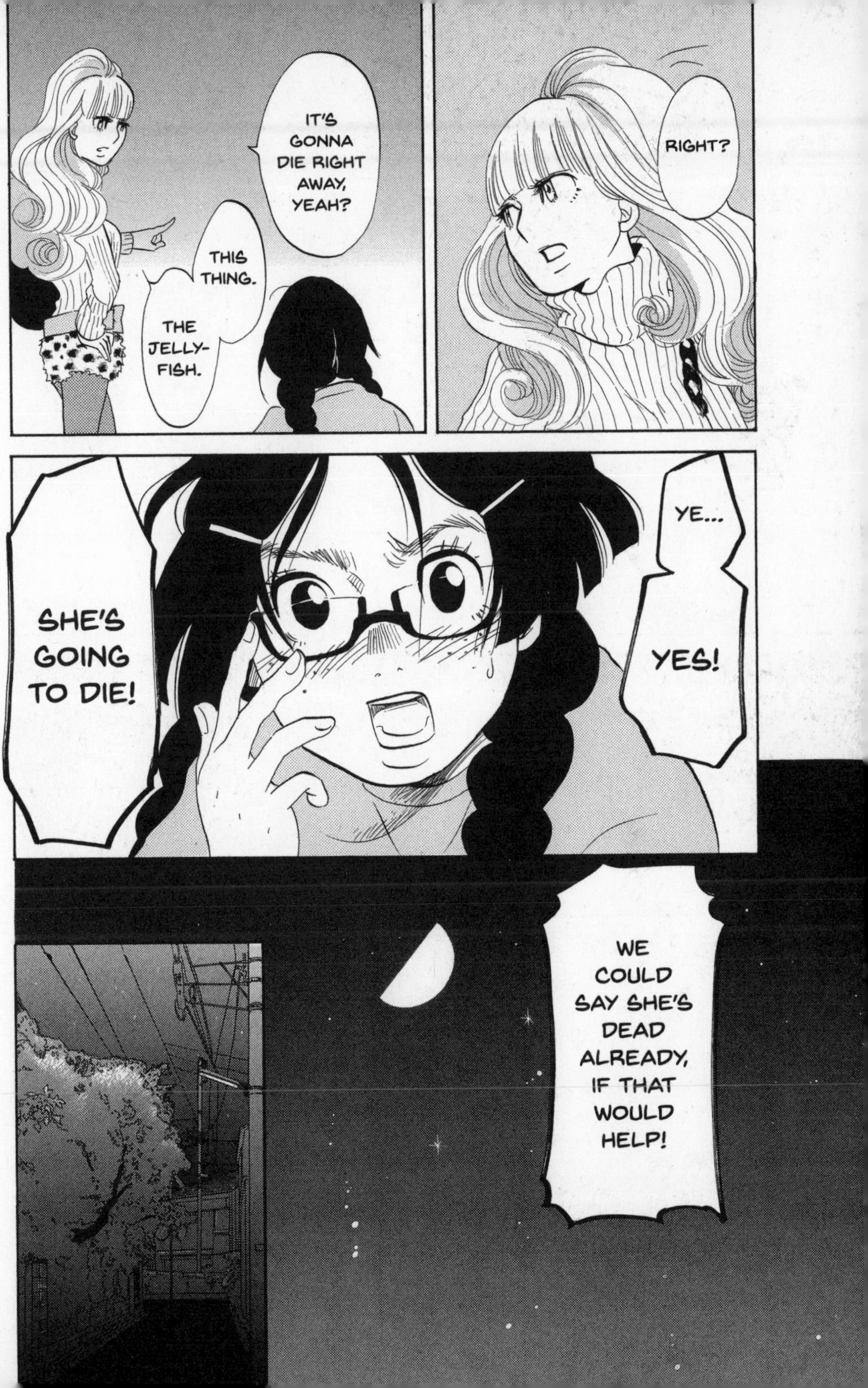
RIGHT?
IT'S GONNA DIE RIGHT AWAY, YEAH?
THIS THING.
THE JELLY-FISH.
YE...
YES!
SHE'S GOING TO DIE!
WE COULD SAY SHE'S DEAD ALREADY, IF THAT WOULD HELP!

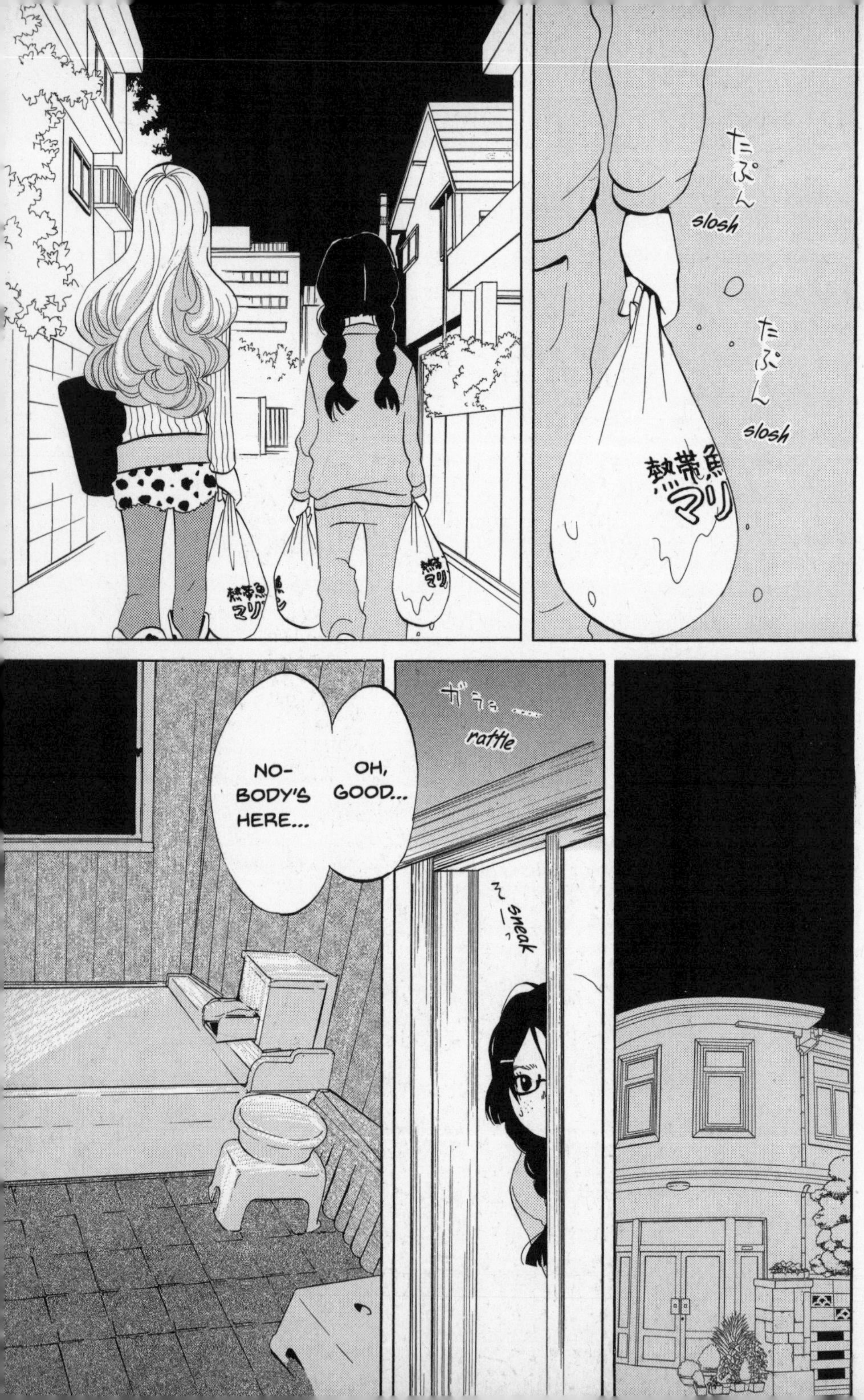
たぷん
slosh
たぷん
slosh
熱帯魚マリ
ガラ…
rattle
そー…
sneak
OH, GOOD...
NOBODY'S HERE...

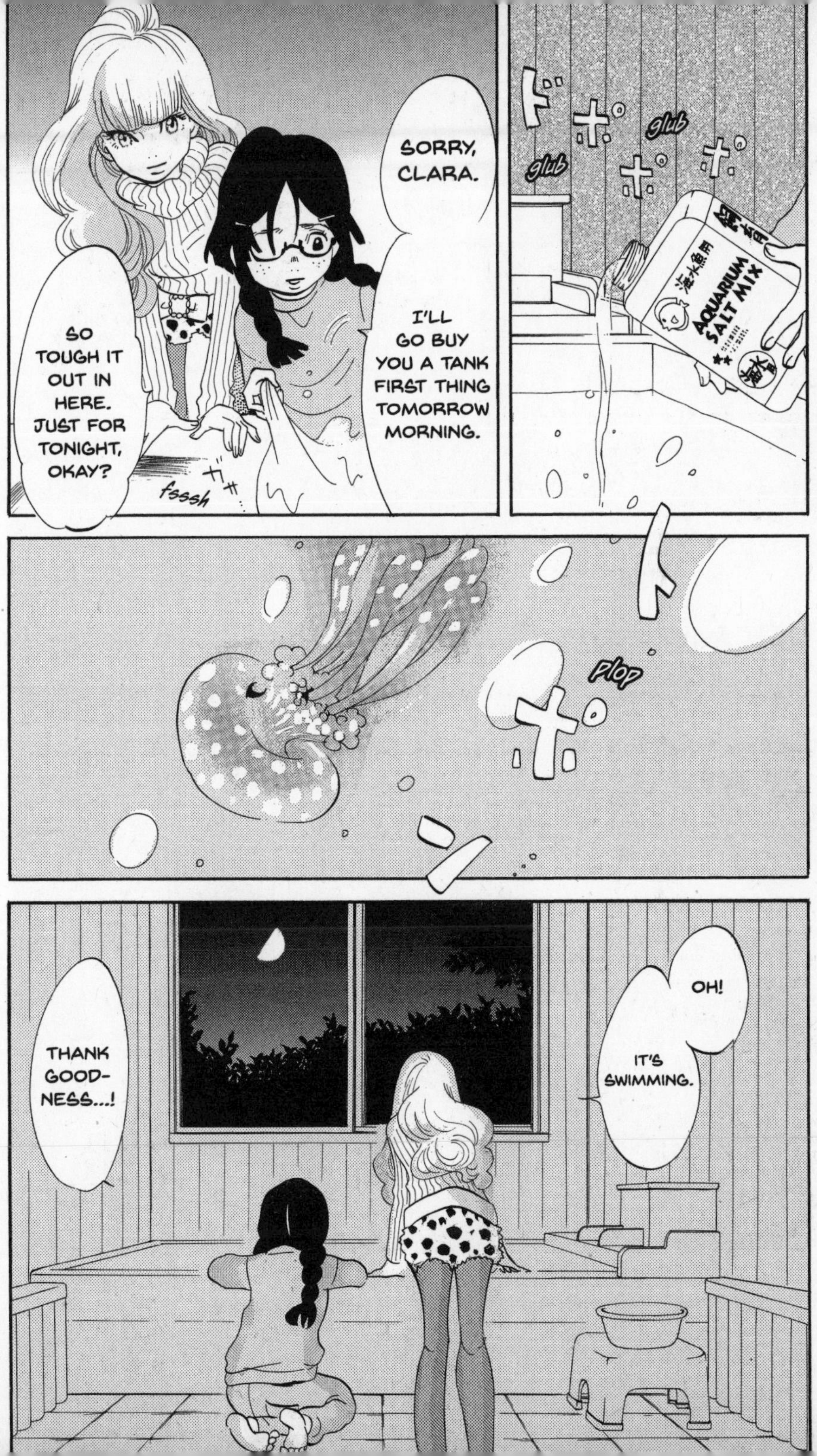
glub
glub
AQUARIUM SALT MIX
SORRY, CLARA.
I'LL GO BUY YOU A TANK FIRST THING TOMORROW MORNING.
SO TOUGH IT OUT IN HERE. JUST FOR TONIGHT, OKAY?
fsssh
plop
OH!
IT'S SWIMMING.
THANK GOODNESS...!

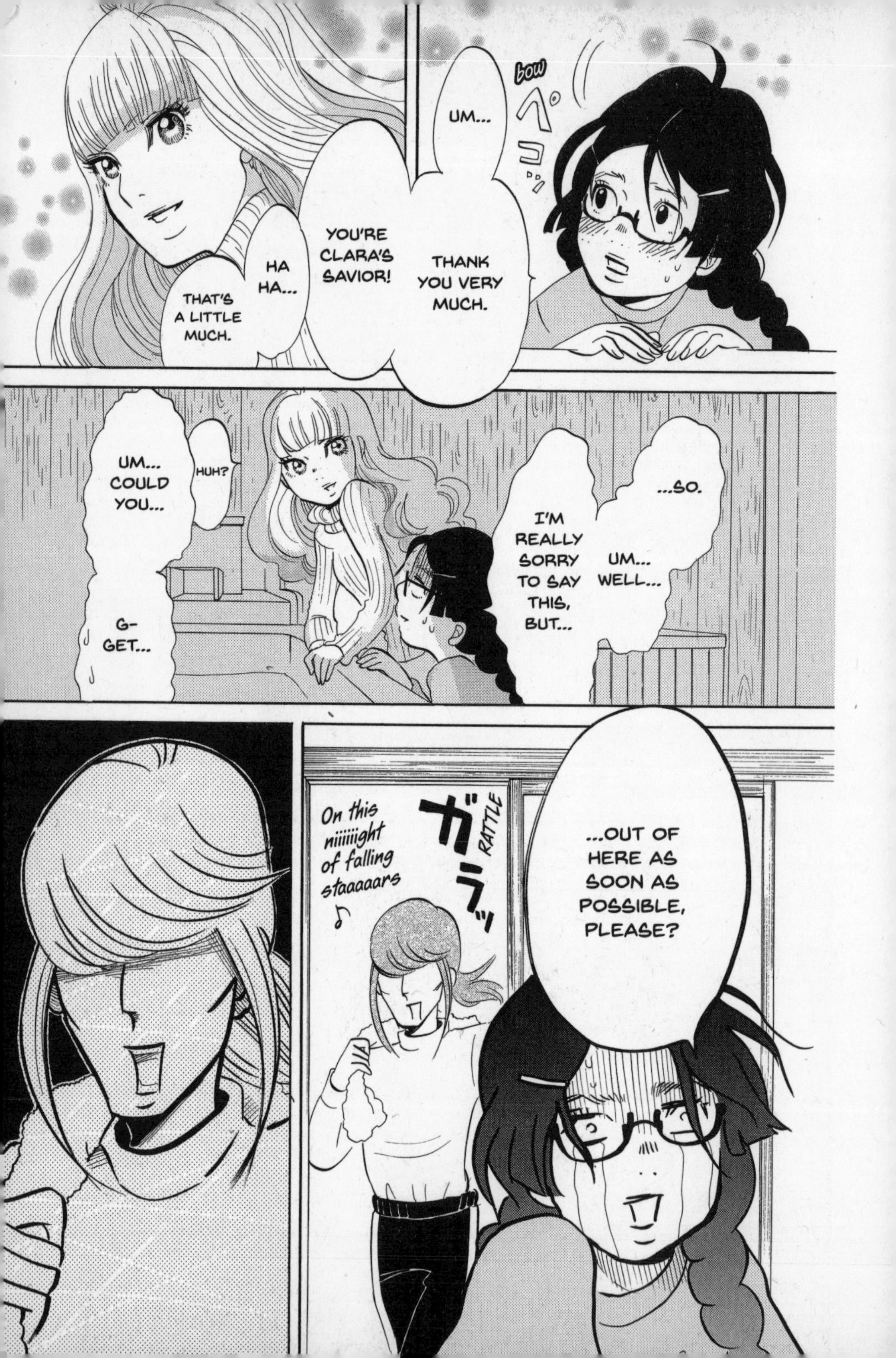
bow
ペコ
UM...
THANK YOU VERY MUCH.
YOU'RE CLARA'S SAVIOR!
HA HA...
THAT'S A LITTLE MUCH.
...SO.
UM... WELL...
I'M REALLY SORRY TO SAY THIS, BUT...
HUH?
UM... COULD YOU...
G- GET...
...OUT OF HERE AS SOON AS POSSIBLE, PLEASE?
ガラッ
RATTLE
On this niiiiiight of falling staaaaars ♪

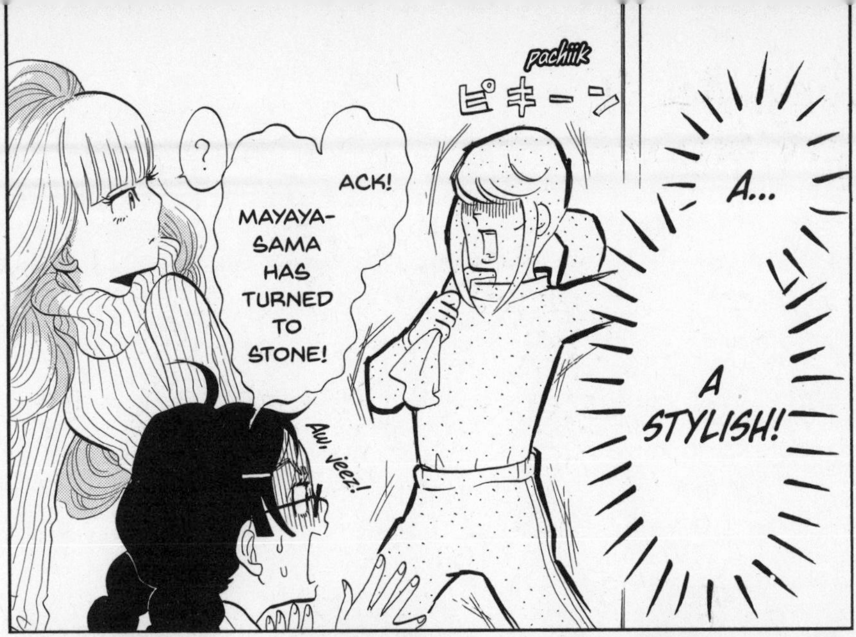
A...
A STYLISH!
pachiik
ピキーン
ACK! MAYAYA-SAMA HAS TURNED TO STONE!
?
Aw, jeez!

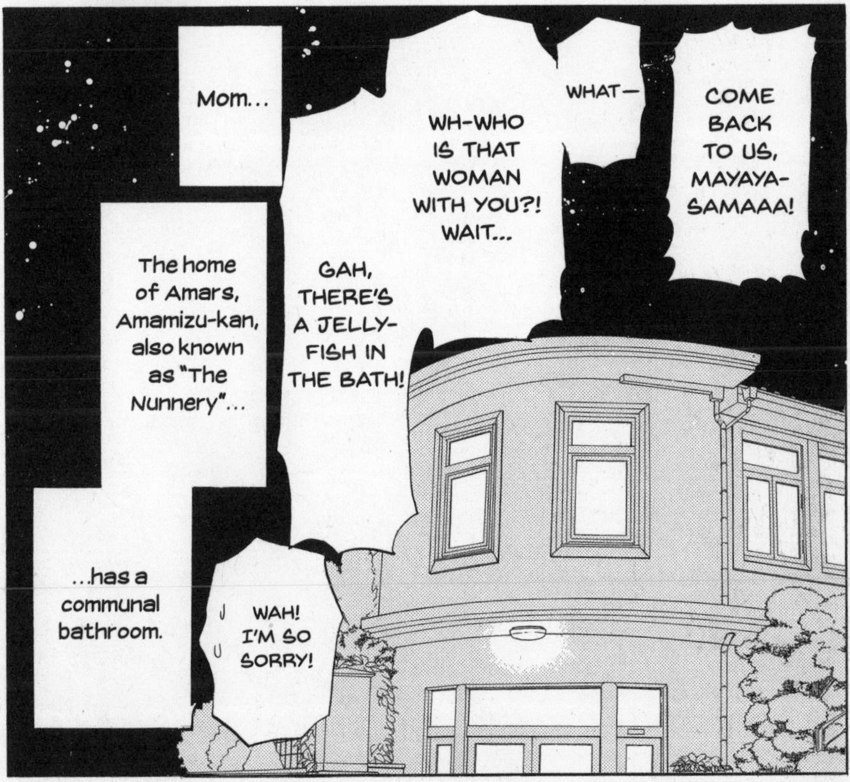
COME BACK TO US, MAYAYA-SAMAAA!
WHAT—
WH-WHO IS THAT WOMAN WITH YOU?! WAIT...
Mom...
GAH, THERE'S A JELLY-FISH IN THE BATH!
The home of Amars, Amamizu-kan, also known as "The Nunnery"...
WAH! I'M SO SORRY!
...has a communal bathroom.

Episode 2
Pretty Woman

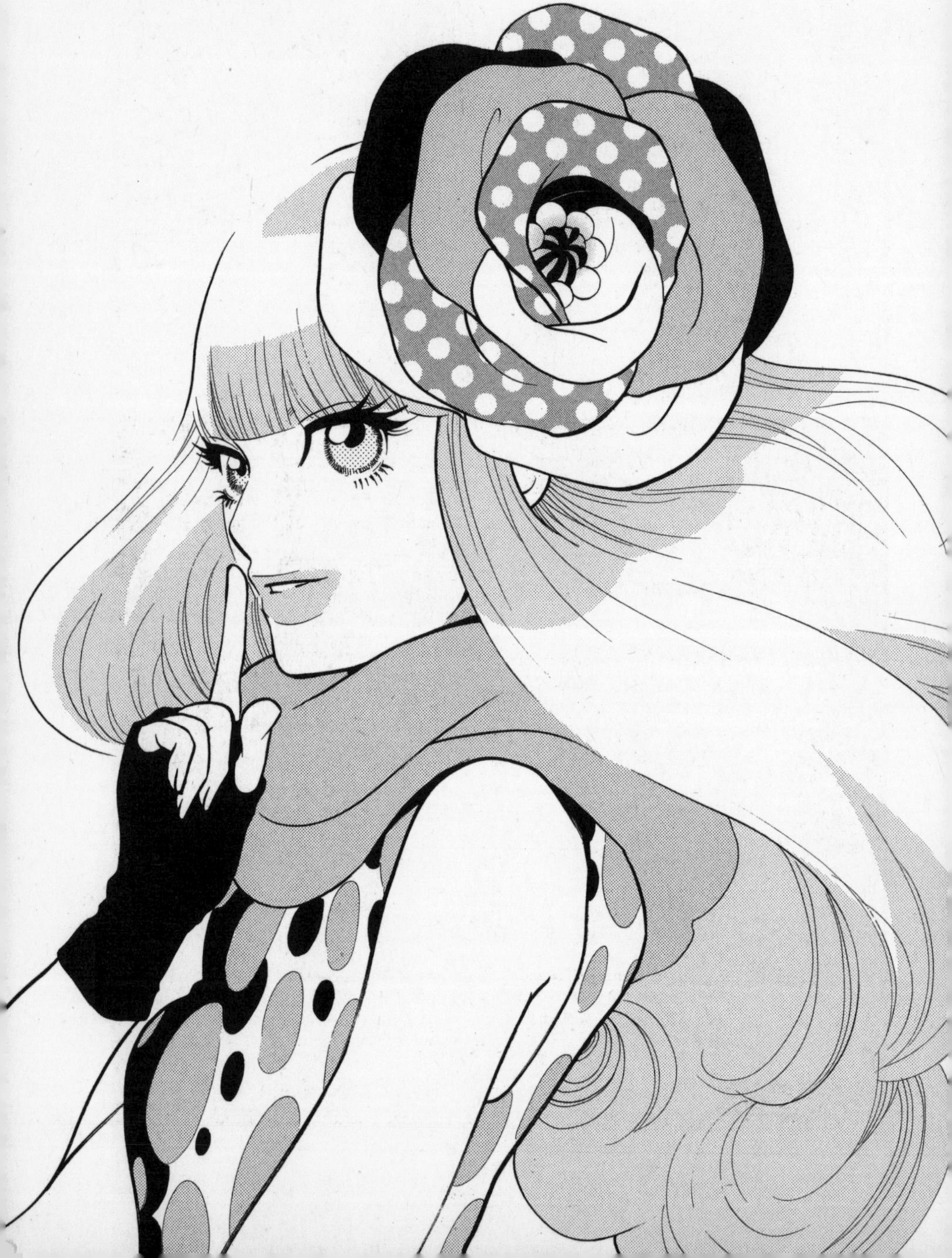

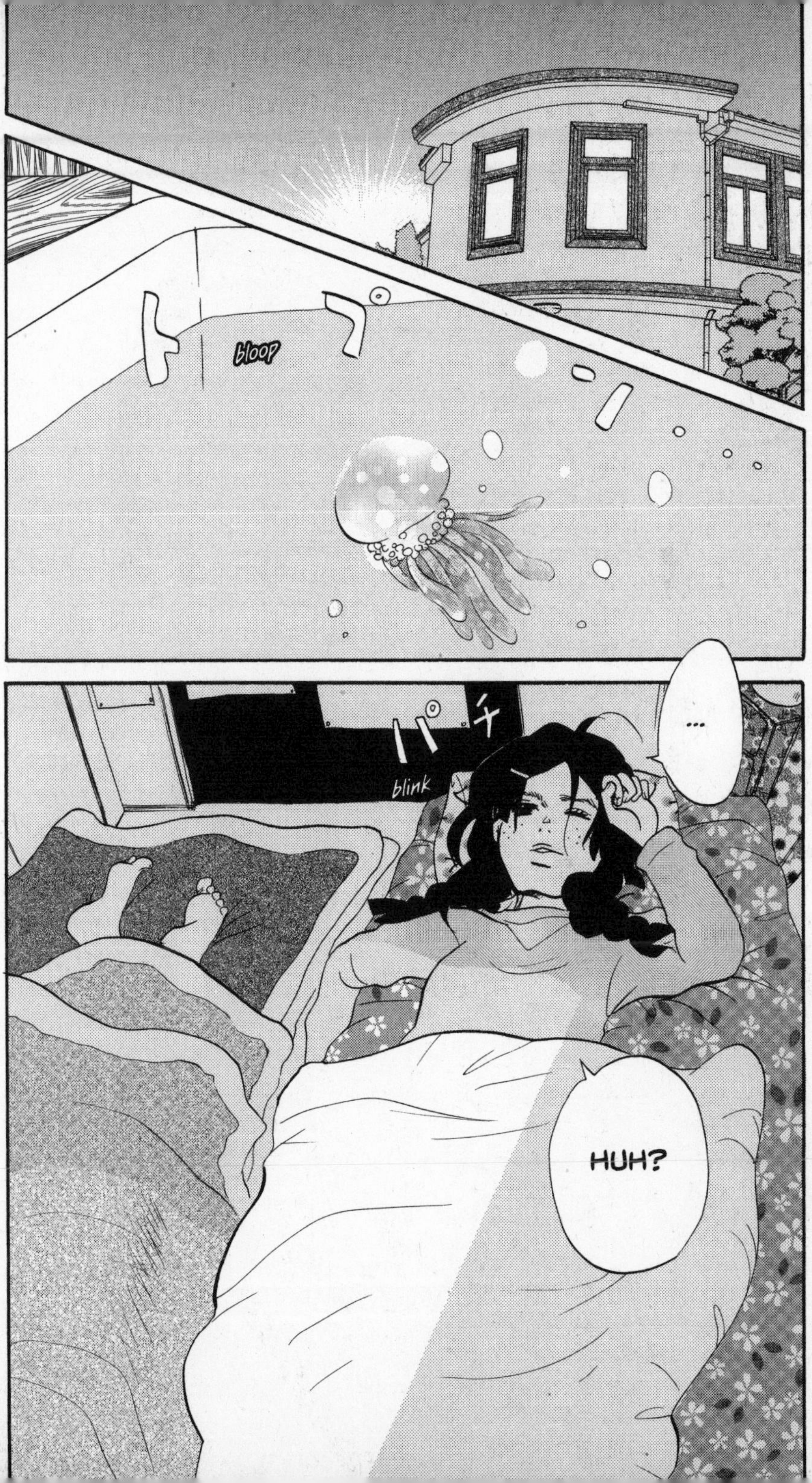
トプーン
bloop
パチ
blink
...
HUH?

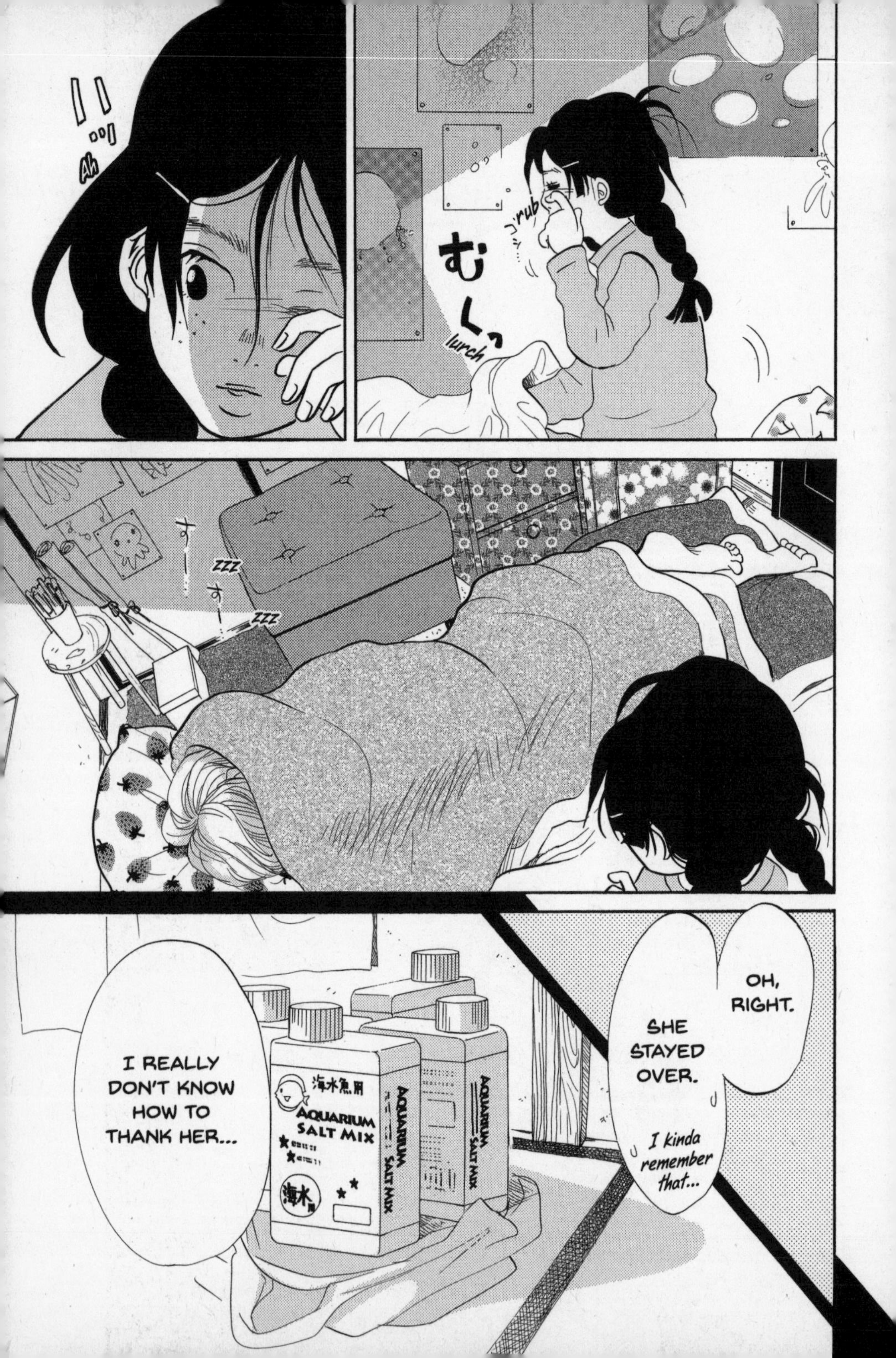
rub
むくっ
lurch
Ah!!
すー…
zzz
すー…
zzz
OH, RIGHT.
SHE STAYED OVER.
I kinda remember that...
I REALLY DON'T KNOW HOW TO THANK HER...
海水魚用
AQUARIUM SALT MIX
海水用
AQUARIUM SALT MIX

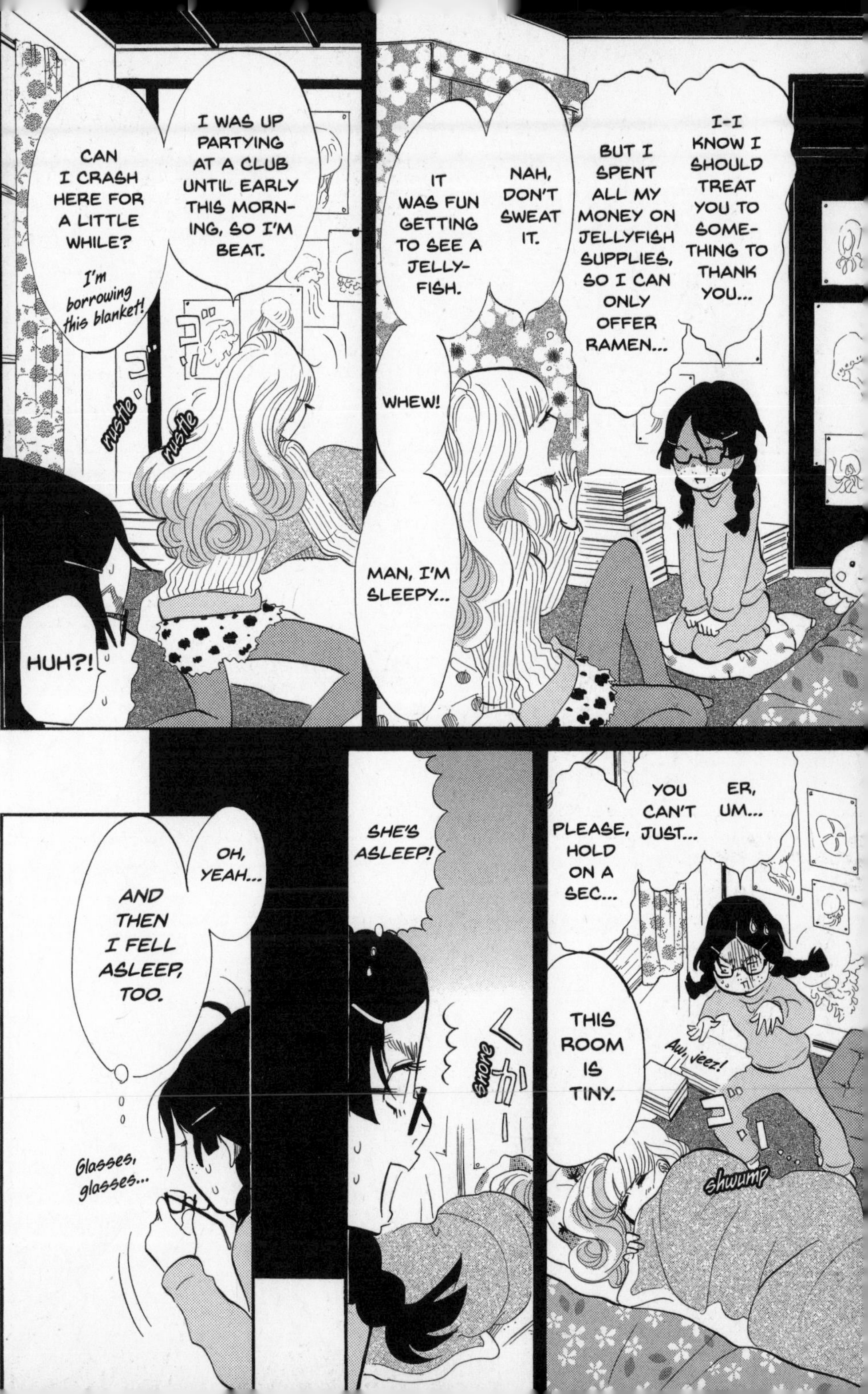
I-I KNOW I SHOULD TREAT YOU TO SOMETHING TO THANK YOU...
BUT I SPENT ALL MY MONEY ON JELLYFISH SUPPLIES, SO I CAN ONLY OFFER RAMEN...
NAH, DON'T SWEAT IT.
IT WAS FUN GETTING TO SEE A JELLYFISH.
WHEW!
MAN, I'M SLEEPY...
I WAS UP PARTYING AT A CLUB UNTIL EARLY THIS MORNING, SO I'M BEAT.
CAN I CRASH HERE FOR A LITTLE WHILE?
I'm borrowing this blanket!
rustle
rustle
HUH?!
ER, UM...
YOU CAN'T JUST...
PLEASE, HOLD ON A SEC...
THIS ROOM IS TINY.
Aw, jeez!
shwump
SHE'S ASLEEP!
snore
OH, YEAH...
AND THEN I FELL ASLEEP, TOO.
Glasses, glasses...

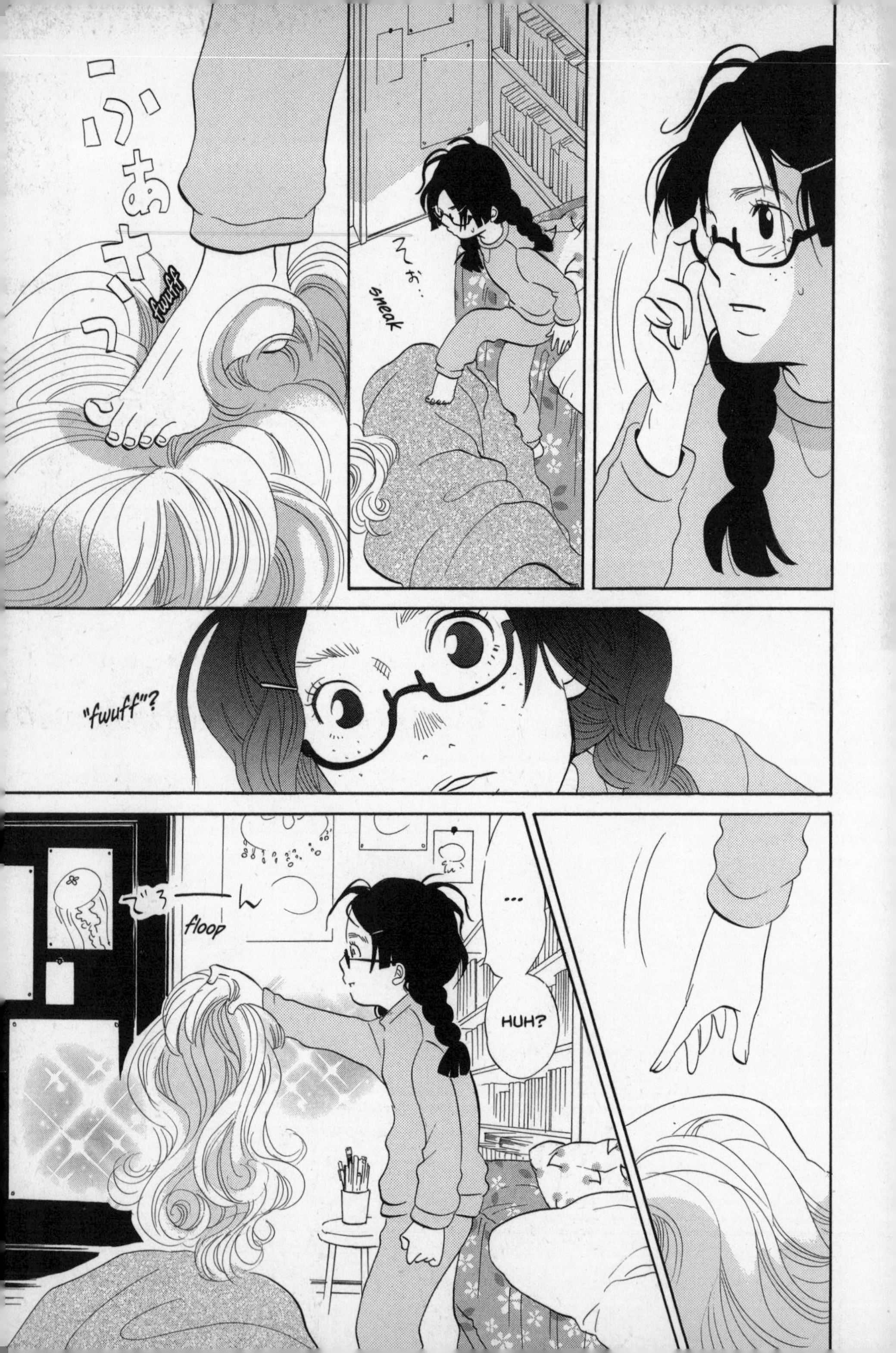

そお…
sneak
ふあさっ
fwuff
"fwuff"?
...
でろーーん
floop
HUH?

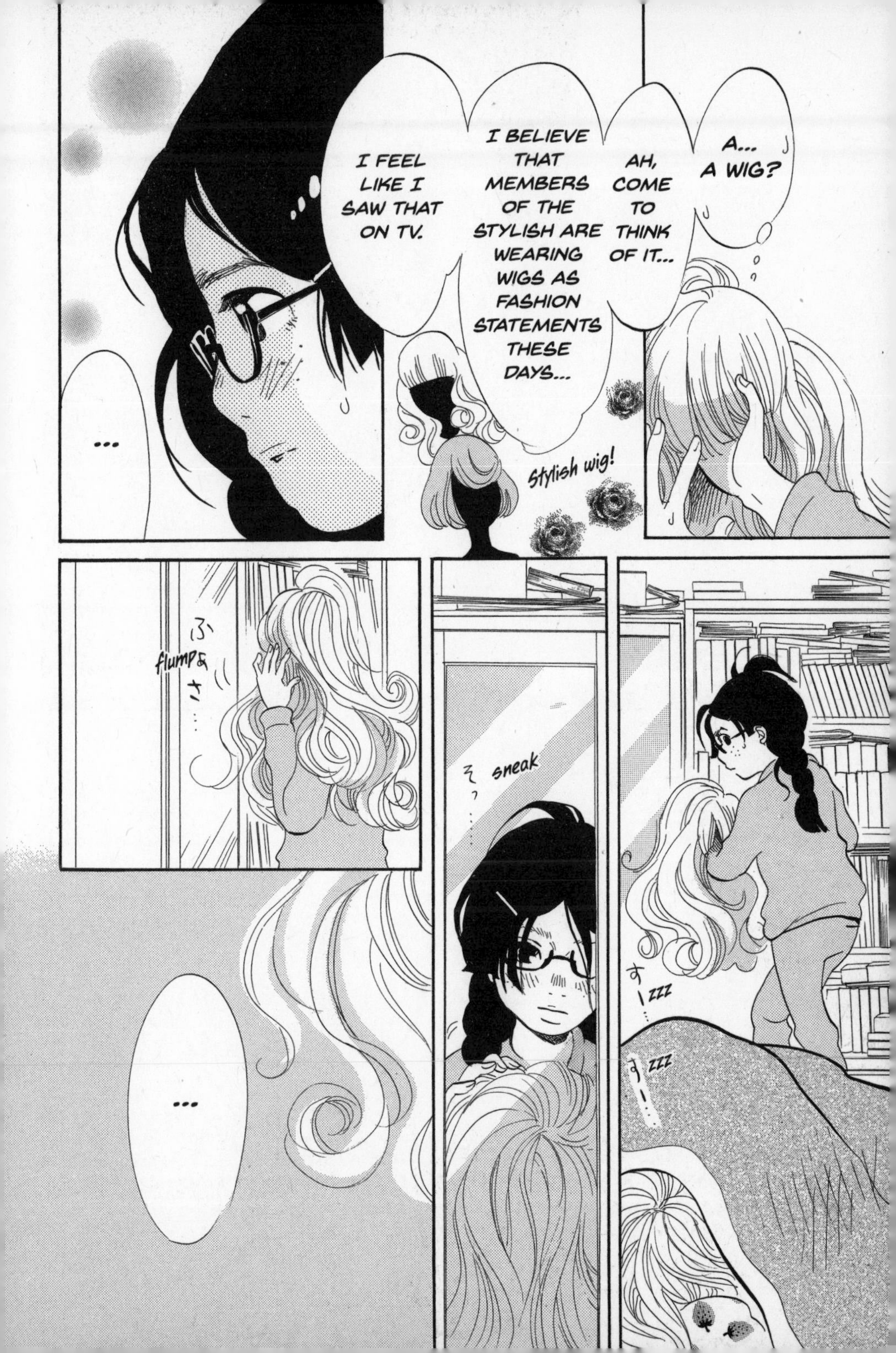
A... A WIG?
AH, COME TO THINK OF IT...
I BELIEVE THAT MEMBERS OF THE STYLISH ARE WEARING WIGS AS FASHION STATEMENTS THESE DAYS...
I FEEL LIKE I SAW THAT ON TV.
Stylish wig!
...
すー… zzz
すー… zzz
そ… sneak
ふぁさ… flump
...

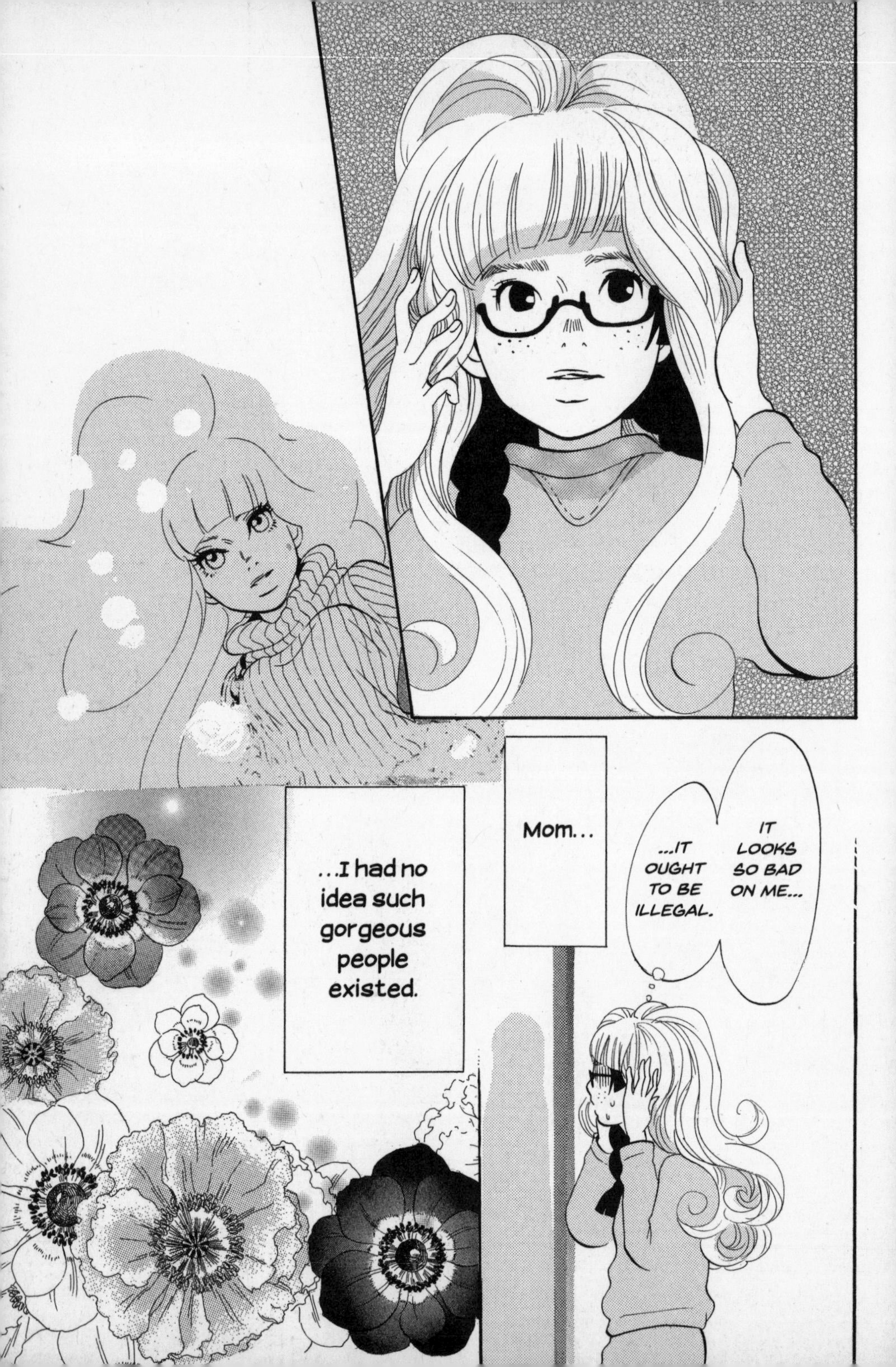
IT LOOKS SO BAD ON ME...
...IT OUGHT TO BE ILLEGAL.
Mom...
...I had no idea such gorgeous people existed.

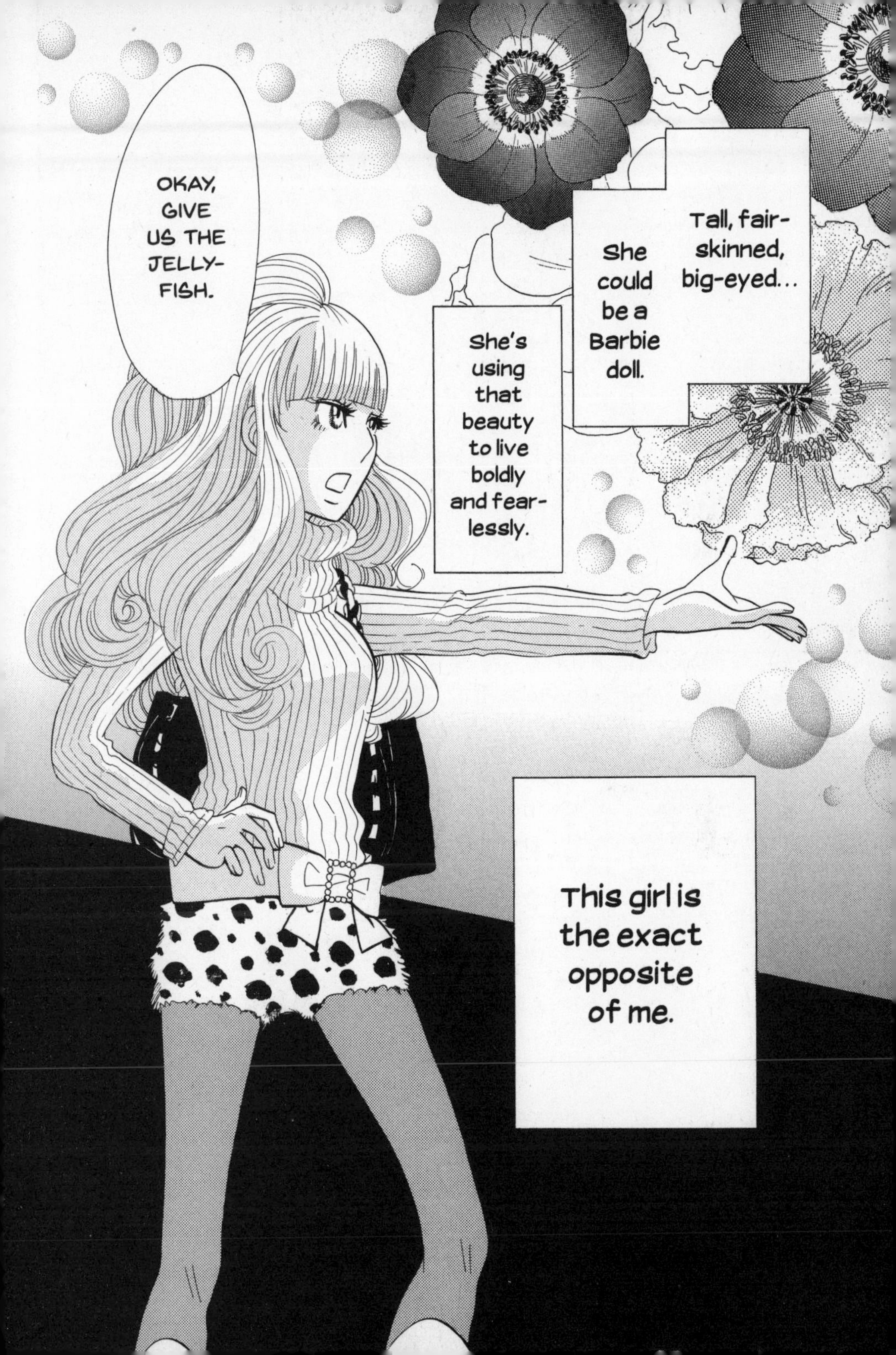
Tall, fair-skinned, big-eyed...
She could be a Barbie doll.
She's using that beauty to live boldly and fearlessly.
OKAY, GIVE US THE JELLY-FISH.
This girl is the exact opposite of me.

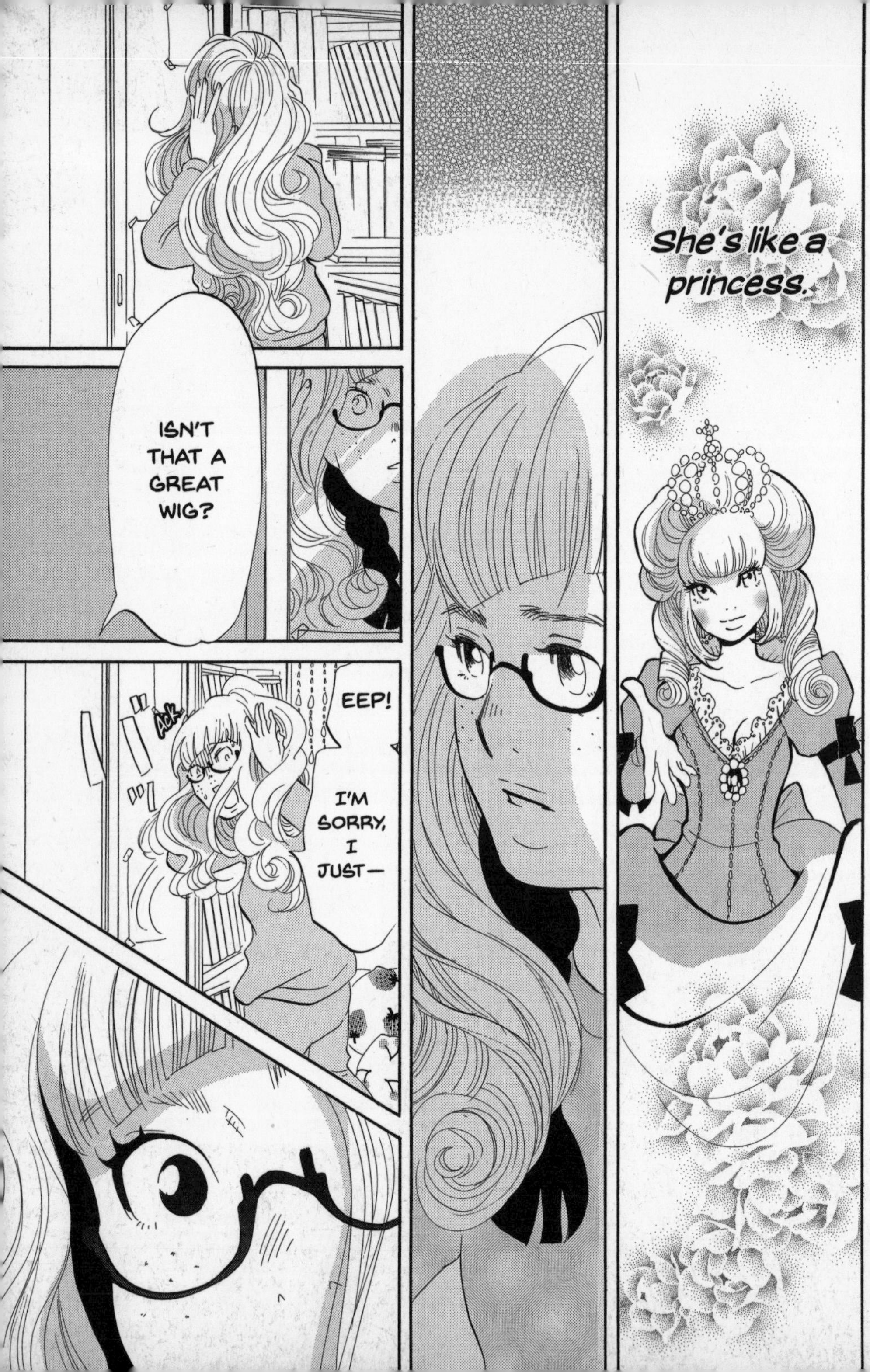
She's like a princess.
ISN'T THAT A GREAT WIG?
EEP!
Ack
I'M SORRY, I JUST—

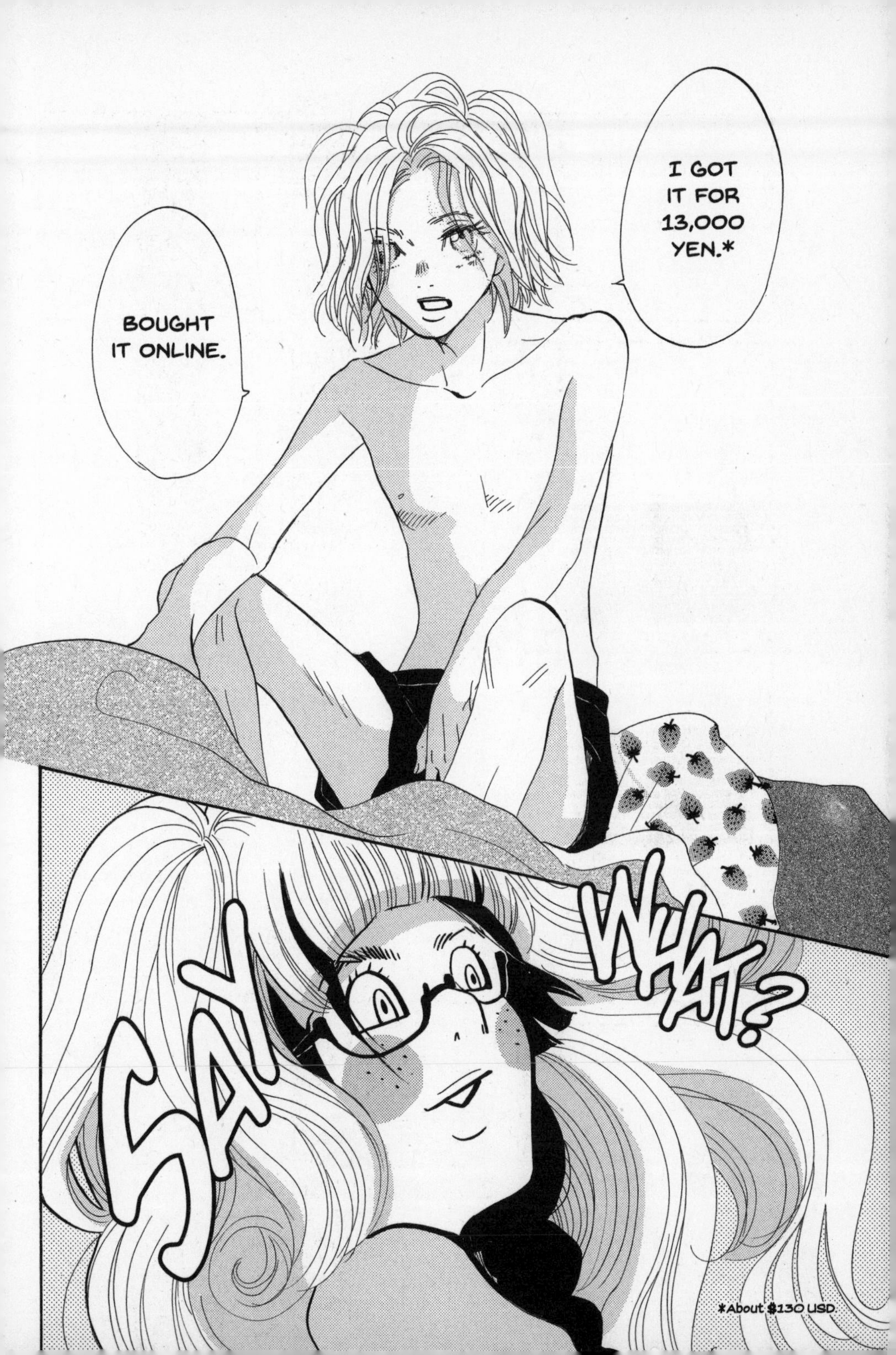
I GOT IT FOR 13,000 YEN.*
BOUGHT IT ONLINE.
SAY WHAT?
*About $130 USD.

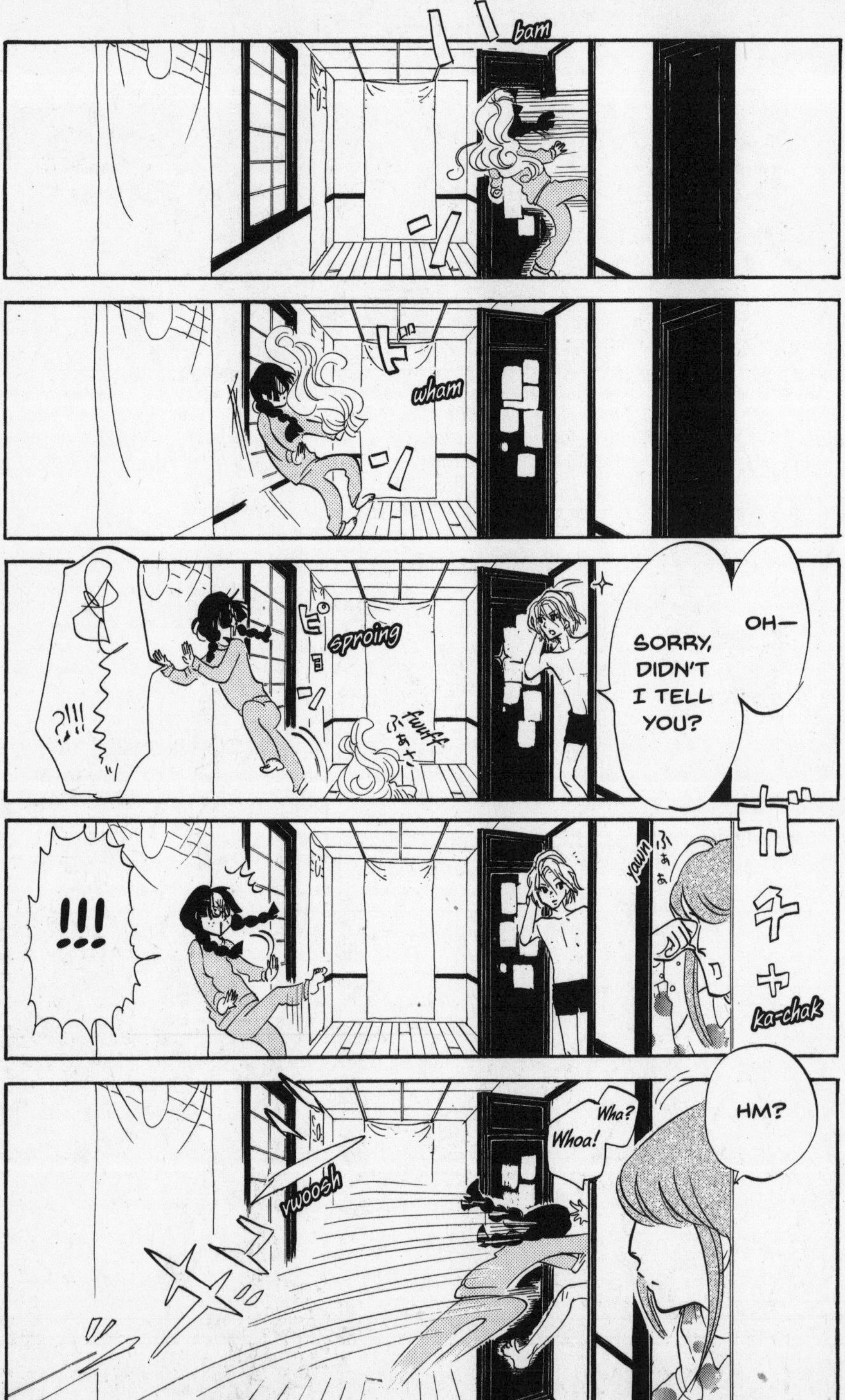

bam
wham
OH—
SORRY, DIDN'T I TELL YOU?
sproing
fwuff
ふぁさ
?!!!
ガチャ
ka-chak
yawn
ふぁぁ
!!!
HM?
Wha?
Whoa!
vwoosh

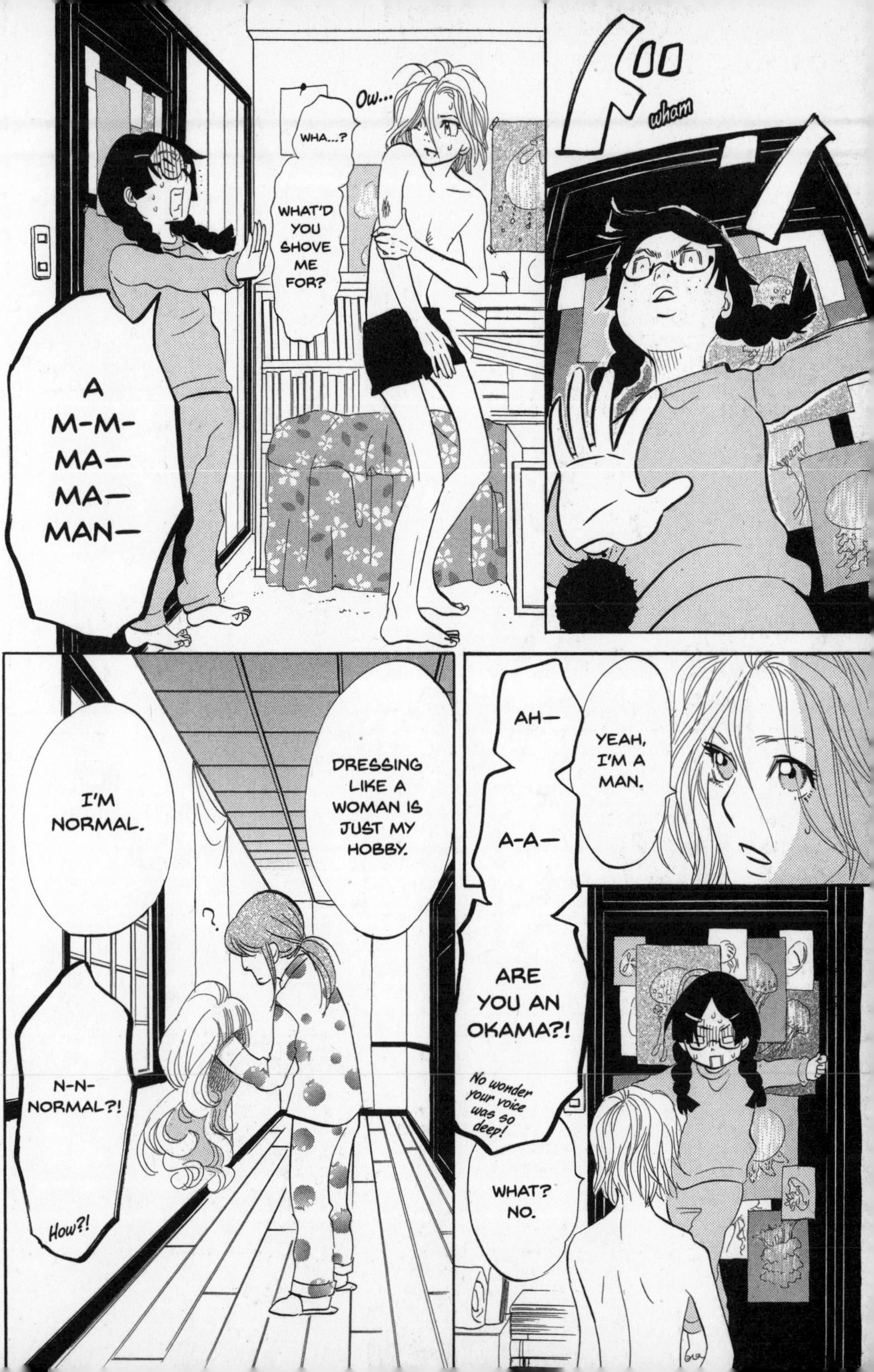

DOO
wham
Ow...
WHA...?
WHAT'D YOU SHOVE ME FOR?
A M-M-MA—MA—MAN—
YEAH, I'M A MAN.
AH—
A-A—
ARE YOU AN OKAMA?!
No wonder your voice was so deep!
WHAT? NO.
DRESSING LIKE A WOMAN IS JUST MY HOBBY.
I'M NORMAL.
?
N-N-NORMAL?!
How?!

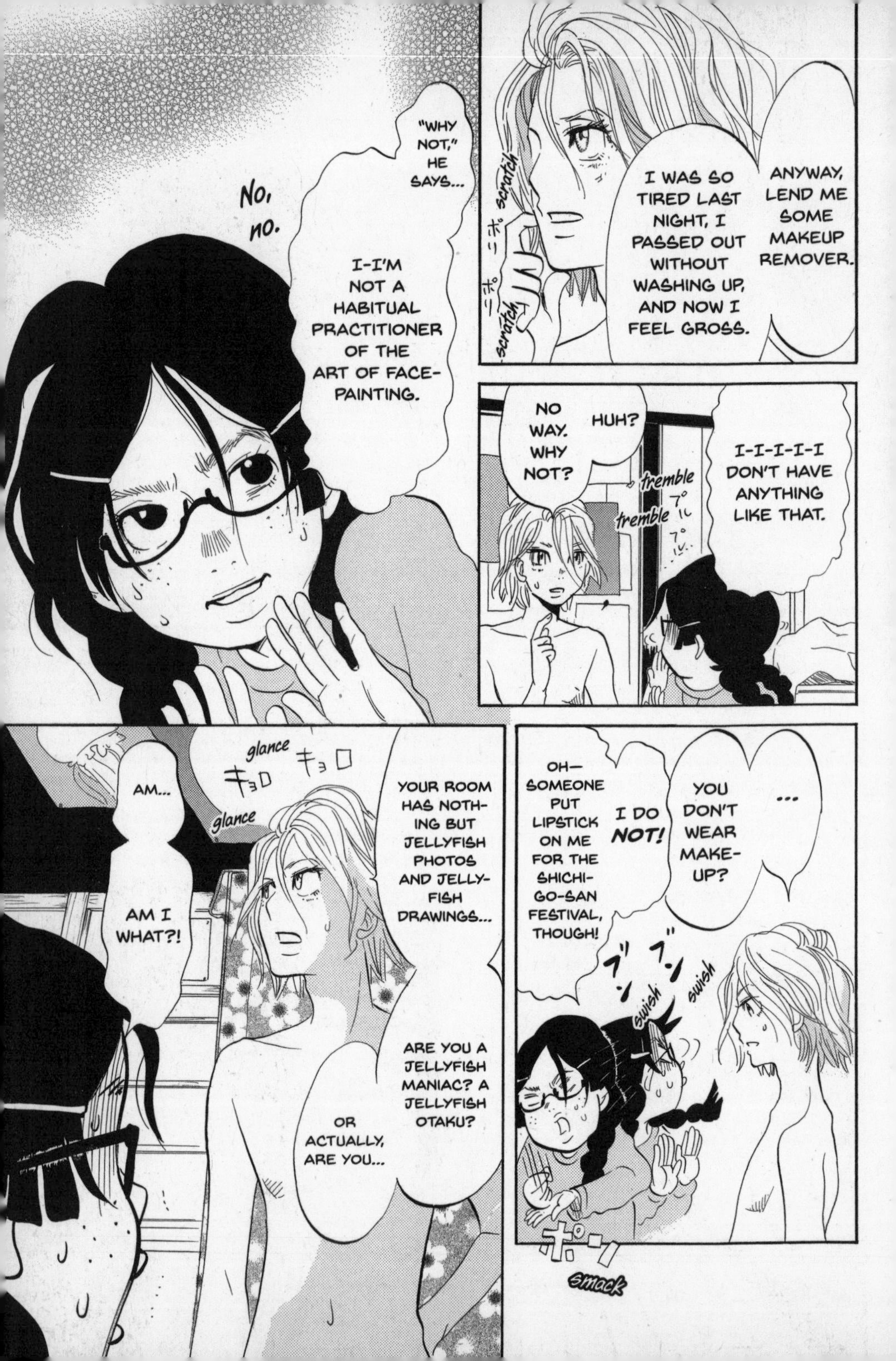
ANYWAY, LEND ME SOME MAKEUP REMOVER.
I WAS SO TIRED LAST NIGHT, I PASSED OUT WITHOUT WASHING UP, AND NOW I FEEL GROSS.
scratch scratch
I-I-I-I-I DON'T HAVE ANYTHING LIKE THAT.
HUH?
NO WAY. WHY NOT?
tremble tremble
"WHY NOT," HE SAYS...
No, no.
I-I'M NOT A HABITUAL PRACTITIONER OF THE ART OF FACE-PAINTING.
...
YOU DON'T WEAR MAKE-UP?
I DO NOT!
OH—SOMEONE PUT LIPSTICK ON ME FOR THE SHICHI-GO-SAN FESTIVAL, THOUGH!
swish swish
smack
glance キョロ
glance キョロ
YOUR ROOM HAS NOTH-ING BUT JELLYFISH PHOTOS AND JELLY-FISH DRAWINGS...
ARE YOU A JELLYFISH MANIAC? A JELLYFISH OTAKU?
OR ACTUALLY, ARE YOU...
AM...
AM I WHAT?!

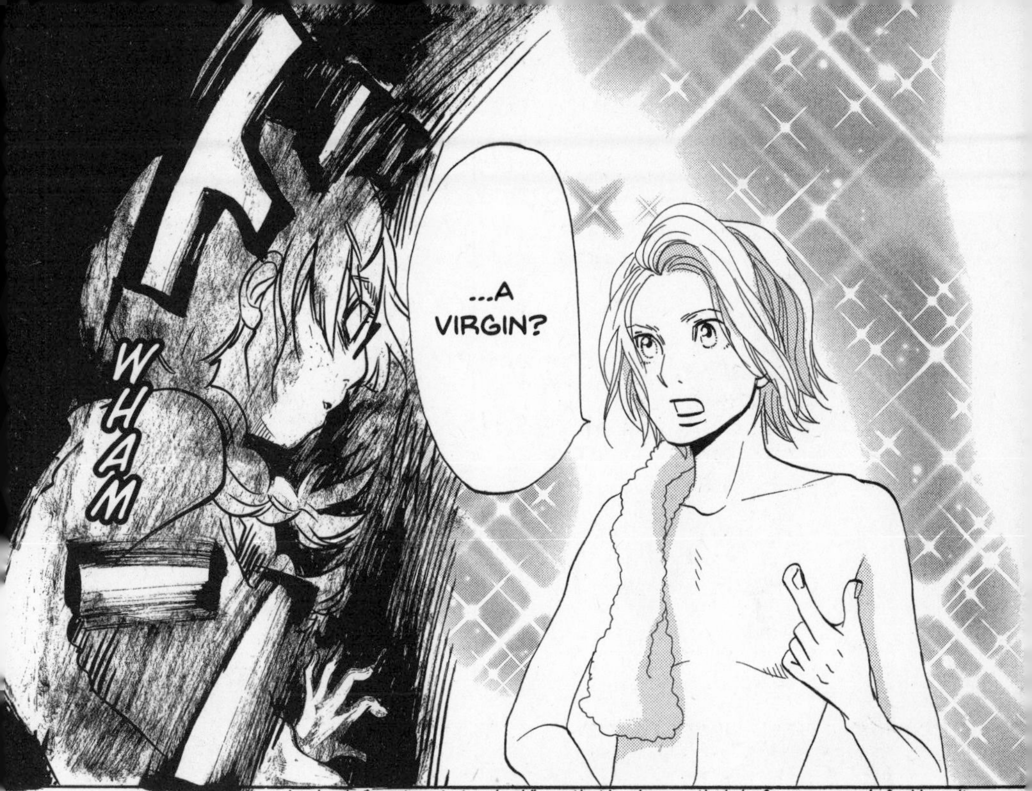
...A VIRGIN?
WHAM

*An iconic department store in Shibuya that has become the hub of young women's fashion culture.

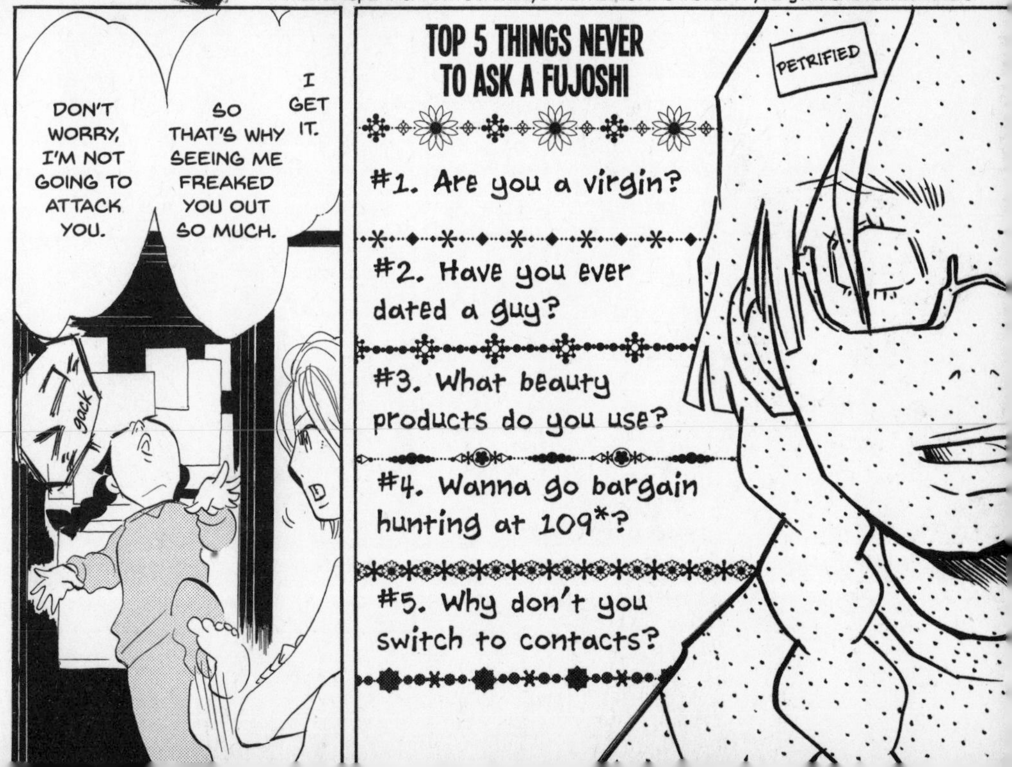
PETRIFIED
TOP 5 THINGS NEVER TO ASK A FUJOSHI
#1. Are you a virgin?
#2. Have you ever dated a guy?
#3. What beauty products do you use?
#4. Wanna go bargain hunting at 109*?
#5. Why don't you switch to contacts?
I GET IT.
SO THAT'S WHY SEEING ME FREAKED YOU OUT SO MUCH.
DON'T WORRY, I'M NOT GOING TO ATTACK YOU.
gack

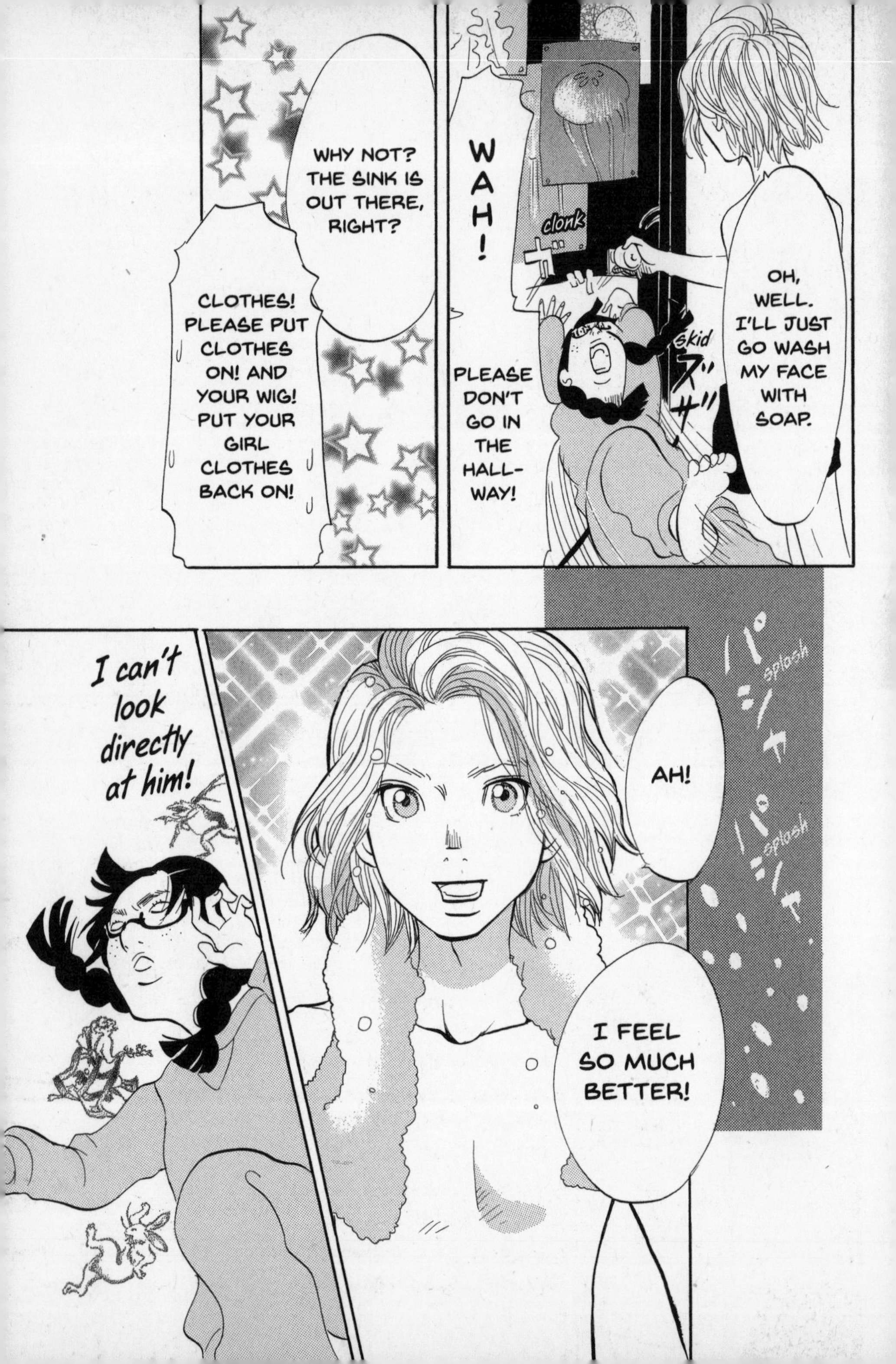

OH, WELL. I'LL JUST GO WASH MY FACE WITH SOAP.
clonk
skid
WAH!
PLEASE DON'T GO IN THE HALLWAY!
WHY NOT? THE SINK IS OUT THERE, RIGHT?
CLOTHES! PLEASE PUT CLOTHES ON! AND YOUR WIG! PUT YOUR GIRL CLOTHES BACK ON!
splash
splash
AH!
I FEEL SO MUCH BETTER!
I can't look directly at him!

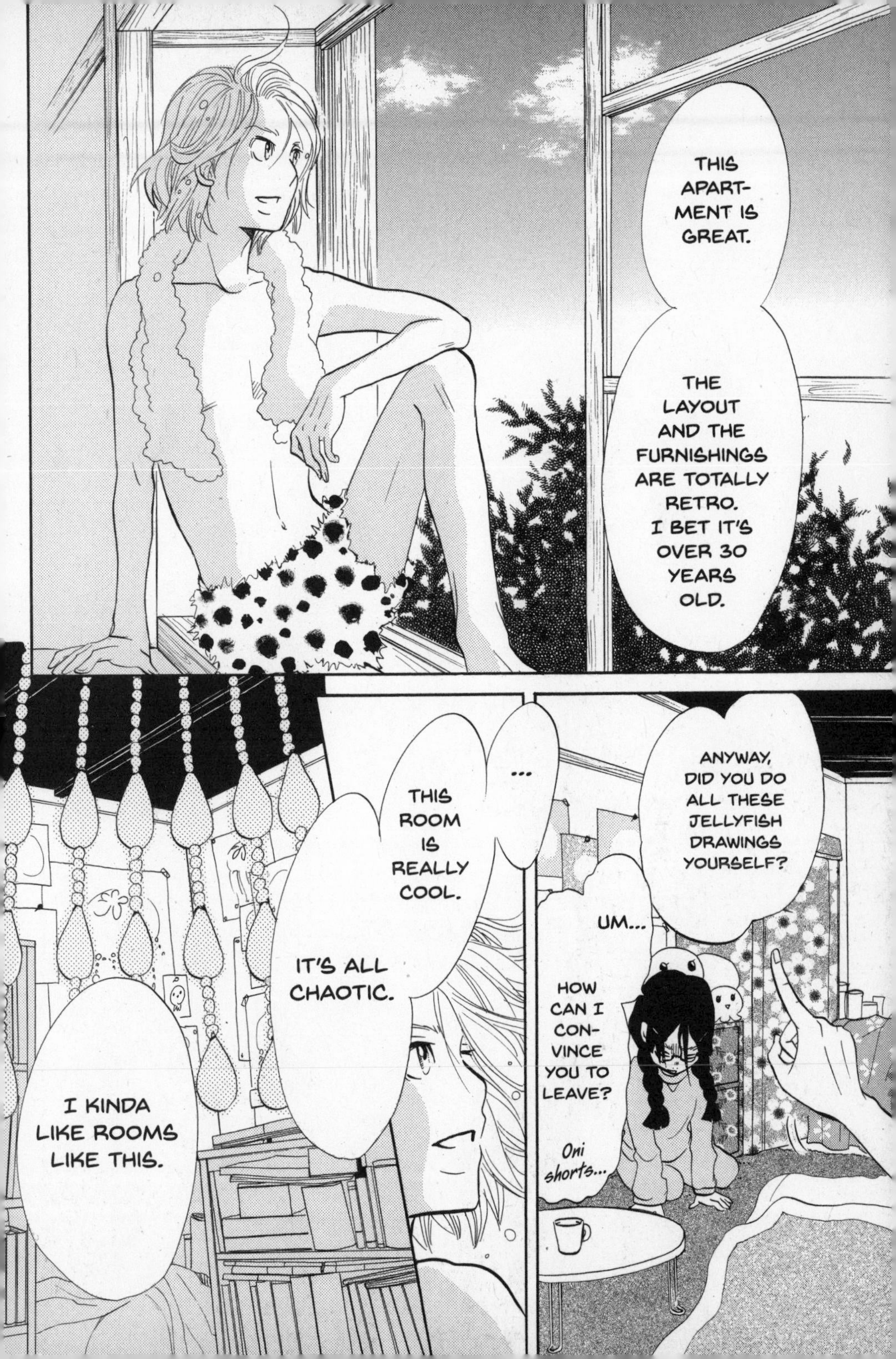
THIS APARTMENT IS GREAT.
THE LAYOUT AND THE FURNISHINGS ARE TOTALLY RETRO. I BET IT'S OVER 30 YEARS OLD.
ANYWAY, DID YOU DO ALL THESE JELLYFISH DRAWINGS YOURSELF?
UM...
HOW CAN I CONVINCE YOU TO LEAVE?
Oni shorts...
...
THIS ROOM IS REALLY COOL.
IT'S ALL CHAOTIC.
I KINDA LIKE ROOMS LIKE THIS.

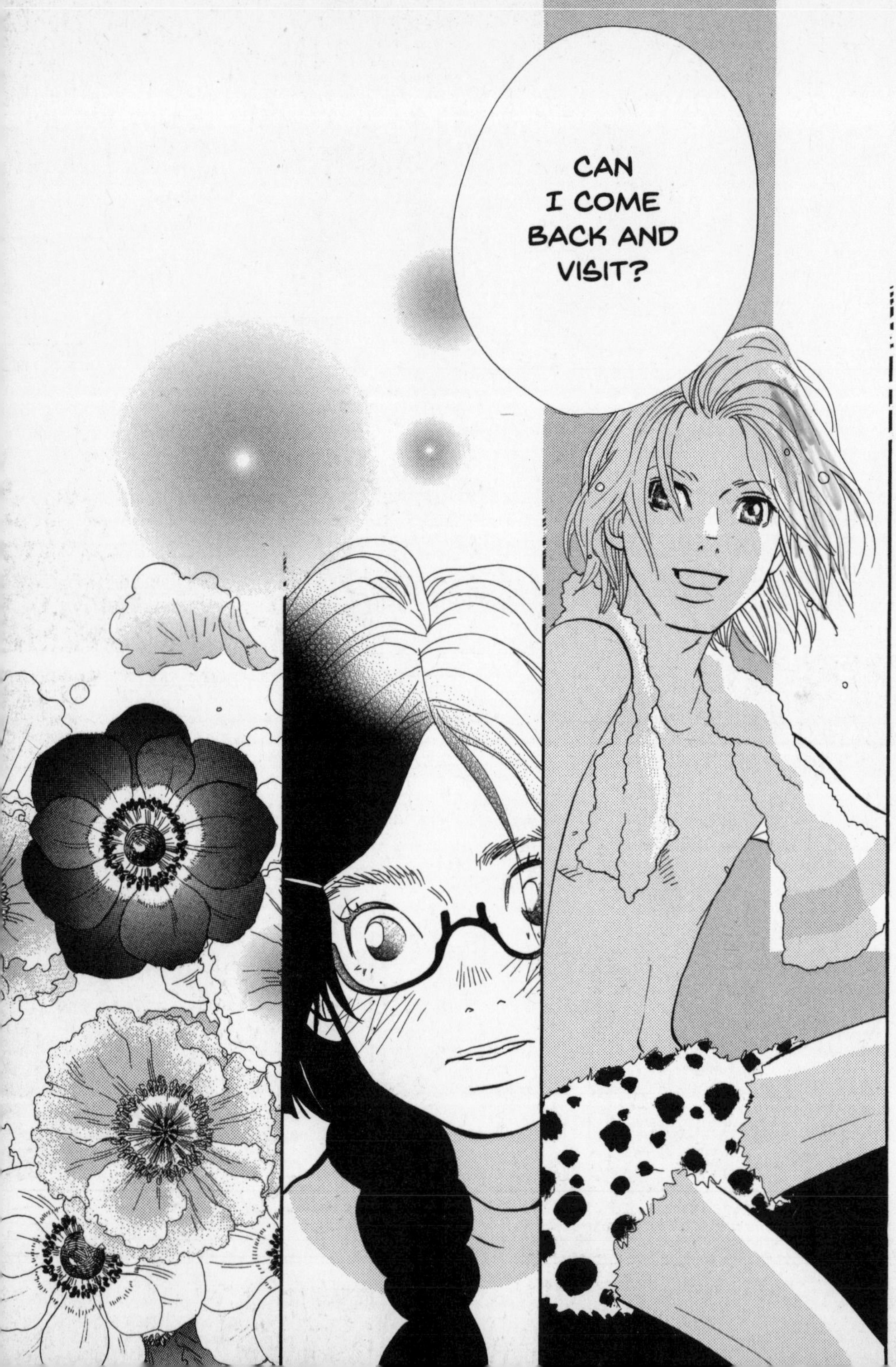
CAN I COME BACK AND VISIT?

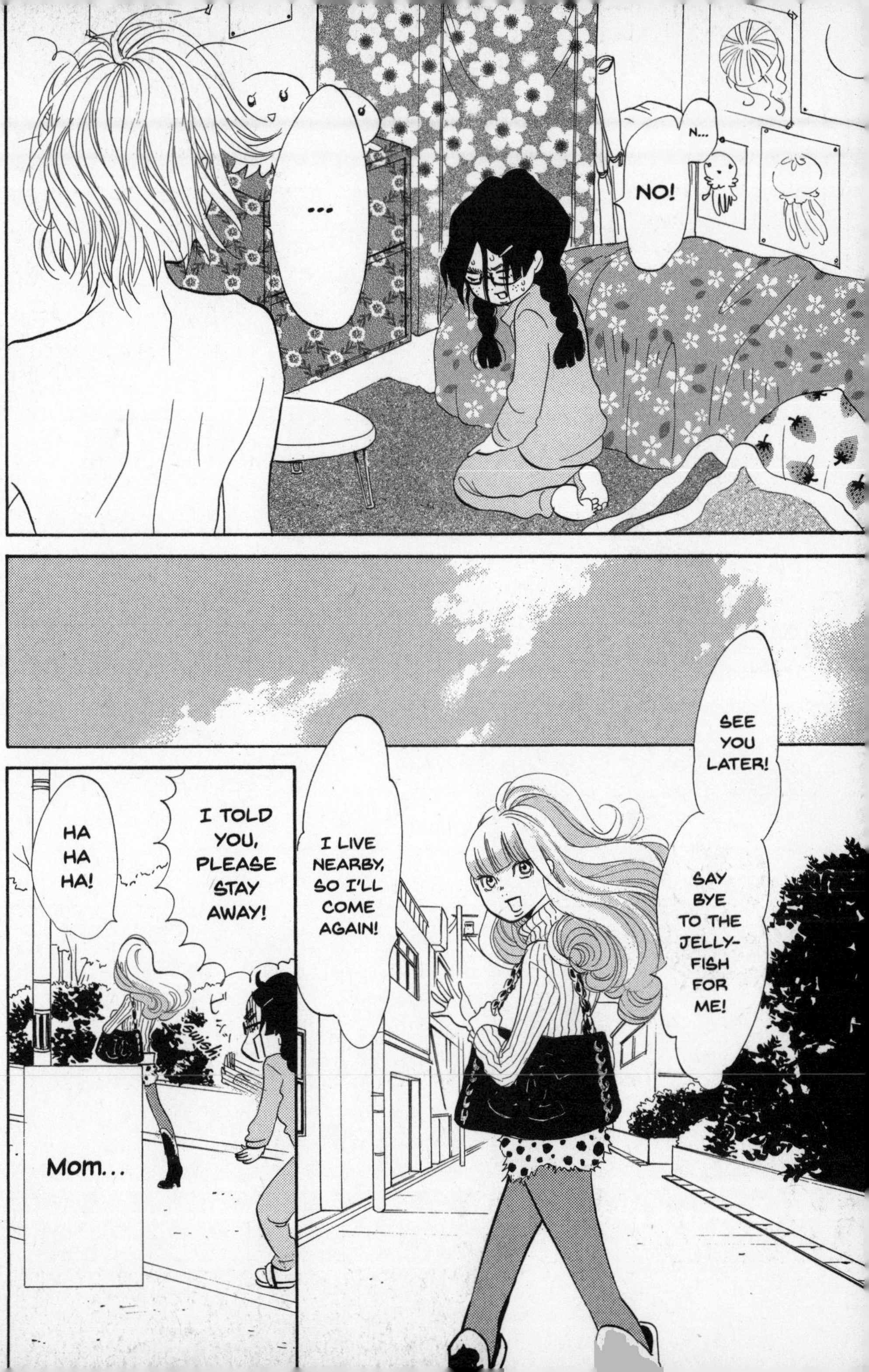
N... NO!
...
SEE YOU LATER!
SAY BYE TO THE JELLY-FISH FOR ME!
I LIVE NEARBY, SO I'LL COME AGAIN!
I TOLD YOU, PLEASE STAY AWAY!
HA HA HA!
SWISH
Mom...

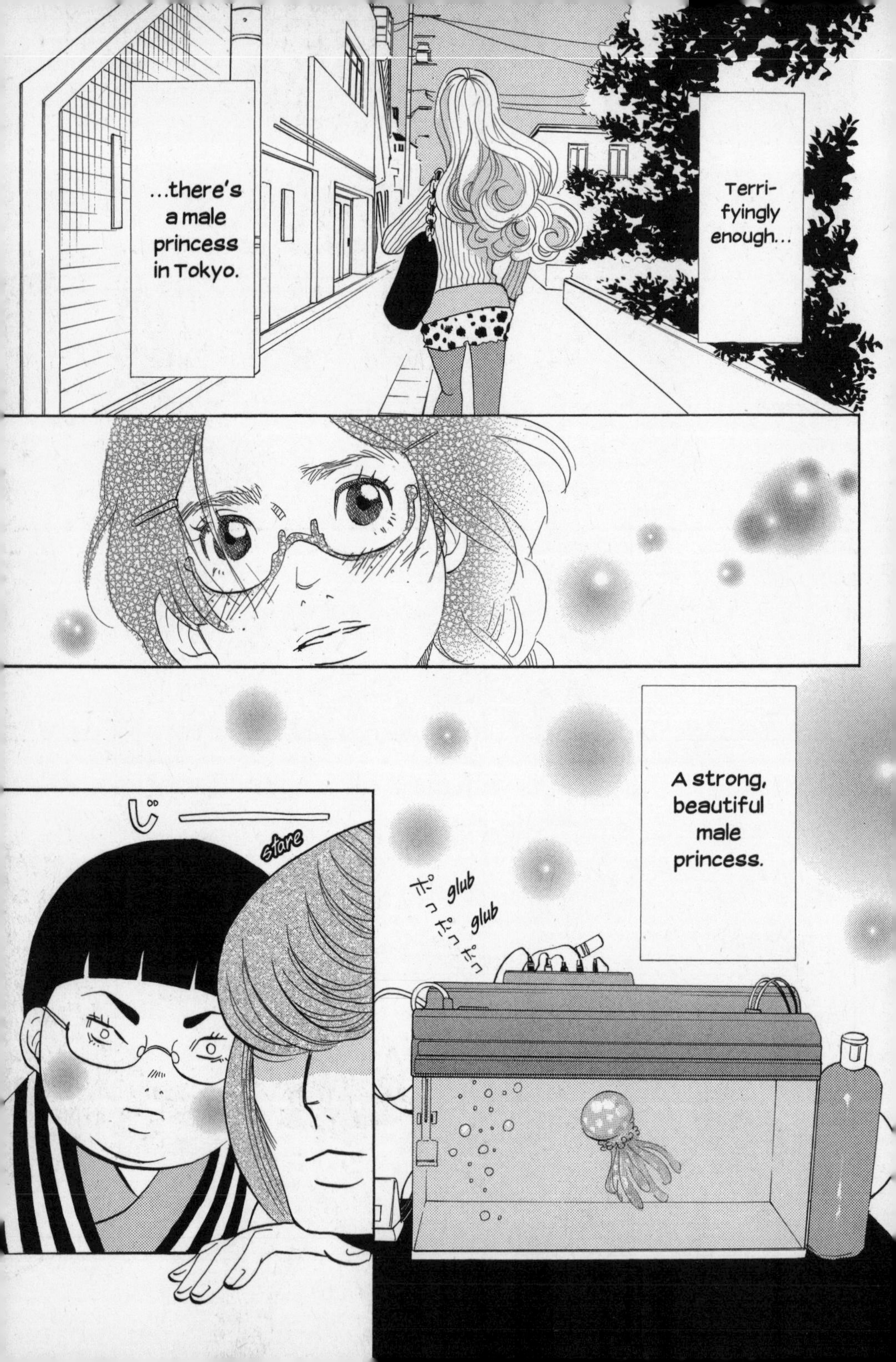
Terri-fyingly enough...
...there's a male princess in Tokyo.
A strong, beautiful male princess.
ポコ ポコ ポコ
glub glub
じ——
stare

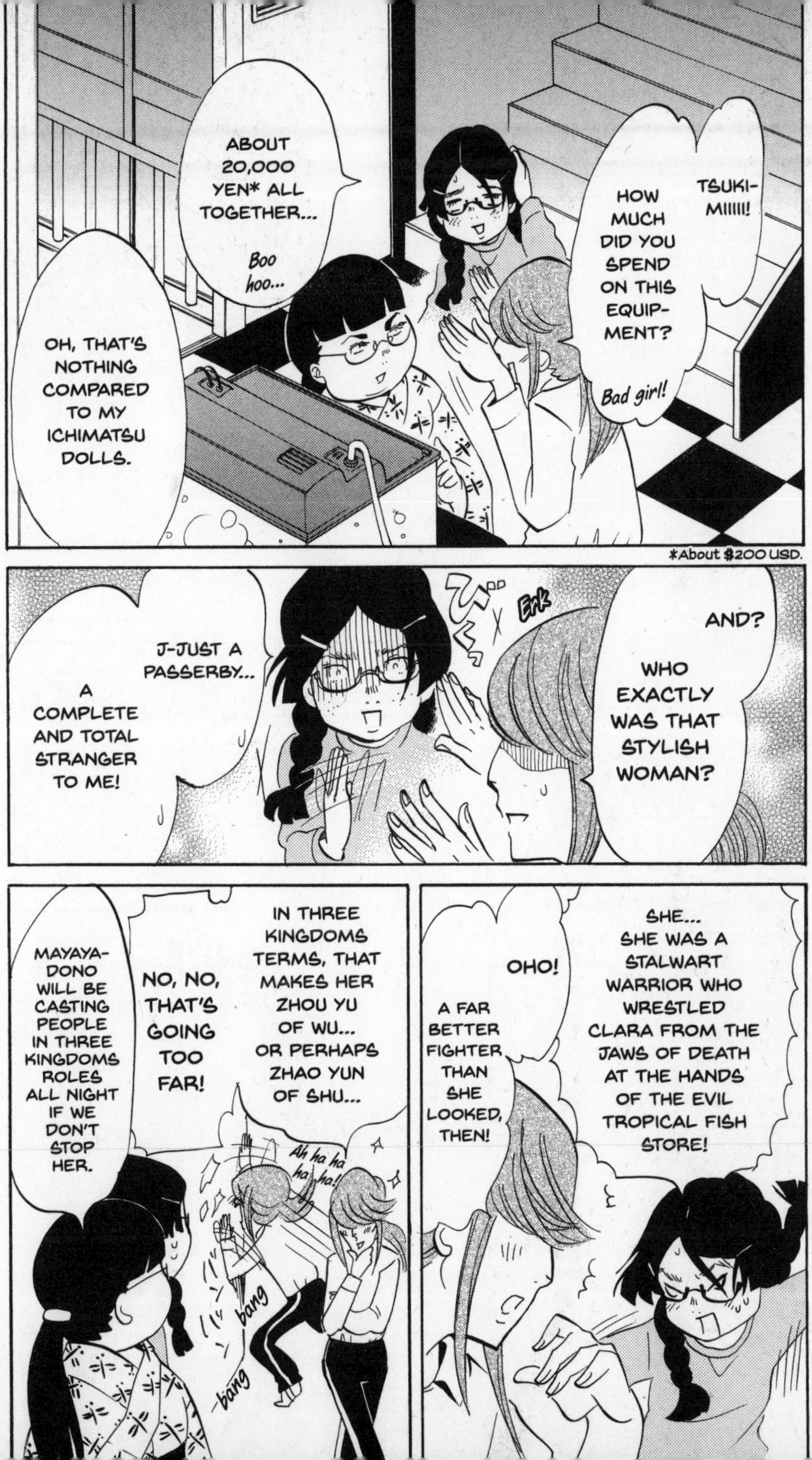
TSUKI-MIIIII!
HOW MUCH DID YOU SPEND ON THIS EQUIPMENT?
Bad girl!
ABOUT 20,000 YEN* ALL TOGETHER...
Boo hoo...
OH, THAT'S NOTHING COMPARED TO MY ICHIMATSU DOLLS.
AND?
WHO EXACTLY WAS THAT STYLISH WOMAN?
Erk
J-JUST A PASSERBY...
A COMPLETE AND TOTAL STRANGER TO ME!
SHE... SHE WAS A STALWART WARRIOR WHO WRESTLED CLARA FROM THE JAWS OF DEATH AT THE HANDS OF THE EVIL TROPICAL FISH STORE!
OHO!
A FAR BETTER FIGHTER THAN SHE LOOKED, THEN!
IN THREE KINGDOMS TERMS, THAT MAKES HER ZHOU YU OF WU... OR PERHAPS ZHAO YUN OF SHU...
Ah ha ha ha ha!
NO, NO, THAT'S GOING TOO FAR!
bang
bang
MAYAYA-DONO WILL BE CASTING PEOPLE IN THREE KINGDOMS ROLES ALL NIGHT IF WE DON'T STOP HER.
*About $200 USD.

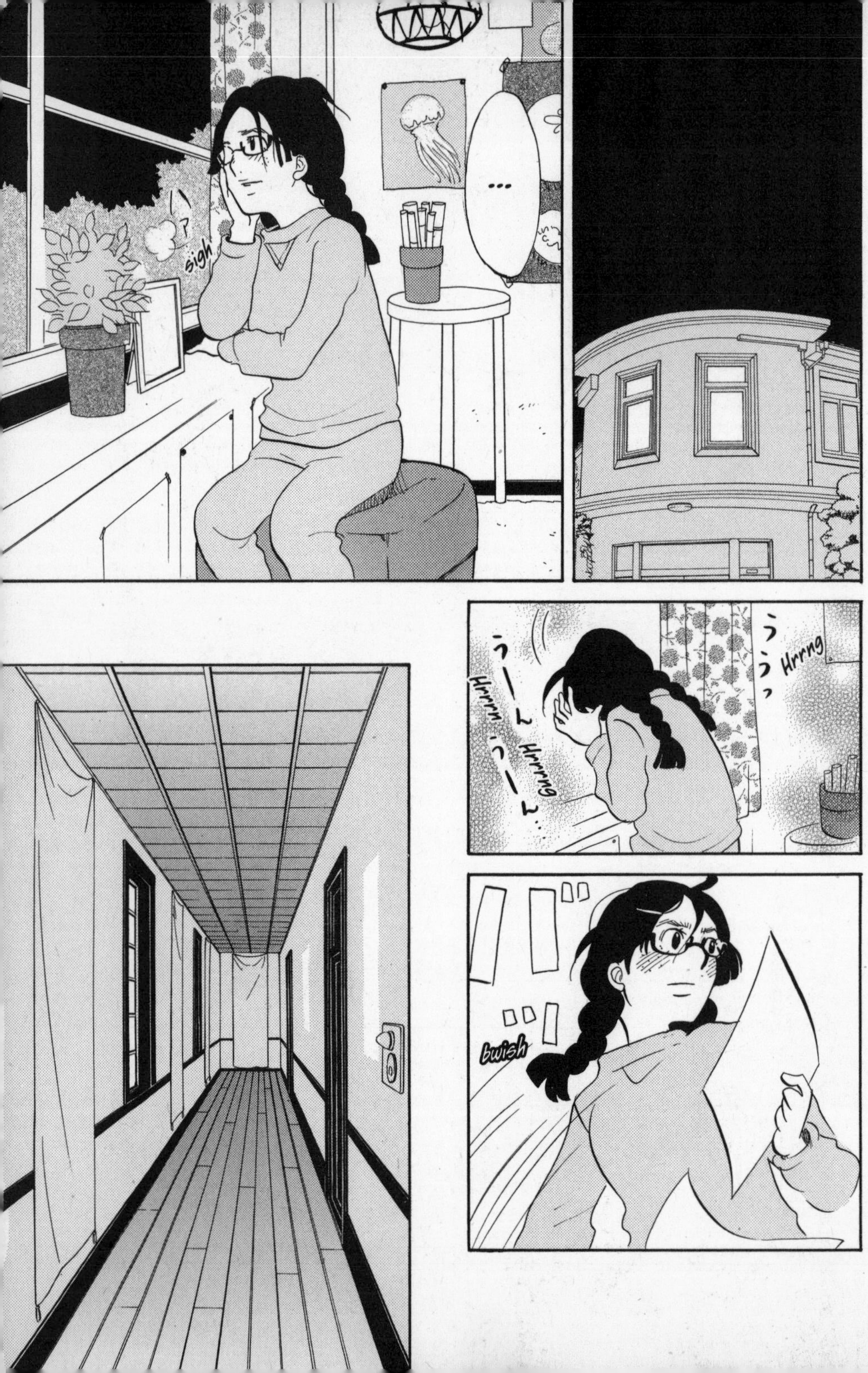
...
ハァ
sigh
うぅっ
Hrrng
うーん
Hrrrn
うーん…
Hrrrng
bwish

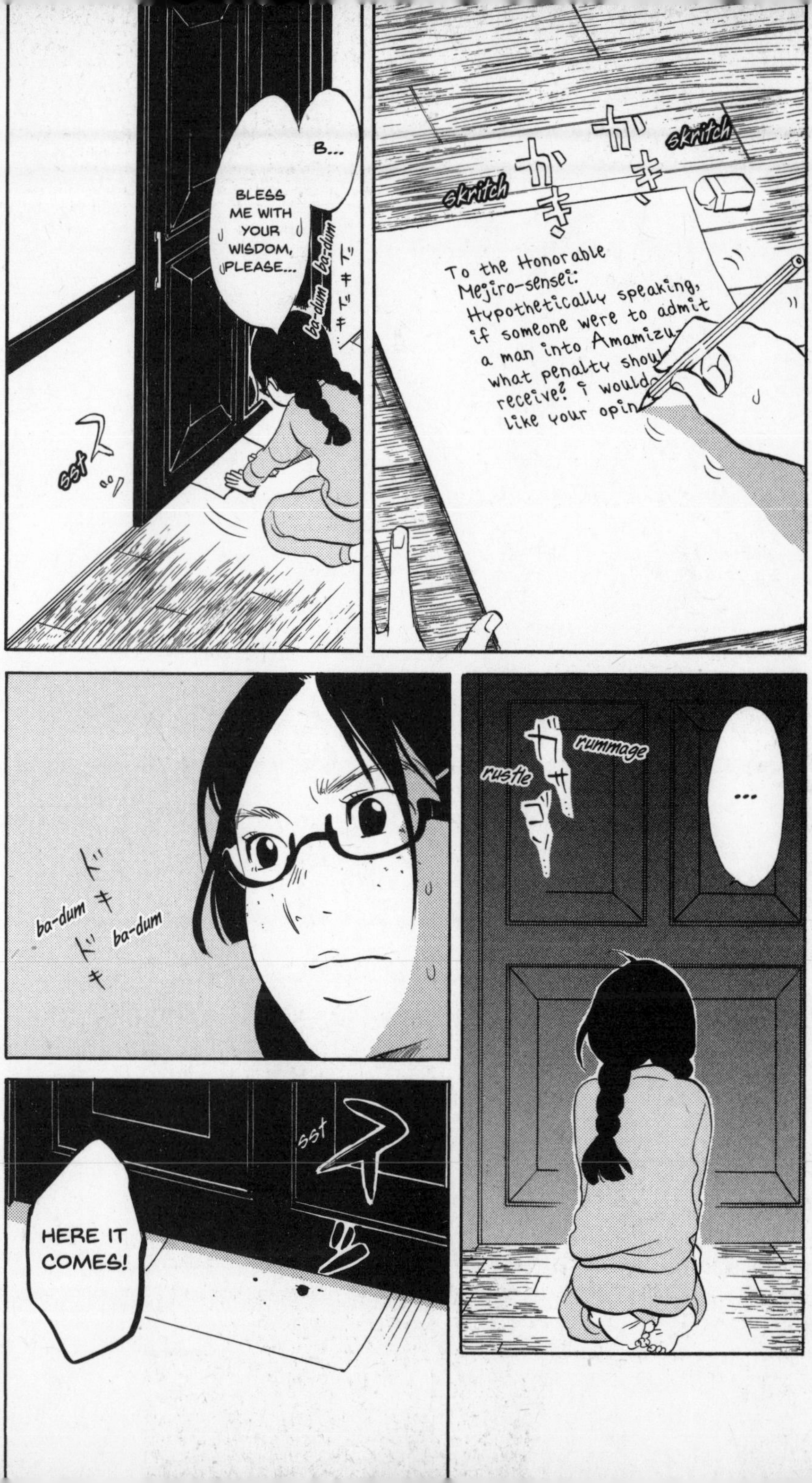
skritch
skritch
To the Honorable
Mejiro-sensei:
Hypothetically speaking,
if someone were to admit
a man into Amamizu-
what penalty shoul
receive? I would
like your opin
B...
BLESS ME WITH YOUR WISDOM, PLEASE...
ba-dum ba-dum
sst
rustle
rummage
...
ba-dum
ba-dum
sst
HERE IT COMES!

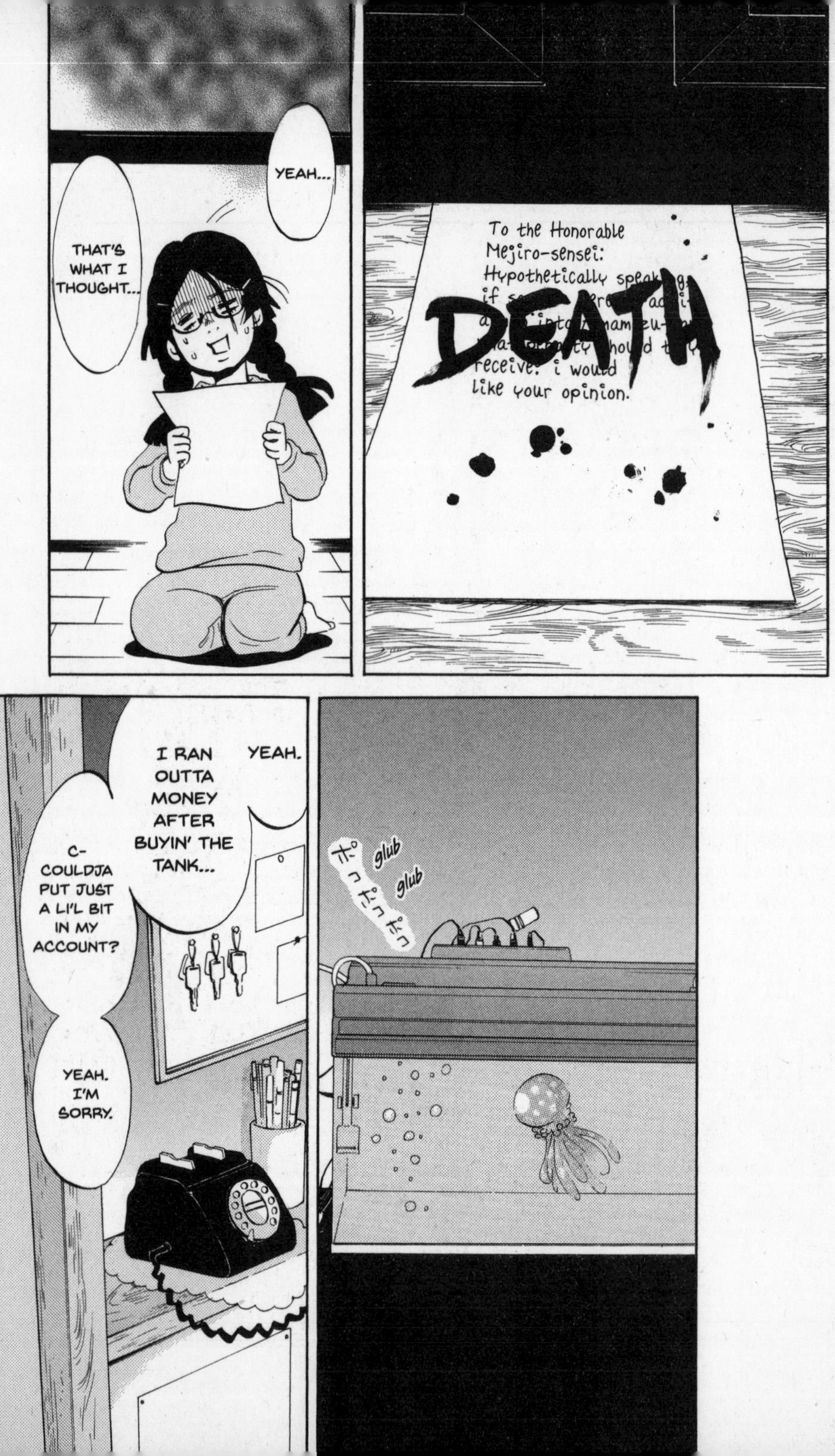
To the Honorable
Mejiro-sensei:
DEATH
receive. i would
like your opinion.
YEAH...
THAT'S WHAT I THOUGHT...
ポコポコポコ
glub
glub
YEAH.
I RAN OUTTA MONEY AFTER BUYIN' THE TANK...
C-COULDJA PUT JUST A LI'L BIT IN MY ACCOUNT?
YEAH. I'M SORRY.

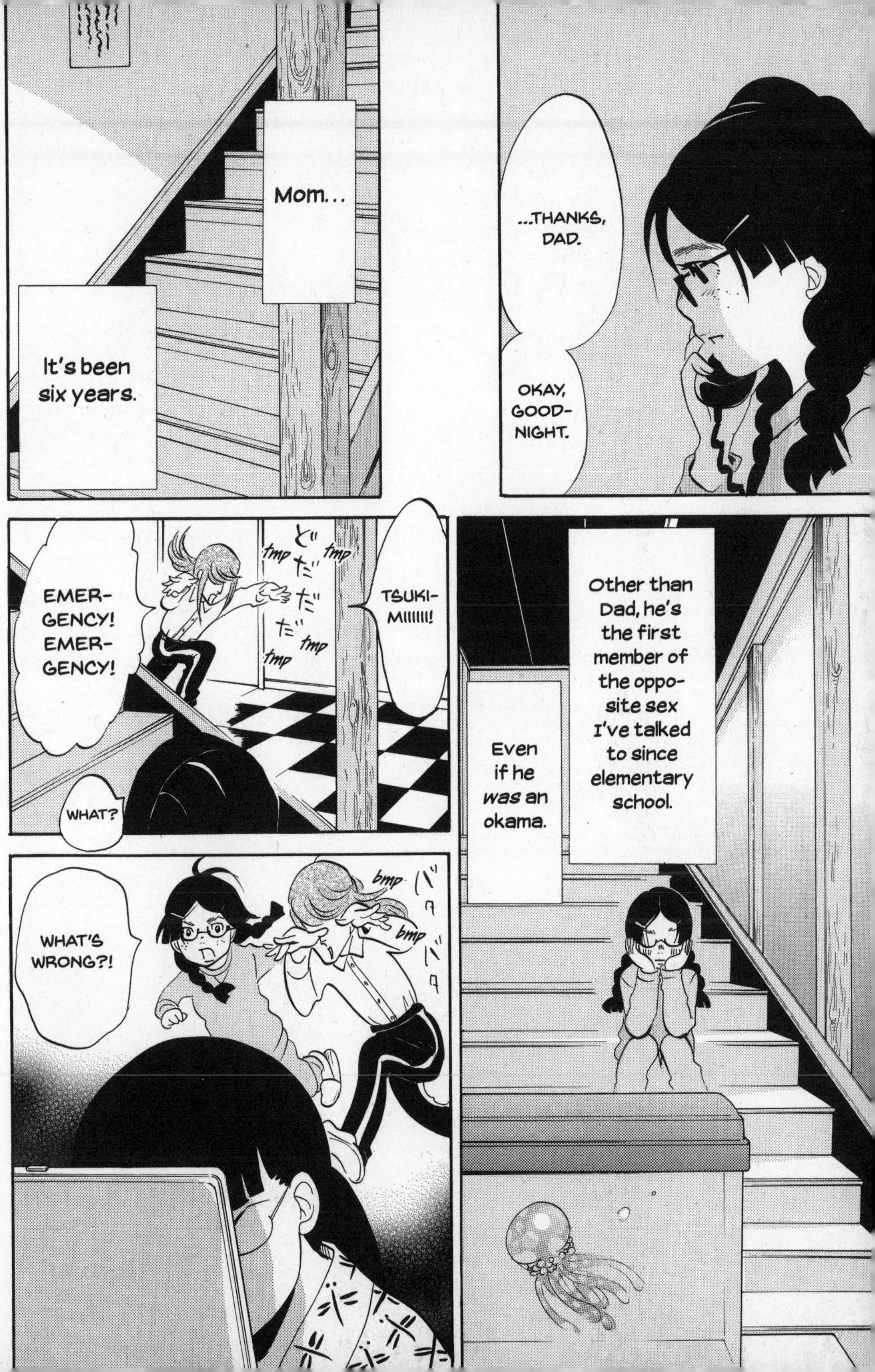
...THANKS, DAD.
OKAY, GOOD-NIGHT.
Mom...
It's been six years.
Other than Dad, he's the first member of the opposite sex I've talked to since elementary school.
Even if he was an okama.
TSUKI-MIIIIII!
どだだだ
tmp tmp tmp tmp
EMER-GENCY! EMER-GENCY!
WHAT?
バタバタ
bmp bmp
WHAT'S WRONG?!

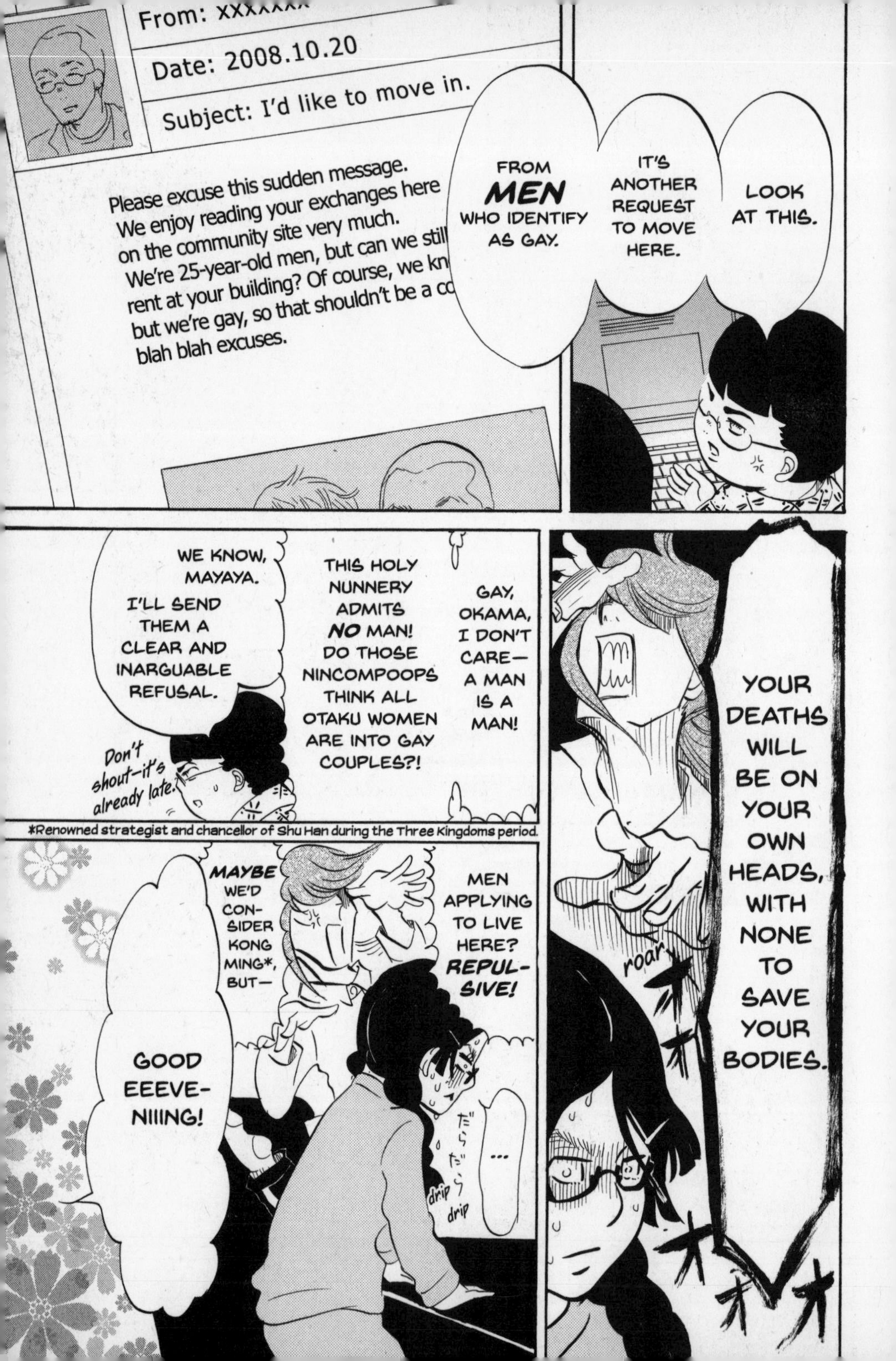
LOOK AT THIS.
IT'S ANOTHER REQUEST TO MOVE HERE.
FROM MEN WHO IDENTIFY AS GAY.
From: XXXXXX
Date: 2008.10.20
Subject: I'd like to move in.
Please excuse this sudden message.
We enjoy reading your exchanges here
on the community site very much.
We're 25-year-old men, but can we still
rent at your building? Of course, we kn
but we're gay, so that shouldn't be a co
blah blah excuses.
YOUR DEATHS WILL BE ON YOUR OWN HEADS, WITH NONE TO SAVE YOUR BODIES.
roar
GAY, OKAMA, I DON'T CARE— A MAN IS A MAN!
THIS HOLY NUNNERY ADMITS NO MAN! DO THOSE NINCOMPOOPS THINK ALL OTAKU WOMEN ARE INTO GAY COUPLES?!
WE KNOW, MAYAYA. I'LL SEND THEM A CLEAR AND INARGUABLE REFUSAL.
Don't shout—it's already late.
MEN APPLYING TO LIVE HERE? REPULSIVE!
MAYBE WE'D CONSIDER KONG MING*, BUT—
...
だらだら
drip drip
GOOD EEEVENIIING!

*Renowned strategist and chancellor of Shu Han during the Three Kingdoms period.

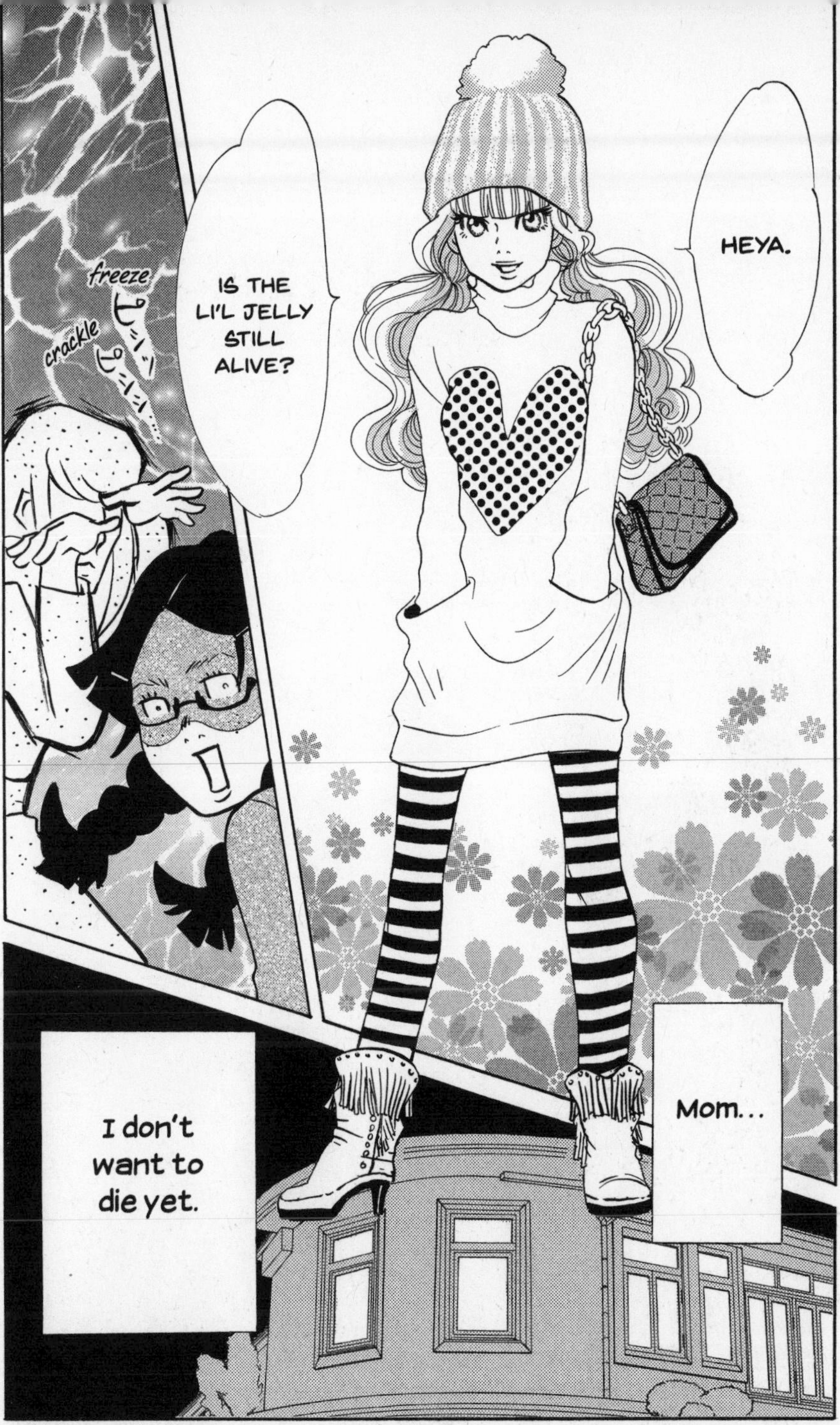

HEYA.
IS THE LI'L JELLY STILL ALIVE?
freeze
crackle
Mom...
I don't want to die yet.

Episode 3
Sukiyaki Western Django

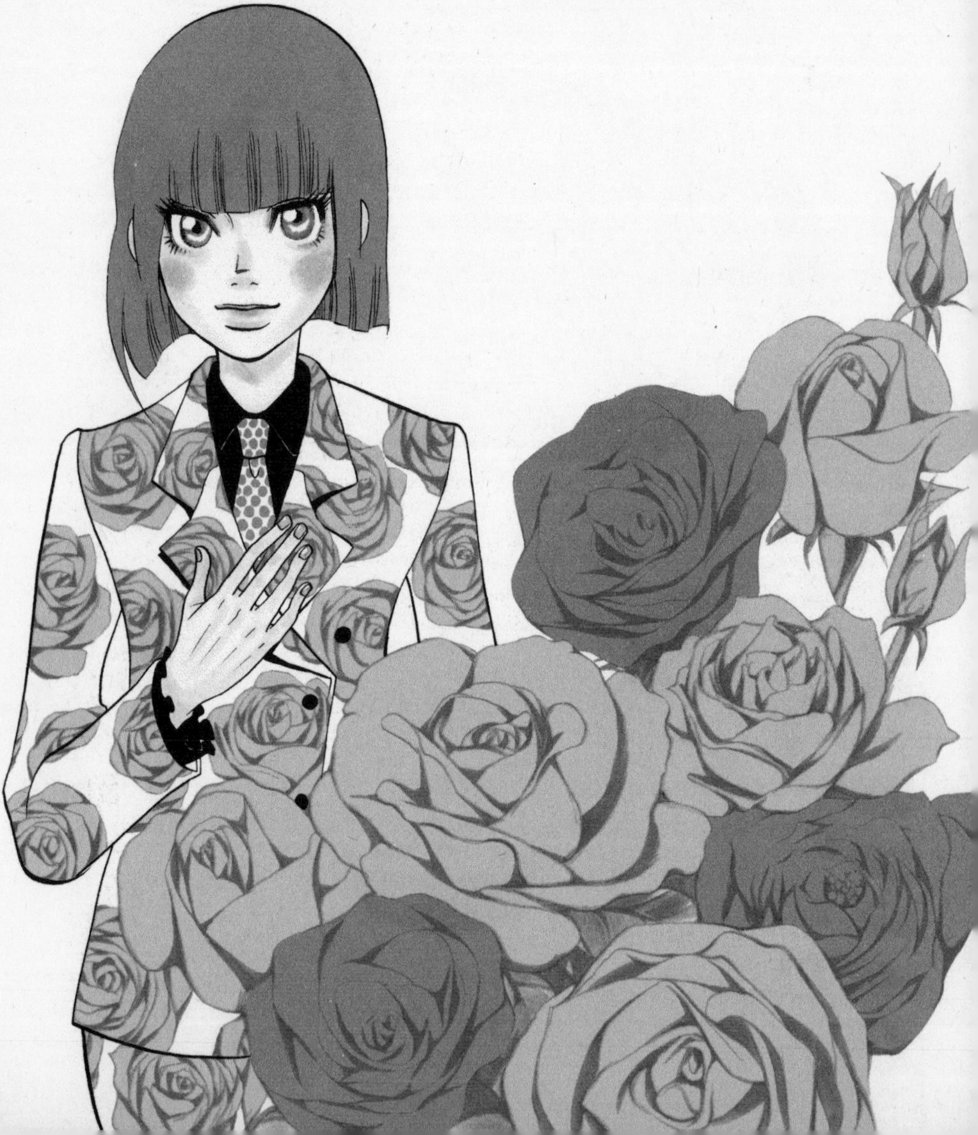

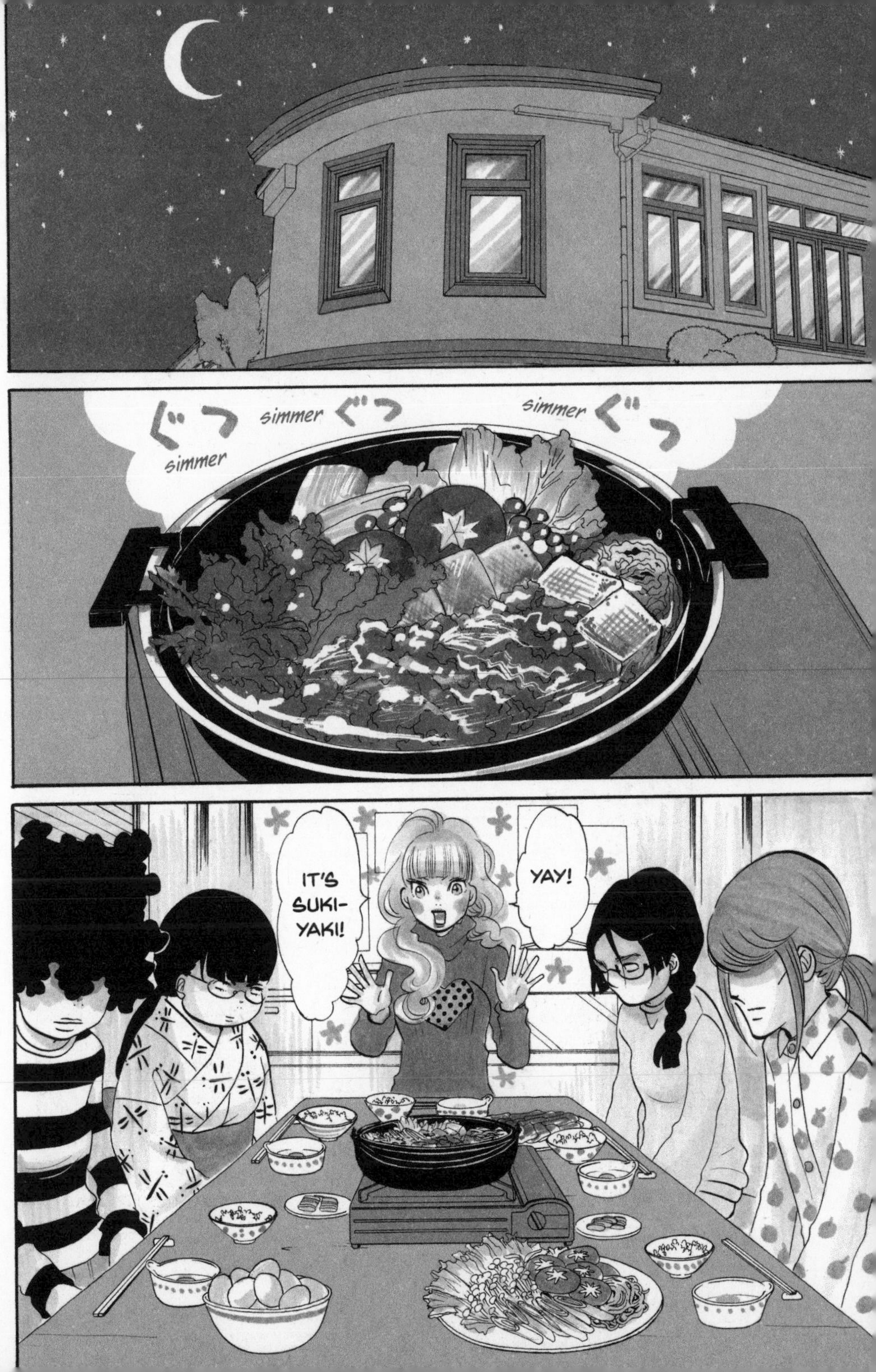
simmer
ぐつ
simmer
ぐつ
ぐつ
simmer
YAY!
IT'S SUKI-YAKI!

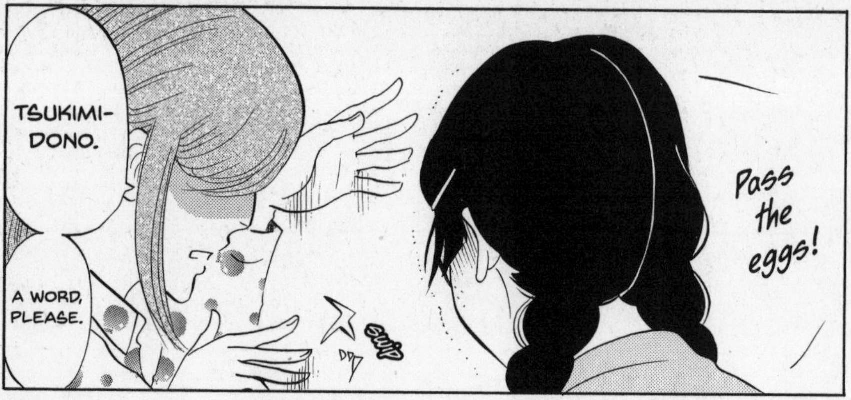
Pass the eggs!
TSUKIMI-DONO.
swip
A WORD, PLEASE.
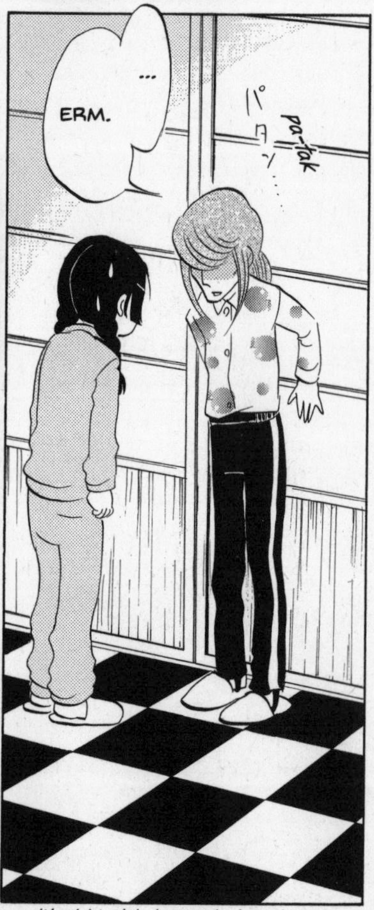
...
ERM.
pa-tak
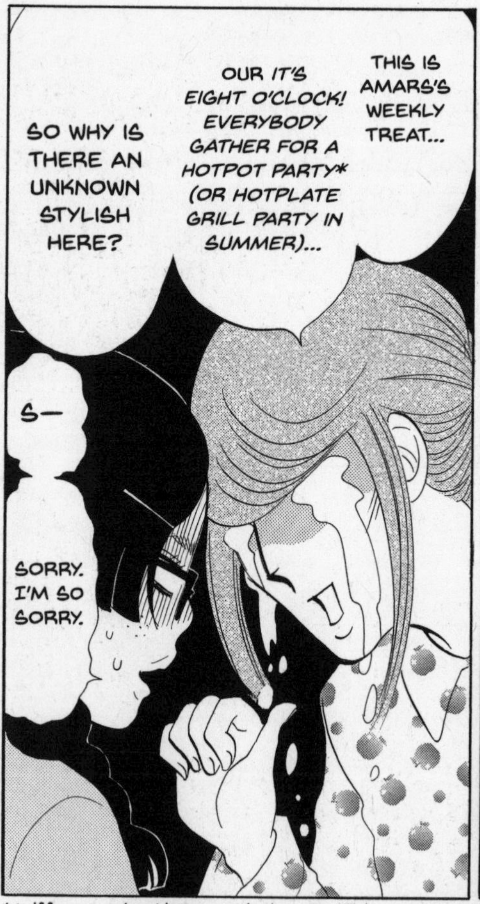
THIS IS AMARS'S WEEKLY TREAT...
OUR *IT'S EIGHT O'CLOCK! EVERYBODY GATHER FOR A HOTPOT PARTY** (OR HOTPLATE GRILL PARTY IN SUMMER)...
SO WHY IS THERE AN UNKNOWN STYLISH HERE?
S—
SORRY. I'M SO SORRY.

*A riff on a prominent '70s comedy show, *Hachiji da yo, Zenin shugo*, or *It's Eight O'Clock, Everybody Gather!*

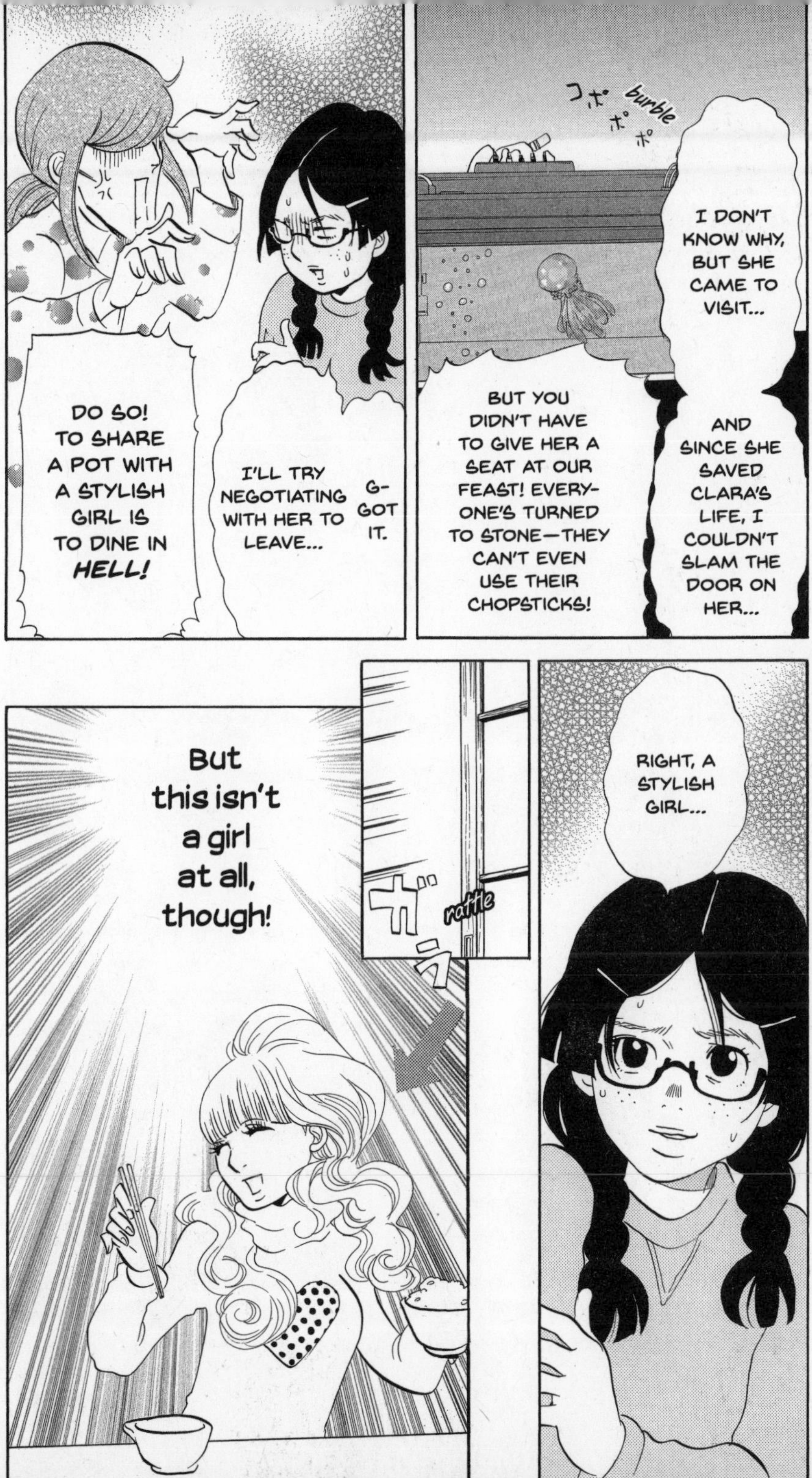
burble
I DON'T KNOW WHY, BUT SHE CAME TO VISIT...
AND SINCE SHE SAVED CLARA'S LIFE, I COULDN'T SLAM THE DOOR ON HER...
BUT YOU DIDN'T HAVE TO GIVE HER A SEAT AT OUR FEAST! EVERYONE'S TURNED TO STONE—THEY CAN'T EVEN USE THEIR CHOPSTICKS!
G-GOT IT.
I'LL TRY NEGOTIATING WITH HER TO LEAVE...
DO SO! TO SHARE A POT WITH A STYLISH GIRL IS TO DINE IN ***HELL!***
RIGHT, A STYLISH GIRL...
rattle
But this isn't a girl at all, though!

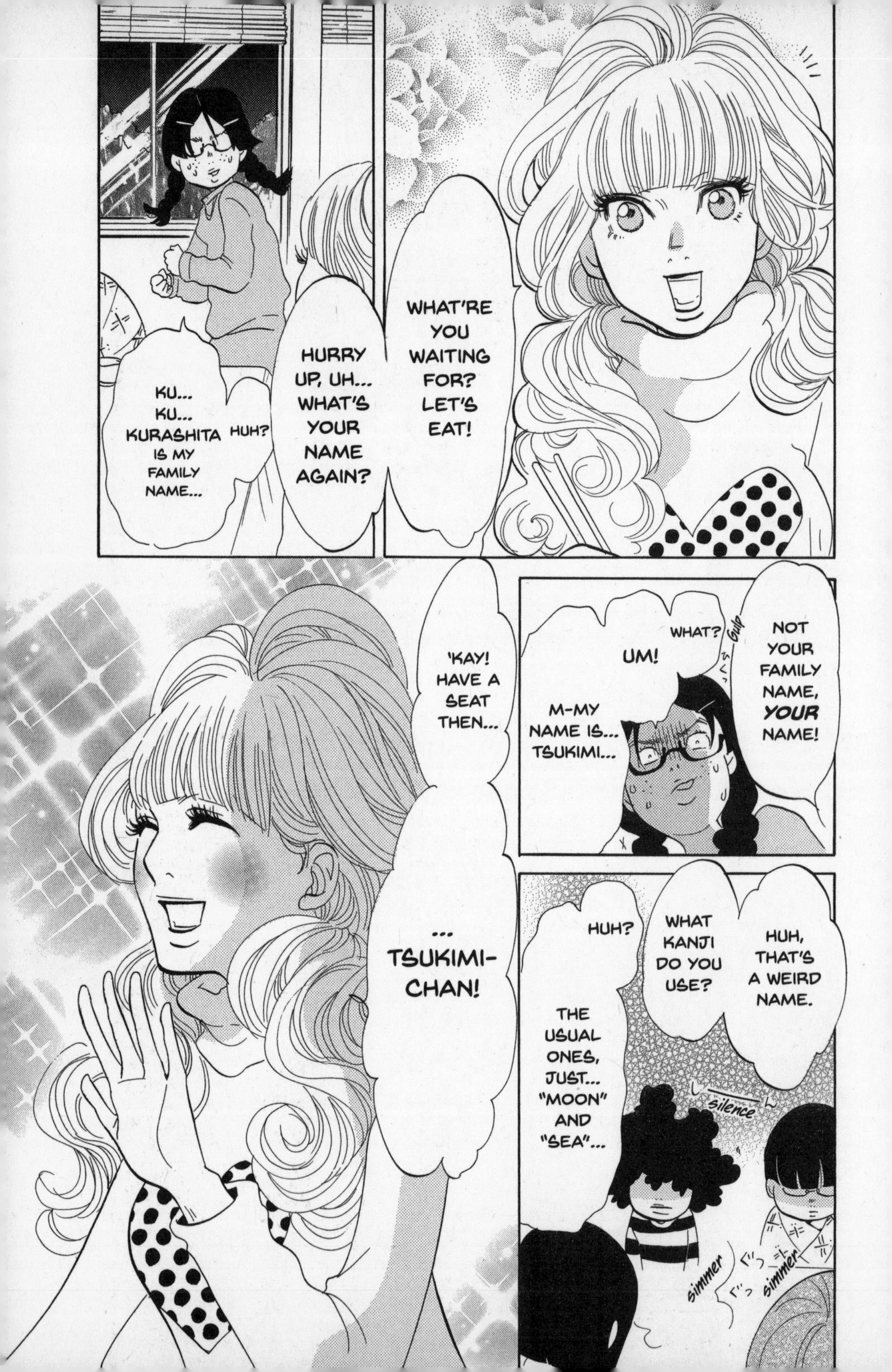
WHAT'RE YOU WAITING FOR? LET'S EAT!
HURRY UP, UH... WHAT'S YOUR NAME AGAIN?
HUH?
KU... KU... KURASHITA IS MY FAMILY NAME...
NOT YOUR FAMILY NAME, ***YOUR*** NAME!
Gulp
WHAT?
UM!
M-MY NAME IS... TSUKIMI...
HUH, THAT'S A WEIRD NAME.
WHAT KANJI DO YOU USE?
HUH?
THE USUAL ONES, JUST... "MOON" AND "SEA"...
silence
simmer
simmer
'KAY! HAVE A SEAT THEN...
... TSUKIMI-CHAN!

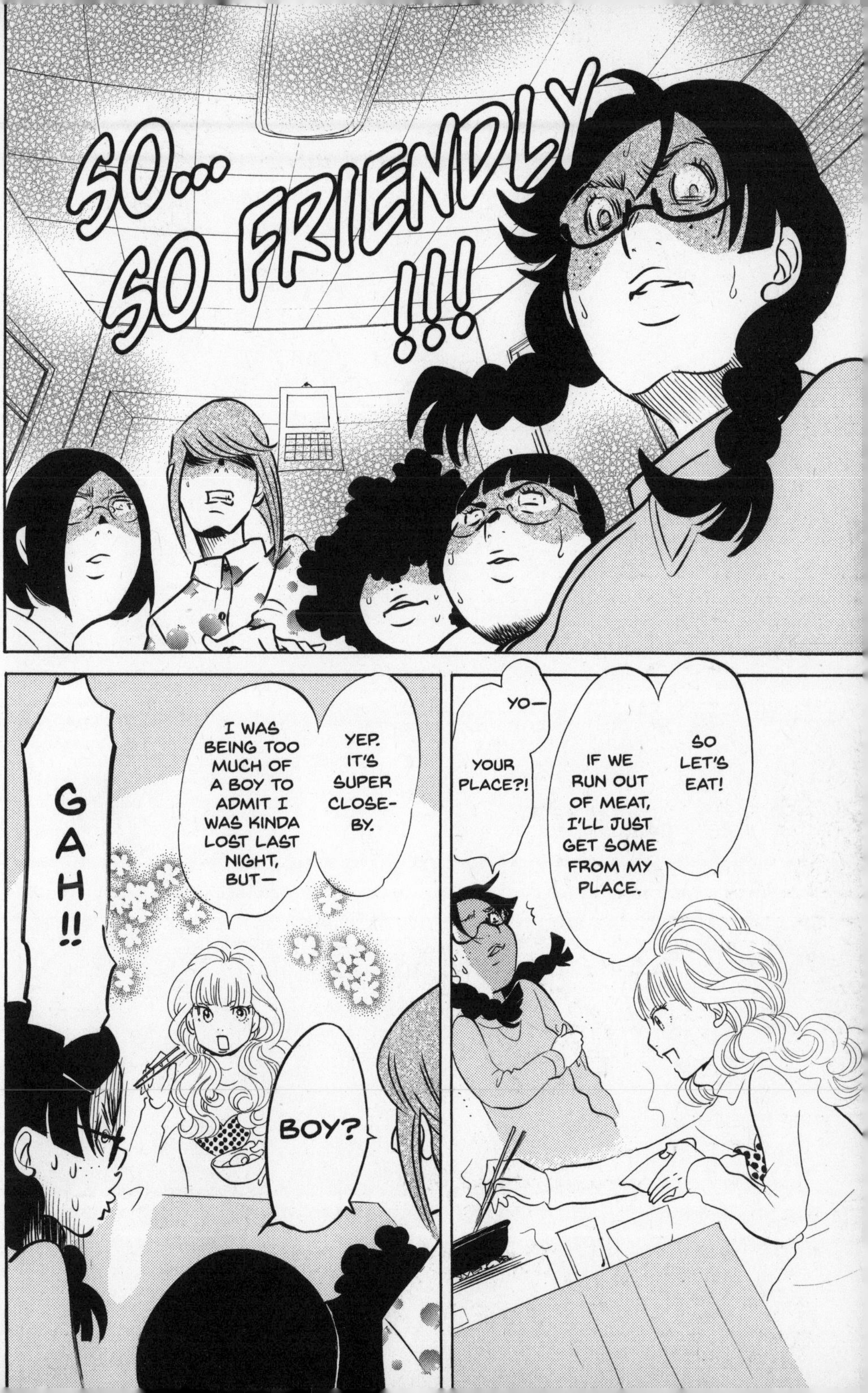
SO... SO FRIENDLY!!!
SO LET'S EAT!
IF WE RUN OUT OF MEAT, I'LL JUST GET SOME FROM MY PLACE.
YO— YOUR PLACE?!
YEP. IT'S SUPER CLOSE-BY.
I WAS BEING TOO MUCH OF A BOY TO ADMIT I WAS KINDA LOST LAST NIGHT, BUT—
BOY?
GAH!!

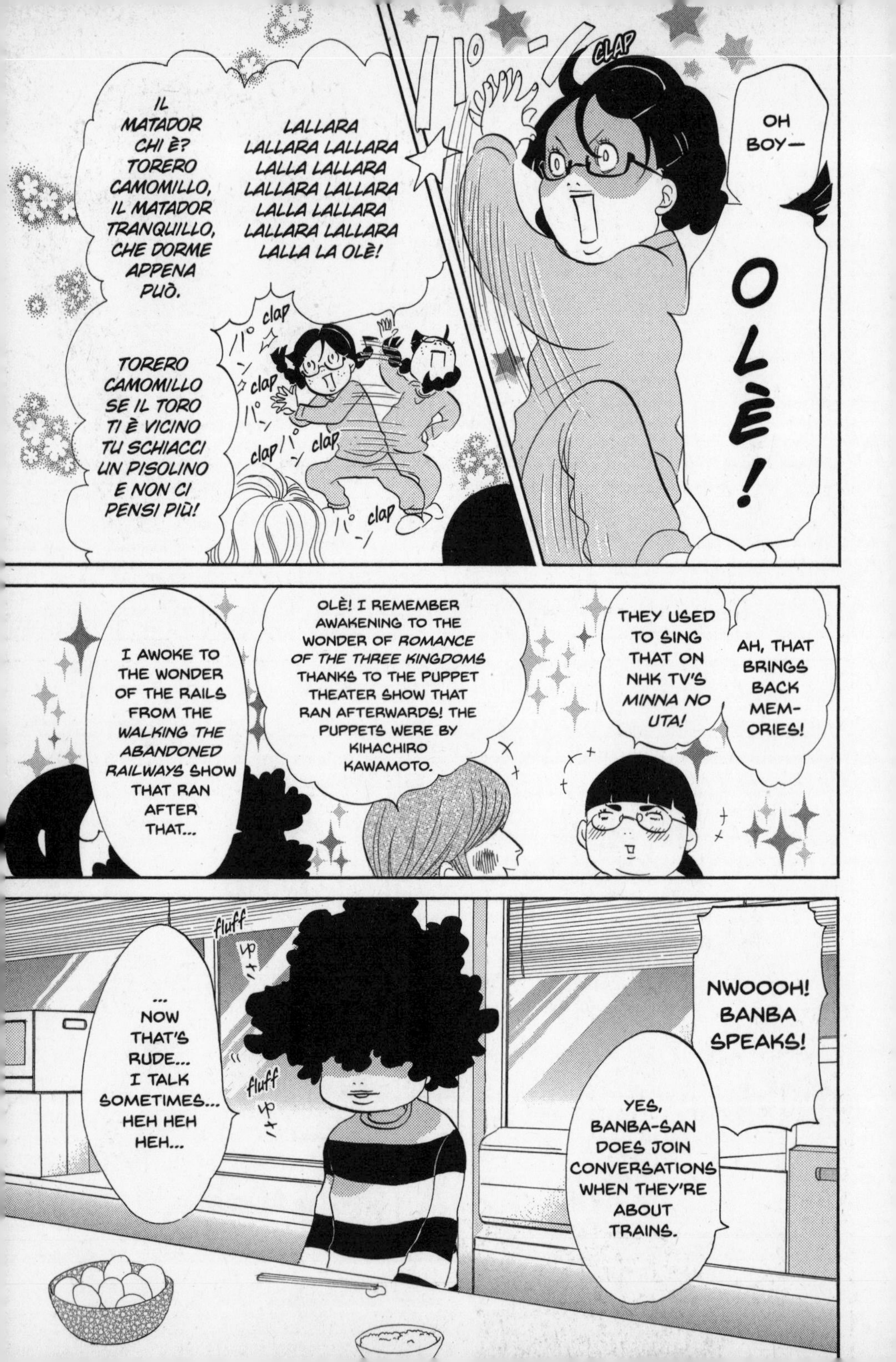

OH BOY—
CLAP
OLÈ!
LALLARA LALLARA LALLARA LALLA LALLARA LALLARA LALLARA LALLA LALLARA LALLARA LALLARA LALLA LA OLÈ!
IL MATADOR CHI È? TORERO CAMOMILLO, IL MATADOR TRANQUILLO, CHE DORME APPENA PUÒ.
clap
clap
TORERO CAMOMILLO SE IL TORO TI È VICINO TU SCHIACCI UN PISOLINO E NON CI PENSI PIÙ!
clap
clap
clap
AH, THAT BRINGS BACK MEM-ORIES!
THEY USED TO SING THAT ON NHK TV'S MINNA NO UTA!
OLÈ! I REMEMBER AWAKENING TO THE WONDER OF ROMANCE OF THE THREE KINGDOMS THANKS TO THE PUPPET THEATER SHOW THAT RAN AFTERWARDS! THE PUPPETS WERE BY KIHACHIRO KAWAMOTO.
I AWOKE TO THE WONDER OF THE RAILS FROM THE WALKING THE ABANDONED RAILWAYS SHOW THAT RAN AFTER THAT...
NWOOOH! BANBA SPEAKS!
YES, BANBA-SAN DOES JOIN CONVERSATIONS WHEN THEY'RE ABOUT TRAINS.
fluff
fluff
... NOW THAT'S RUDE... I TALK SOMETIMES... HEH HEH HEH...

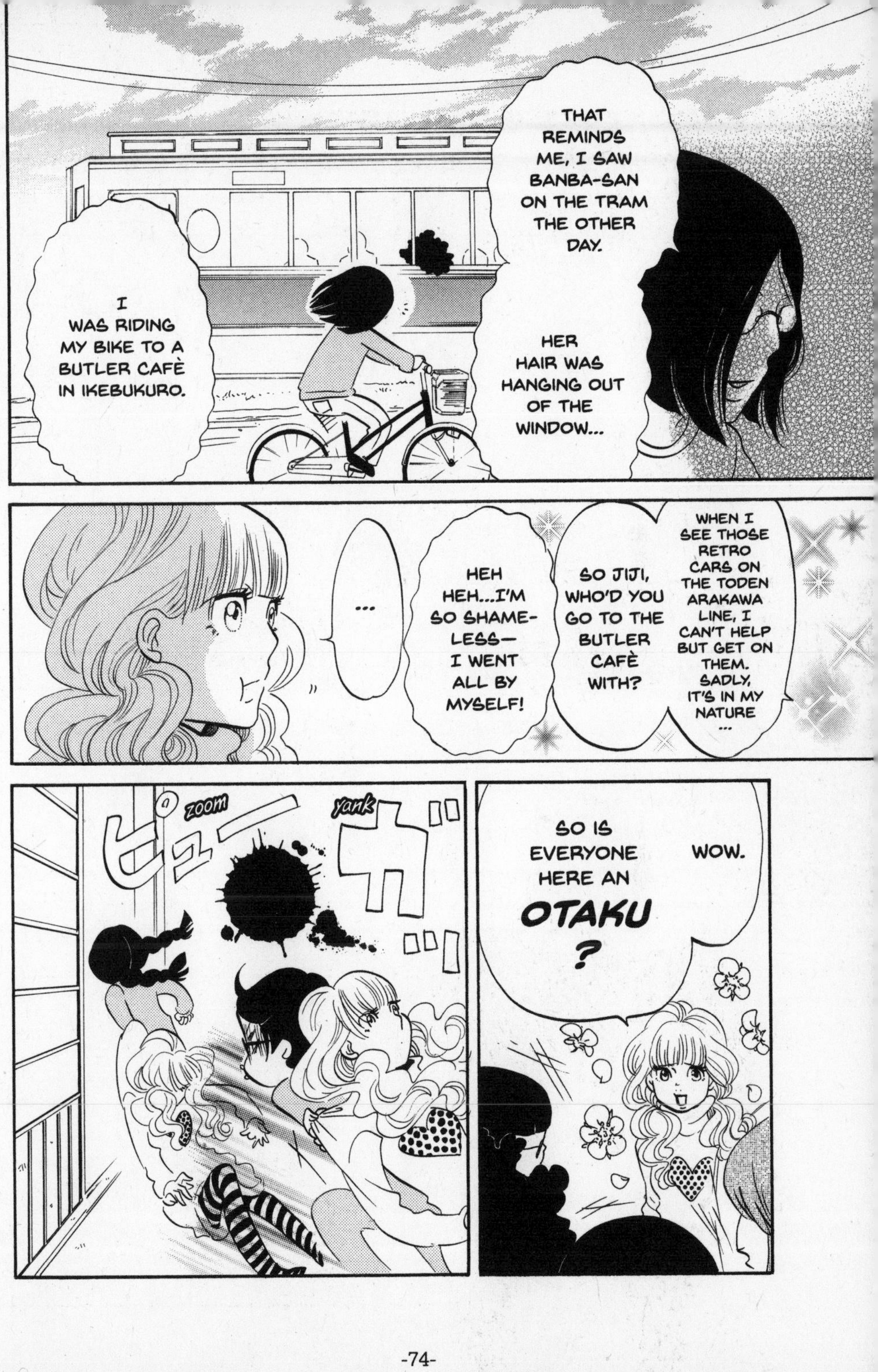
THAT REMINDS ME, I SAW BANBA-SAN ON THE TRAM THE OTHER DAY.
HER HAIR WAS HANGING OUT OF THE WINDOW...
I WAS RIDING MY BIKE TO A BUTLER CAFÈ IN IKEBUKURO.
WHEN I SEE THOSE RETRO CARS ON THE TODEN ARAKAWA LINE, I CAN'T HELP BUT GET ON THEM. SADLY, IT'S IN MY NATURE...
SO JIJI, WHO'D YOU GO TO THE BUTLER CAFÈ WITH?
HEH HEH...I'M SO SHAME-LESS— I WENT ALL BY MYSELF!
...
WOW.
SO IS EVERYONE HERE AN OTAKU?
ガッ
yank
ピュー
zoom

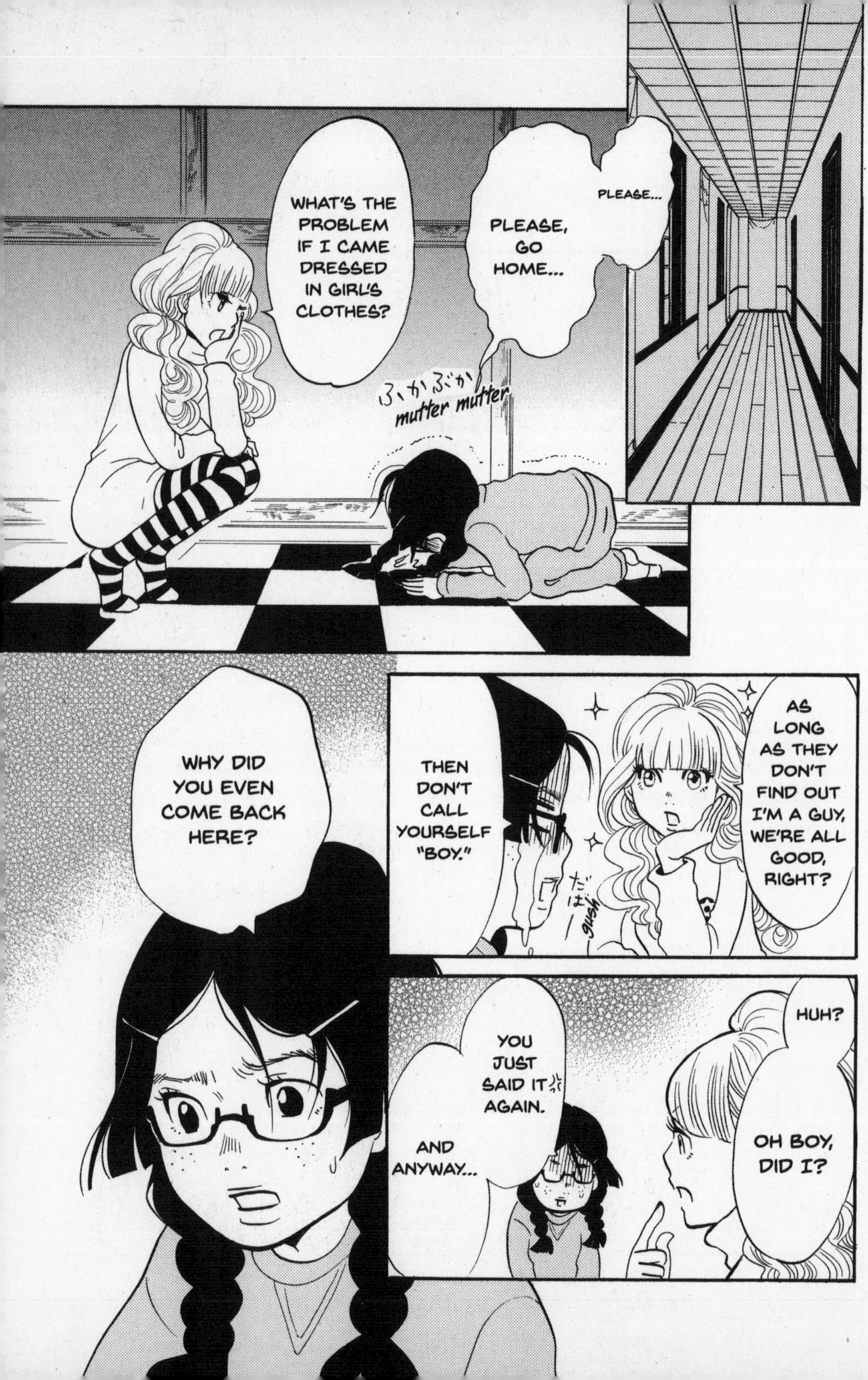
PLEASE...
PLEASE, GO HOME...
ふかぶか
mutter mutter
WHAT'S THE PROBLEM IF I CAME DRESSED IN GIRL'S CLOTHES?
AS LONG AS THEY DON'T FIND OUT I'M A GUY, WE'RE ALL GOOD, RIGHT?
THEN DON'T CALL YOURSELF "BOY."
だはー
gush
HUH?
OH BOY, DID I?
YOU JUST SAID IT AGAIN.
AND ANYWAY...
WHY DID YOU EVEN COME BACK HERE?

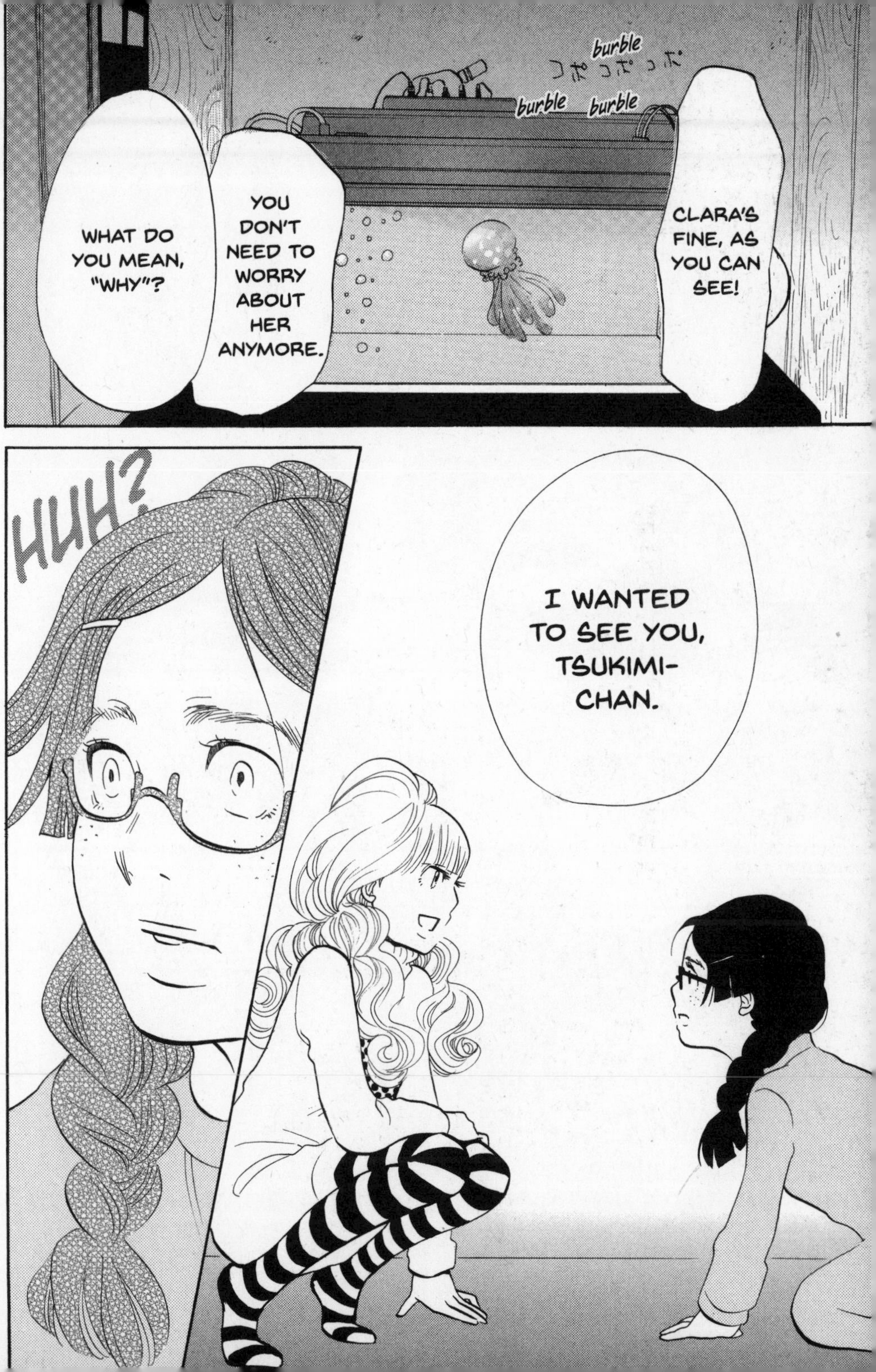
burble
burble
burble
CLARA'S FINE, AS YOU CAN SEE!
YOU DON'T NEED TO WORRY ABOUT HER ANYMORE.
WHAT DO YOU MEAN, "WHY"?
I WANTED TO SEE YOU, TSUKIMI-CHAN.
HUH?

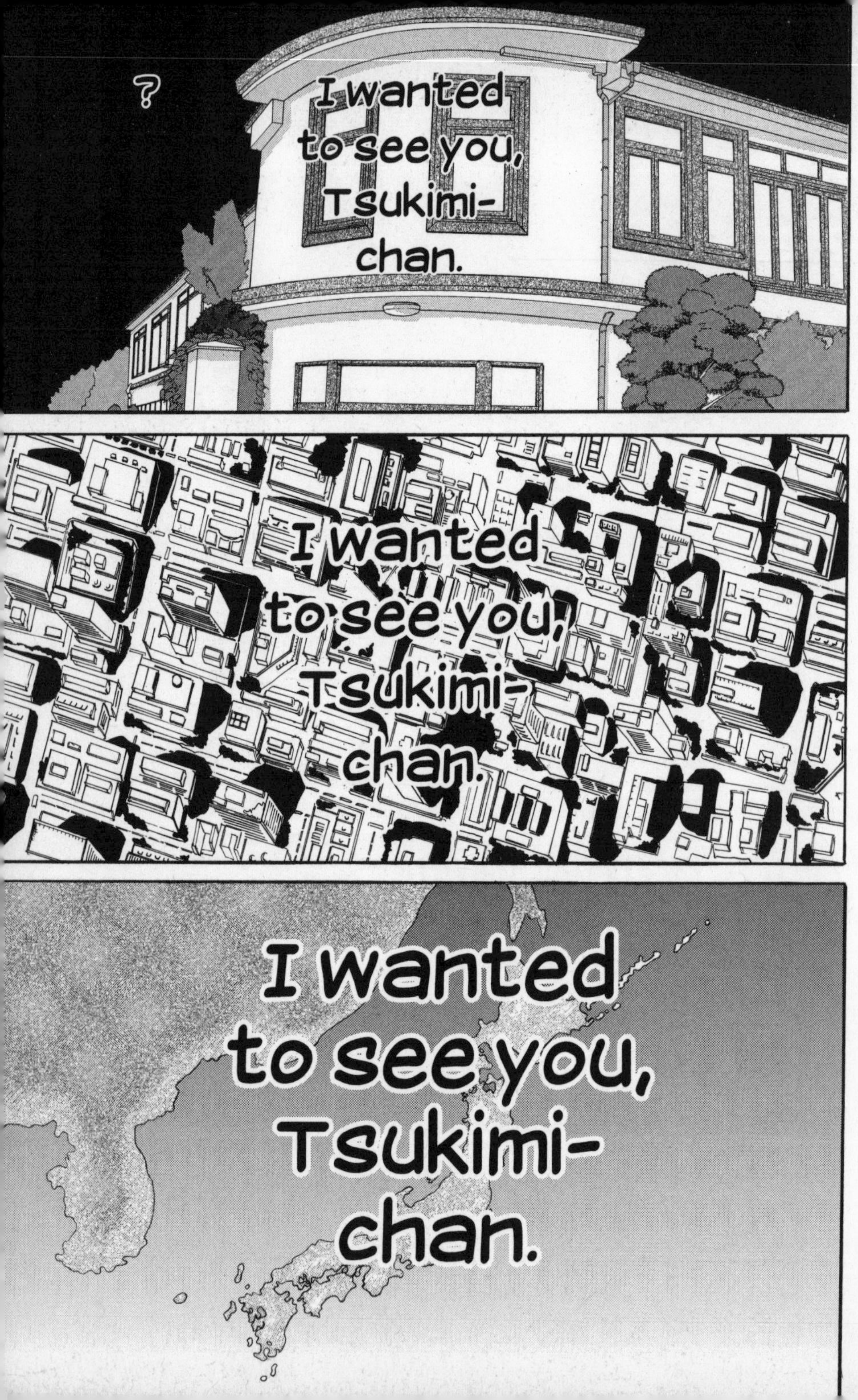
I wanted to see you, Tsukimi-chan.
?
I wanted to see you, Tsukimi-chan.
I wanted to see you, Tsukimi-chan.

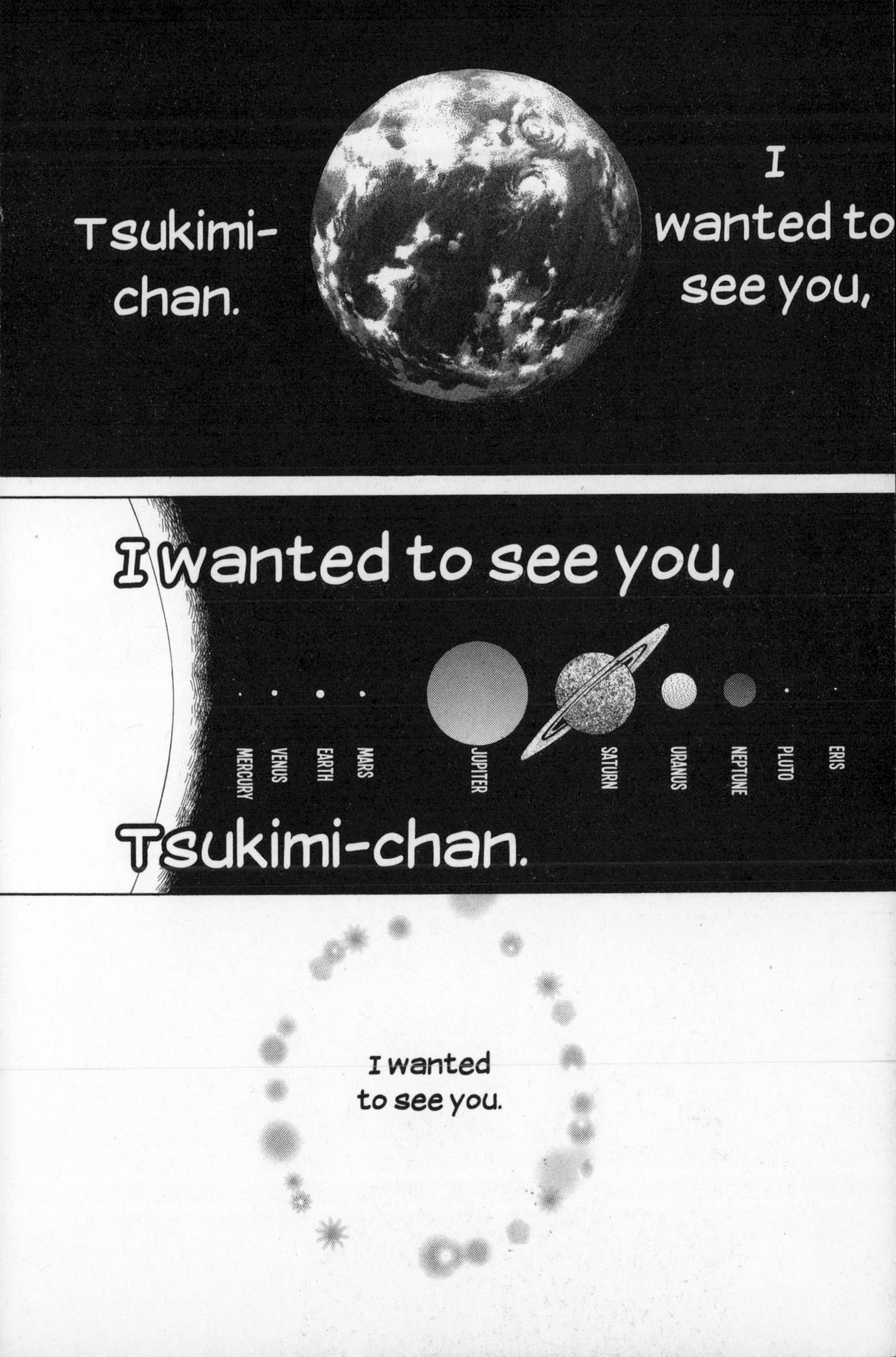
I wanted to see you,
Tsukimi-chan.
I wanted to see you,
MERCURY
VENUS
EARTH
MARS
JUPITER
SATURN
URANUS
NEPTUNE
PLUTO
ERIS
Tsukimi-chan.
I wanted to see you.

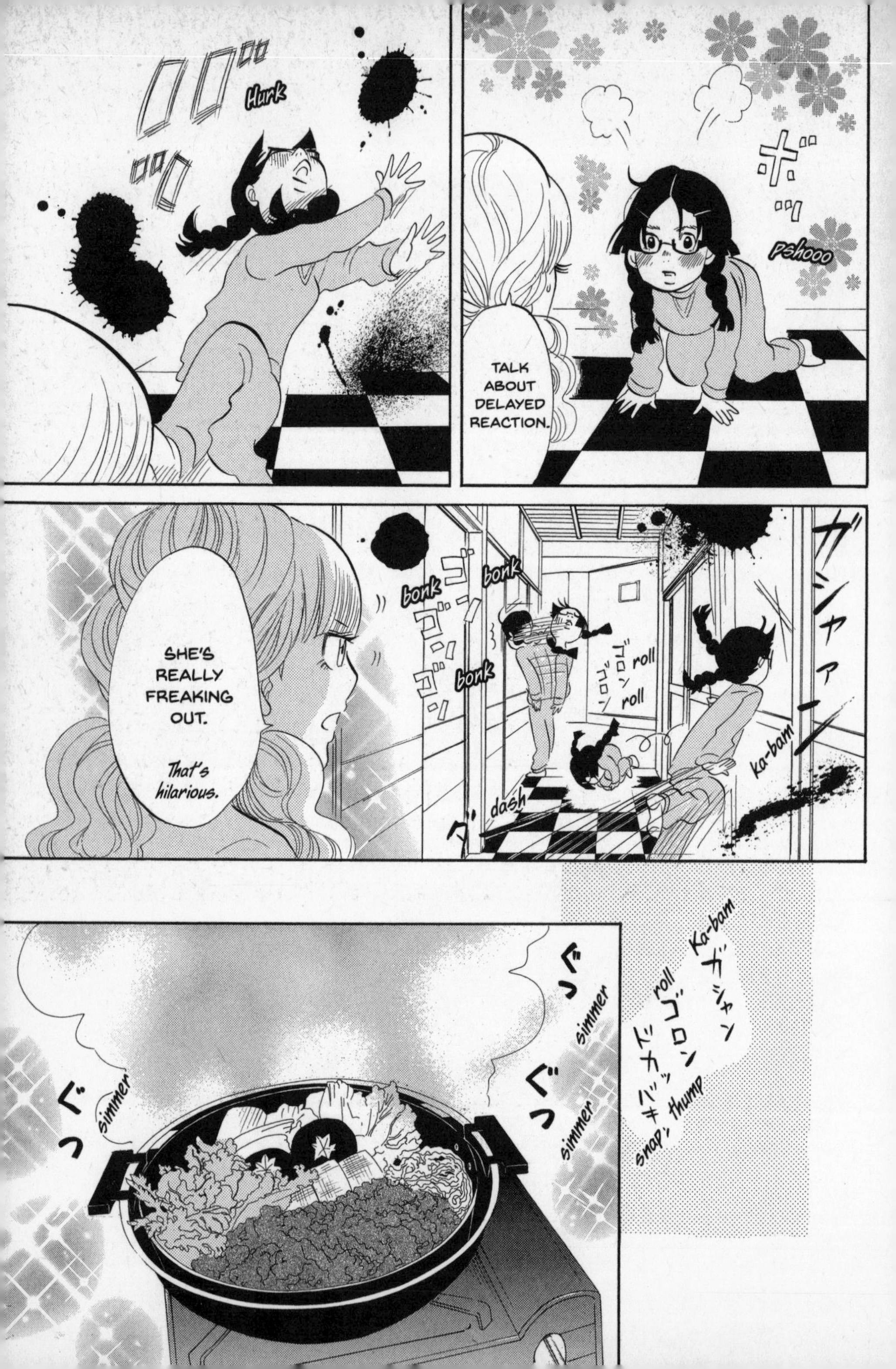
ボッ
pshooo
TALK ABOUT DELAYED REACTION.
Hurk
ガシャアーン
ka-bam
ゴロンゴロン
roll roll
ダ
dash
ゴン ゴン ゴン
bonk bonk bonk
SHE'S REALLY FREAKING OUT.
That's hilarious.
Ka-bam
ガシャン
roll
ゴロン
ドカッ バキ
snap, thump
ぐつ ぐつ
simmer simmer
ぐつ
simmer

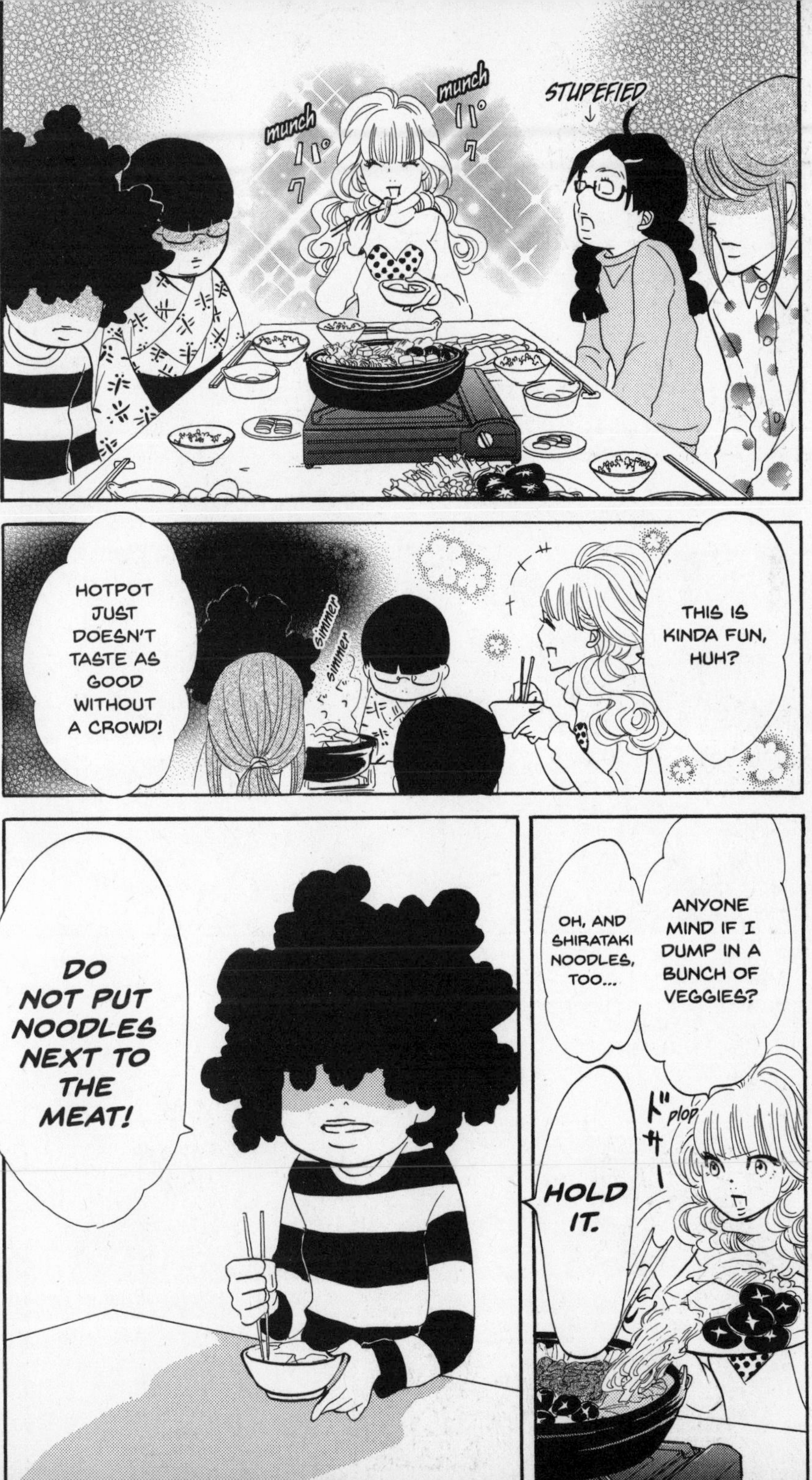
STUPEFIED
munch パク
munch パク
THIS IS KINDA FUN, HUH?
simmer
simmer
HOTPOT JUST DOESN'T TASTE AS GOOD WITHOUT A CROWD!
ANYONE MIND IF I DUMP IN A BUNCH OF VEGGIES?
OH, AND SHIRATAKI NOODLES, TOO...
ドサー plop
HOLD IT.
DO NOT PUT NOODLES NEXT TO THE MEAT!

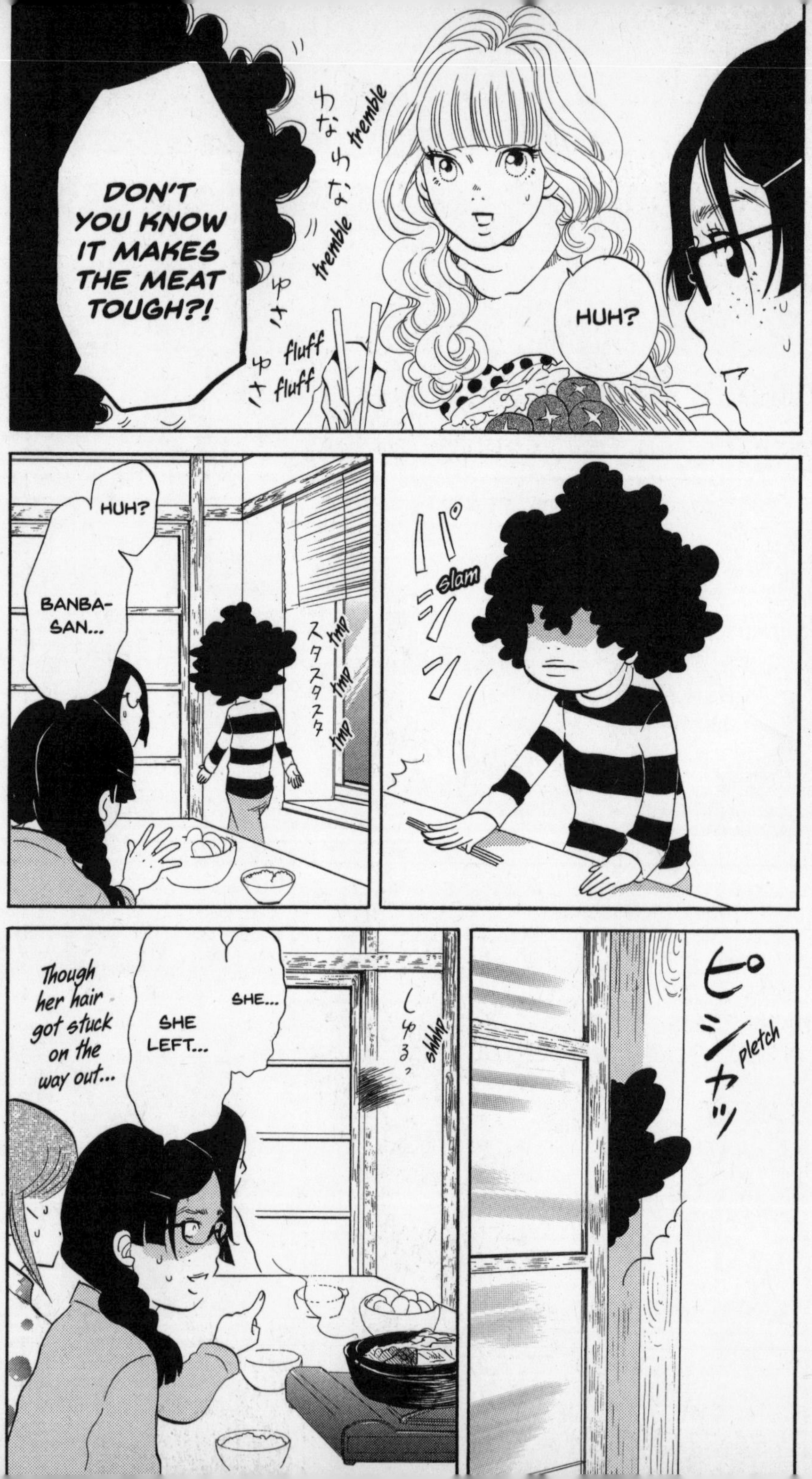
HUH?
わなわな
tremble
tremble
ゆさゆさ
fluff
fluff
DON'T YOU KNOW IT MAKES THE MEAT TOUGH?!
パシン
slam
スタスタスタ
tmp
tmp
tmp
HUH?
BANBA-SAN...
ピシャッ
pletch
しゅるっ
shhhp
SHE...
SHE LEFT...
Though her hair got stuck on the way out...

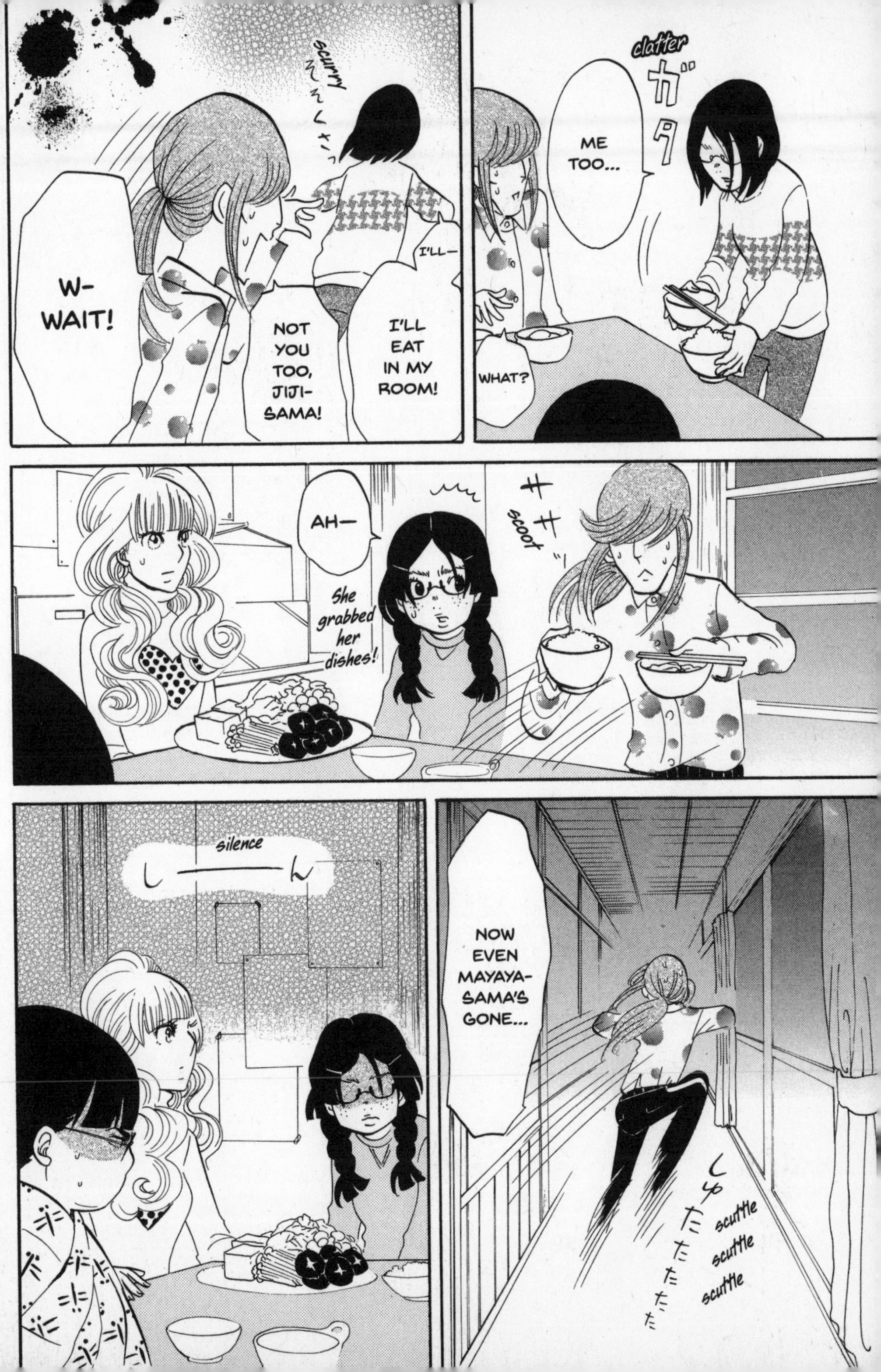
clatter
ガタ
ME TOO...
WHAT?
scurry
そそくさっ
I'LL—
I'LL EAT IN MY ROOM!
NOT YOU TOO, JIJI-SAMA!
W-WAIT!
キキッ
scoot
AH—
She grabbed her dishes!
NOW EVEN MAYAYA-SAMA'S GONE...
しゅたたたたた
scuttle
scuttle
scuttle
silence
しーん

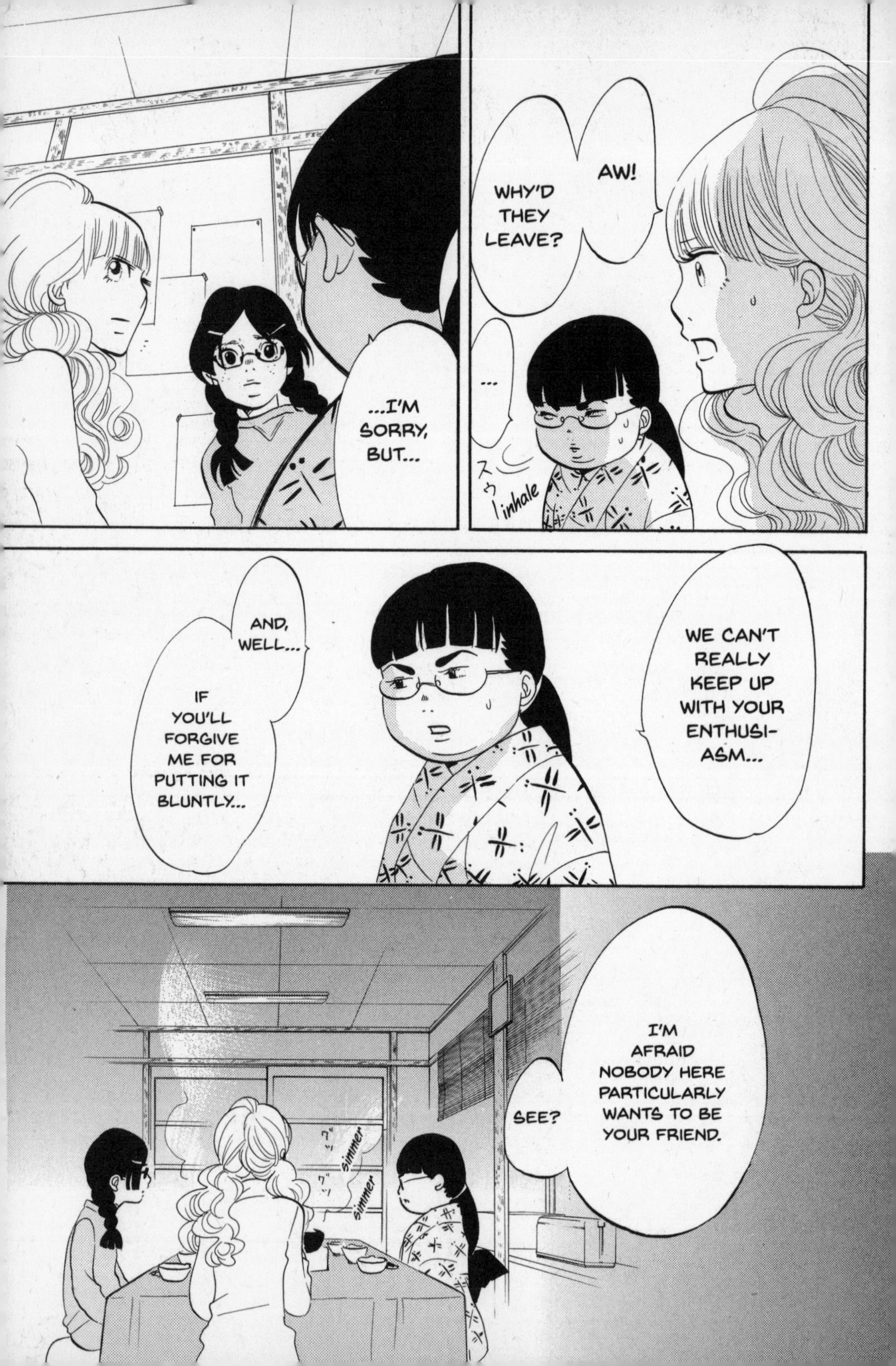
AW!
WHY'D THEY LEAVE?
...
スゥ inhale
...I'M SORRY, BUT...
WE CAN'T REALLY KEEP UP WITH YOUR ENTHUSI-ASM...
AND, WELL...
IF YOU'LL FORGIVE ME FOR PUTTING IT BLUNTLY...
I'M AFRAID NOBODY HERE PARTICULARLY WANTS TO BE YOUR FRIEND.
SEE?
simmer
simmer

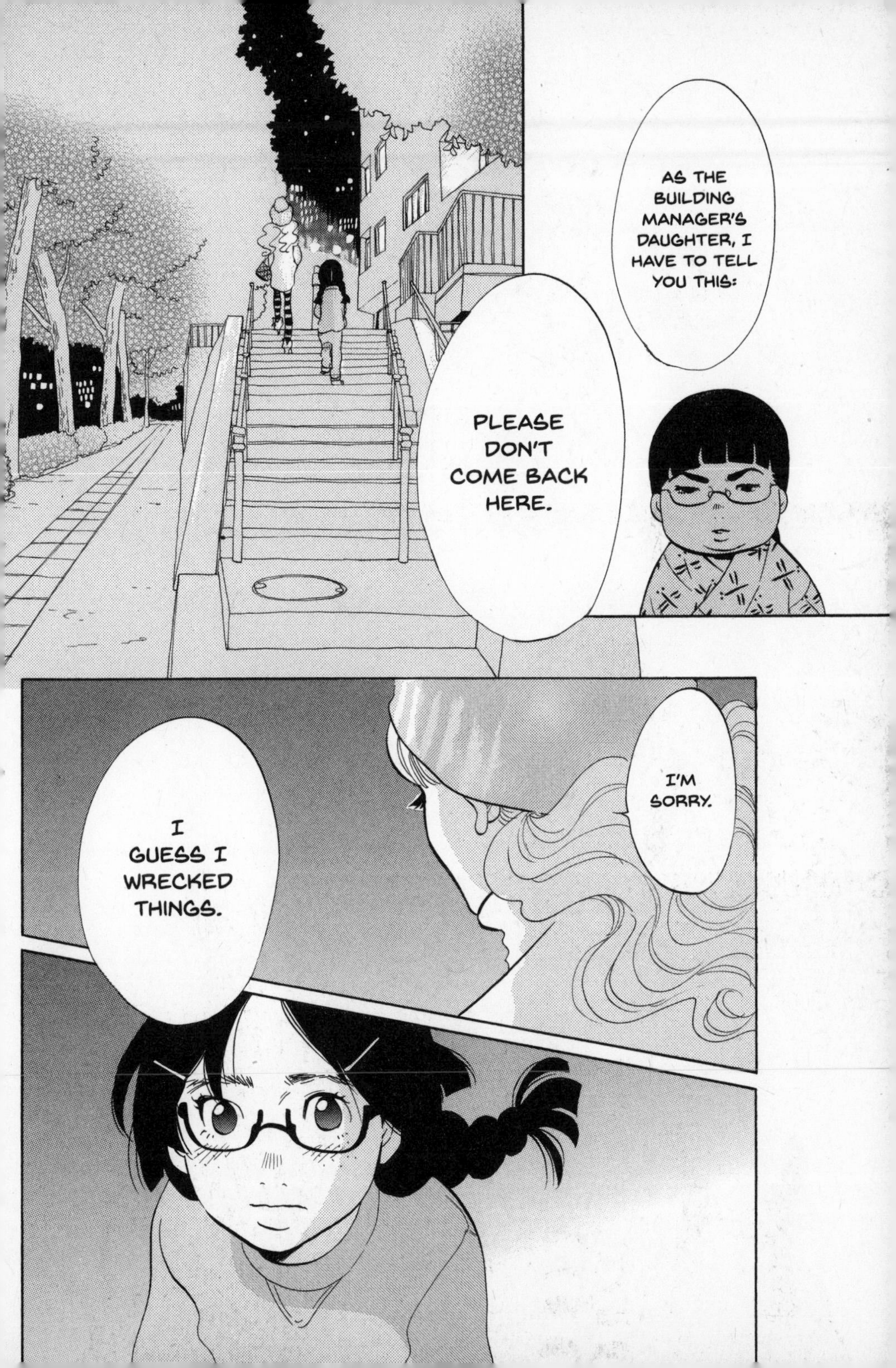
AS THE BUILDING MANAGER'S DAUGHTER, I HAVE TO TELL YOU THIS:
PLEASE DON'T COME BACK HERE.
I'M SORRY.
I GUESS I WRECKED THINGS.

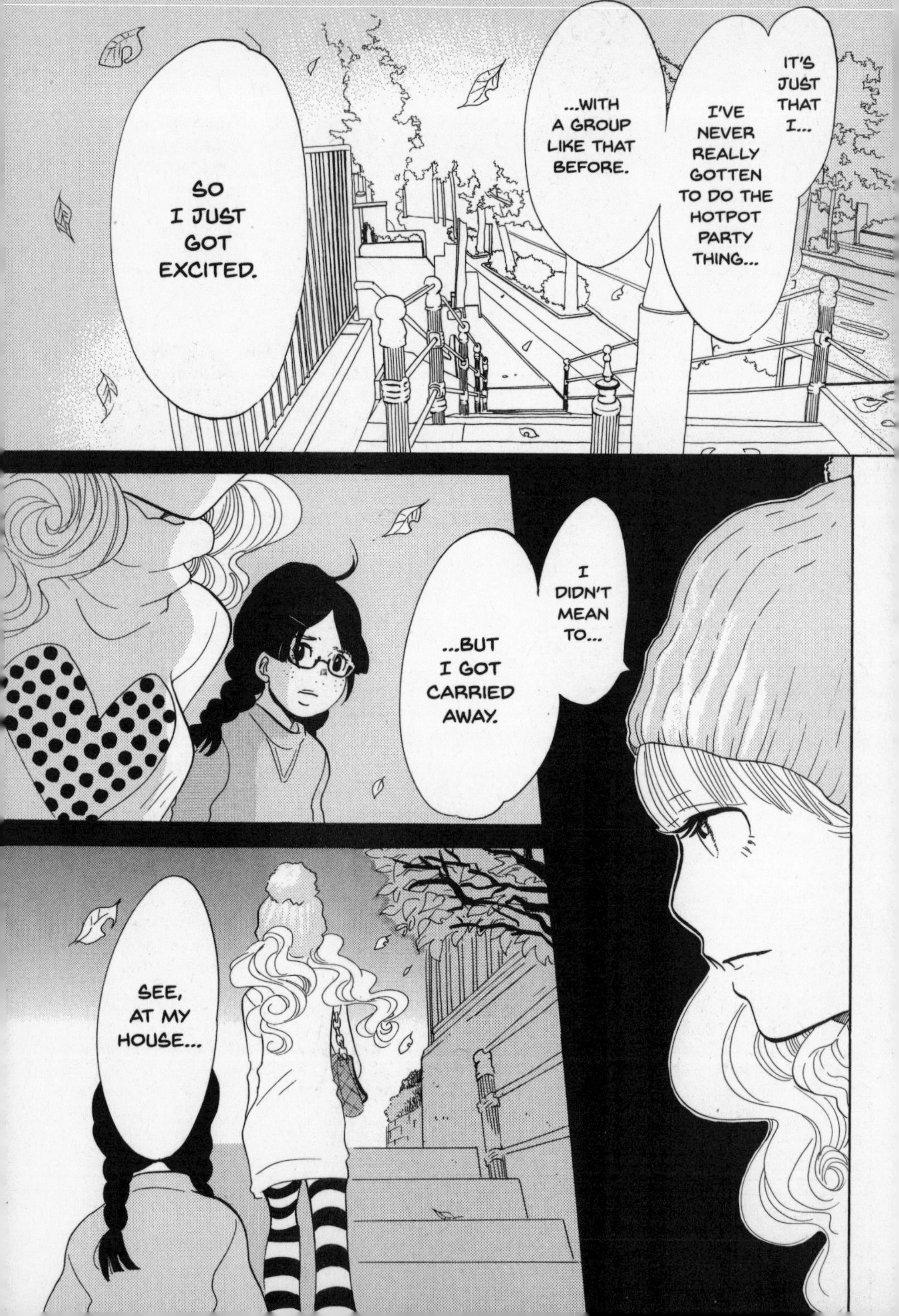
IT'S JUST THAT I...
I'VE NEVER REALLY GOTTEN TO DO THE HOTPOT PARTY THING...
...WITH A GROUP LIKE THAT BEFORE.
SO I JUST GOT EXCITED.
I DIDN'T MEAN TO...
...BUT I GOT CARRIED AWAY.
SEE, AT MY HOUSE...

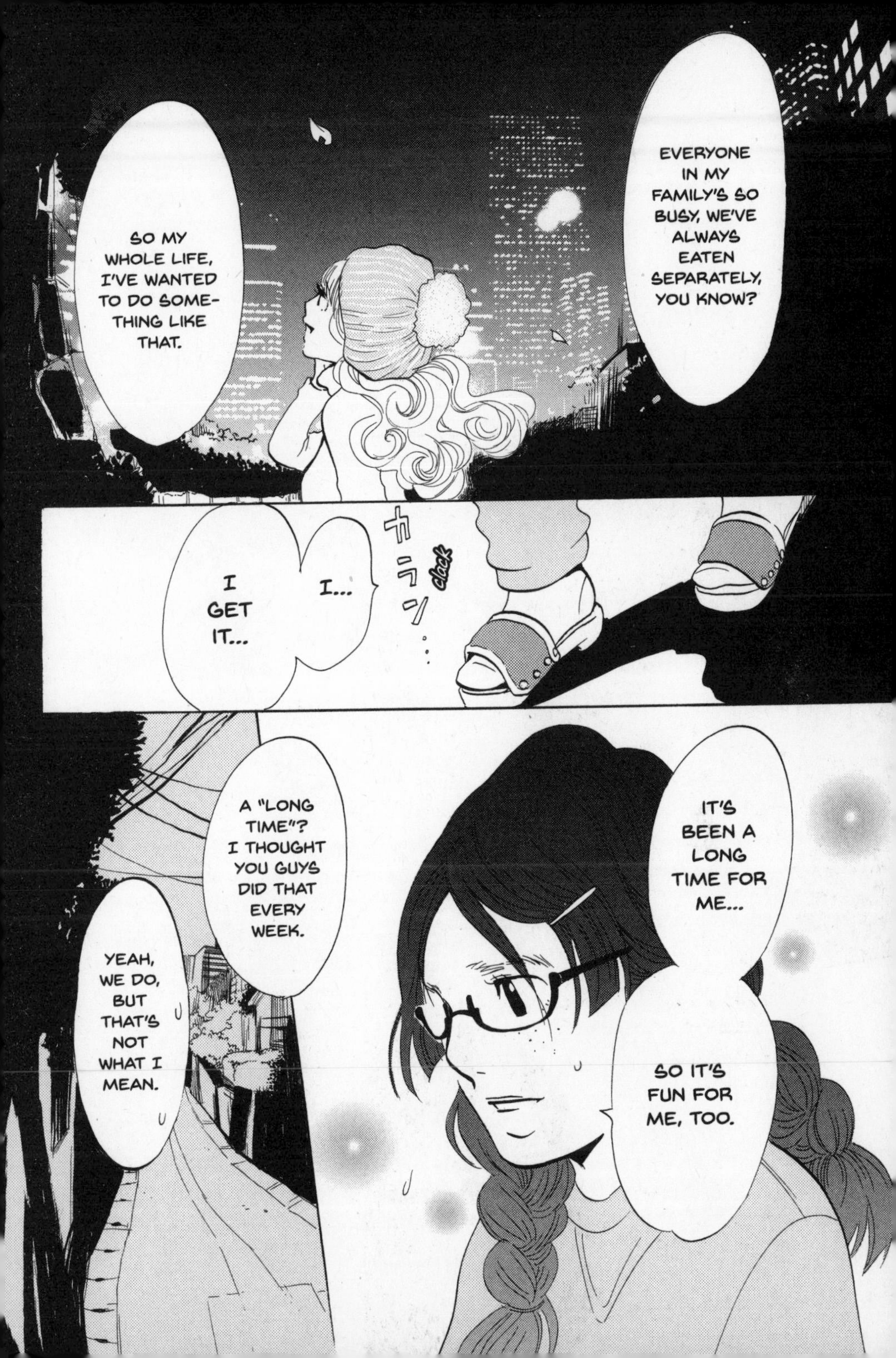
EVERYONE IN MY FAMILY'S SO BUSY, WE'VE ALWAYS EATEN SEPARATELY, YOU KNOW?
SO MY WHOLE LIFE, I'VE WANTED TO DO SOME-THING LIKE THAT.
カラン
clack
I...
I GET IT...
IT'S BEEN A LONG TIME FOR ME...
SO IT'S FUN FOR ME, TOO.
A "LONG TIME"? I THOUGHT YOU GUYS DID THAT EVERY WEEK.
YEAH, WE DO, BUT THAT'S NOT WHAT I MEAN.

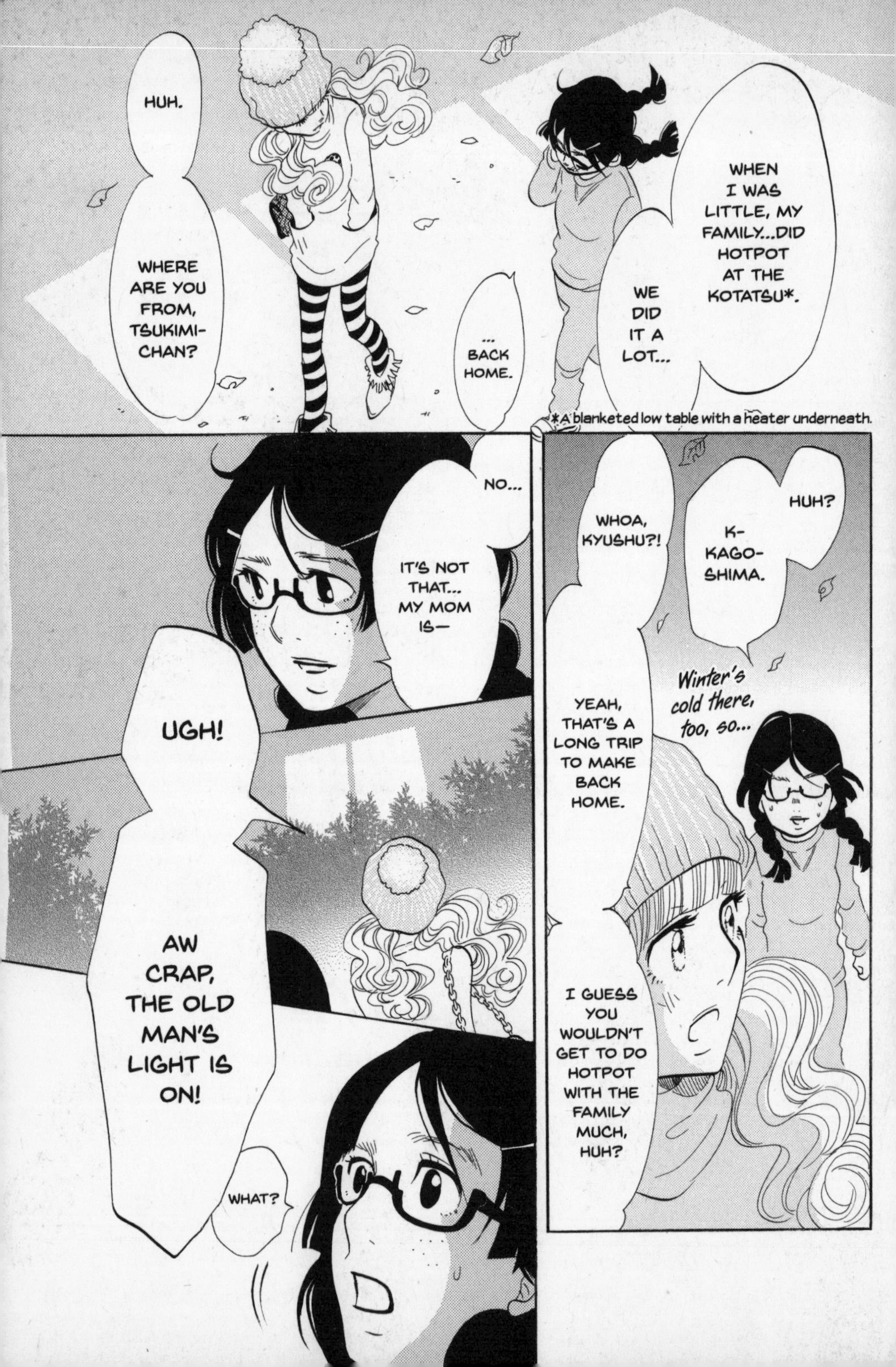
WHEN I WAS LITTLE, MY FAMILY...DID HOTPOT AT THE KOTATSU*.
WE DID IT A LOT...
...BACK HOME.
HUH.
WHERE ARE YOU FROM, TSUKIMI-CHAN?
HUH?
K-KAGOSHIMA.
WHOA, KYUSHU?!
YEAH, THAT'S A LONG TRIP TO MAKE BACK HOME.
Winter's cold there, too, so...
I GUESS YOU WOULDN'T GET TO DO HOTPOT WITH THE FAMILY MUCH, HUH?
NO...
IT'S NOT THAT... MY MOM IS—
UGH!
AW CRAP, THE OLD MAN'S LIGHT IS ON!
WHAT?
*A blanketed low table with a heater underneath.

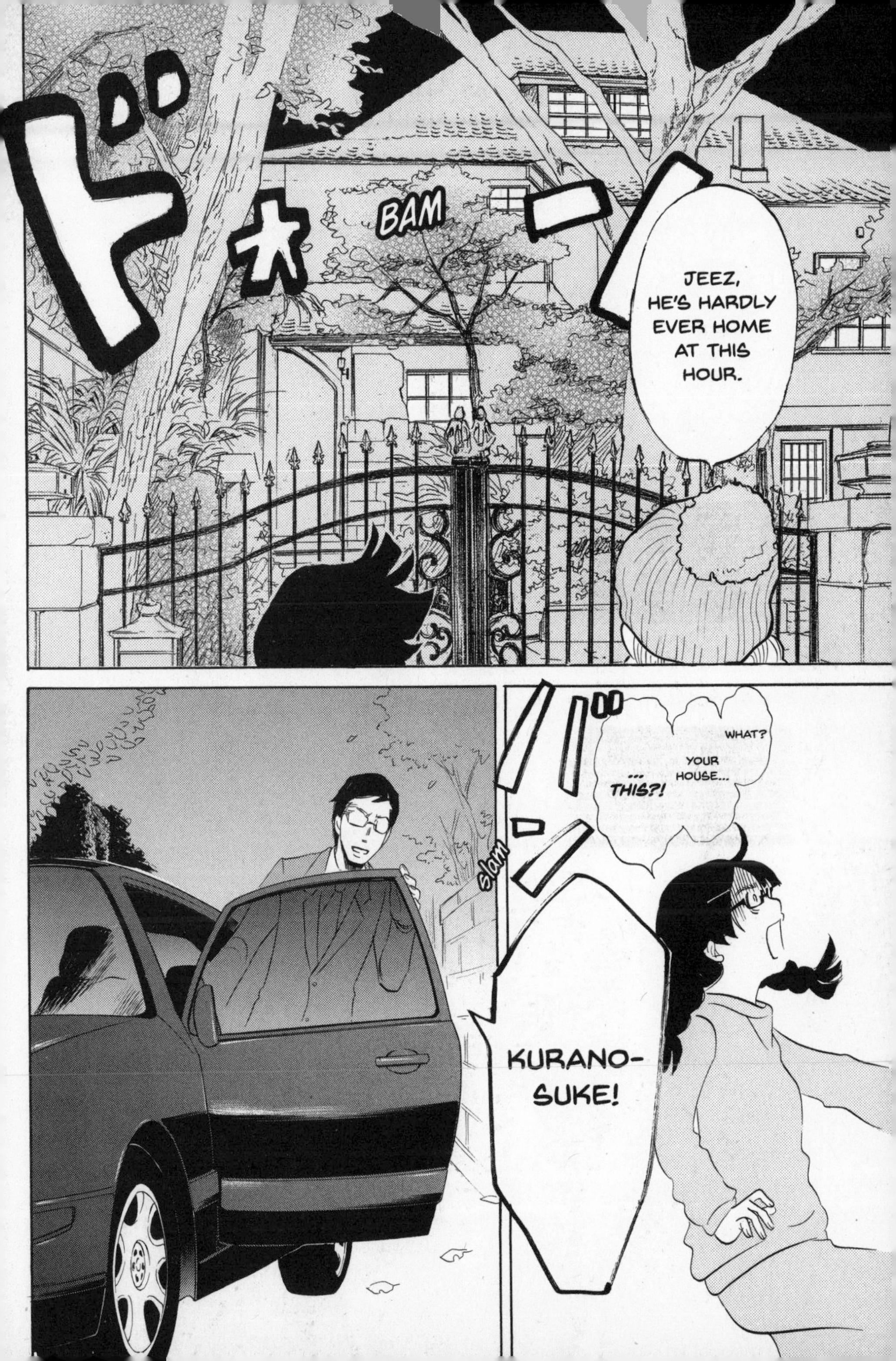
BAM
JEEZ, HE'S HARDLY EVER HOME AT THIS HOUR.
WHAT?
YOUR HOUSE...
...THIS?!
KURANO-SUKE!
slam

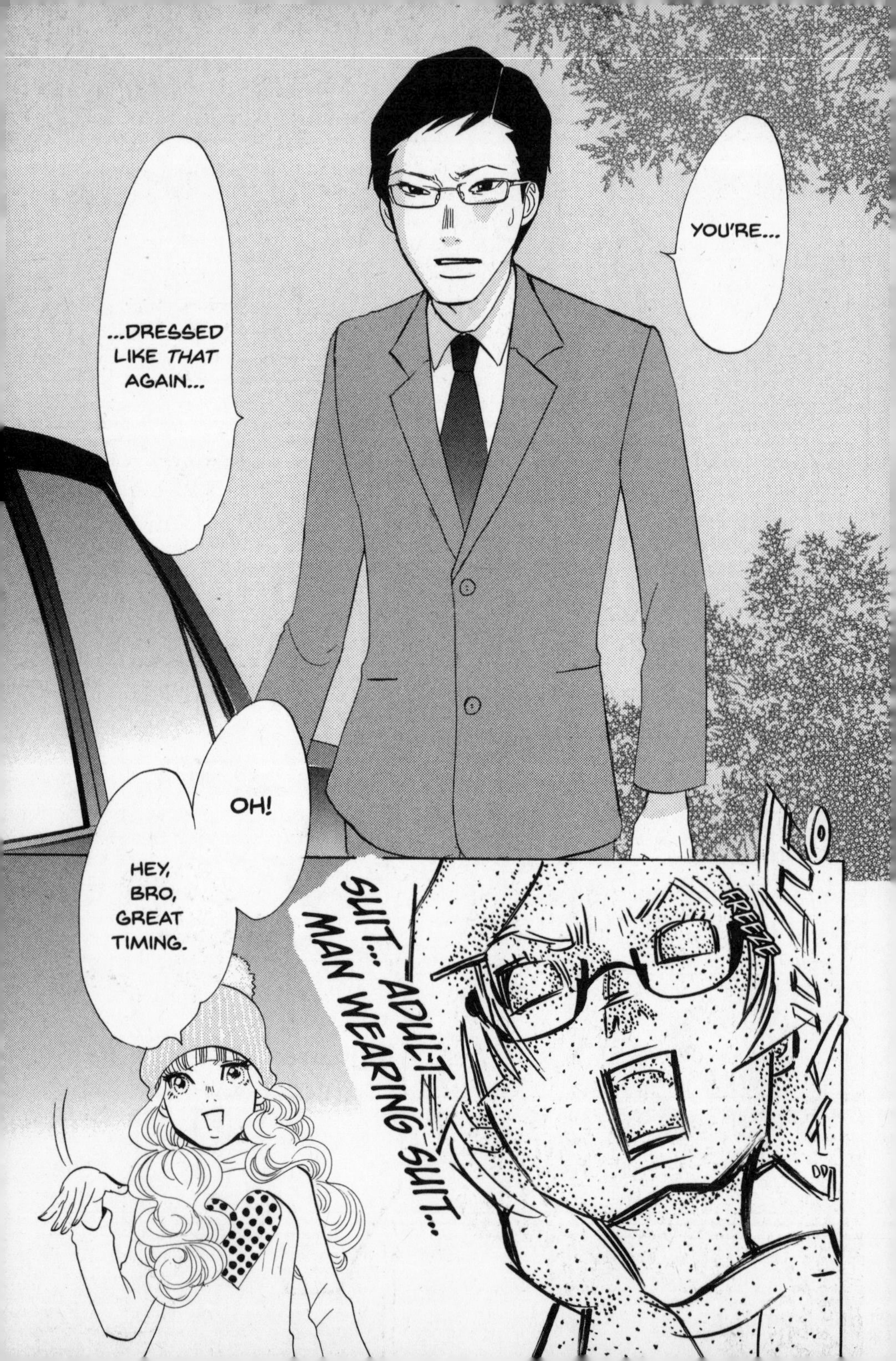
YOU'RE...
...DRESSED LIKE THAT AGAIN...
OH!
HEY, BRO, GREAT TIMING.
FREEZE
SUIT... ADULT MAN WEARING SUIT...

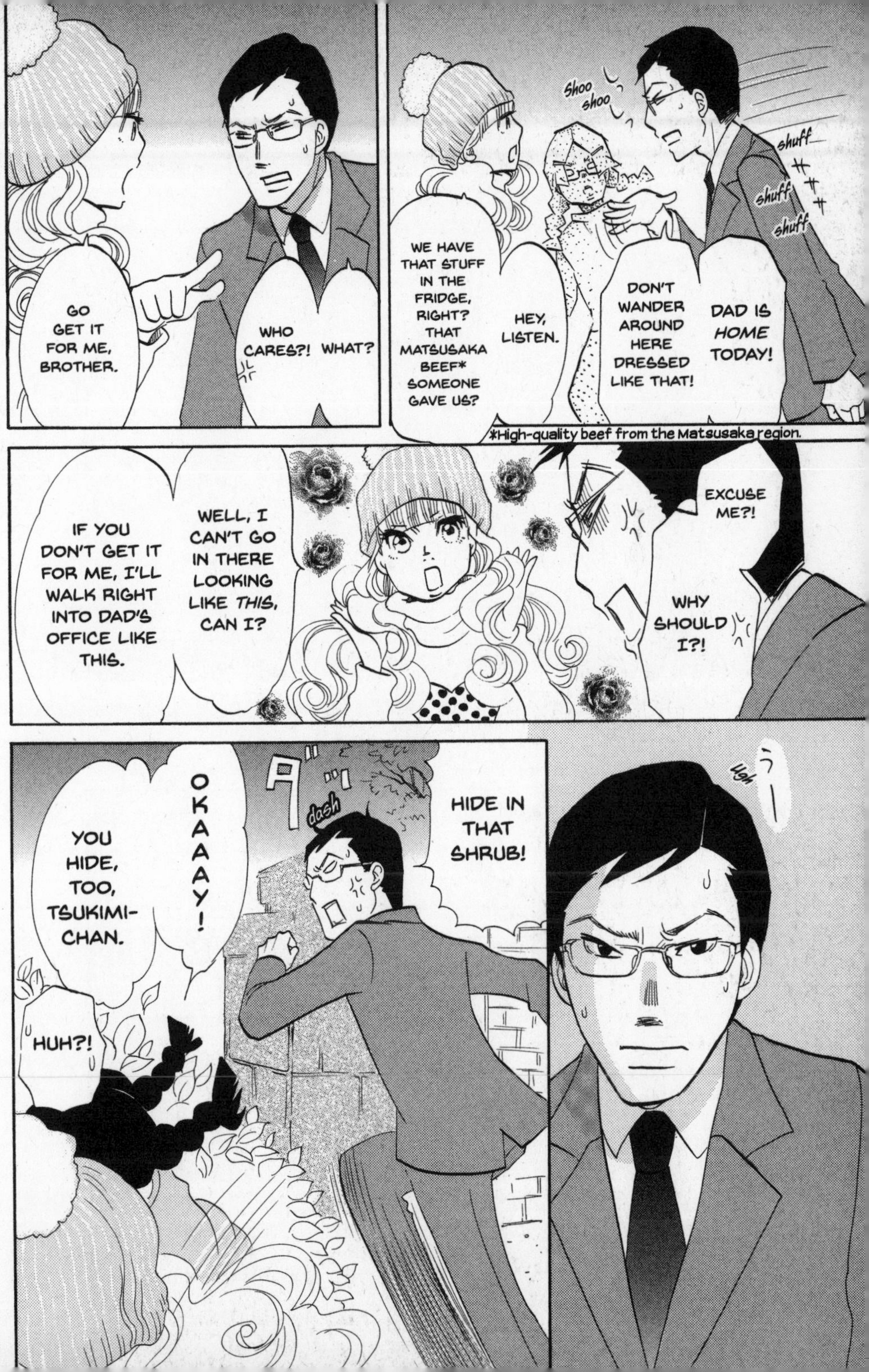
Shoo shoo
shuff shuff shuff
DAD IS HOME TODAY!
DON'T WANDER AROUND HERE DRESSED LIKE THAT!
HEY, LISTEN.
WE HAVE THAT STUFF IN THE FRIDGE, RIGHT? THAT MATSUSAKA BEEF* SOMEONE GAVE US?
WHAT?
WHO CARES?!
GO GET IT FOR ME, BROTHER.
EXCUSE ME?!
WHY SHOULD I?!
WELL, I CAN'T GO IN THERE LOOKING LIKE *THIS*, CAN I?
IF YOU DON'T GET IT FOR ME, I'LL WALK RIGHT INTO DAD'S OFFICE LIKE THIS.
Ugh
HIDE IN THAT SHRUB!
dash
OKAAAY!
YOU HIDE, TOO, TSUKIMI-CHAN.
HUH?!
*High-quality beef from the Matsusaka region.

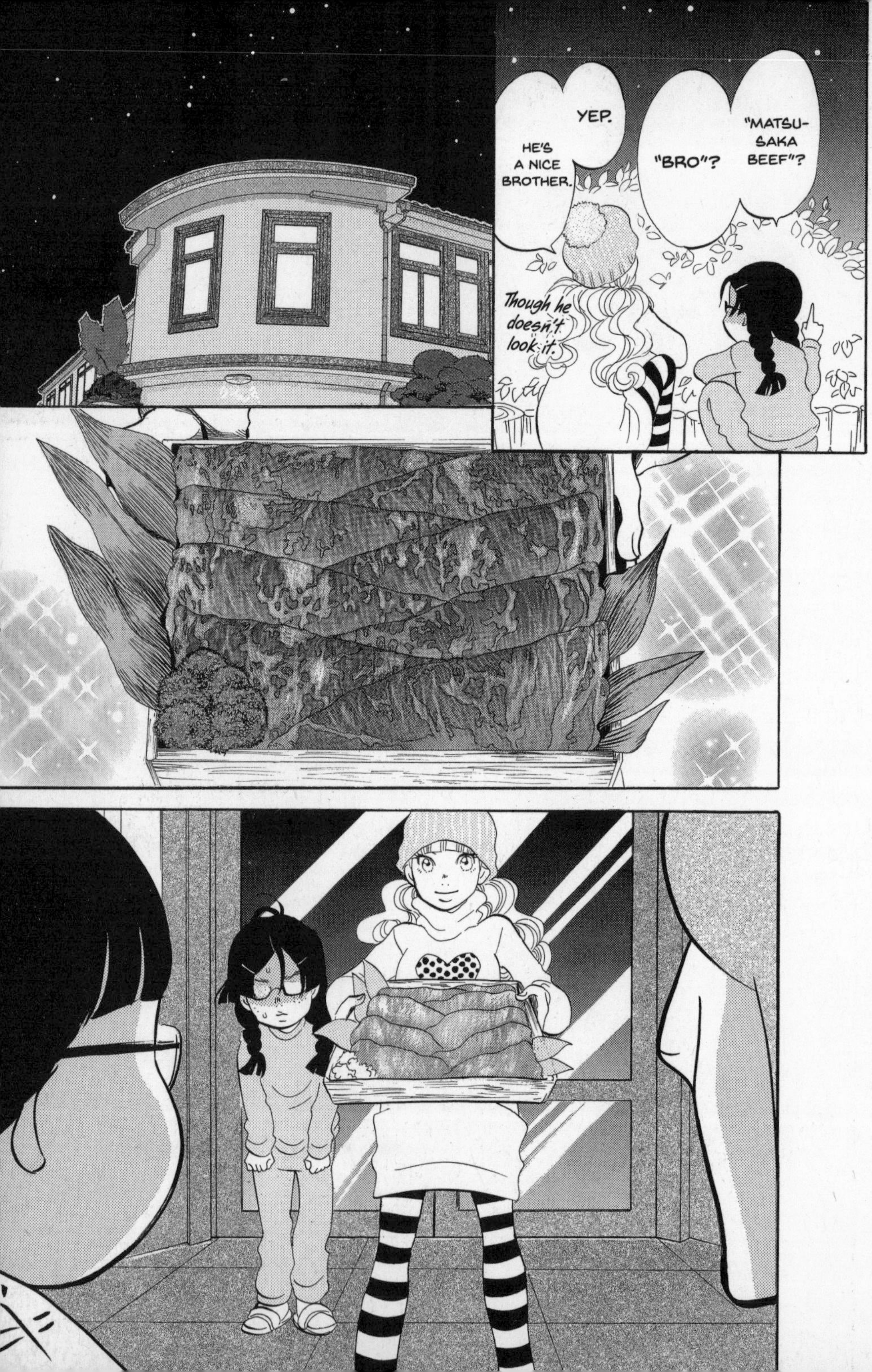
"MATSU-SAKA BEEF"?
"BRO"?
YEP.
HE'S A NICE BROTHER.
Though he doesn't look it.

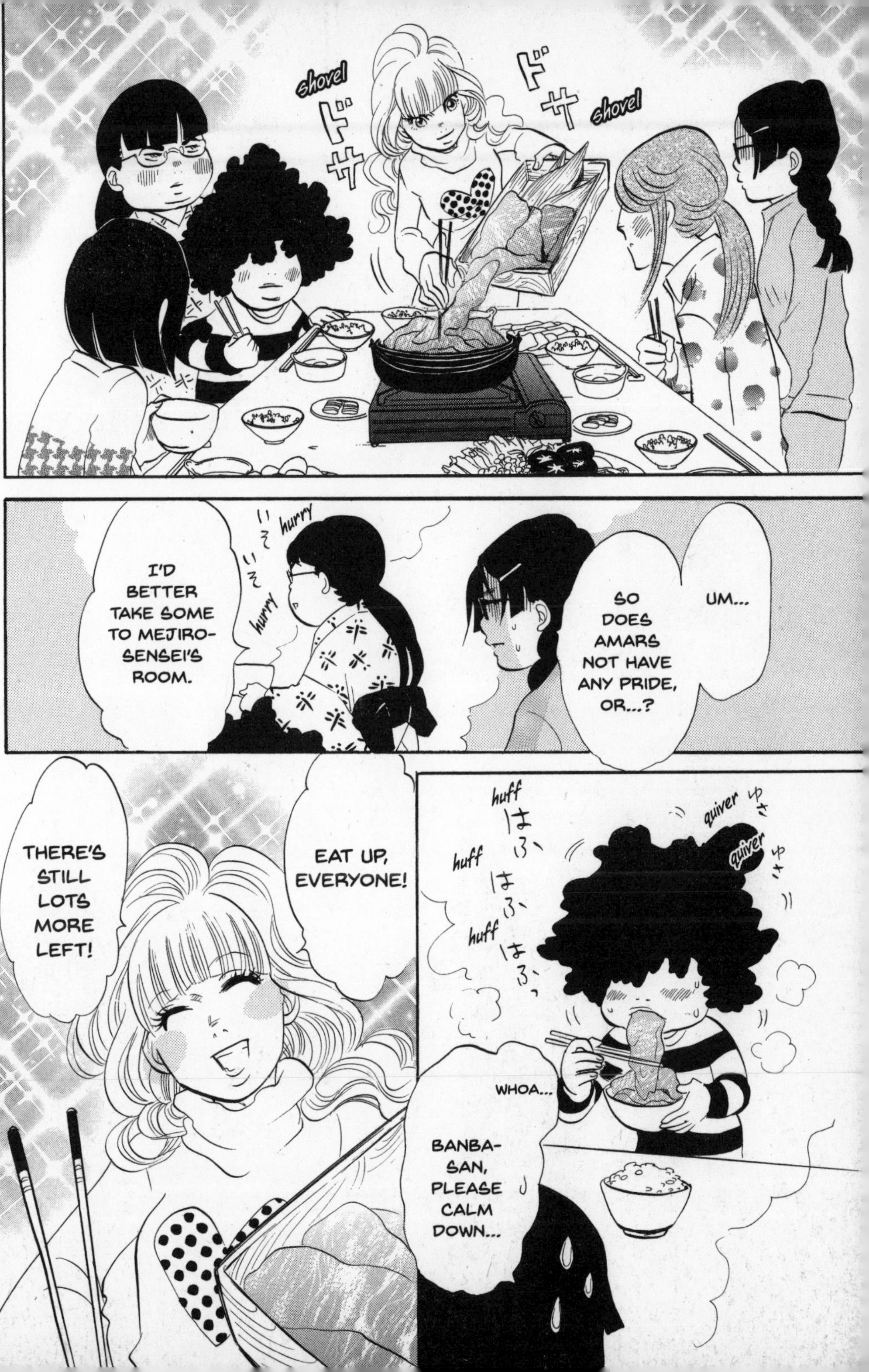
shovel
ドサ
ドサ
shovel
UM...
SO DOES AMARS NOT HAVE ANY PRIDE, OR...?
hurry いそ
いそ hurry
I'D BETTER TAKE SOME TO MEJIRO-SENSEI'S ROOM.
quiver ゆさ
ゆさ quiver
huff はふ
huff はふ
huff はふ
WHOA...
BANBA-SAN, PLEASE CALM DOWN...
EAT UP, EVERYONE!
THERE'S STILL LOTS MORE LEFT!

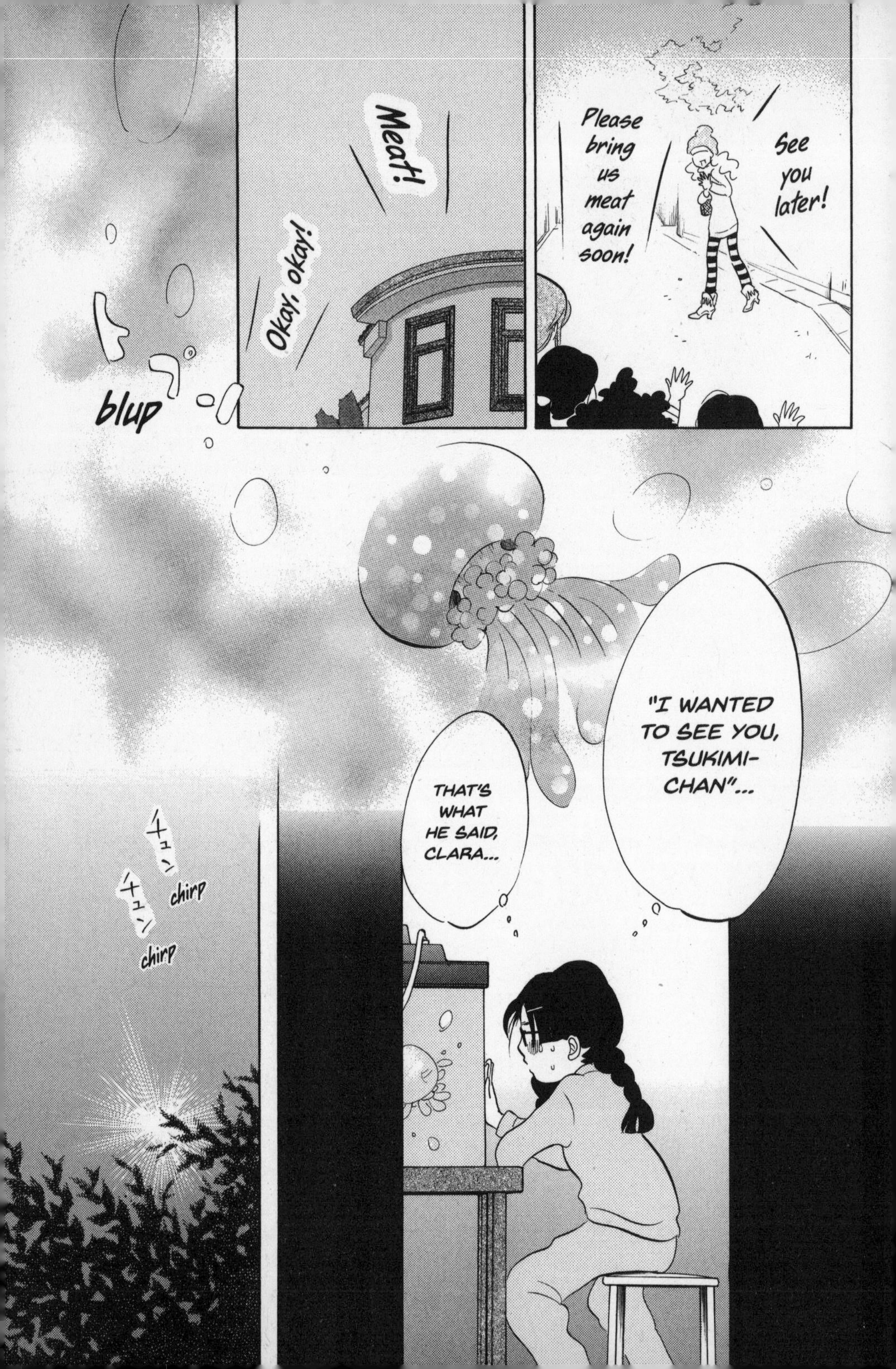
See you later!
Please bring us meat again soon!
Meat!
Okay, okay!
blup
"I WANTED TO SEE YOU, TSUKIMI-CHAN"...
THAT'S WHAT HE SAID, CLARA...
チュン
chirp
チュン
chirp

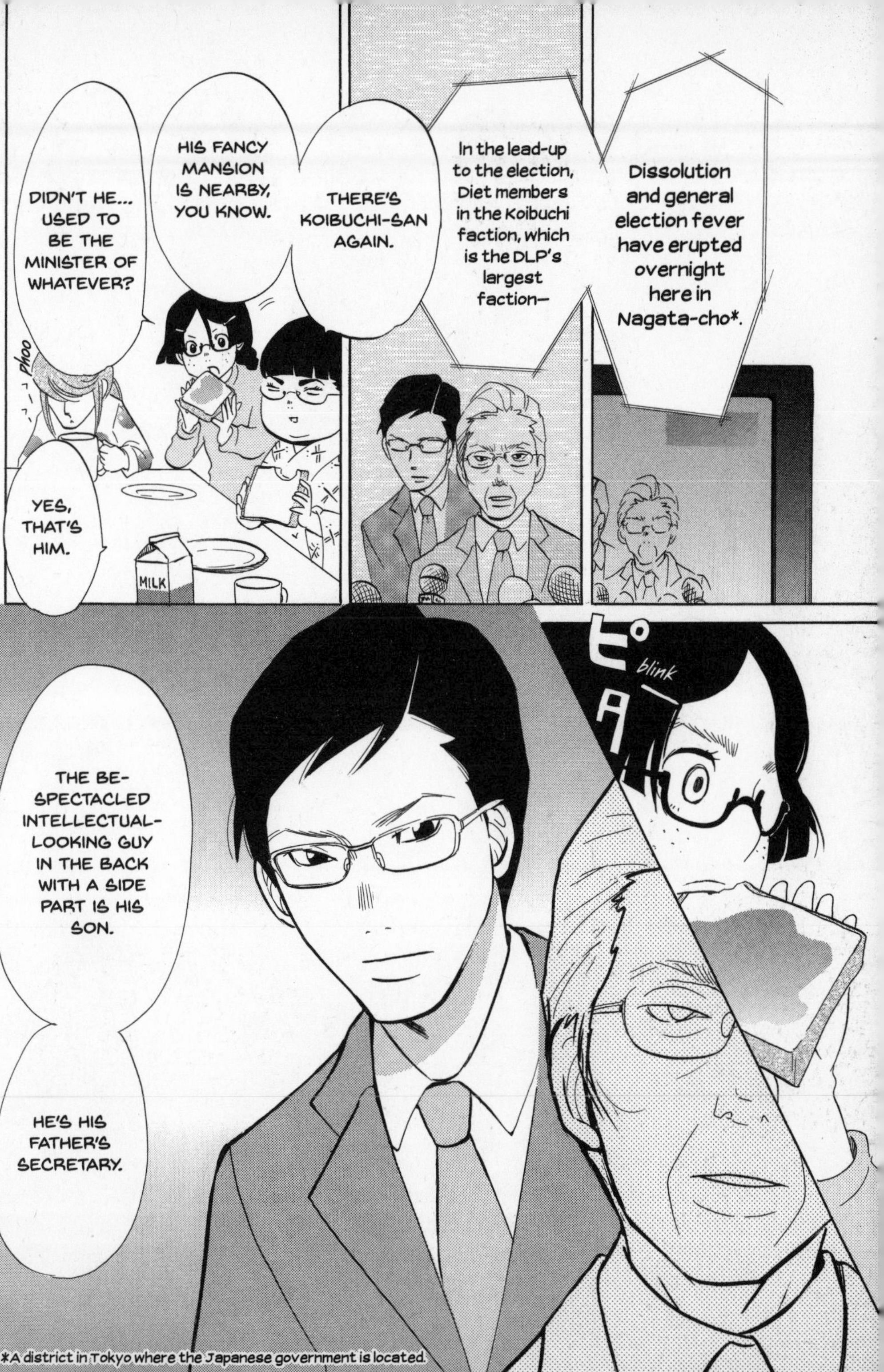
Dissolution and general election fever have erupted overnight here in Nagata-cho*.
In the lead-up to the election, Diet members in the Koibuchi faction, which is the DLP's largest faction—
THERE'S KOIBUCHI-SAN AGAIN.
HIS FANCY MANSION IS NEARBY, YOU KNOW.
DIDN'T HE... USED TO BE THE MINISTER OF WHATEVER?
phoo
YES, THAT'S HIM.
MILK
blink
THE BE-SPECTACLED INTELLECTUAL-LOOKING GUY IN THE BACK WITH A SIDE PART IS HIS SON.
HE'S HIS FATHER'S SECRETARY.

*A district in Tokyo where the Japanese government is located.

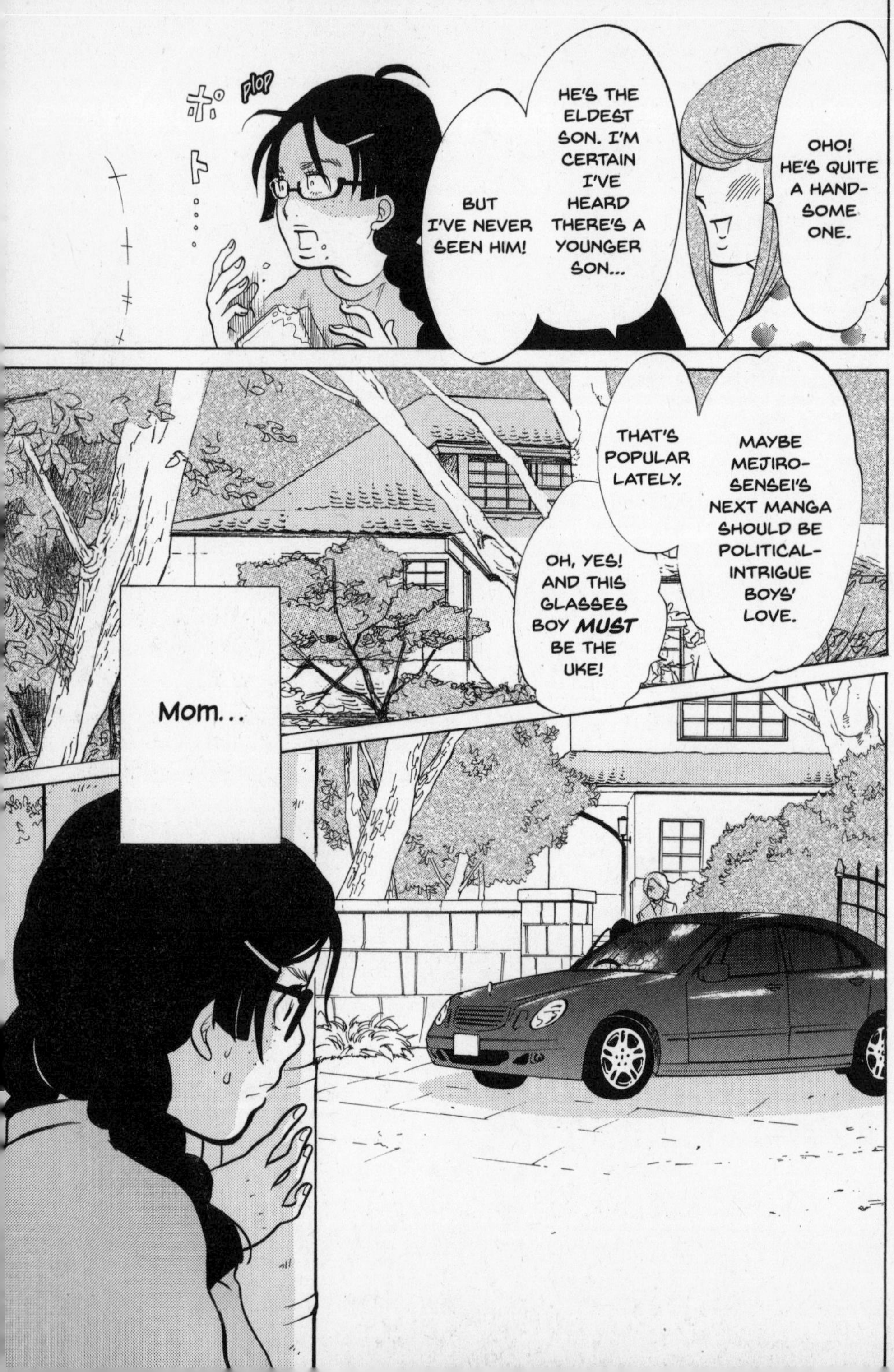
OHO! HE'S QUITE A HAND-SOME ONE.
HE'S THE ELDEST SON. I'M CERTAIN I'VE HEARD THERE'S A YOUNGER SON...
BUT I'VE NEVER SEEN HIM!
ポト....
plop
MAYBE MEJIRO-SENSEI'S NEXT MANGA SHOULD BE POLITICAL-INTRIGUE BOYS' LOVE.
THAT'S POPULAR LATELY.
OH, YES! AND THIS GLASSES BOY **MUST** BE THE UKE!
Mom...

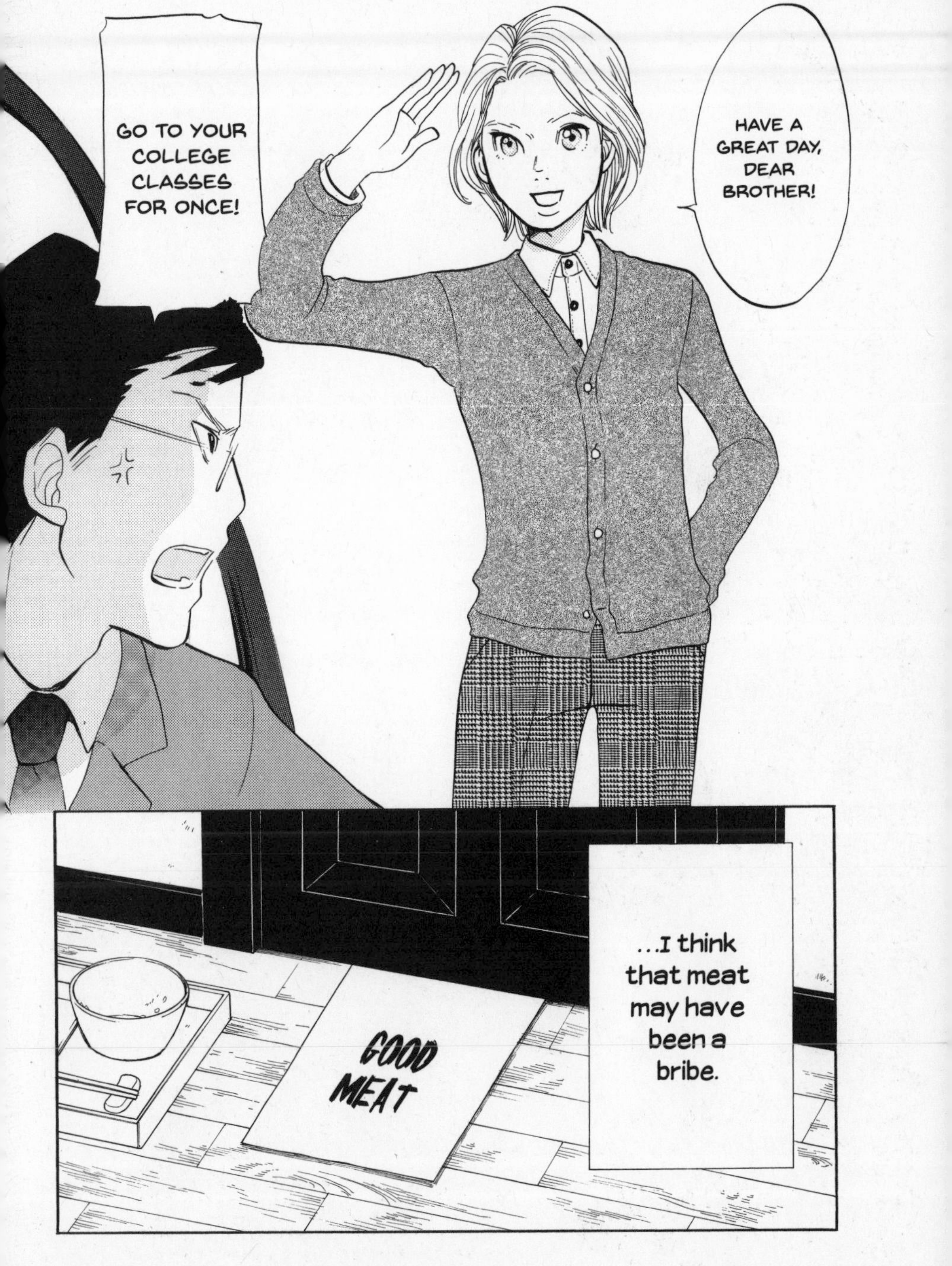
HAVE A GREAT DAY, DEAR BROTHER!
GO TO YOUR COLLEGE CLASSES FOR ONCE!
...I think that meat may have been a bribe.
GOOD MEAT

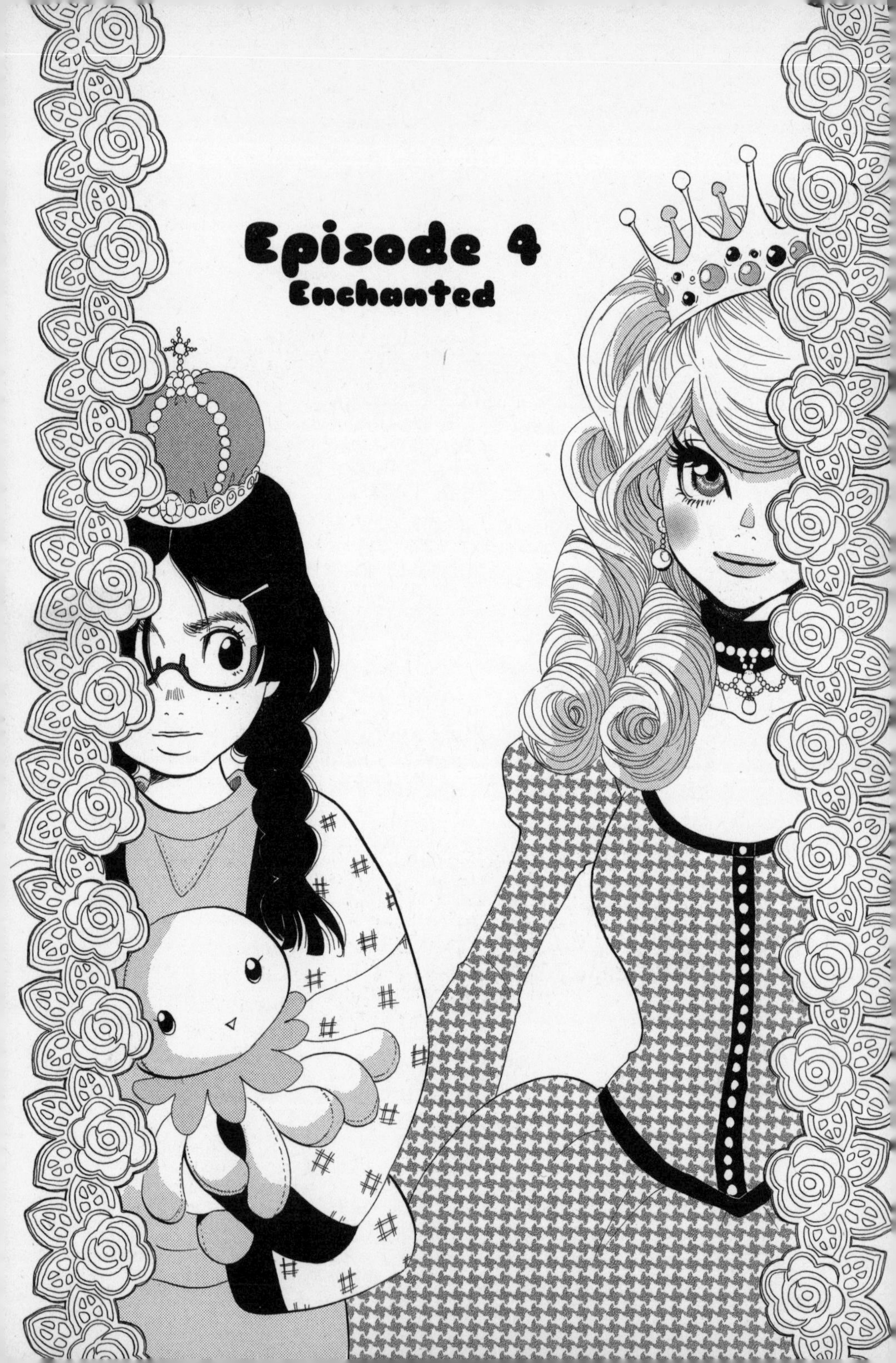
Episode 4
Enchanted

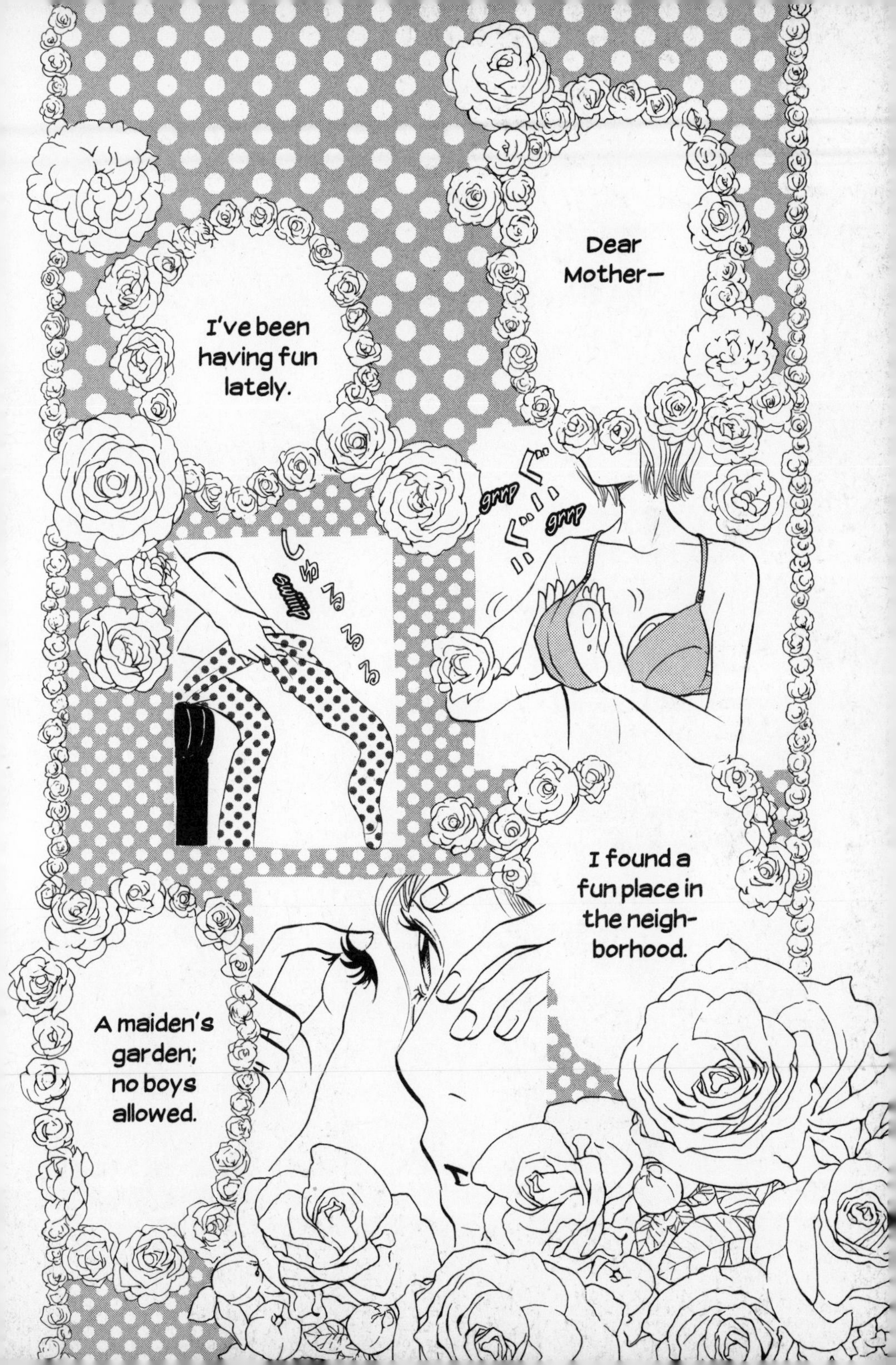
Dear Mother—
I've been having fun lately.
grrp
grrp
しゅるるる
swiiiip
I found a fun place in the neigh-borhood.
A maiden's garden; no boys allowed.

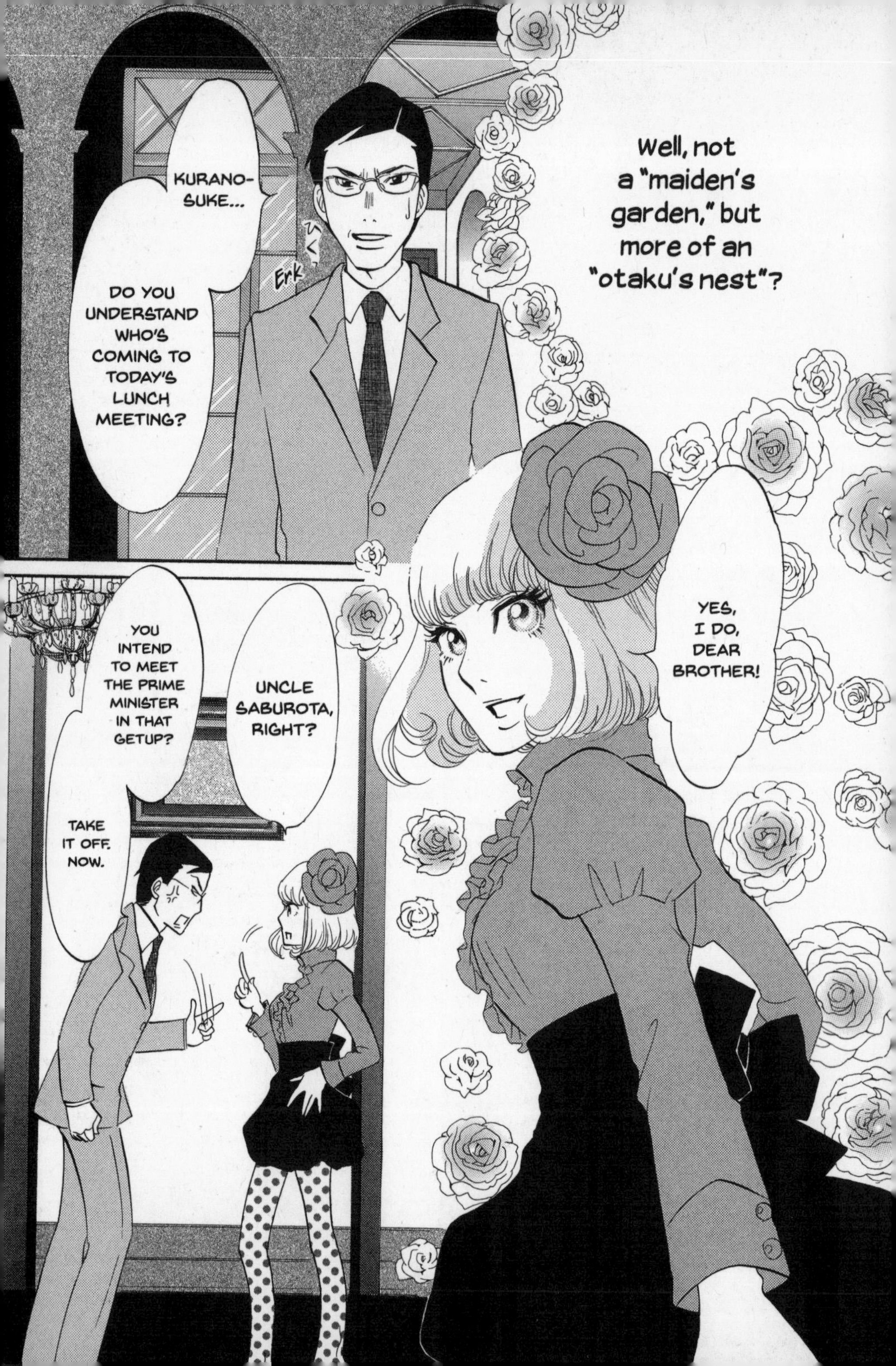
Well, not a "maiden's garden," but more of an "otaku's nest"?
KURANOSUKE...
Erk
DO YOU UNDERSTAND WHO'S COMING TO TODAY'S LUNCH MEETING?
YES, I DO, DEAR BROTHER!
UNCLE SABUROTA, RIGHT?
YOU INTEND TO MEET THE PRIME MINISTER IN THAT GETUP?
TAKE IT OFF. NOW.

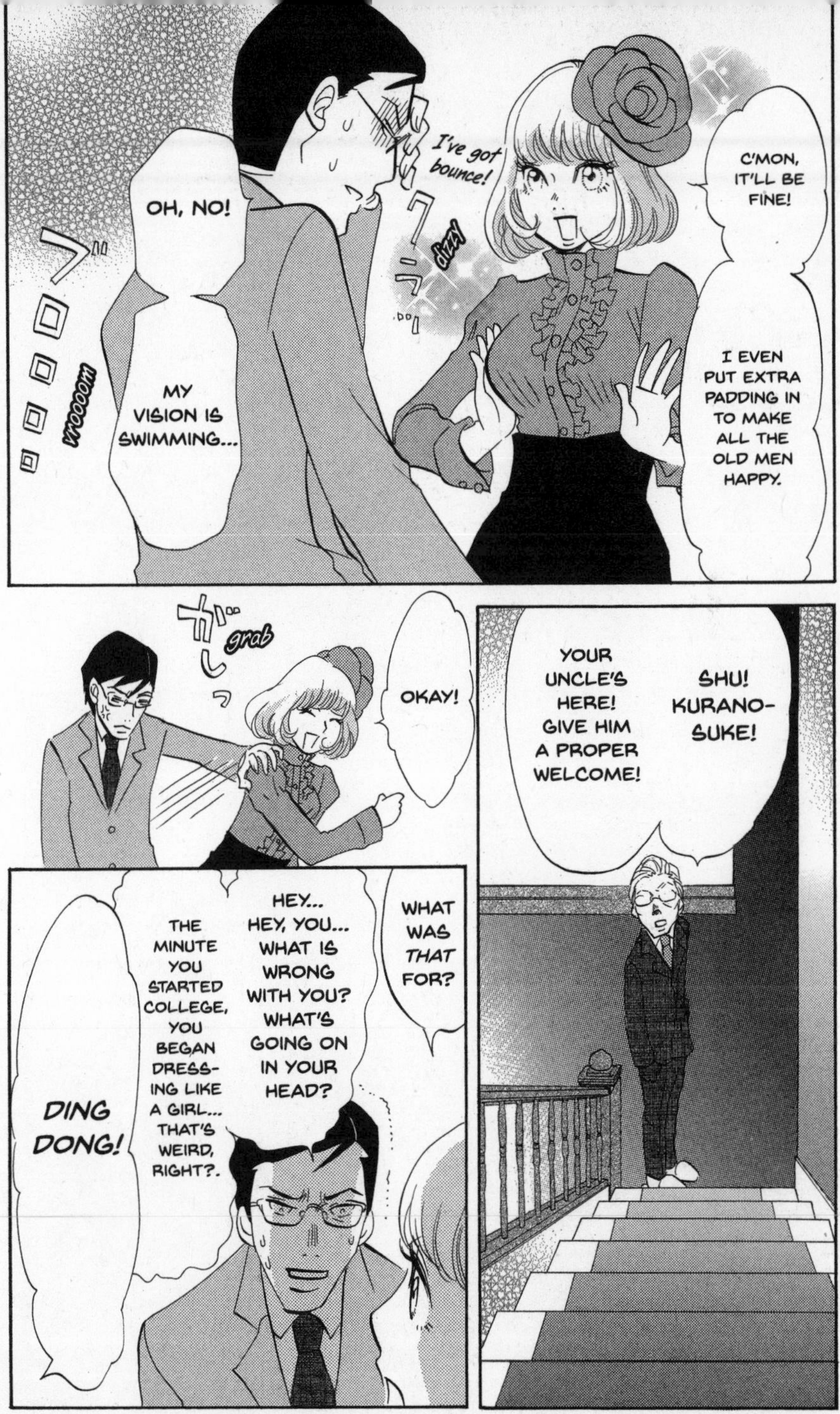
C'MON, IT'LL BE FINE!
I EVEN PUT EXTRA PADDING IN TO MAKE ALL THE OLD MEN HAPPY.
I've got bounce!
dizzy
OH, NO!
MY VISION IS SWIMMING...
WOOOOM
SHU! KURANO-SUKE!
YOUR UNCLE'S HERE! GIVE HIM A PROPER WELCOME!
OKAY!
grab
WHAT WAS THAT FOR?
HEY... HEY, YOU... WHAT IS WRONG WITH YOU? WHAT'S GOING ON IN YOUR HEAD?
THE MINUTE YOU STARTED COLLEGE, YOU BEGAN DRESS-ING LIKE A GIRL... THAT'S WEIRD, RIGHT?.
DING DONG!

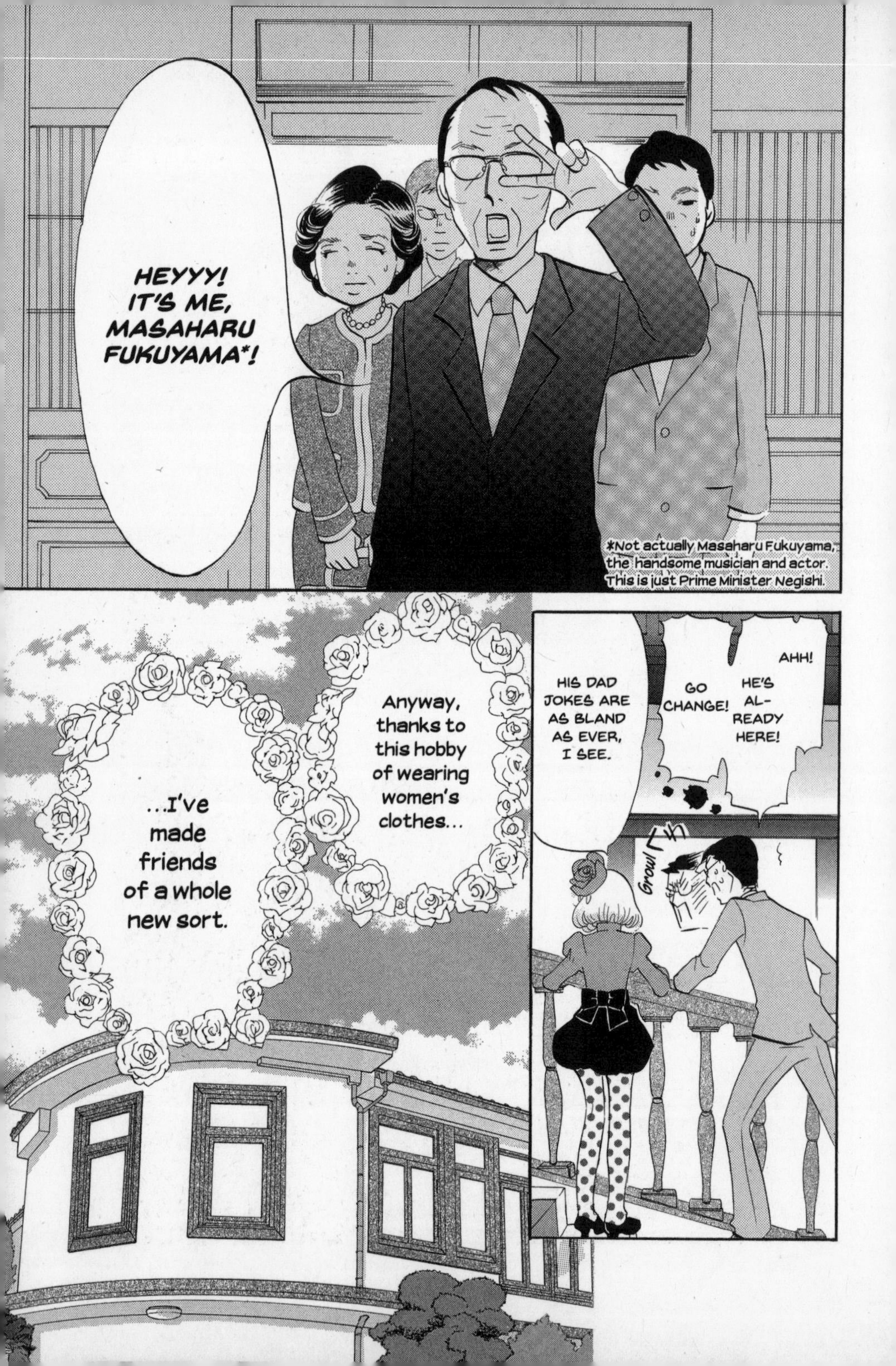
HEYYY! IT'S ME, MASAHARU FUKUYAMA*!
*Not actually Masaharu Fukuyama, the handsome musician and actor. This is just Prime Minister Negishi.
AHH! HE'S AL-READY HERE!
GO CHANGE!
HIS DAD JOKES ARE AS BLAND AS EVER, I SEE.
Growl
Anyway, thanks to this hobby of wearing women's clothes...
...I've made friends of a whole new sort.

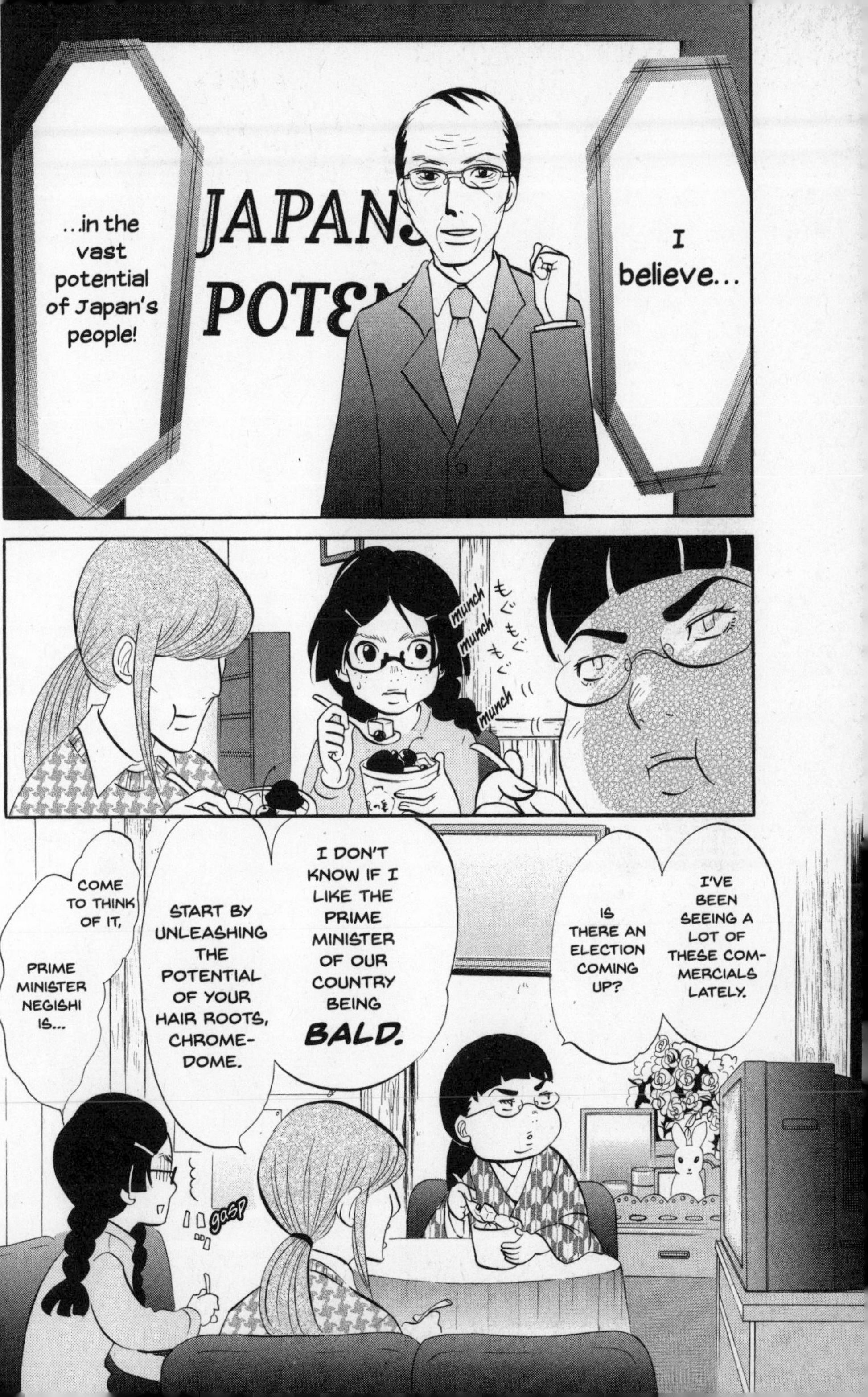
I believe...
...in the vast potential of Japan's people!
munch munch munch
もぐもぐもぐ
I'VE BEEN SEEING A LOT OF THESE COMMERCIALS LATELY.
IS THERE AN ELECTION COMING UP?
I DON'T KNOW IF I LIKE THE PRIME MINISTER OF OUR COUNTRY BEING **BALD.**
START BY UNLEASHING THE POTENTIAL OF YOUR HAIR ROOTS, CHROME-DOME.
COME TO THINK OF IT,
PRIME MINISTER NEGISHI IS...
gasp

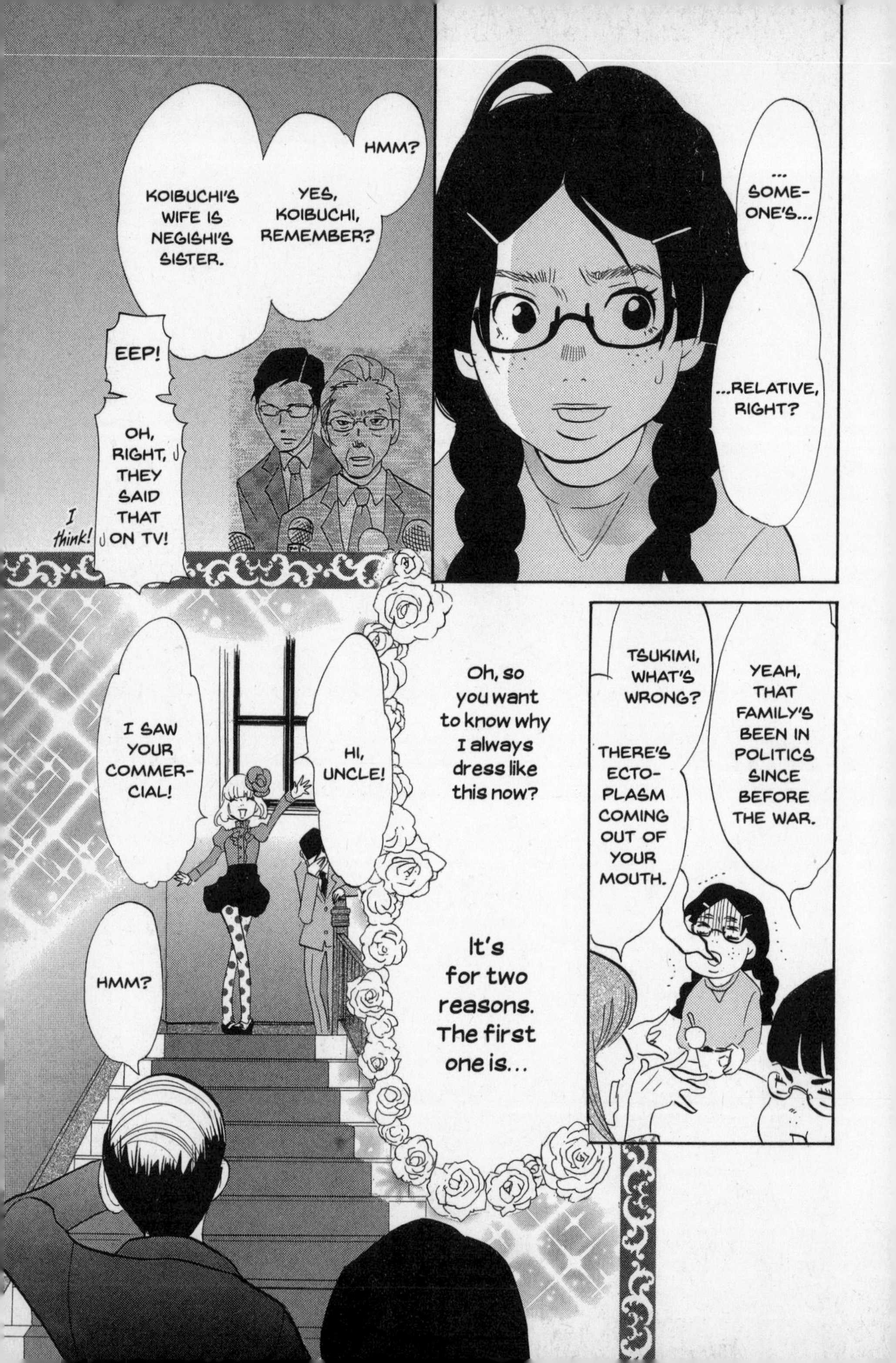
... SOME-ONE'S...
...RELATIVE, RIGHT?
HMM?
YES, KOIBUCHI, REMEMBER?
KOIBUCHI'S WIFE IS NEGISHI'S SISTER.
EEP!
OH, RIGHT, THEY SAID THAT ON TV!
I think!
YEAH, THAT FAMILY'S BEEN IN POLITICS SINCE BEFORE THE WAR.
TSUKIMI, WHAT'S WRONG?
THERE'S ECTO-PLASM COMING OUT OF YOUR MOUTH.
Oh, so you want to know why I always dress like this now?
HI, UNCLE!
I SAW YOUR COMMERCIAL!
It's for two reasons. The first one is...
HMM?

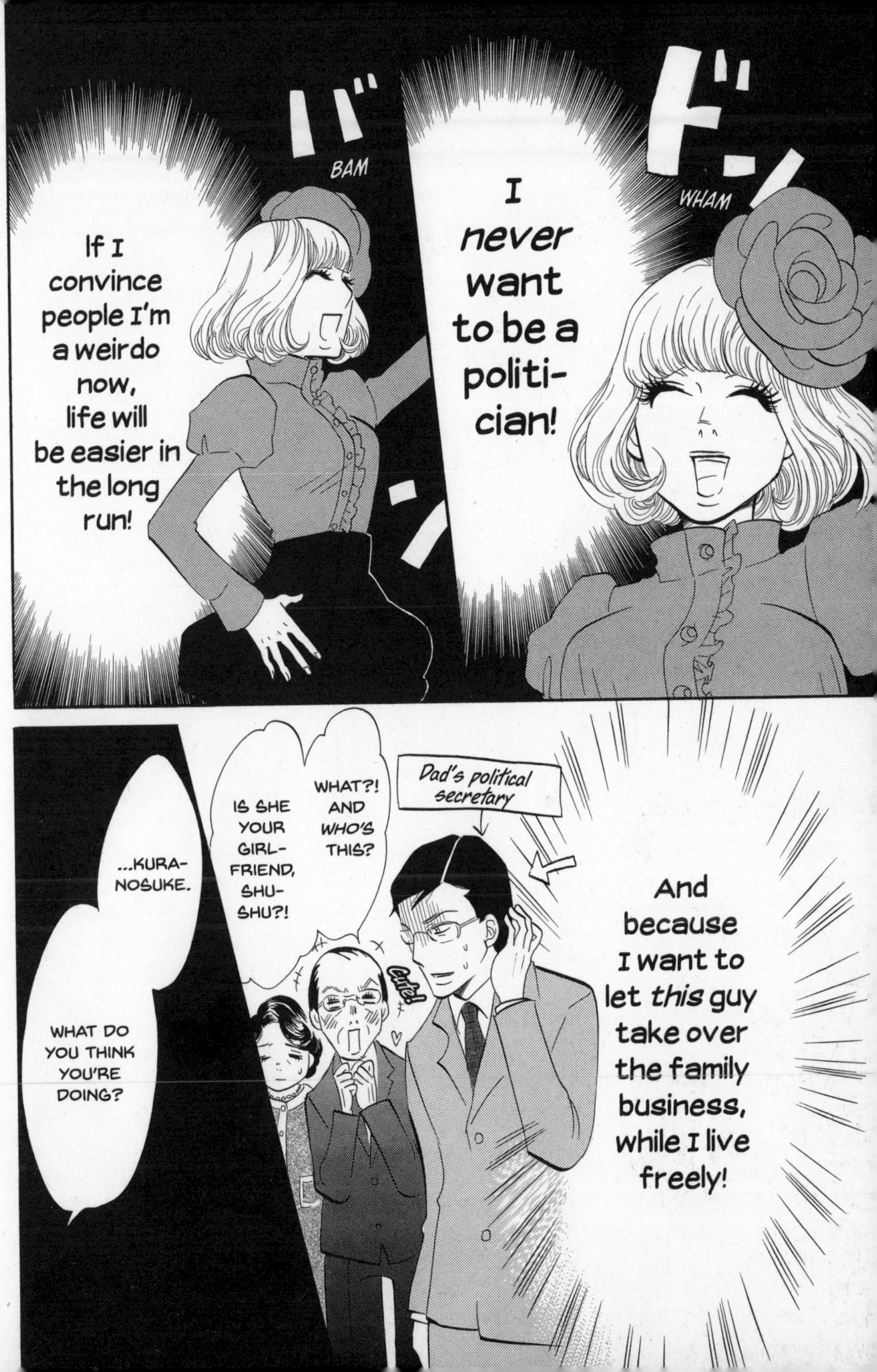
WHAM
I *never* want to be a politi-cian!
BAM
If I convince people I'm a weirdo now, life will be easier in the long run!
And because I want to let *this* guy take over the family business, while I live freely!
Dad's political secretary
WHAT?! AND WHO'S THIS?
IS SHE YOUR GIRL-FRIEND, SHU-SHU?!
Cute!
...KURA-NOSUKE.
WHAT DO YOU THINK YOU'RE DOING?

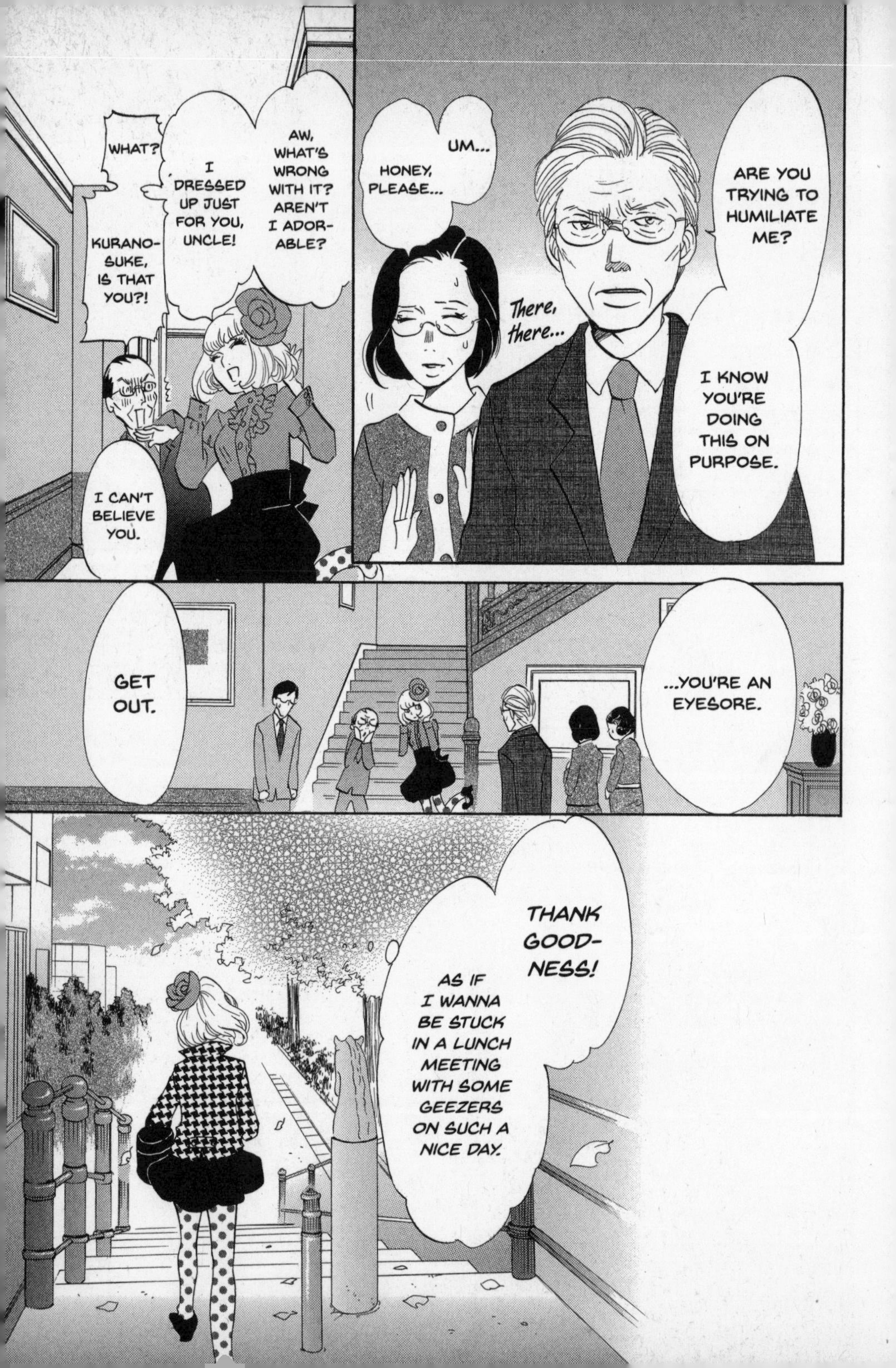
ARE YOU TRYING TO HUMILIATE ME?
I KNOW YOU'RE DOING THIS ON PURPOSE.
UM...
HONEY, PLEASE...
There, there...
AW, WHAT'S WRONG WITH IT? AREN'T I ADORABLE?
I DRESSED UP JUST FOR YOU, UNCLE!
WHAT?
KURANOSUKE, IS THAT YOU?!
I CAN'T BELIEVE YOU.
...YOU'RE AN EYESORE.
GET OUT.
THANK GOODNESS!
AS IF I WANNA BE STUCK IN A LUNCH MEETING WITH SOME GEEZERS ON SUCH A NICE DAY.

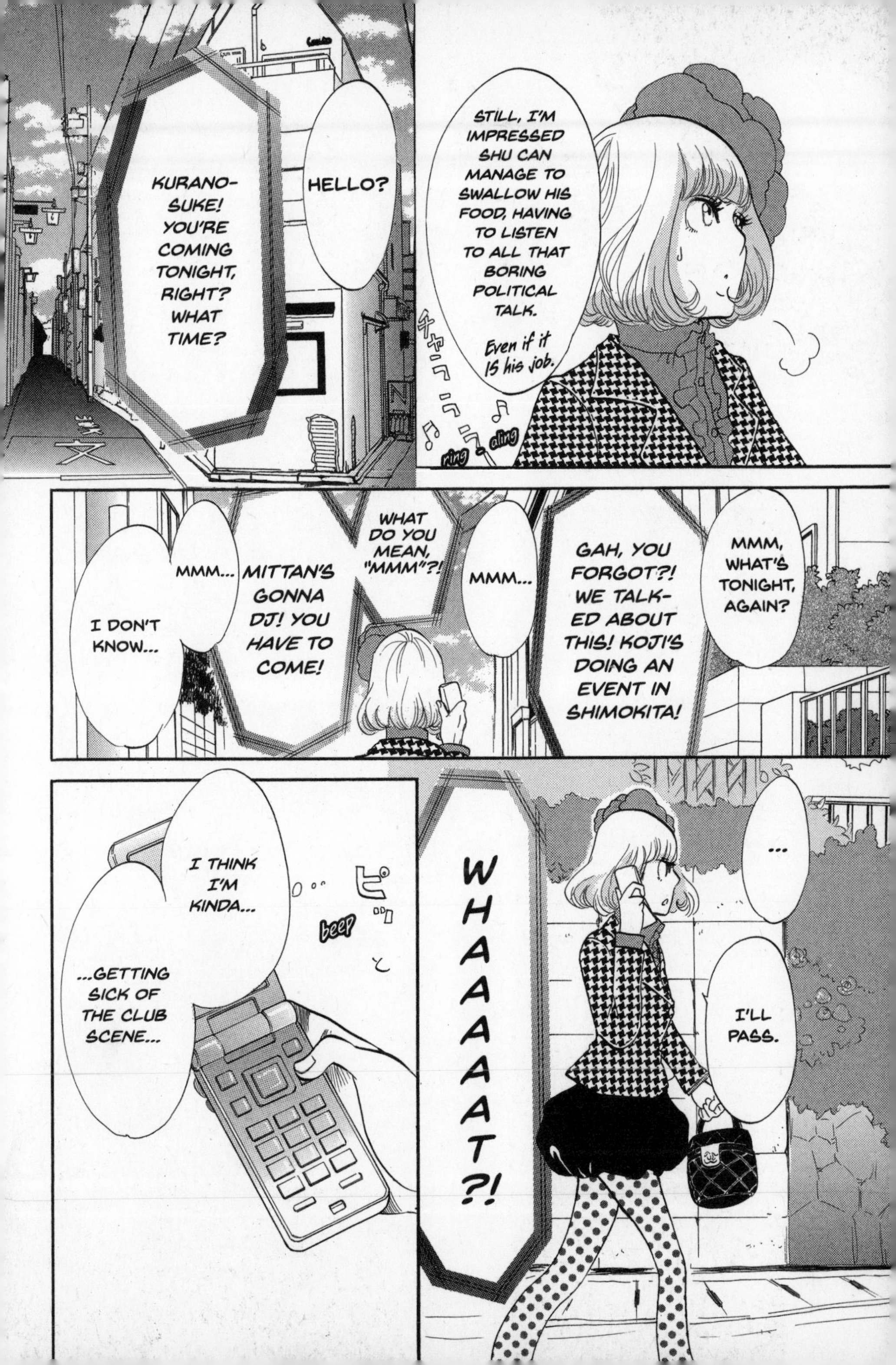
STILL, I'M IMPRESSED SHU CAN MANAGE TO SWALLOW HIS FOOD, HAVING TO LISTEN TO ALL THAT BORING POLITICAL TALK.
Even if it IS his job.
ring-aling
HELLO?
KURANO-SUKE! YOU'RE COMING TONIGHT, RIGHT? WHAT TIME?
MMM, WHAT'S TONIGHT, AGAIN?
GAH, YOU FORGOT?! WE TALK-ED ABOUT THIS! KOJI'S DOING AN EVENT IN SHIMOKITA!
MMM...
WHAT DO YOU MEAN, "MMM"?!
MITTAN'S GONNA DJ! YOU HAVE TO COME!
MMM...
I DON'T KNOW...
...
I'LL PASS.
WHAAAAAT?!
I THINK I'M KINDA...
...GETTING SICK OF THE CLUB SCENE...
beep

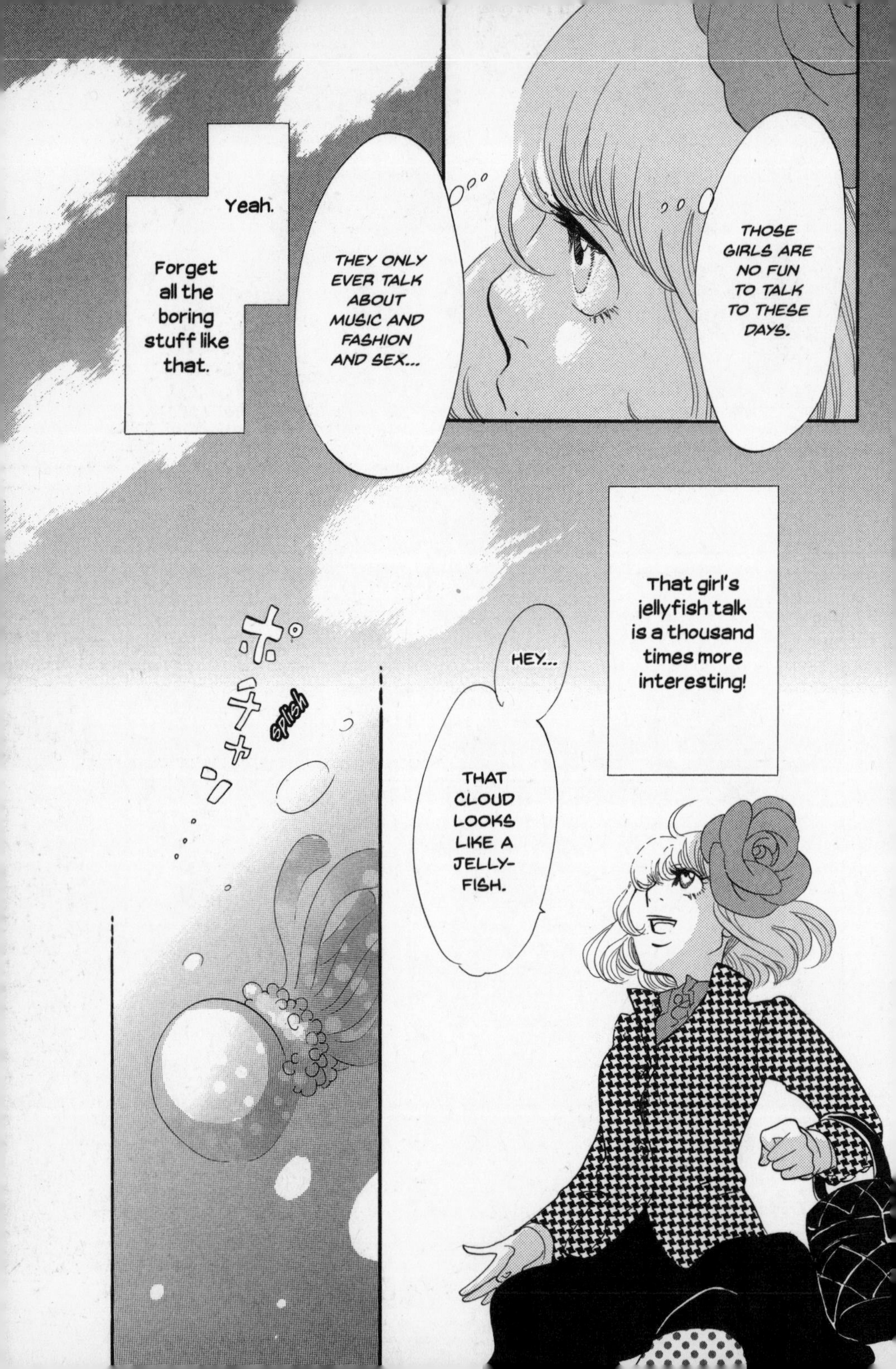
THOSE GIRLS ARE NO FUN TO TALK TO THESE DAYS.
THEY ONLY EVER TALK ABOUT MUSIC AND FASHION AND SEX...
Yeah.
Forget all the boring stuff like that.
That girl's jellyfish talk is a thousand times more interesting!
HEY...
THAT CLOUD LOOKS LIKE A JELLY-FISH.
ポチャン
splish

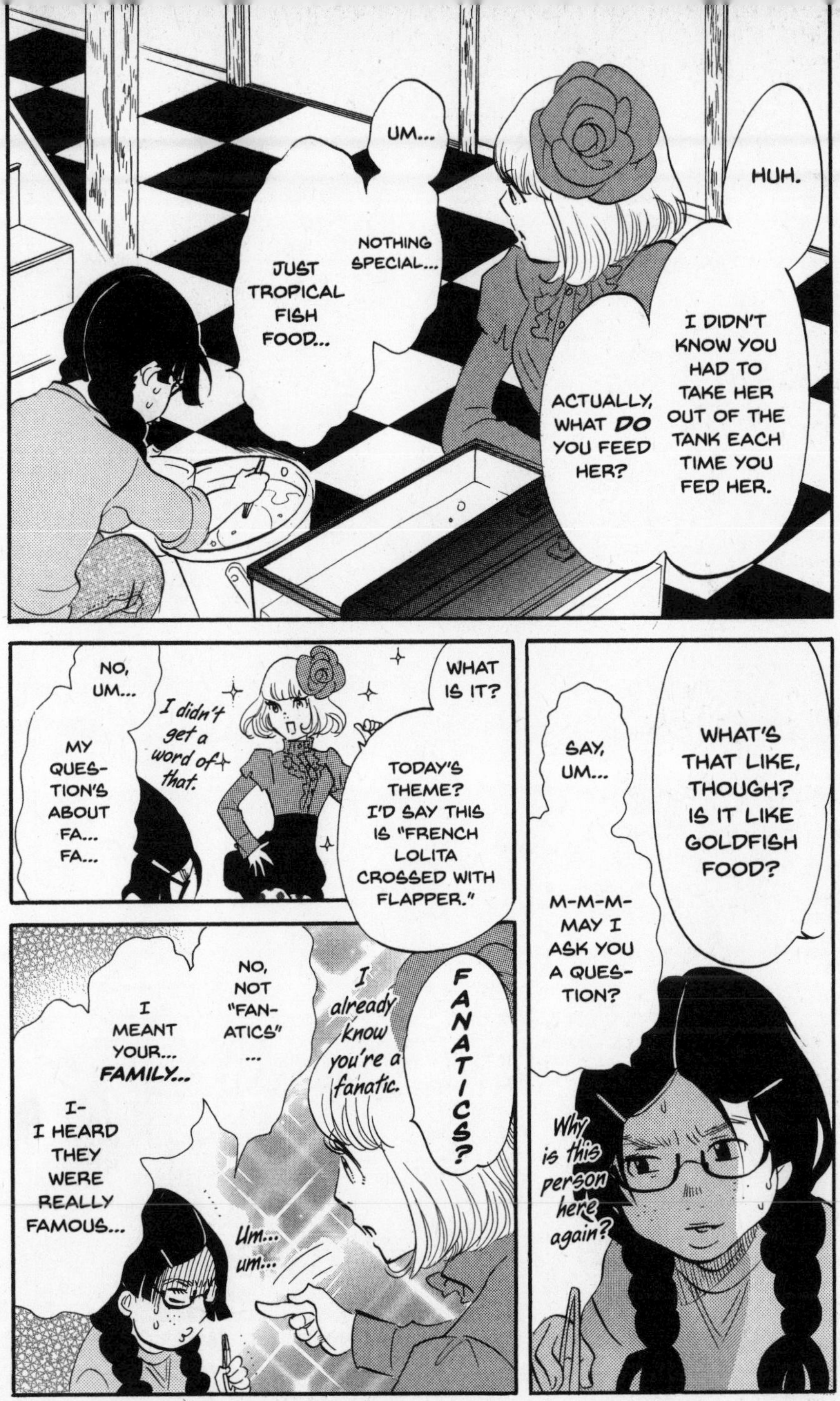
HUH.
I DIDN'T KNOW YOU HAD TO TAKE HER OUT OF THE TANK EACH TIME YOU FED HER.
ACTUALLY, WHAT **DO** YOU FEED HER?
UM...
NOTHING SPECIAL...
JUST TROPICAL FISH FOOD...
WHAT'S THAT LIKE, THOUGH? IS IT LIKE GOLDFISH FOOD?
SAY, UM...
M-M-M-MAY I ASK YOU A QUESTION?
Why is this person here again?
WHAT IS IT?
TODAY'S THEME? I'D SAY THIS IS "FRENCH LOLITA CROSSED WITH FLAPPER."
I didn't get a word of that.
NO, UM...
MY QUES-TION'S ABOUT FA... FA...
FANATICS?
I already know you're a fanatic.
NO, NOT "FAN-ATICS" ...
I MEANT YOUR... **FAMILY...**
I- I HEARD THEY WERE REALLY FAMOUS...
Um... um...

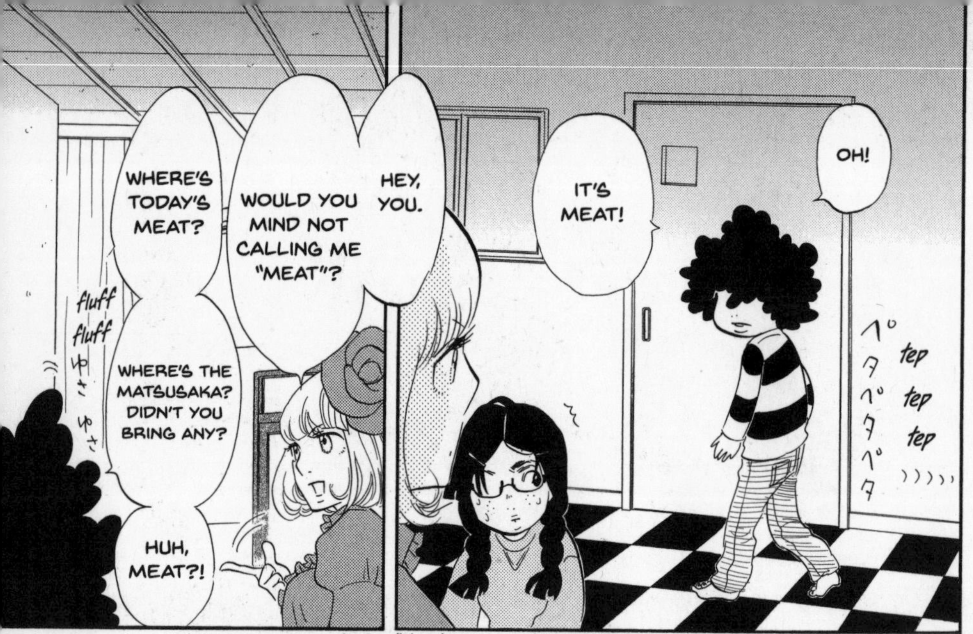
OH!
tep tep tep
IT'S MEAT!
HEY, YOU.
WOULD YOU MIND NOT CALLING ME "MEAT"?
WHERE'S TODAY'S MEAT?
fluff fluff
WHERE'S THE MATSUSAKA? DIDN'T YOU BRING ANY?
HUH, MEAT?!

*A traditional Japanese dessert of jelly, sweet red bean, fruits, topped with syrup.

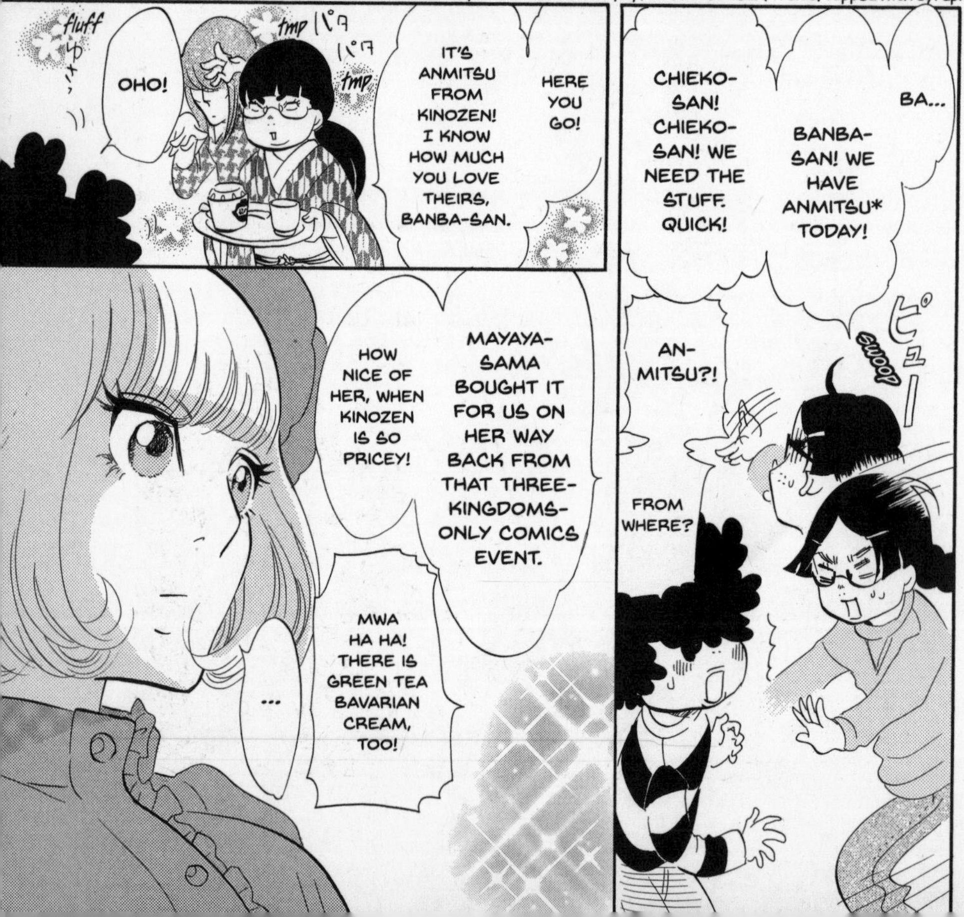
BA...
BANBA-SAN! WE HAVE ANMITSU* TODAY!
CHIEKO-SAN! CHIEKO-SAN! WE NEED THE STUFF. QUICK!
HERE YOU GO!
IT'S ANMITSU FROM KINOZEN! I KNOW HOW MUCH YOU LOVE THEIRS, BANBA-SAN.
tmp tmp
fluff
OHO!
swoop
AN-MITSU?!
FROM WHERE?
MAYAYA-SAMA BOUGHT IT FOR US ON HER WAY BACK FROM THAT THREE-KINGDOMS-ONLY COMICS EVENT.
HOW NICE OF HER, WHEN KINOZEN IS SO PRICEY!
MWA HA HA! THERE IS GREEN TEA BAVARIAN CREAM, TOO!
...

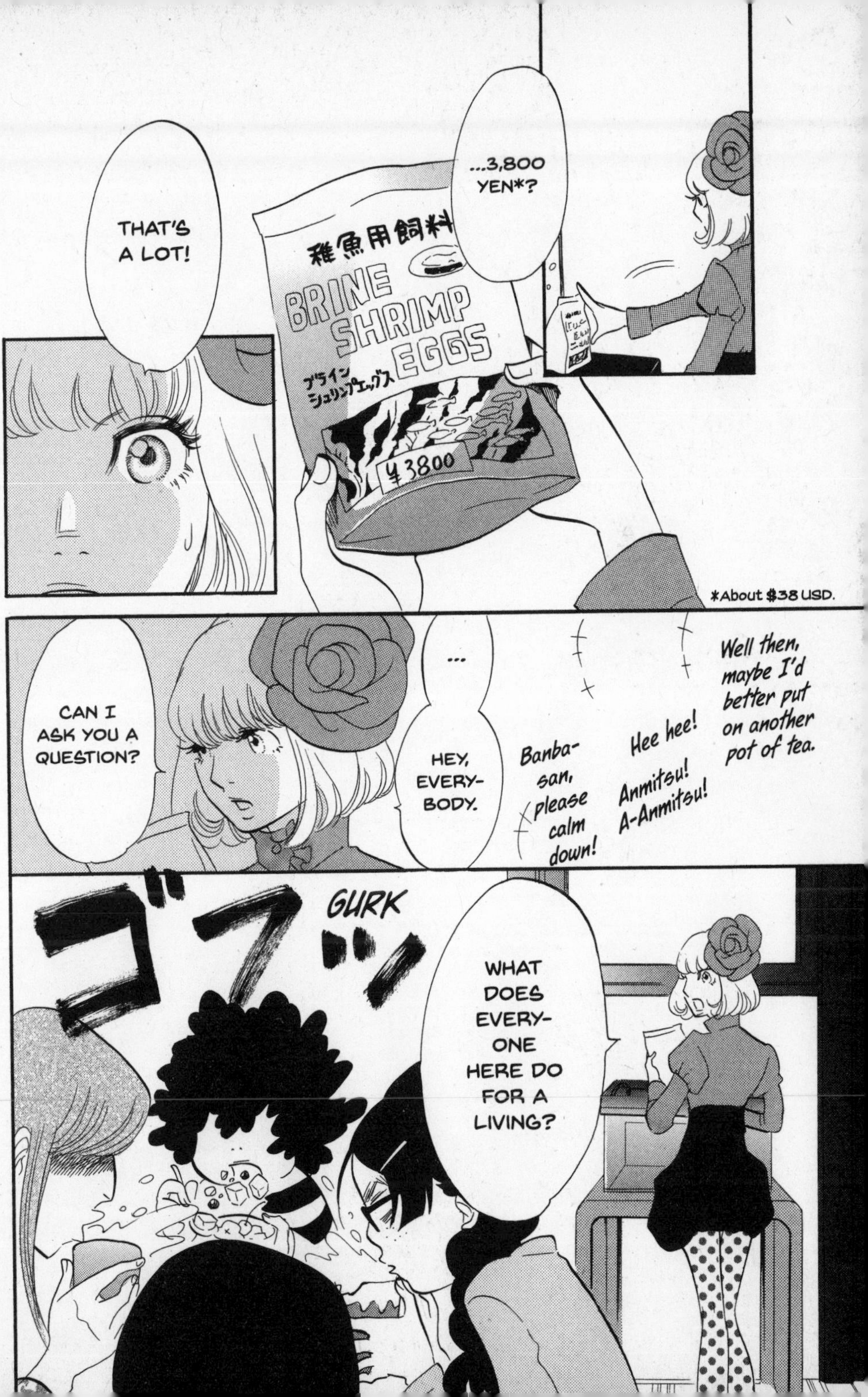
...3,800 YEN*?
THAT'S A LOT!
稚魚用飼料
BRINE SHRIMP EGGS
ブラインシュリンプエッグス
¥3800
Well then, maybe I'd better put on another pot of tea.
Hee hee!
Anmitsu! A-Anmitsu!
Banba-san, please calm down!
...
HEY, EVERY-BODY.
CAN I ASK YOU A QUESTION?
WHAT DOES EVERY-ONE HERE DO FOR A LIVING?
GURK
ゴブッ
*About $38 USD.

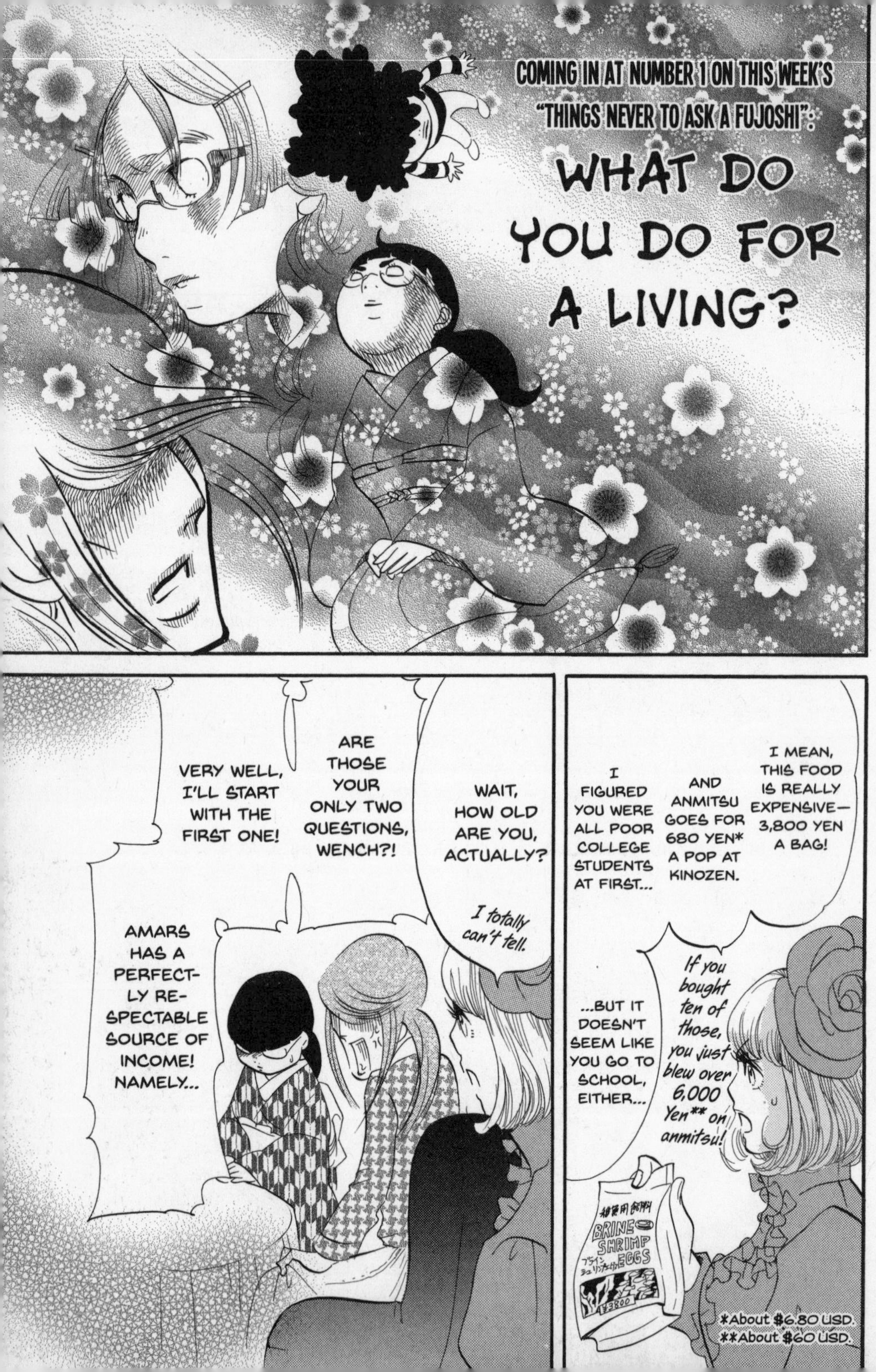
COMING IN AT NUMBER 1 ON THIS WEEK'S "THINGS NEVER TO ASK A FUJOSHI":
WHAT DO YOU DO FOR A LIVING?
I MEAN, THIS FOOD IS REALLY EXPENSIVE— 3,800 YEN A BAG!
AND ANMITSU GOES FOR 680 YEN* A POP AT KINOZEN.
I FIGURED YOU WERE ALL POOR COLLEGE STUDENTS AT FIRST...
If you bought ten of those, you just blew over 6,000 Yen** on anmitsu!
...BUT IT DOESN'T SEEM LIKE YOU GO TO SCHOOL, EITHER...
BRINE SHRIMP EGGS
¥3800
WAIT, HOW OLD ARE YOU, ACTUALLY?
I totally can't tell.
ARE THOSE YOUR ONLY TWO QUESTIONS, WENCH?!
VERY WELL, I'LL START WITH THE FIRST ONE!
AMARS HAS A PERFECTLY RESPECTABLE SOURCE OF INCOME! NAMELY...
*About $6.80 USD.
**About $60 USD.

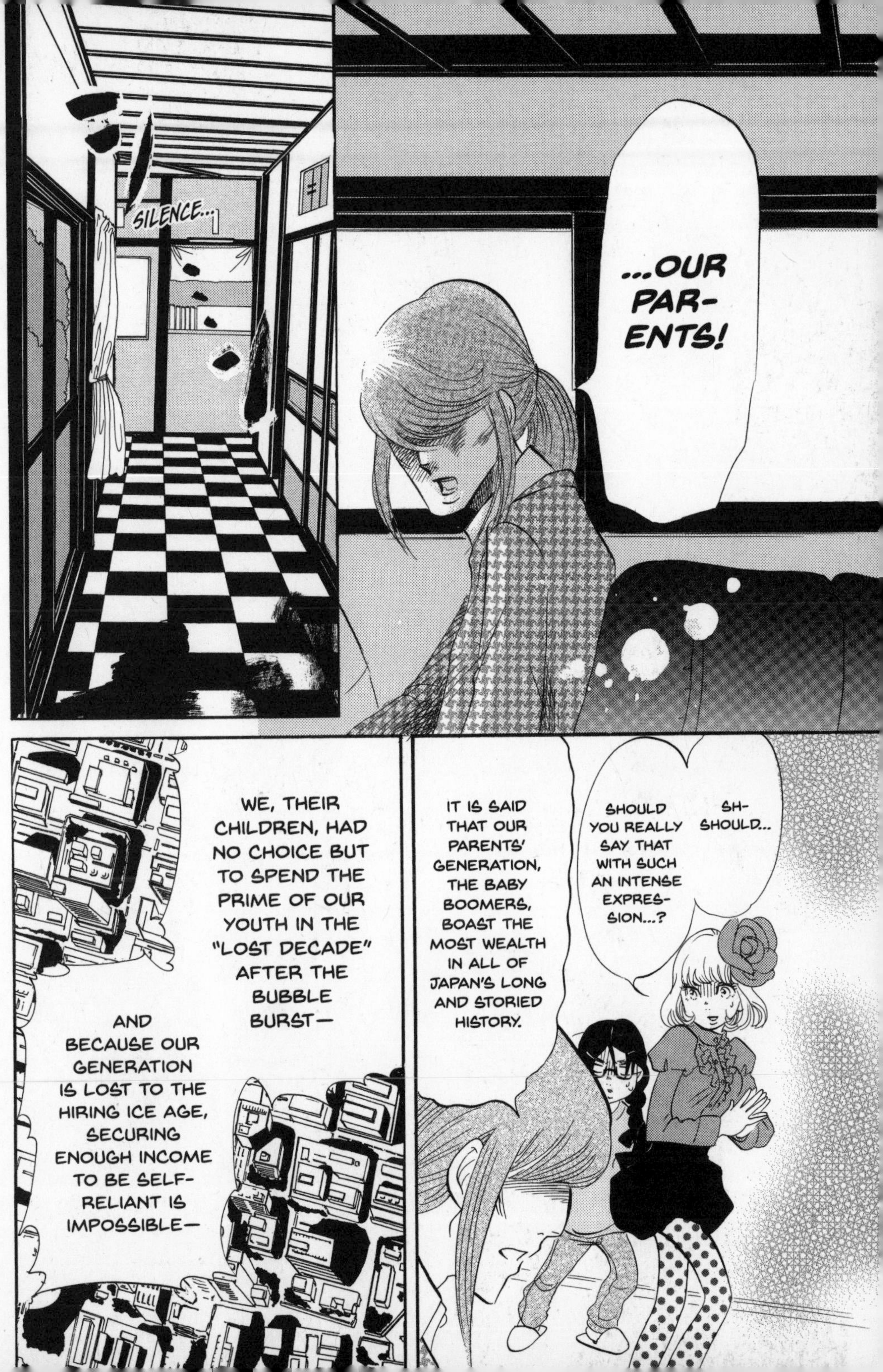
...OUR PAR- ENTS!
SILENCE...
SH- SHOULD...
SHOULD YOU REALLY SAY THAT WITH SUCH AN INTENSE EXPRES- SION...?
IT IS SAID THAT OUR PARENTS' GENERATION, THE BABY BOOMERS, BOAST THE MOST WEALTH IN ALL OF JAPAN'S LONG AND STORIED HISTORY.
WE, THEIR CHILDREN, HAD NO CHOICE BUT TO SPEND THE PRIME OF OUR YOUTH IN THE "LOST DECADE" AFTER THE BUBBLE BURST—
AND BECAUSE OUR GENERATION IS LOST TO THE HIRING ICE AGE, SECURING ENOUGH INCOME TO BE SELF- RELIANT IS IMPOSSIBLE—

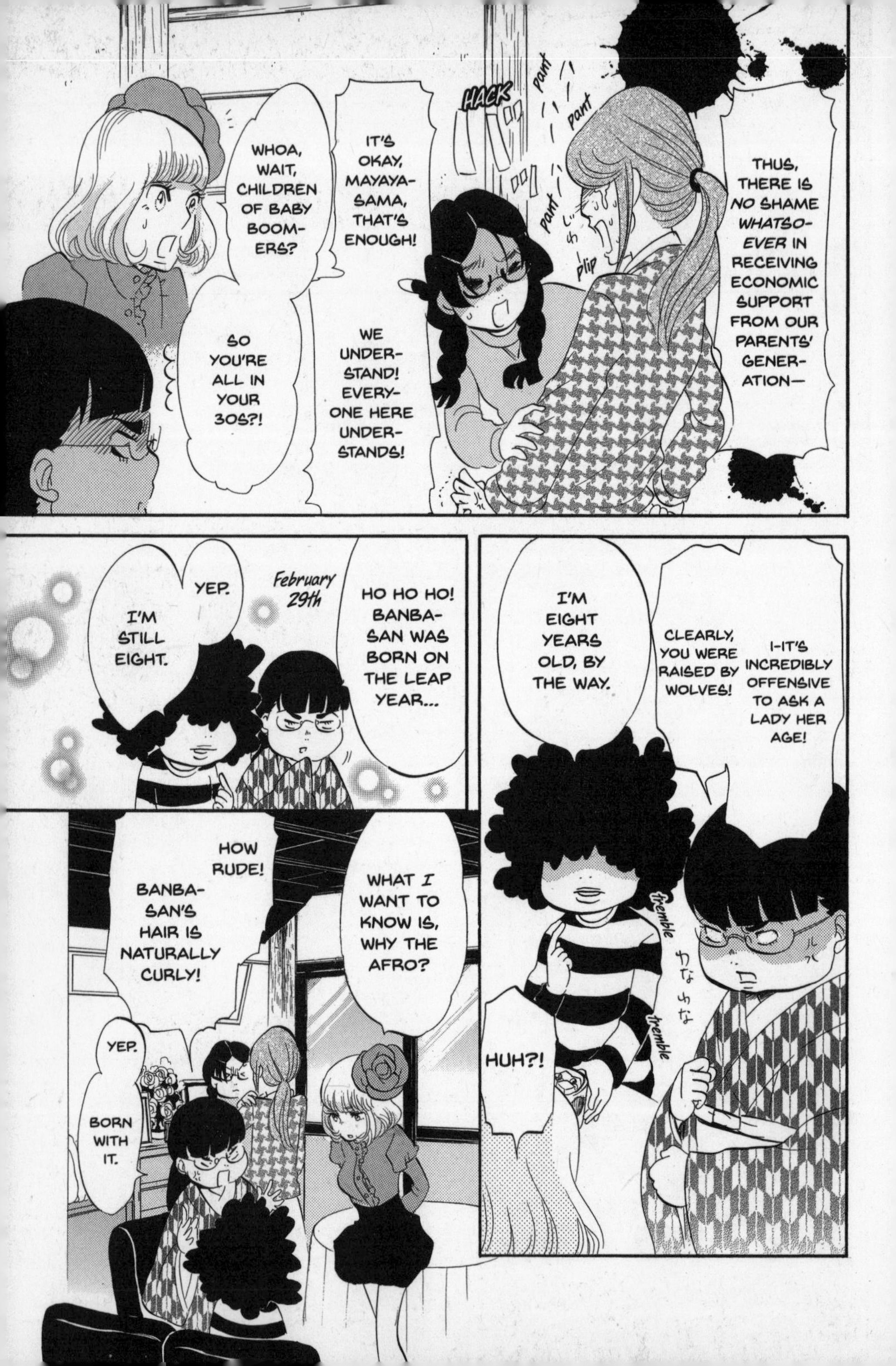
THUS, THERE IS NO SHAME *WHATSOEVER* IN RECEIVING ECONOMIC SUPPORT FROM OUR PARENTS' GENERATION—
HACK
pant
pant
pant
plip
IT'S OKAY, MAYAYA-SAMA, THAT'S ENOUGH!
WE UNDERSTAND! EVERYONE HERE UNDERSTANDS!
WHOA, WAIT, CHILDREN OF BABY BOOMERS?
SO YOU'RE ALL IN YOUR 30S?!
I-IT'S INCREDIBLY OFFENSIVE TO ASK A LADY HER AGE!
CLEARLY, YOU WERE RAISED BY WOLVES!
I'M EIGHT YEARS OLD, BY THE WAY.
tremble
tremble
HUH?!
HO HO HO! BANBA-SAN WAS BORN ON THE LEAP YEAR...
February 29th
YEP.
I'M STILL EIGHT.
WHAT *I* WANT TO KNOW IS, WHY THE AFRO?
HOW RUDE! BANBA-SAN'S HAIR IS NATURALLY CURLY!
YEP.
BORN WITH IT.

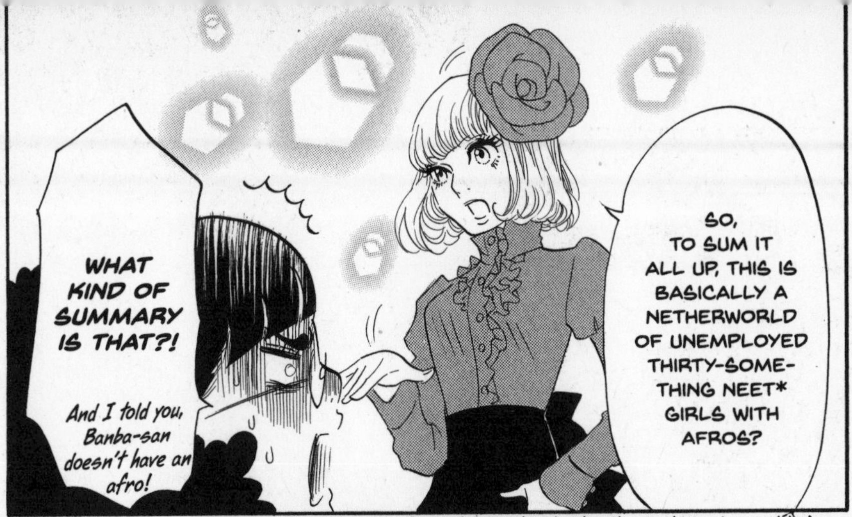
SO, TO SUM IT ALL UP, THIS IS BASICALLY A NETHERWORLD OF UNEMPLOYED THIRTY-SOME-THING NEET* GIRLS WITH AFROS?
WHAT KIND OF SUMMARY IS THAT?!
And I told you, Banba-san doesn't have an afro!

*People who are: unemployed, not students, not in training for employment (Not in Education, Employment, or Training).

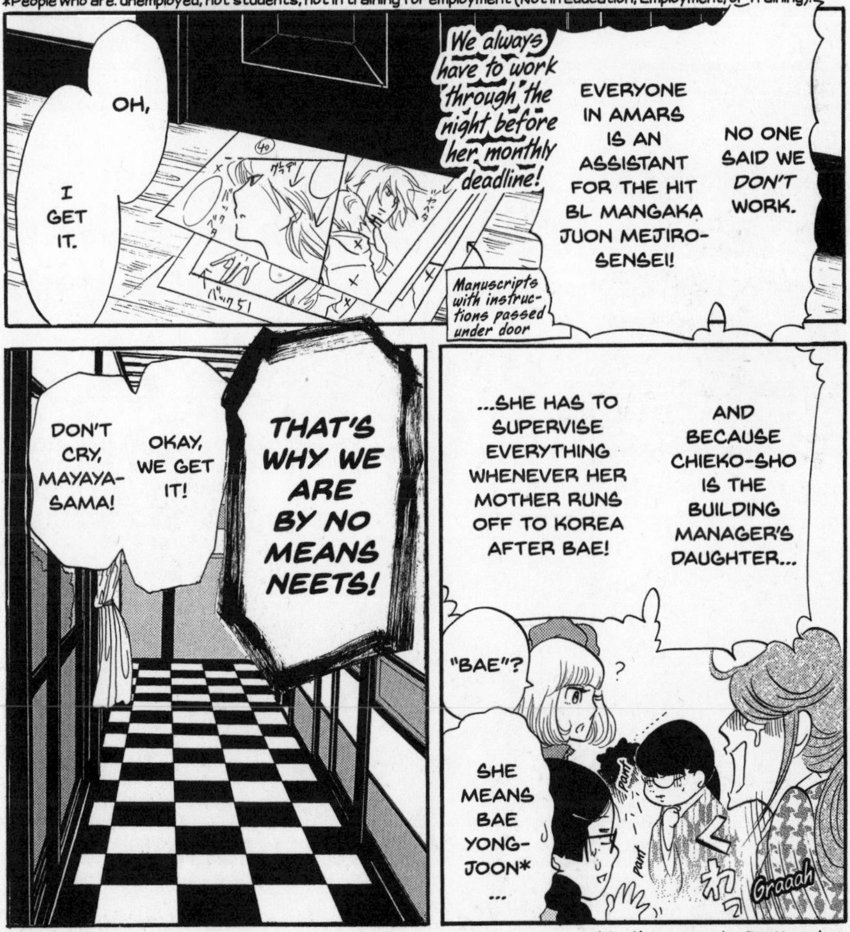
NO ONE SAID WE DON'T WORK.
EVERYONE IN AMARS IS AN ASSISTANT FOR THE HIT BL MANGAKA JUON MEJIRO-SENSEI!
We always have to work through the night before her monthly deadline!
Manuscripts with instructions passed under door
OH, I GET IT.
AND BECAUSE CHIEKO-SHO IS THE BUILDING MANAGER'S DAUGHTER...
...SHE HAS TO SUPERVISE EVERYTHING WHENEVER HER MOTHER RUNS OFF TO KOREA AFTER BAE!
"BAE"?
SHE MEANS BAE YONG-JOON* ...
pant
pant
Graaah
THAT'S WHY WE ARE BY NO MEANS NEETS!
OKAY, WE GET IT!
DON'T CRY, MAYAYA-SAMA!

*South Korean actor Bae Yong-joon.

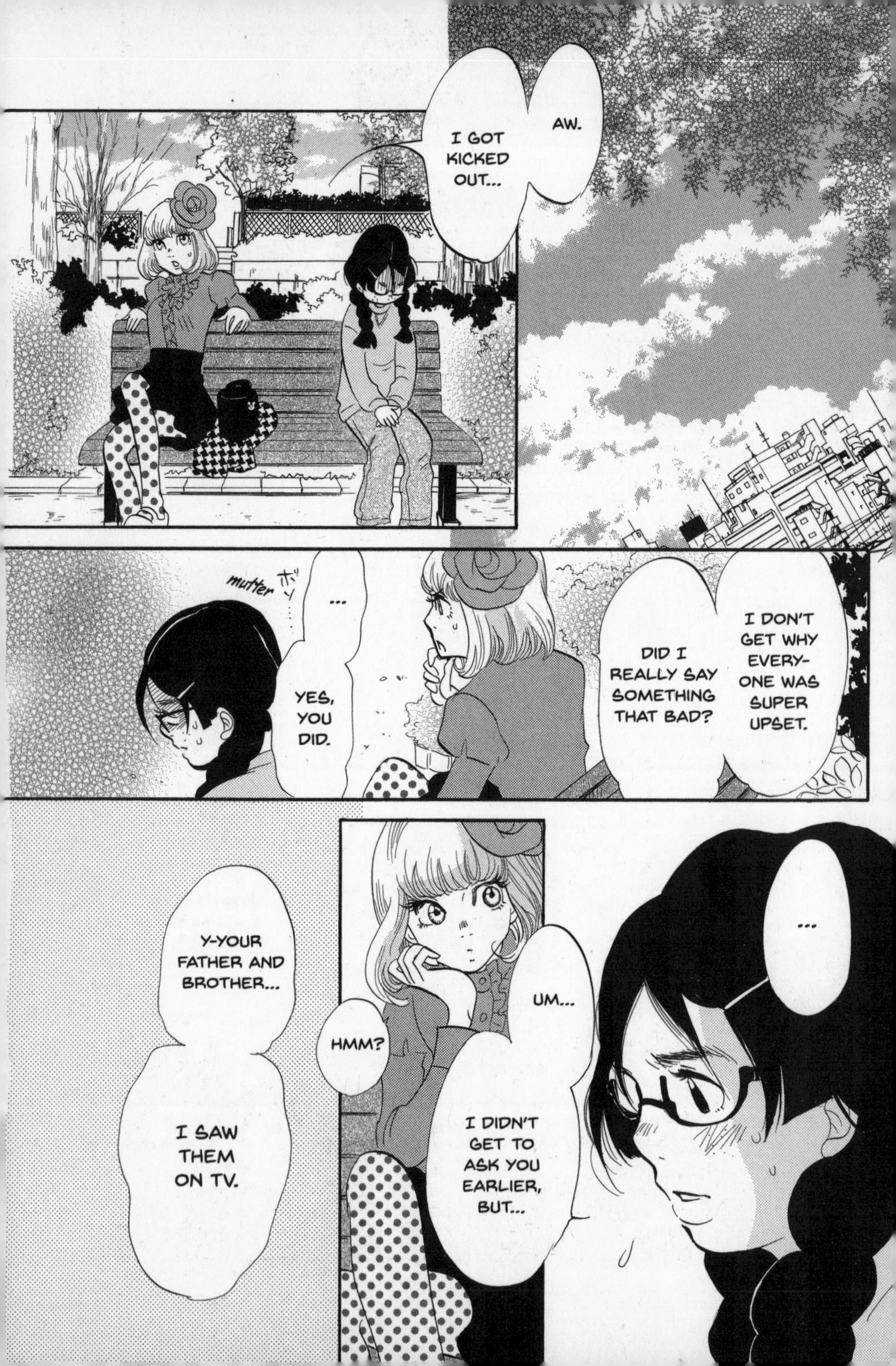
AW.
I GOT KICKED OUT...
I DON'T GET WHY EVERY-ONE WAS SUPER UPSET.
DID I REALLY SAY SOMETHING THAT BAD?
...
YES, YOU DID.
mutter ボソ
...
UM...
I DIDN'T GET TO ASK YOU EARLIER, BUT...
HMM?
Y-YOUR FATHER AND BROTHER...
I SAW THEM ON TV.

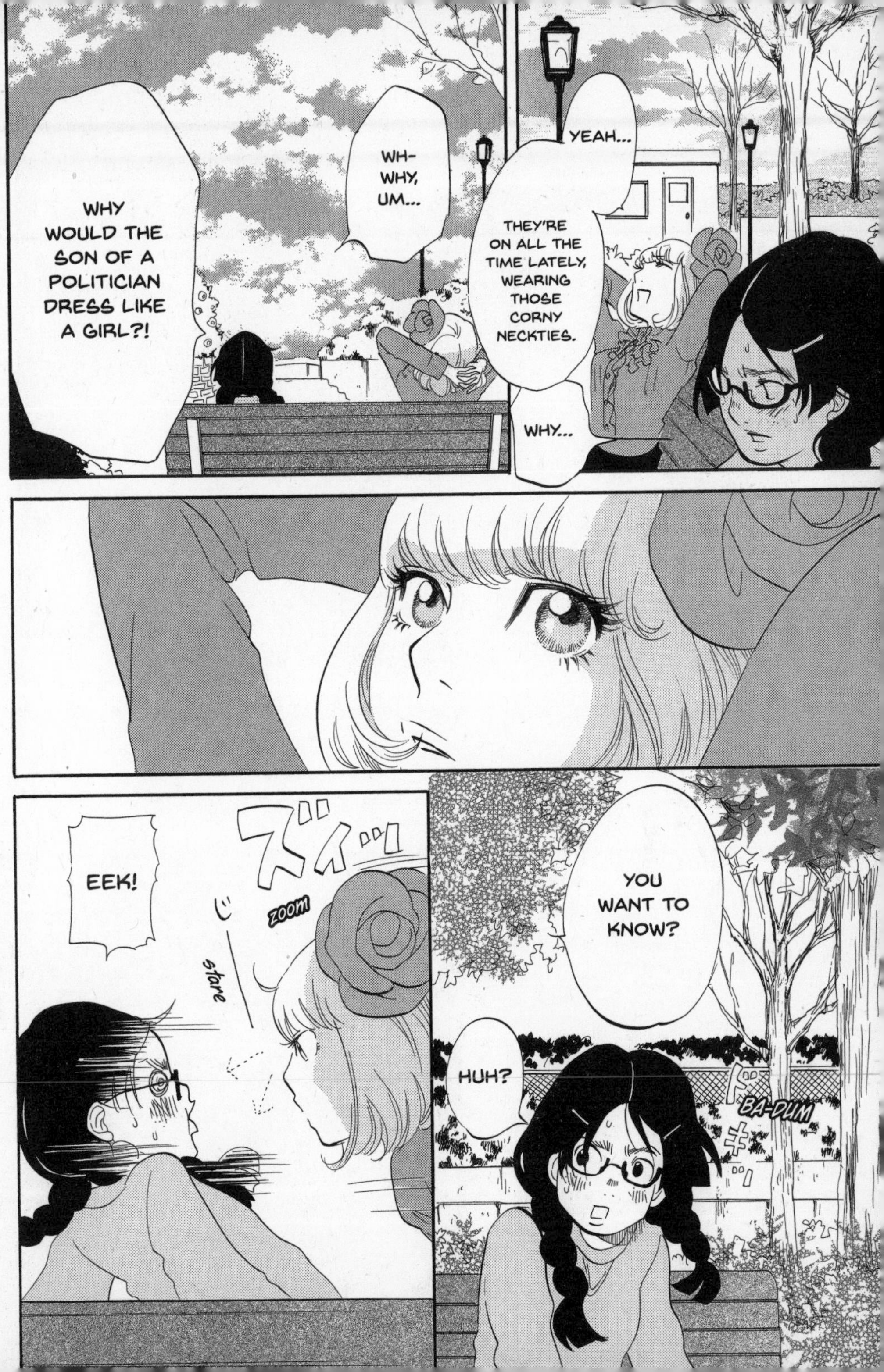
YEAH...
THEY'RE ON ALL THE TIME LATELY, WEARING THOSE CORNY NECKTIES.
WHY...
WH-WHY, UM...
WHY WOULD THE SON OF A POLITICIAN DRESS LIKE A GIRL?!
YOU WANT TO KNOW?
BA-DUM
HUH?
ZOOM
stare
EEK!

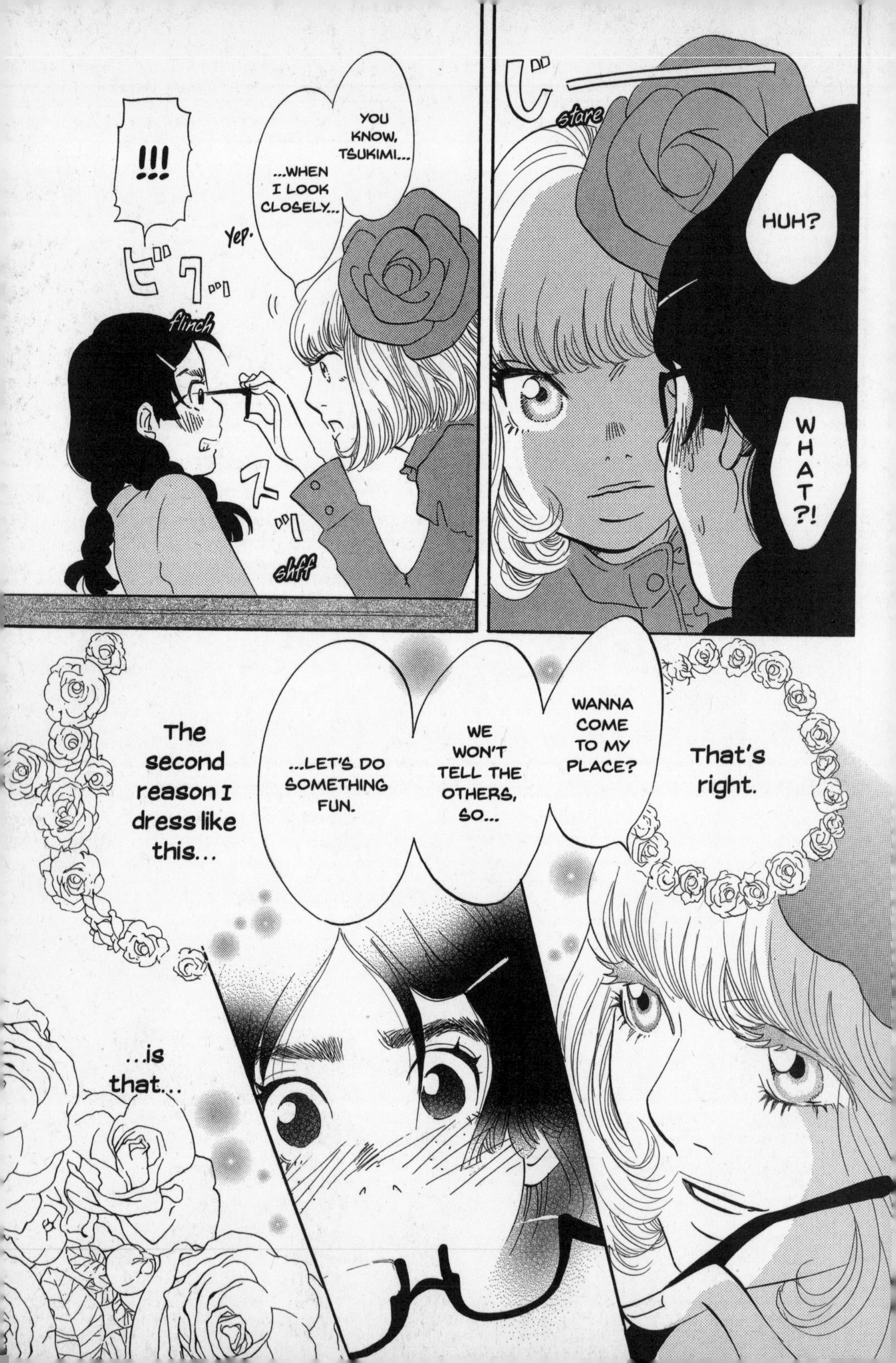
じー
stare
HUH?
WHAT?!
YOU KNOW, TSUKIMI...
...WHEN I LOOK CLOSELY...
!!!
Yep.
ビクッ
flinch
スッ
shff
That's right.
WANNA COME TO MY PLACE?
WE WON'T TELL THE OTHERS, SO...
...LET'S DO SOMETHING FUN.
The second reason I dress like this...
...is that...

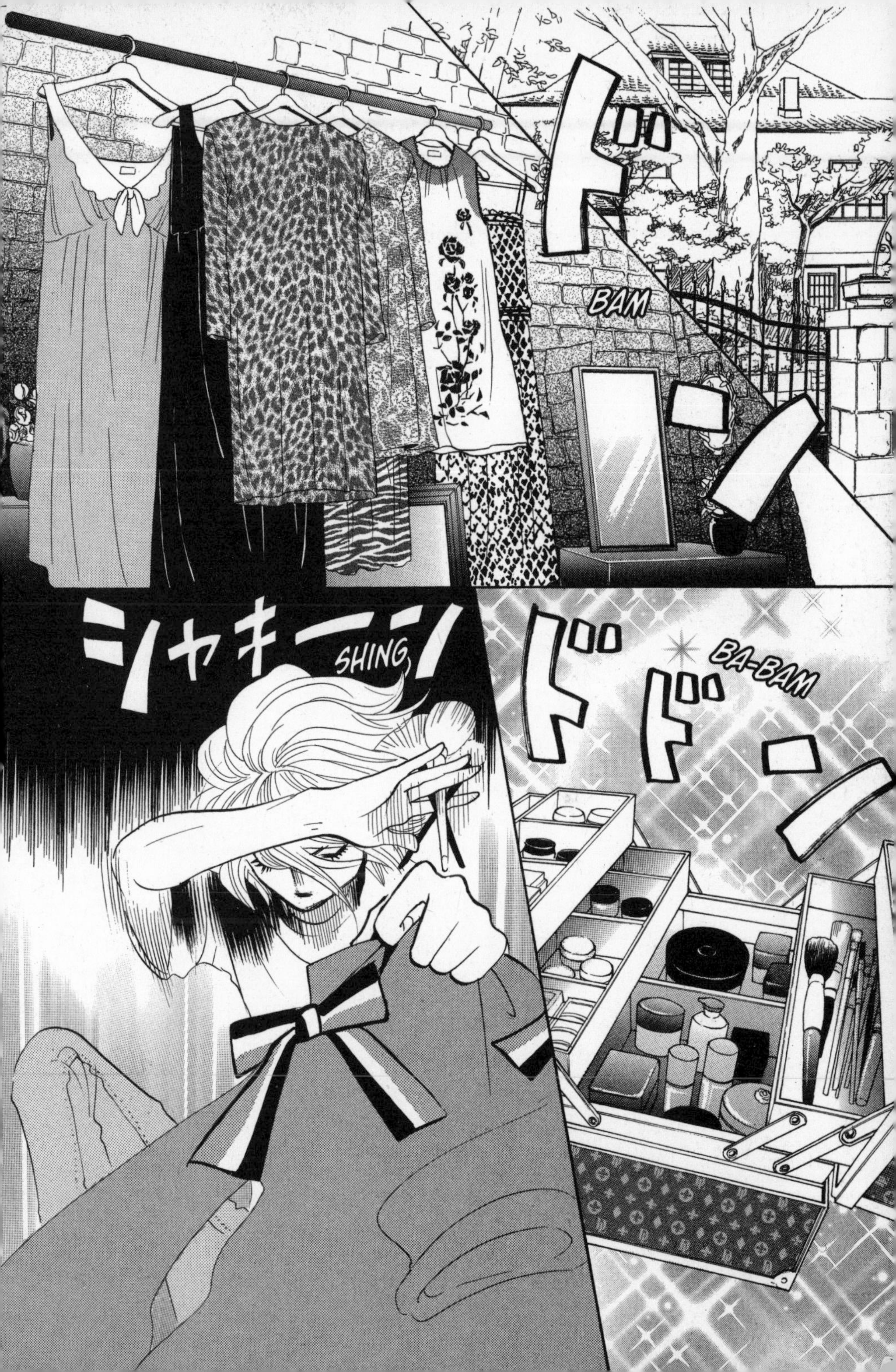

ドーン
BAM
ドドーン
BA-BAM
シャキーン
SHING

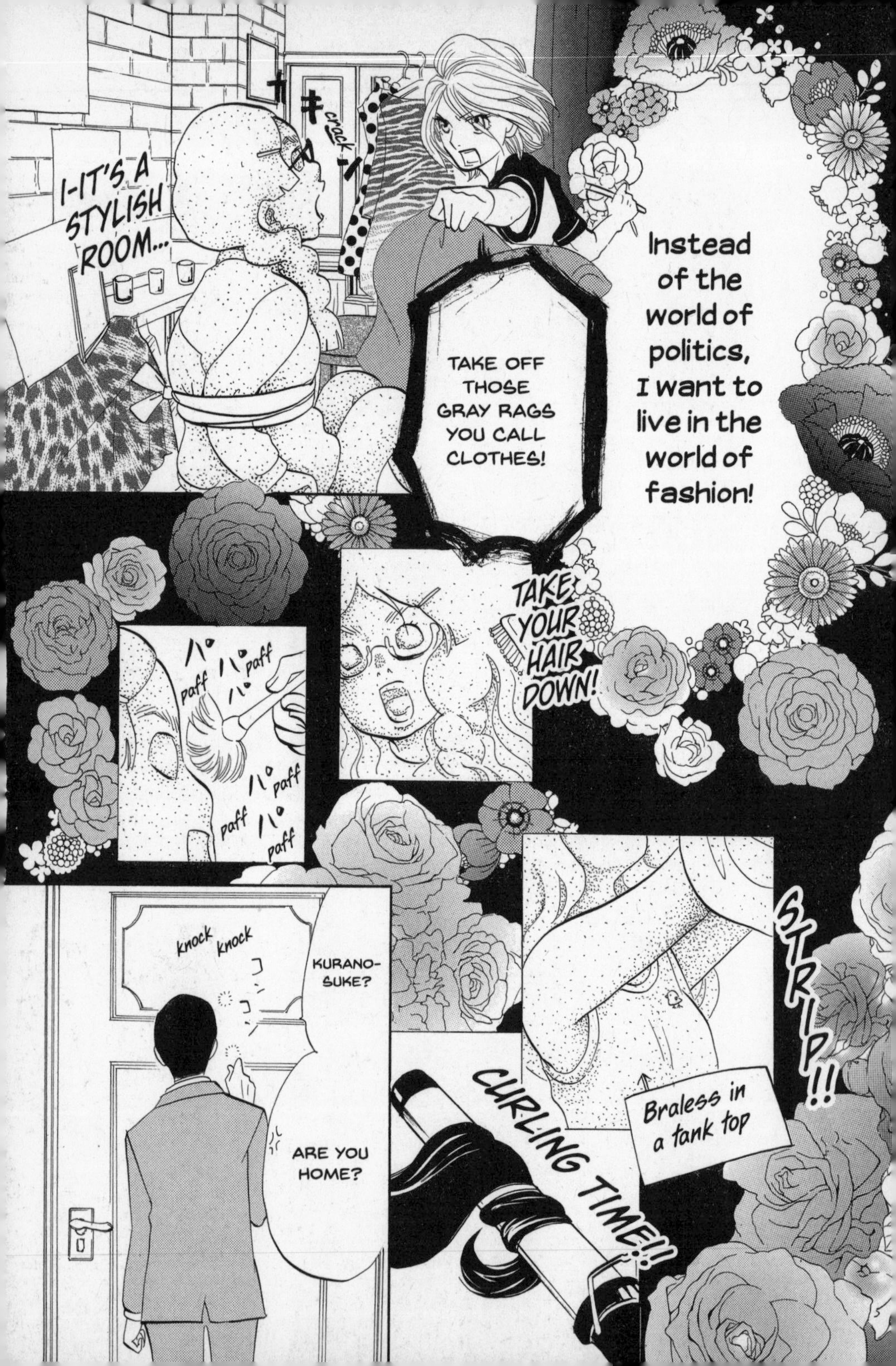
Instead of the world of politics, I want to live in the world of fashion!
TAKE OFF THOSE GRAY RAGS YOU CALL CLOTHES!
crack
I-IT'S A STYLISH ROOM...
TAKE YOUR HAIR DOWN!
paff
paff
paff
paff
paff
paff
STRIP!!
Braless in a tank top
CURLING TIME!!
knock knock
KURANO-SUKE?
ARE YOU HOME?

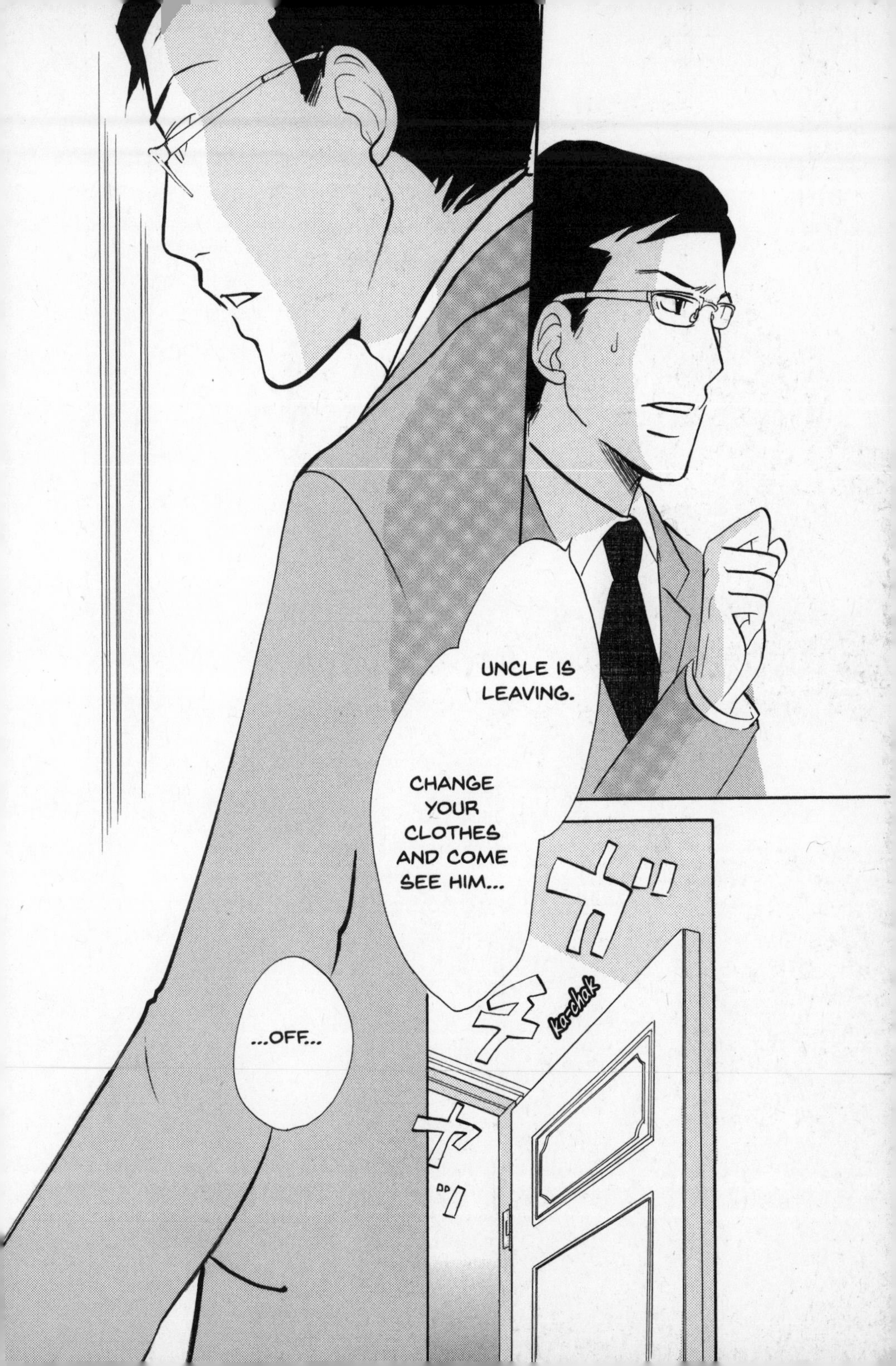
UNCLE IS LEAVING.
CHANGE YOUR CLOTHES AND COME SEE HIM...
ka-chak
...OFF...

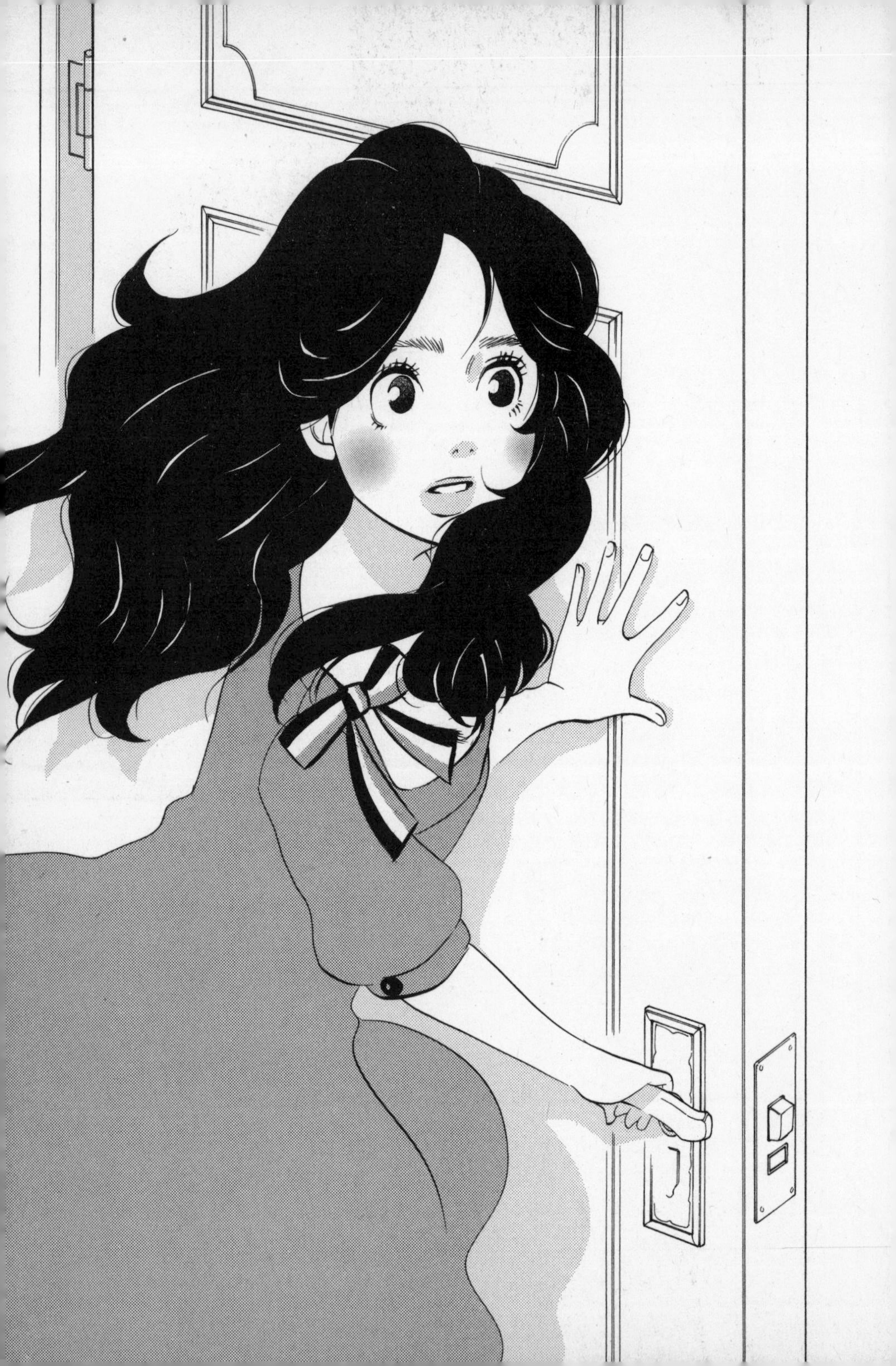

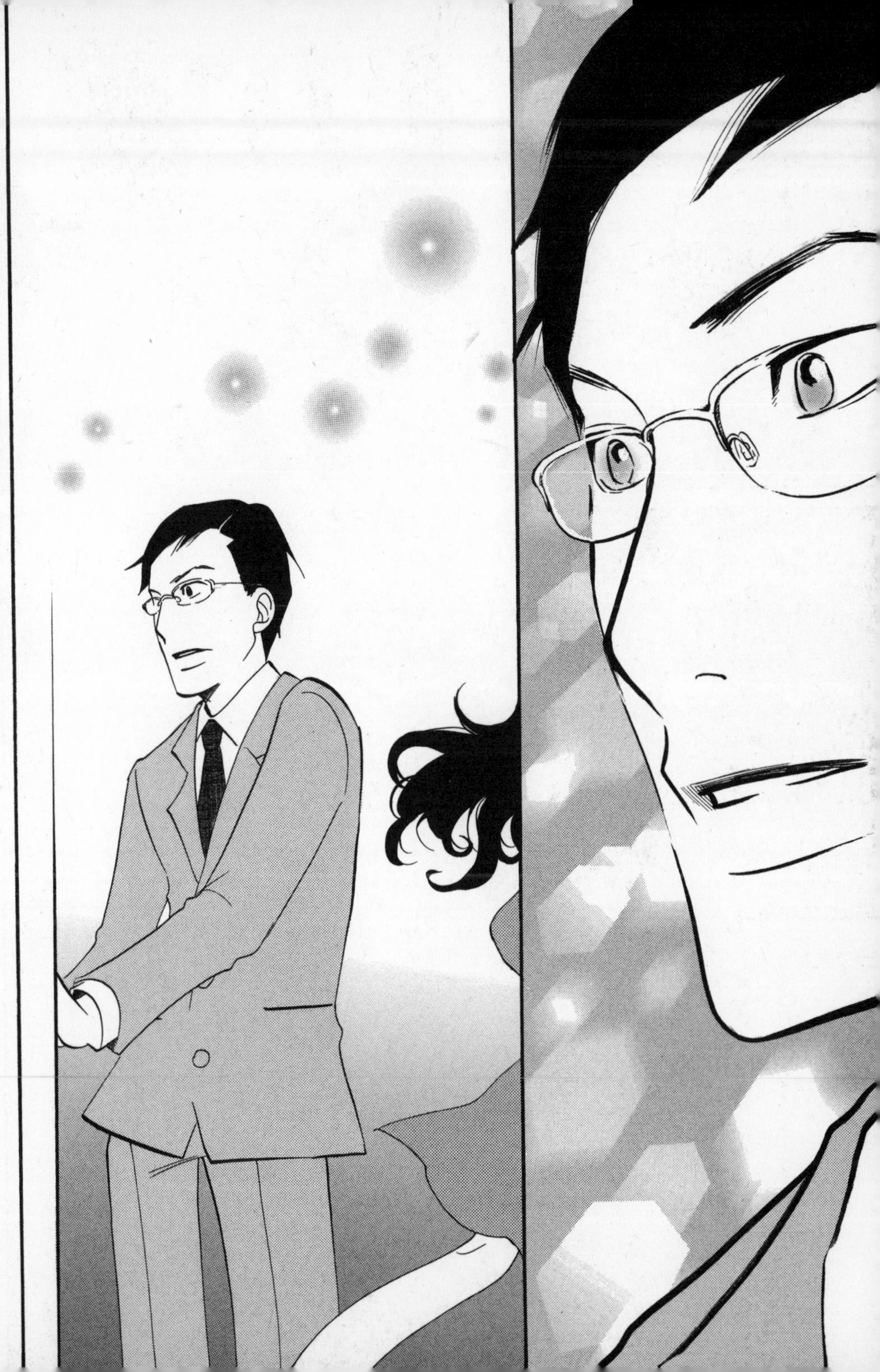

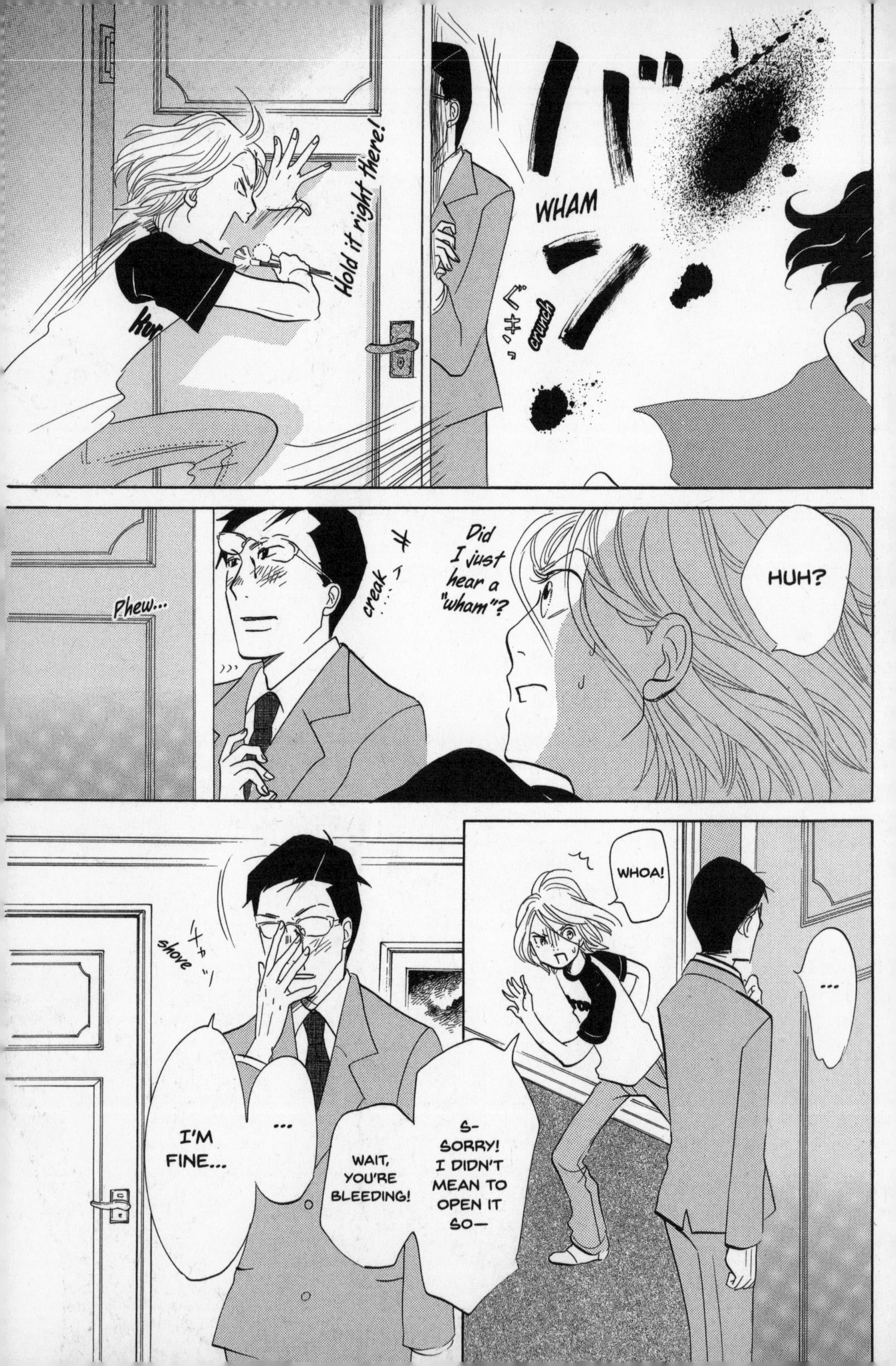
WHAM
crunch
Hold it right there!
HUH?
Did I just hear a "wham"?
creak
Phew...
WHOA!
...
S-SORRY! I DIDN'T MEAN TO OPEN IT SO—
WAIT, YOU'RE BLEEDING!
...
I'M FINE...
shove

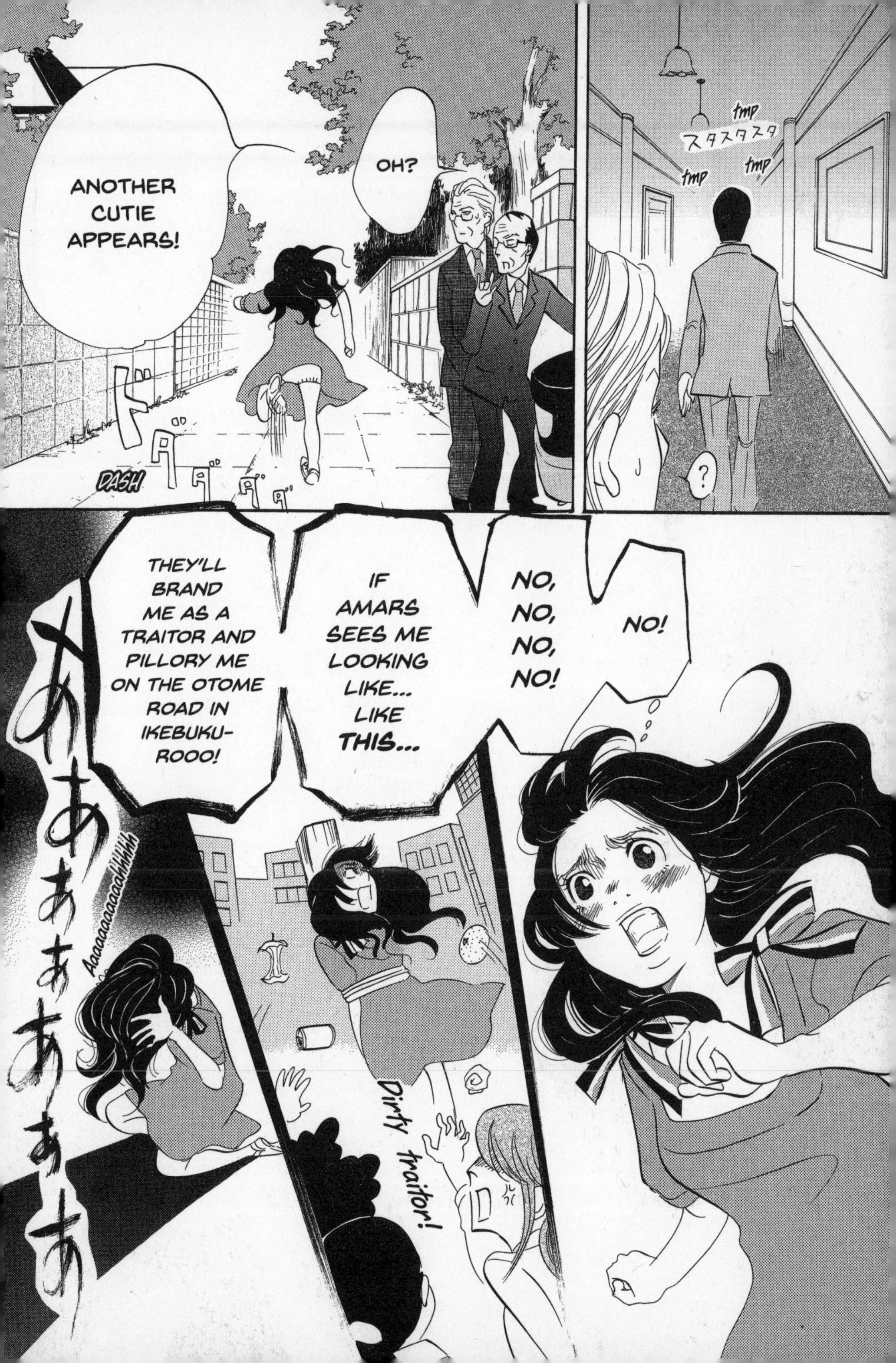

tmp
スタスタスタ
tmp
tmp
?
OH?
ANOTHER CUTIE APPEARS!
DASH
NO!
NO, NO, NO, NO!
IF AMARS SEES ME LOOKING LIKE... LIKE THIS...
THEY'LL BRAND ME AS A TRAITOR AND PILLORY ME ON THE OTOME ROAD IN IKEBUKU-ROOO!
Aaaaaaaaaahhhhh
Dirty traitor!

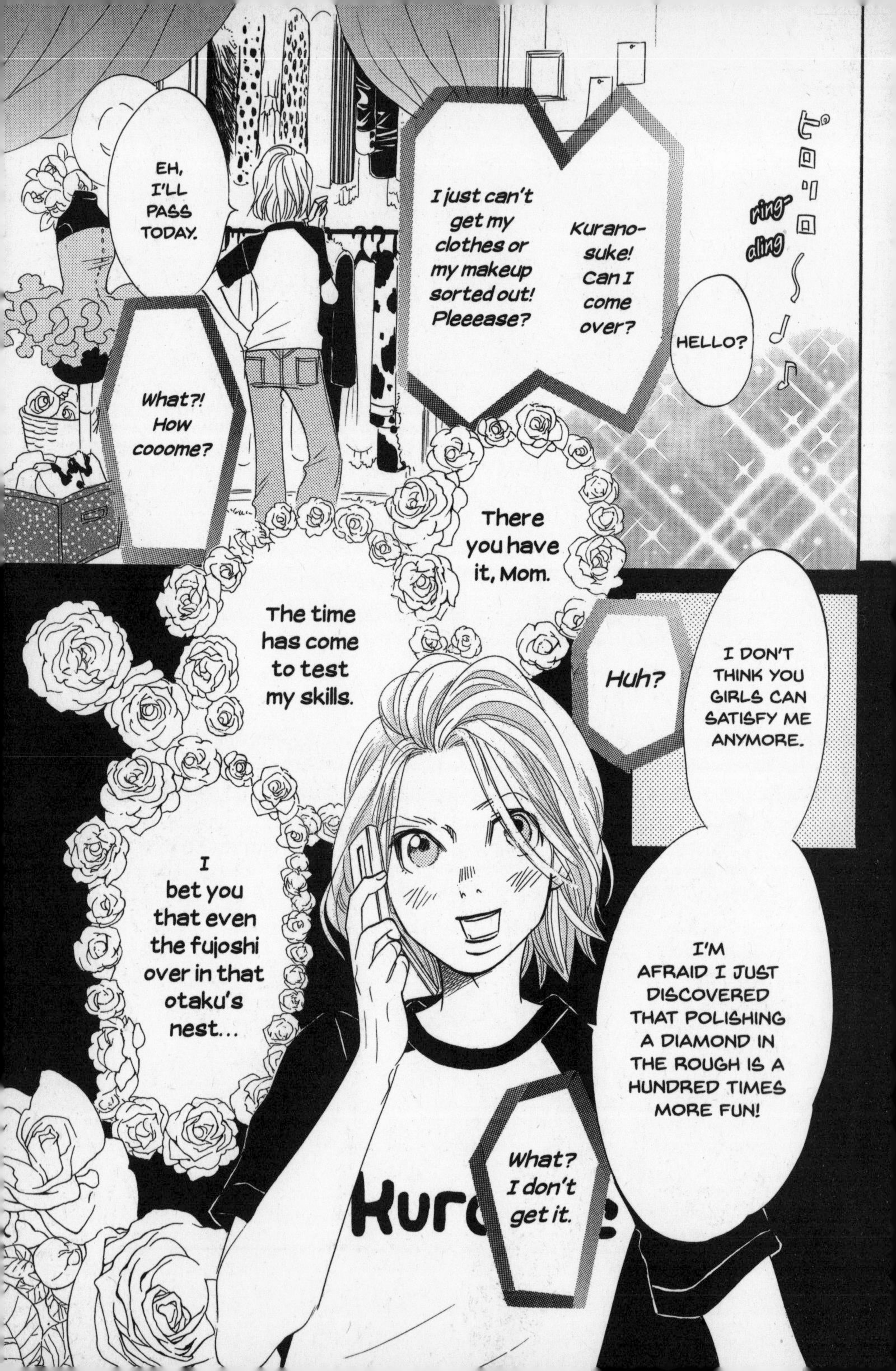
ピロリロ～♪
ring-aling
HELLO?
Kurano-suke! Can I come over?
I just can't get my clothes or my makeup sorted out! Pleeease?
EH, I'LL PASS TODAY.
What?! How cooome?
I DON'T THINK YOU GIRLS CAN SATISFY ME ANYMORE.
Huh?
I'M AFRAID I JUST DISCOVERED THAT POLISHING A DIAMOND IN THE ROUGH IS A HUNDRED TIMES MORE FUN!
What? I don't get it.
There you have it, Mom.
The time has come to test my skills.
I bet you that even the fujoshi over in that otaku's nest...
Kuro

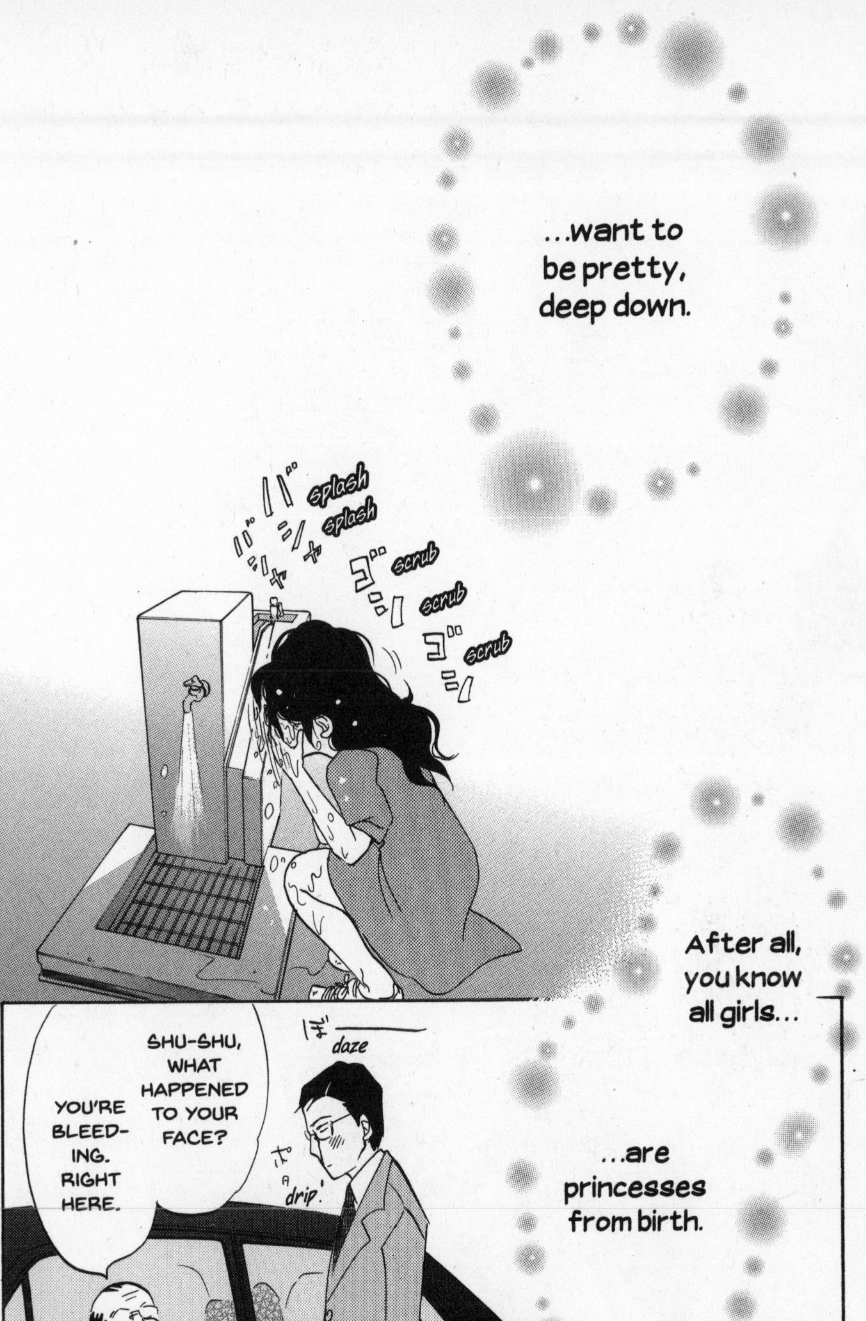
...want to be pretty, deep down.
splash
splash
scrub
scrub
scrub
After all, you know all girls...
...are princesses from birth.
daze
drip
SHU-SHU, WHAT HAPPENED TO YOUR FACE?
YOU'RE BLEED-ING. RIGHT HERE.

Episode 5
Vampires from Amars

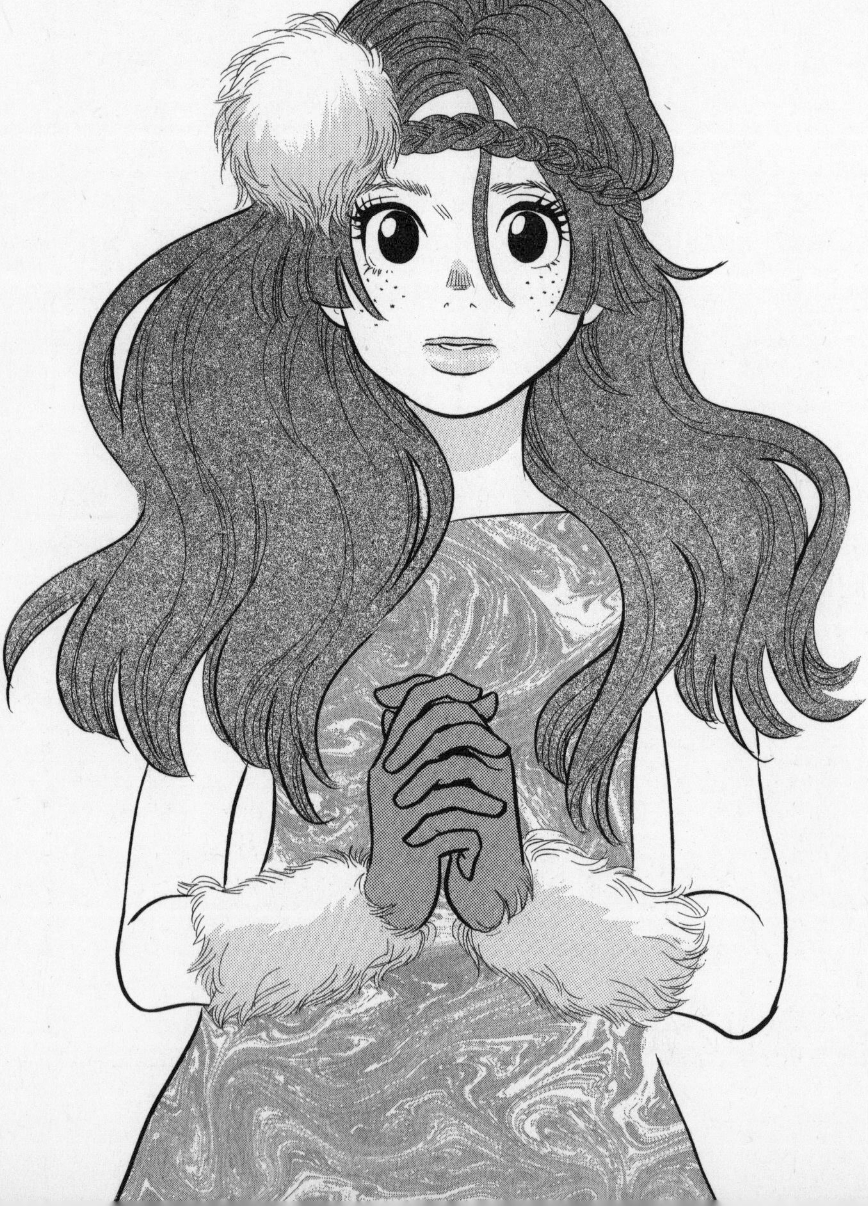

高田の森児童公園
ザーッ
zsssh
ザバ
ザバ
splosh
splosh
Mom...
ゴシゴシゴシゴシゴシゴシゴシゴシ
scrub
scrub
scrub
scrub
I stand corrected. That person is ***not*** a princess.
ザー
zsssh

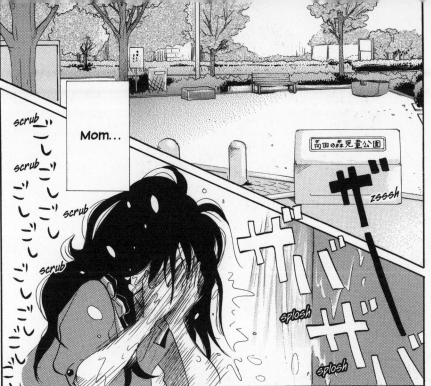

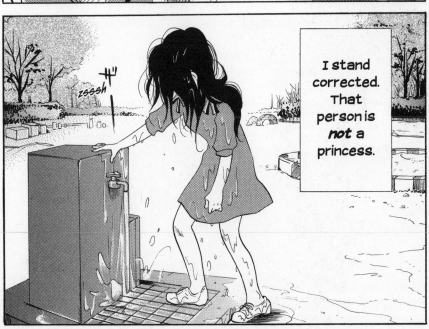

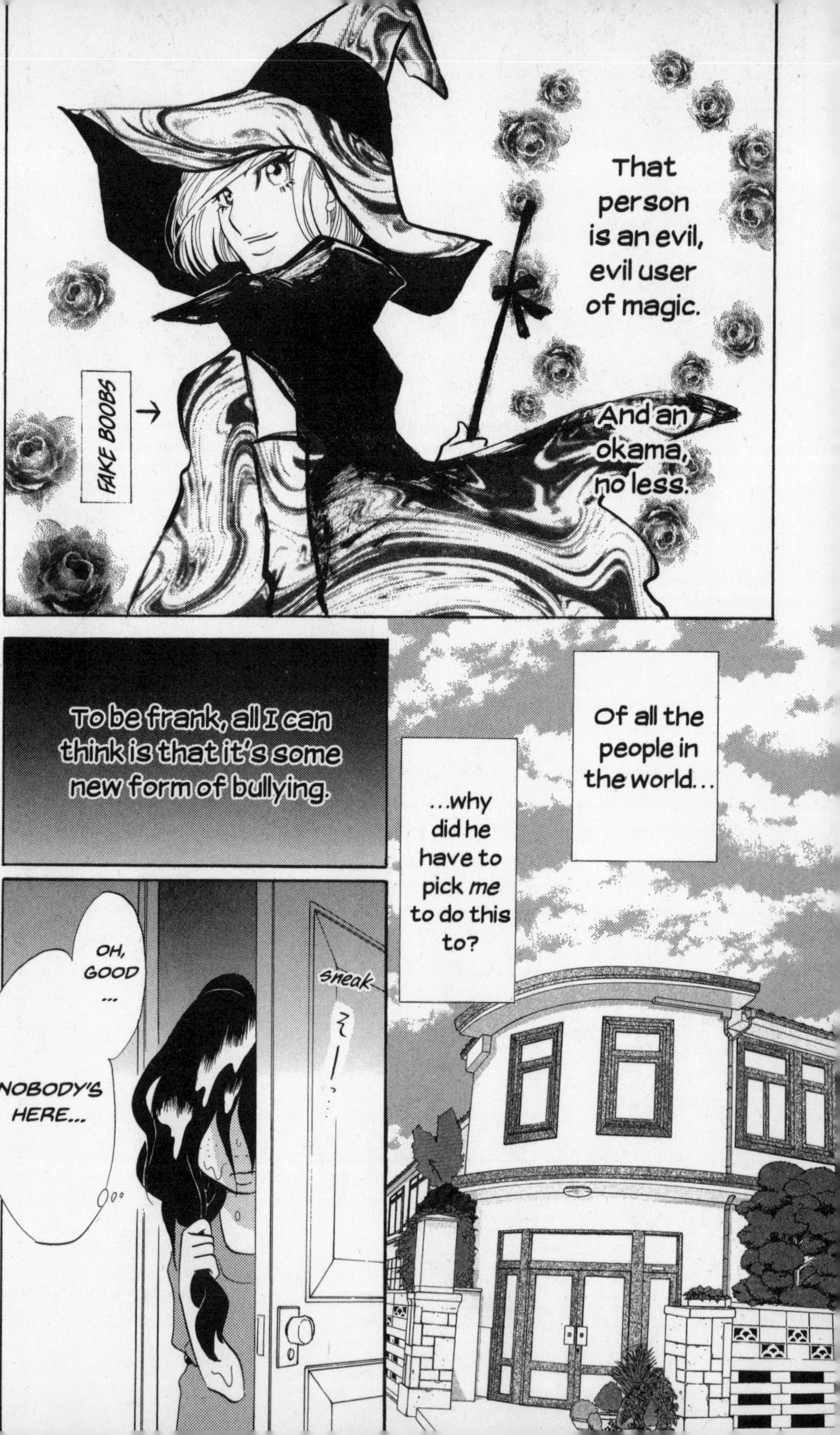
That person is an evil, evil user of magic.
And an okama, no less.
FAKE BOOBS
Of all the people in the world...
...why did he have to pick *me* to do this to?
To be frank, all I can think is that it's some new form of bullying.
sneak
OH, GOOD... NOBODY'S HERE...

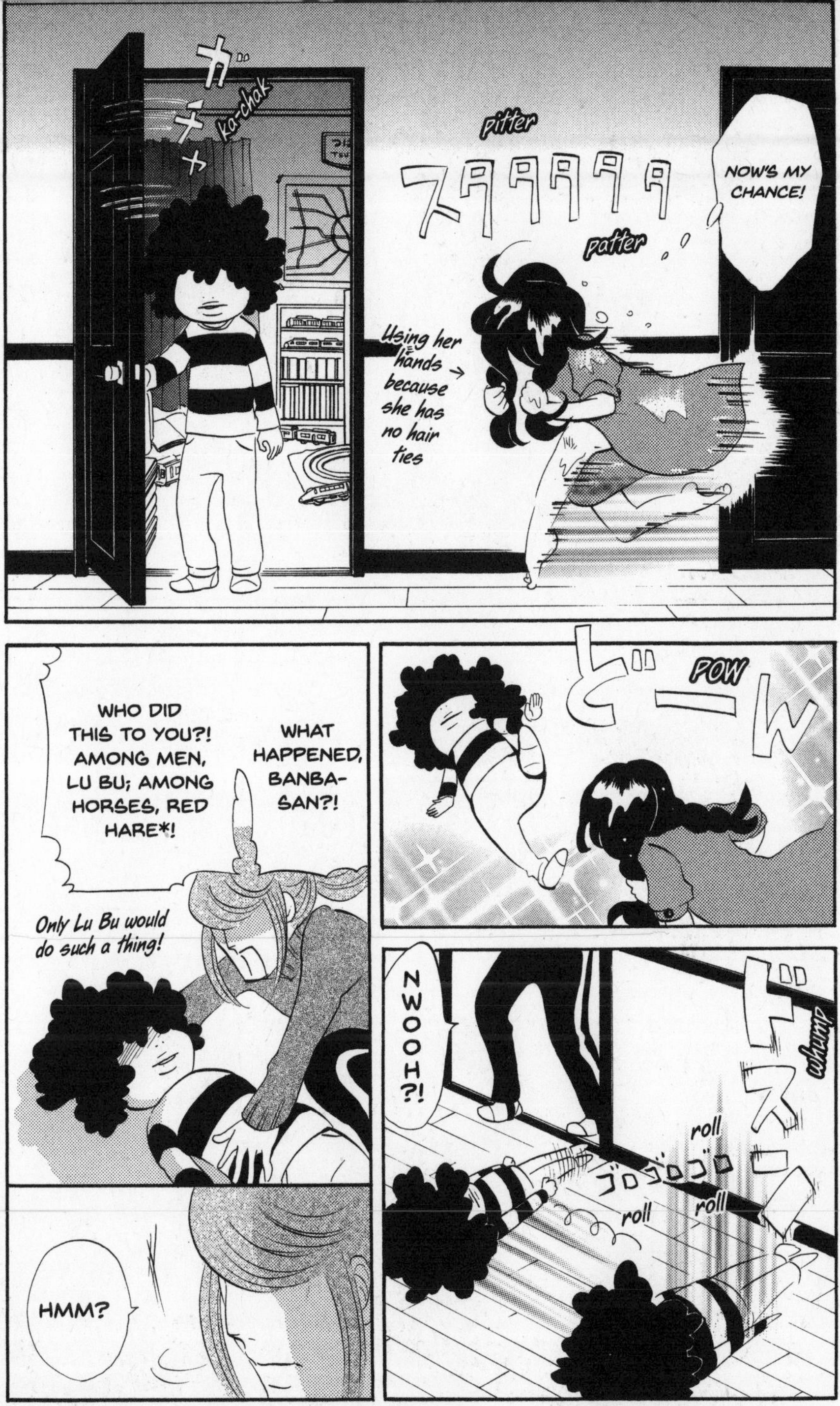
NOW'S MY CHANCE!
pitter
スタタタタタ
patter
Using her hands because she has no hair ties
ガチャ
ka-chak
どーん
POW
NWOOOH?!
ドスッ
whump
ゴロゴロ
roll
roll
roll
WHAT HAPPENED, BANBA-SAN?!
WHO DID THIS TO YOU?! AMONG MEN, LU BU; AMONG HORSES, RED HARE*!
Only Lu Bu would do such a thing!
HMM?

*A quote from *Records of the Three Kingdoms* about the warlord, Lu Bu, who had a reputation as a traitor and rode his infamous horse, the Red Hare.

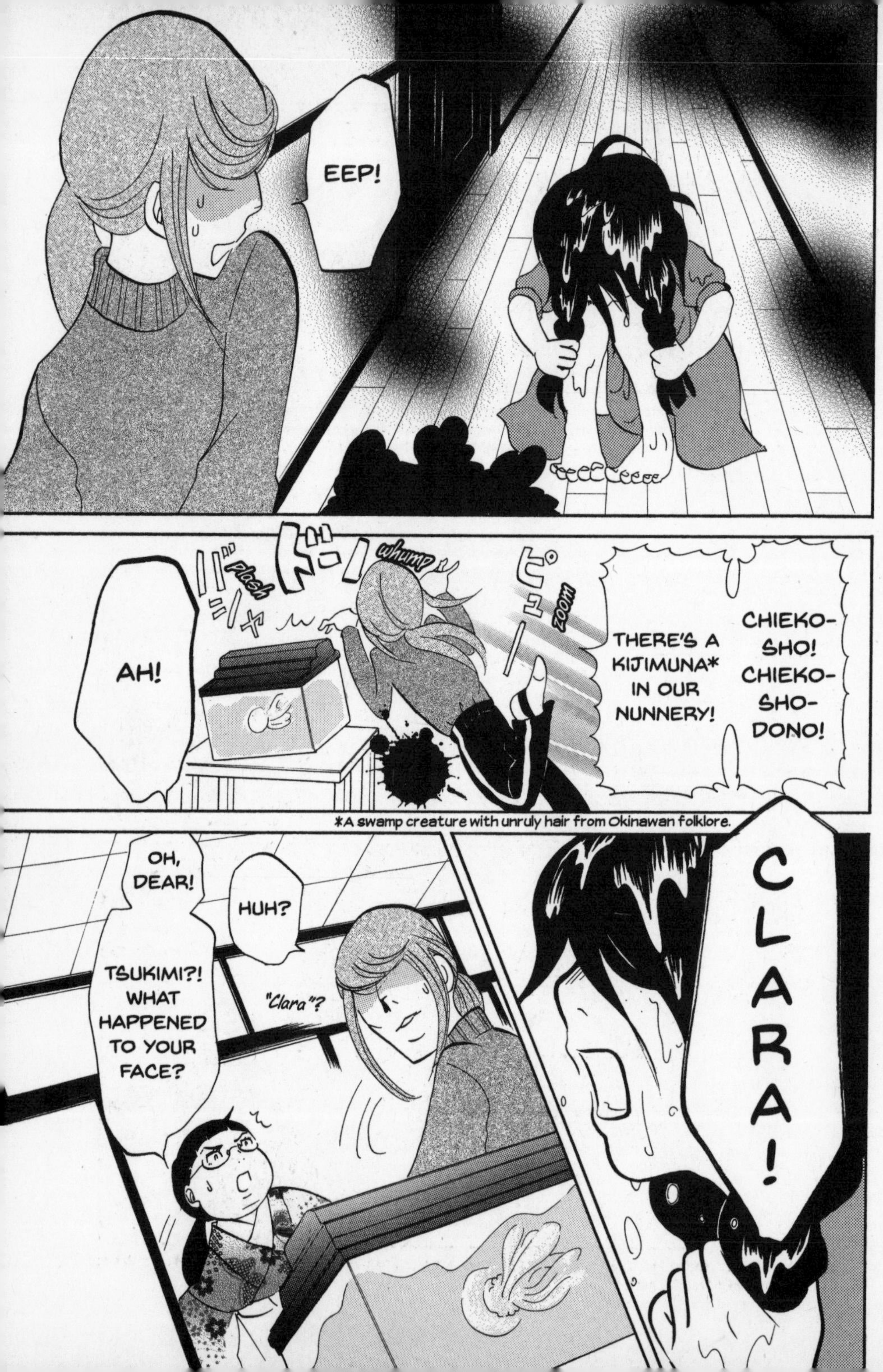
EEP!
CHIEKO-SHO! CHIEKO-SHO-DONO!
THERE'S A KIJIMUNA* IN OUR NUNNERY!
zoom
whump
plash
AH!
CLARA!
HUH?
OH, DEAR!
TSUKIMI?! WHAT HAPPENED TO YOUR FACE?
"Clara"?
*A swamp creature with unruly hair from Okinawan folklore.

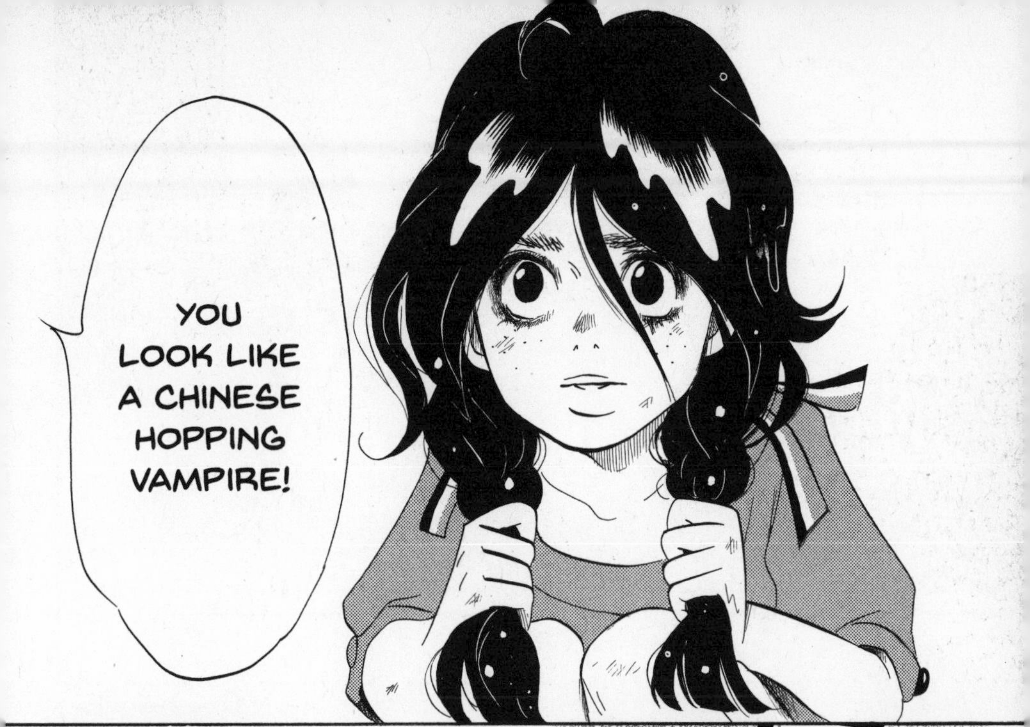
YOU LOOK LIKE A CHINESE HOPPING VAMPIRE!

*A Hong Kong movie from 1985.

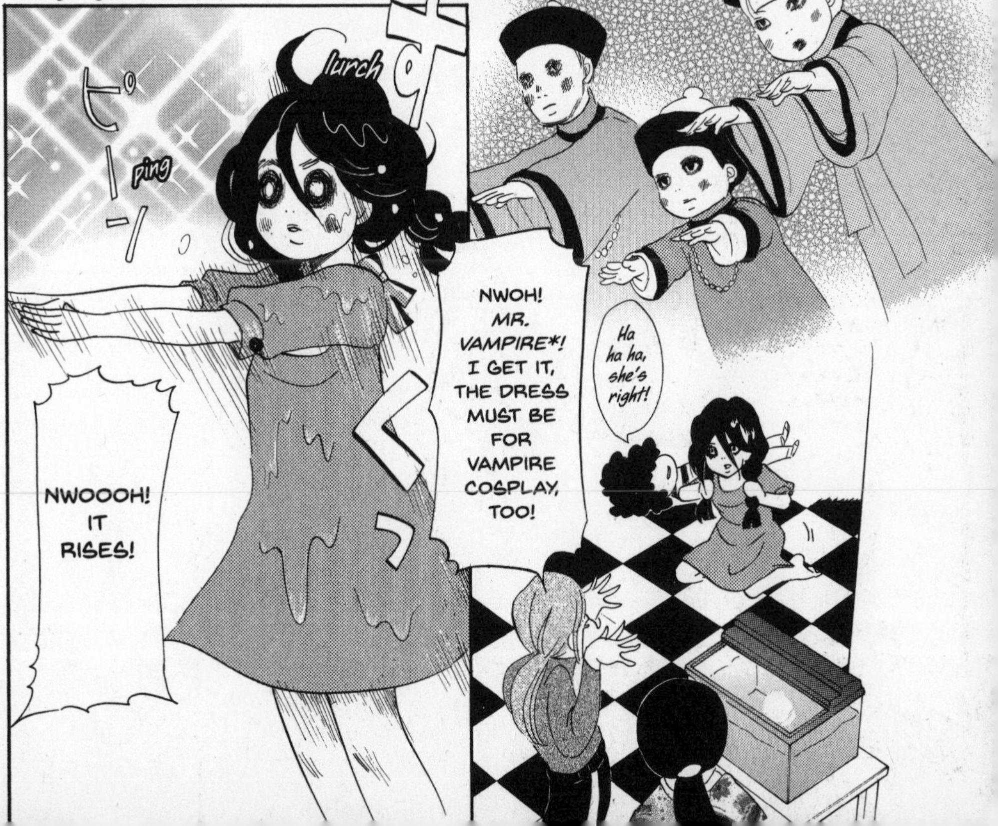
lurch
ping
NWOH! MR. VAMPIRE*! I GET IT, THE DRESS MUST BE FOR VAMPIRE COSPLAY, TOO!
Ha ha ha, she's right!
NWOOOH! IT RISES!

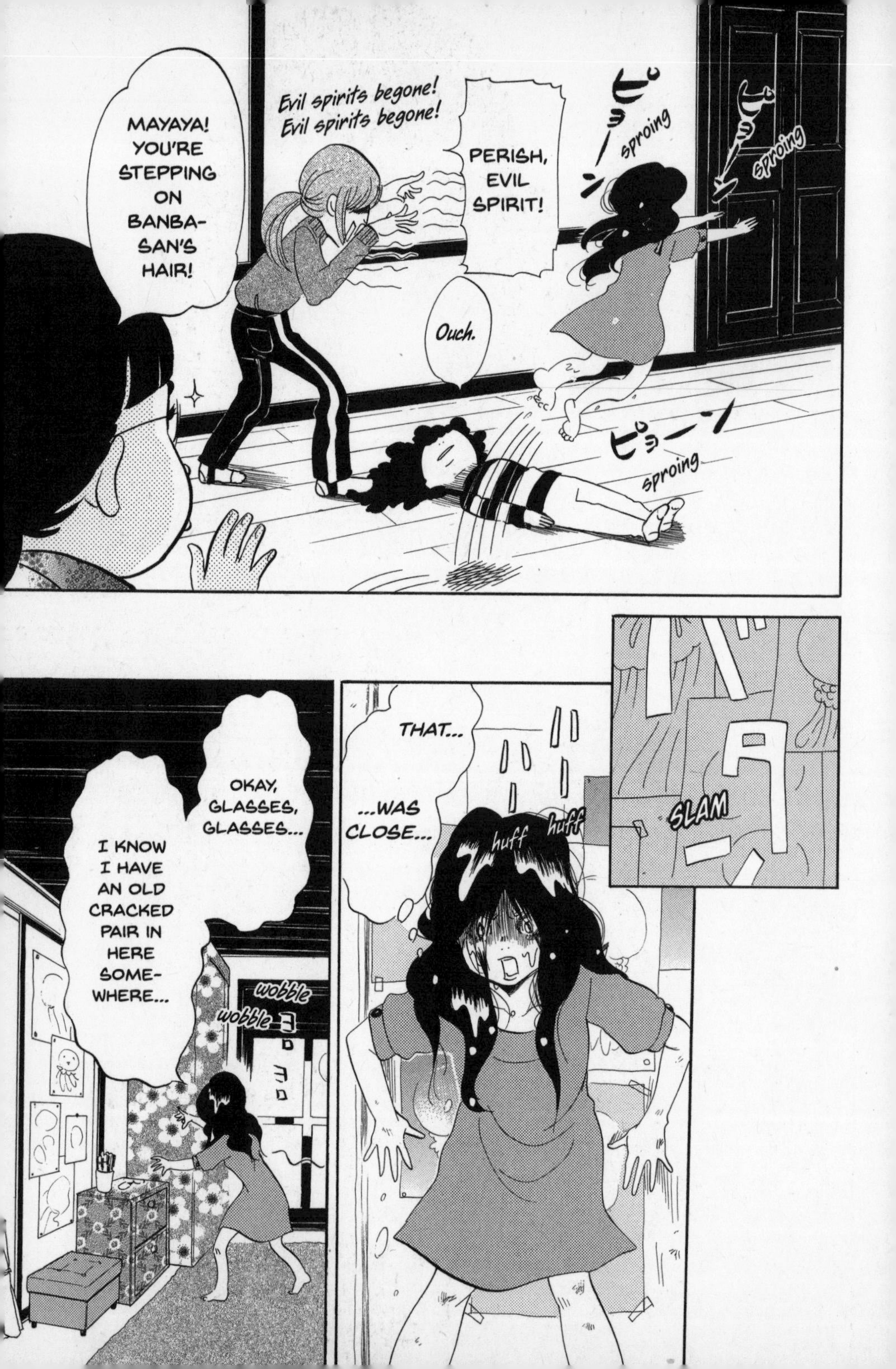
sproing
sproing
PERISH, EVIL SPIRIT!
Evil spirits begone! Evil spirits begone!
Ouch.
MAYAYA! YOU'RE STEPPING ON BANBA-SAN'S HAIR!
sproing
SLAM
THAT...
...WAS CLOSE...
huff
huff
OKAY, GLASSES, GLASSES...
I KNOW I HAVE AN OLD CRACKED PAIR IN HERE SOMEWHERE...
wobble
wobble

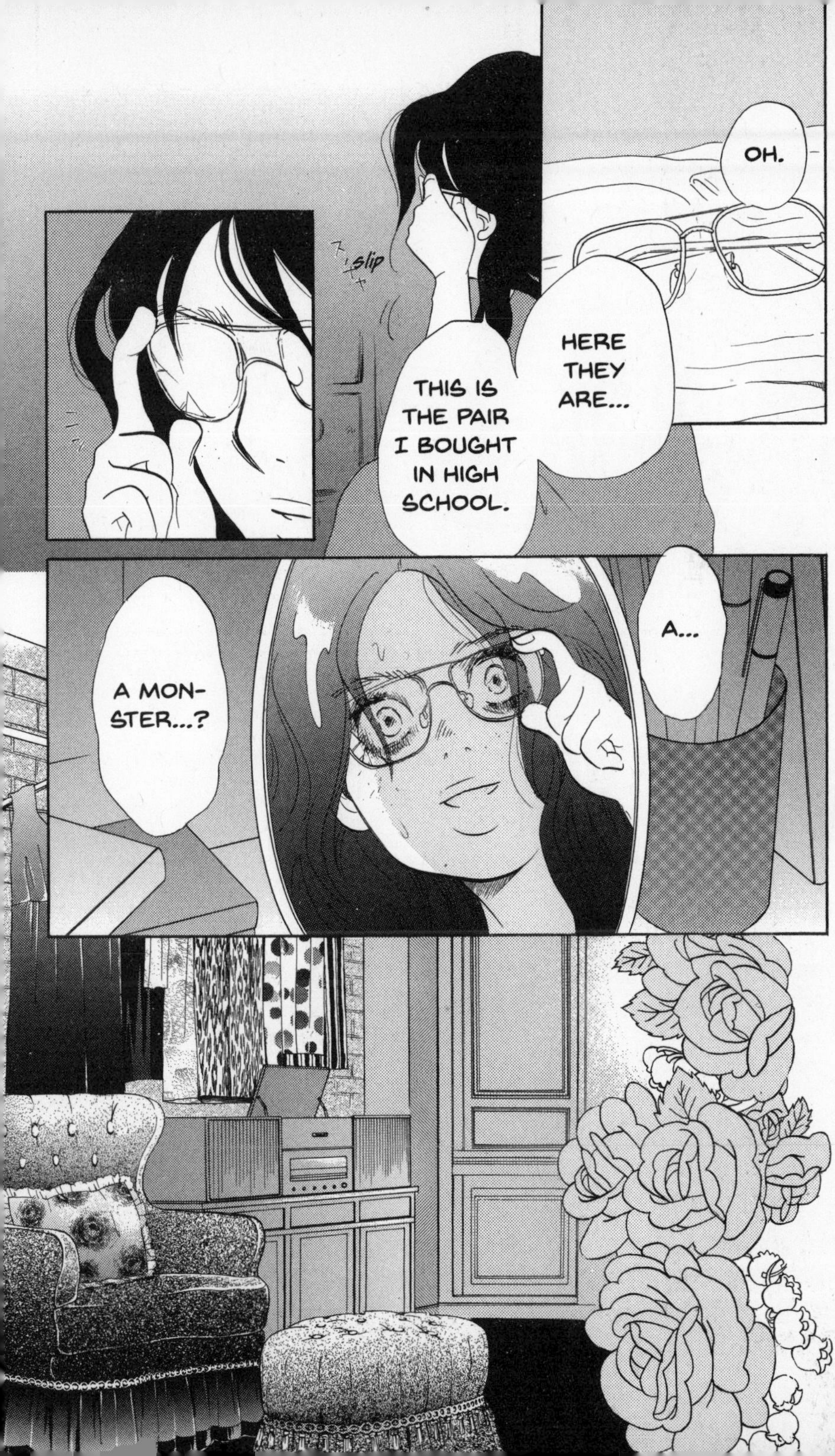
OH.
HERE THEY ARE...
slip
THIS IS THE PAIR I BOUGHT IN HIGH SCHOOL.
A...
A MON-STER...?

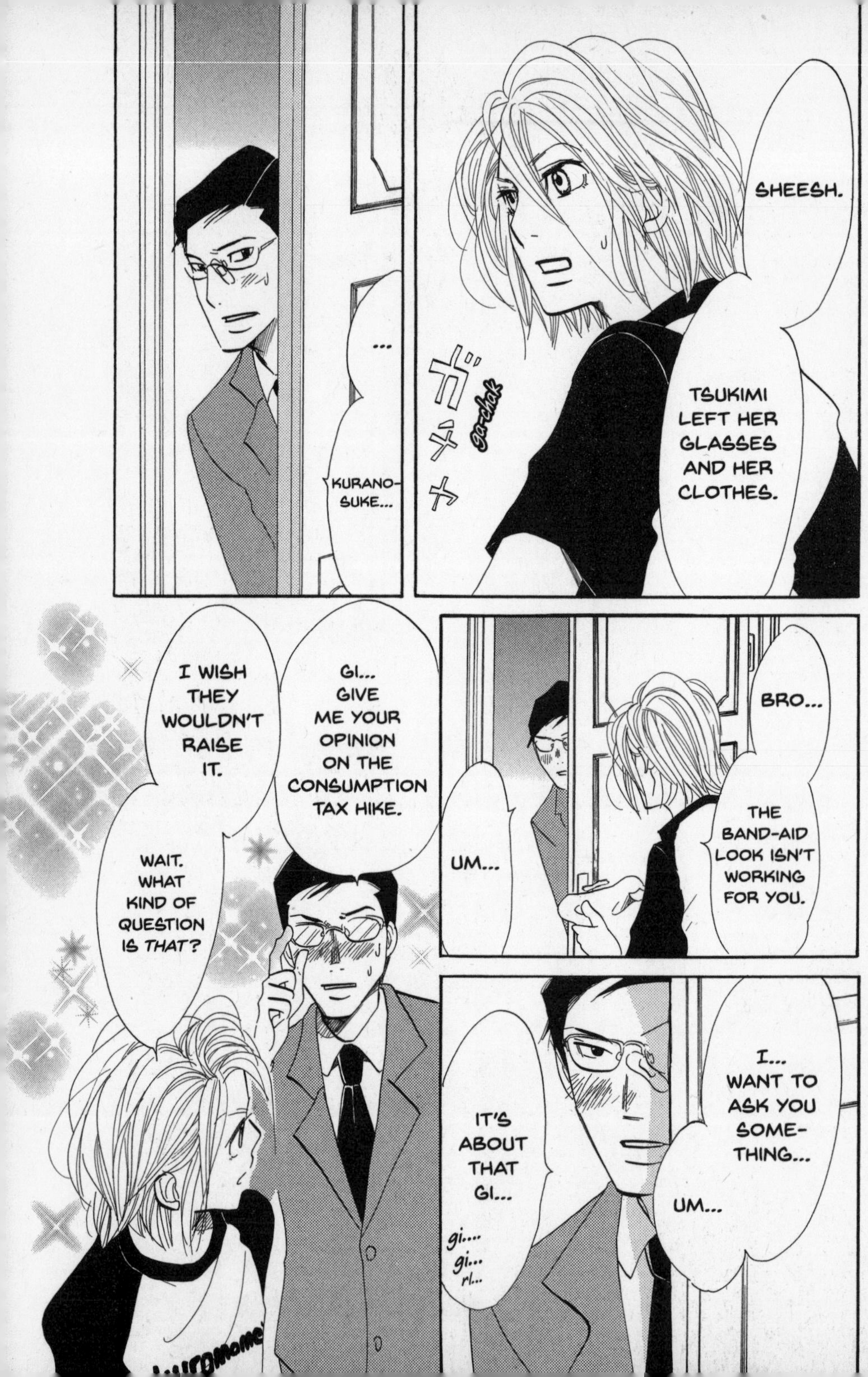
SHEESH.
TSUKIMI LEFT HER GLASSES AND HER CLOTHES.
ガチャ
ga-chak
...
KURANO-SUKE...
BRO...
THE BAND-AID LOOK ISN'T WORKING FOR YOU.
UM...
I... WANT TO ASK YOU SOME-THING...
UM...
IT'S ABOUT THAT GI...
gi.... gi... rl...
GI... GIVE ME YOUR OPINION ON THE CONSUMPTION TAX HIKE.
I WISH THEY WOULDN'T RAISE IT.
WAIT. WHAT KIND OF QUESTION IS *THAT*?

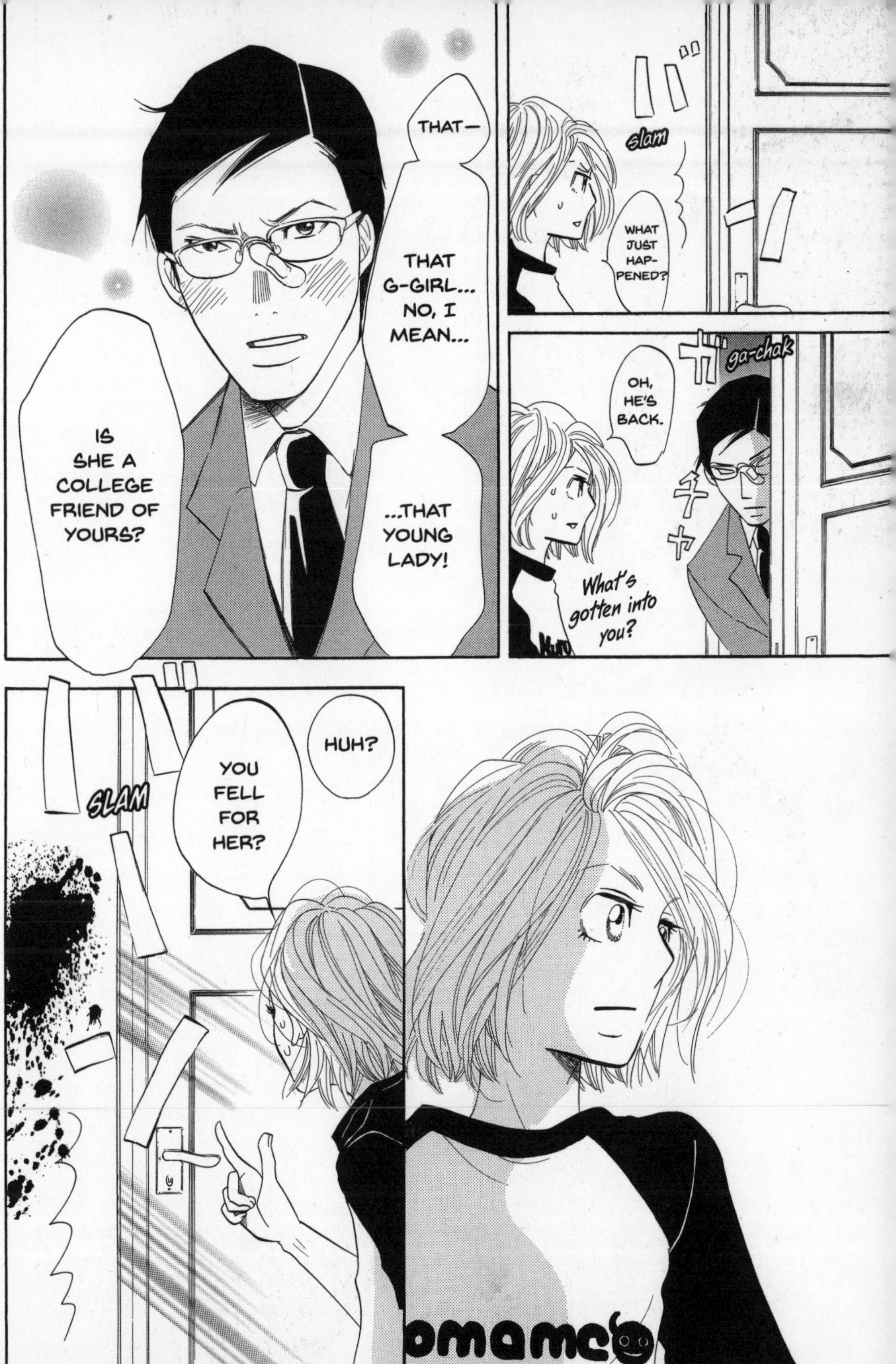
slam
WHAT JUST HAPPENED?
ga-chak
OH, HE'S BACK.
What's gotten into you?
THAT—
THAT G-GIRL... NO, I MEAN...
...THAT YOUNG LADY!
IS SHE A COLLEGE FRIEND OF YOURS?
SLAM
HUH?
YOU FELL FOR HER?

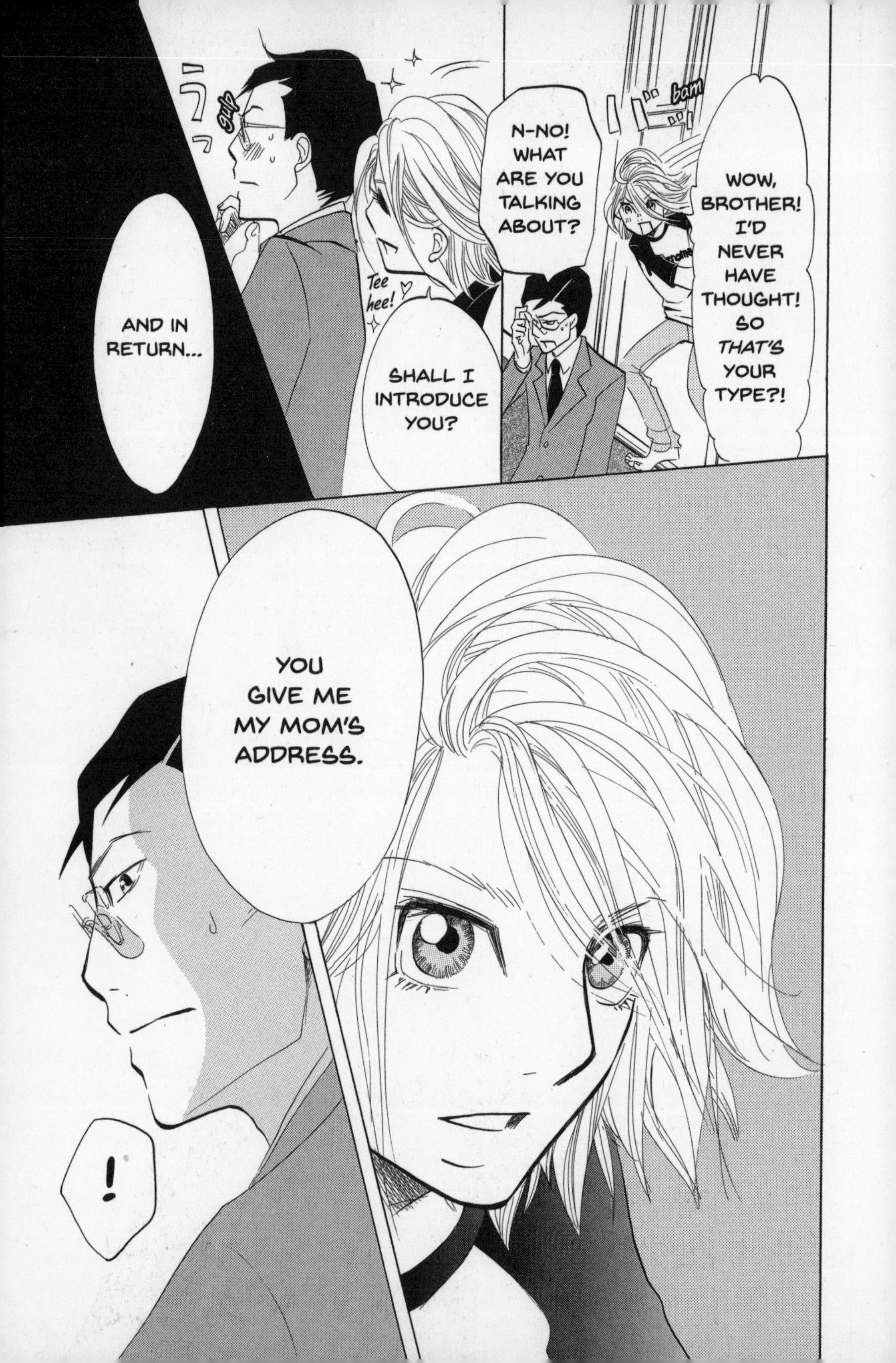
bam
WOW, BROTHER! I'D NEVER HAVE THOUGHT! SO *THAT'S* YOUR TYPE?!
N-NO! WHAT ARE YOU TALKING ABOUT?
Tee hee!
SHALL I INTRODUCE YOU?
gulp
AND IN RETURN...
YOU GIVE ME MY MOM'S ADDRESS.
!

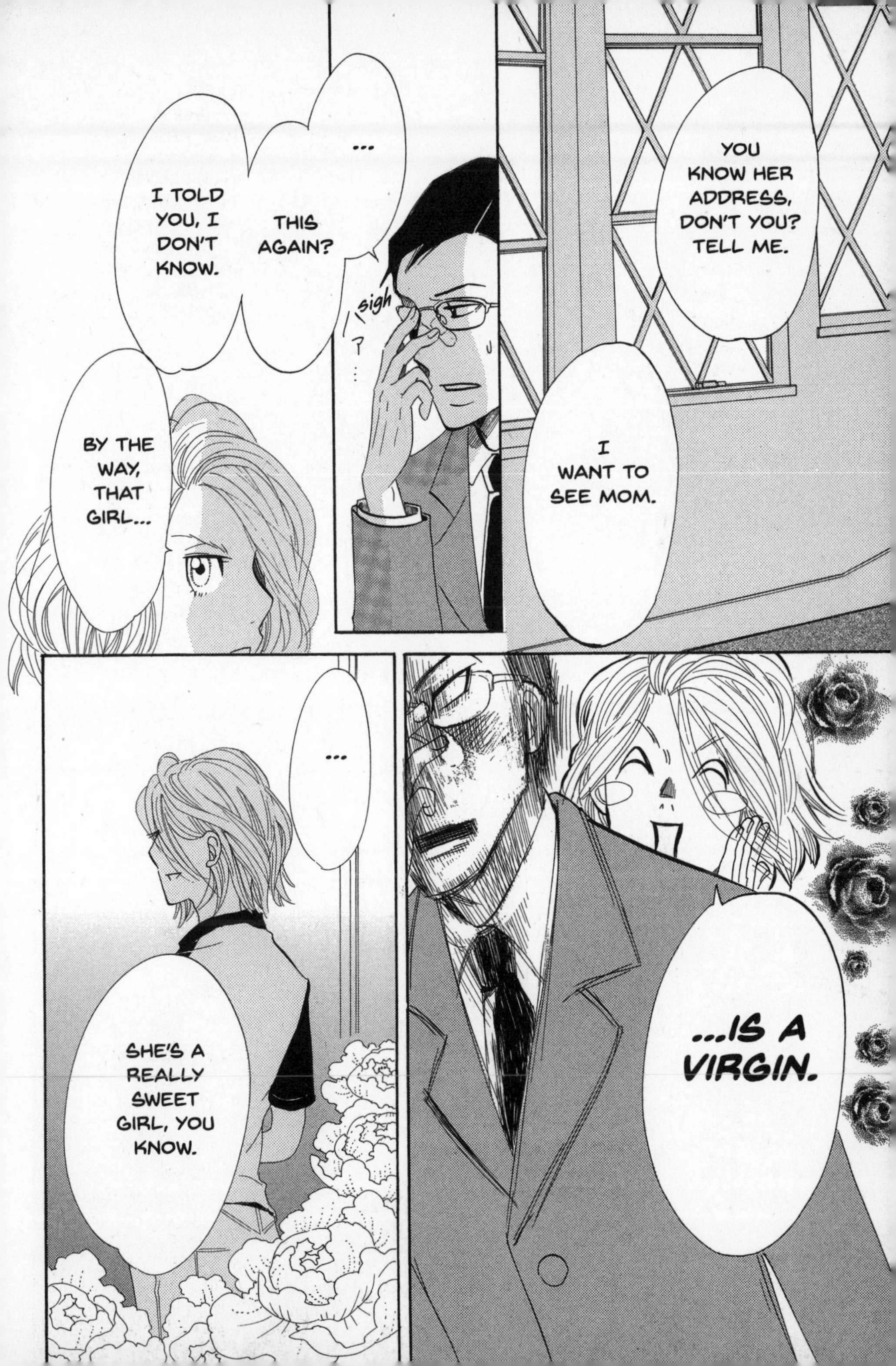
YOU KNOW HER ADDRESS, DON'T YOU? TELL ME.
I WANT TO SEE MOM.
...
THIS AGAIN?
sigh
I TOLD YOU, I DON'T KNOW.
BY THE WAY, THAT GIRL...
...IS A VIRGIN.
...
SHE'S A REALLY SWEET GIRL, YOU KNOW.

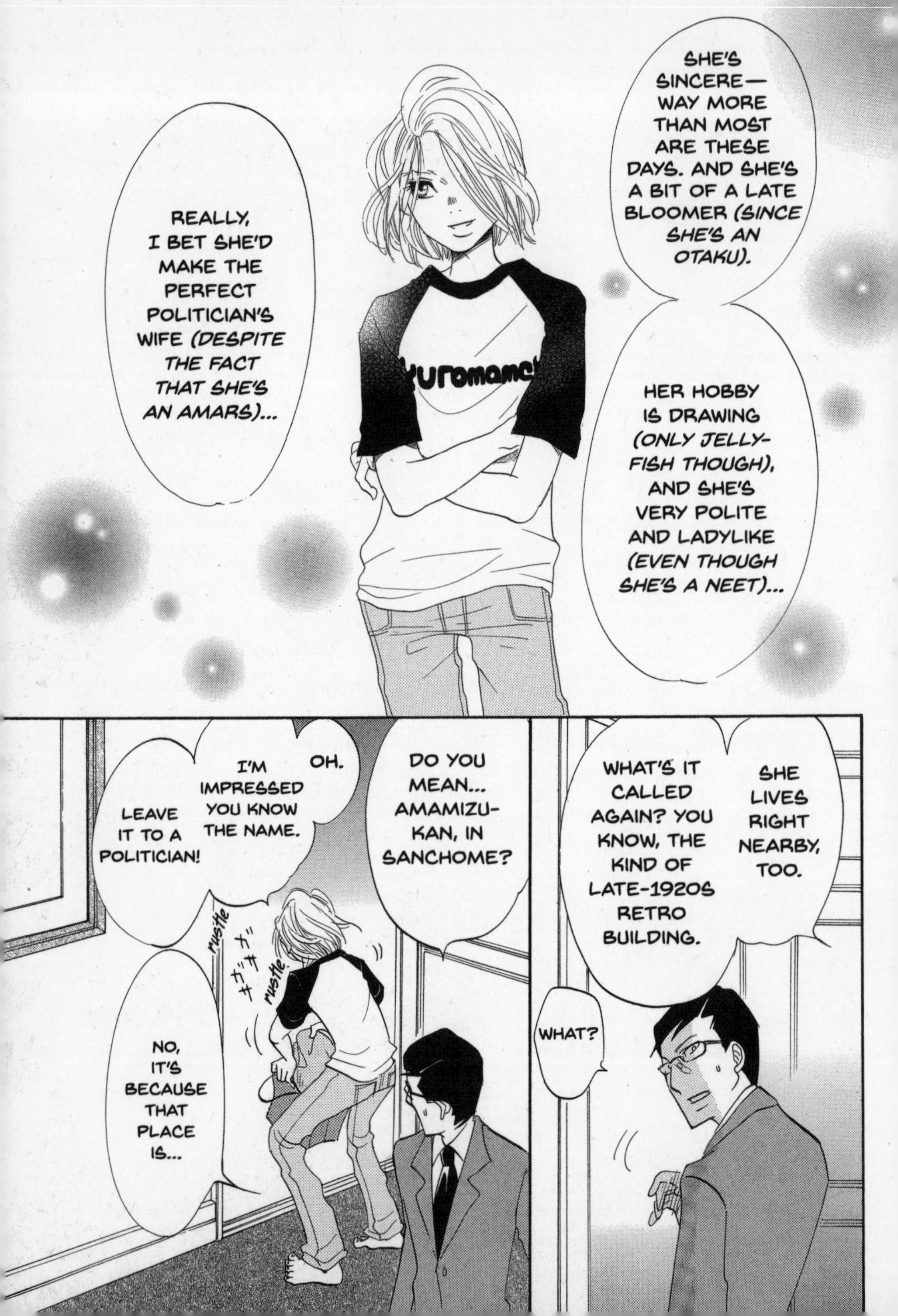
SHE'S SINCERE—WAY MORE THAN MOST ARE THESE DAYS. AND SHE'S A BIT OF A LATE BLOOMER (SINCE SHE'S AN OTAKU).
HER HOBBY IS DRAWING (ONLY JELLY-FISH THOUGH), AND SHE'S VERY POLITE AND LADYLIKE (EVEN THOUGH SHE'S A NEET)...
REALLY, I BET SHE'D MAKE THE PERFECT POLITICIAN'S WIFE (DESPITE THE FACT THAT SHE'S AN AMARS)...
SHE LIVES RIGHT NEARBY, TOO.
WHAT'S IT CALLED AGAIN? YOU KNOW, THE KIND OF LATE-1920S RETRO BUILDING.
WHAT?
DO YOU MEAN... AMAMIZU-KAN, IN SANCHOME?
OH.
I'M IMPRESSED YOU KNOW THE NAME.
LEAVE IT TO A POLITICIAN!
rustle
rustle
NO, IT'S BECAUSE THAT PLACE IS...

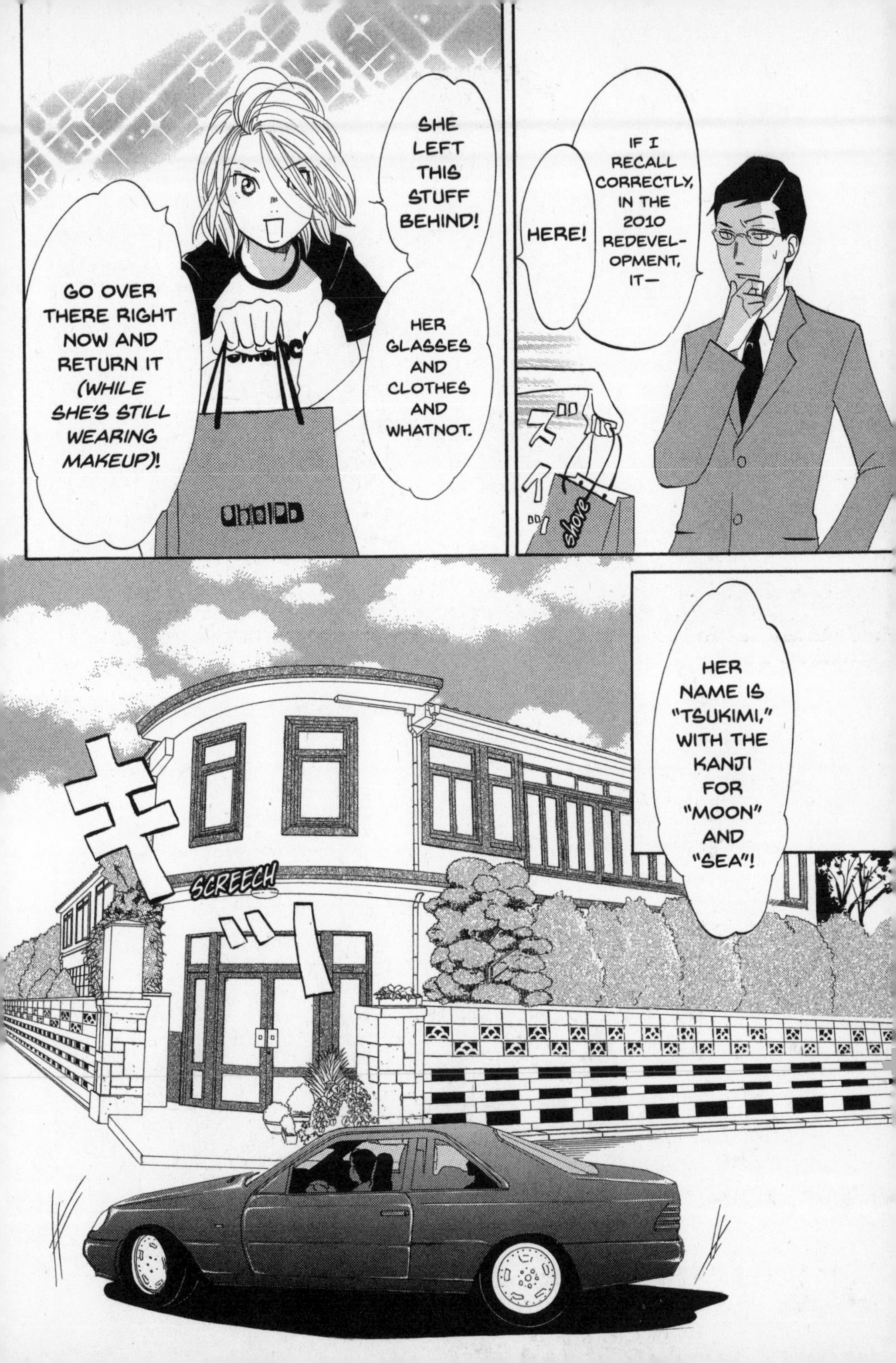
IF I RECALL CORRECTLY, IN THE 2010 REDEVEL-OPMENT, IT—
HERE!
shove
SHE LEFT THIS STUFF BEHIND!
HER GLASSES AND CLOTHES AND WHATNOT.
GO OVER THERE RIGHT NOW AND RETURN IT (WHILE SHE'S STILL WEARING MAKEUP)!
HER NAME IS "TSUKIMI," WITH THE KANJI FOR "MOON" AND "SEA"!
SCREECH

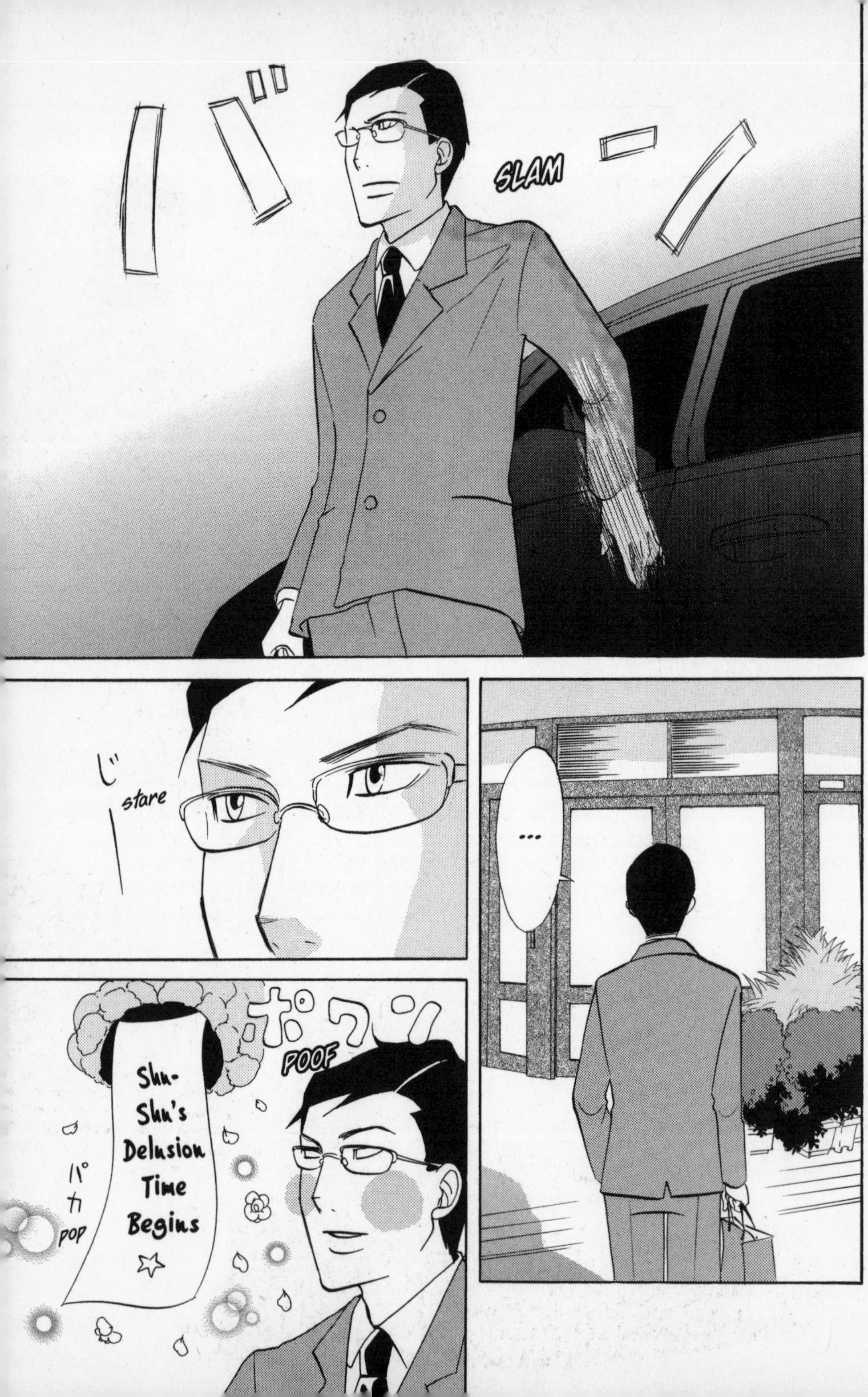
SLAM
...
じー
stare
ポワン
POOF
Shu-Shu's Delusion Time Begins ☆
パカ
pop

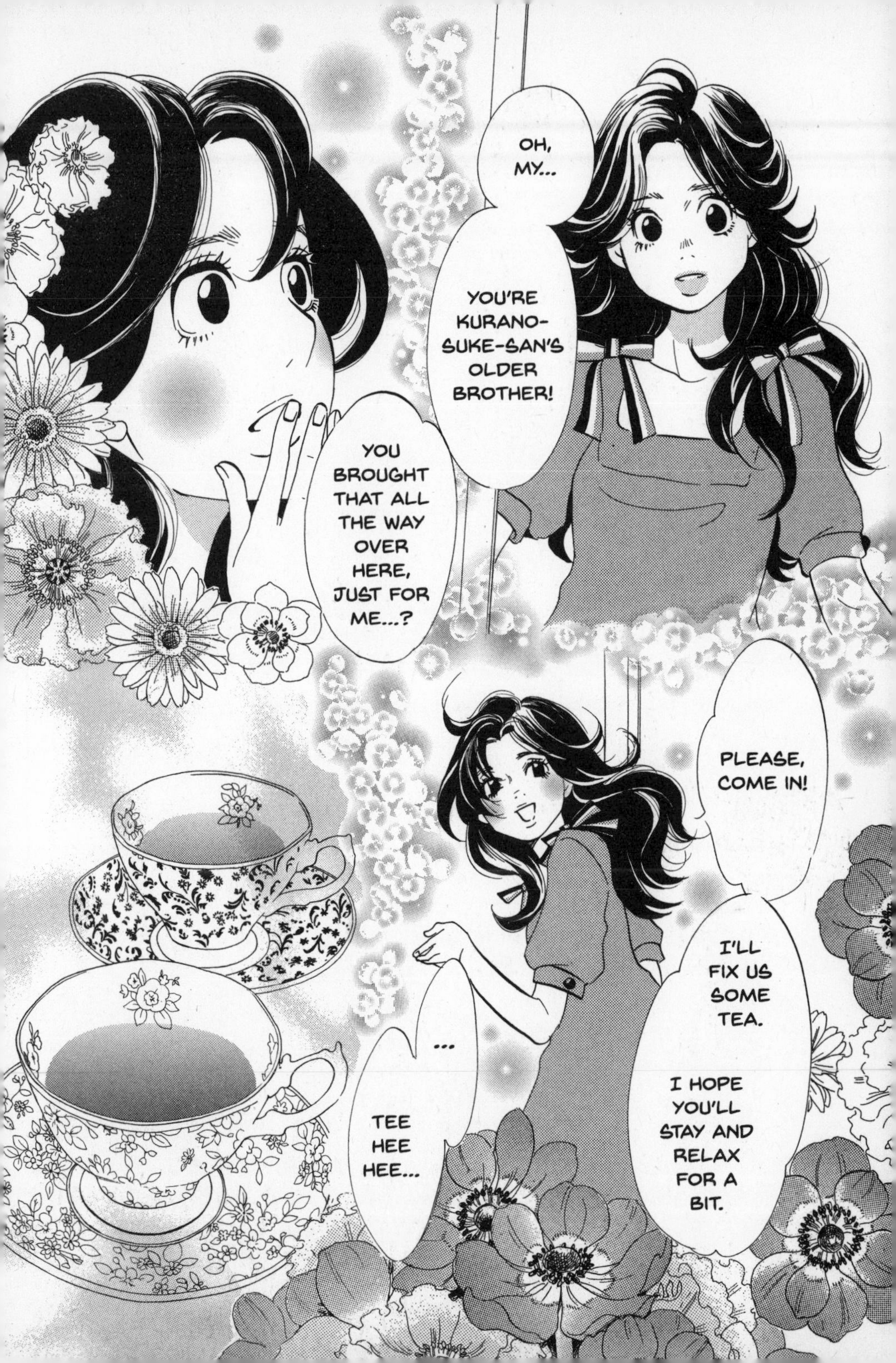
OH, MY...
YOU'RE KURANO-SUKE-SAN'S OLDER BROTHER!
YOU BROUGHT THAT ALL THE WAY OVER HERE, JUST FOR ME...?
PLEASE, COME IN!
I'LL FIX US SOME TEA.
I HOPE YOU'LL STAY AND RELAX FOR A BIT.
...
TEE HEE HEE...

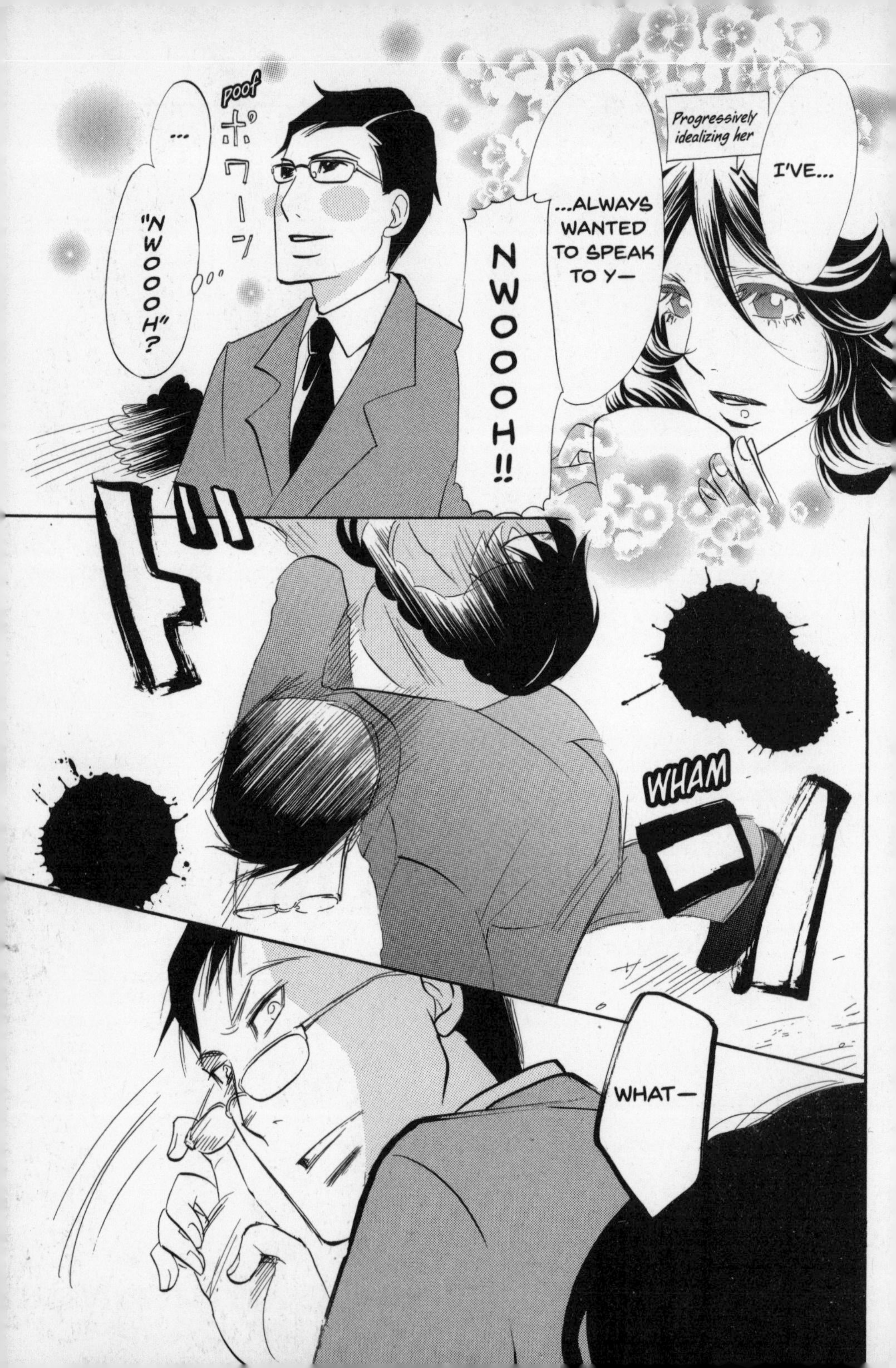
Progressively idealizing her
I'VE...
...ALWAYS WANTED TO SPEAK TO Y—
NWOOOOH!!
poof
ポワーッ
...
"NWOOOOH"?
WHAM
WHAT—

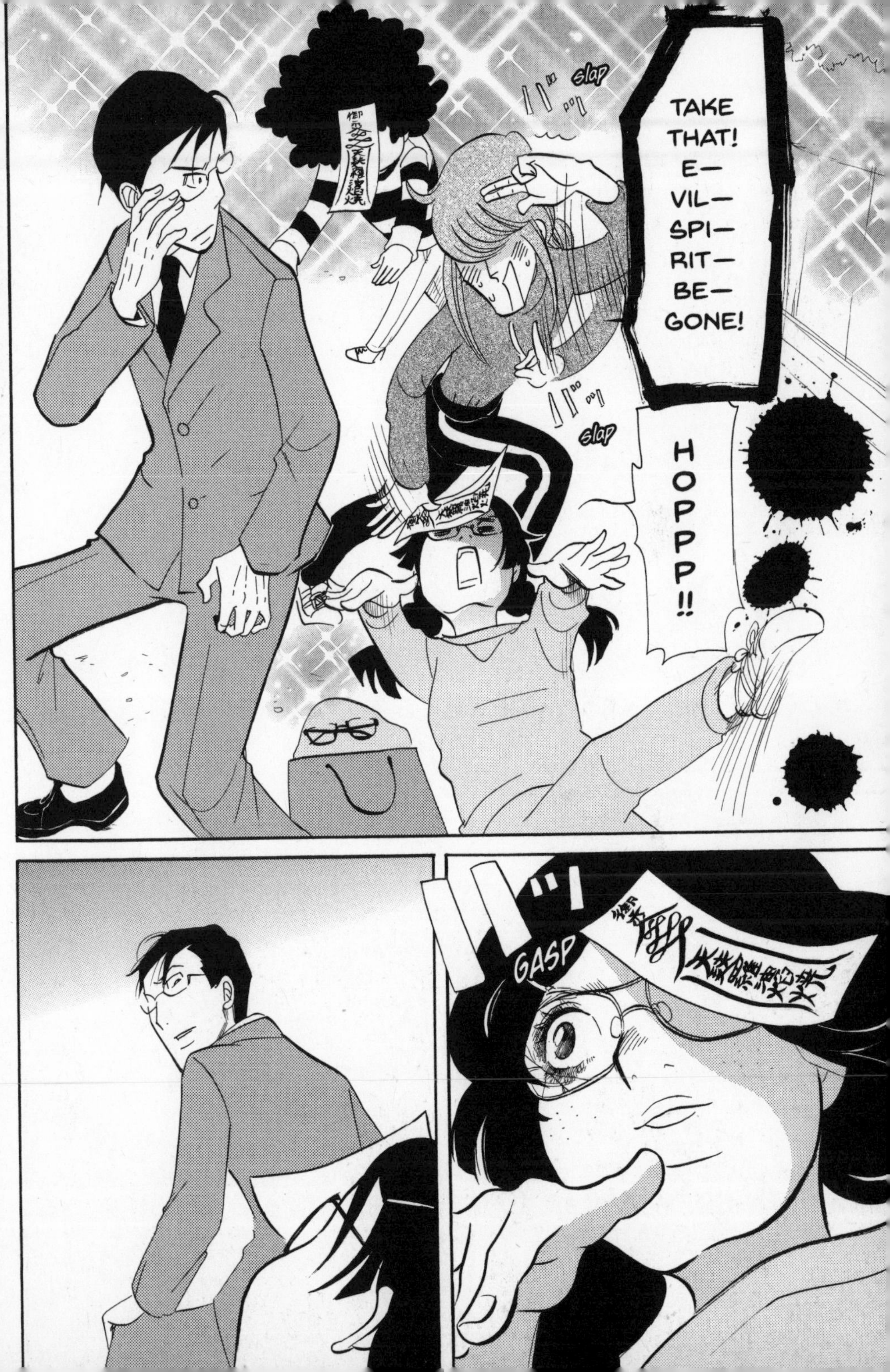
TAKE THAT! E— VIL— SPI— RIT— BE— GONE!
slap
HOPPP!!
slap
GASP

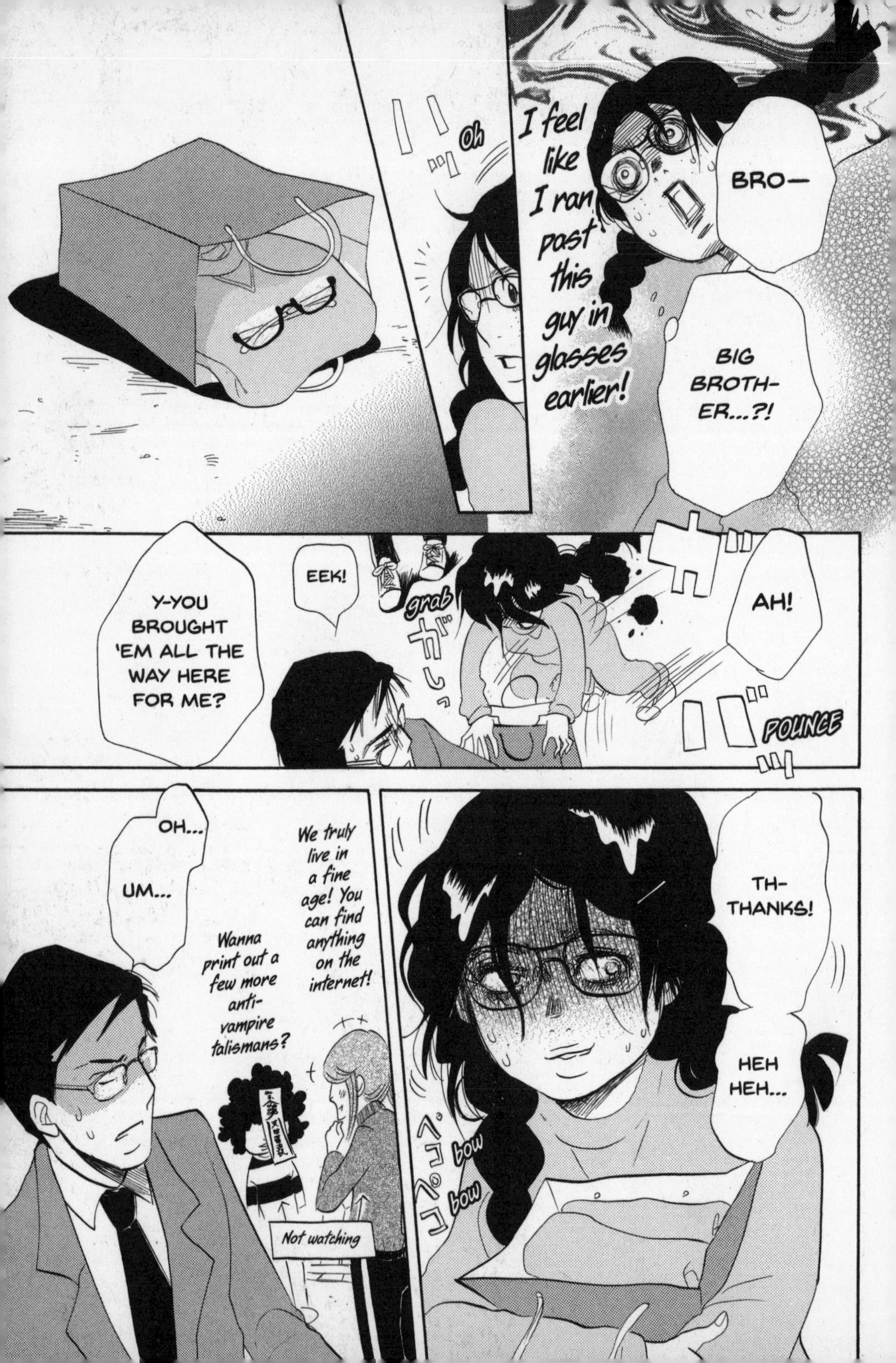
BRO—
BIG BROTH-ER...?!
I feel like I ran past this guy in glasses earlier!
Oh
AH!
POUNCE
grab
EEK!
Y-YOU BROUGHT 'EM ALL THE WAY HERE FOR ME?
TH- THANKS!
HEH HEH...
bow
bow
OH...
UM...
We truly live in a fine age! You can find anything on the internet!
Wanna print out a few more anti-vampire talismans?
Not watching

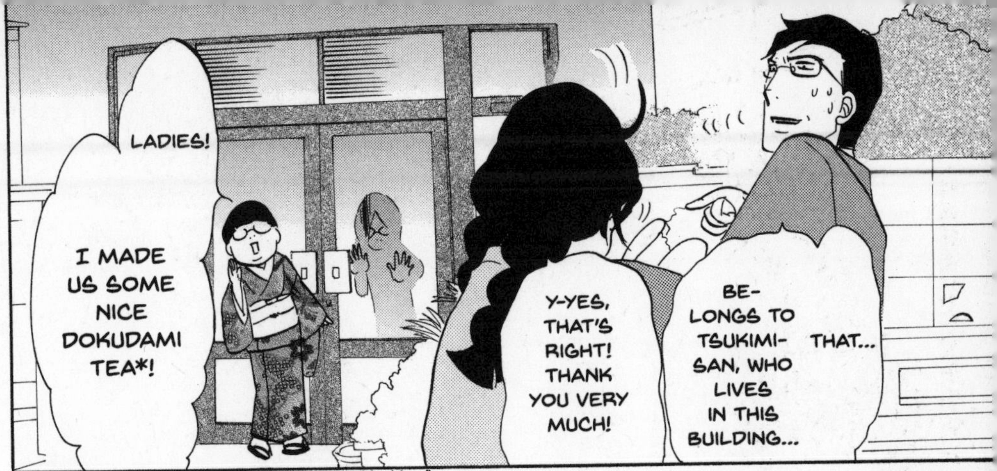
THAT...
BE-LONGS TO TSUKIMI-SAN, WHO LIVES IN THIS BUILDING...
Y-YES, THAT'S RIGHT! THANK YOU VERY MUCH!
LADIES!
I MADE US SOME NICE DOKUDAMI TEA*!

*An herbal tea; literally translates to "poison-blocking."

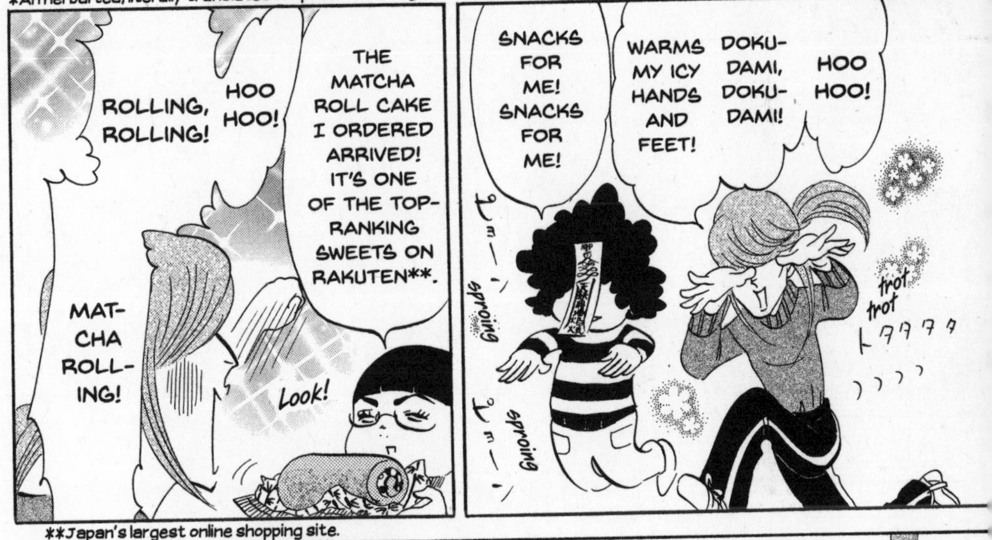
HOO HOO!
DOKU-DAMI, DOKU-DAMI!
WARMS MY ICY HANDS AND FEET!
SNACKS FOR ME! SNACKS FOR ME!
trot trot
sproing
sproing
THE MATCHA ROLL CAKE I ORDERED ARRIVED! IT'S ONE OF THE TOP-RANKING SWEETS ON RAKUTEN**.
HOO HOO!
ROLLING, ROLLING!
Look!
MAT-CHA ROLL-ING!

**Japan's largest online shopping site.

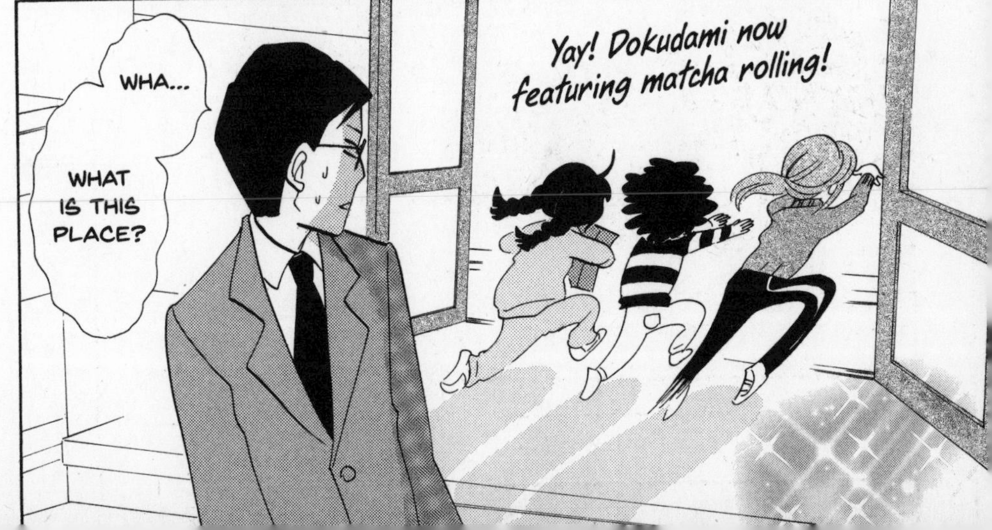
Yay! Dokudami now featuring matcha rolling!
WHA...
WHAT IS THIS PLACE?

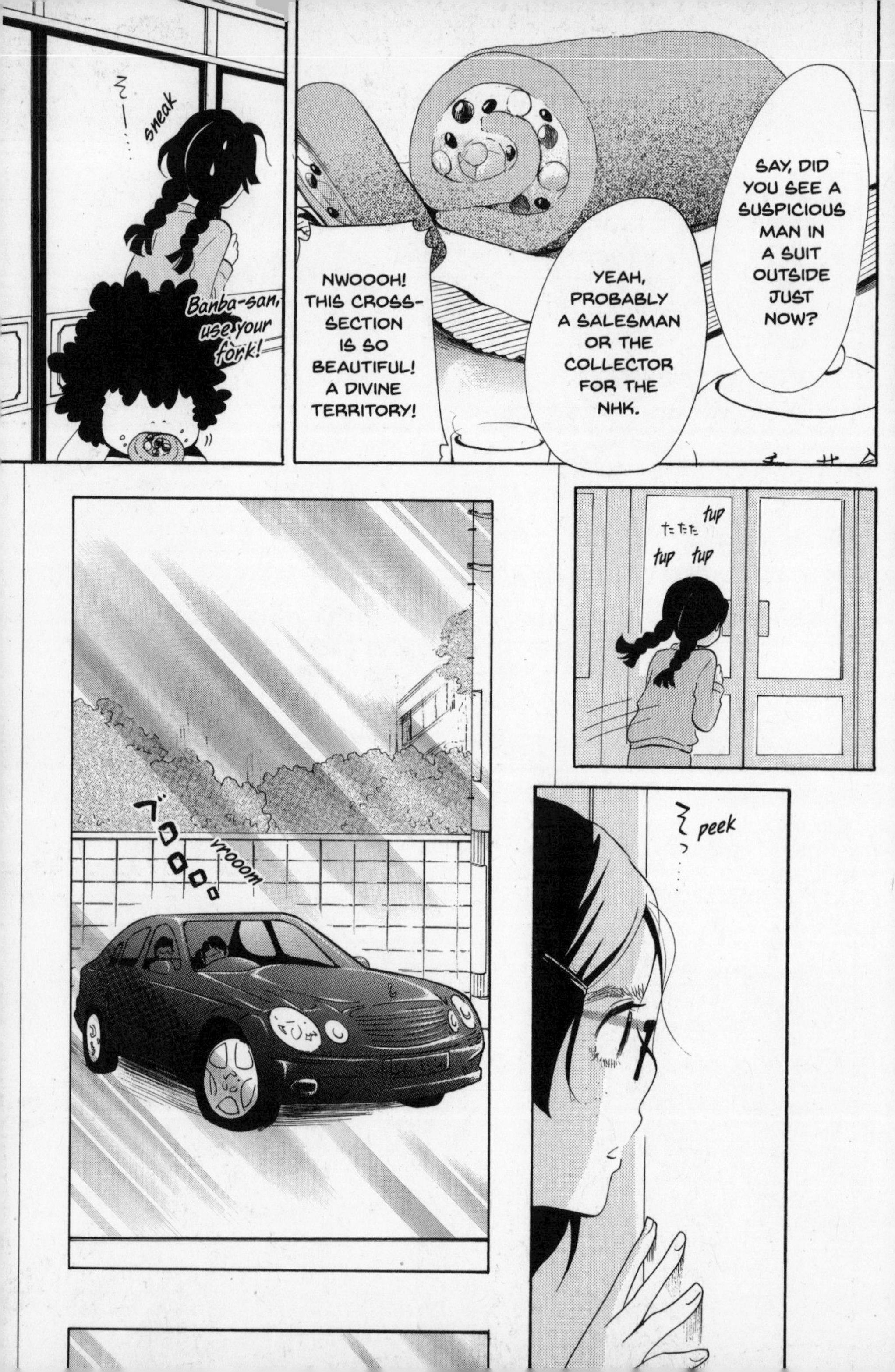
SAY, DID YOU SEE A SUSPICIOUS MAN IN A SUIT OUTSIDE JUST NOW?
YEAH, PROBABLY A SALESMAN OR THE COLLECTOR FOR THE NHK.
NWOOOH! THIS CROSS-SECTION IS SO BEAUTIFUL! A DIVINE TERRITORY!
sneak
Banba-san, use your fork!
たたた
tup
tup tup
peek
vrooom

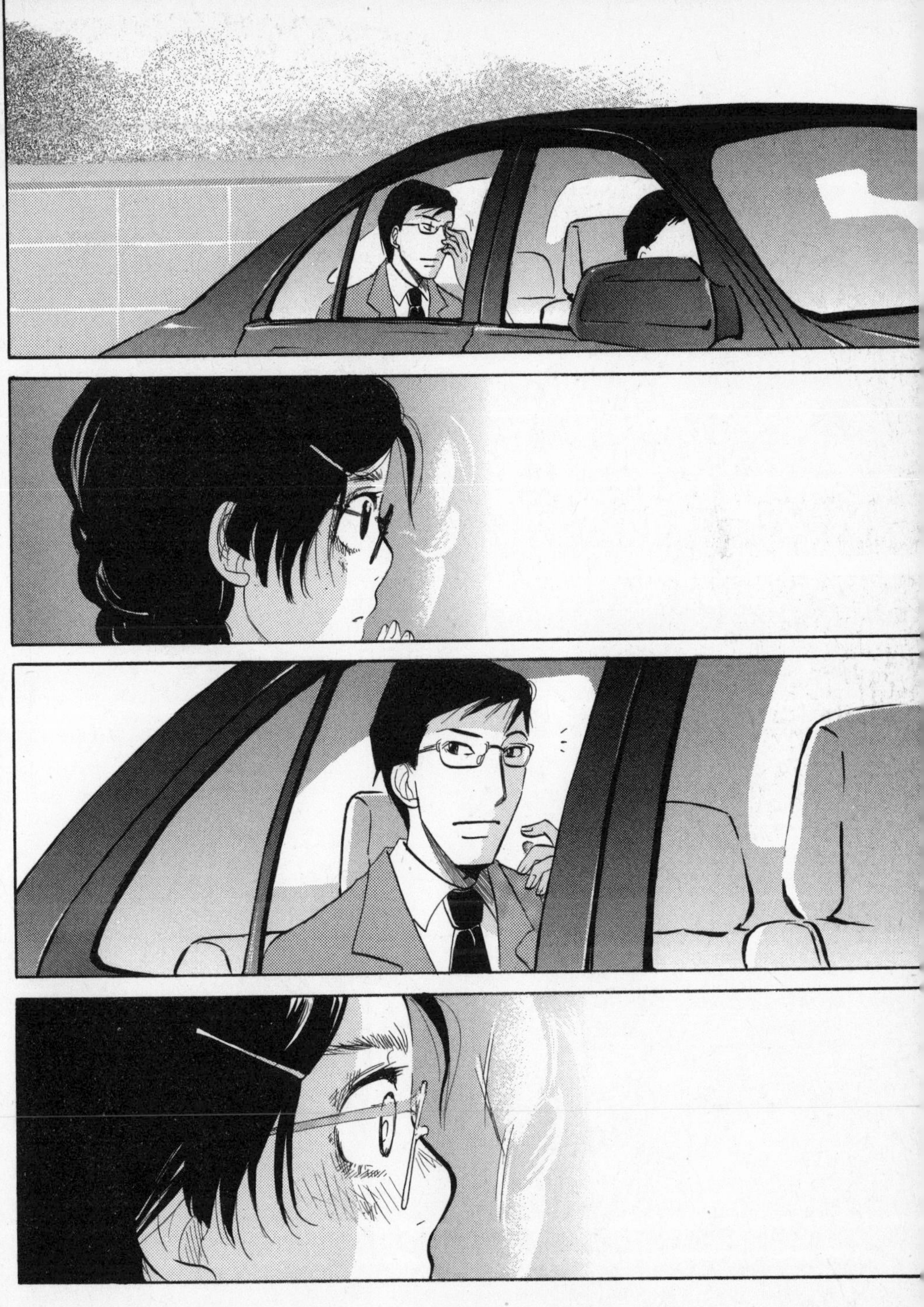

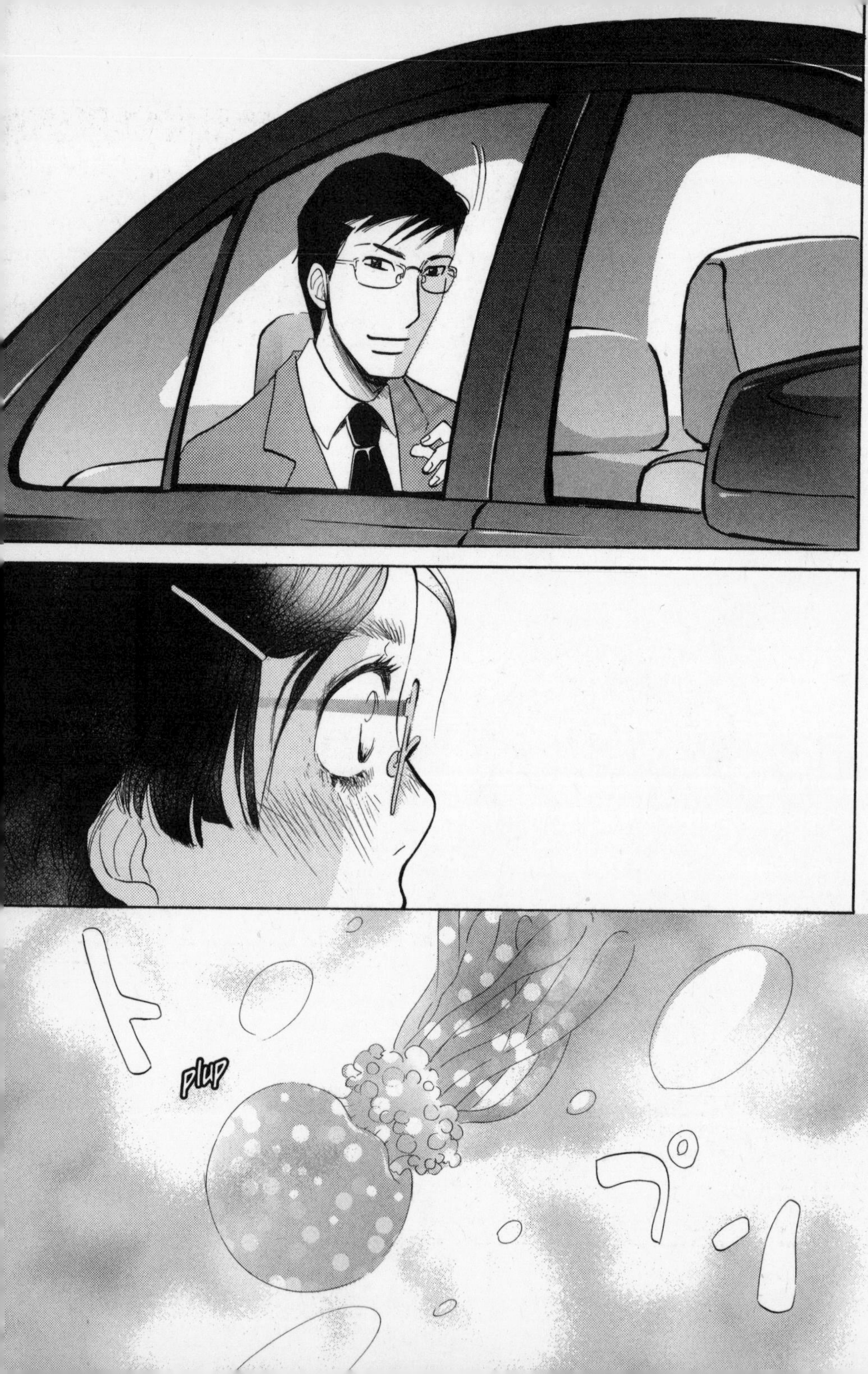
plup

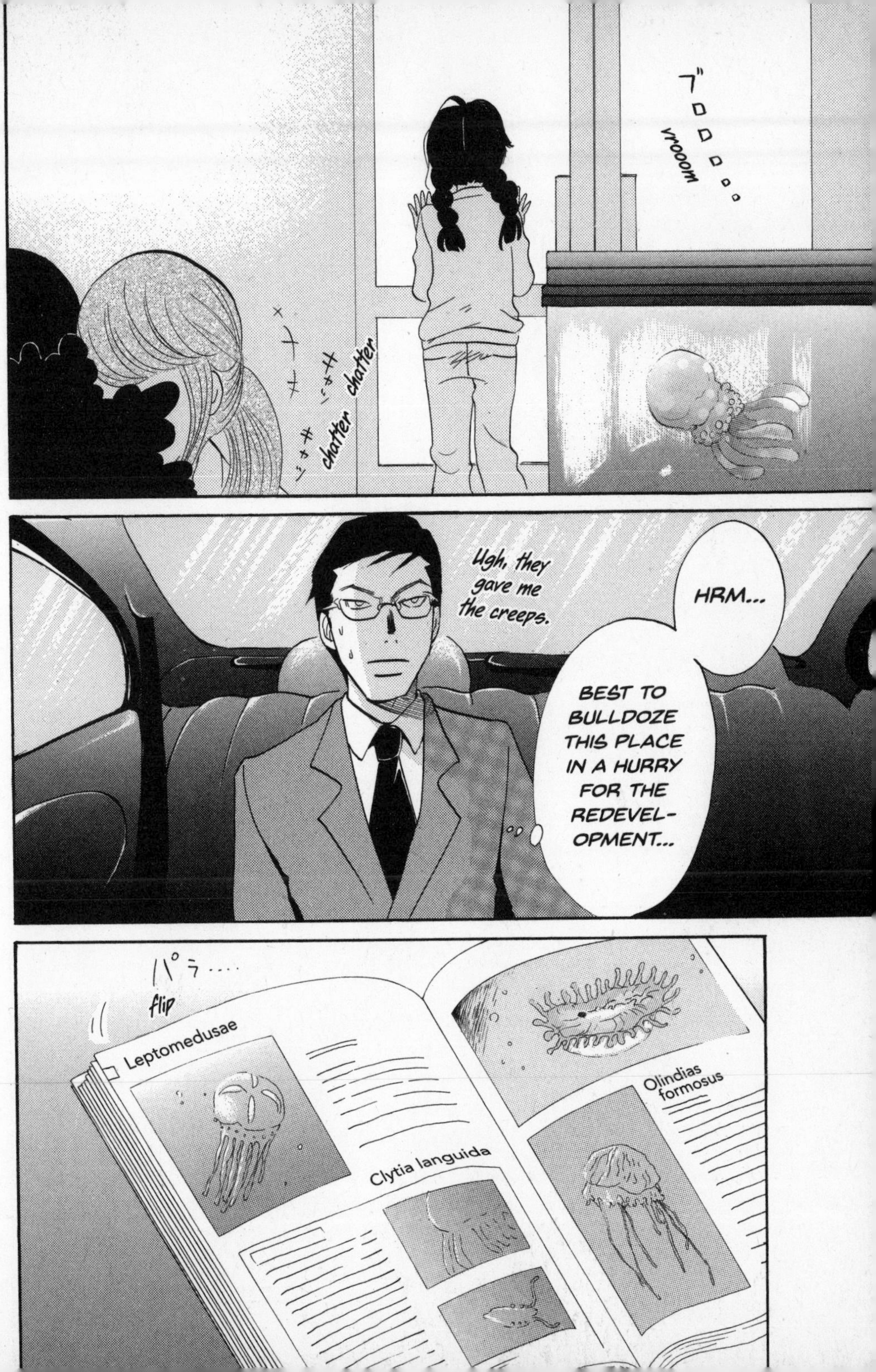
ブロロロ。。。
vroooom
キャッキャッ
chatter chatter
HRM...
BEST TO BULLDOZE THIS PLACE IN A HURRY FOR THE REDEVEL-OPMENT...
Ugh, they gave me the creeps.
パラ....
flip
Olindias formosus
Leptomedusae
Clytia languida

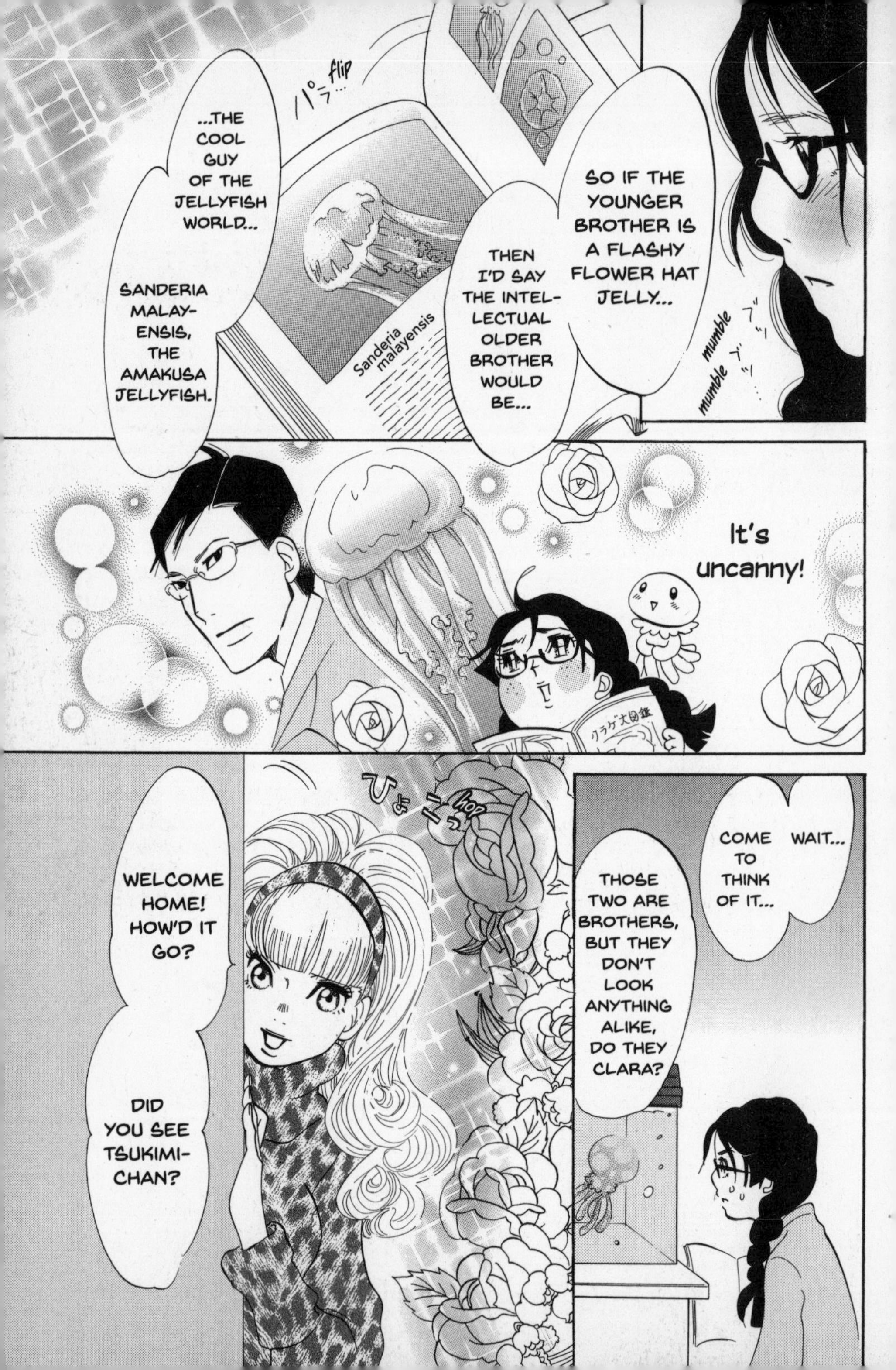
mumble ブツ
mumble ブツ…
SO IF THE YOUNGER BROTHER IS A FLASHY FLOWER HAT JELLY...
THEN I'D SAY THE INTEL-LECTUAL OLDER BROTHER WOULD BE...
flip パラ…
Sanderia malayensis
...THE COOL GUY OF THE JELLYFISH WORLD...
SANDERIA MALAY-ENSIS, THE AMAKUSA JELLYFISH.
It's uncanny!
クラゲ大図鑑
WAIT... COME TO THINK OF IT...
THOSE TWO ARE BROTHERS, BUT THEY DON'T LOOK ANYTHING ALIKE, DO THEY CLARA?
ひょこっ hop
WELCOME HOME! HOW'D IT GO?
DID YOU SEE TSUKIMI-CHAN?

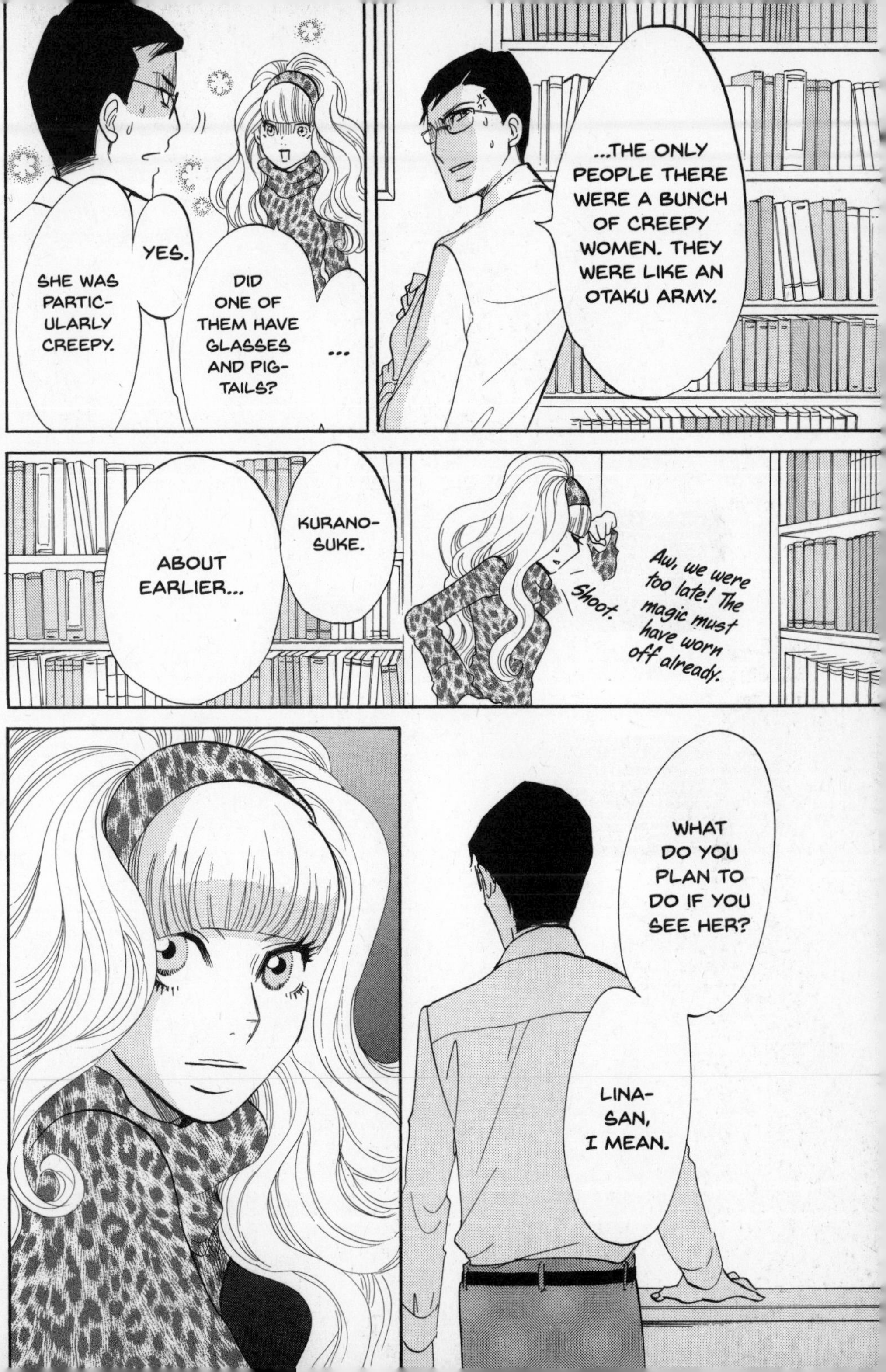
...THE ONLY PEOPLE THERE WERE A BUNCH OF CREEPY WOMEN. THEY WERE LIKE AN OTAKU ARMY.
...
DID ONE OF THEM HAVE GLASSES AND PIG-TAILS?
YES.
SHE WAS PARTIC-ULARLY CREEPY.
Aw, we were too late! The magic must have worn off already.
Shoot.
KURANO-SUKE.
ABOUT EARLIER...
WHAT DO YOU PLAN TO DO IF YOU SEE HER?
LINA-SAN, I MEAN.

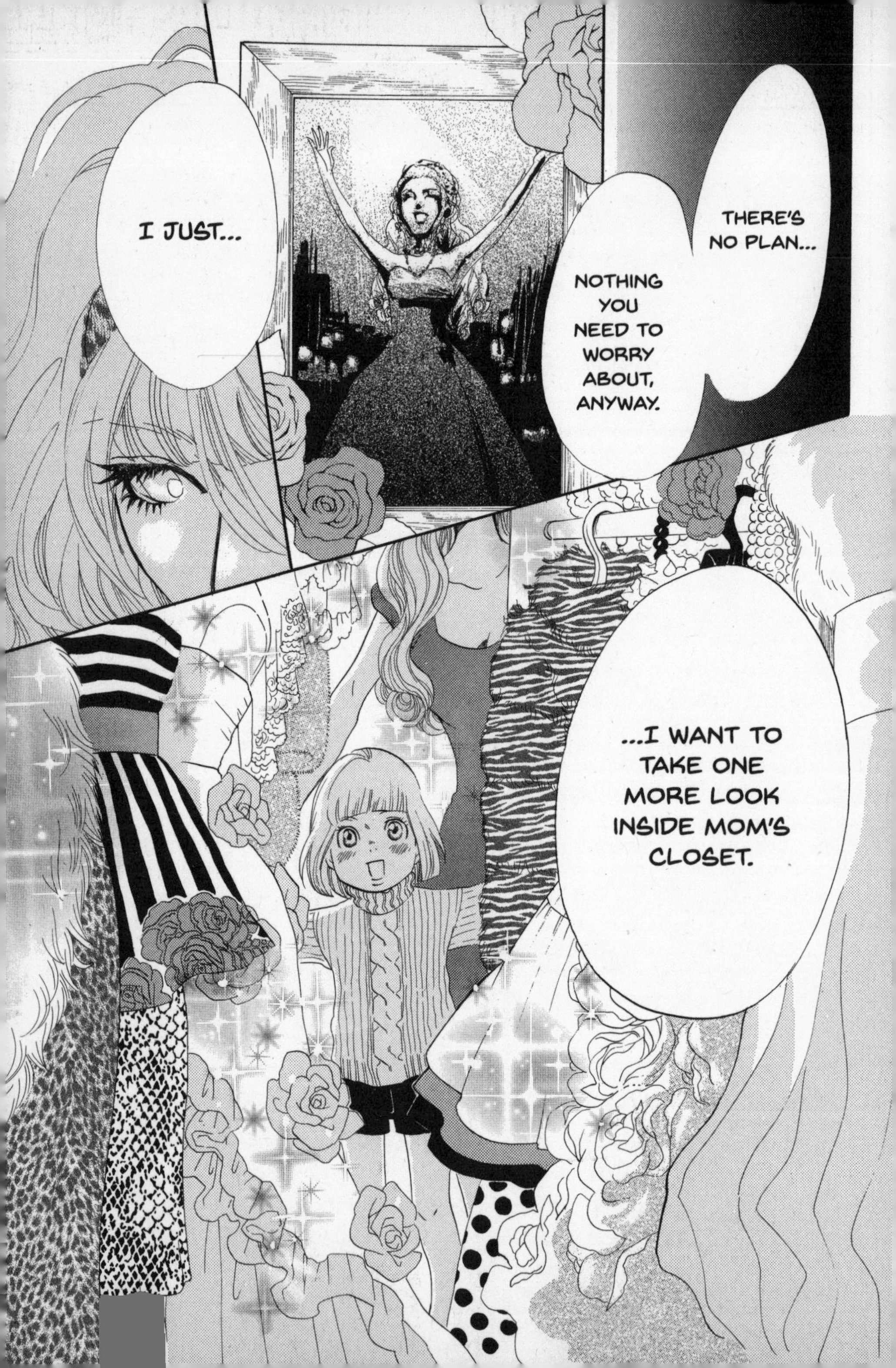
THERE'S NO PLAN...
NOTHING YOU NEED TO WORRY ABOUT, ANYWAY.
I JUST...
...I WANT TO TAKE ONE MORE LOOK INSIDE MOM'S CLOSET.

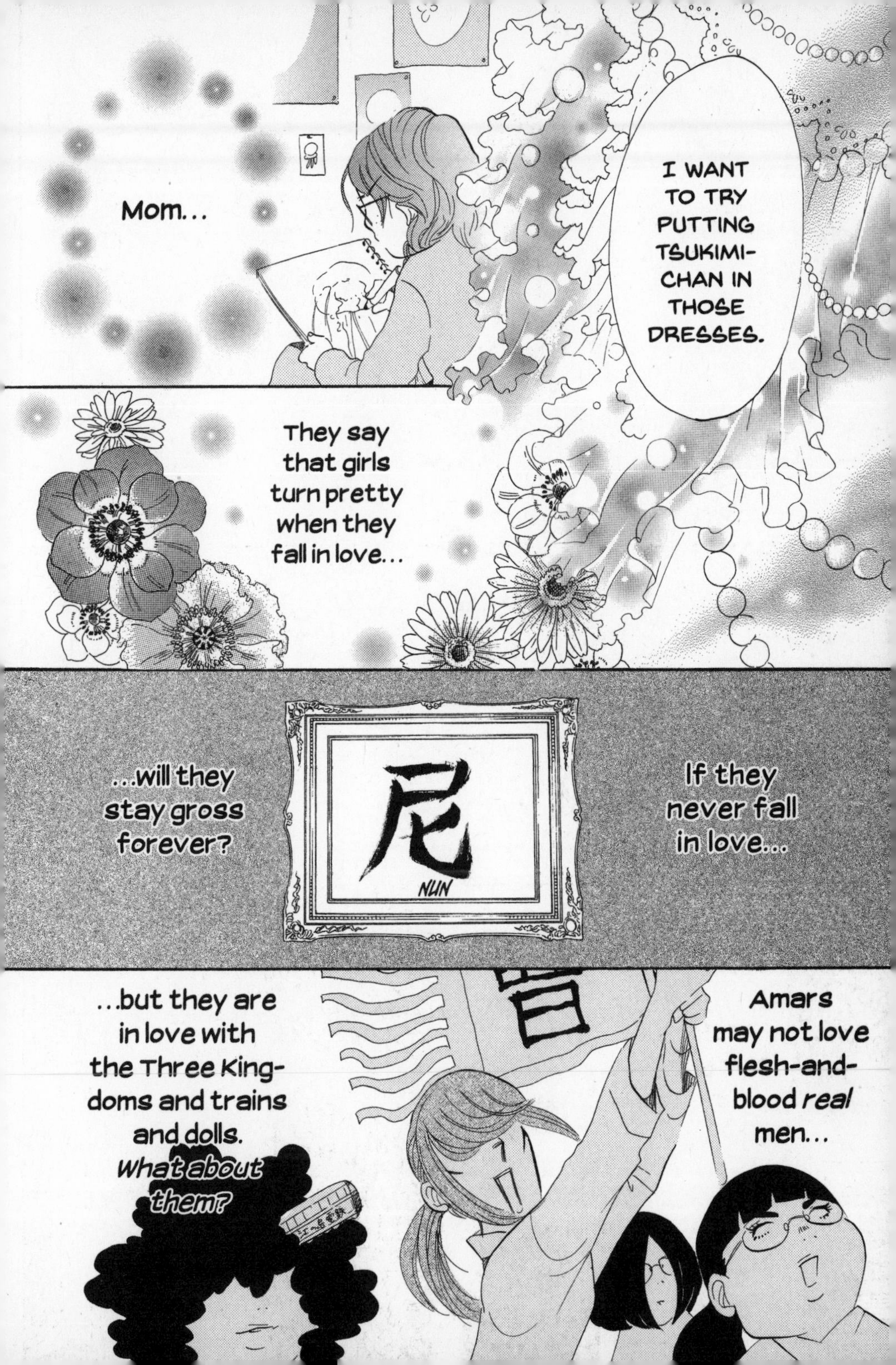
I WANT TO TRY PUTTING TSUKIMI-CHAN IN THOSE DRESSES.
Mom...
They say that girls turn pretty when they fall in love...
If they never fall in love...
尼
NUN
...will they stay gross forever?
Amars may not love flesh-and-blood *real* men...
...but they are in love with the Three King-doms and trains and dolls. *What about them?*

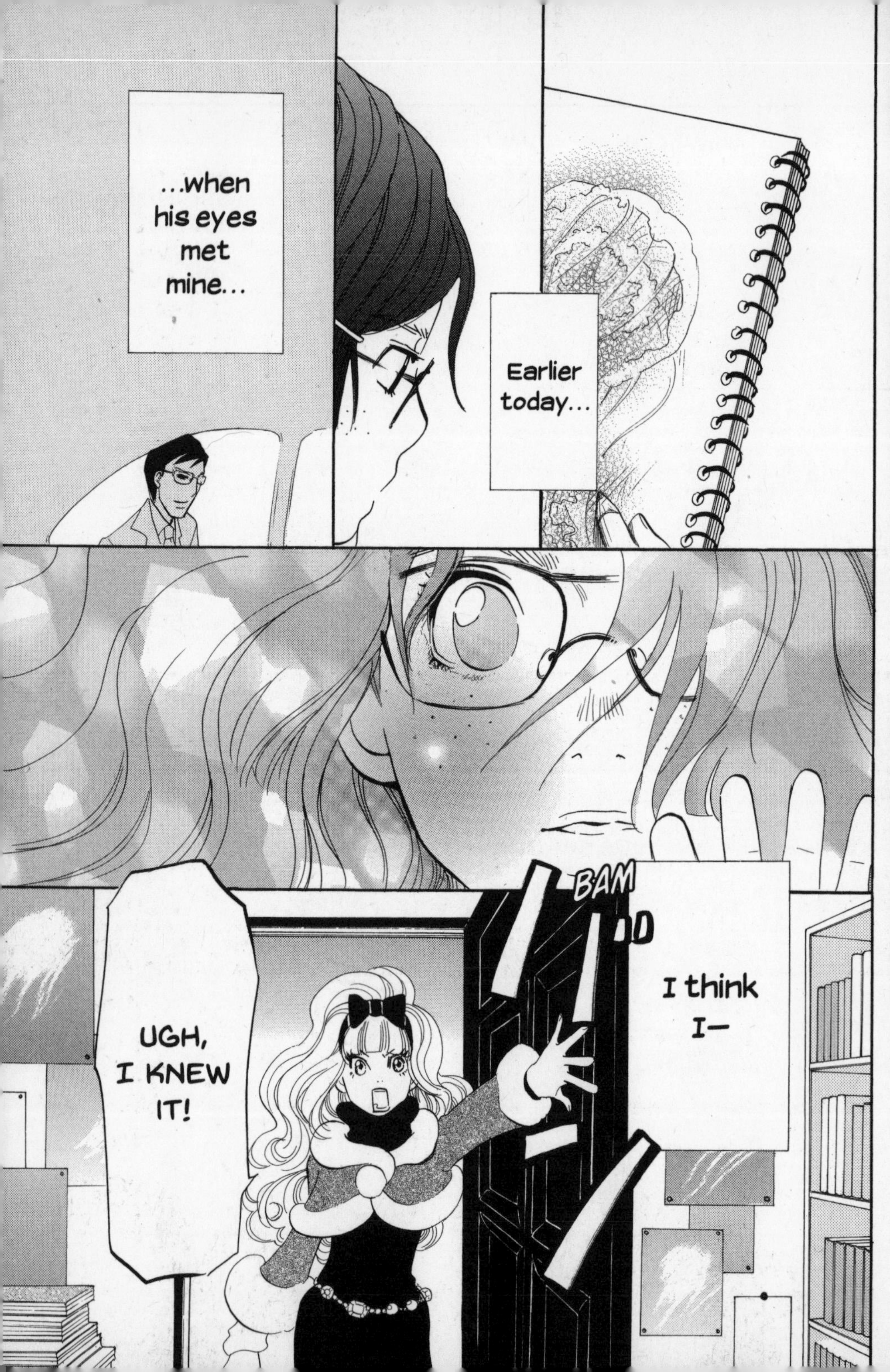
Earlier today...
...when his eyes met mine...
I think I—
BAM
UGH, I KNEW IT!

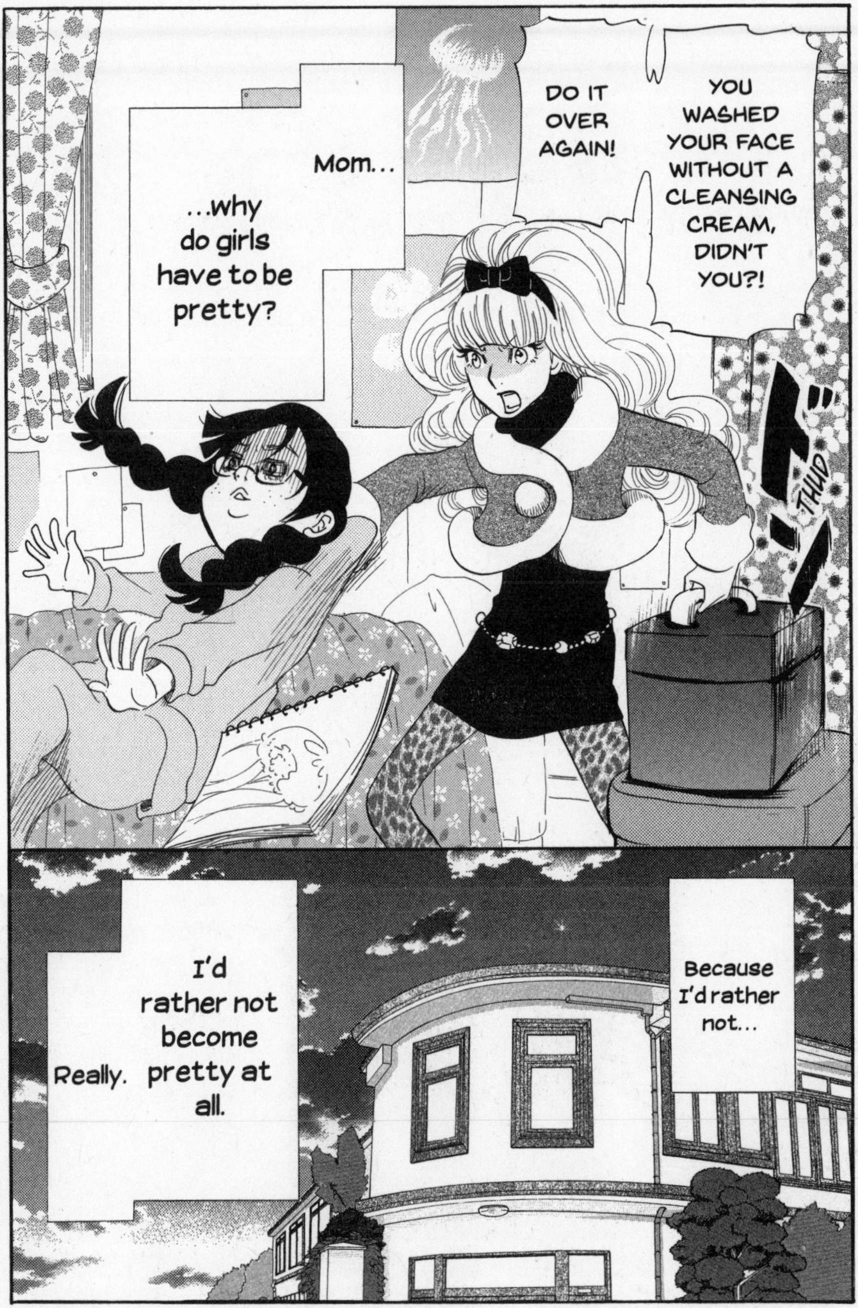
YOU WASHED YOUR FACE WITHOUT A CLEANSING CREAM, DIDN'T YOU?!
DO IT OVER AGAIN!
THUD
Mom...
...why do girls have to be pretty?
Because I'd rather not...
I'd rather not become pretty at all.
Really.

Episode 6
Take Me Out to the Aquarium

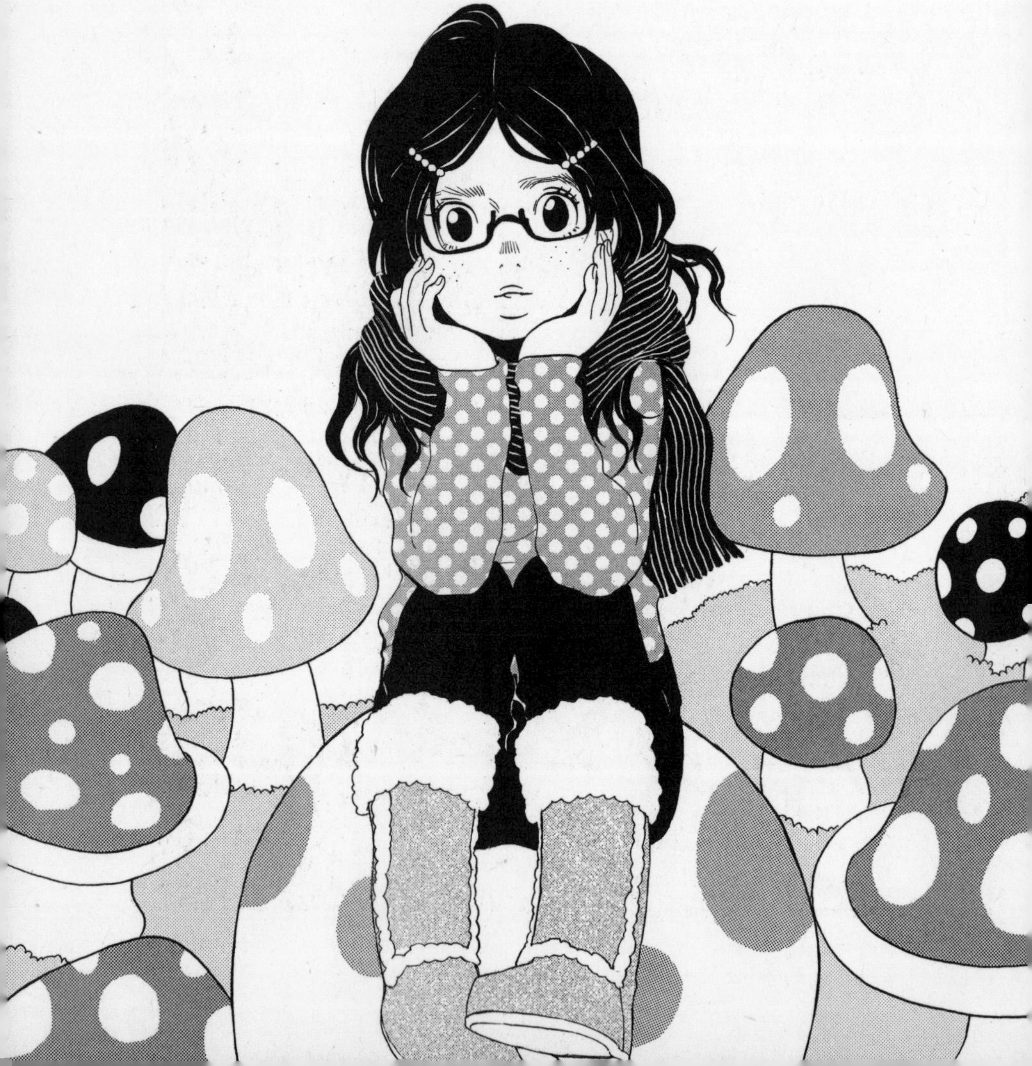

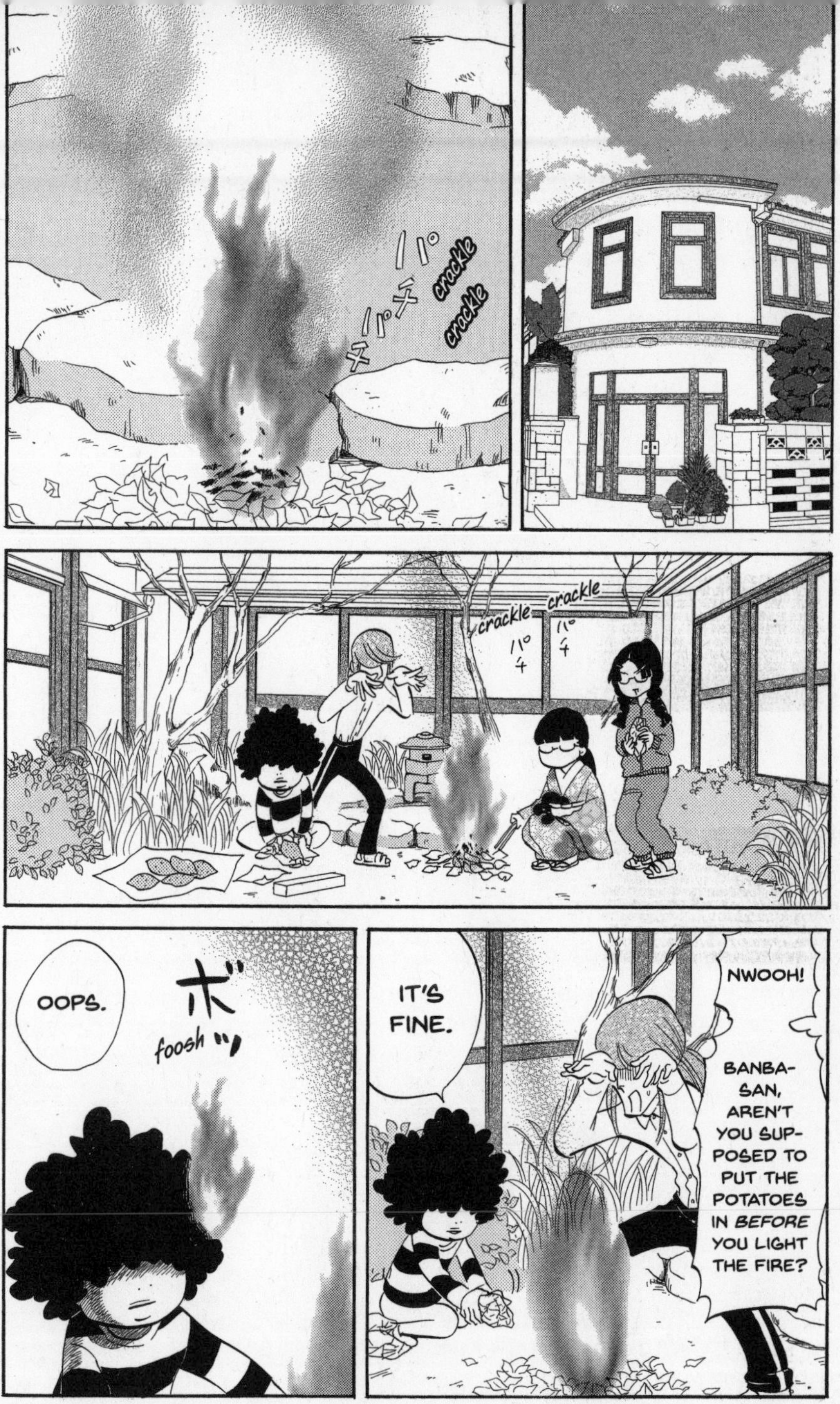
パチパチ
crackle crackle
crackle crackle
パチ
パチ
NWOOH!
IT'S FINE.
BANBA-SAN, AREN'T YOU SUPPOSED TO PUT THE POTATOES IN *BEFORE* YOU LIGHT THE FIRE?
OOPS.
ボッ
foosh

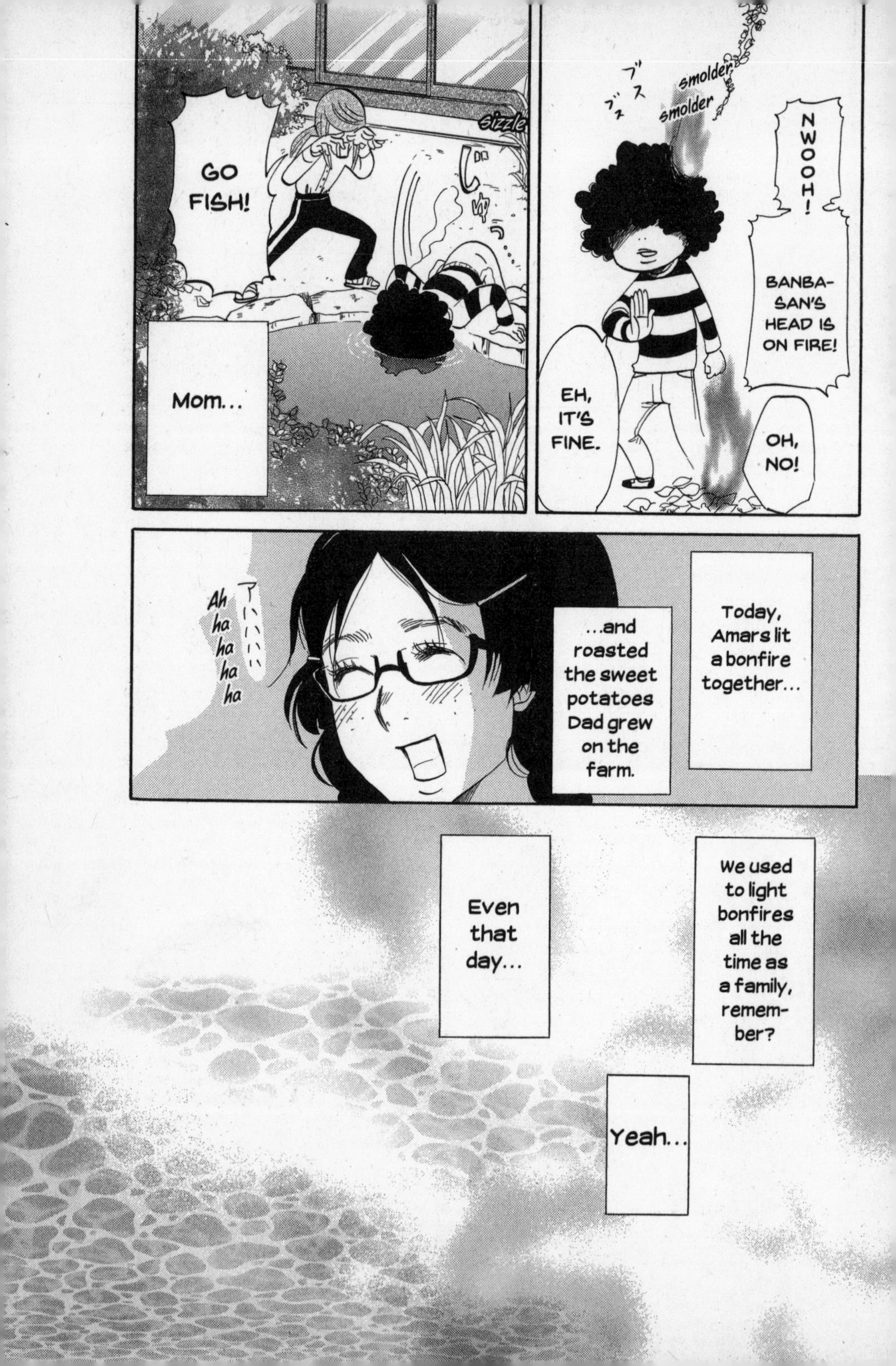
ブスブス
smolder smolder
NWOOOH!
BANBA-SAN'S HEAD IS ON FIRE!
OH, NO!
EH, IT'S FINE.
sizzle
GO FISH!
Mom...
Today, Amars lit a bonfire together...
...and roasted the sweet potatoes Dad grew on the farm.
アハハハハ
Ah ha ha ha ha
We used to light bonfires all the time as a family, remember?
Even that day...
Yeah...

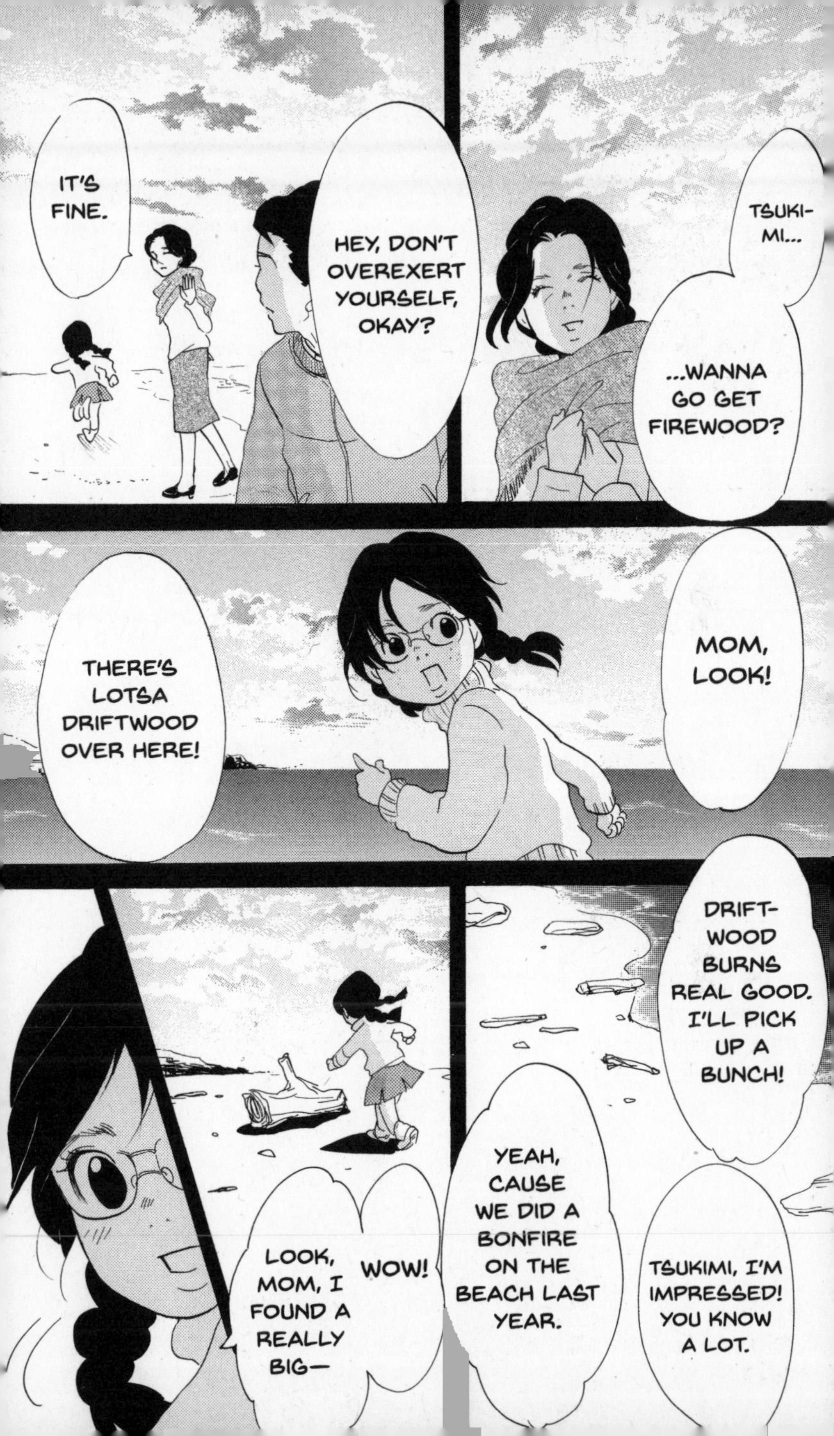
TSUKI-MI...
...WANNA GO GET FIREWOOD?
HEY, DON'T OVEREXERT YOURSELF, OKAY?
IT'S FINE.
MOM, LOOK!
THERE'S LOTSA DRIFTWOOD OVER HERE!
DRIFT-WOOD BURNS REAL GOOD. I'LL PICK UP A BUNCH!
TSUKIMI, I'M IMPRESSED! YOU KNOW A LOT.
YEAH, CAUSE WE DID A BONFIRE ON THE BEACH LAST YEAR.
WOW!
LOOK, MOM, I FOUND A REALLY BIG—

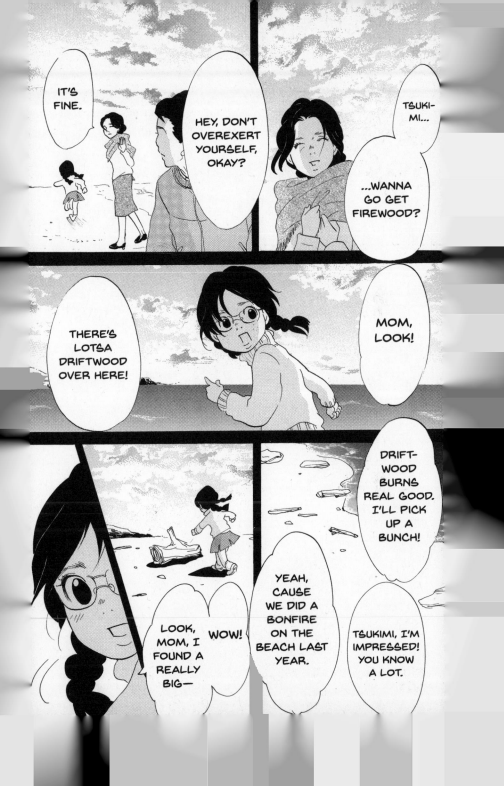

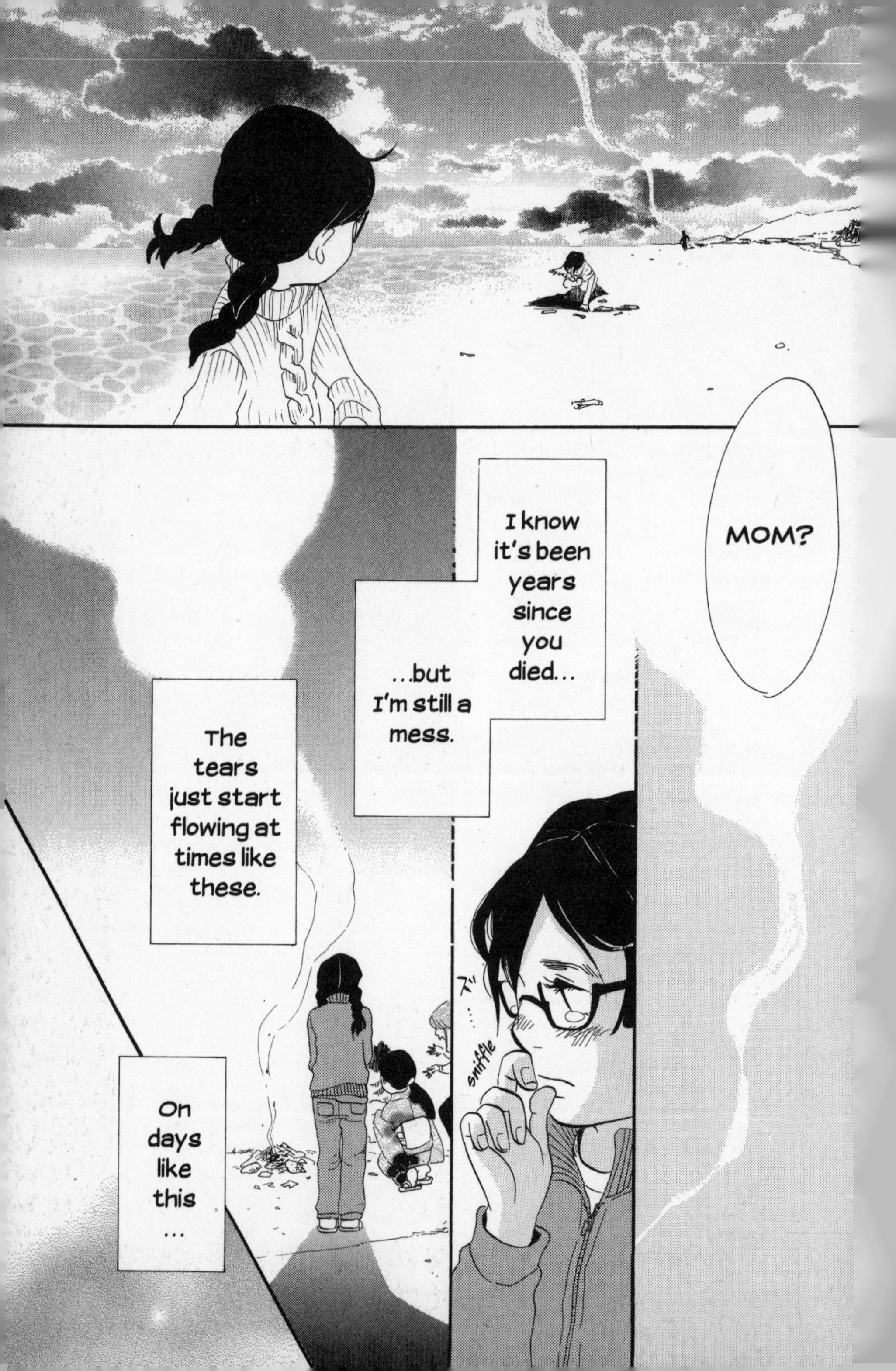
MOM?
I know it's been years since you died...
...but I'm still a mess.
ズ...
sniffle
The tears just start flowing at times like these.
On days like this ...

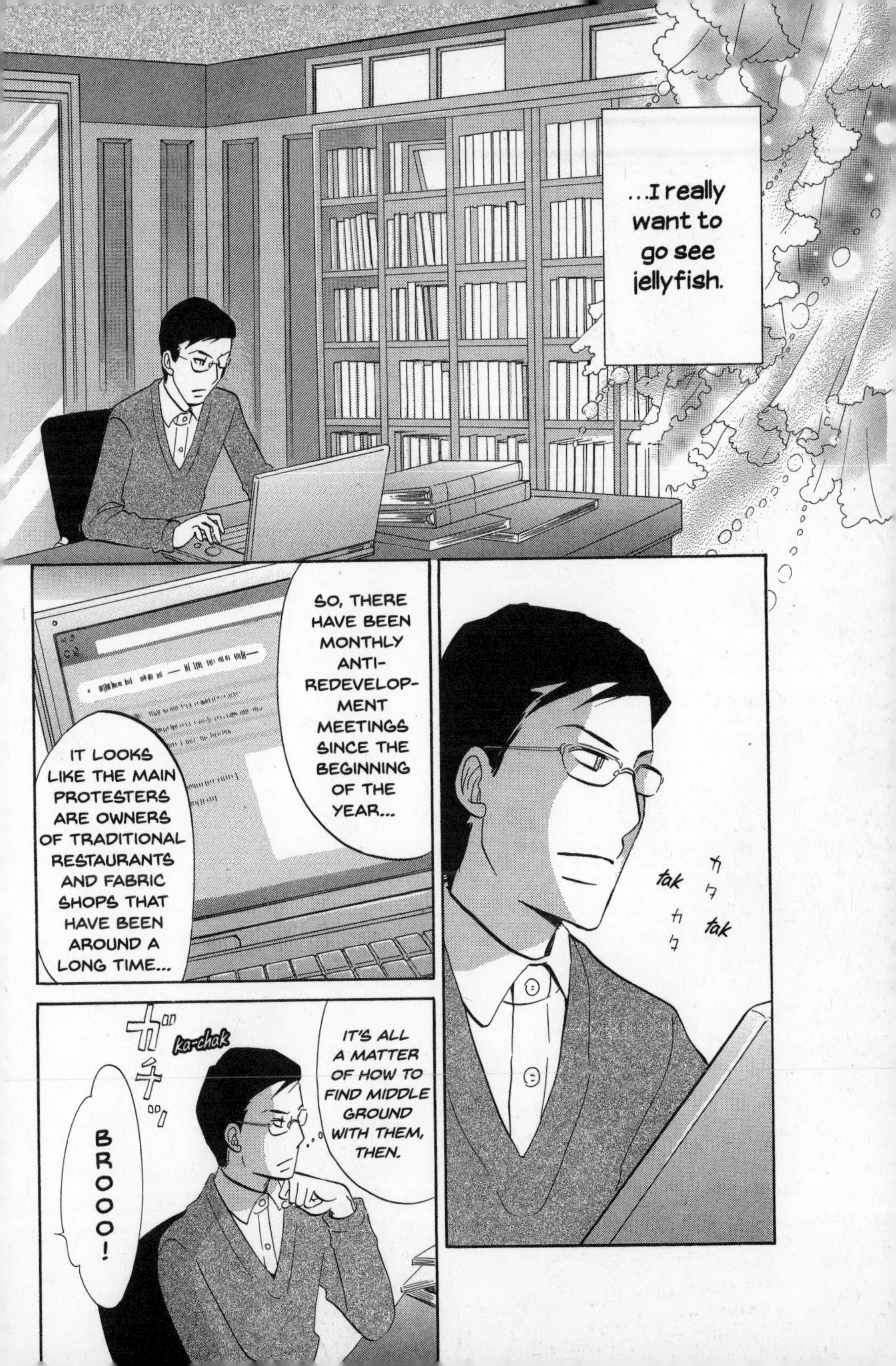
...I really want to go see jellyfish.
tak tak
SO, THERE HAVE BEEN MONTHLY ANTI-REDEVELOPMENT MEETINGS SINCE THE BEGINNING OF THE YEAR...
IT LOOKS LIKE THE MAIN PROTESTERS ARE OWNERS OF TRADITIONAL RESTAURANTS AND FABRIC SHOPS THAT HAVE BEEN AROUND A LONG TIME...
IT'S ALL A MATTER OF HOW TO FIND MIDDLE GROUND WITH THEM, THEN.
ka-chak
BROOO!

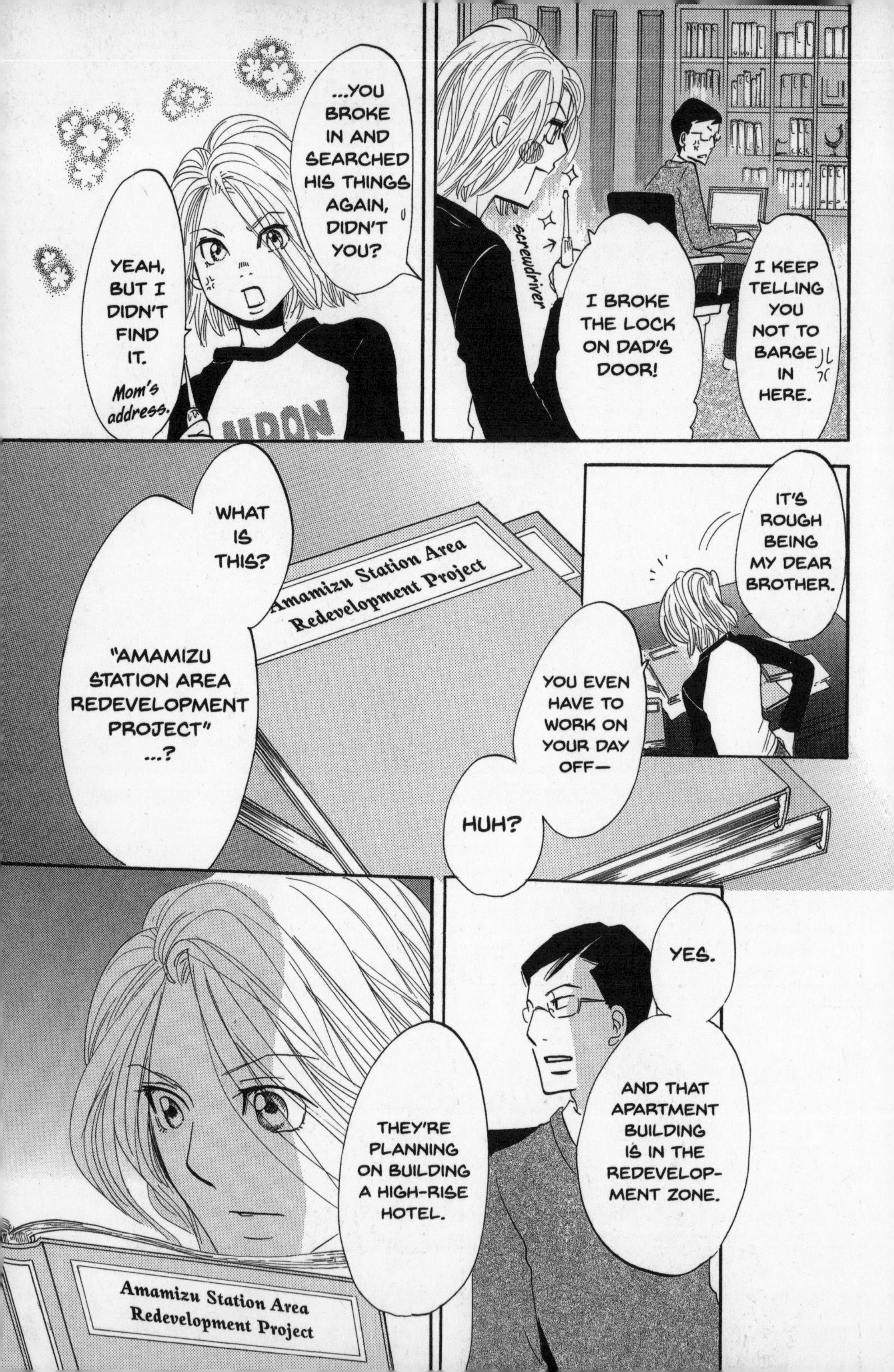
I KEEP TELLING YOU NOT TO BARGE IN HERE.
I BROKE THE LOCK ON DAD'S DOOR!
screwdriver
...YOU BROKE IN AND SEARCHED HIS THINGS AGAIN, DIDN'T YOU?
YEAH, BUT I DIDN'T FIND IT. Mom's address.
IT'S ROUGH BEING MY DEAR BROTHER.
YOU EVEN HAVE TO WORK ON YOUR DAY OFF—
HUH?
WHAT IS THIS?
Amamizu Station Area Redevelopment Project
"AMAMIZU STATION AREA REDEVELOPMENT PROJECT" ...?
YES.
THEY'RE PLANNING ON BUILDING A HIGH-RISE HOTEL.
AND THAT APARTMENT BUILDING IS IN THE REDEVELOPMENT ZONE.
Amamizu Station Area Redevelopment Project

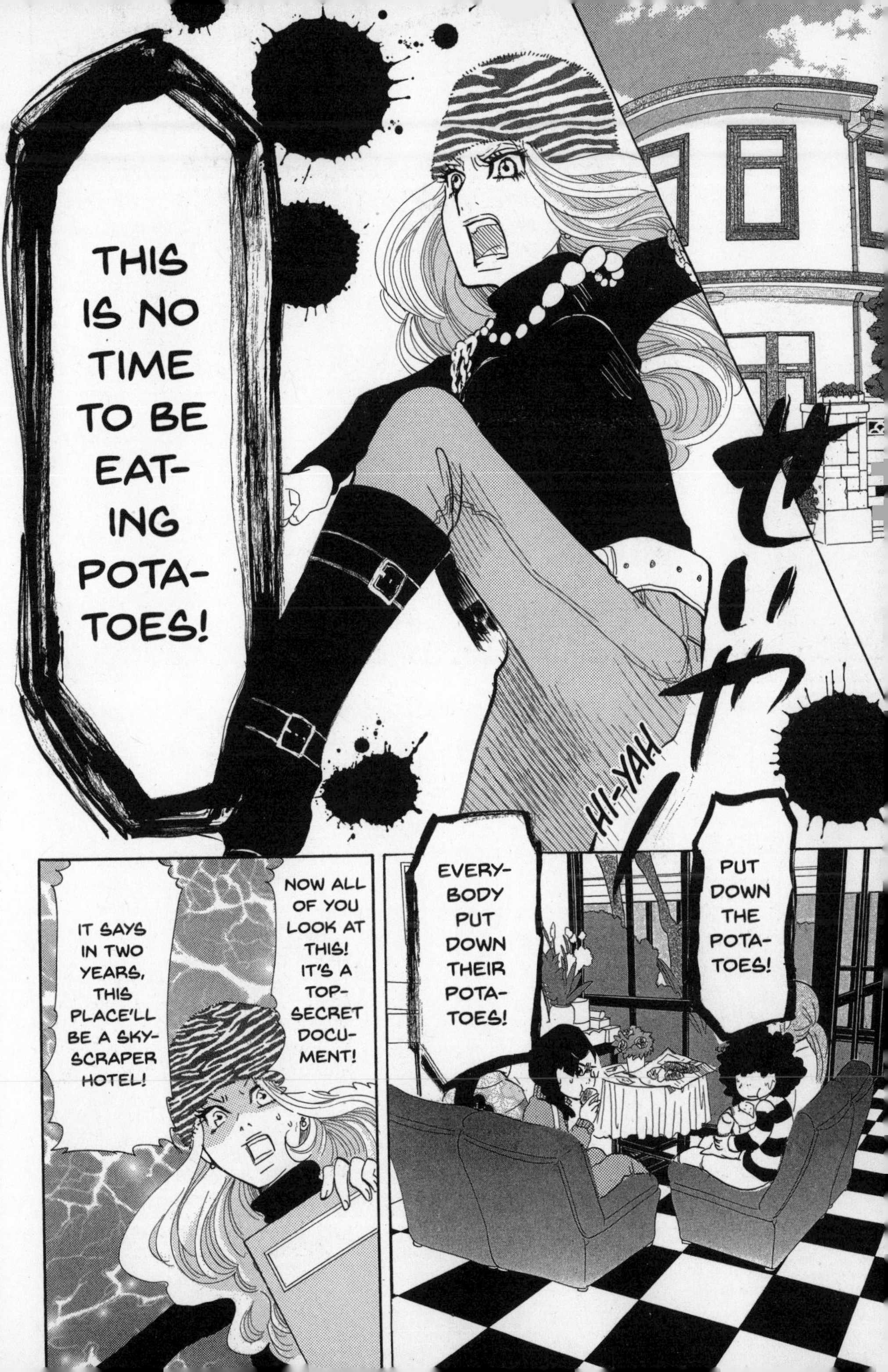
THIS IS NO TIME TO BE EATING POTATOES!
HI-YAH
PUT DOWN THE POTATOES!
EVERYBODY PUT DOWN THEIR POTATOES!
NOW ALL OF YOU LOOK AT THIS! IT'S A TOP-SECRET DOCUMENT!
IT SAYS IN TWO YEARS, THIS PLACE'LL BE A SKYSCRAPER HOTEL!

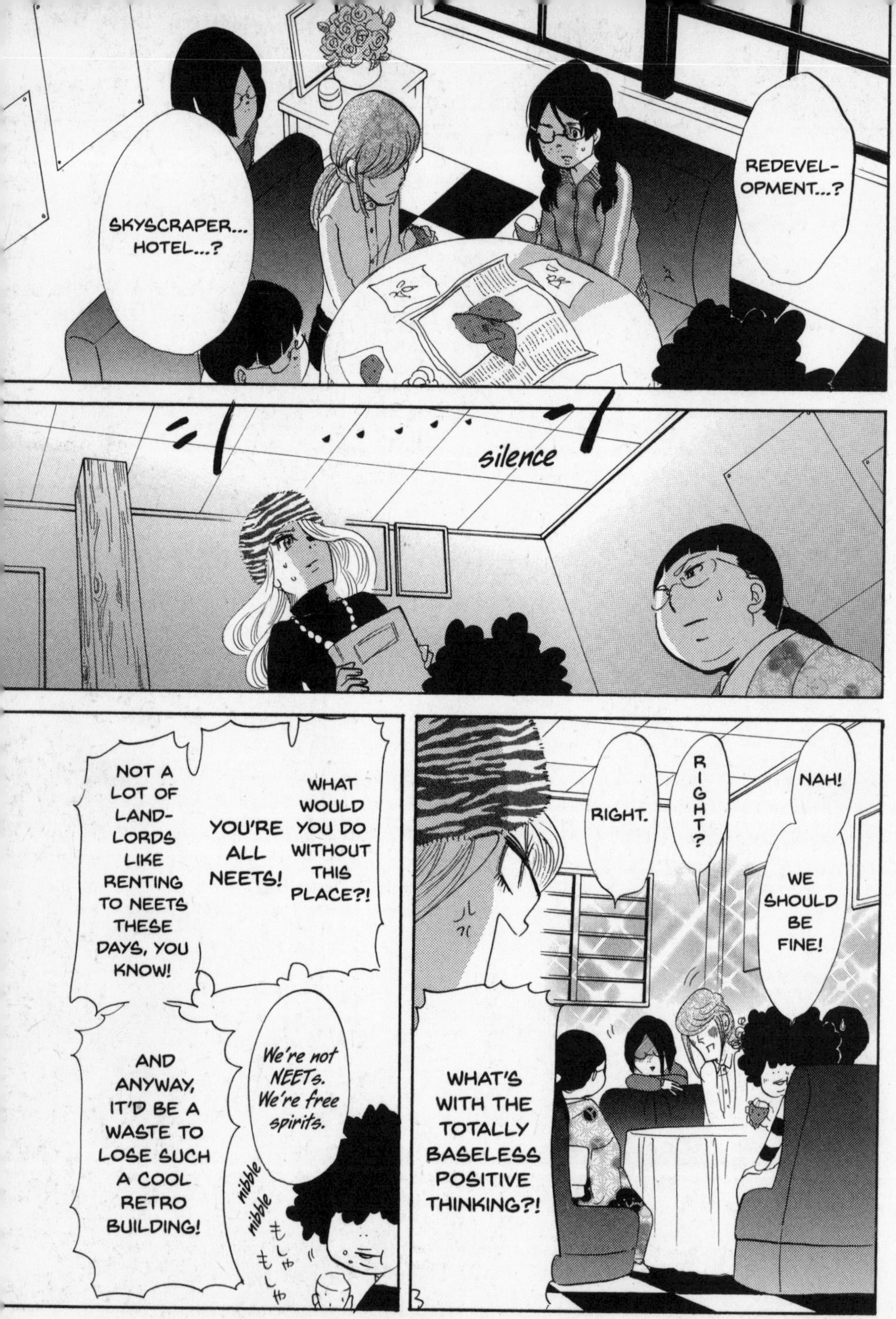

REDEVEL-
OPMENT...?
SKYSCRAPER... HOTEL...?
silence
NAH!
RIGHT?
RIGHT.
WE SHOULD BE FINE!
WHAT'S WITH THE TOTALLY BASELESS POSITIVE THINKING?!
WHAT WOULD YOU DO WITHOUT THIS PLACE?!
YOU'RE ALL NEETS!
NOT A LOT OF LAND-
LORDS LIKE RENTING TO NEETS THESE DAYS, YOU KNOW!
We're not NEETs. We're free spirits.
AND ANYWAY, IT'D BE A WASTE TO LOSE SUCH A COOL RETRO BUILDING!
nibble nibble
もしゃもしゃ

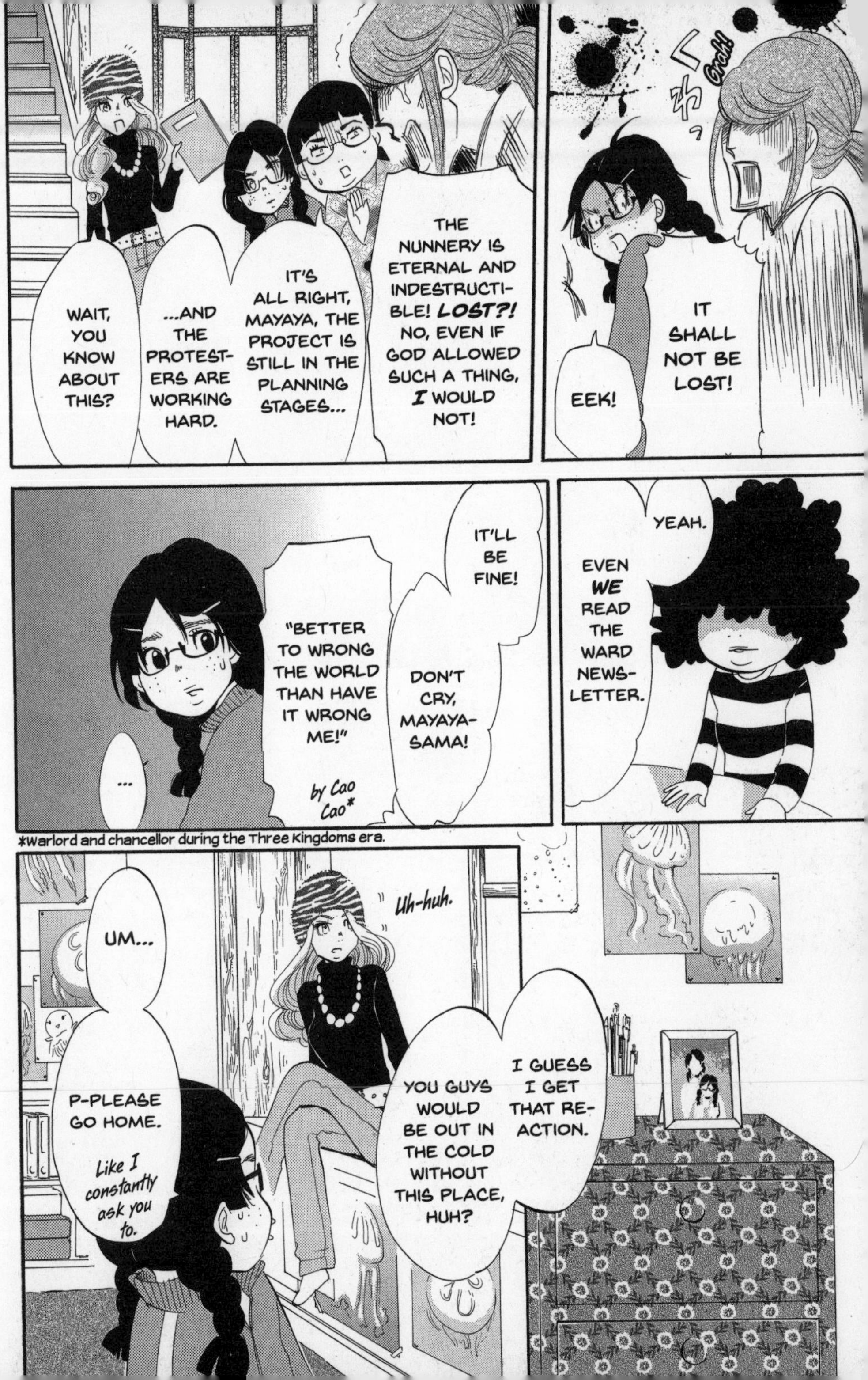
Grah!
IT SHALL NOT BE LOST!
EEK!
THE NUNNERY IS ETERNAL AND INDESTRUCTIBLE! *LOST?!* NO, EVEN IF GOD ALLOWED SUCH A THING, *I* WOULD NOT!
IT'S ALL RIGHT, MAYAYA, THE PROJECT IS STILL IN THE PLANNING STAGES...
...AND THE PROTESTERS ARE WORKING HARD.
WAIT, YOU KNOW ABOUT THIS?
YEAH.
EVEN **WE** READ THE WARD NEWSLETTER.
IT'LL BE FINE!
DON'T CRY, MAYAYA-SAMA!
"BETTER TO WRONG THE WORLD THAN HAVE IT WRONG ME!"
by Cao Cao*
...
Uh-huh.
I GUESS I GET THAT REACTION.
YOU GUYS WOULD BE OUT IN THE COLD WITHOUT THIS PLACE, HUH?
UM...
P-PLEASE GO HOME.
Like I constantly ask you to.
*Warlord and chancellor during the Three Kingdoms era.

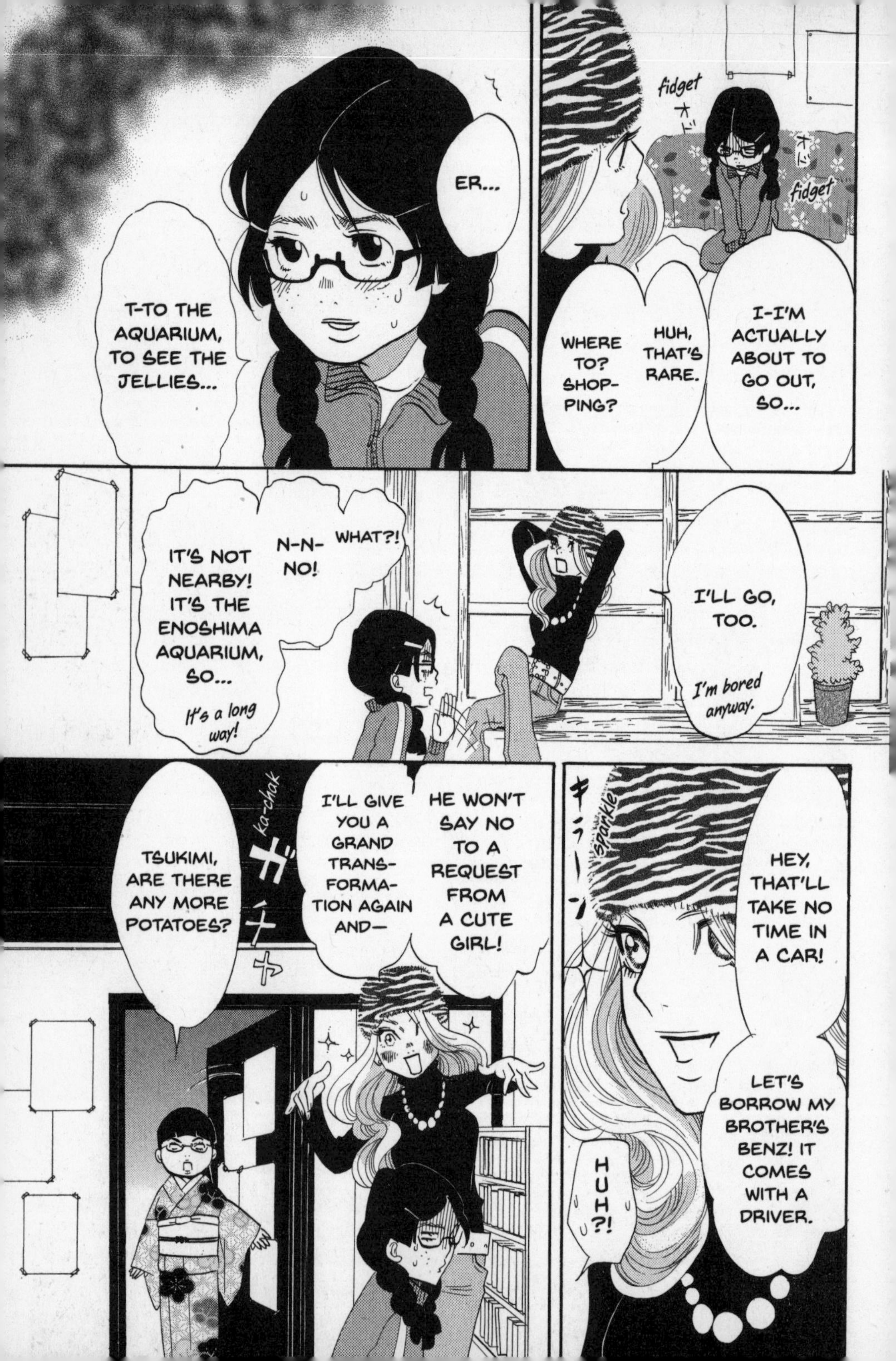
fidget
fidget
I-I'M ACTUALLY ABOUT TO GO OUT, SO...
HUH, THAT'S RARE.
WHERE TO? SHOPPING?
ER...
T-TO THE AQUARIUM, TO SEE THE JELLIES...
I'LL GO, TOO.
I'm bored anyway.
WHAT?!
N-N-NO!
IT'S NOT NEARBY! IT'S THE ENOSHIMA AQUARIUM, SO...
It's a long way!
sparkle
HEY, THAT'LL TAKE NO TIME IN A CAR!
LET'S BORROW MY BROTHER'S BENZ! IT COMES WITH A DRIVER.
HUH?!
HE WON'T SAY NO TO A REQUEST FROM A CUTE GIRL!
I'LL GIVE YOU A GRAND TRANSFORMATION AGAIN AND—
ka-chak
TSUKIMI, ARE THERE ANY MORE POTATOES?

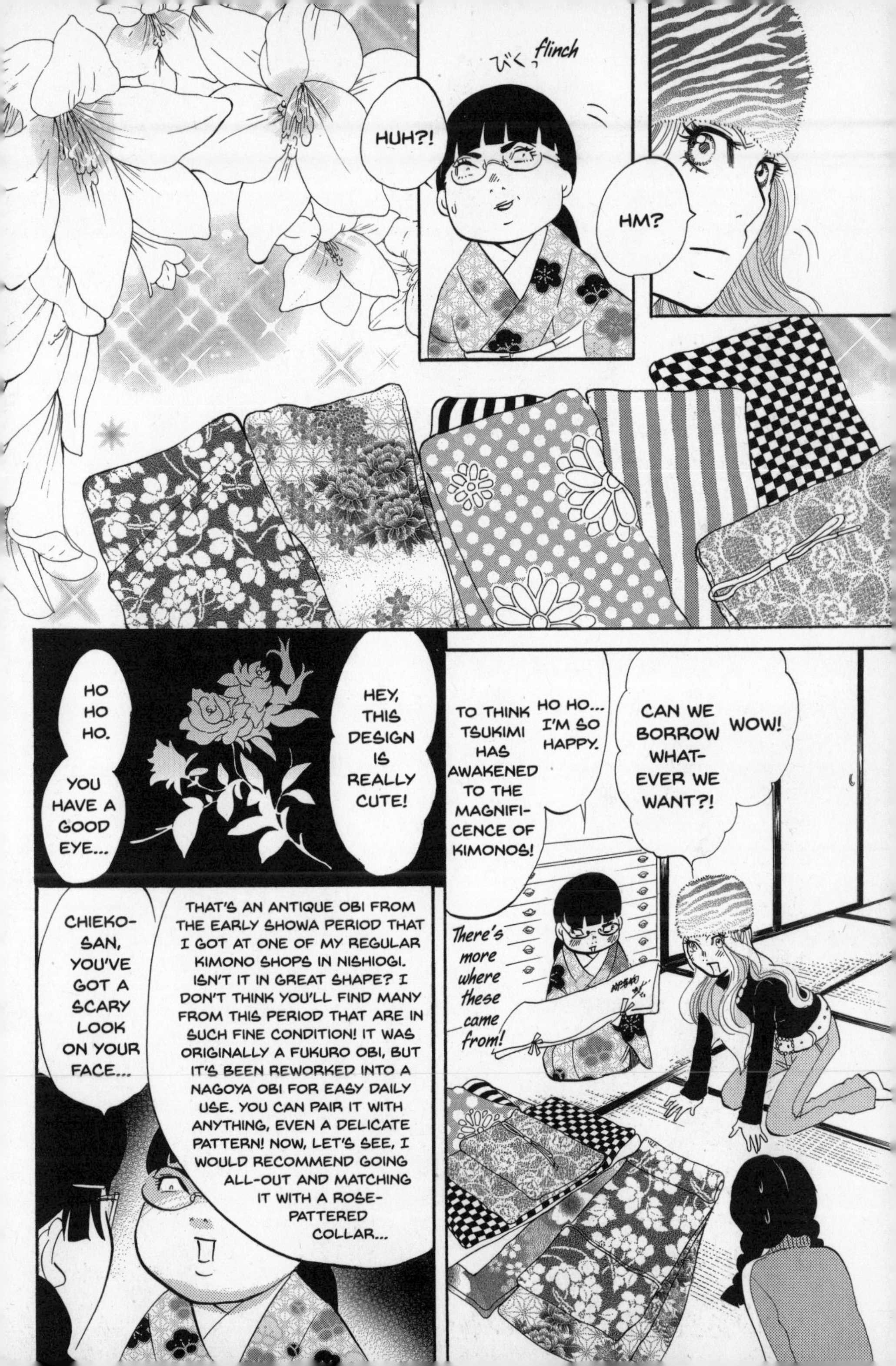
HM?
びくっ flinch
HUH?!
WOW!
CAN WE BORROW WHAT-EVER WE WANT?!
HO HO... I'M SO HAPPY.
TO THINK TSUKIMI HAS AWAKENED TO THE MAGNIFI-CENCE OF KIMONOS!
There's more where these came from!
HEY, THIS DESIGN IS REALLY CUTE!
HO HO HO.
YOU HAVE A GOOD EYE...
THAT'S AN ANTIQUE OBI FROM THE EARLY SHOWA PERIOD THAT I GOT AT ONE OF MY REGULAR KIMONO SHOPS IN NISHIOGI. ISN'T IT IN GREAT SHAPE? I DON'T THINK YOU'LL FIND MANY FROM THIS PERIOD THAT ARE IN SUCH FINE CONDITION! IT WAS ORIGINALLY A FUKURO OBI, BUT IT'S BEEN REWORKED INTO A NAGOYA OBI FOR EASY DAILY USE. YOU CAN PAIR IT WITH ANYTHING, EVEN A DELICATE PATTERN! NOW, LET'S SEE, I WOULD RECOMMEND GOING ALL-OUT AND MATCHING IT WITH A ROSE-PATTERED COLLAR...
CHIEKO-SAN, YOU'VE GOT A SCARY LOOK ON YOUR FACE...

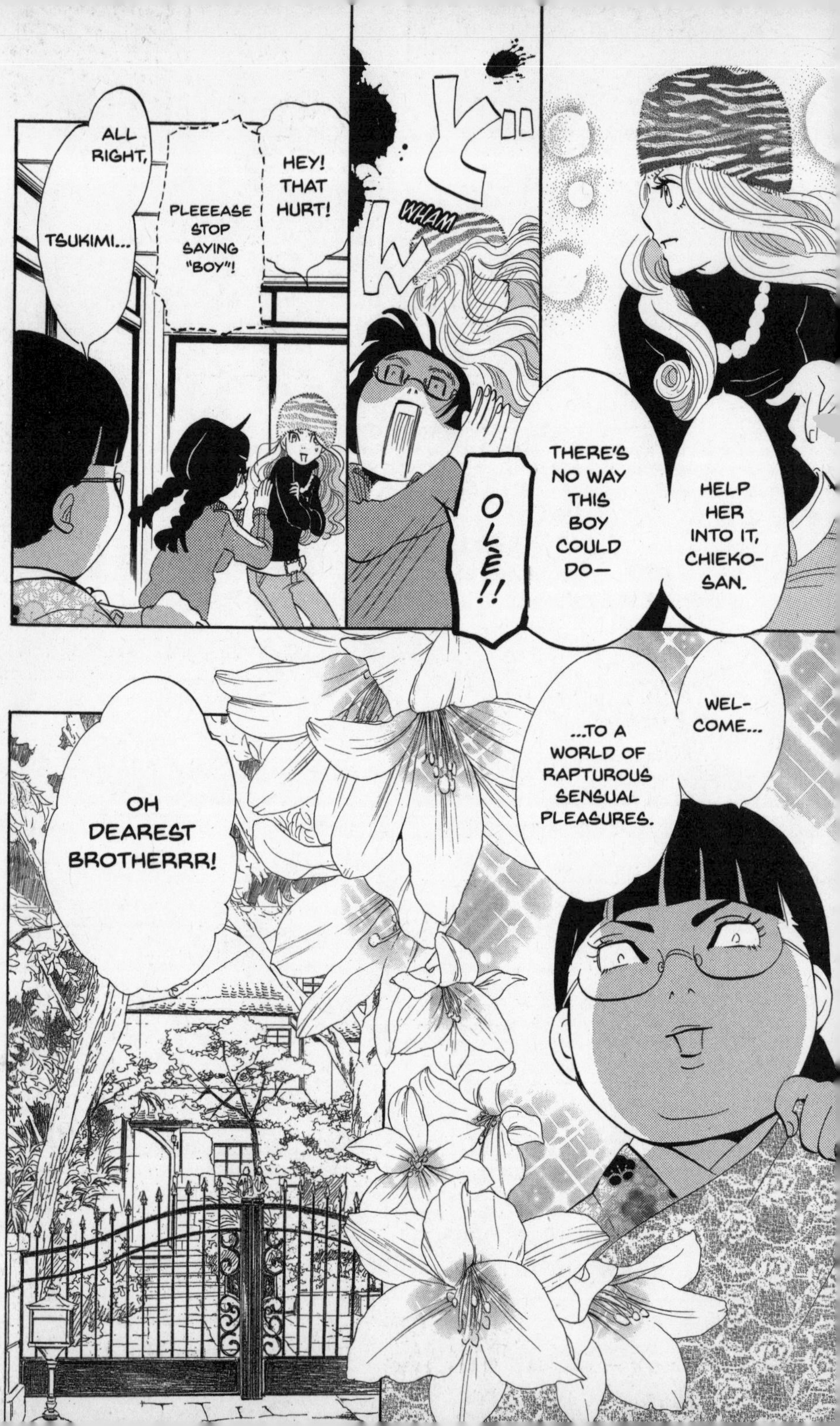
HELP HER INTO IT, CHIEKO-SAN.
THERE'S NO WAY THIS BOY COULD DO—
OLÈ!!
WHAM
HEY! THAT HURT!
PLEEEASE STOP SAYING "BOY"!
ALL RIGHT, TSUKIMI...
WEL-COME...
...TO A WORLD OF RAPTUROUS SENSUAL PLEASURES.
OH DEAREST BROTHERRR!

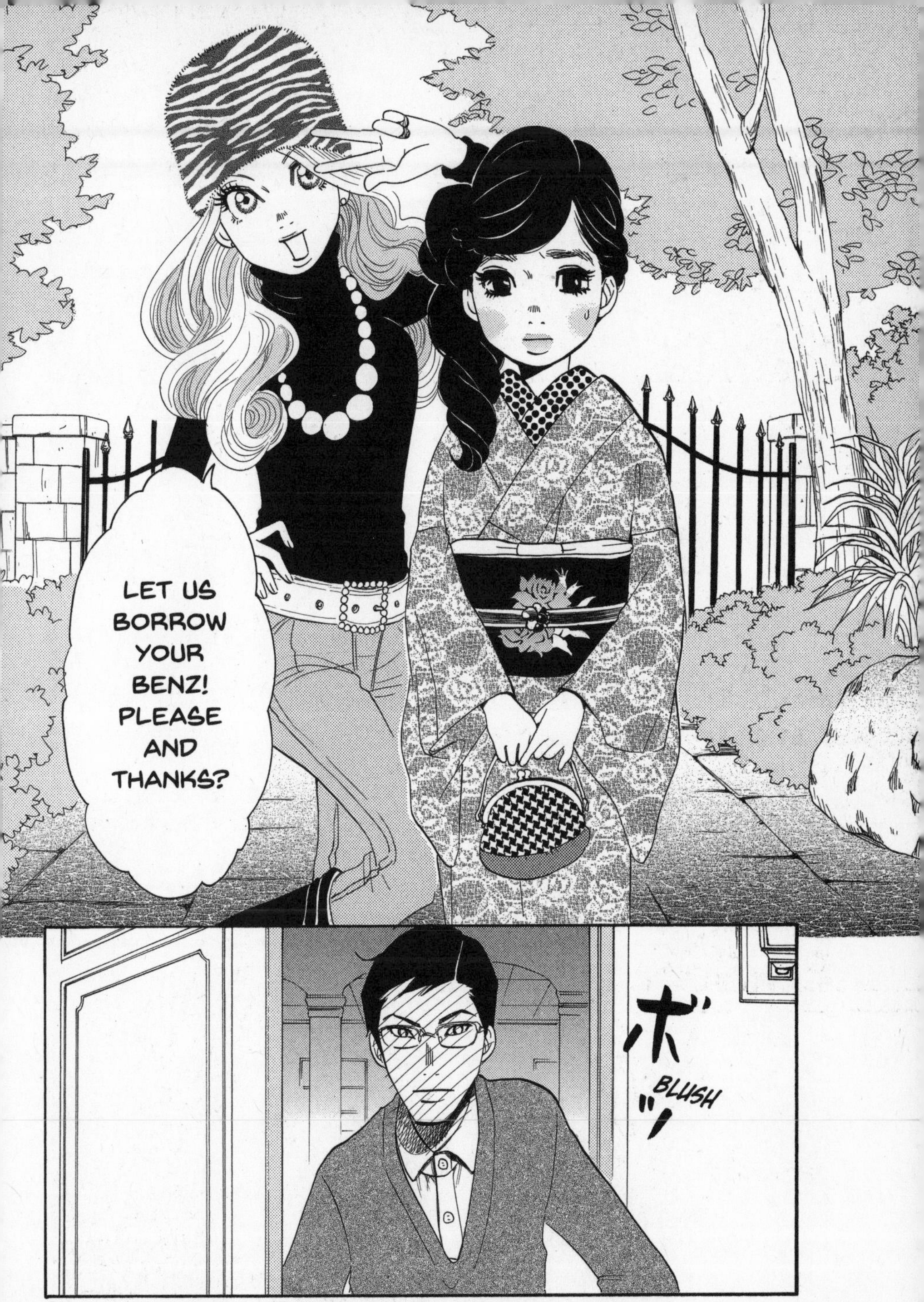
LET US BORROW YOUR BENZ! PLEASE AND THANKS?
ボッ
BLUSH

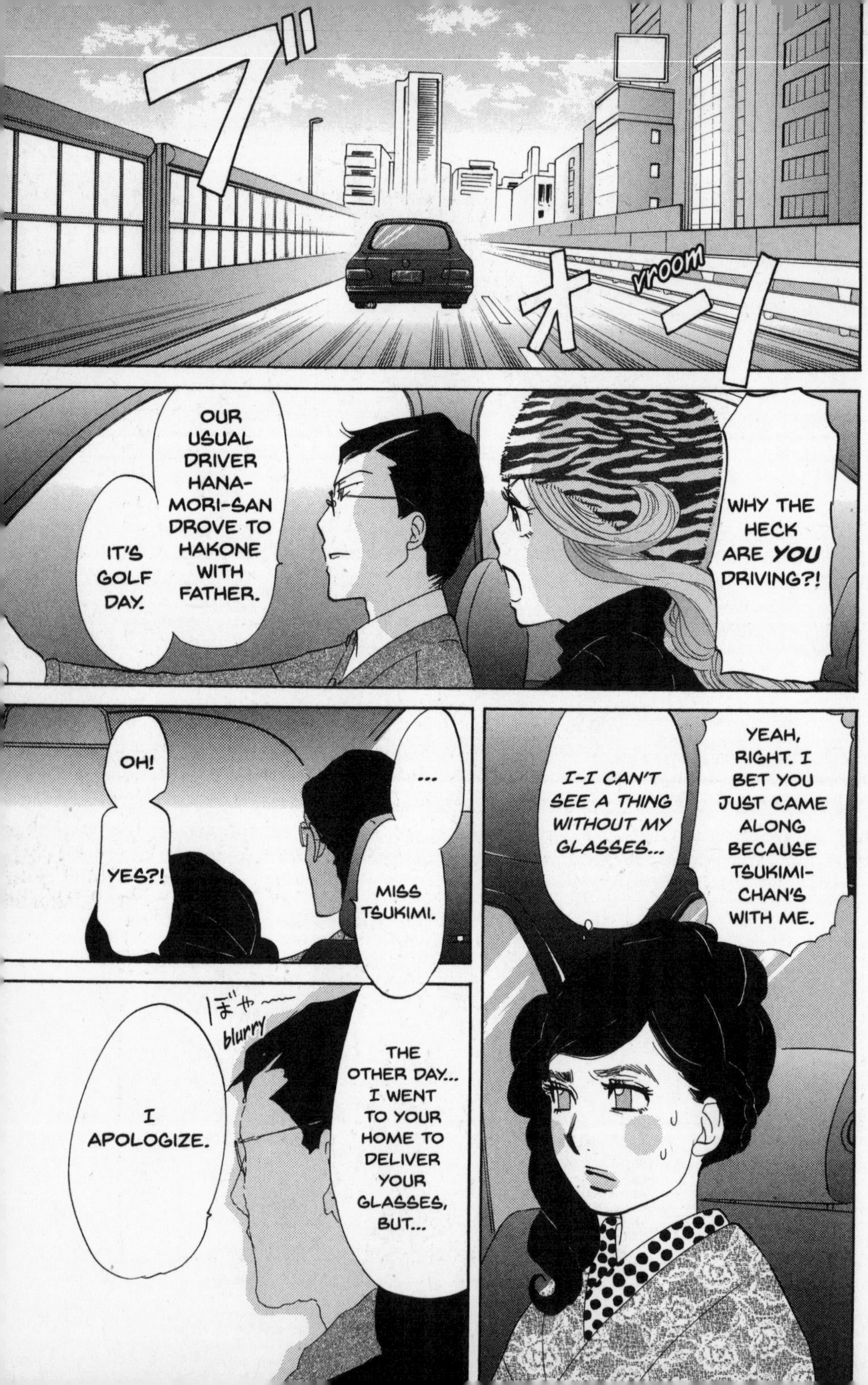
vroom
WHY THE HECK ARE YOU DRIVING?!
OUR USUAL DRIVER HANA-MORI-SAN DROVE TO HAKONE WITH FATHER.
IT'S GOLF DAY.
YEAH, RIGHT. I BET YOU JUST CAME ALONG BECAUSE TSUKIMI-CHAN'S WITH ME.
I-I CAN'T SEE A THING WITHOUT MY GLASSES...
...
MISS TSUKIMI.
OH!
YES?!
THE OTHER DAY... I WENT TO YOUR HOME TO DELIVER YOUR GLASSES, BUT...
ぼや～～
blurry
I APOLOGIZE.

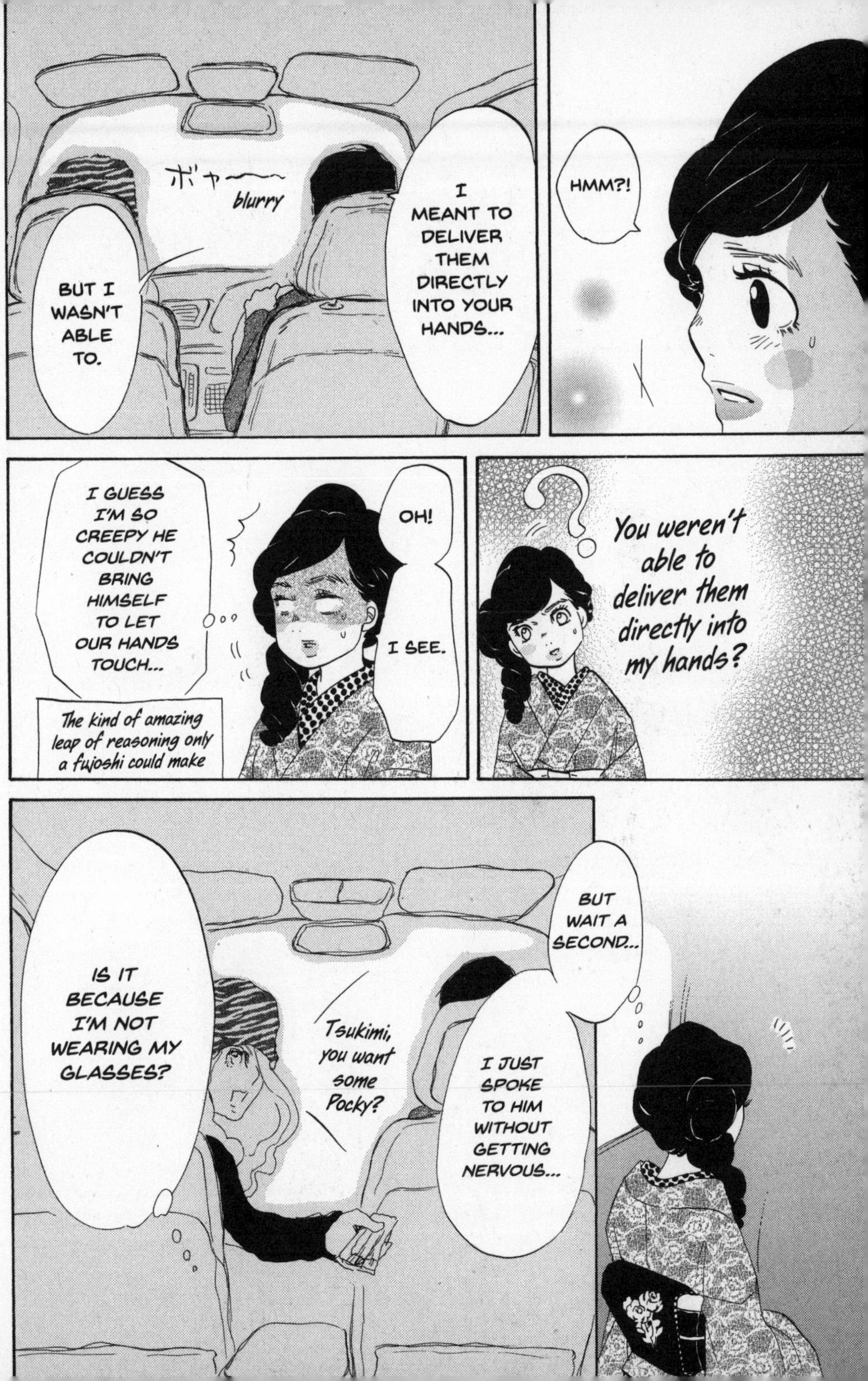
HMM?!
I MEANT TO DELIVER THEM DIRECTLY INTO YOUR HANDS...
ボヤ〜〜
blurry
BUT I WASN'T ABLE TO.
You weren't able to deliver them directly into my hands?
OH!
I SEE.
I GUESS I'M SO CREEPY HE COULDN'T BRING HIMSELF TO LET OUR HANDS TOUCH...
The kind of amazing leap of reasoning only a fujoshi could make
BUT WAIT A SECOND...
I JUST SPOKE TO HIM WITHOUT GETTING NERVOUS...
Tsukimi, you want some Pocky?
IS IT BECAUSE I'M NOT WEARING MY GLASSES?

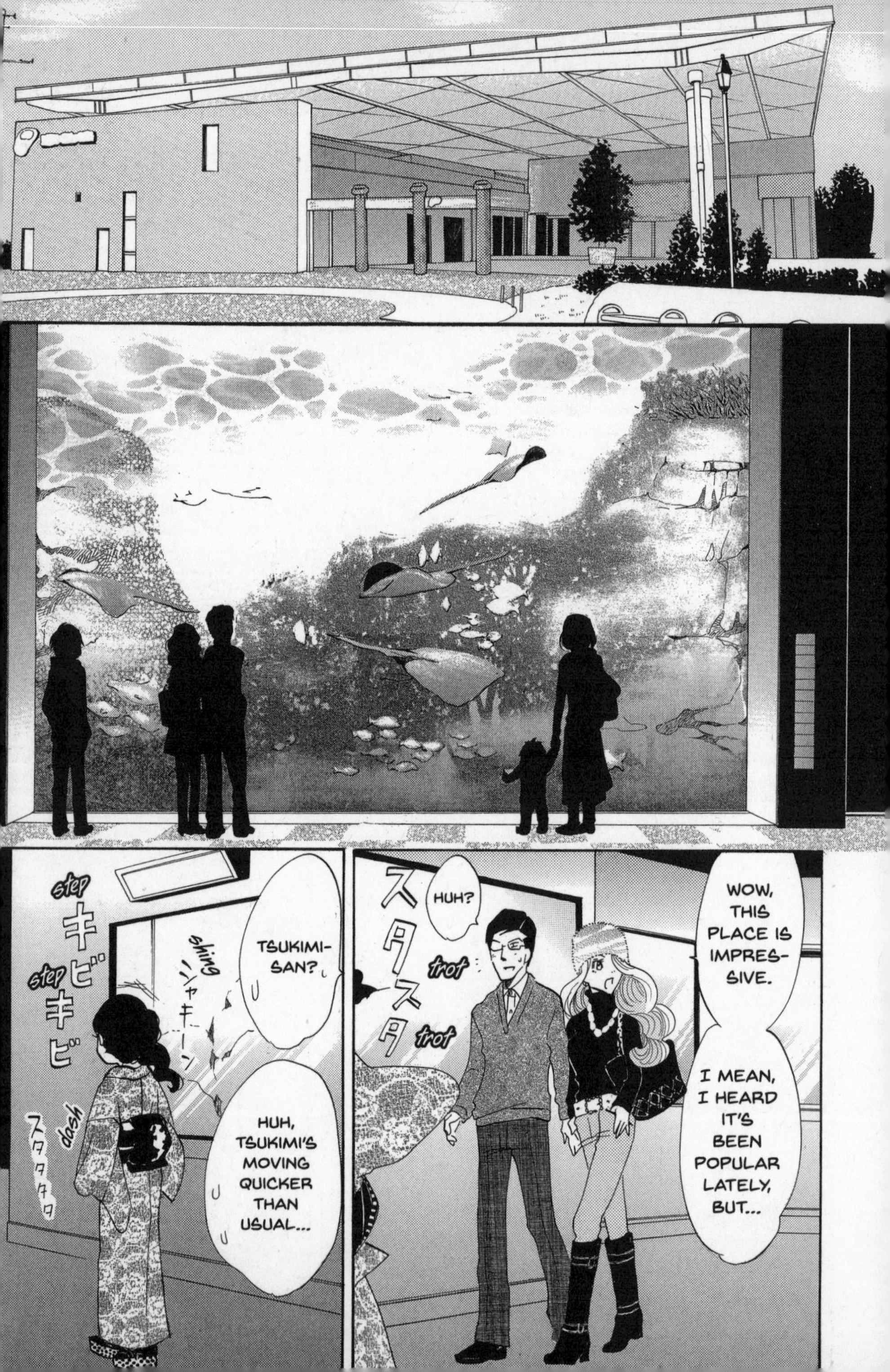
WOW, THIS PLACE IS IMPRESSIVE.
I MEAN, I HEARD IT'S BEEN POPULAR LATELY, BUT...
HUH?
スタスタ
trot trot
TSUKIMI-SAN?
HUH, TSUKIMI'S MOVING QUICKER THAN USUAL...
シャキーン
shing
キビキビ
step step
スタタタタ
dash

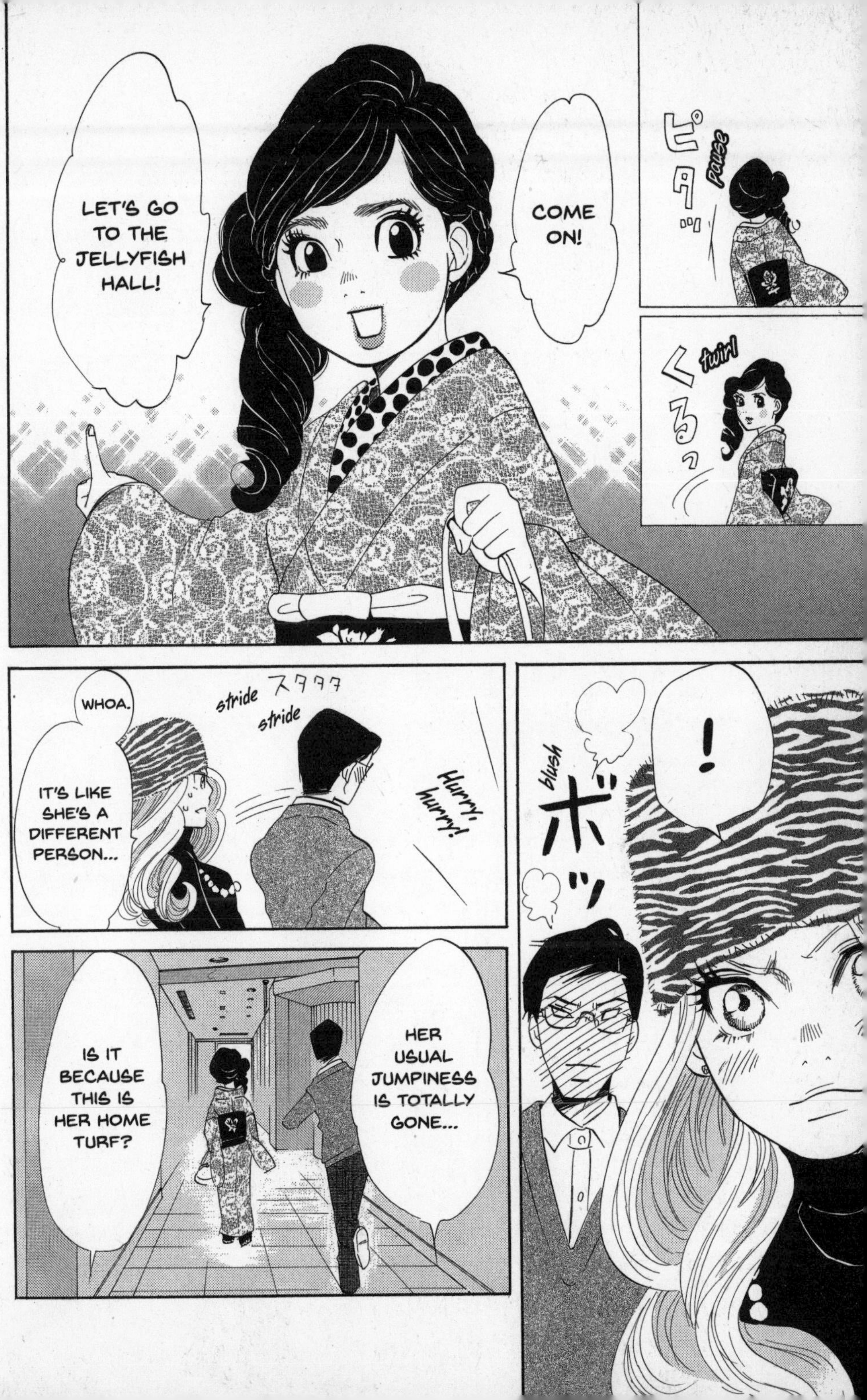
ピタッ
Pause
くるっ
twirl
COME ON!
LET'S GO TO THE JELLYFISH HALL!
!
ボッ
blush
Hurry, hurry!
stride
stride
スタタタ
WHOA.
IT'S LIKE SHE'S A DIFFERENT PERSON...
HER USUAL JUMPINESS IS TOTALLY GONE...
IS IT BECAUSE THIS IS HER HOME TURF?

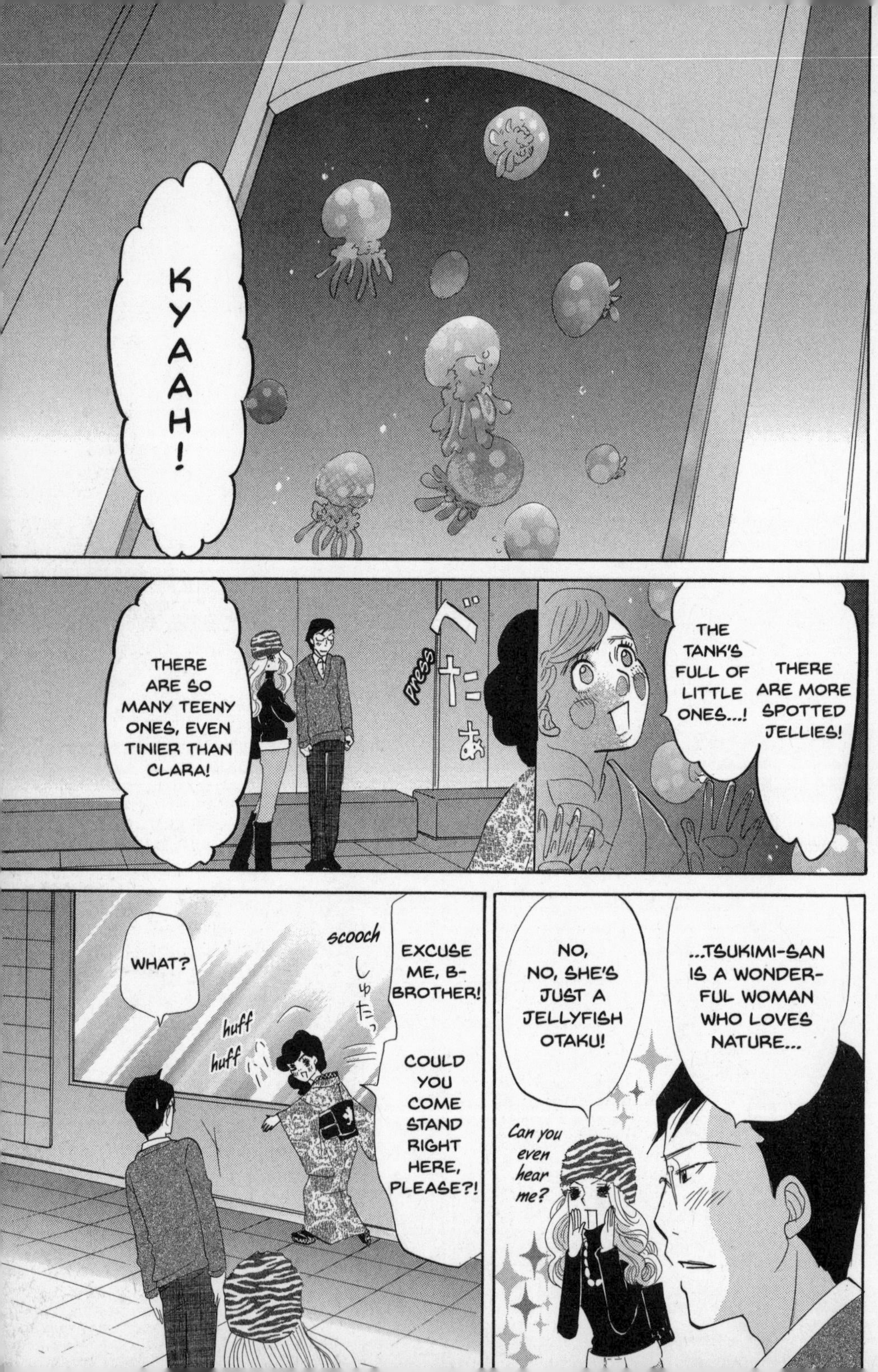
KYAAH!
THERE ARE MORE SPOTTED JELLIES!
THE TANK'S FULL OF LITTLE ONES...!
press
THERE ARE SO MANY TEENY ONES, EVEN TINIER THAN CLARA!
...TSUKIMI-SAN IS A WONDERFUL WOMAN WHO LOVES NATURE...
NO, NO, SHE'S JUST A JELLYFISH OTAKU!
Can you even hear me?
EXCUSE ME, B-BROTHER!
COULD YOU COME STAND RIGHT HERE, PLEASE?!
scooch
huff huff
WHAT?

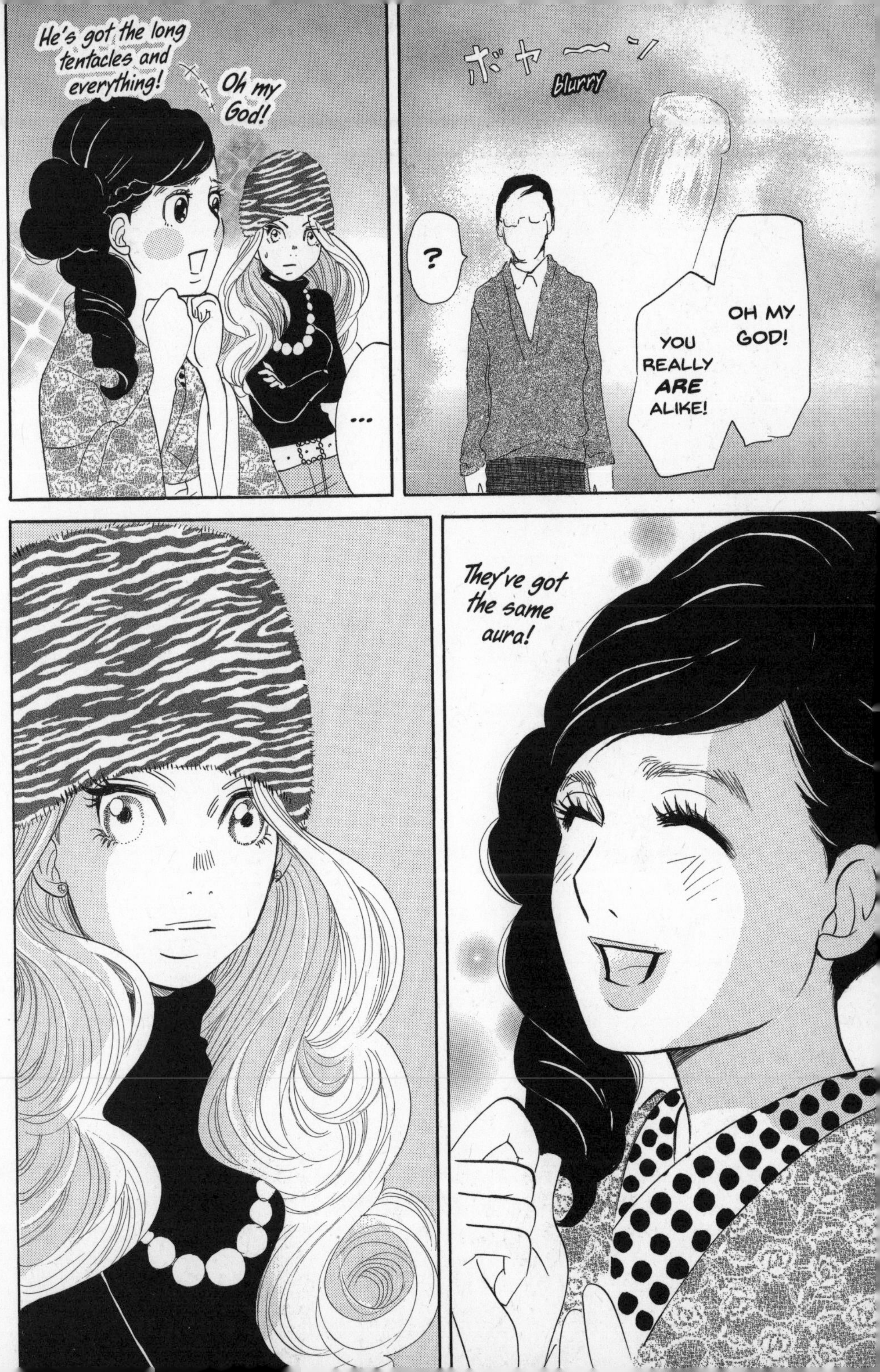

ボヤ〜ン
blurry
?
OH MY GOD! YOU REALLY ARE ALIKE!
He's got the long tentacles and everything!
Oh my God!
...
They've got the same aura!

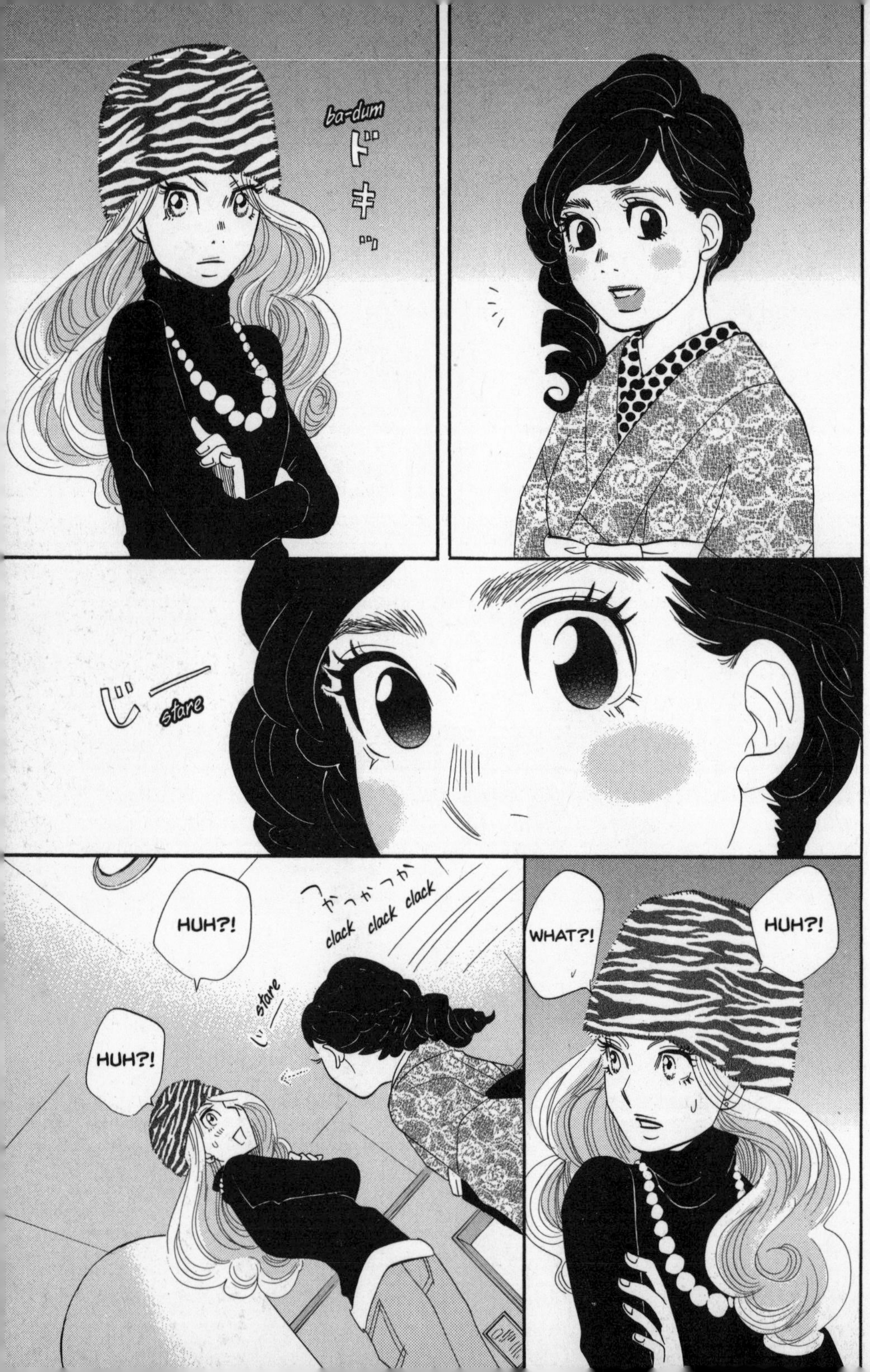
ba-dum
ドキッ
じー
stare
HUH?!
WHAT?!
HUH?!
カッカッカッ
clack clack clack
じー
stare
HUH?!

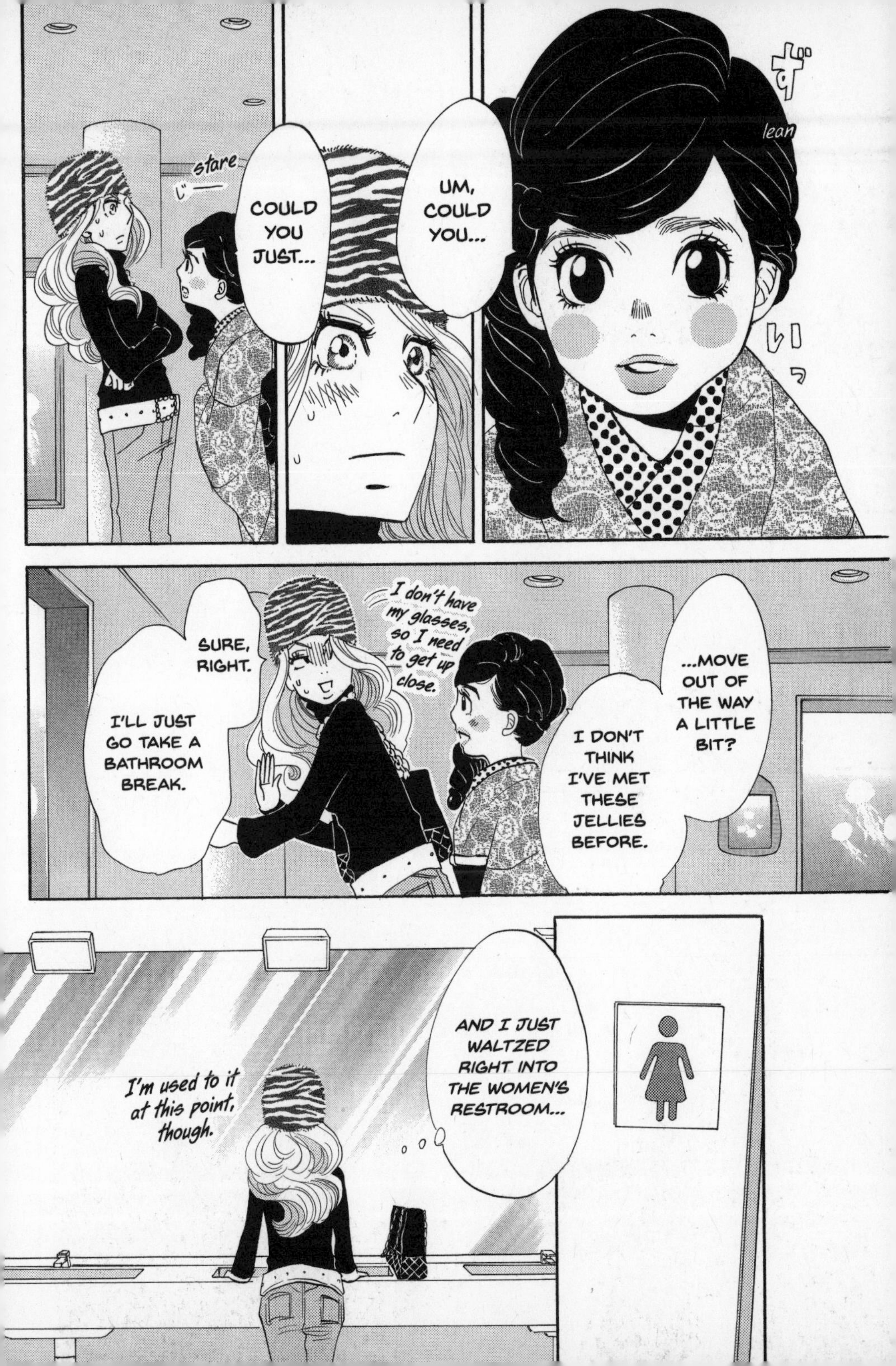
lean
UM, COULD YOU...
COULD YOU JUST...
stare
...MOVE OUT OF THE WAY A LITTLE BIT?
I DON'T THINK I'VE MET THESE JELLIES BEFORE.
I don't have my glasses, so I need to get up close.
SURE, RIGHT.
I'LL JUST GO TAKE A BATHROOM BREAK.
AND I JUST WALTZED RIGHT INTO THE WOMEN'S RESTROOM...
I'm used to it at this point, though.

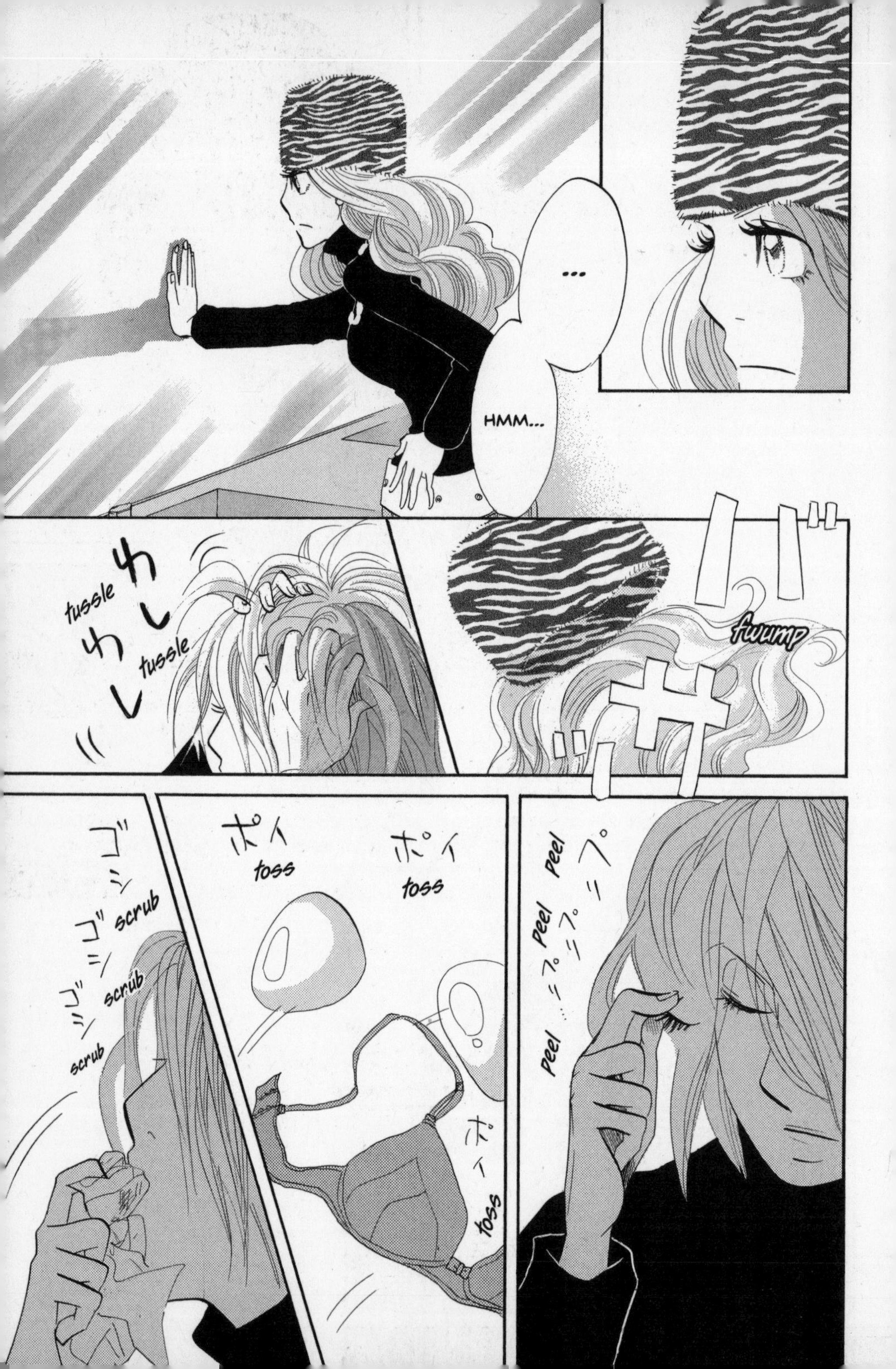

...
HMM...
fwump
わしわし
tussle
tussle
ペリッペリッ
peel
peel
peel
peel
ポイ
toss
ポイ
toss
ポイ
toss
ゴシゴシ
scrub
scrub
scrub

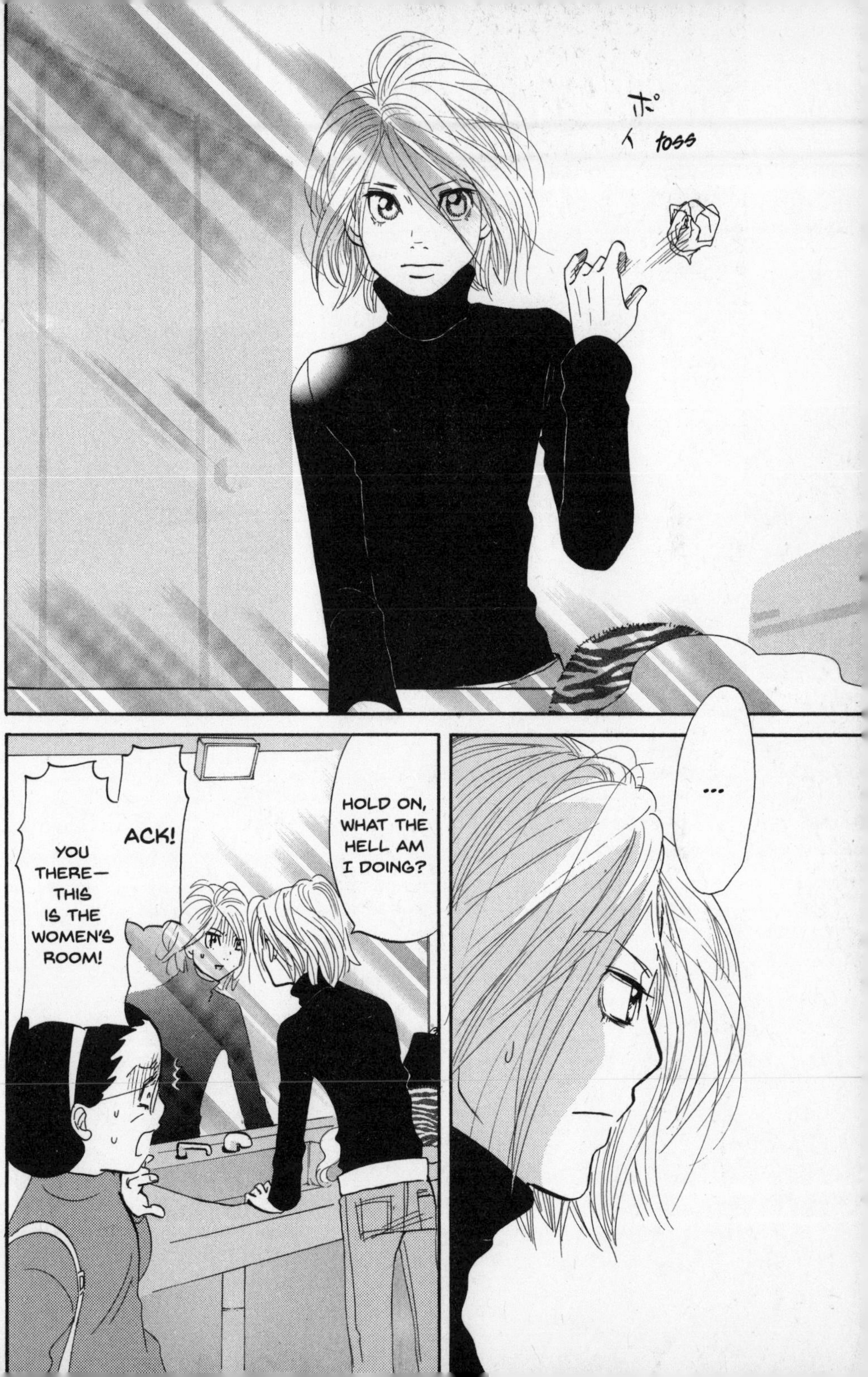
ポイ toss
...
HOLD ON, WHAT THE HELL AM I DOING?
ACK!
YOU THERE—THIS IS THE WOMEN'S ROOM!

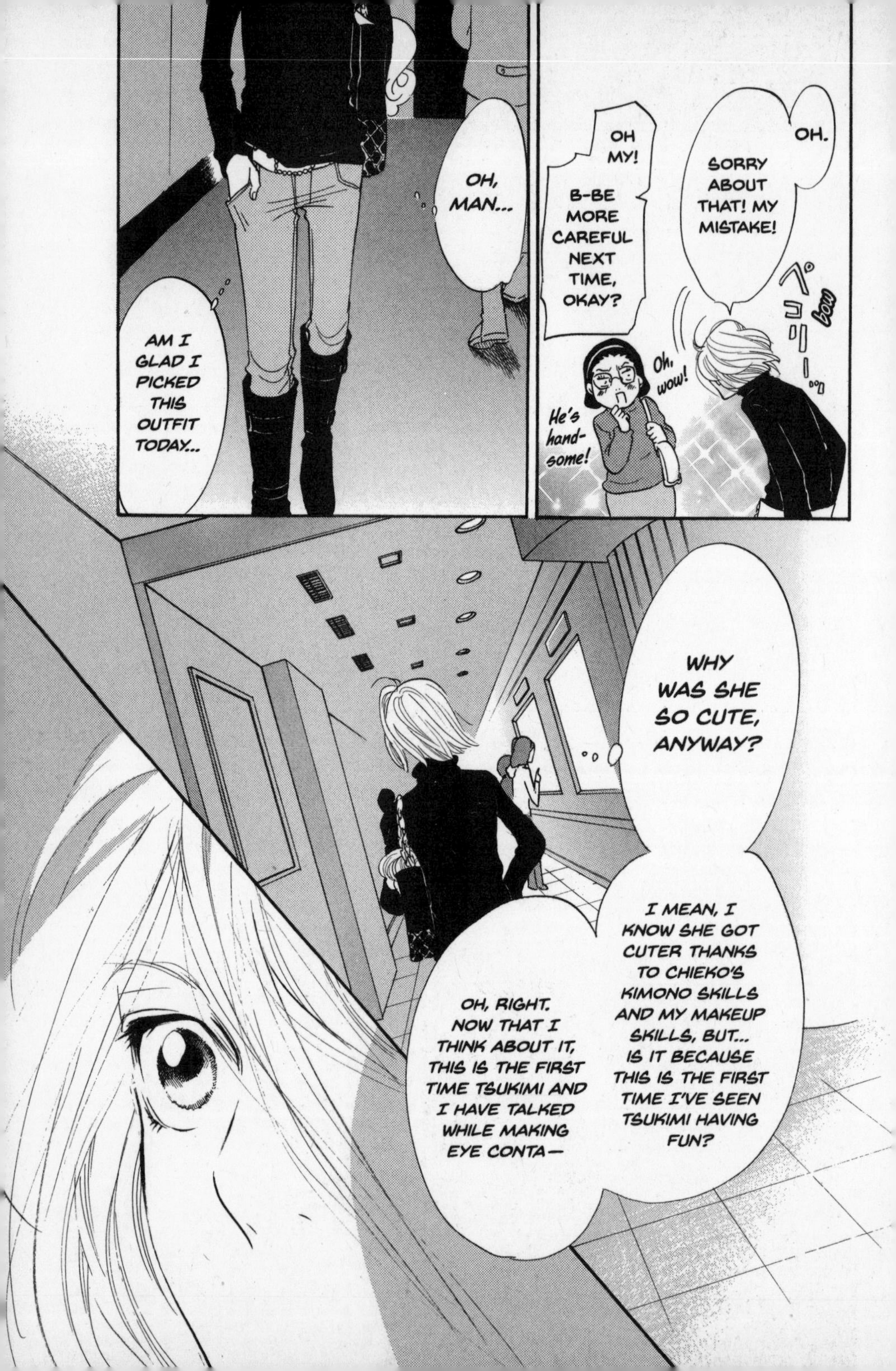
OH.
SORRY ABOUT THAT! MY MISTAKE!
bow
OH MY!
B-BE MORE CAREFUL NEXT TIME, OKAY?
Oh, wow!
He's handsome!
OH, MAN...
AM I GLAD I PICKED THIS OUTFIT TODAY...
WHY WAS SHE SO CUTE, ANYWAY?
I MEAN, I KNOW SHE GOT CUTER THANKS TO CHIEKO'S KIMONO SKILLS AND MY MAKEUP SKILLS, BUT... IS IT BECAUSE THIS IS THE FIRST TIME I'VE SEEN TSUKIMI HAVING FUN?
OH, RIGHT. NOW THAT I THINK ABOUT IT, THIS IS THE FIRST TIME TSUKIMI AND I HAVE TALKED WHILE MAKING EYE CONTA—

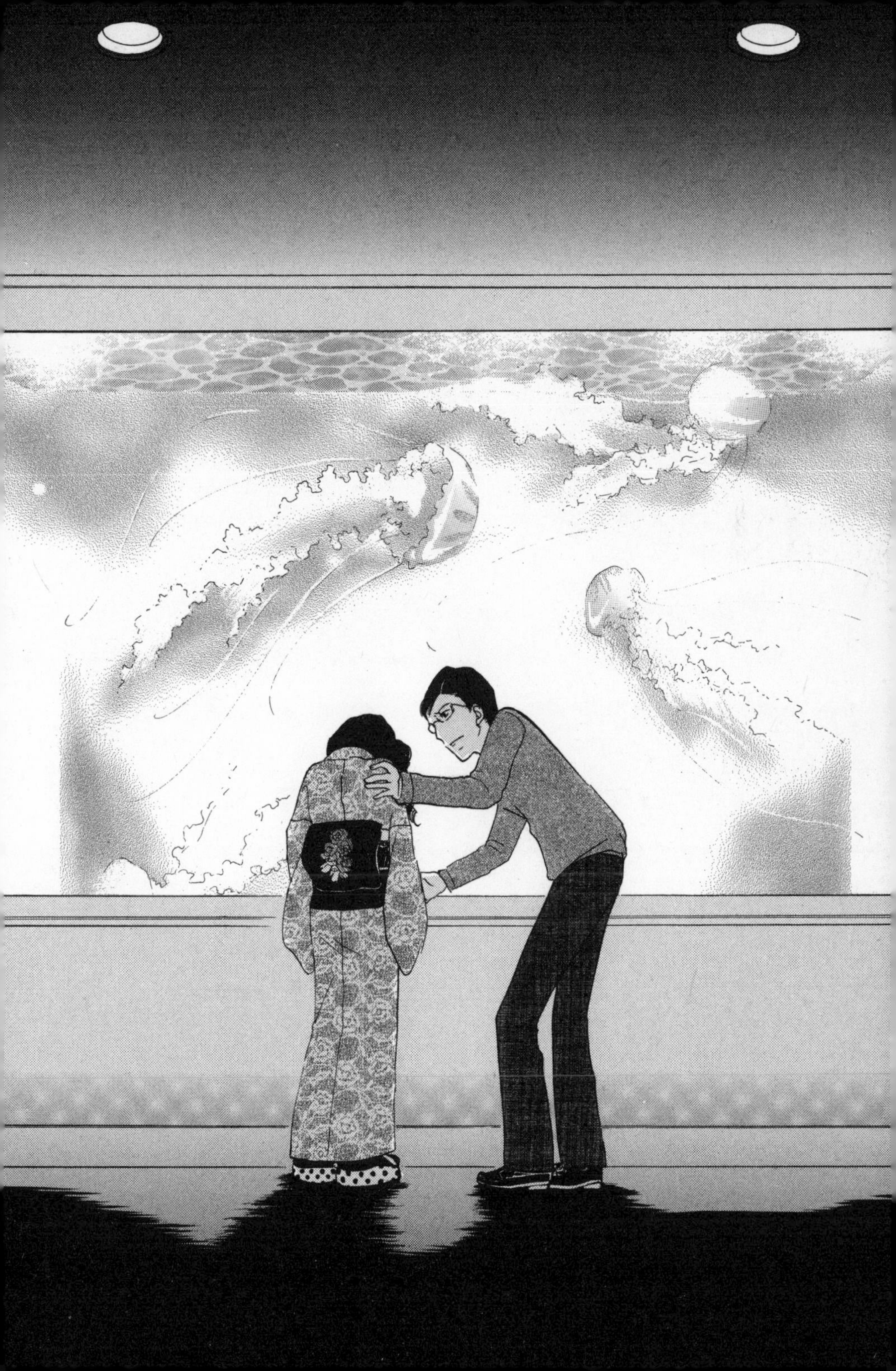

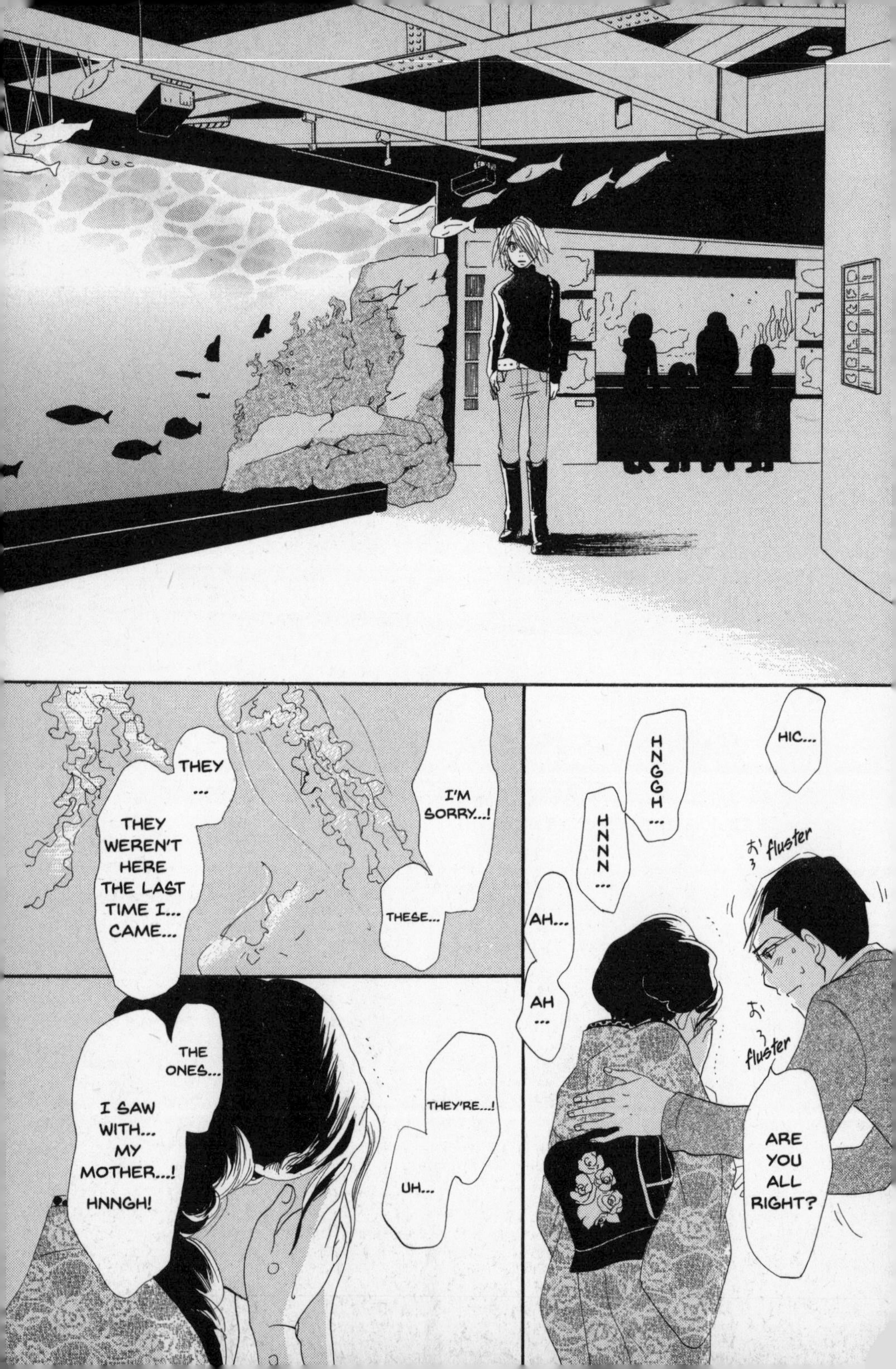
HIC...
HNGGH...
HNNN...
おろ fluster
AH...
AH...
おろ fluster
ARE YOU ALL RIGHT?
I'M SORRY...!
THESE...
THEY... THEY WEREN'T HERE THE LAST TIME I... CAME...
THEY'RE...!
UH...
THE ONES... I SAW WITH... MY MOTHER...!
HNNGH!

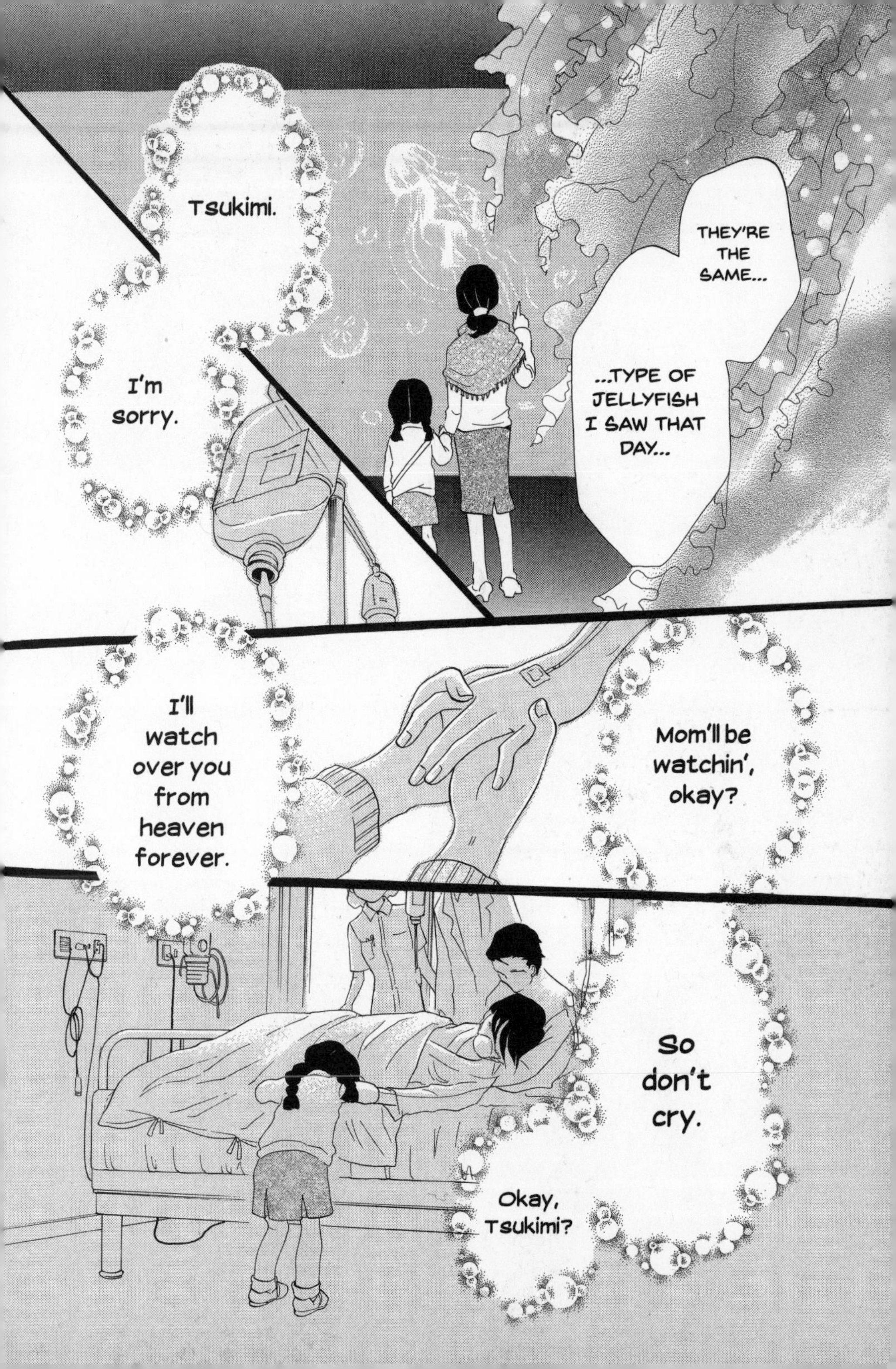
THEY'RE THE SAME...
...TYPE OF JELLYFISH I SAW THAT DAY...
Tsukimi.
I'm sorry.
Mom'll be watchin', okay?
I'll watch over you from heaven forever.
So don't cry.
Okay, Tsukimi?

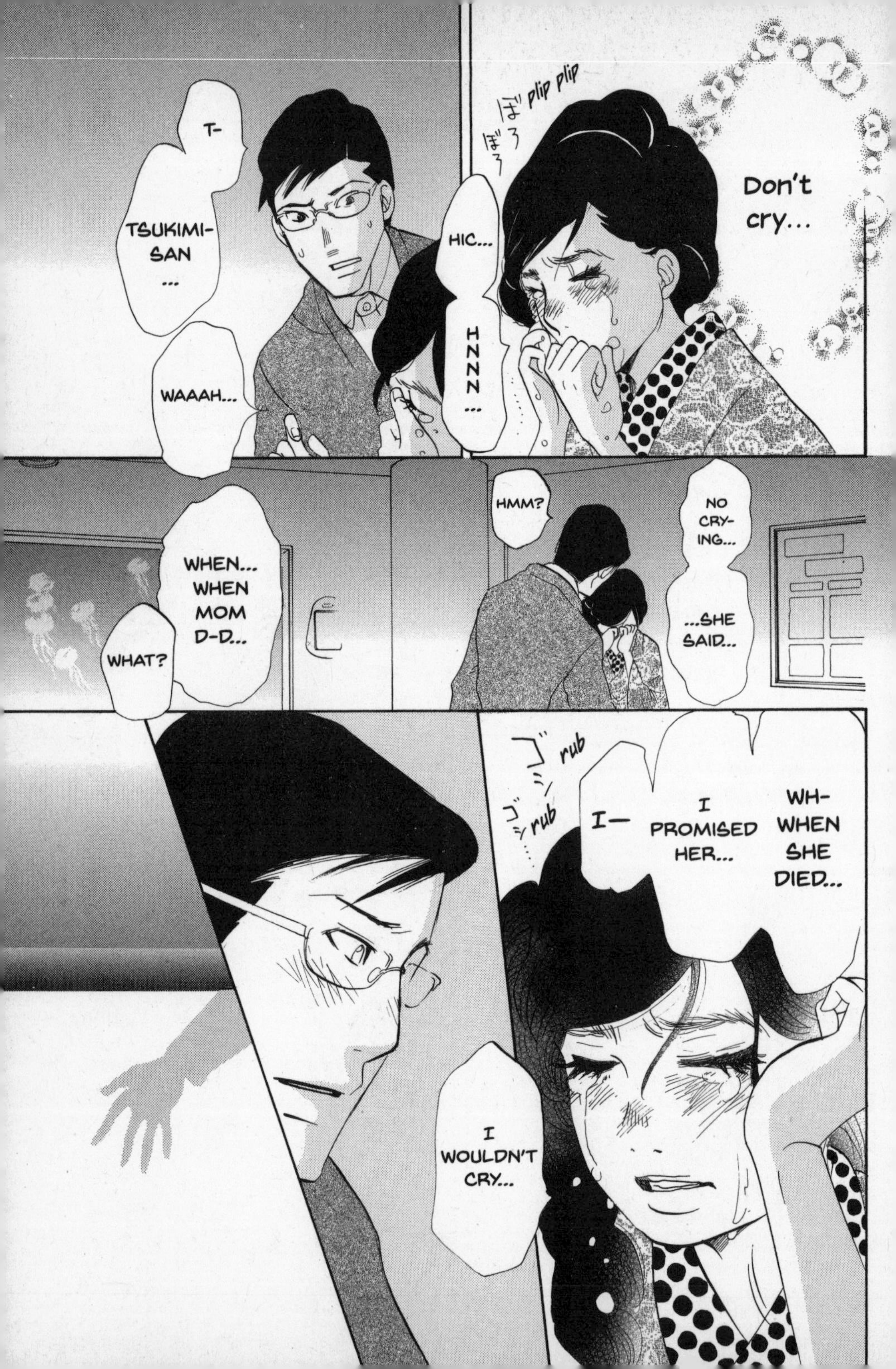
Don't cry…
ぼろぼろ plip plip
HIC…
HNNN…
T-
TSUKIMI-SAN…
WAAAH…
NO CRY-ING…
…SHE SAID…
HMM?
WHEN… WHEN MOM D-D…
WHAT?
WH- WHEN SHE DIED…
I PROMISED HER…
I—
ゴシ rub ゴシ rub
I WOULDN'T CRY…

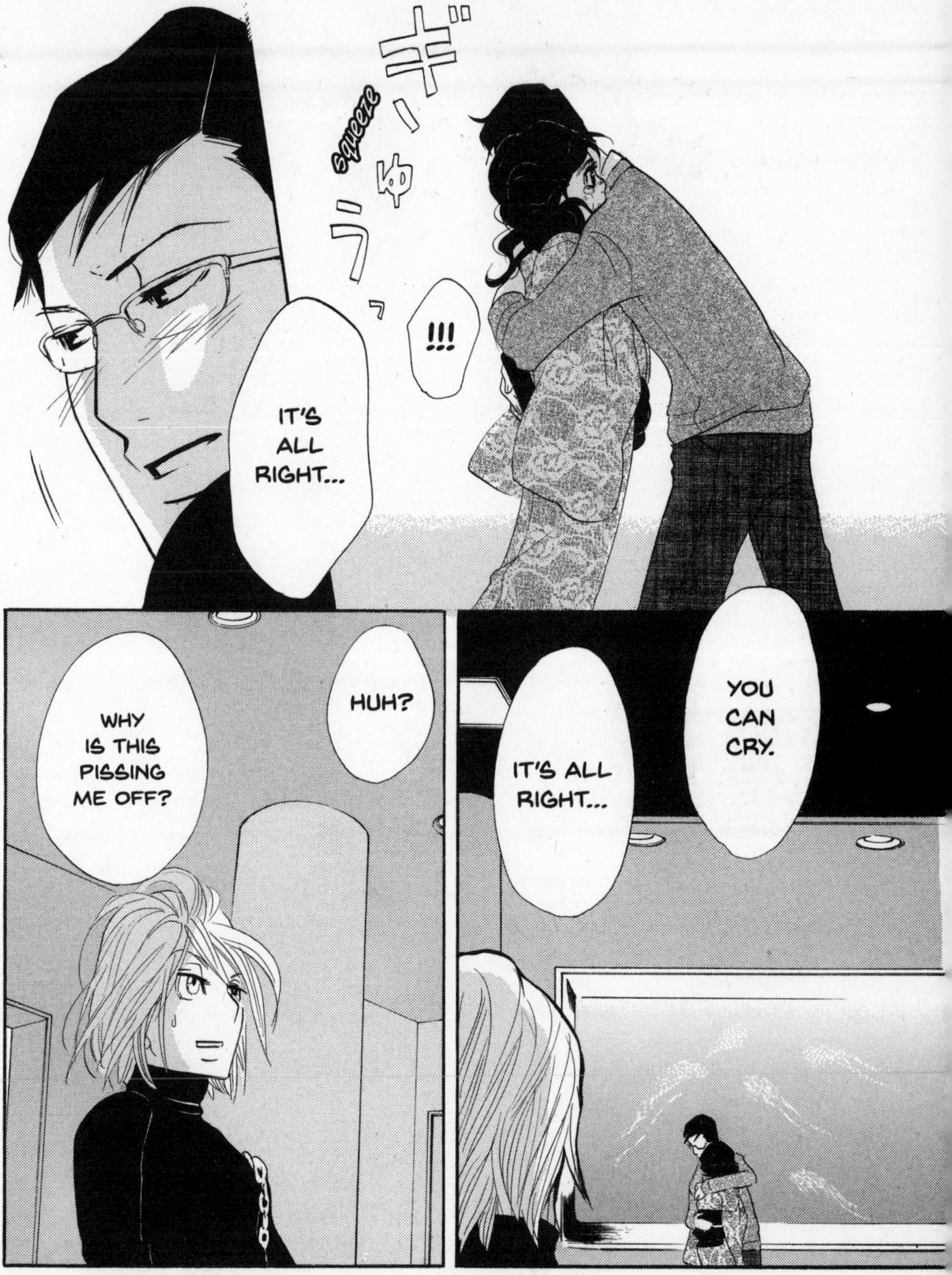
ギゅうッ
squeeze
!!!
IT'S ALL RIGHT...
YOU CAN CRY.
IT'S ALL RIGHT...
HUH?
WHY IS THIS PISSING ME OFF?

Bonus Manga: "Jelly, Higashimura, Barcelona"

I'll dare to draw a true, non-fiction autobiographical manga here...

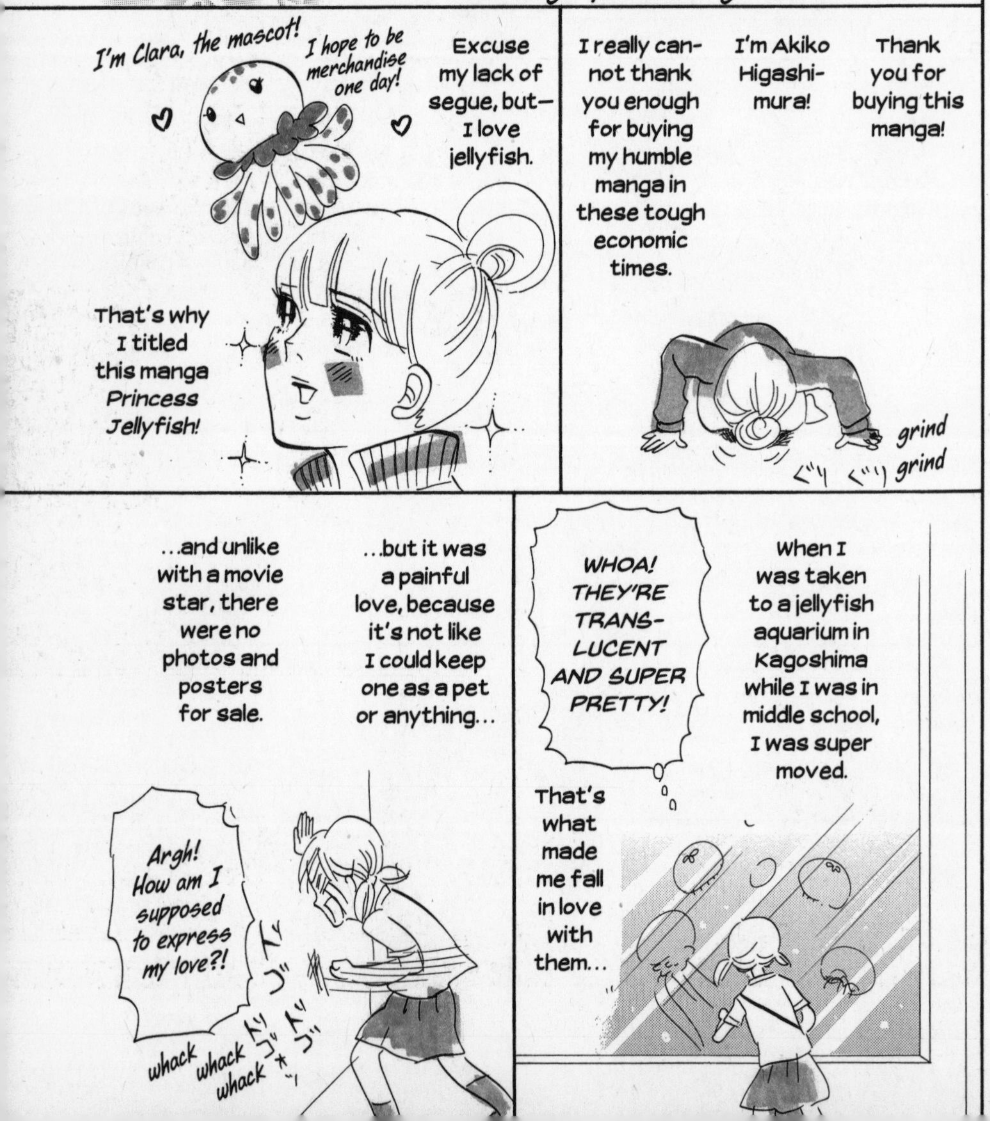
Thank you for buying this manga!
I'm Akiko Higashi-mura!
I really can-not thank you enough for buying my humble manga in these tough economic times.
grind grind
ぐり ぐり
Excuse my lack of segue, but— I love jellyfish.
I hope to be merchandise one day!
I'm Clara, the mascot!
That's why I titled this manga Princess Jellyfish!
When I was taken to a jellyfish aquarium in Kagoshima while I was in middle school, I was super moved.
WHOA! THEY'RE TRANS-LUCENT AND SUPER PRETTY!
That's what made me fall in love with them...
...but it was a painful love, because it's not like I could keep one as a pet or anything...
...and unlike with a movie star, there were no photos and posters for sale.
Argh! How am I supposed to express my love?!
whack whack whack

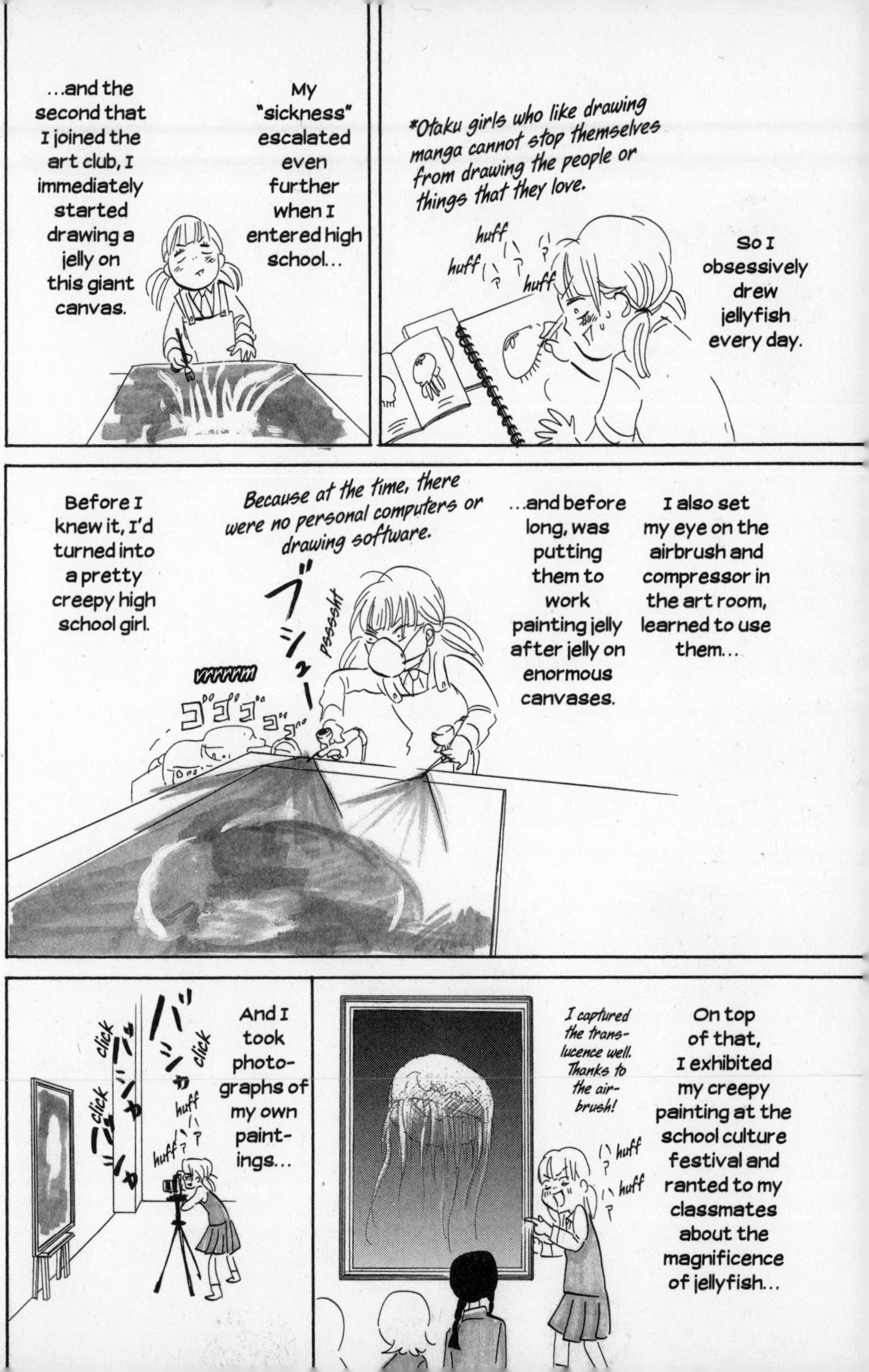
So I obsessively drew jellyfish every day.
*Otaku girls who like drawing manga cannot stop themselves from drawing the people or things that they love.
huff
huff
huff
My "sickness" escalated even further when I entered high school...
...and the second that I joined the art club, I immediately started drawing a jelly on this giant canvas.
I also set my eye on the airbrush and compressor in the art room, learned to use them...
...and before long, was putting them to work painting jelly after jelly on enormous canvases.
Because at the time, there were no personal computers or drawing software.
pssssht
vrrrrrm
Before I knew it, I'd turned into a pretty creepy high school girl.
On top of that, I exhibited my creepy painting at the school culture festival and ranted to my classmates about the magnificence of jellyfish...
I captured the translucence well. Thanks to the airbrush!
huff
huff
And I took photographs of my own paintings...
click
click
click
huff
huff

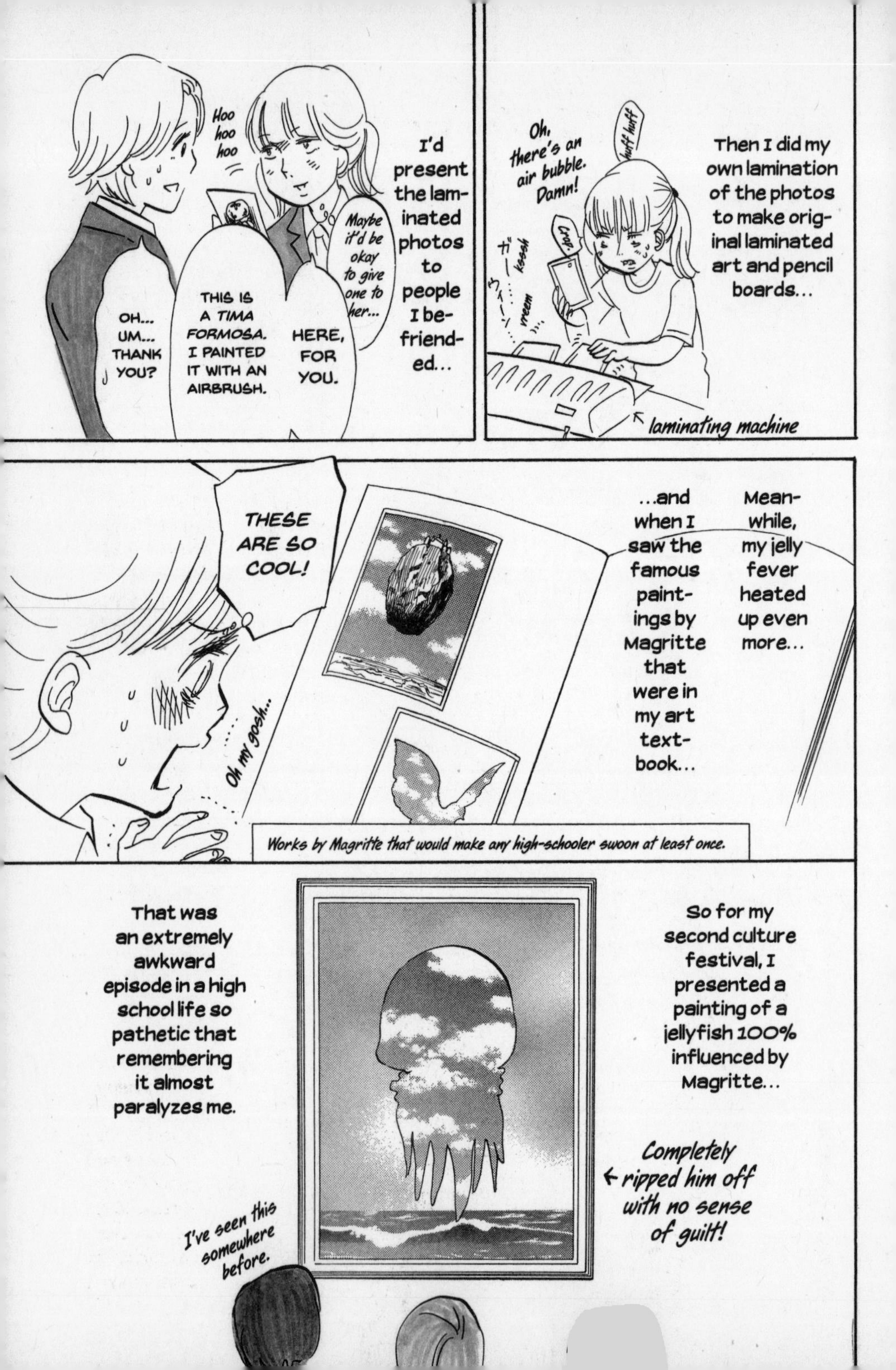
Then I did my own lamination of the photos to make original laminated art and pencil boards...
huff huff
Oh, there's an air bubble. Damn!
Crop.
kssh
vreem
laminating machine
I'd present the laminated photos to people I befriended...
Maybe it'd be okay to give one to her...
Hoo hoo hoo
HERE, FOR YOU.
THIS IS A TIMA FORMOSA. I PAINTED IT WITH AN AIRBRUSH.
OH... UM... THANK YOU?
Meanwhile, my jelly fever heated up even more...
...and when I saw the famous paintings by Magritte that were in my art textbook...
THESE ARE SO COOL!
Oh my gosh...
Works by Magritte that would make any high-schooler swoon at least once.
So for my second culture festival, I presented a painting of a jellyfish 100% influenced by Magritte...
Completely ripped him off with no sense of guilt!
I've seen this somewhere before.
That was an extremely awkward episode in a high school life so pathetic that remembering it almost paralyzes me.

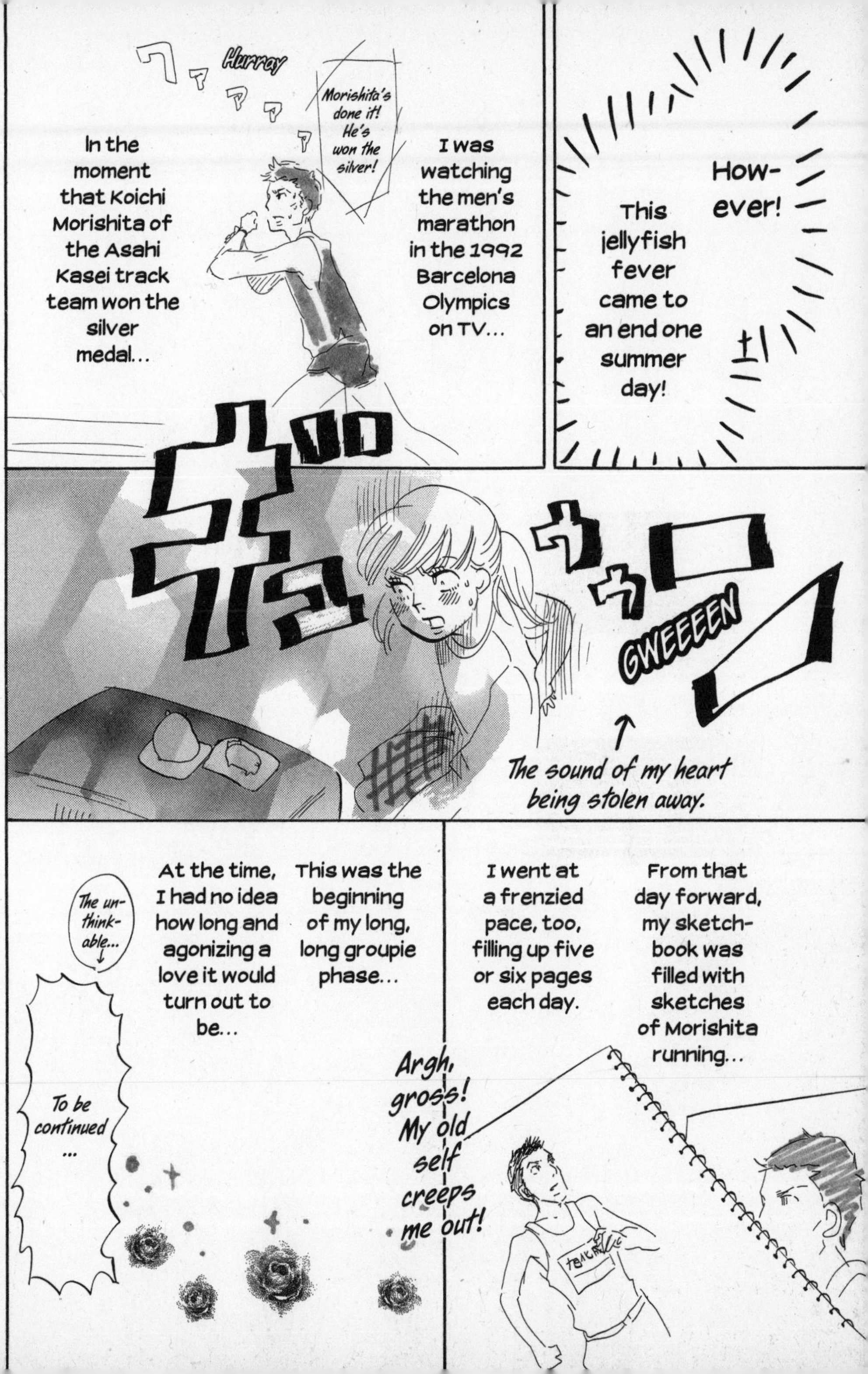

However!
This jellyfish fever came to an end one summer day!
I was watching the men's marathon in the 1992 Barcelona Olympics on TV...
Hurray
Morishita's done it! He's won the silver!
In the moment that Koichi Morishita of the Asahi Kasei track team won the silver medal...
GWEEEEN
The sound of my heart being stolen away.
From that day forward, my sketch-book was filled with sketches of Morishita running...
I went at a frenzied pace, too, filling up five or six pages each day.
Argh, gross! My old self creeps me out!
This was the beginning of my long, long groupie phase...
At the time, I had no idea how long and agonizing a love it would turn out to be...
The un-thinkable...
To be continued ...

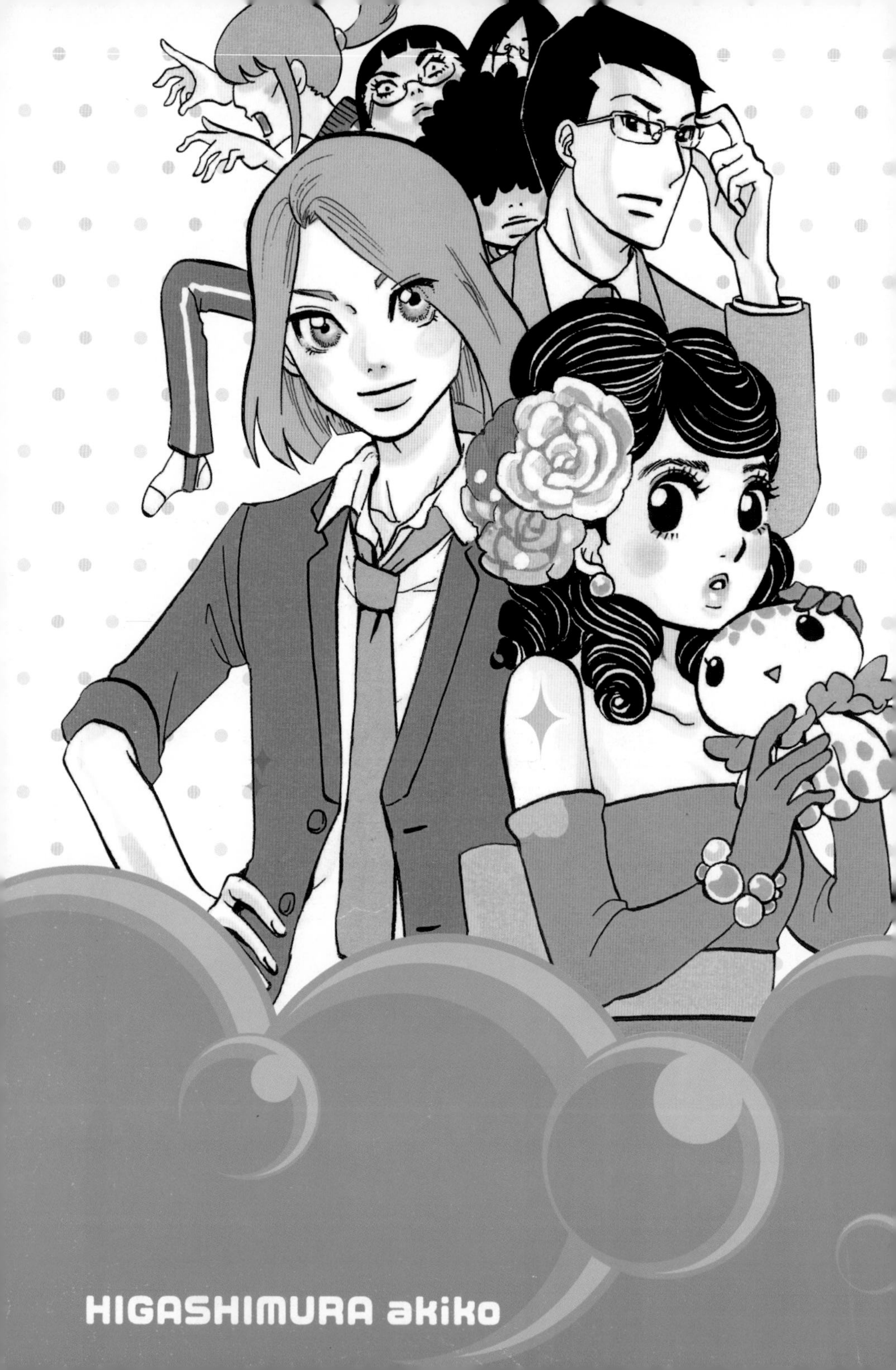

HIGASHIMURA akiko

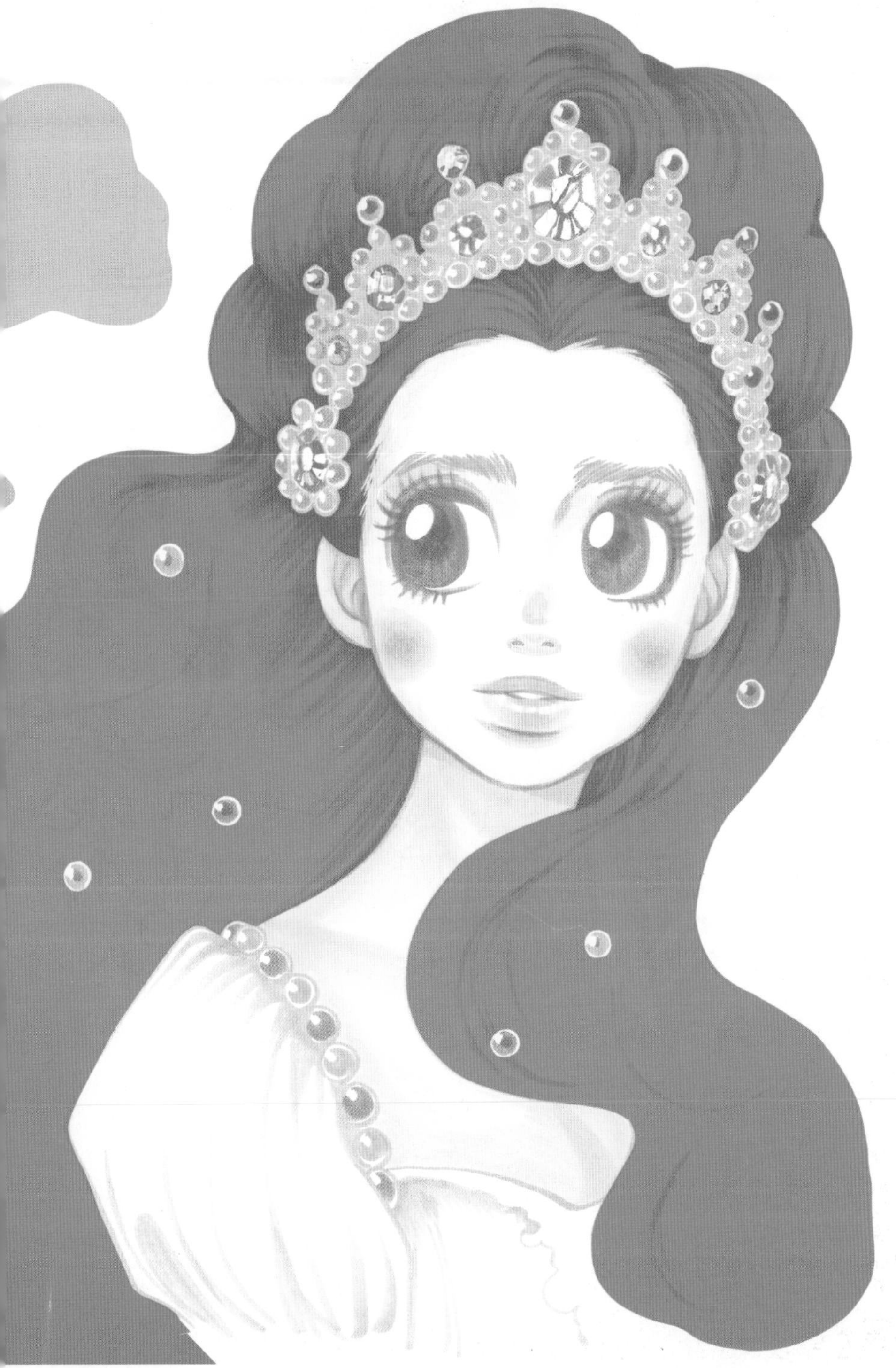

Episode 7
Clear and Present Danger

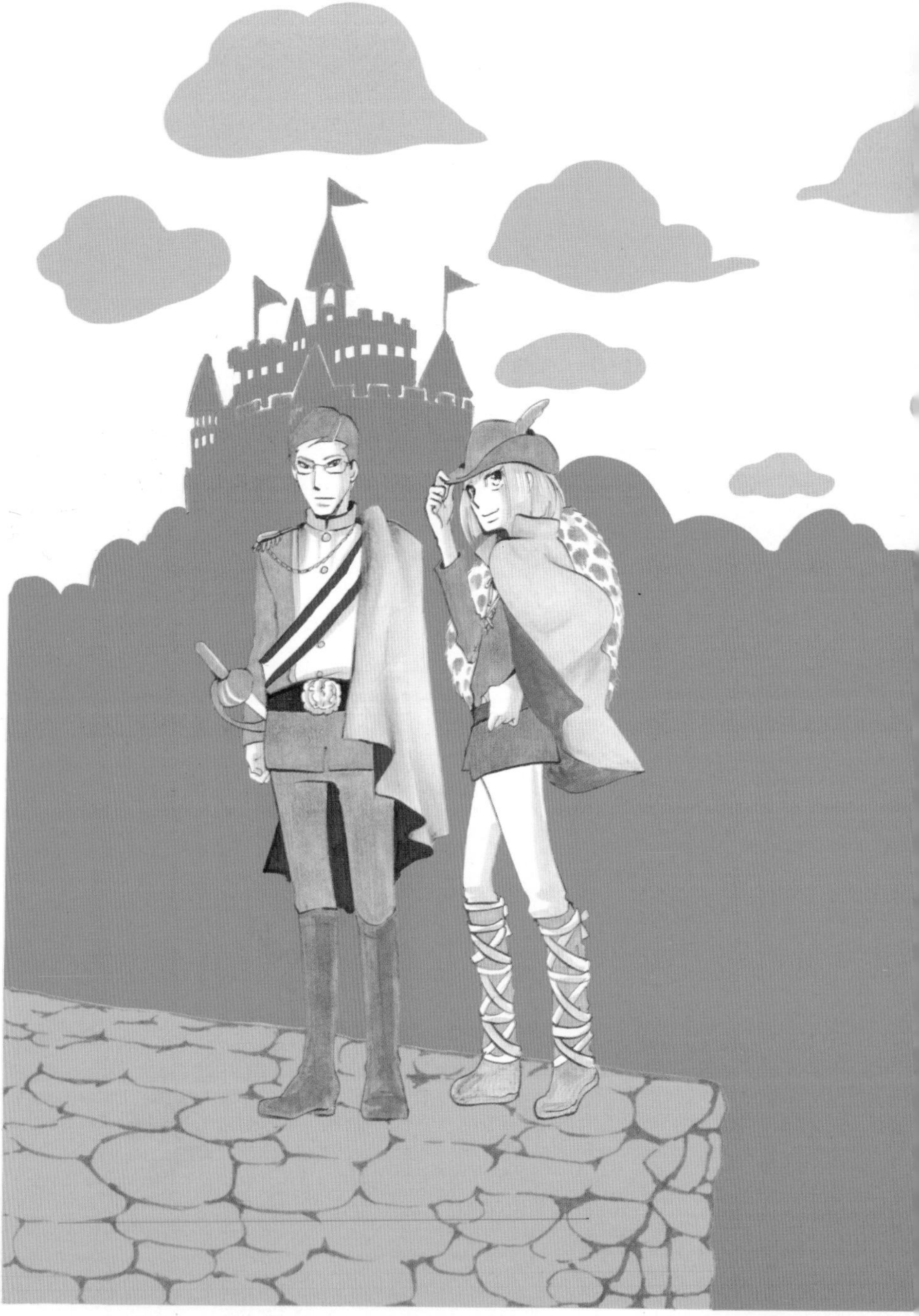

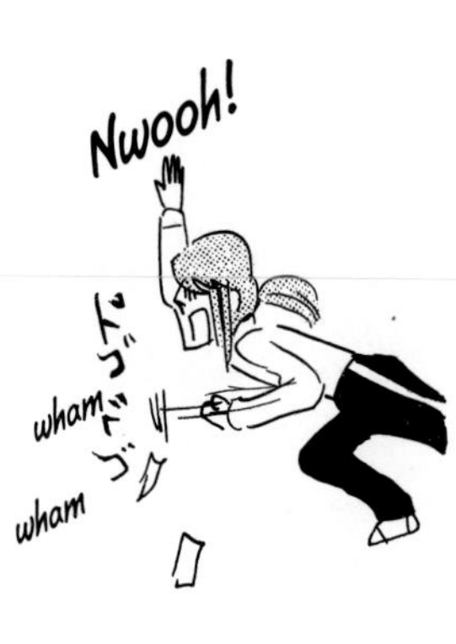
Nwooh!
wham
wham

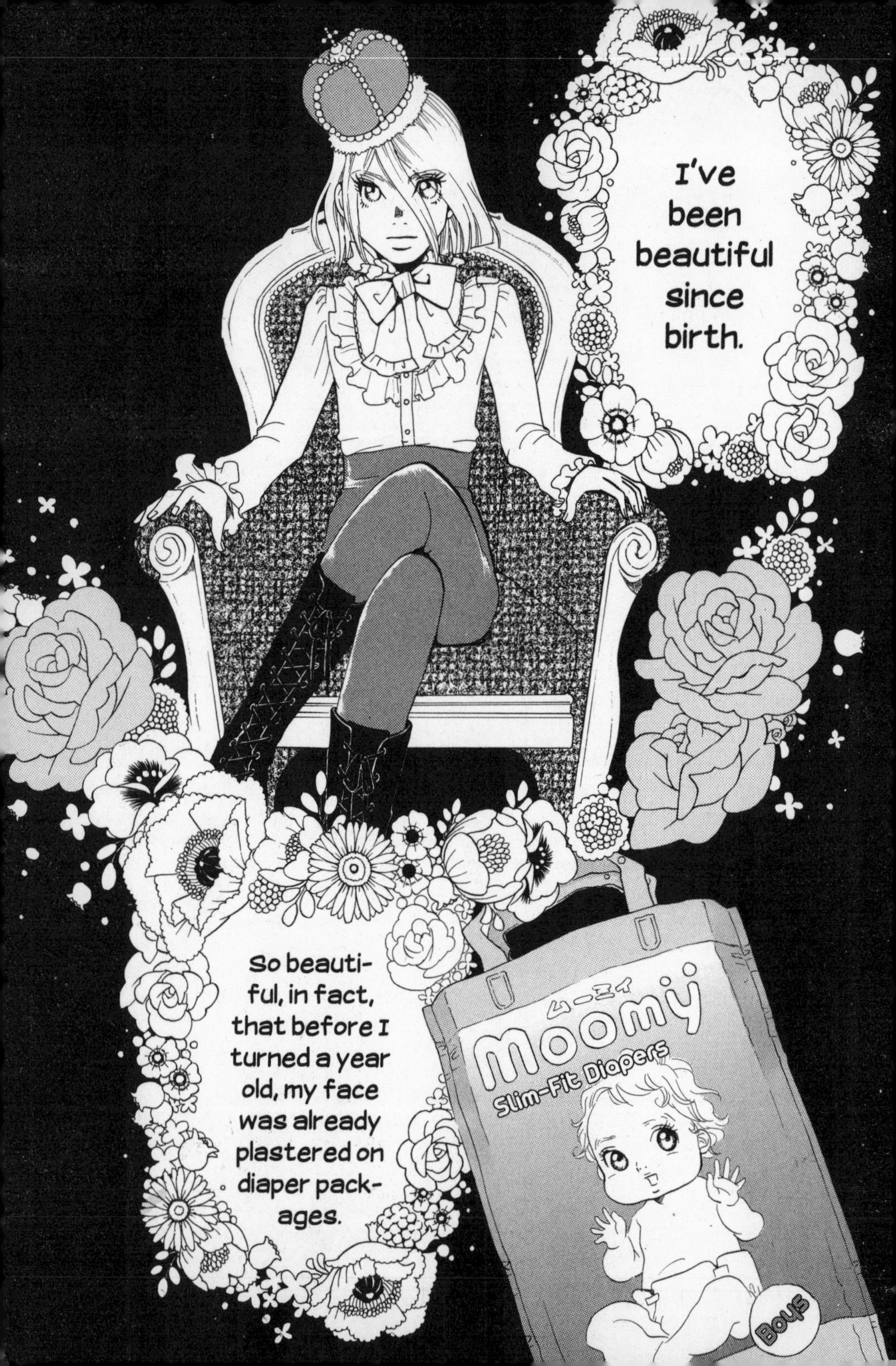
I've been beautiful since birth.
So beautiful, in fact, that before I turned a year old, my face was already plastered on diaper packages.
ムーミィ
Moomy
Slim-Fit Diapers
Boys

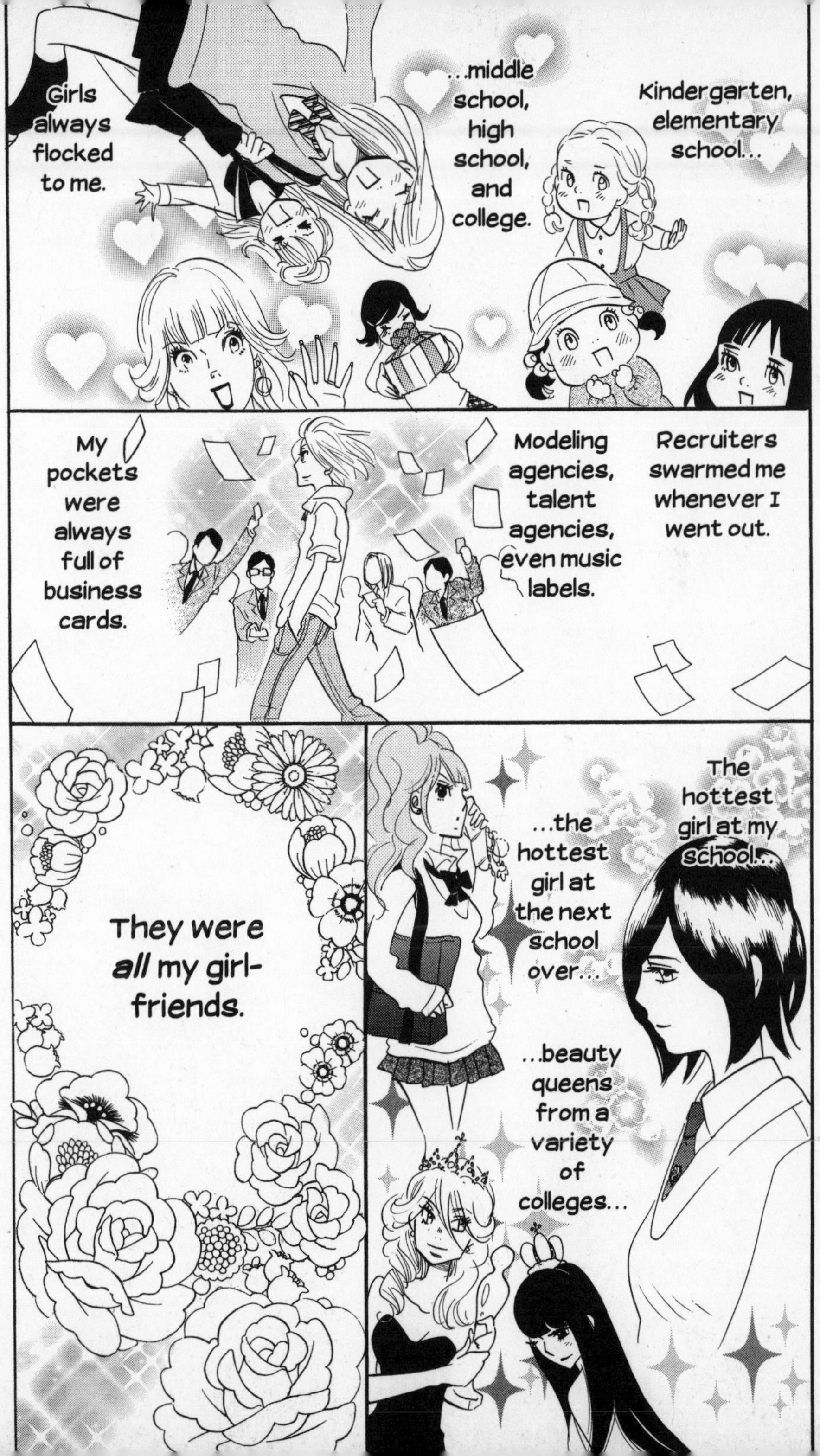
Kindergarten, elementary school...
...middle school, high school, and college.
Girls always flocked to me.
Recruiters swarmed me whenever I went out.
Modeling agencies, talent agencies, even music labels.
My pockets were always full of business cards.
The hottest girl at my school...
...the hottest girl at the next school over...
...beauty queens from a variety of colleges...
They were *all* my girl-friends.

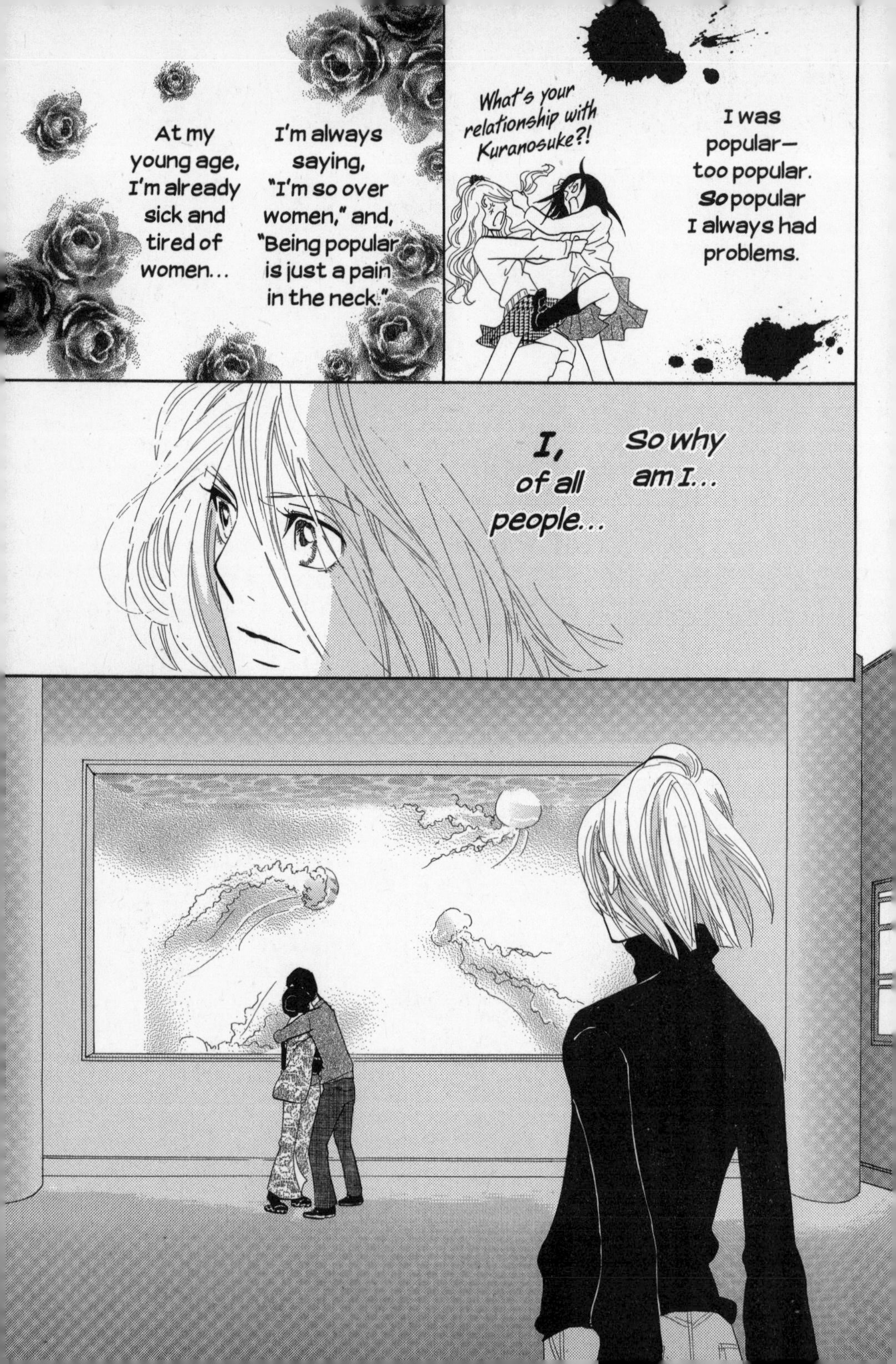
I was popular—too popular. So popular I always had problems.
What's your relationship with Kuranosuke?!
I'm always saying, "I'm so over women," and, "Being popular is just a pain in the neck."
At my young age, I'm already sick and tired of women...
So why am I...
I, of all people...

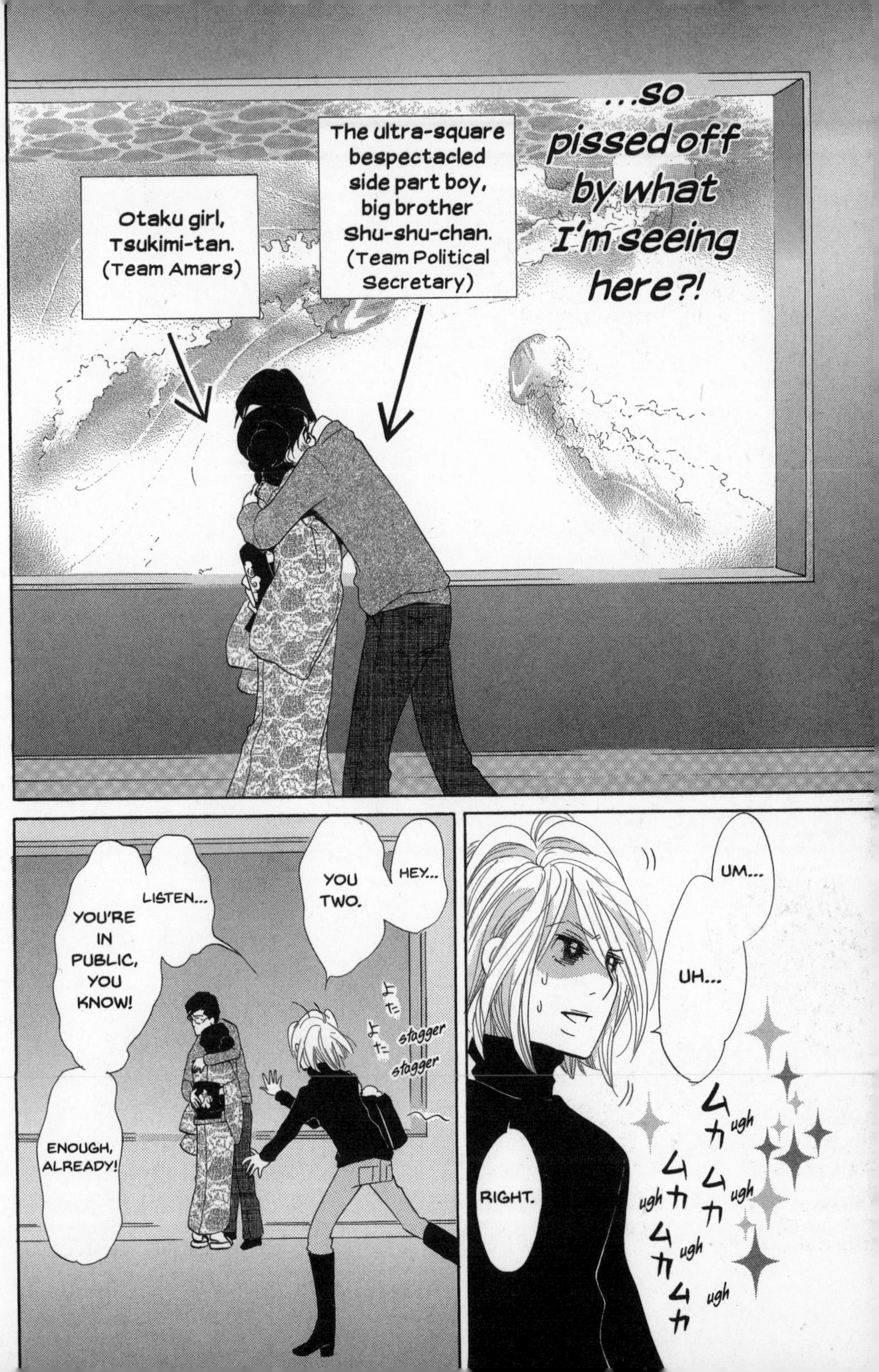
...so pissed off by what I'm seeing here?!
The ultra-square bespectacled side part boy, big brother Shu-shu-chan. (Team Political Secretary)
Otaku girl, Tsukimi-tan. (Team Amars)
UM...
UH...
RIGHT.
ムカ ugh
ムカ ugh
ムカ ugh
ムカ ugh
ムカ ugh
HEY...
YOU TWO.
よた stagger
よた stagger
LISTEN...
YOU'RE IN PUBLIC, YOU KNOW!
ENOUGH, ALREADY!

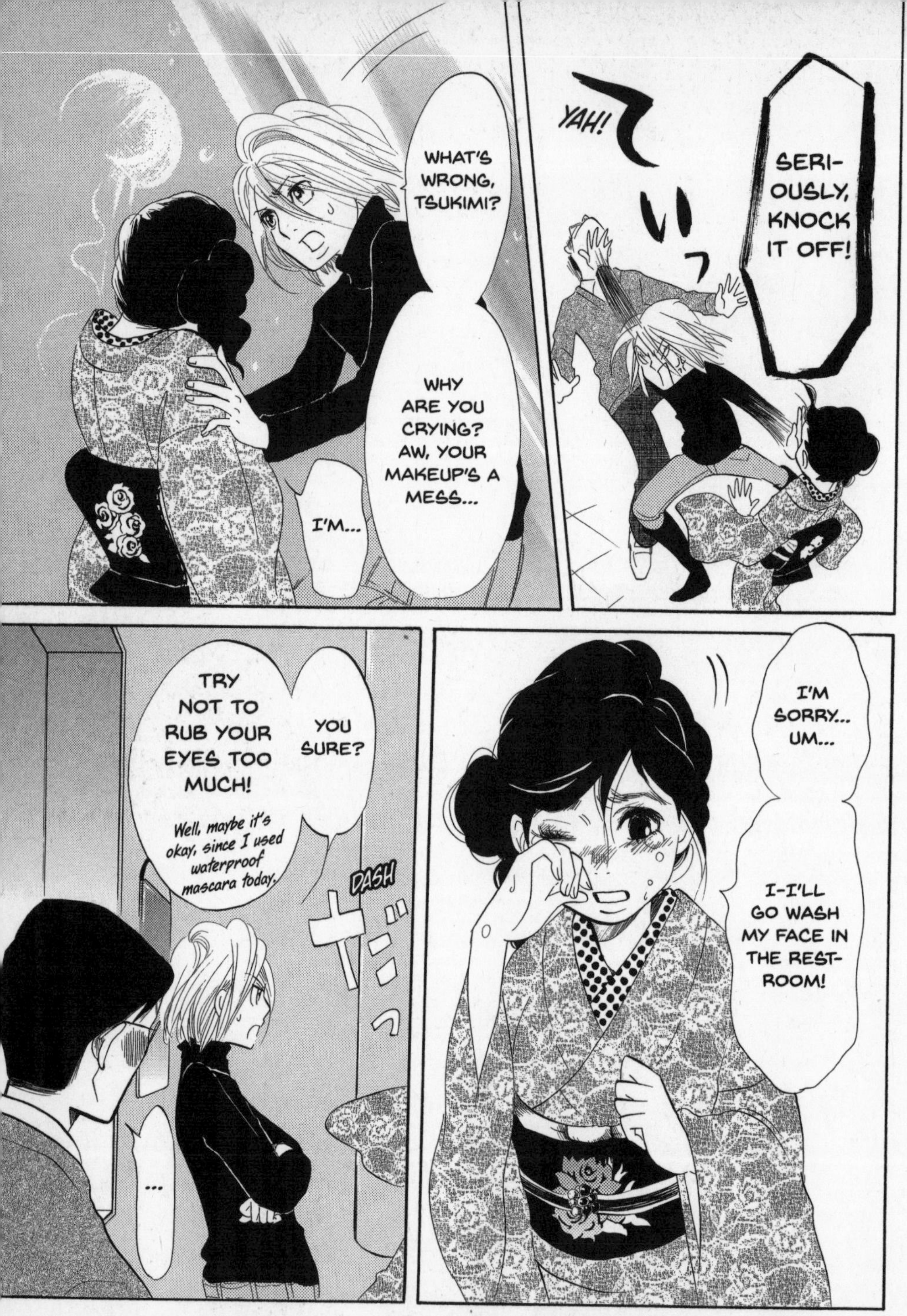
SERIOUSLY, KNOCK IT OFF!
YAH!
WHAT'S WRONG, TSUKIMI?
WHY ARE YOU CRYING? AW, YOUR MAKEUP'S A MESS...
I'M...
I'M SORRY... UM...
I-I'LL GO WASH MY FACE IN THE RESTROOM!
DASH
TRY NOT TO RUB YOUR EYES TOO MUCH!
Well, maybe it's okay, since I used waterproof mascara today.
YOU SURE?
...

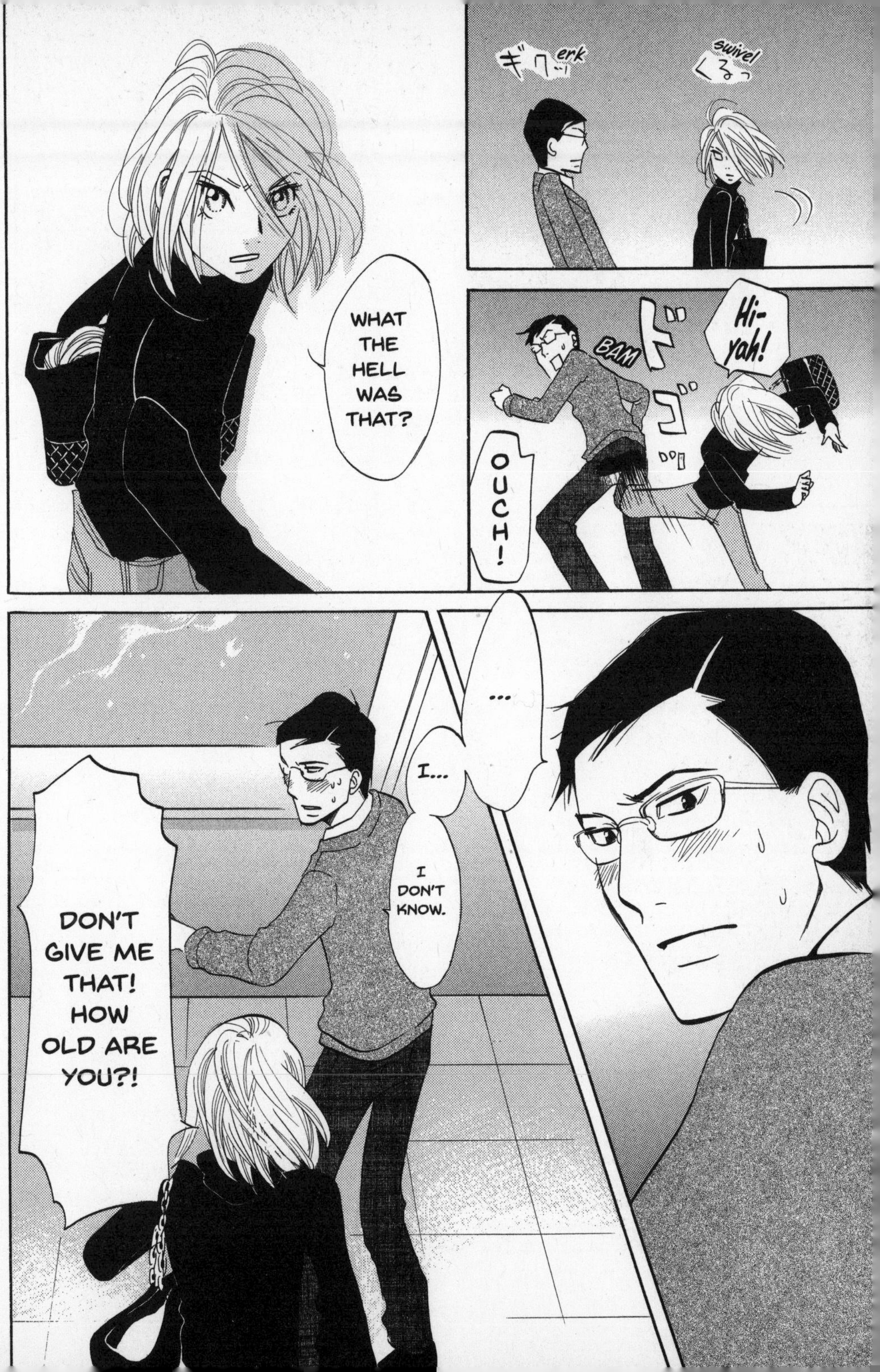
erk
swivel
Hi-yah!
BAM
OUCH!
WHAT THE HELL WAS THAT?
...
I...
I DON'T KNOW.
DON'T GIVE ME THAT! HOW OLD ARE YOU?!

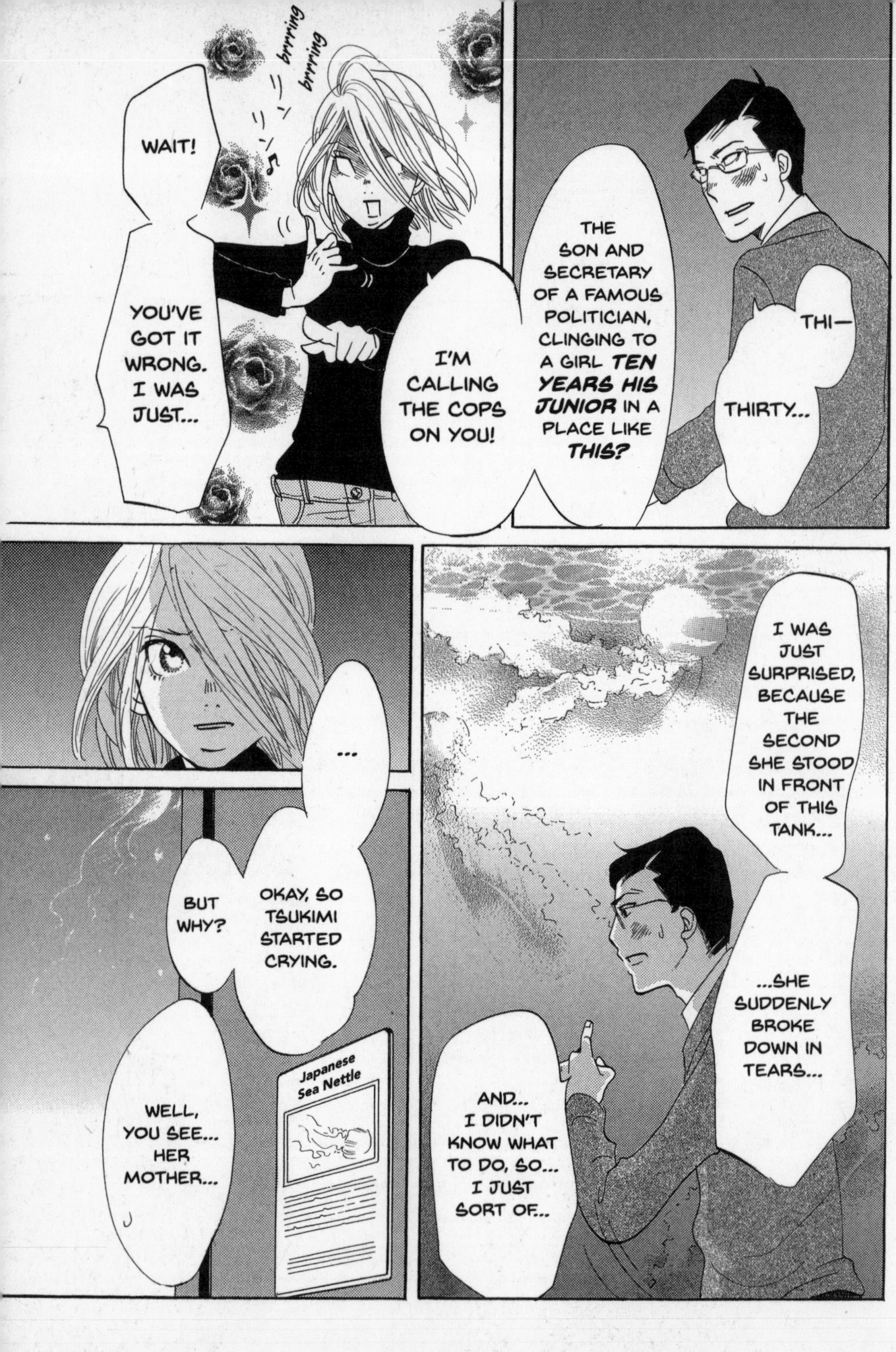
THI—
THIRTY...
THE SON AND SECRETARY OF A FAMOUS POLITICIAN, CLINGING TO A GIRL **TEN YEARS HIS JUNIOR** IN A PLACE LIKE **THIS?**
I'M CALLING THE COPS ON YOU!
brrring
brrring
WAIT!
YOU'VE GOT IT WRONG. I WAS JUST...
I WAS JUST SURPRISED, BECAUSE THE SECOND SHE STOOD IN FRONT OF THIS TANK...
...SHE SUDDENLY BROKE DOWN IN TEARS...
AND... I DIDN'T KNOW WHAT TO DO, SO... I JUST SORT OF...
...
OKAY, SO TSUKIMI STARTED CRYING.
BUT WHY?
Japanese Sea Nettle
WELL, YOU SEE... HER MOTHER...

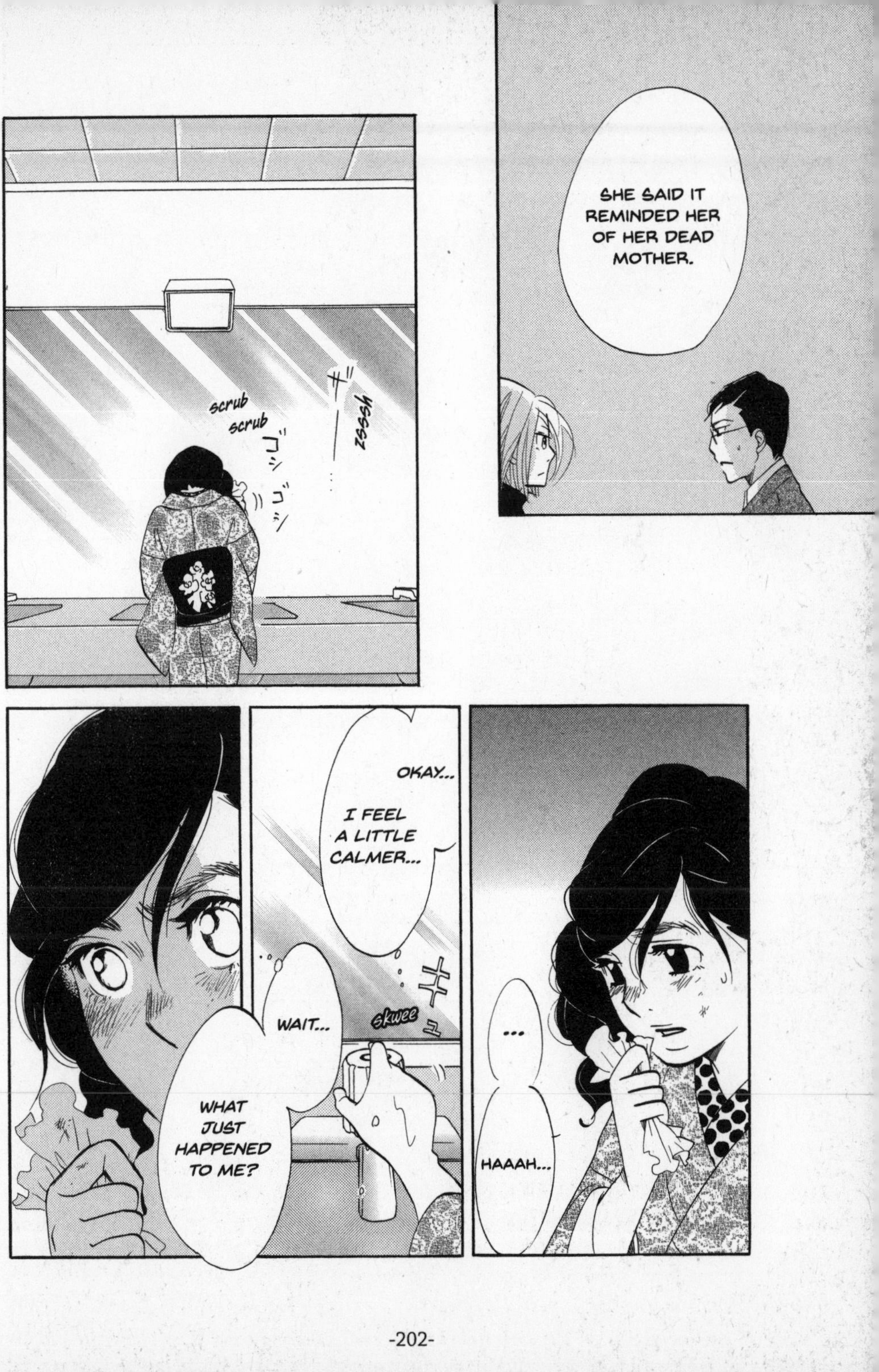
SHE SAID IT REMINDED HER OF HER DEAD MOTHER.
scrub scrub
zsssh
...
HAAAH...
OKAY...
I FEEL A LITTLE CALMER...
skwee
WAIT...
WHAT JUST HAPPENED TO ME?

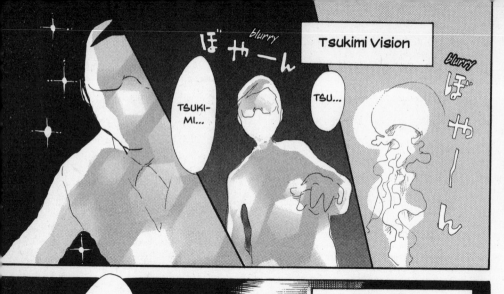

Tsukimi Vision
blurry
ぼやーん
TSU...
blurry
ぼやーん
TSUKI-MI...
Sensation on Tsukimi's Back
IT'S ALL RIGHT.
YOU CAN CRY.
Full-Body Sensations
IT'S ALL RIGHT...

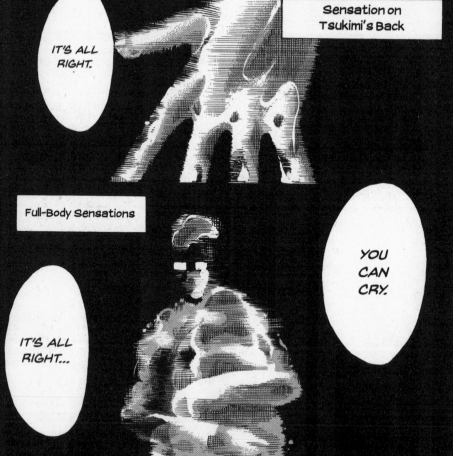

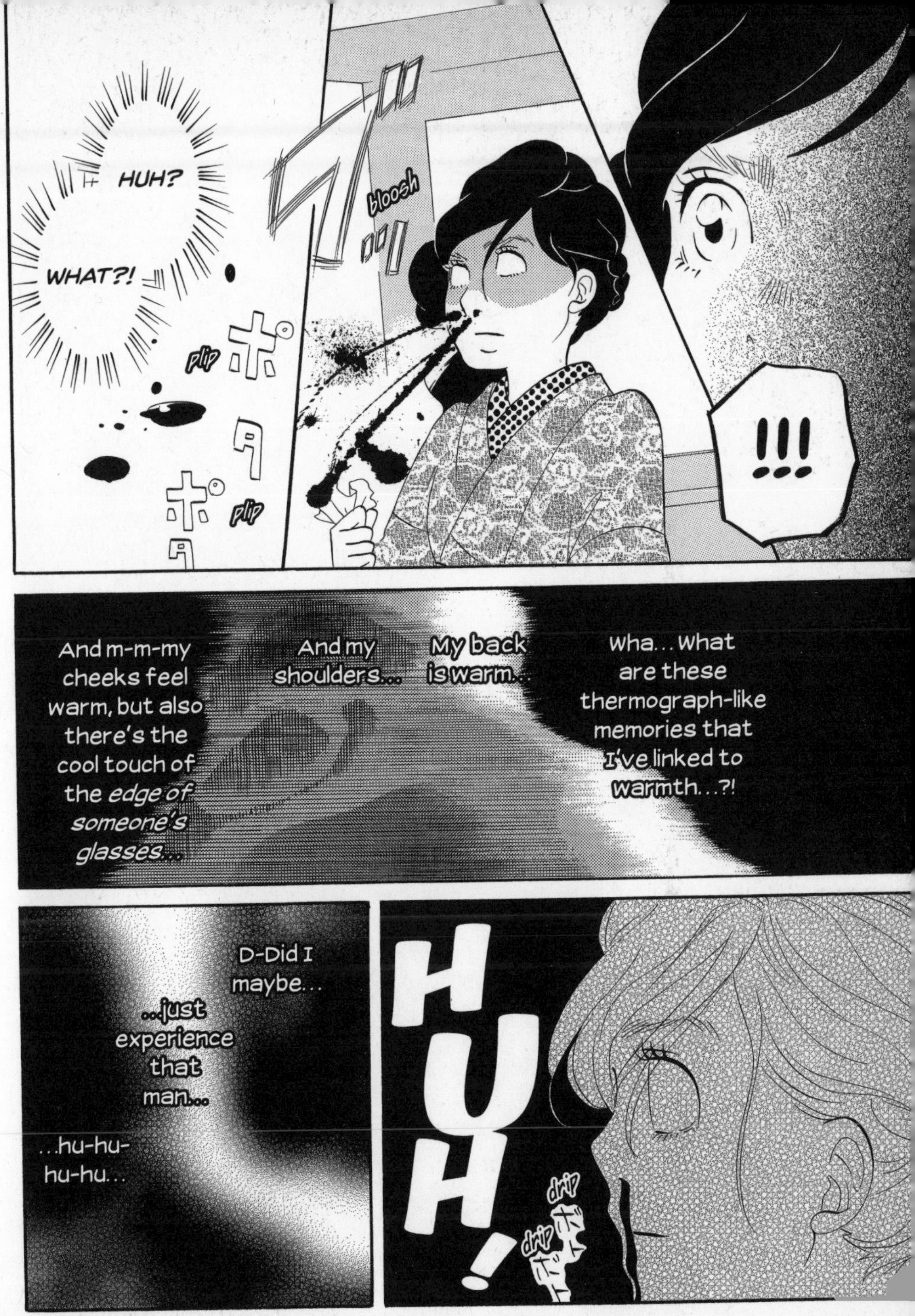
!!!
bloosh
HUH?
WHAT?!
plip
plip
Wha... What are these thermograph-like memories that I've linked to warmth...?!
My back is warm...
And my shoulders...
And m-m-my cheeks feel warm, but also there's the cool touch of the *edge of someone's glasses*...
HUH!
drip
drip
D-Did I maybe...
...just experience that man...
...hu-hu-hu-hu...

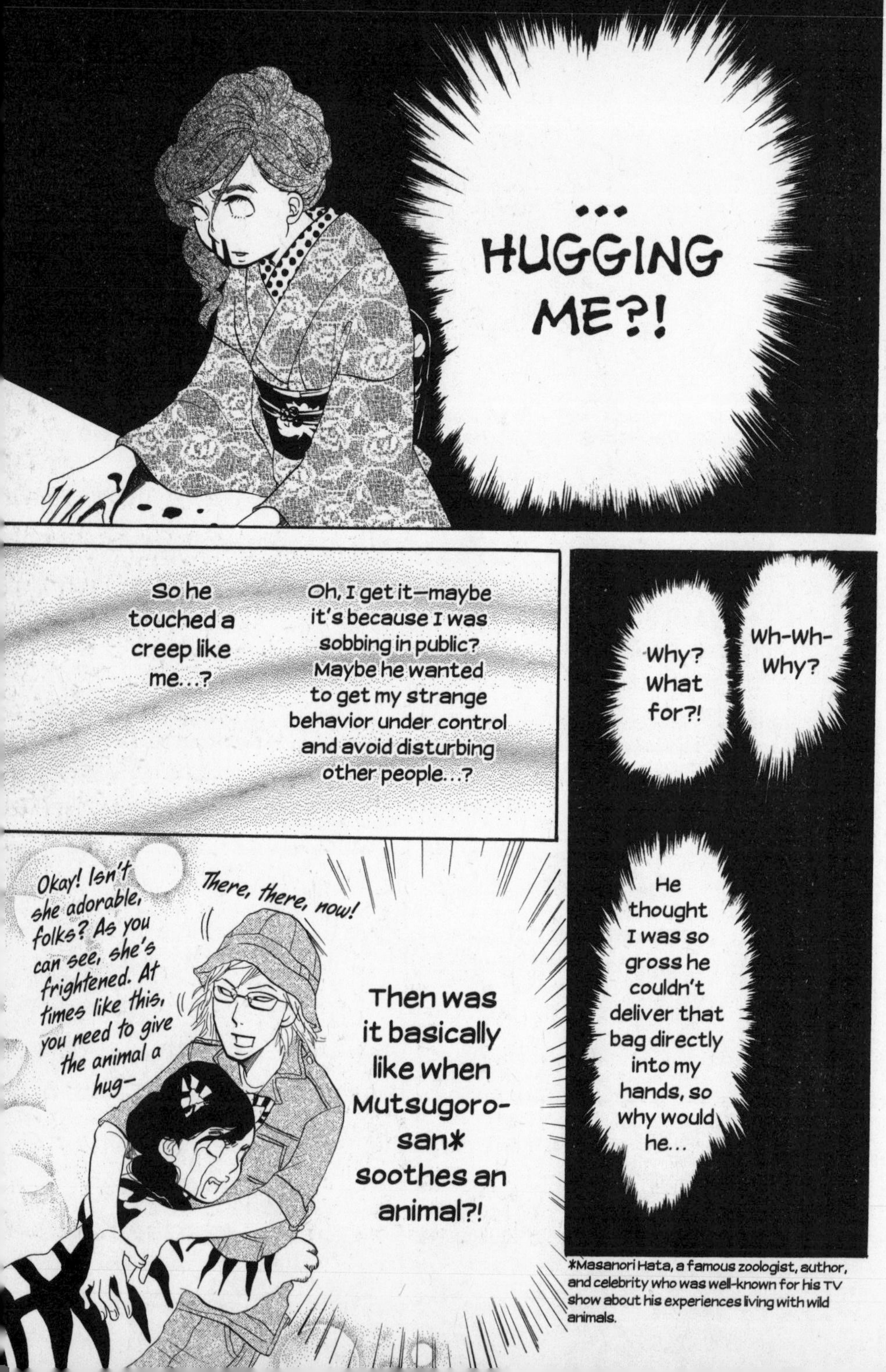
...HUGGING ME?!
Wh-Wh-Why?
Why? What for?!
He thought I was so gross he couldn't deliver that bag directly into my hands, so why would he...
Oh, I get it—maybe it's because I was sobbing in public? Maybe he wanted to get my strange behavior under control and avoid disturbing other people...?
So he touched a creep like me...?
Then was it basically like when Mutsugoro-san* soothes an animal?!
There, there, now!
Okay! Isn't she adorable, folks? As you can see, she's frightened. At times like this, you need to give the animal a hug—

*Masanori Hata, a famous zoologist, author, and celebrity who was well-known for his TV show about his experiences living with wild animals.

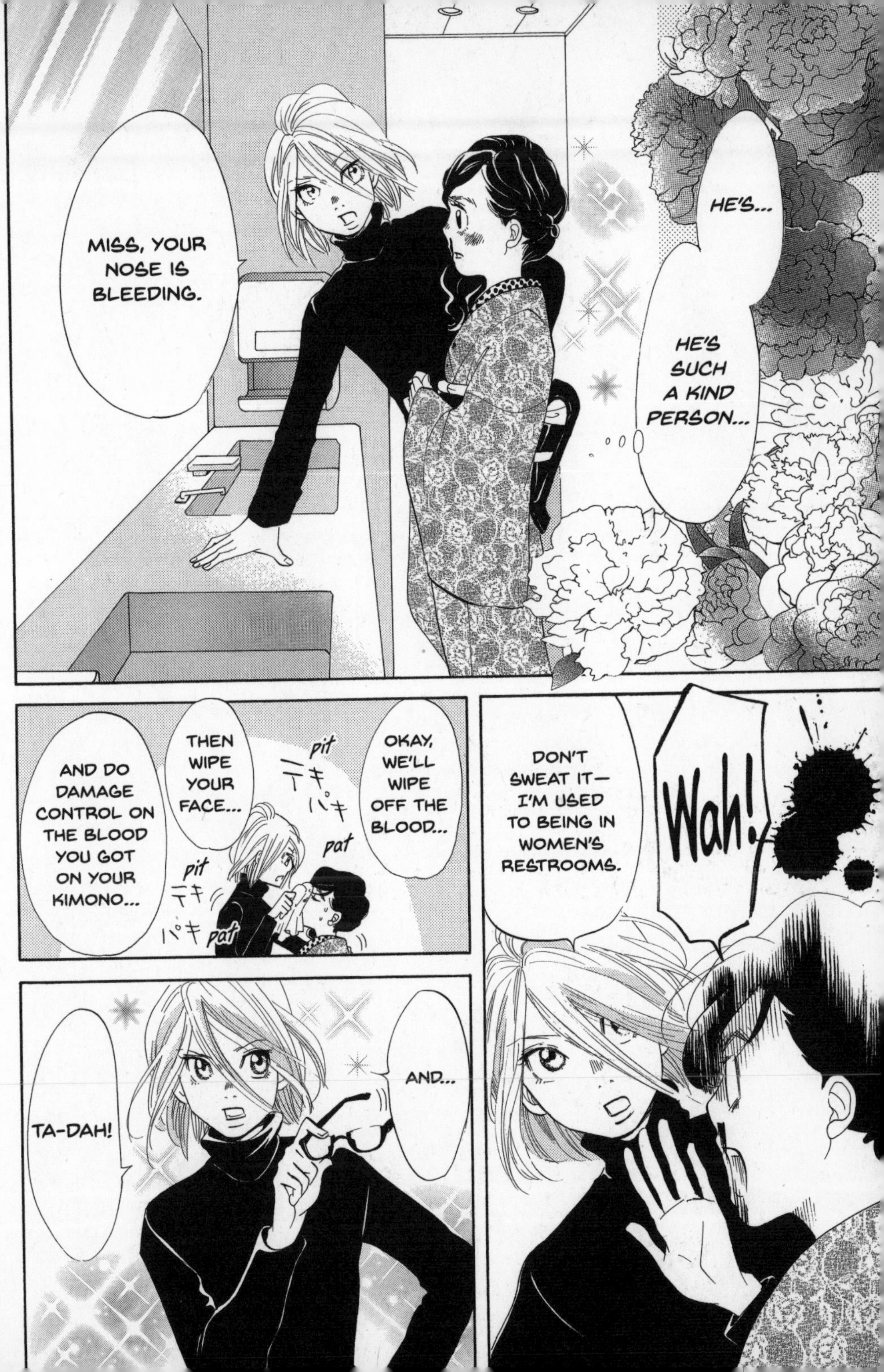
HE'S...
HE'S SUCH A KIND PERSON...
MISS, YOUR NOSE IS BLEEDING.
Wah!
DON'T SWEAT IT—I'M USED TO BEING IN WOMEN'S RESTROOMS.
OKAY, WE'LL WIPE OFF THE BLOOD...
pit テキ パキ pat
THEN WIPE YOUR FACE...
pit テキ パキ pat
AND DO DAMAGE CONTROL ON THE BLOOD YOU GOT ON YOUR KIMONO...
AND...
TA-DAH!

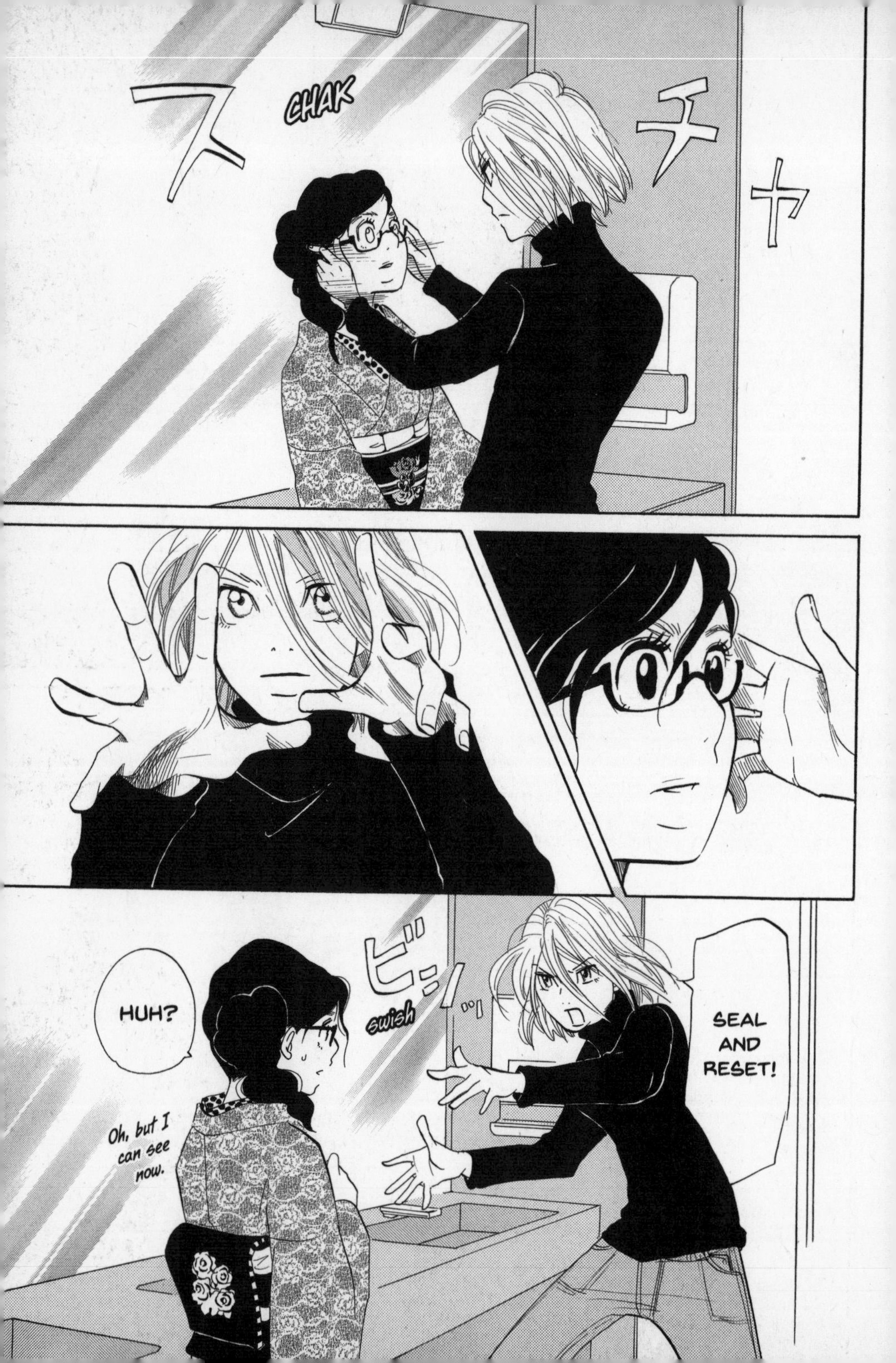

スチャ
CHAK
SEAL AND RESET!
swish
HUH?
Oh, but I can see now.

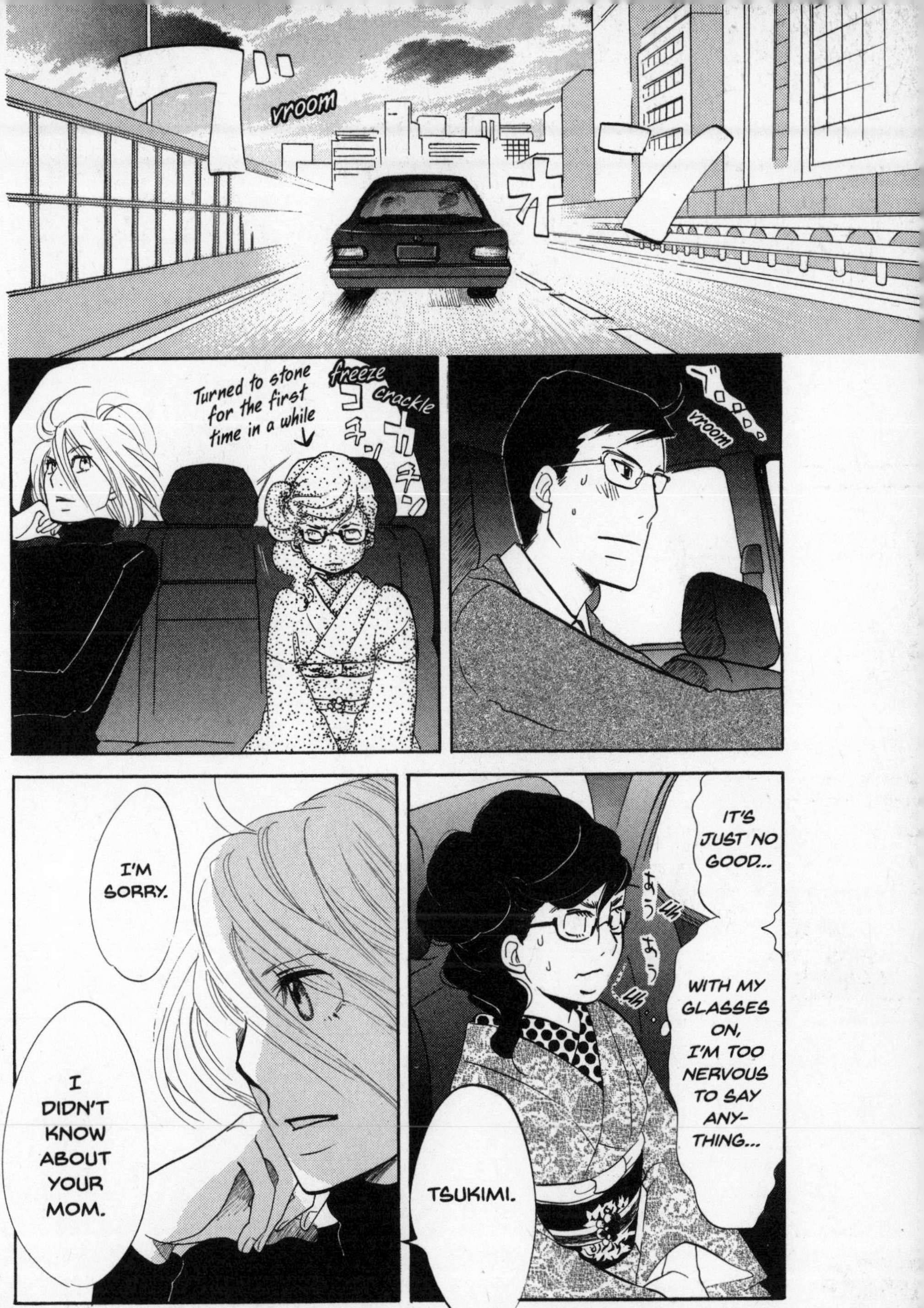
vroom
vroom
Turned to stone for the first time in a while
freeze
crackle
IT'S JUST NO GOOD...
WITH MY GLASSES ON, I'M TOO NERVOUS TO SAY ANY-THING...
TSUKIMI.
I'M SORRY.
I DIDN'T KNOW ABOUT YOUR MOM.

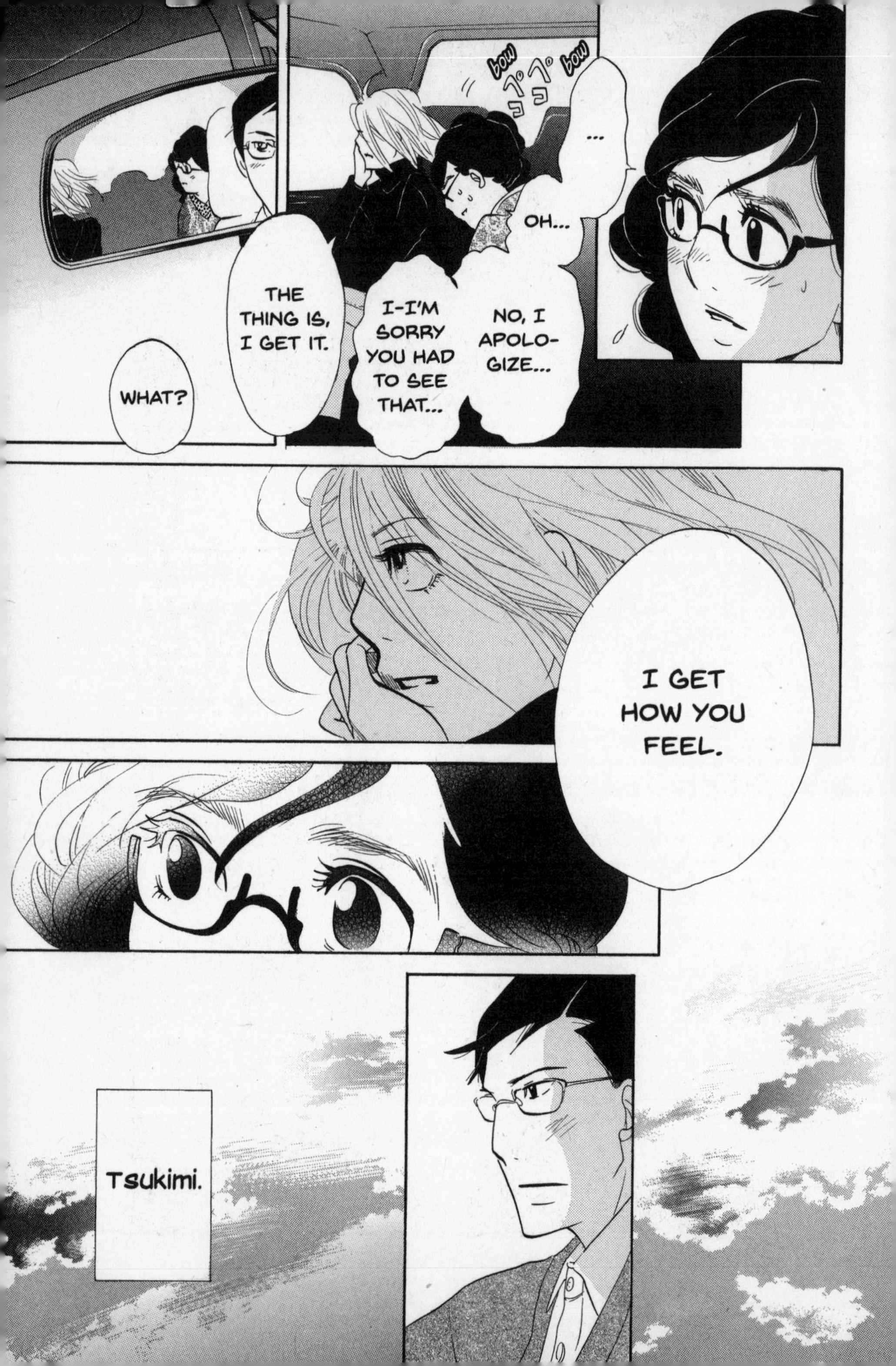
bow bow
...
OH...
NO, I APOLOGIZE...
I-I'M SORRY YOU HAD TO SEE THAT...
THE THING IS, I GET IT.
WHAT?
I GET HOW YOU FEEL.
Tsukimi.

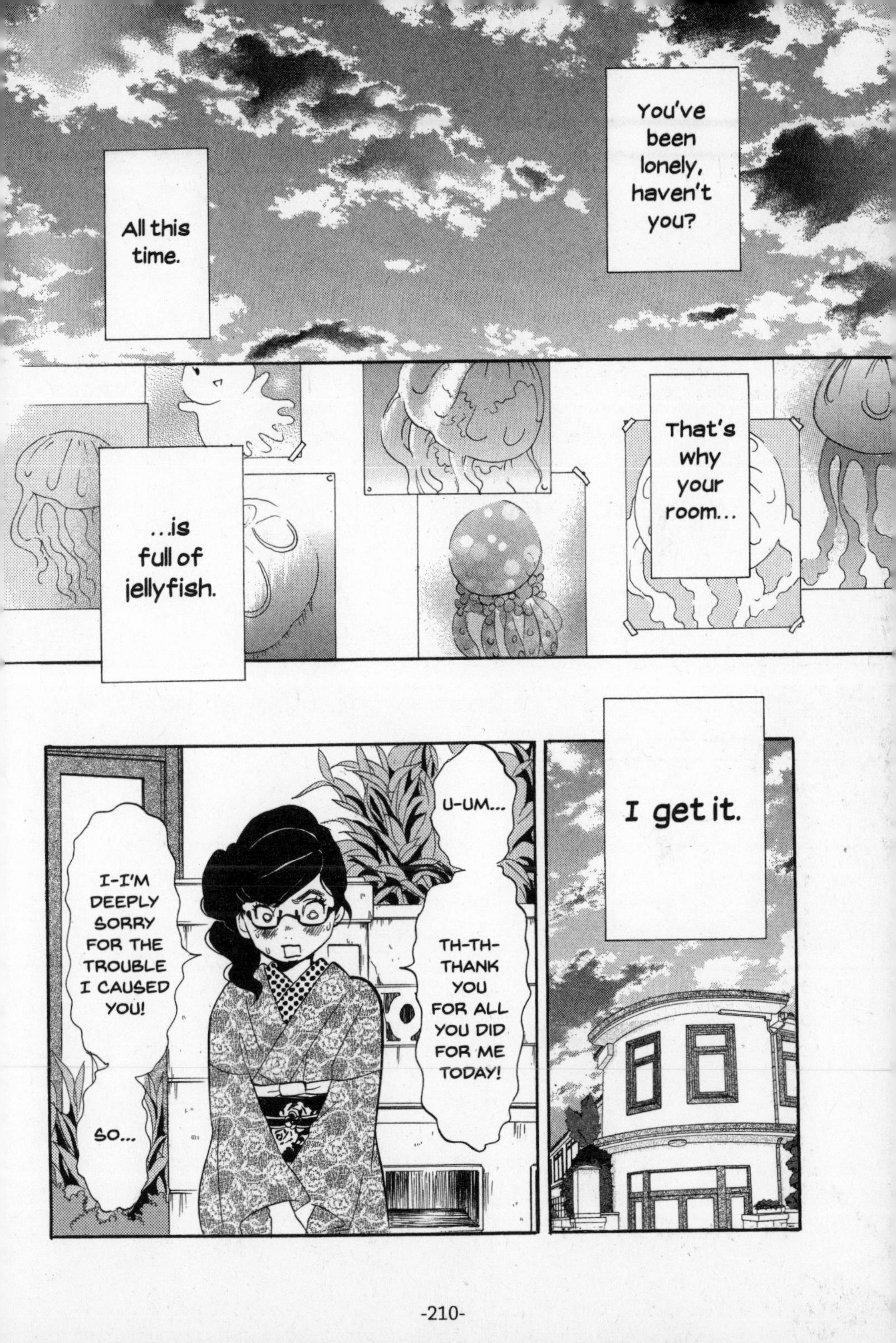
You've been lonely, haven't you?
All this time.
That's why your room...
...is full of jellyfish.
I get it.
U-UM...
TH-TH-THANK YOU FOR ALL YOU DID FOR ME TODAY!
I-I'M DEEPLY SORRY FOR THE TROUBLE I CAUSED YOU!
SO...

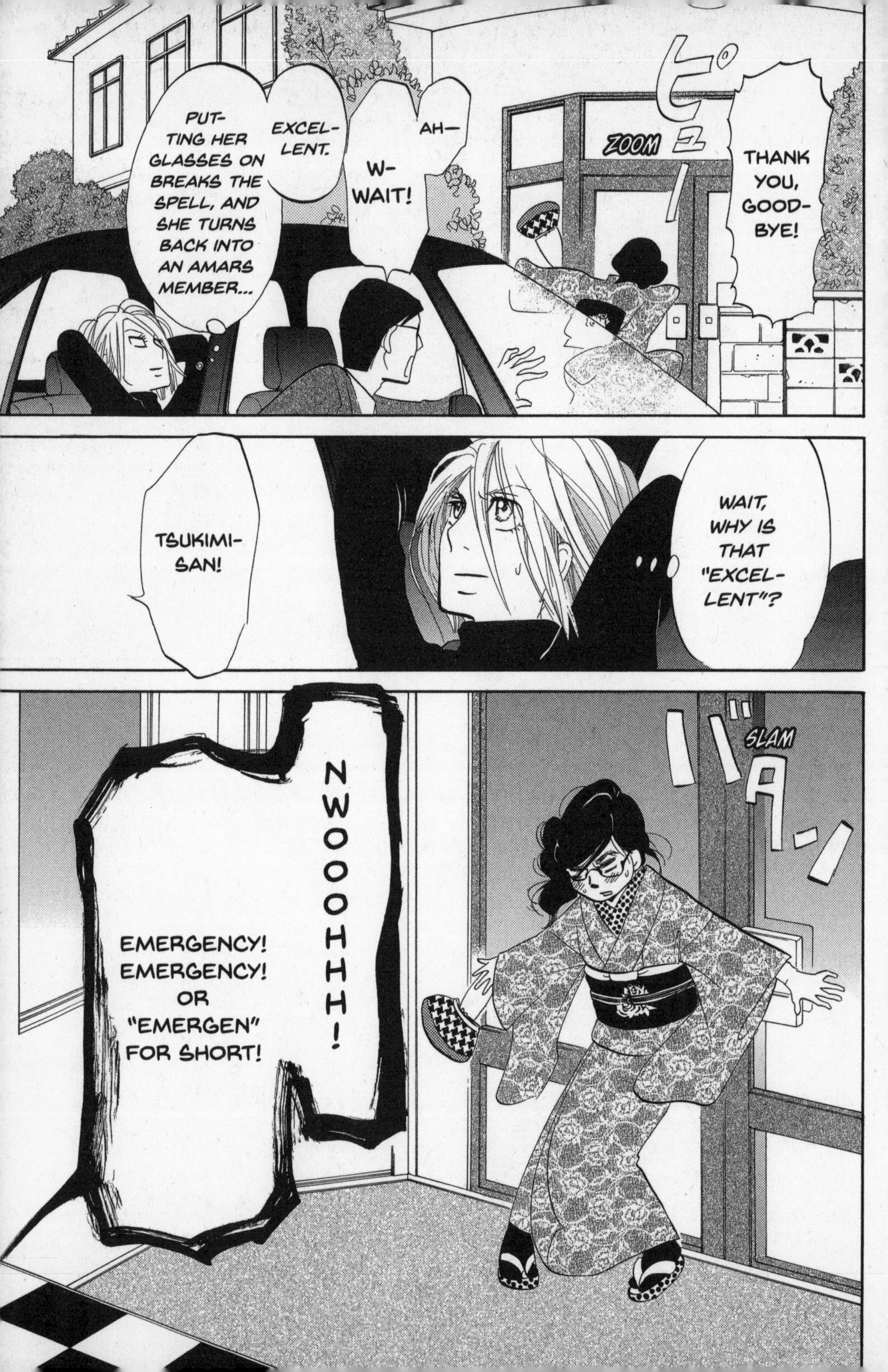
THANK YOU, GOOD-BYE!
ZOOM
AH— W-WAIT!
EXCEL-LENT.
PUT-TING HER GLASSES ON BREAKS THE SPELL, AND SHE TURNS BACK INTO AN AMARS MEMBER...
WAIT, WHY IS THAT "EXCEL-LENT"?
TSUKIMI-SAN!
SLAM
NWOOOOHHH!
EMERGENCY! EMERGENCY! OR "EMERGEN" FOR SHORT!

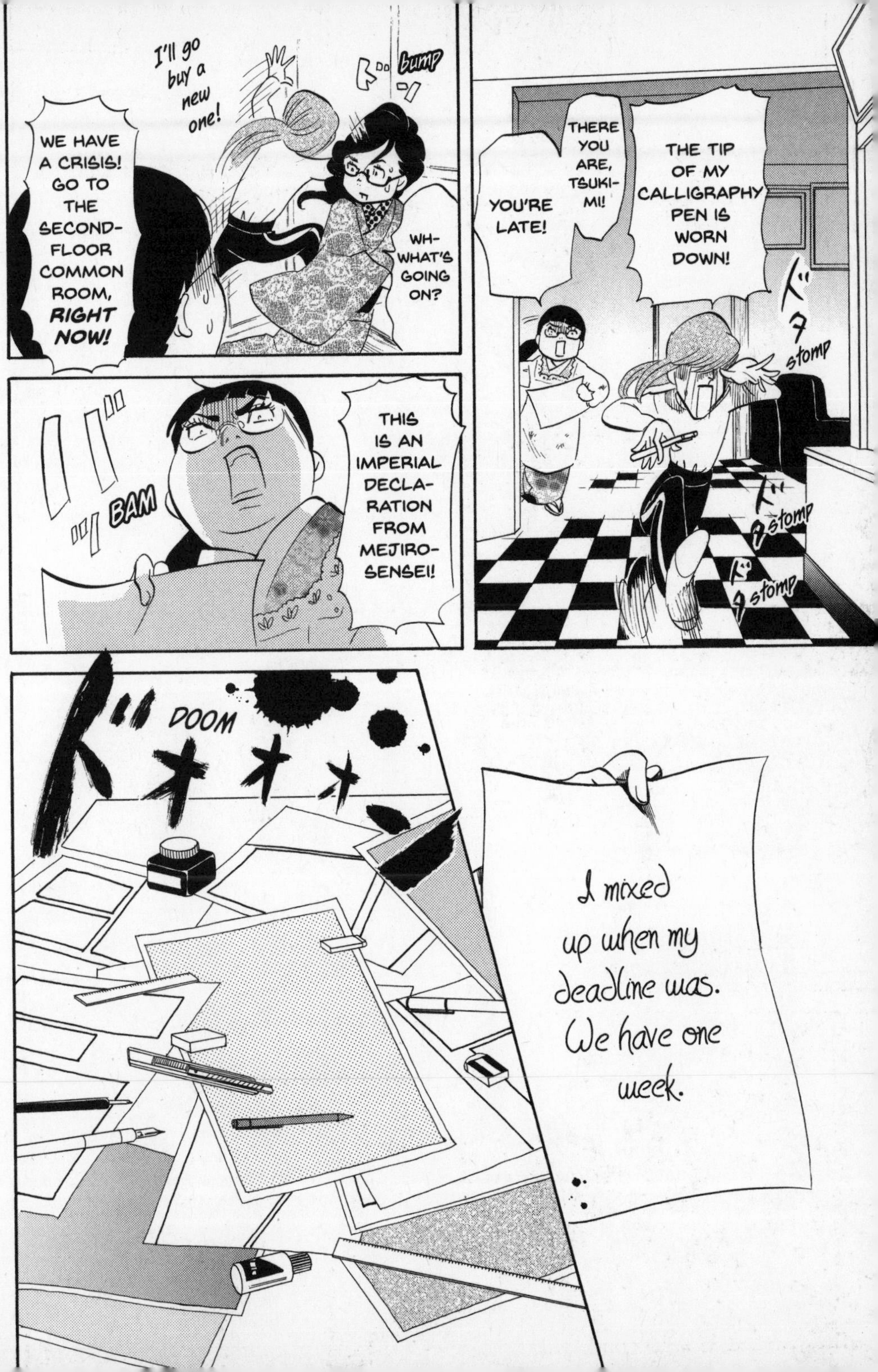
THE TIP OF MY CALLIGRAPHY PEN IS WORN DOWN!
THERE YOU ARE, TSUKIMI!
YOU'RE LATE!
ドタ stomp
ドタ stomp
ドタ stomp
ドン bump
I'll go buy a new one!
WH-WHAT'S GOING ON?
WE HAVE A CRISIS! GO TO THE SECOND-FLOOR COMMON ROOM, **RIGHT NOW!**
THIS IS AN IMPERIAL DECLARATION FROM MEJIRO-SENSEI!
BAM
ドオオオ DOOM
I mixed up when my deadline was. We have one week.

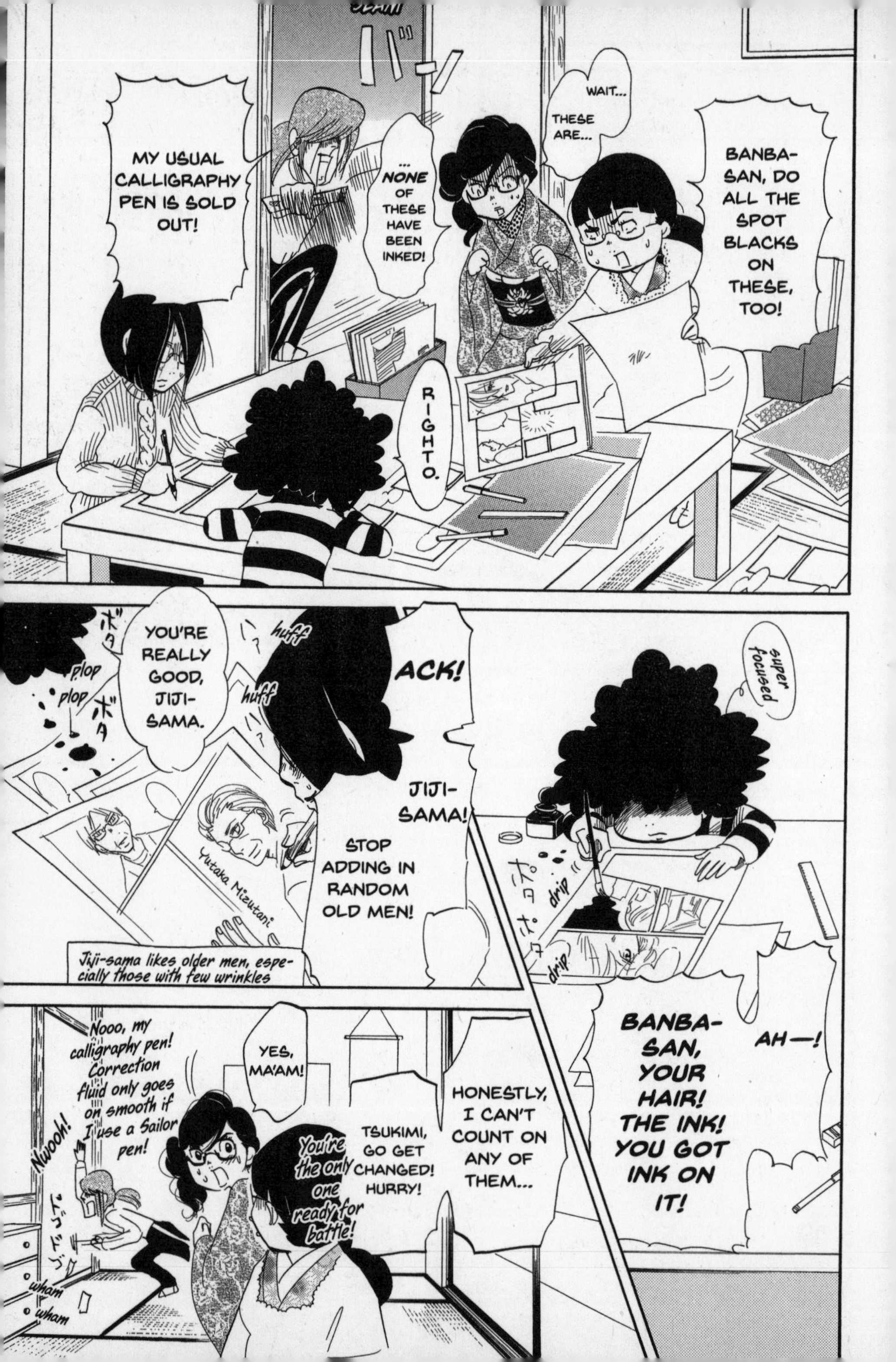
BANBA-SAN, DO ALL THE SPOT BLACKS ON THESE, TOO!
WAIT... THESE ARE...
... NONE OF THESE HAVE BEEN INKED!
MY USUAL CALLIGRAPHY PEN IS SOLD OUT!
RIGHTO.
super focused
drip
drip
AH—!
BANBA-SAN, YOUR HAIR! THE INK! YOU GOT INK ON IT!
ACK!
JIJI-SAMA!
STOP ADDING IN RANDOM OLD MEN!
huff
huff
YOU'RE REALLY GOOD, JIJI-SAMA.
plop
plop
Yutaka Mizutani
Jiji-sama likes older men, especially those with few wrinkles
HONESTLY, I CAN'T COUNT ON ANY OF THEM...
TSUKIMI, GO GET CHANGED! HURRY!
YES, MA'AM!
You're the only one ready for battle!
Nooo, my calligraphy pen! Correction fluid only goes on smooth if I use a Sailor pen!
Nwooh!
wham
wham

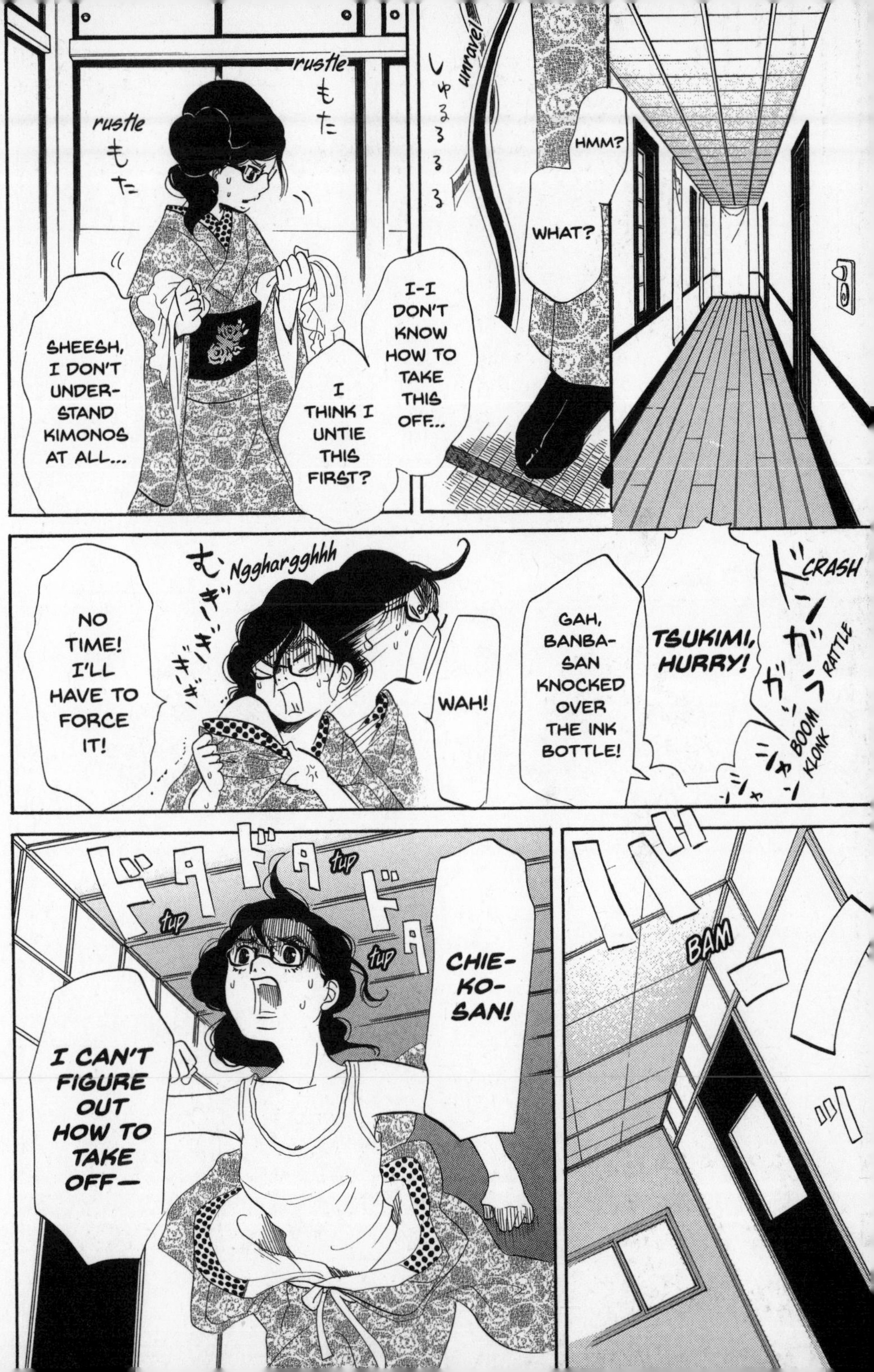
unravel
HMM?
WHAT?
rustle
rustle
I-I DON'T KNOW HOW TO TAKE THIS OFF...
I THINK I UNTIE THIS FIRST?
SHEESH, I DON'T UNDER-STAND KIMONOS AT ALL...
CRASH
RATTLE
BOOM KLONK
TSUKIMI, HURRY!
GAH, BANBA-SAN KNOCKED OVER THE INK BOTTLE!
WAH!
Ngghargghhh
NO TIME! I'LL HAVE TO FORCE IT!
BAM
tup
tup
tup
CHIE-KO-SAN!
I CAN'T FIGURE OUT HOW TO TAKE OFF—

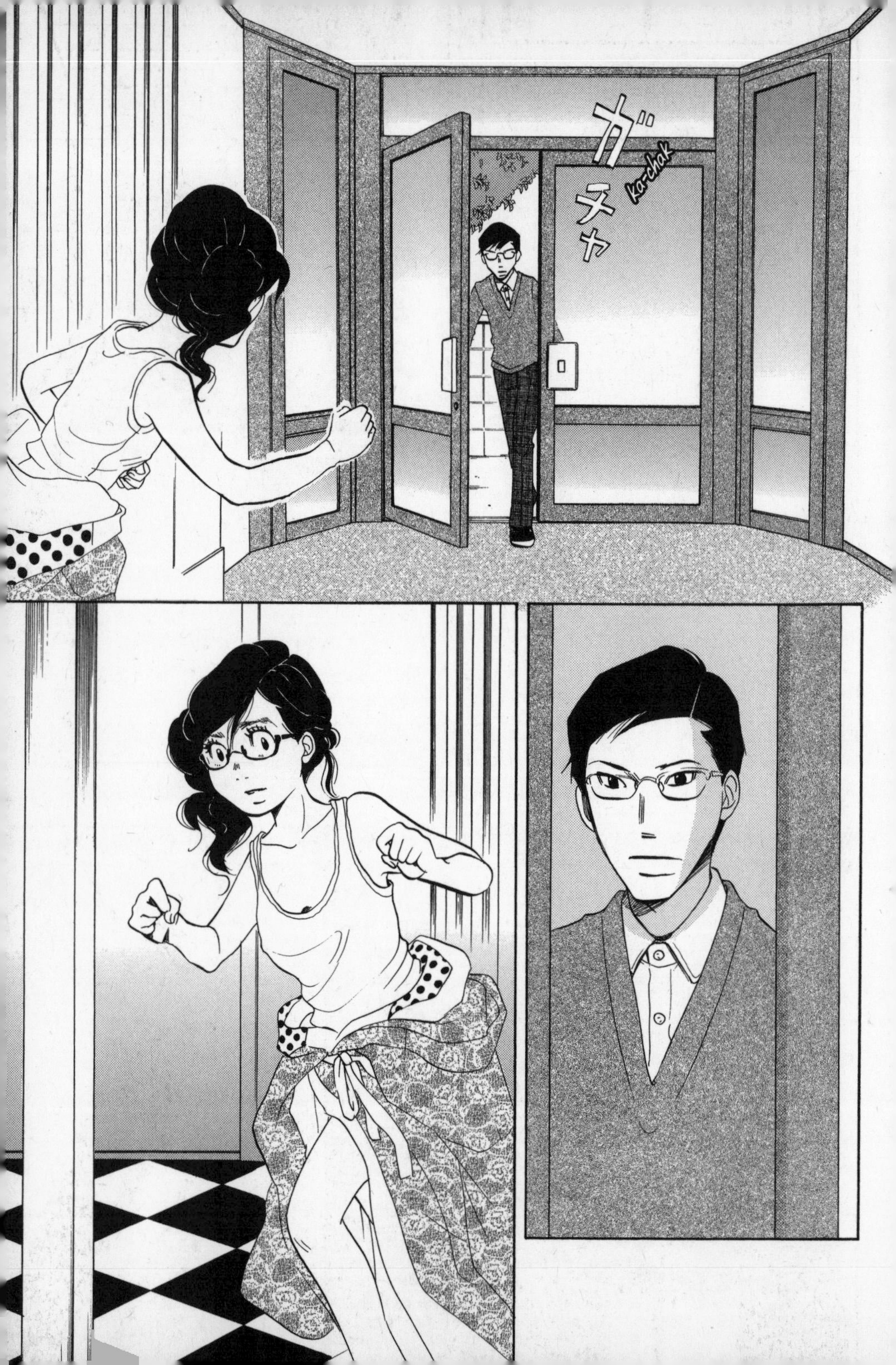
ガチャ
ka-chak

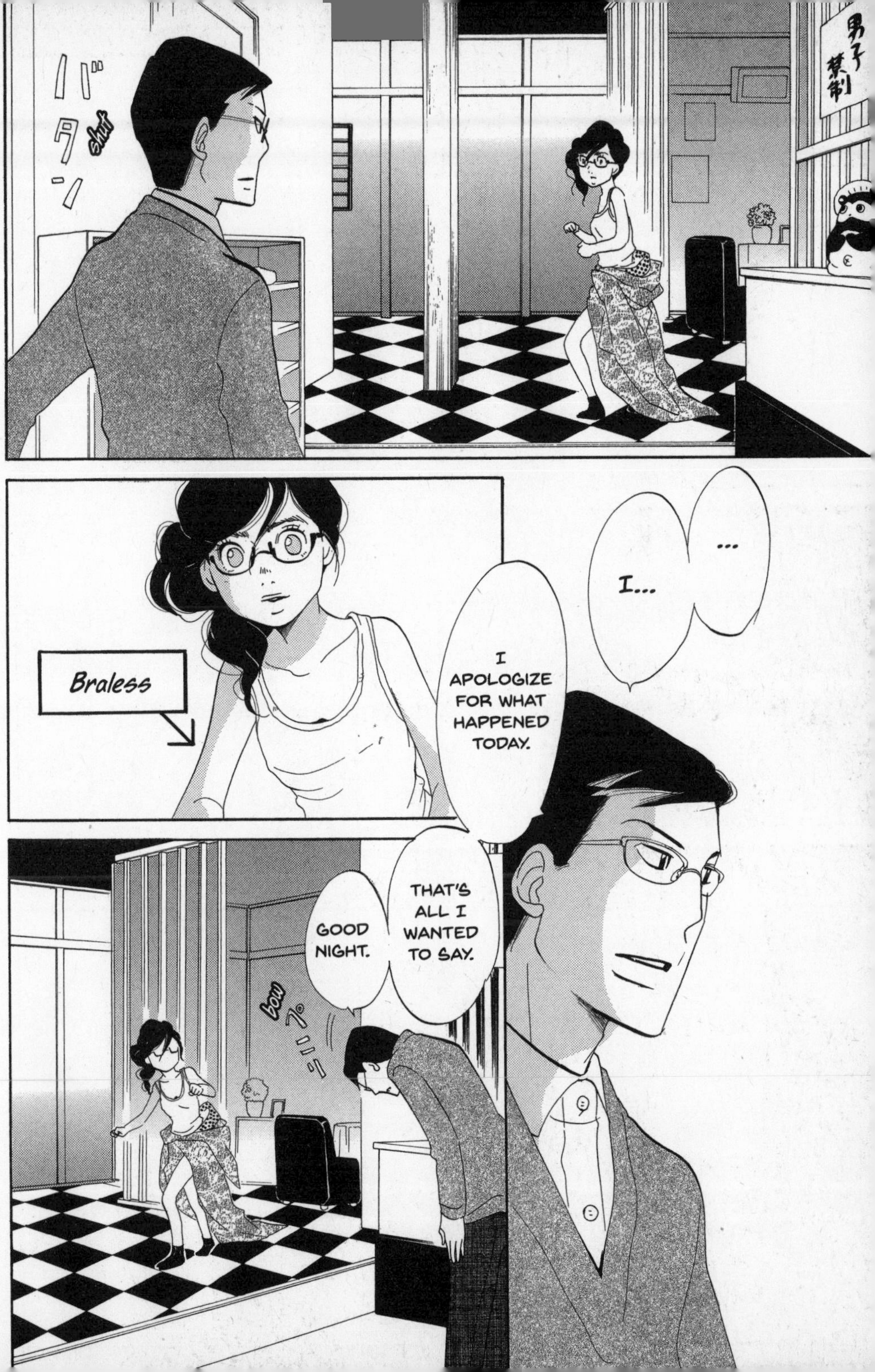
男子禁制
バタン
shut
...
I...
I APOLOGIZE FOR WHAT HAPPENED TODAY.
THAT'S ALL I WANTED TO SAY.
GOOD NIGHT.
Braless
ペこ
bow

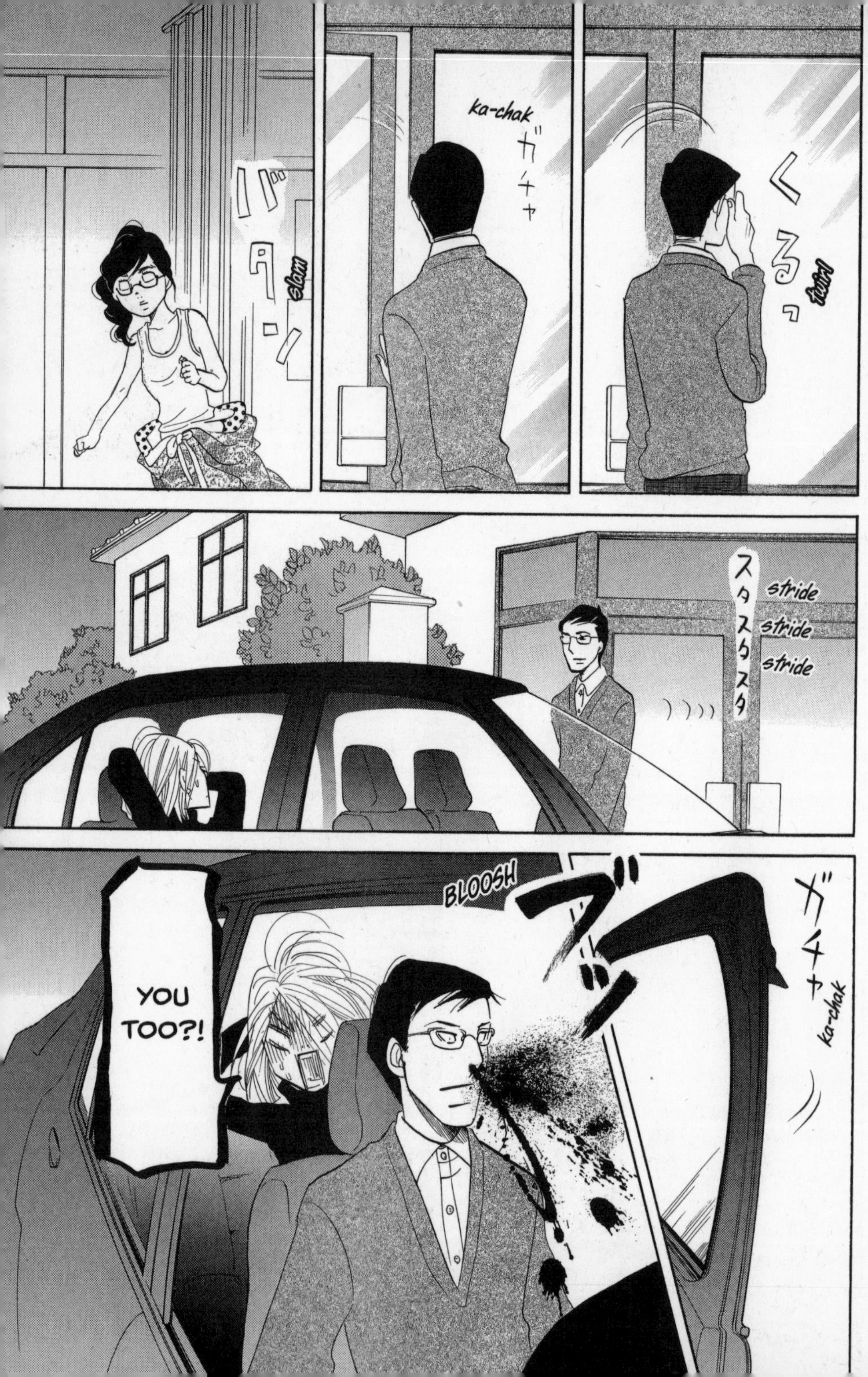

くるっ
twirl
ka-chak
ガチャ
バターン
slam
スタスタスタ
stride
stride
stride
ガチャ
ka-chak
ブッ
BLOOSH
YOU TOO?!

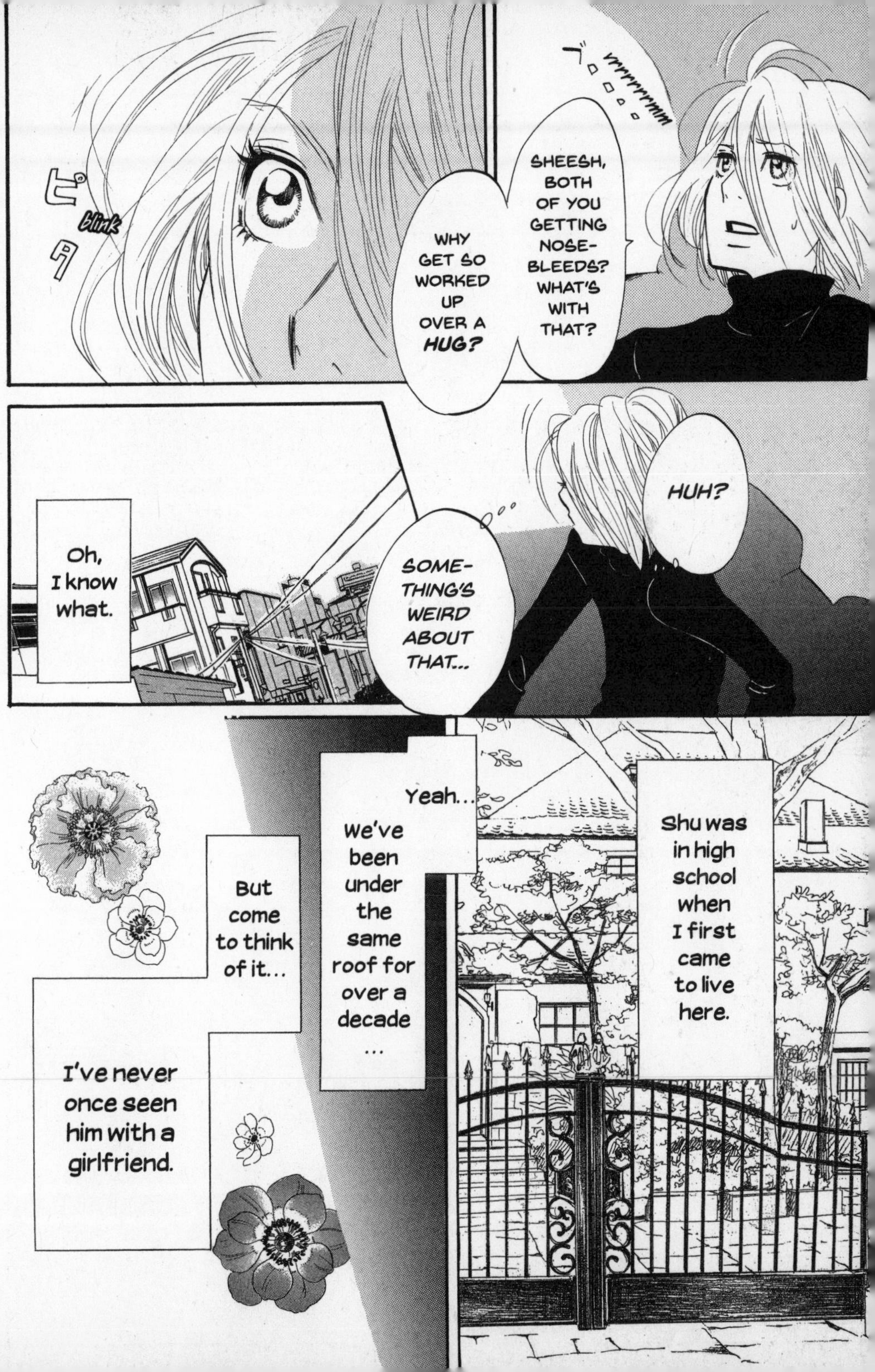
SHEESH, BOTH OF YOU GETTING NOSE-BLEEDS? WHAT'S WITH THAT?
WHY GET SO WORKED UP OVER A HUG?
blink
HUH?
SOME-THING'S WEIRD ABOUT THAT...
Oh, I know what.
Shu was in high school when I first came to live here.
Yeah...
We've been under the same roof for over a decade...
But come to think of it...
I've never once seen him with a girlfriend.

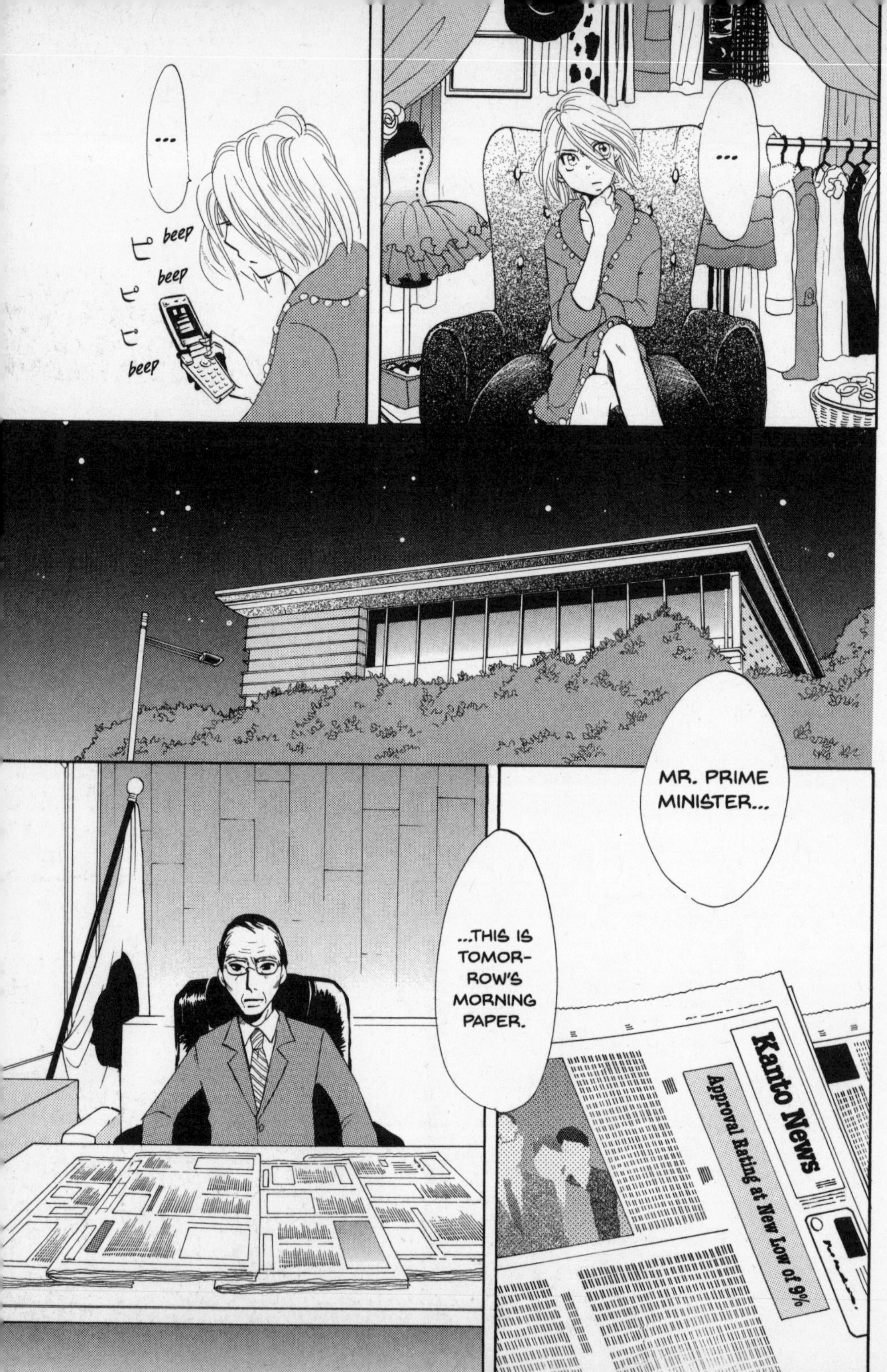
...
...
ピピピ
beep beep beep
MR. PRIME MINISTER...
...THIS IS TOMOR-ROW'S MORNING PAPER.
Kanto News
Approval Rating at New Low of 9%

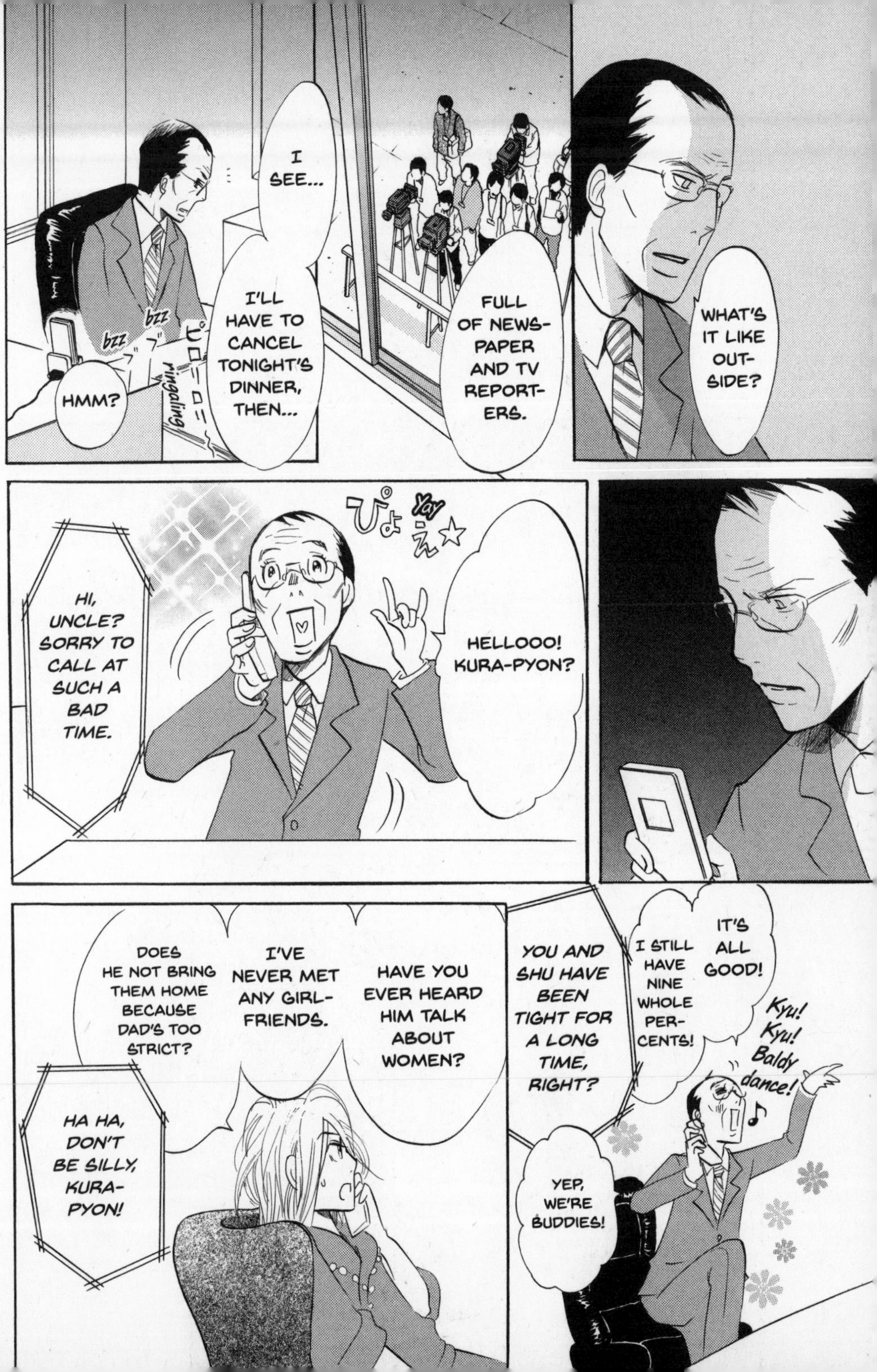
WHAT'S IT LIKE OUT-SIDE?
FULL OF NEWS-PAPER AND TV REPORT-ERS.
I SEE...
I'LL HAVE TO CANCEL TONIGHT'S DINNER, THEN...
bzz
bzz
ringaling
HMM?
Yay
HELLOOO! KURA-PYON?
HI, UNCLE? SORRY TO CALL AT SUCH A BAD TIME.
IT'S ALL GOOD!
I STILL HAVE NINE WHOLE PER-CENTS!
Kyu! Kyu! Baldy dance!
YOU AND SHU HAVE BEEN TIGHT FOR A LONG TIME, RIGHT?
YEP, WE'RE BUDDIES!
HAVE YOU EVER HEARD HIM TALK ABOUT WOMEN?
I'VE NEVER MET ANY GIRL-FRIENDS.
DOES HE NOT BRING THEM HOME BECAUSE DAD'S TOO STRICT?
HA HA, DON'T BE SILLY, KURA-PYON!

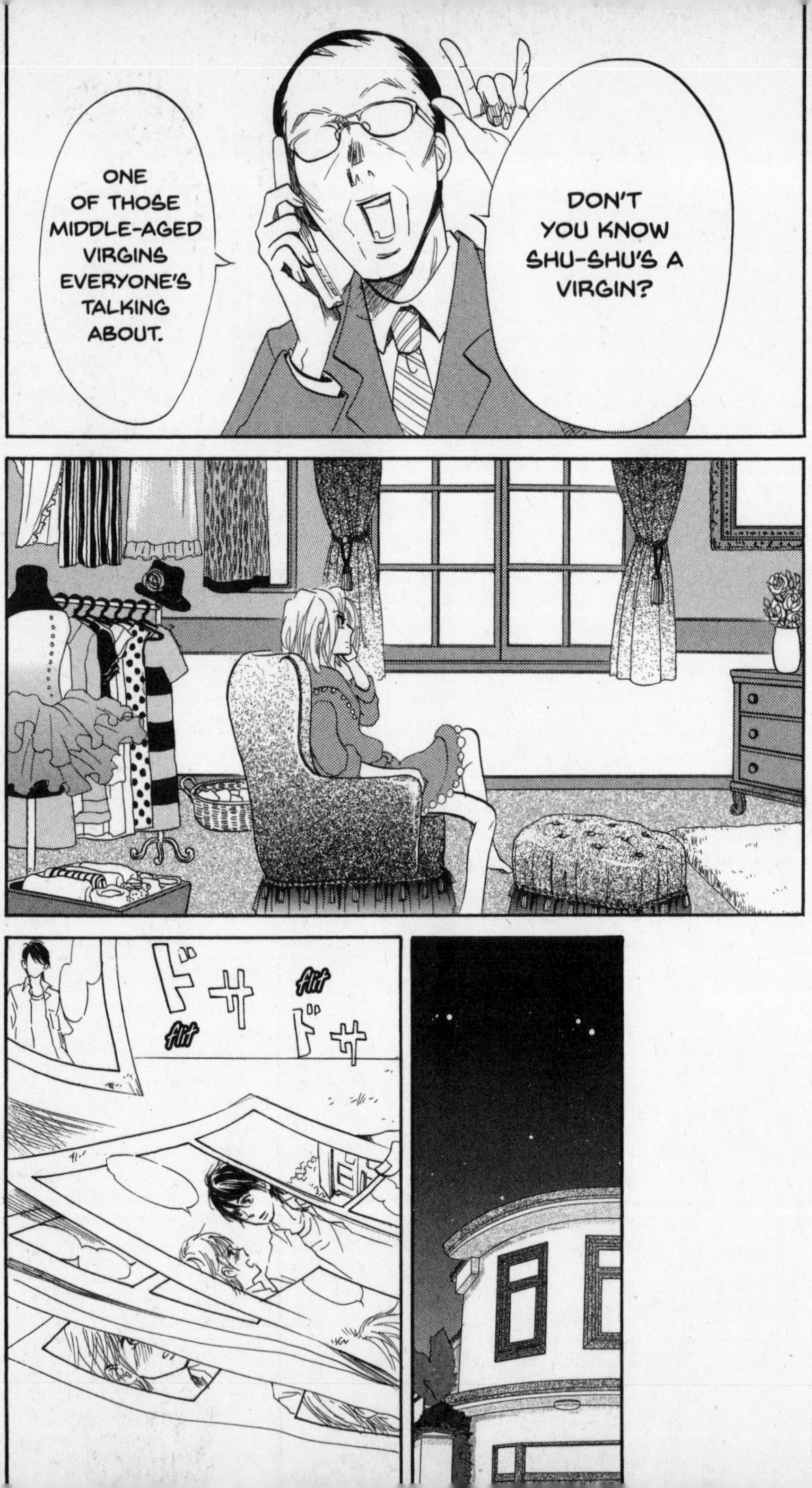
DON'T YOU KNOW SHU-SHU'S A VIRGIN?
ONE OF THOSE MIDDLE-AGED VIRGINS EVERYONE'S TALKING ABOUT.
flit
ドサ
ドサ
flit

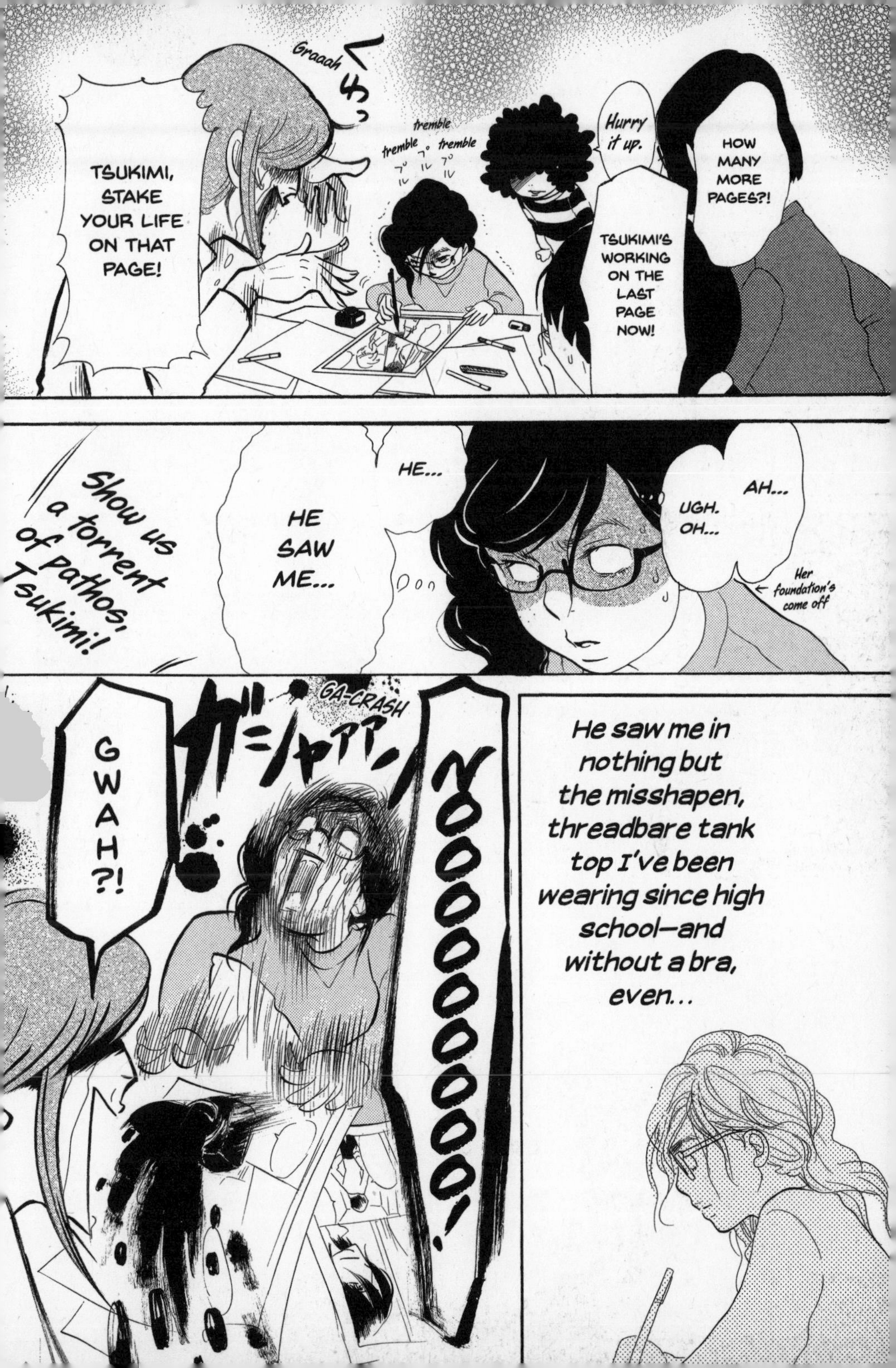
HOW MANY MORE PAGES?!
Hurry it up.
TSUKIMI'S WORKING ON THE LAST PAGE NOW!
tremble tremble tremble
Graaah
TSUKIMI, STAKE YOUR LIFE ON THAT PAGE!
AH... UGH. OH...
Her foundation's come off
HE...
HE SAW ME...
Show us a torrent of pathos, Tsukimi!
He saw me in nothing but the misshapen, threadbare tank top I've been wearing since high school—and without a bra, even...
GA-CRASH
NOOOOOOOOOOOO!
GWAH?!

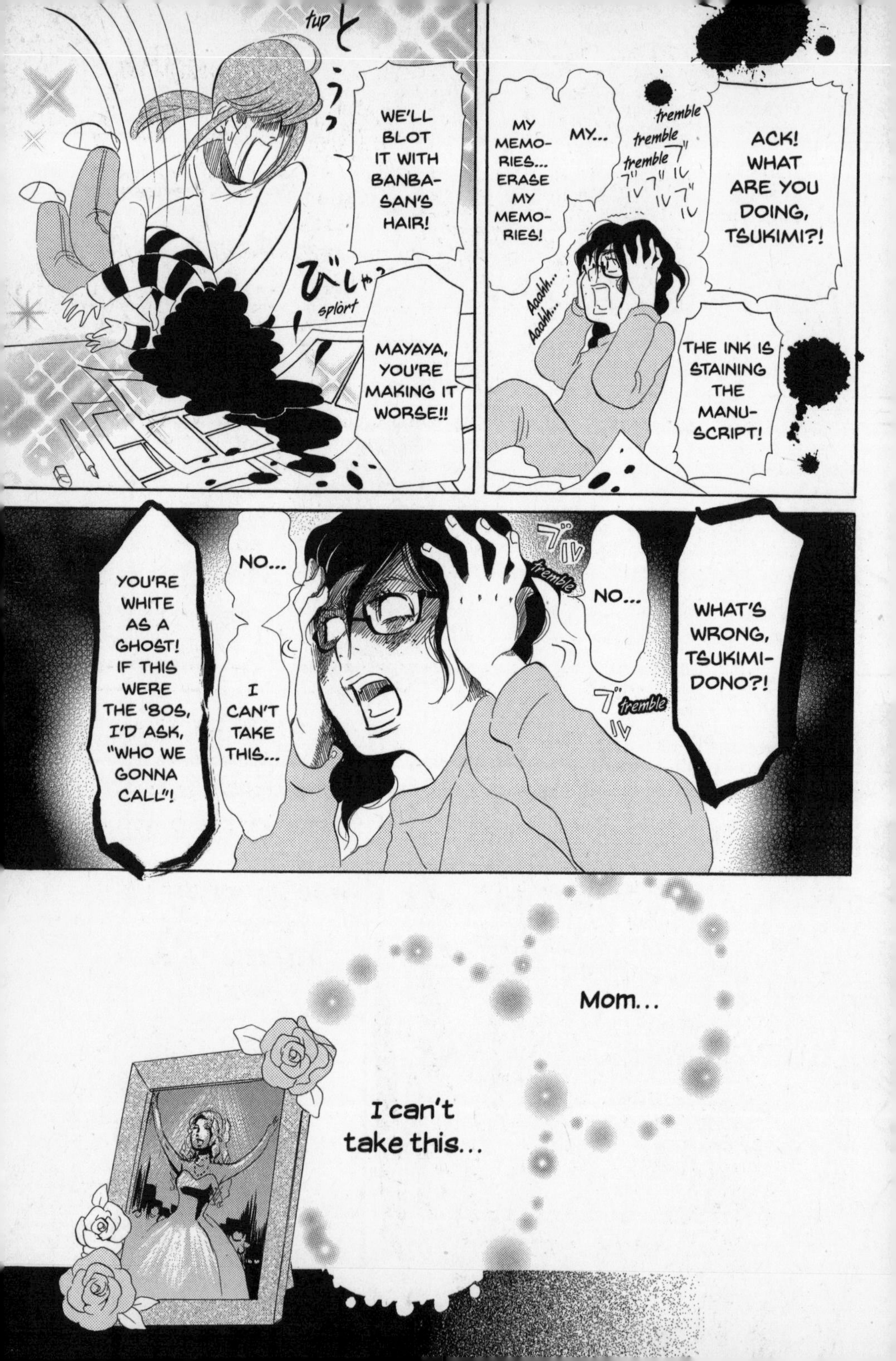

ACK! WHAT ARE YOU DOING, TSUKIMI?!
tremble
tremble
tremble
MY...
MY MEMORIES... ERASE MY MEMORIES!
Aaahh... Aaahh...
THE INK IS STAINING THE MANUSCRIPT!
tup
WE'LL BLOT IT WITH BANBA-SAN'S HAIR!
splort
MAYAYA, YOU'RE MAKING IT WORSE!!
WHAT'S WRONG, TSUKIMI-DONO?!
tremble
NO...
tremble
NO...
I CAN'T TAKE THIS...
YOU'RE WHITE AS A GHOST! IF THIS WERE THE '80S, I'D ASK, "WHO WE GONNA CALL"!
Mom...
I can't take this...

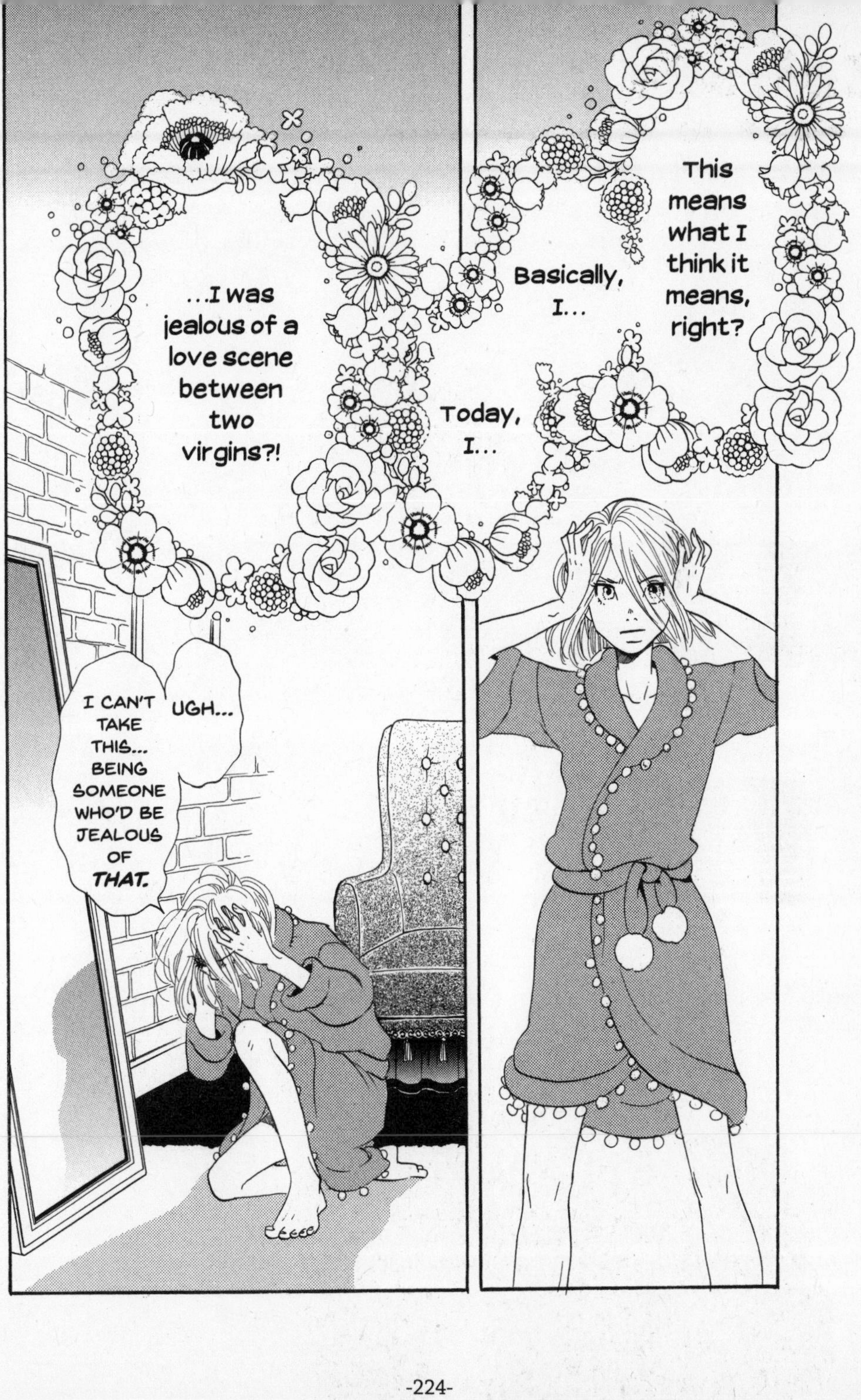
This means what I think it means, right?
Basically, I...
Today, I...
...I was jealous of a love scene between two virgins?!
UGH...
I CAN'T TAKE THIS... BEING SOMEONE WHO'D BE JEALOUS OF *THAT.*

Episode 8
I Want to Be a Jellyfish

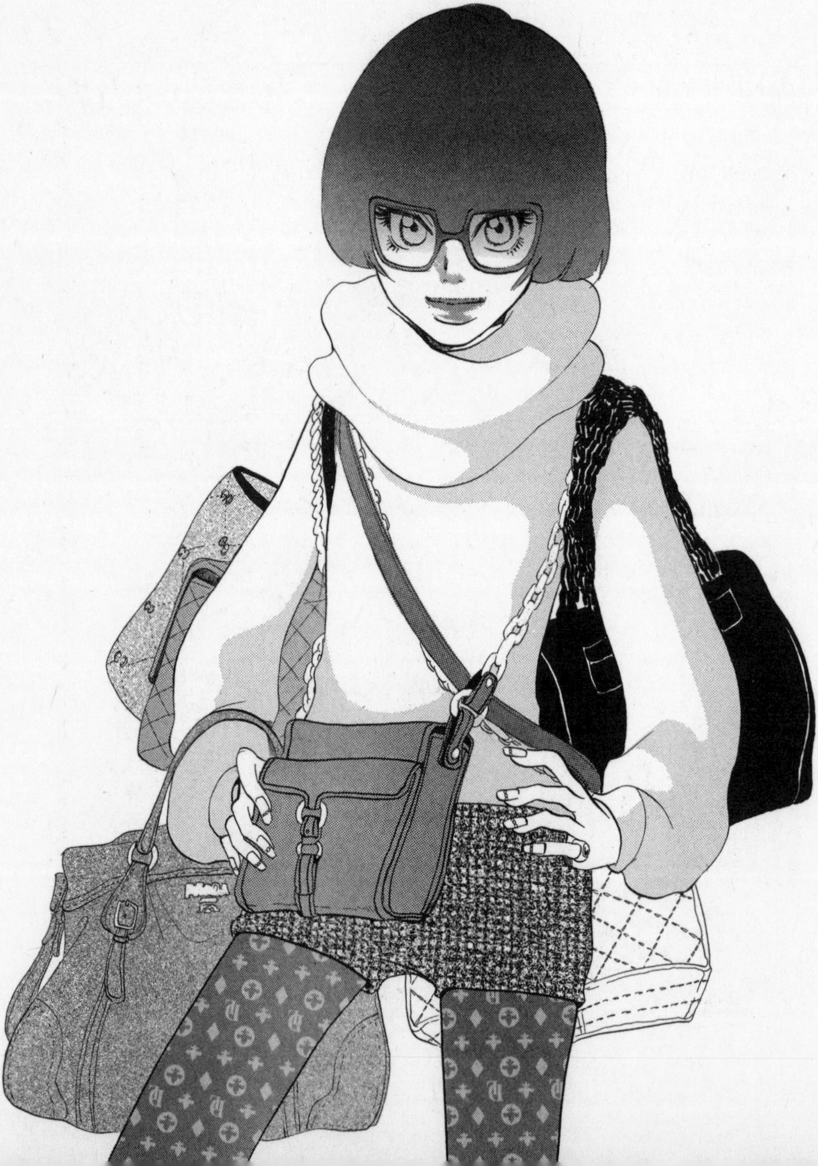

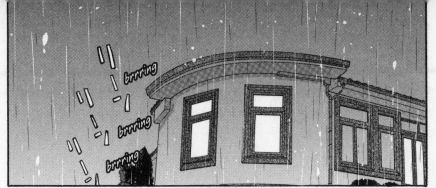

brrring
brrring
brrring
WHAT?
MOTHER, WHAT ARE YOU SAYING?
RIGHT, SO, I DECIDED TO SELL!
PEOPLE HAVE BEEN WANTING TO BUY FOR **YEARS...**
...BUT IT WAS SO HARD TO MAKE UP MY MIND...

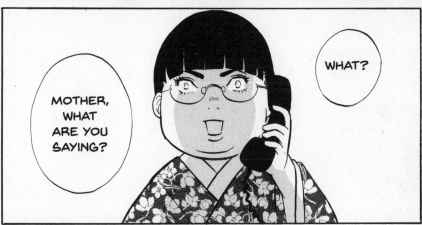

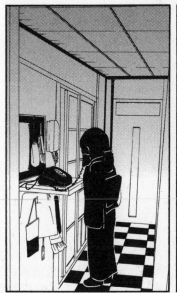

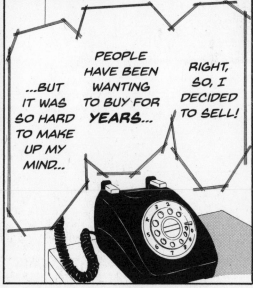

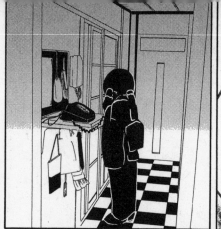

NOW I THINK I'LL QUIT BEING A LANDLADY AND STUDY KOREAN HERE IN KOREA!
I WANT TO MASTER KOREAN NOW, SO WHEN I RUN INTO YONG-SAMA* ON THE STREET SOMEDAY, I CAN STRIKE UP A CONVERSATION WITH HIM!
*Hardcore Japanese fans call Bae Yong-joon this.
SO YOU TELL THE BOARDERS FOR ME, OKAY, HONEY?
TELL THEM, "AMAMIZU-KAN WILL BE GONE IN A YEAR. SORRY!"
zssh
blup

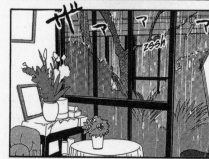

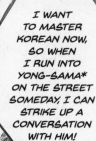

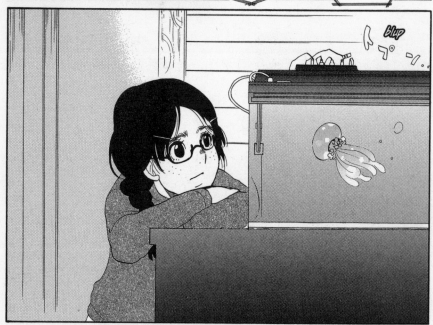

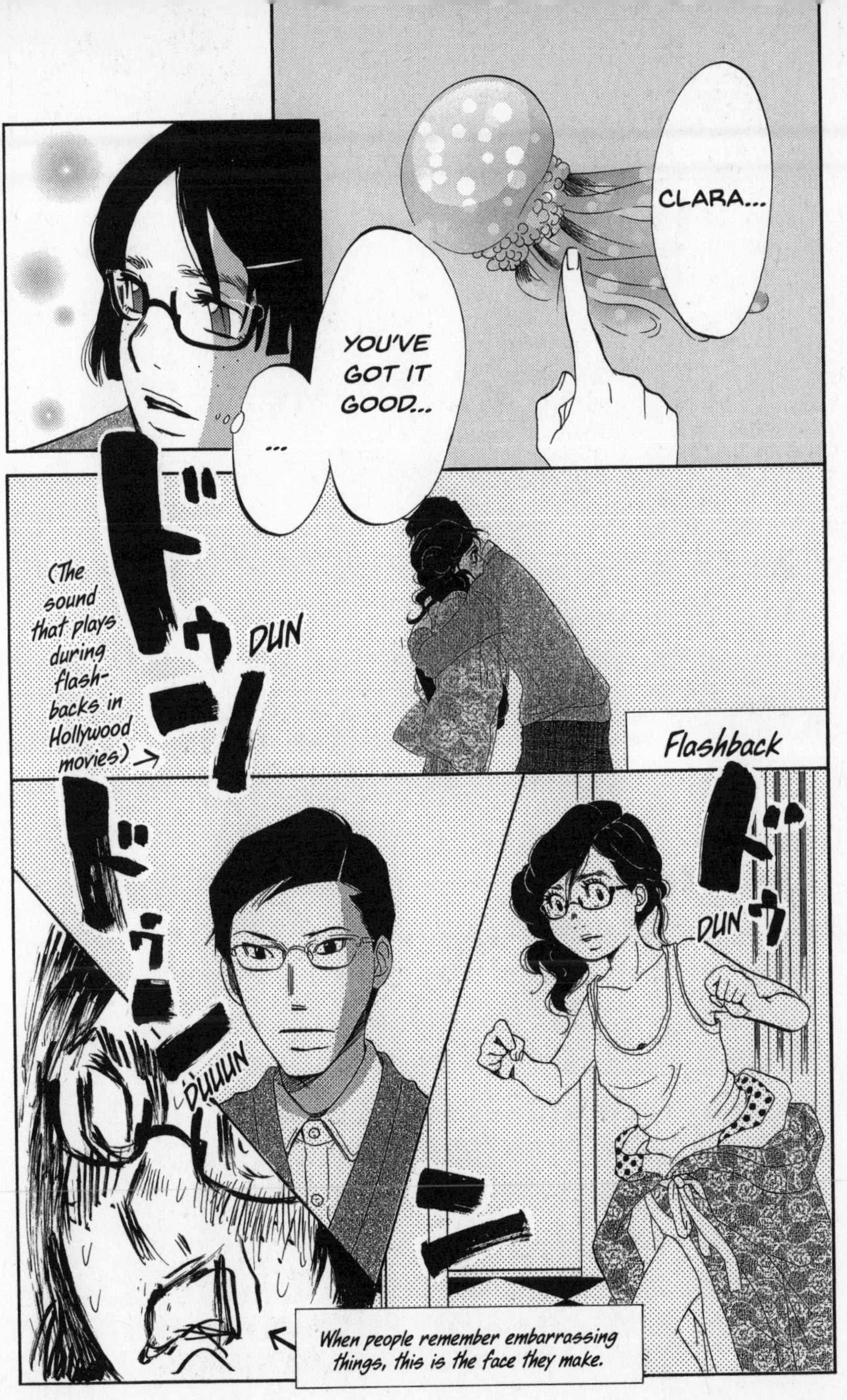

CLARA...
YOU'VE GOT IT GOOD...
...
Flashback
DUN
(The sound that plays during flash-backs in Hollywood movies)
DUN
DUUUN
When people remember embarrassing things, this is the face they make.

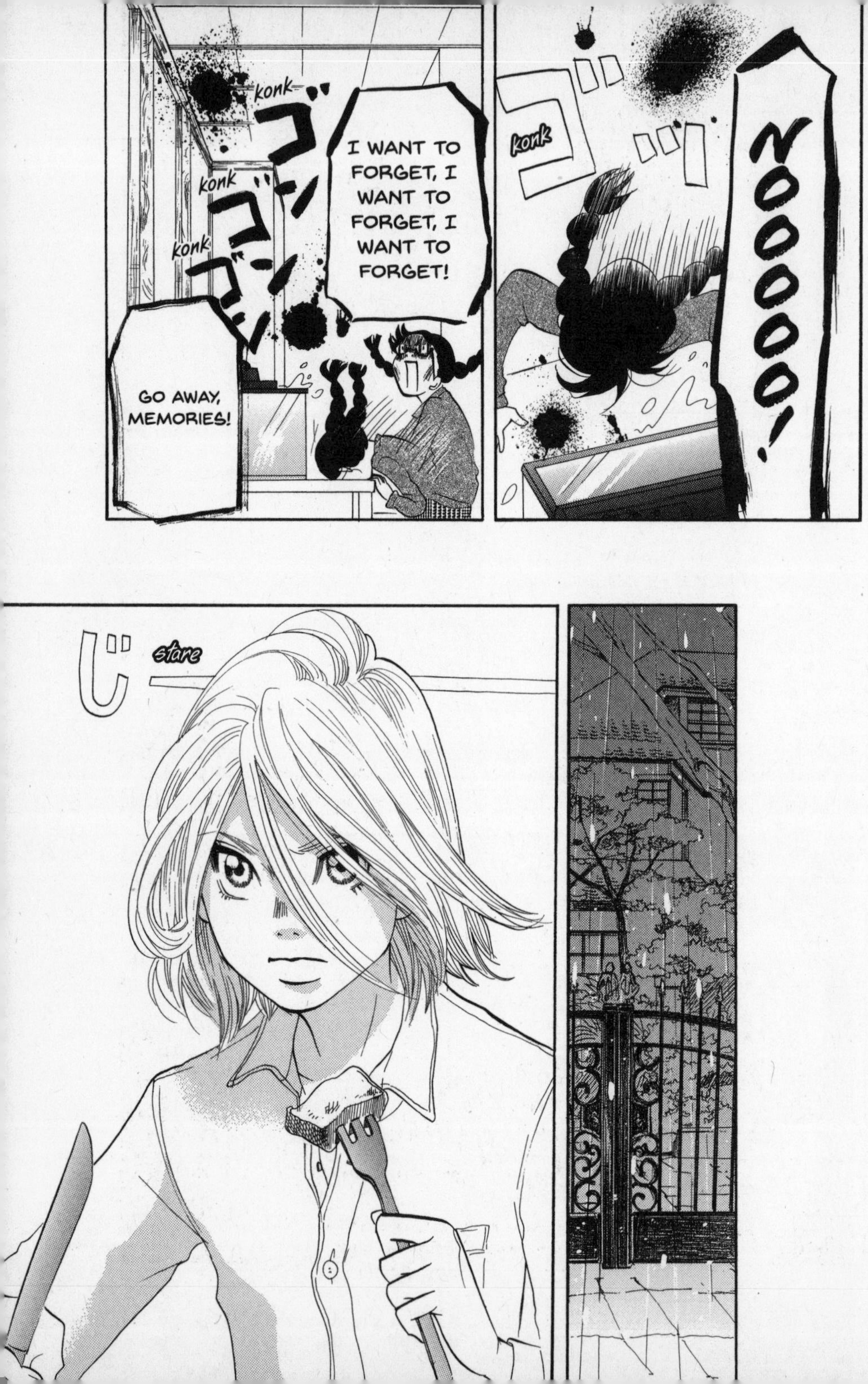
konk
NOOOOOO!
I WANT TO FORGET, I WANT TO FORGET, I WANT TO FORGET!
konk
konk
konk
GO AWAY, MEMORIES!
じー
stare

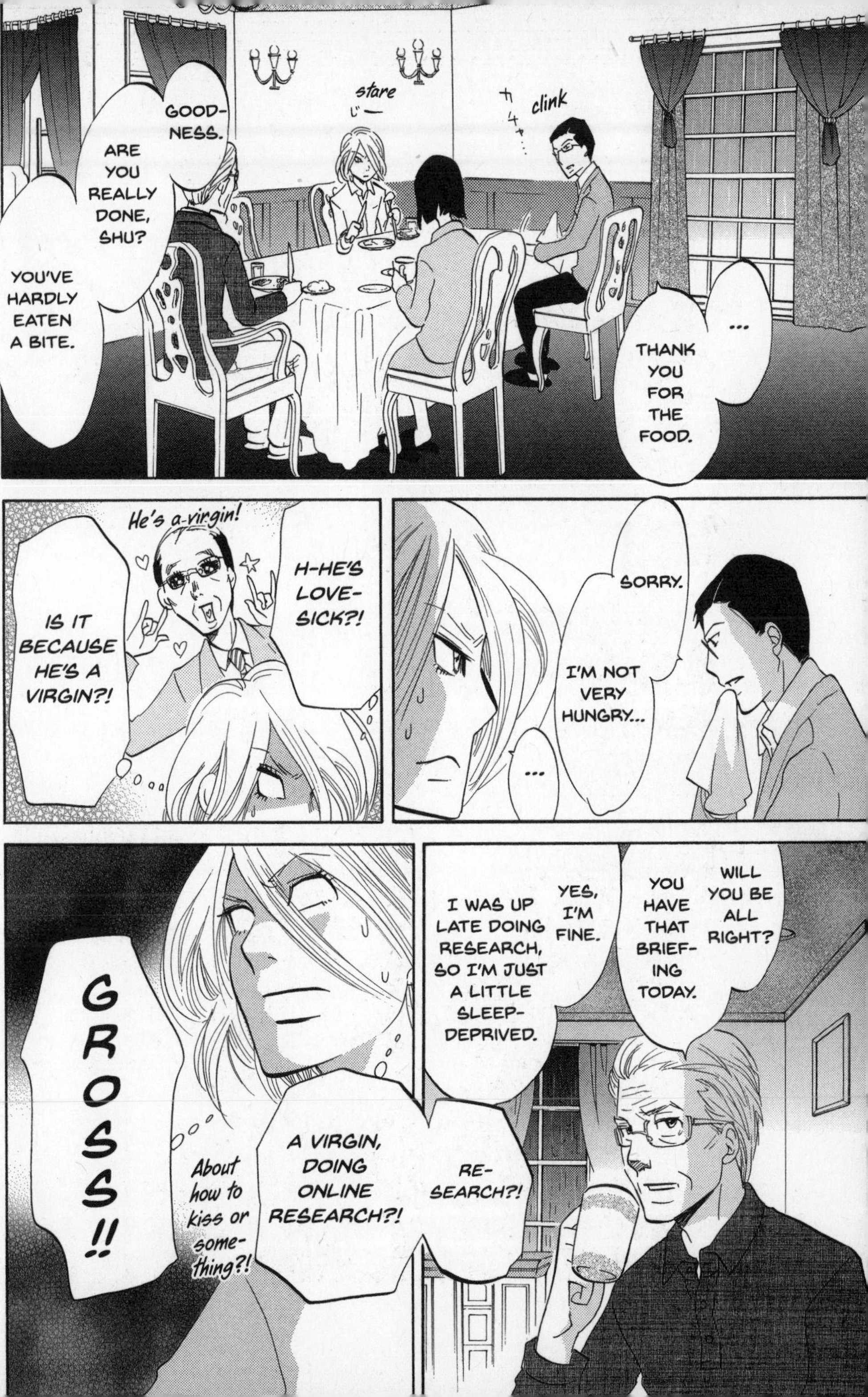
...
THANK YOU FOR THE FOOD.
clink
カチャ…
stare
じー
GOODNESS.
ARE YOU REALLY DONE, SHU?
YOU'VE HARDLY EATEN A BITE.
SORRY.
I'M NOT VERY HUNGRY...
...
H-HE'S LOVE-SICK?!
He's a virgin!
IS IT BECAUSE HE'S A VIRGIN?!
WILL YOU BE ALL RIGHT?
YOU HAVE THAT BRIEF-ING TODAY.
YES, I'M FINE.
I WAS UP LATE DOING RESEARCH, SO I'M JUST A LITTLE SLEEP-DEPRIVED.
RE-SEARCH?!
A VIRGIN, DOING ONLINE RESEARCH?!
About how to kiss or some-thing?!
GROSS!!

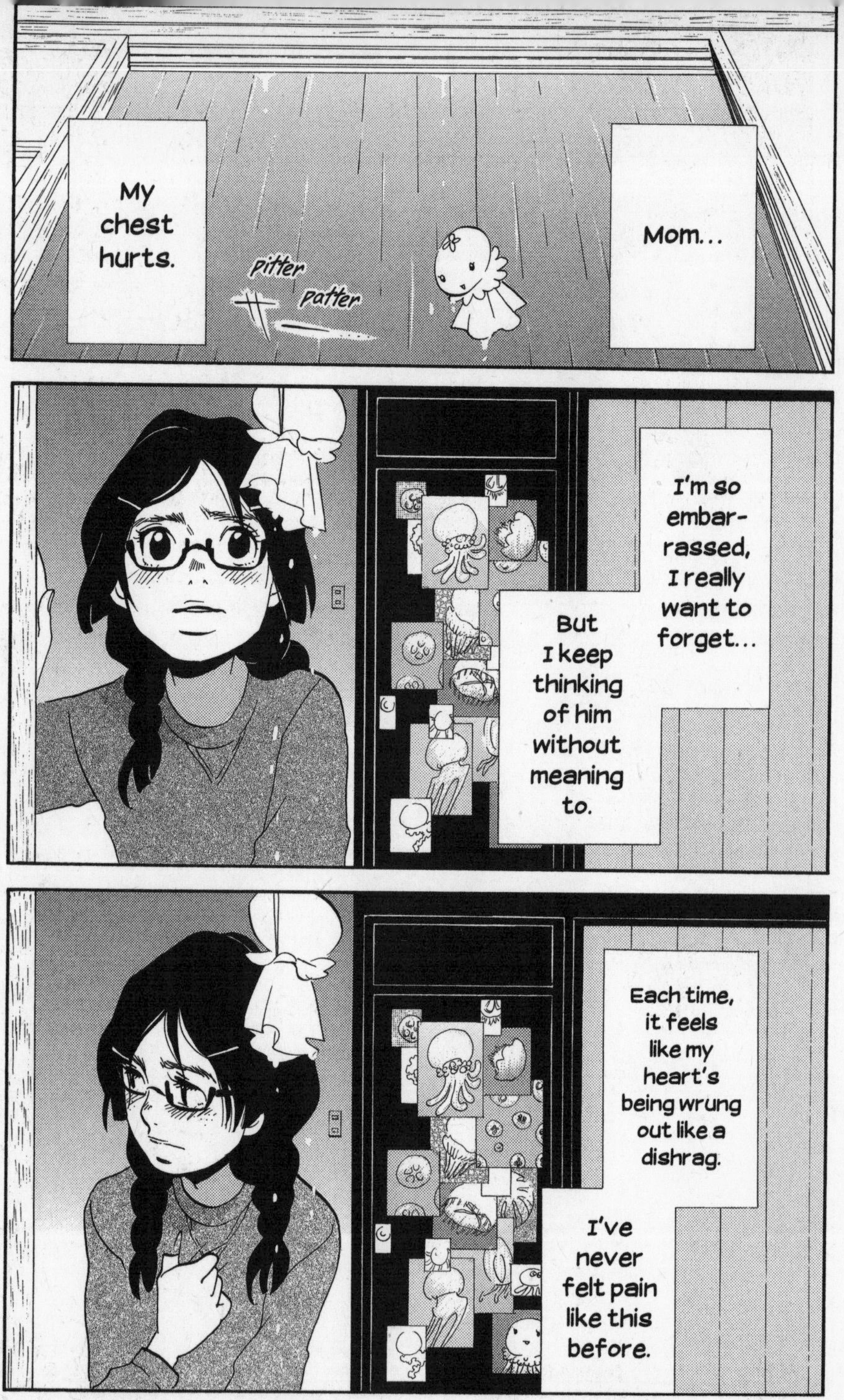
Mom…
My chest hurts.
pitter patter
I'm so embar-rassed, I really want to forget…
But I keep thinking of him without meaning to.
Each time, it feels like my heart's being wrung out like a dishrag.
I've never felt pain like this before.

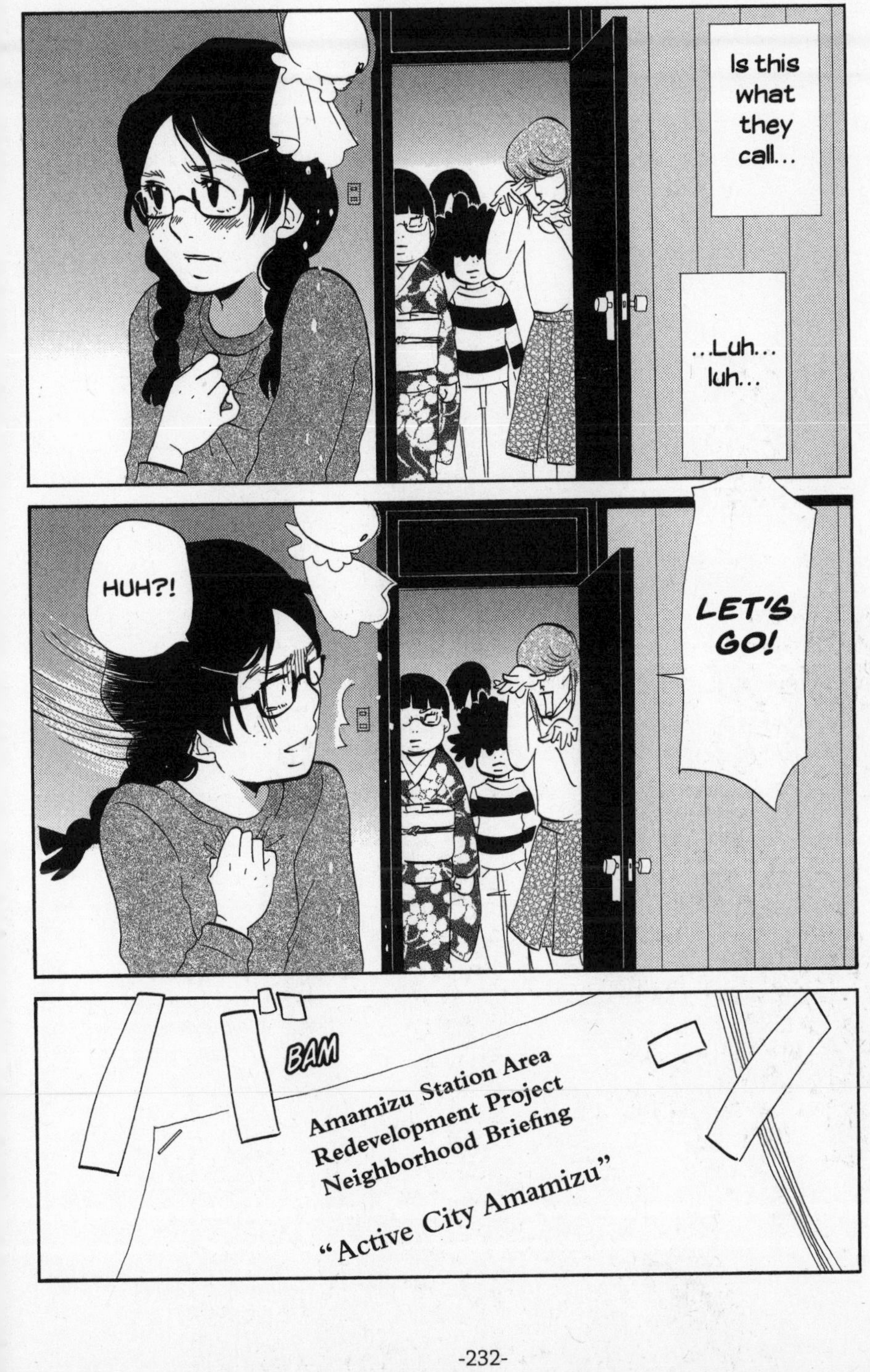

Is this what they call...
...Luh... luh...
LET'S GO!
HUH?!
BAM
Amamizu Station Area Redevelopment Project Neighborhood Briefing
"Active City Amamizu"

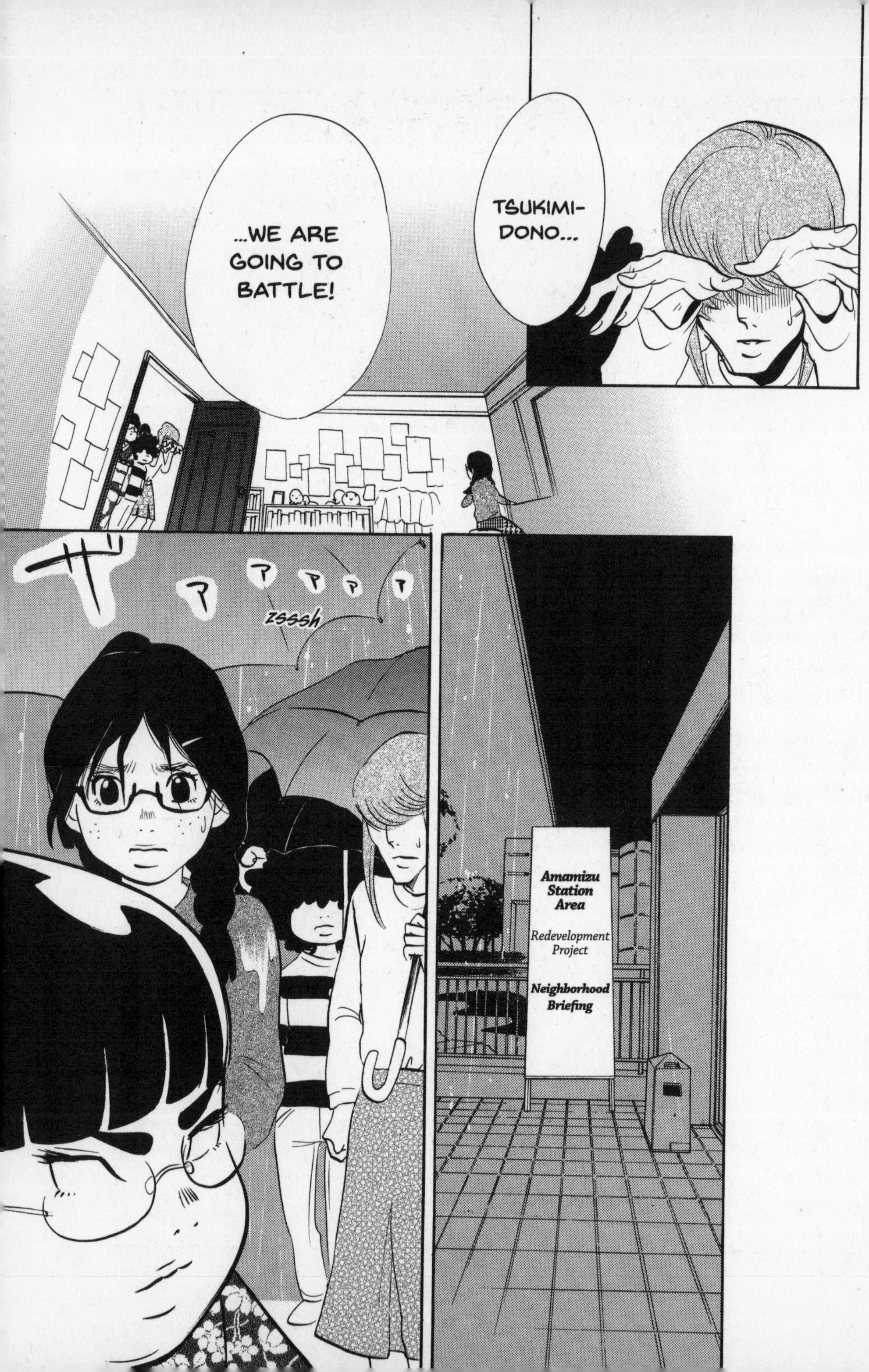
TSUKIMI-DONO...
...WE ARE GOING TO BATTLE!
Amamizu Station Area
Redevelopment Project
Neighborhood Briefing
ザァァァァァ
zsssh

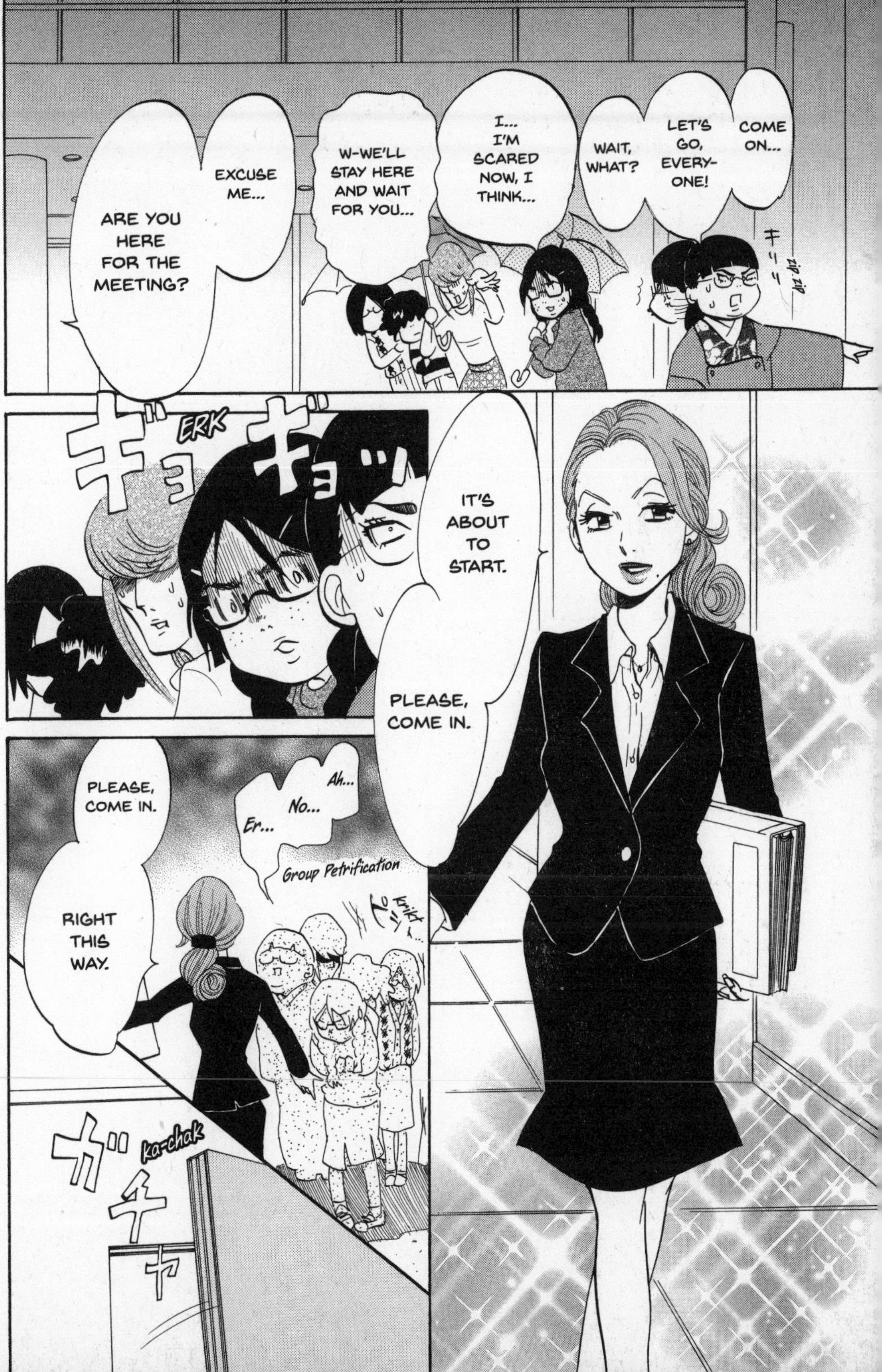
COME ON...
zip zip
LET'S GO, EVERYONE!
WAIT, WHAT?
I... I'M SCARED NOW, I THINK...
W-WE'LL STAY HERE AND WAIT FOR YOU...
EXCUSE ME...
ARE YOU HERE FOR THE MEETING?
IT'S ABOUT TO START.
PLEASE, COME IN.
ERK
PLEASE, COME IN.
RIGHT THIS WAY.
Ah... No... Er...
Group Petrification
ka-chak

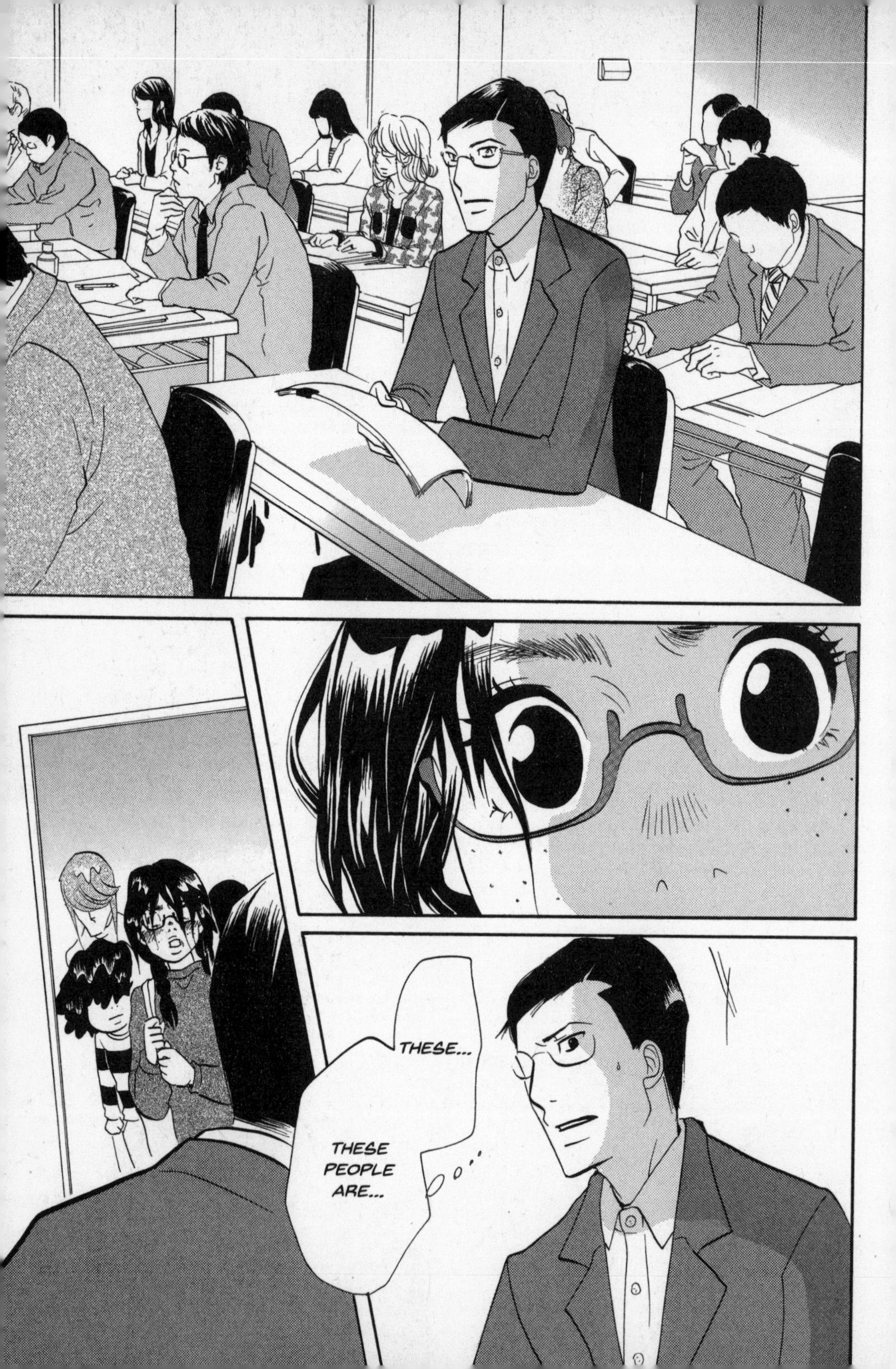
THESE...
THESE PEOPLE ARE...

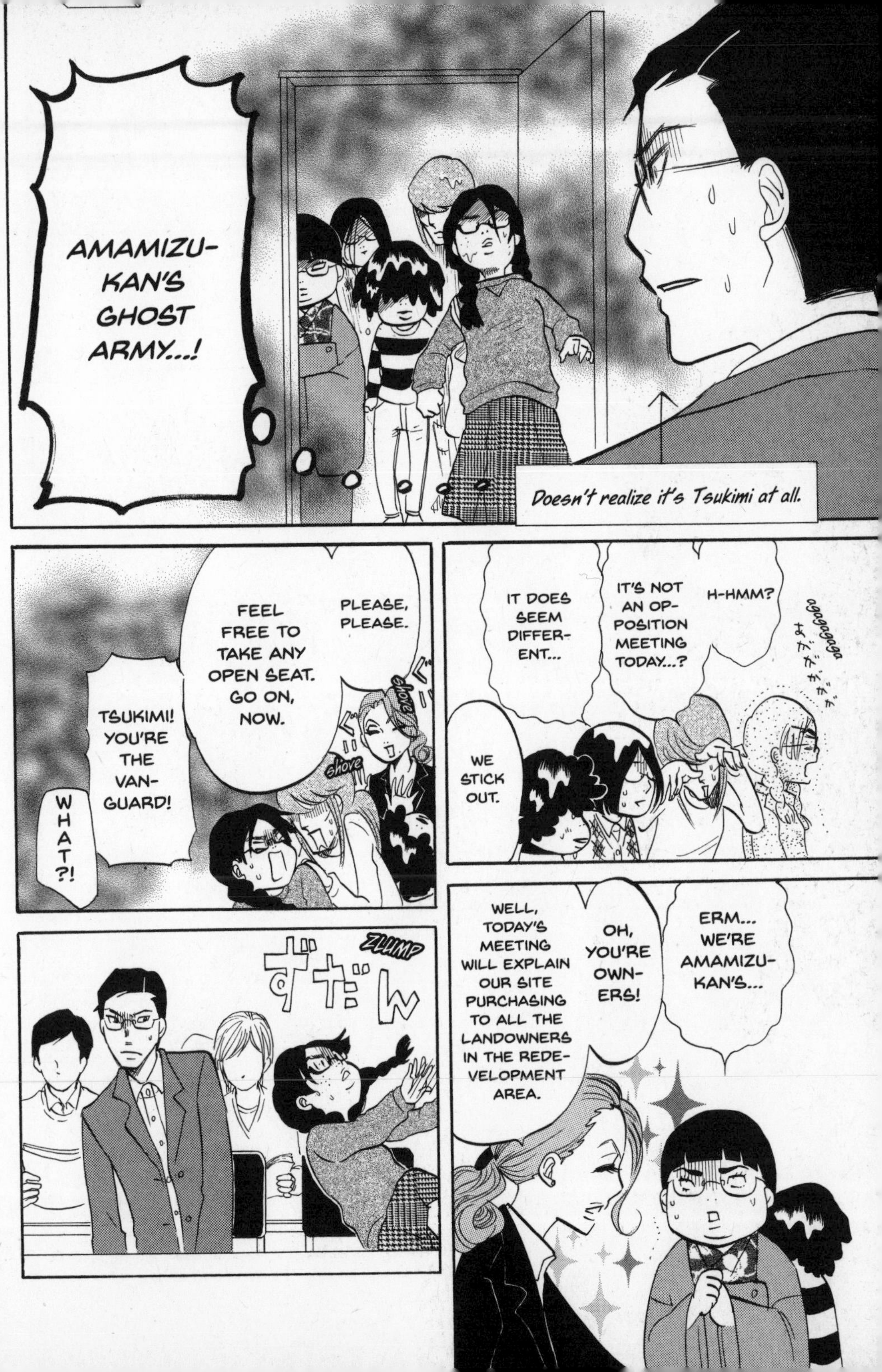
AMAMIZU-KAN'S GHOST ARMY...!
Doesn't realize it's Tsukimi at all.
H-HMM?
IT'S NOT AN OPPOSITION MEETING TODAY...?
IT DOES SEEM DIFFERENT...
agagagaga
WE STICK OUT.
PLEASE, PLEASE.
FEEL FREE TO TAKE ANY OPEN SEAT. GO ON, NOW.
shove
shove
TSUKIMI! YOU'RE THE VANGUARD!
WHAT?!
ERM... WE'RE AMAMIZU-KAN'S...
OH, YOU'RE OWNERS!
WELL, TODAY'S MEETING WILL EXPLAIN OUR SITE PURCHASING TO ALL THE LANDOWNERS IN THE REDEVELOPMENT AREA.
ずだん
ZLUMP

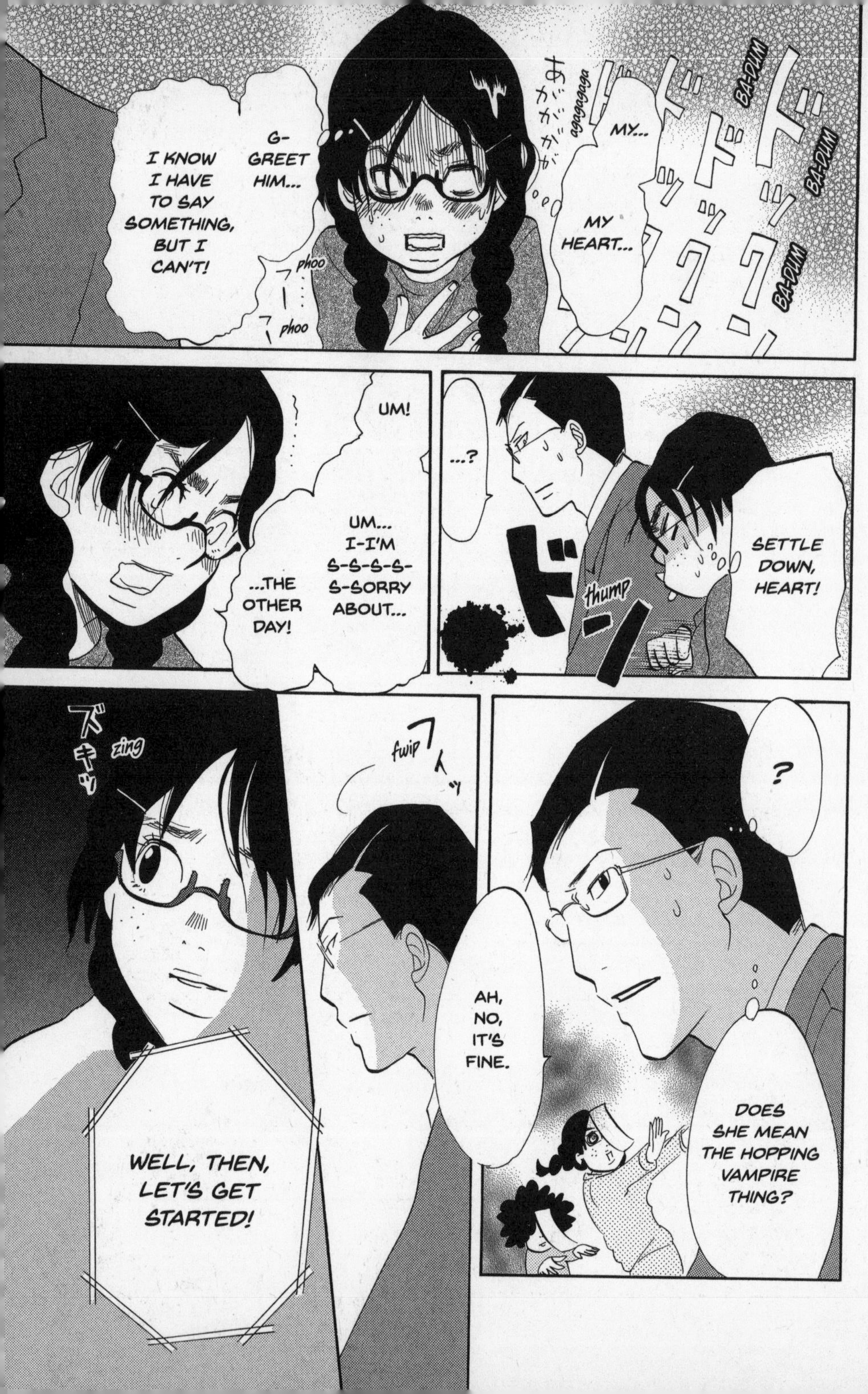

ドドドクンドクン
BA-DUMP
BA-DUMP
BA-DUMP
BA-DUMP
MY... MY HEART...
あががががが
agagagaga
G-GREET HIM...
I KNOW I HAVE TO SAY SOMETHING, BUT I CAN'T!
フーフー
phoo
phoo
SETTLE DOWN, HEART!
ドンッ
thump
...?
UM!
UM... I-I'M S-S-S-S-S-SORRY ABOUT...
...THE OTHER DAY!
?
DOES SHE MEAN THE HOPPING VAMPIRE THING?
フイッ
fwip
AH, NO, IT'S FINE.
ズキッ
zing
WELL, THEN, LET'S GET STARTED!

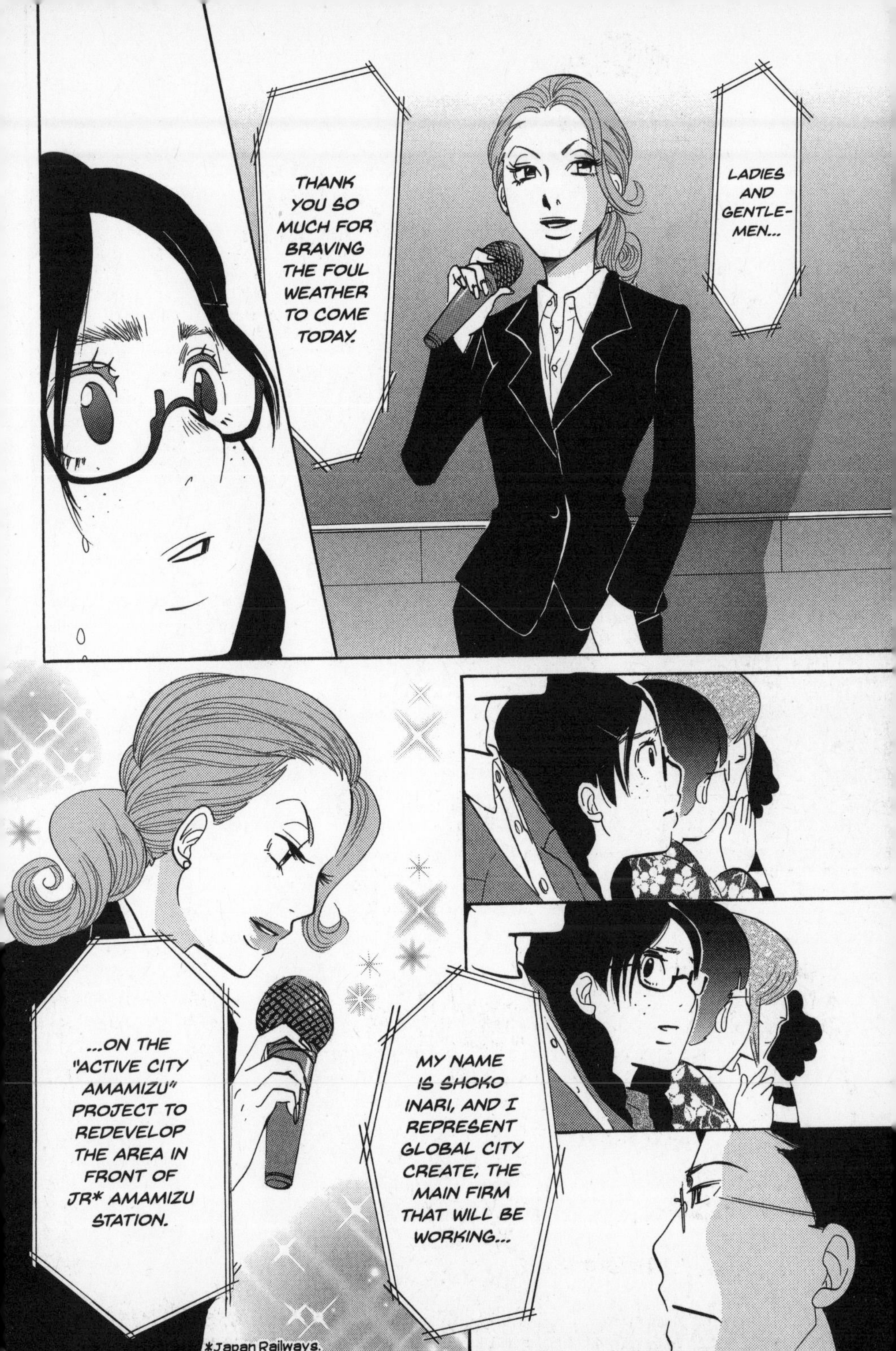
LADIES AND GENTLE-MEN...
THANK YOU SO MUCH FOR BRAVING THE FOUL WEATHER TO COME TODAY.
MY NAME IS SHOKO INARI, AND I REPRESENT GLOBAL CITY CREATE, THE MAIN FIRM THAT WILL BE WORKING...
...ON THE "ACTIVE CITY AMAMIZU" PROJECT TO REDEVELOP THE AREA IN FRONT OF JR* AMAMIZU STATION.

*Japan Railways.

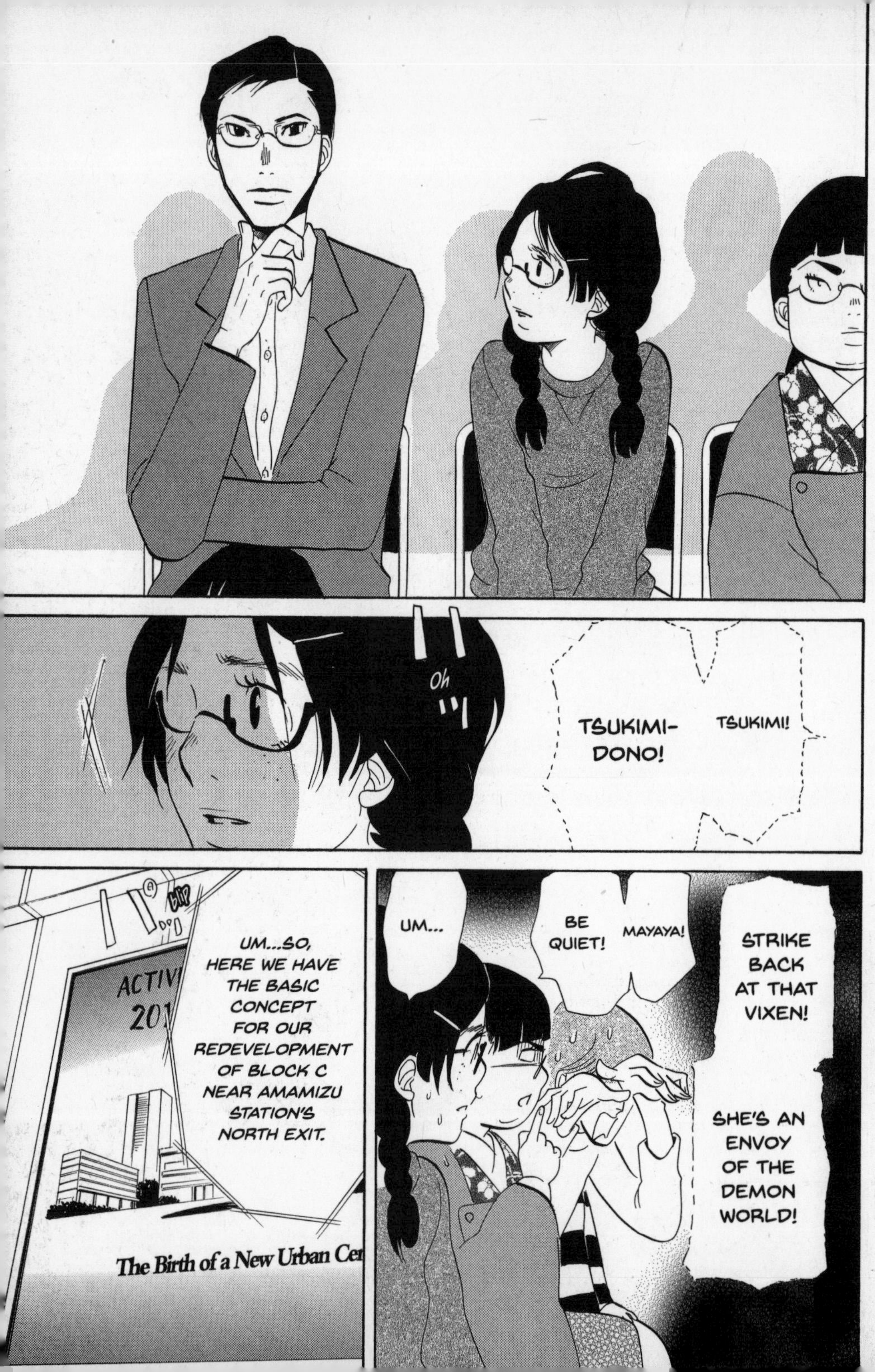
TSUKIMI!
TSUKIMI-DONO!
Oh
STRIKE BACK AT THAT VIXEN!
SHE'S AN ENVOY OF THE DEMON WORLD!
MAYAYA!
BE QUIET!
UM...
blip
UM...SO, HERE WE HAVE THE BASIC CONCEPT FOR OUR REDEVELOPMENT OF BLOCK C NEAR AMAMIZU STATION'S NORTH EXIT.
ACTIV
201
The Birth of a New Urban Cen

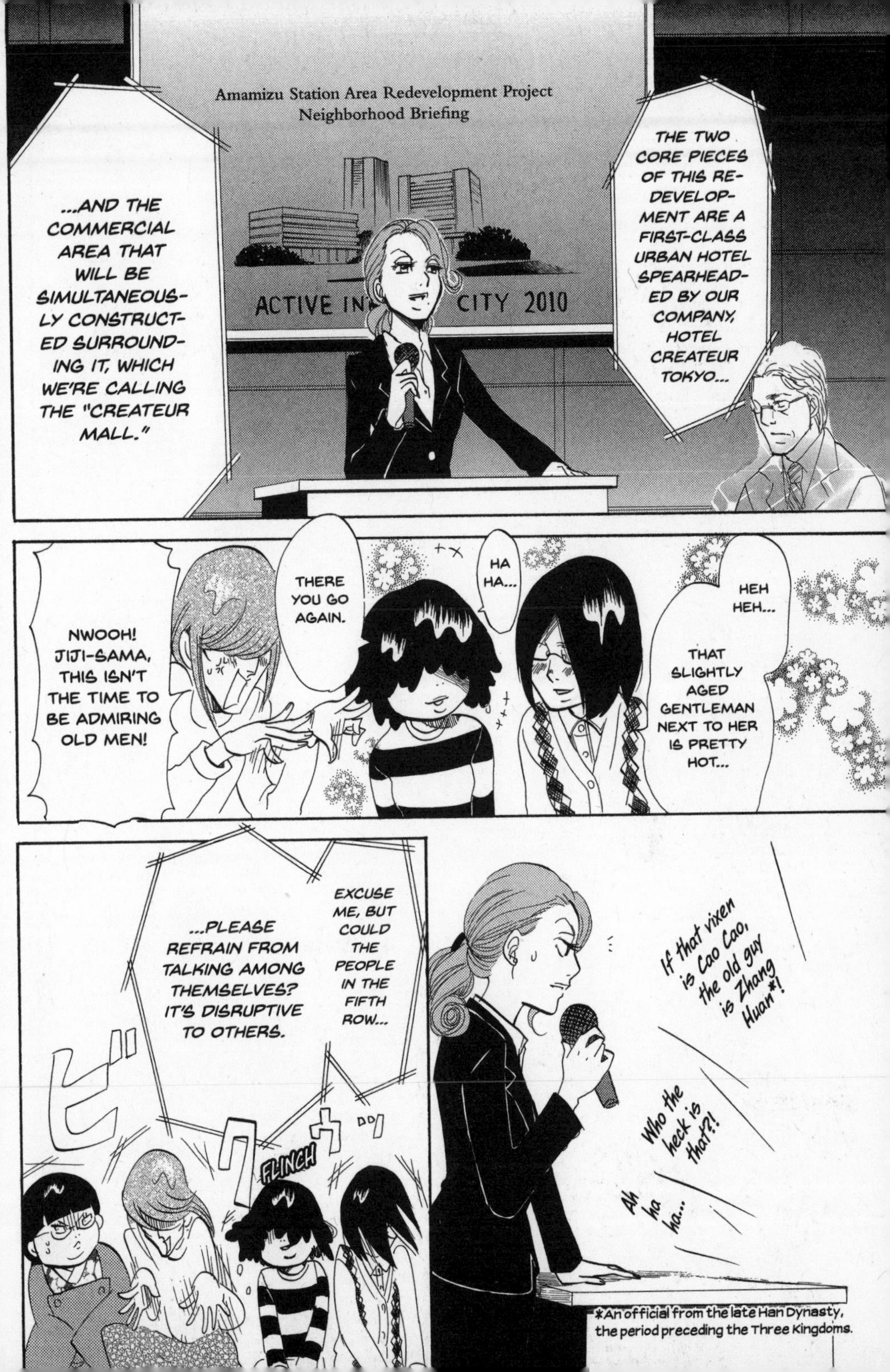
Amamizu Station Area Redevelopment Project
Neighborhood Briefing
ACTIVE IN
CITY 2010
THE TWO CORE PIECES OF THIS RE-DEVELOP-MENT ARE A FIRST-CLASS URBAN HOTEL SPEARHEAD-ED BY OUR COMPANY, HOTEL CREATEUR TOKYO...
...AND THE COMMERCIAL AREA THAT WILL BE SIMULTANEOUS-LY CONSTRUCT-ED SURROUND-ING IT, WHICH WE'RE CALLING THE "CREATEUR MALL."
HEH HEH...
THAT SLIGHTLY AGED GENTLEMAN NEXT TO HER IS PRETTY HOT...
HA HA...
THERE YOU GO AGAIN.
NWOOH! JIJI-SAMA, THIS ISN'T THE TIME TO BE ADMIRING OLD MEN!
If that vixen is Cao Cao, the old guy is Zhang Huan*!
Who the heck is that?!
Ah ha ha...
*An official from the late Han Dynasty, the period preceding the Three Kingdoms.
EXCUSE ME, BUT COULD THE PEOPLE IN THE FIFTH ROW...
...PLEASE REFRAIN FROM TALKING AMONG THEMSELVES? IT'S DISRUPTIVE TO OTHERS.
FLINCH

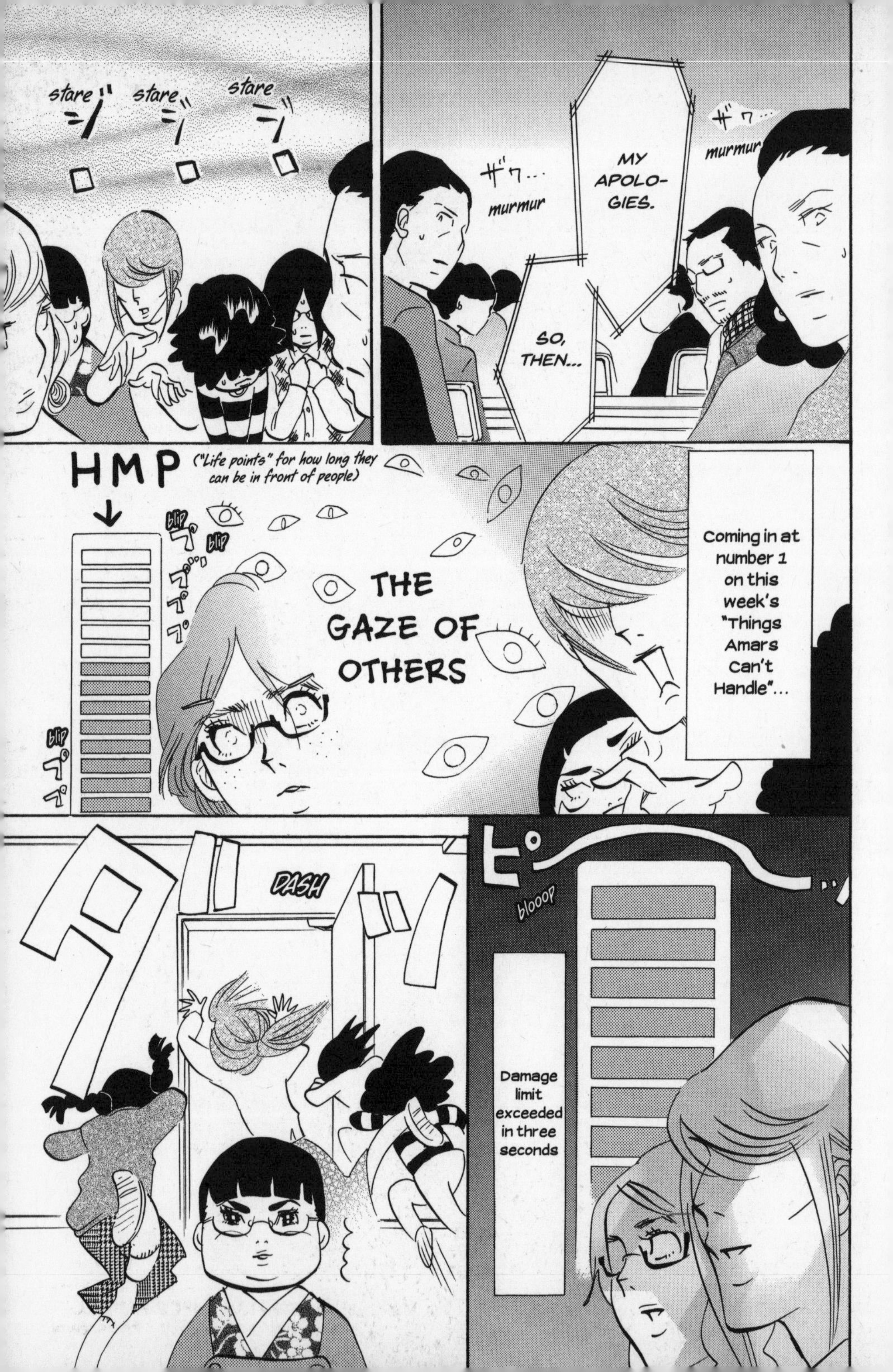
murmur
MY APOLOGIES.
murmur
SO, THEN...
stare
stare
stare
Coming in at number 1 on this week's "Things Amars Can't Handle"...
THE GAZE OF OTHERS
HMP ("Life points" for how long they can be in front of people)
blip
blip
blip
bloooop
Damage limit exceeded in three seconds
DASH

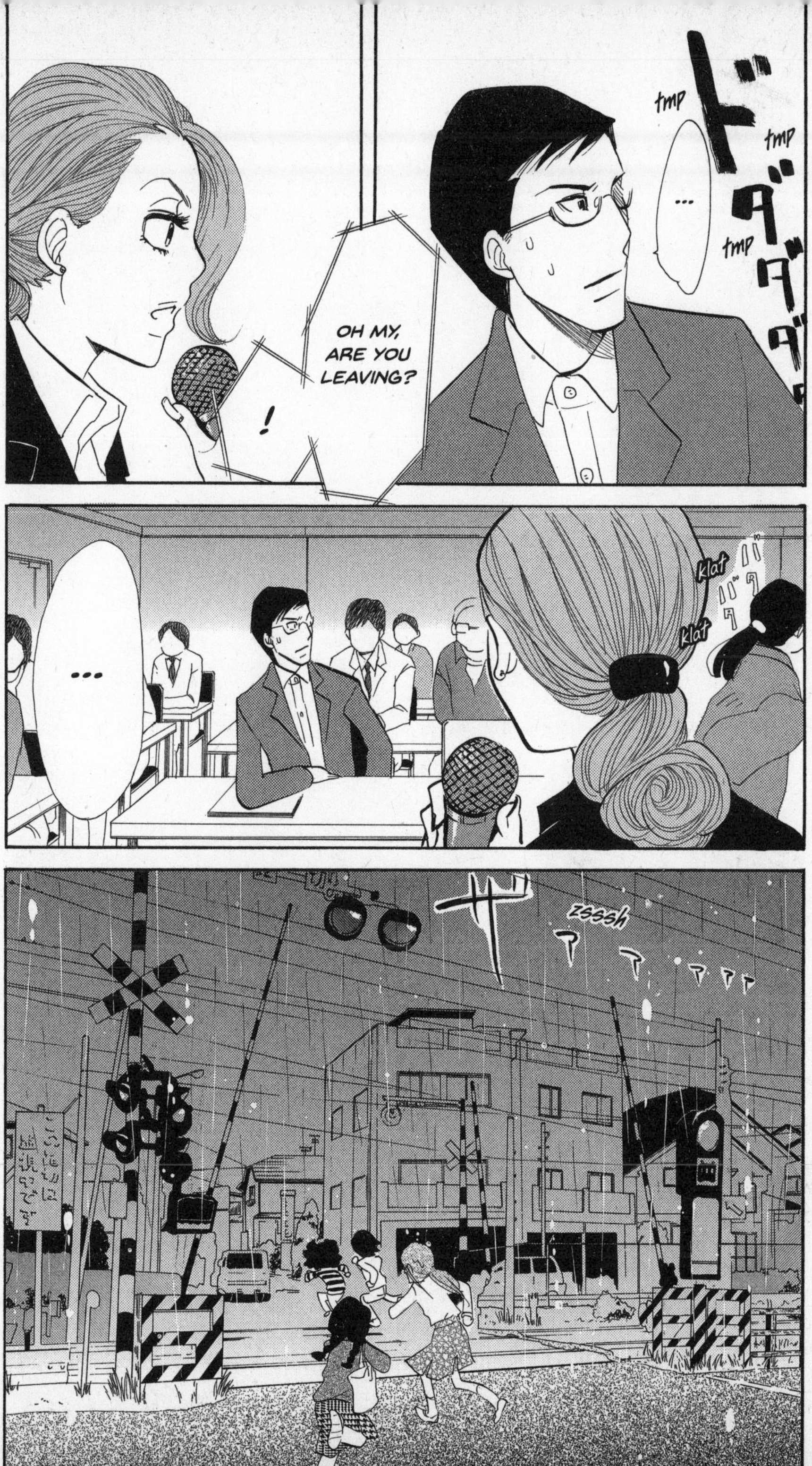
ドダダダ
tmp
tmp
tmp
...
OH MY, ARE YOU LEAVING?
!
バタバタ
klat
klat
...
ザァァァァ
zsssh

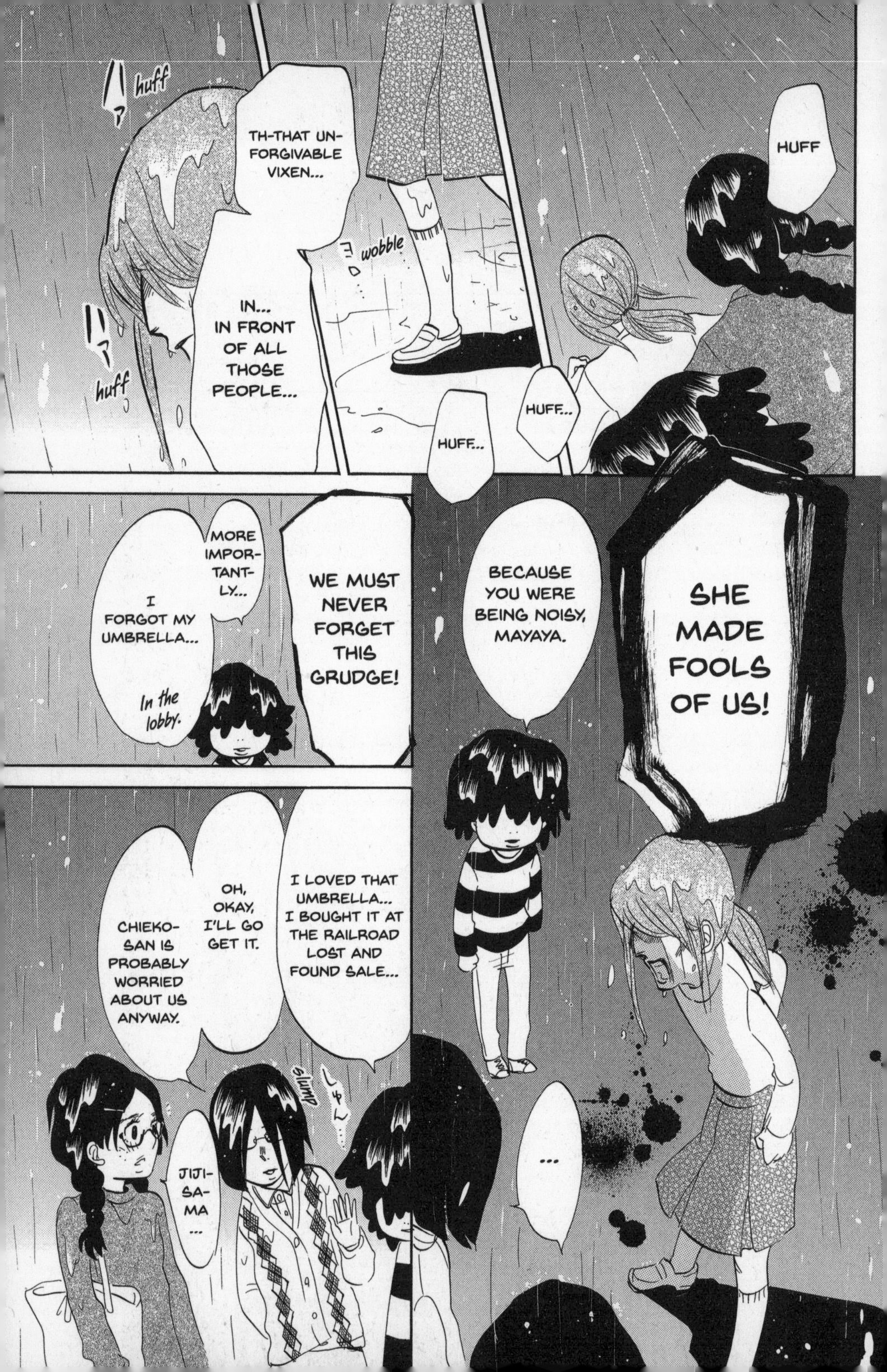
HUFF
HUFF...
HUFF...
huff
TH-THAT UNFORGIVABLE VIXEN...
wobble
IN... IN FRONT OF ALL THOSE PEOPLE...
huff
SHE MADE FOOLS OF US!
BECAUSE YOU WERE BEING NOISY, MAYAYA.
...
WE MUST NEVER FORGET THIS GRUDGE!
MORE IMPORTANTLY...
I FORGOT MY UMBRELLA...
In the lobby.
I LOVED THAT UMBRELLA... I BOUGHT IT AT THE RAILROAD LOST AND FOUND SALE...
OH, OKAY, I'LL GO GET IT.
CHIEKO-SAN IS PROBABLY WORRIED ABOUT US ANYWAY.
slump
JIJI-SAMA...

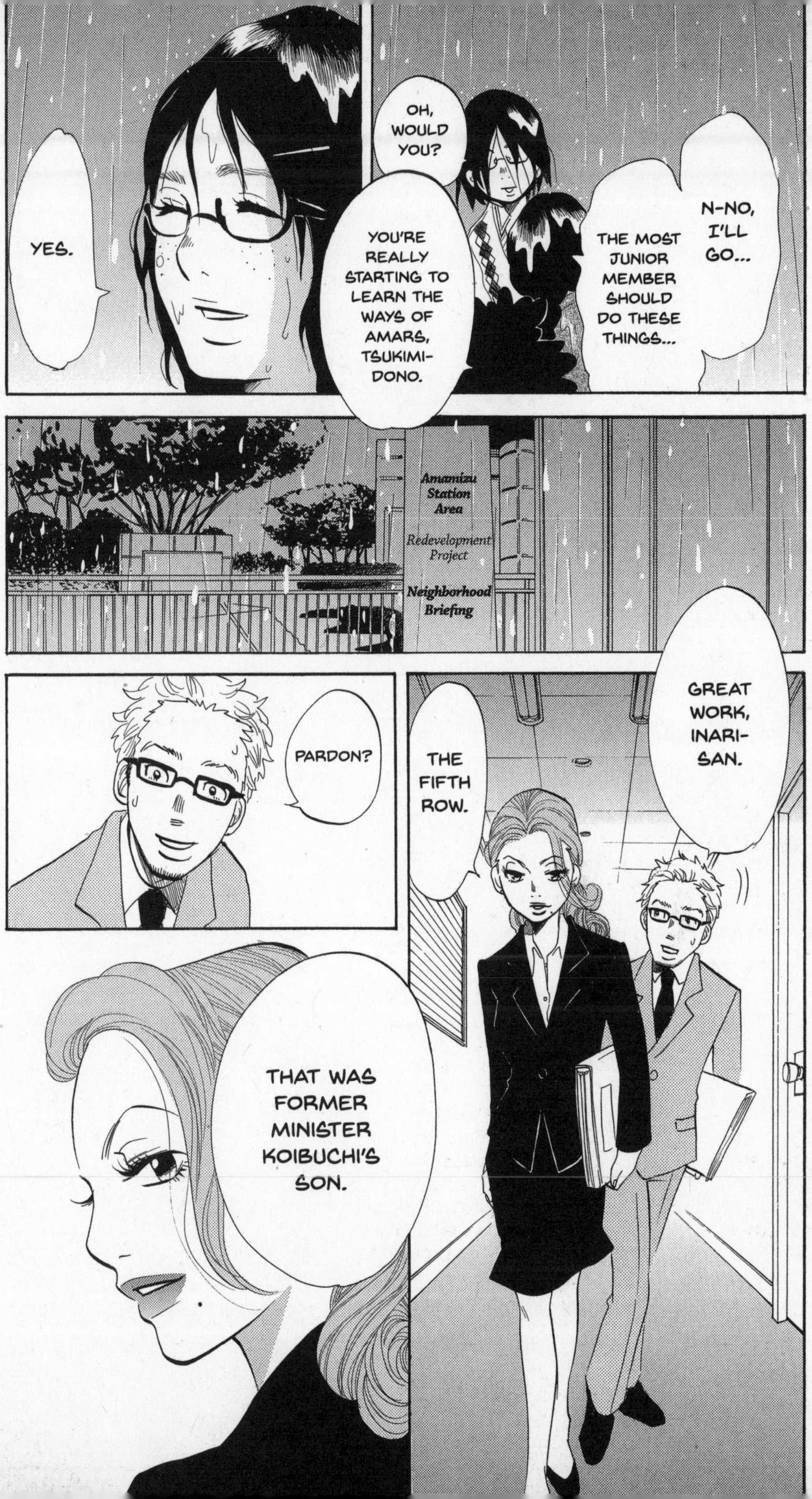
N-NO, I'LL GO...
THE MOST JUNIOR MEMBER SHOULD DO THESE THINGS...
OH, WOULD YOU?
YOU'RE REALLY STARTING TO LEARN THE WAYS OF AMARS, TSUKIMI-DONO.
YES.
Amamizu Station Area
Redevelopment Project
Neighborhood Briefing
GREAT WORK, INARI-SAN.
THE FIFTH ROW.
PARDON?
THAT WAS FORMER MINISTER KOIBUCHI'S SON.

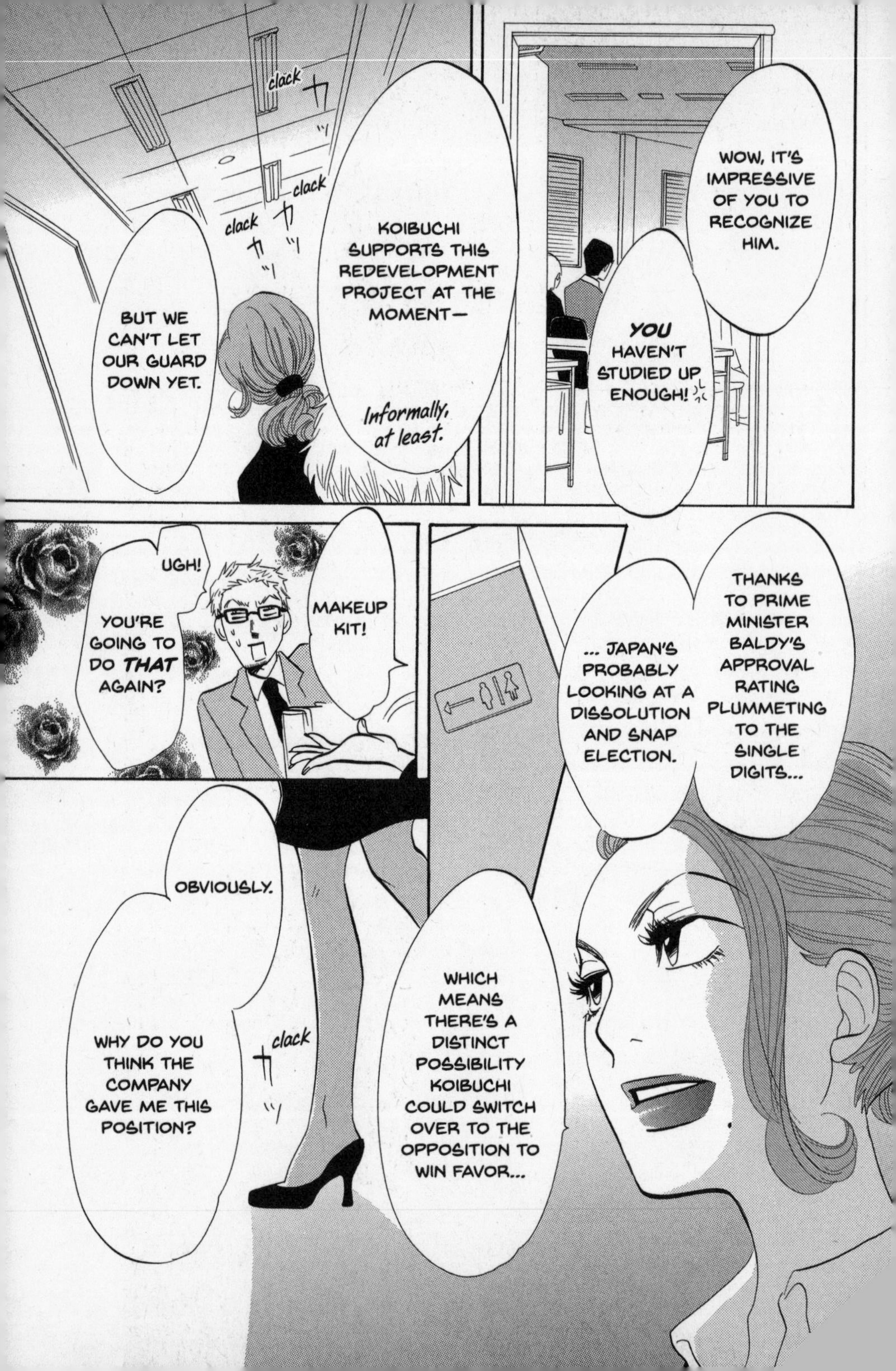
WOW, IT'S IMPRESSIVE OF YOU TO RECOGNIZE HIM.
YOU HAVEN'T STUDIED UP ENOUGH!
KOIBUCHI SUPPORTS THIS REDEVELOPMENT PROJECT AT THE MOMENT— *Informally, at least.*
clack
clack
clack
BUT WE CAN'T LET OUR GUARD DOWN YET.
THANKS TO PRIME MINISTER BALDY'S APPROVAL RATING PLUMMETING TO THE SINGLE DIGITS...
... JAPAN'S PROBABLY LOOKING AT A DISSOLUTION AND SNAP ELECTION.
MAKEUP KIT!
UGH!
YOU'RE GOING TO DO *THAT* AGAIN?
WHICH MEANS THERE'S A DISTINCT POSSIBILITY KOIBUCHI COULD SWITCH OVER TO THE OPPOSITION TO WIN FAVOR...
clack
OBVIOUSLY.
WHY DO YOU THINK THE COMPANY GAVE ME THIS POSITION?

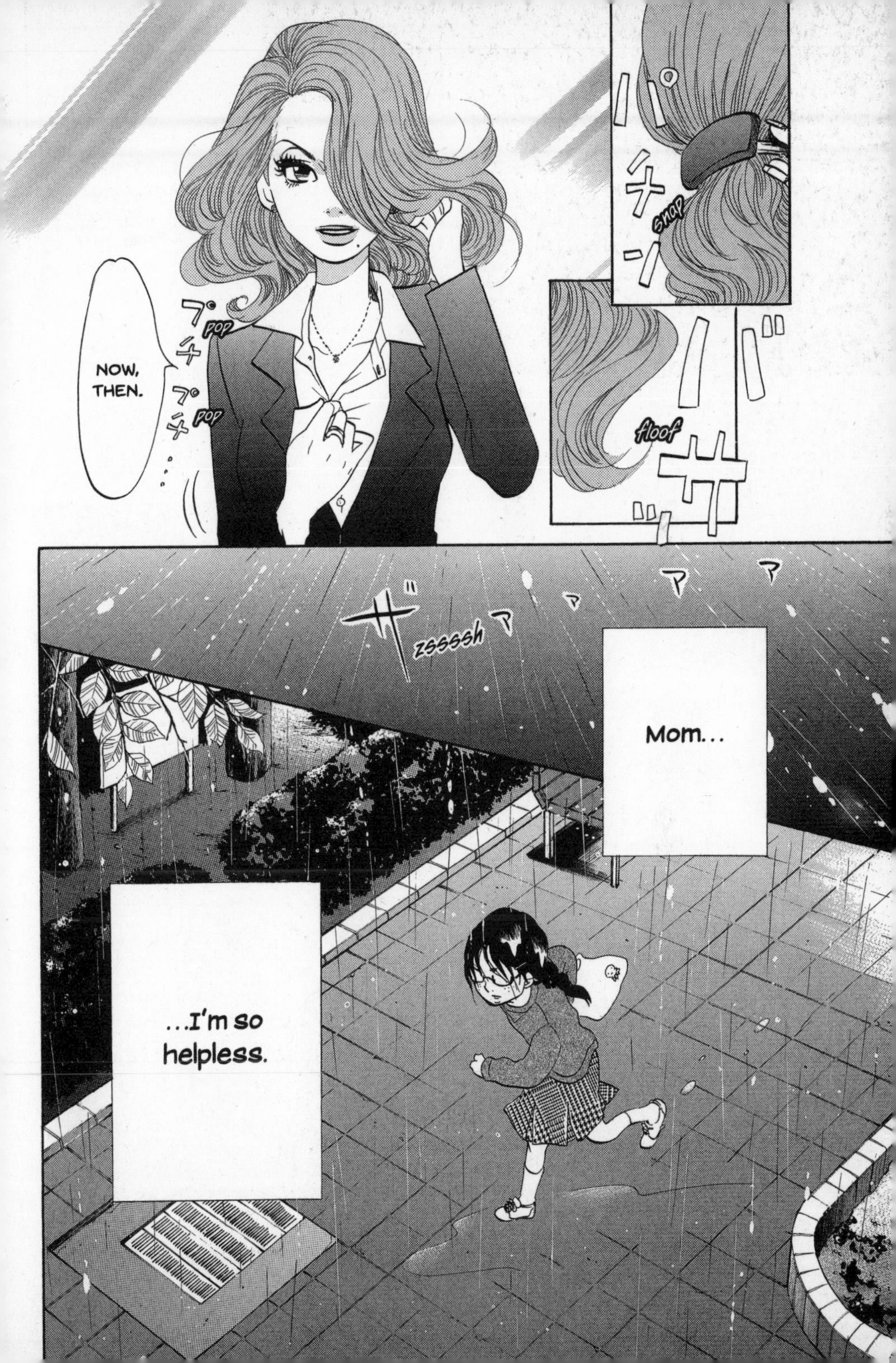

パチン
snap
バサッ
floof
プチプチ…
pop
pop
NOW, THEN.
ザアアアア
zssssh
Mom...
...I'm so helpless.

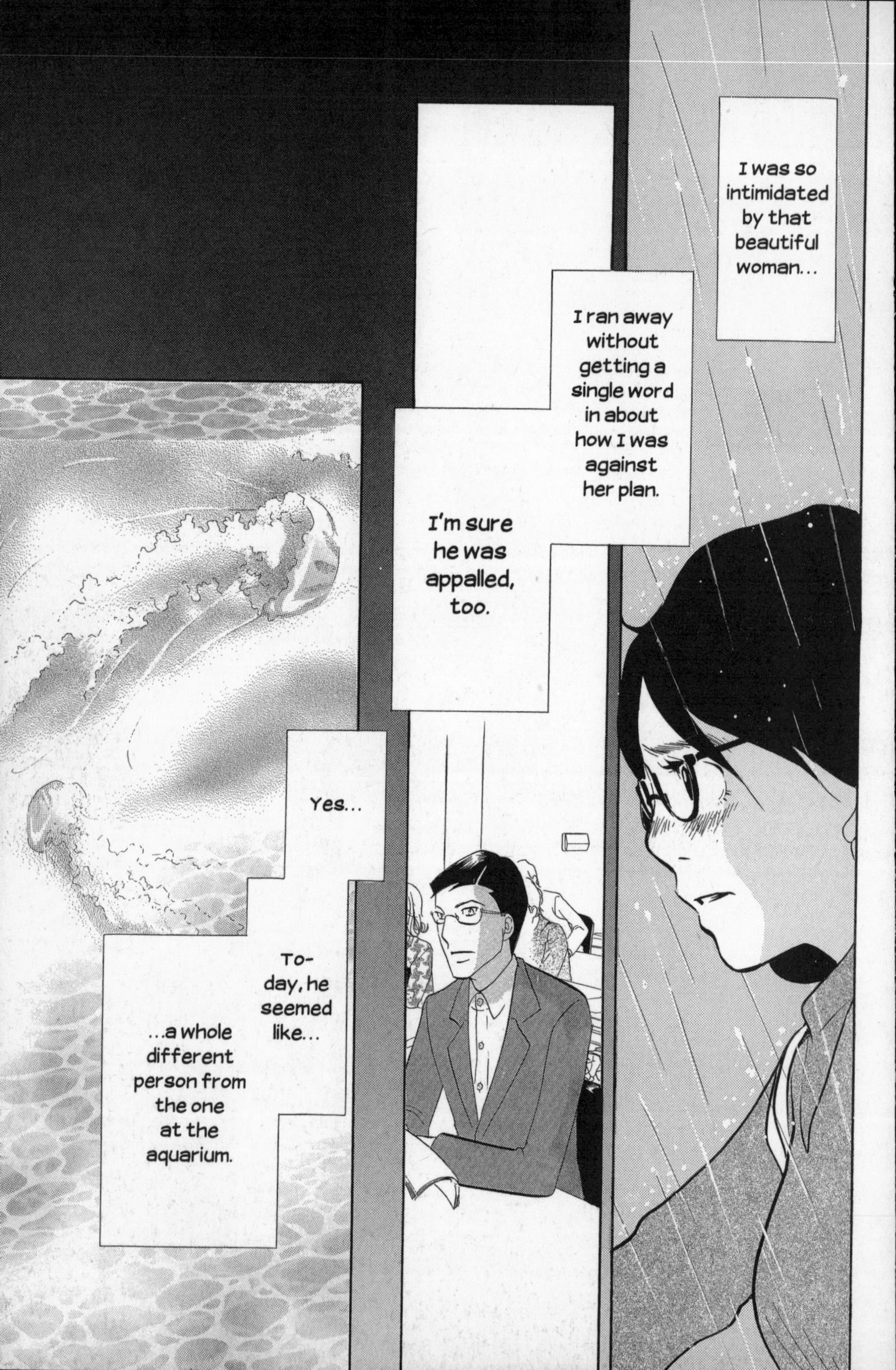
I was so intimidated by that beautiful woman...
I ran away without getting a single word in about how I was against her plan.
I'm sure he was appalled, too.
Yes...
To-day, he seemed like...
...a whole different person from the one at the aquarium.

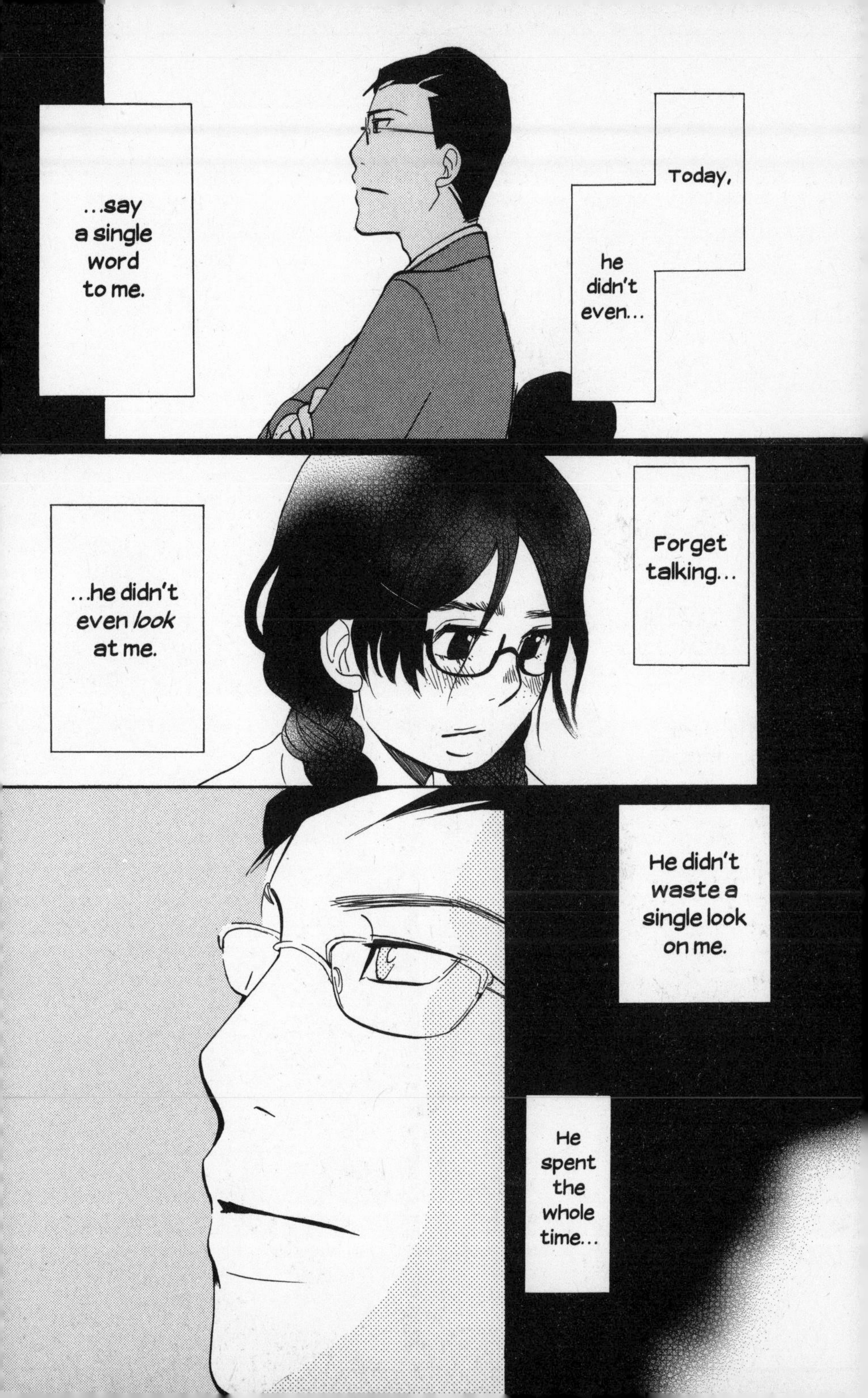
Today,
he didn't even...
...say a single word to me.
Forget talking...
...he didn't even *look* at me.
He didn't waste a single look on me.
He spent the whole time...

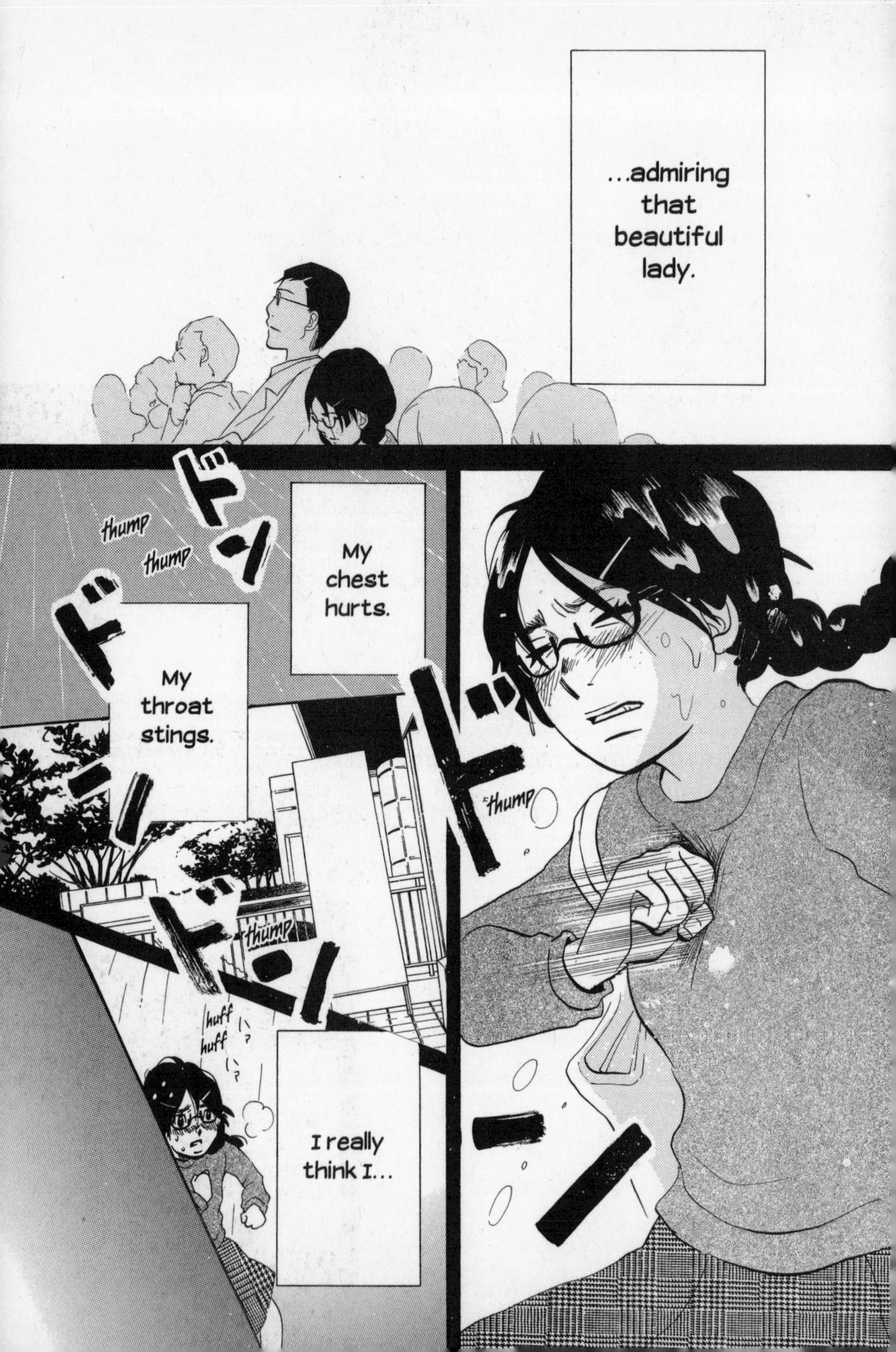
...admiring that beautiful lady.
thump
My chest hurts.
thump
thump
My throat stings.
thump
huff
huff
I really think I...

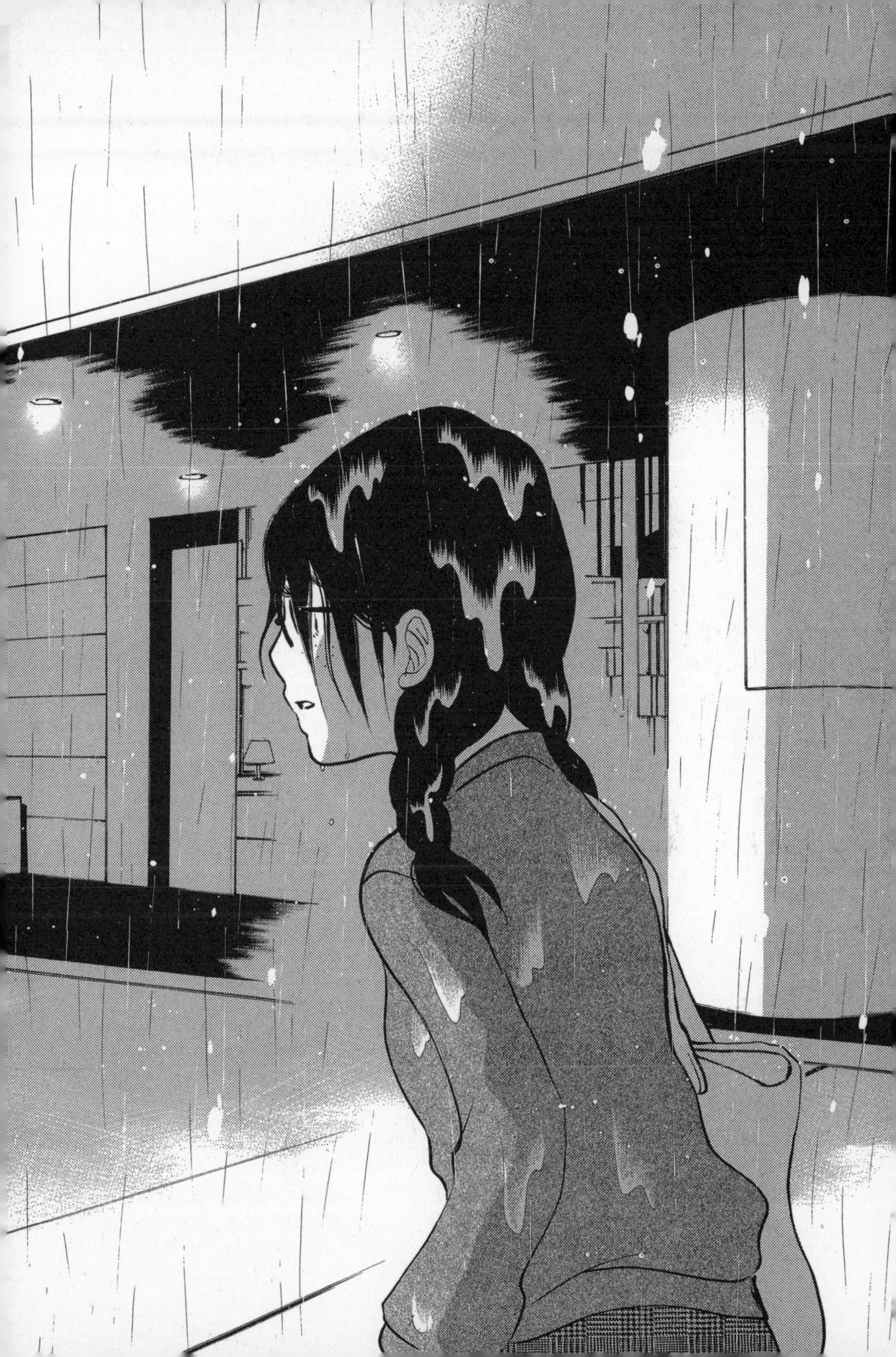

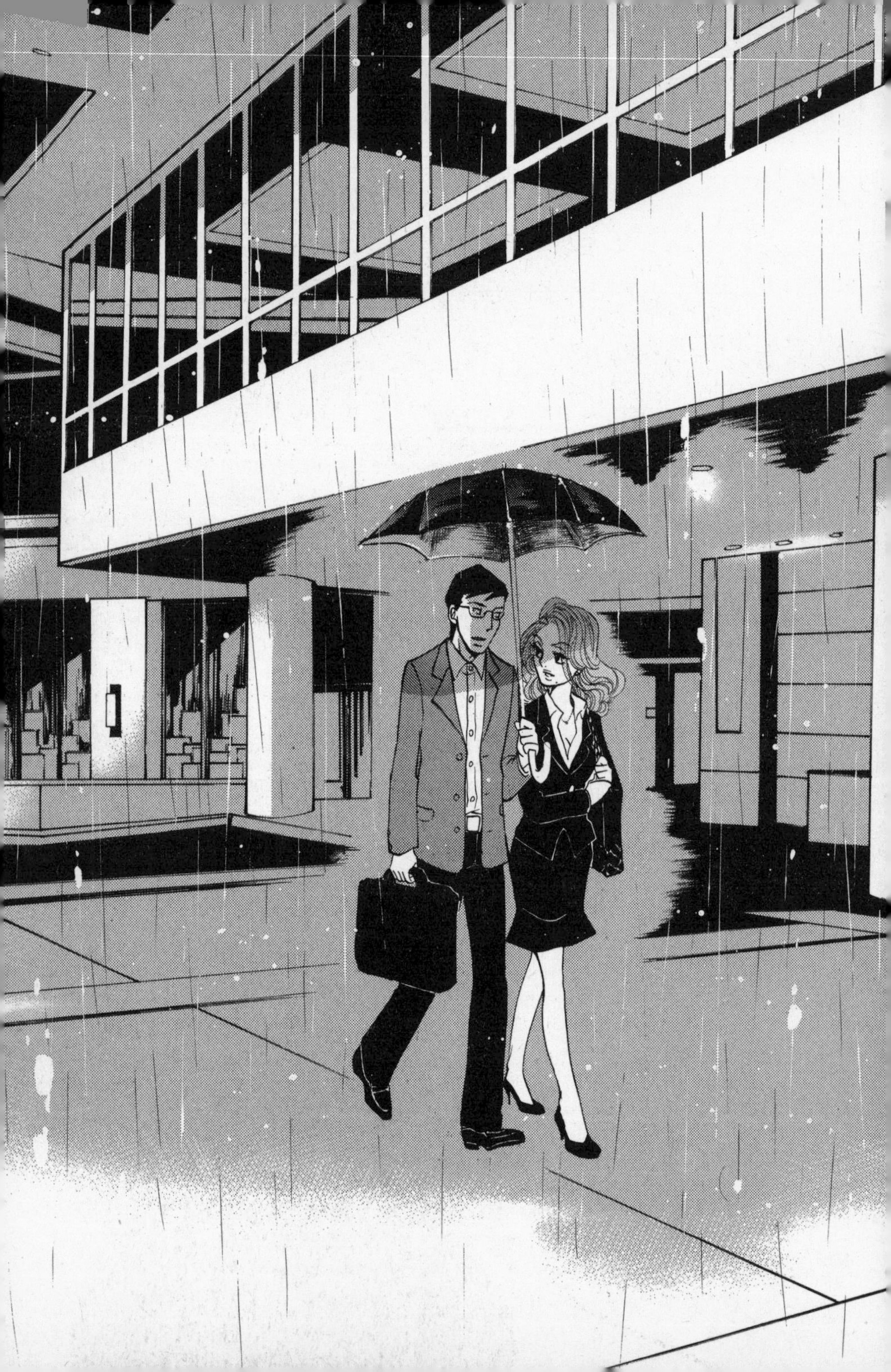

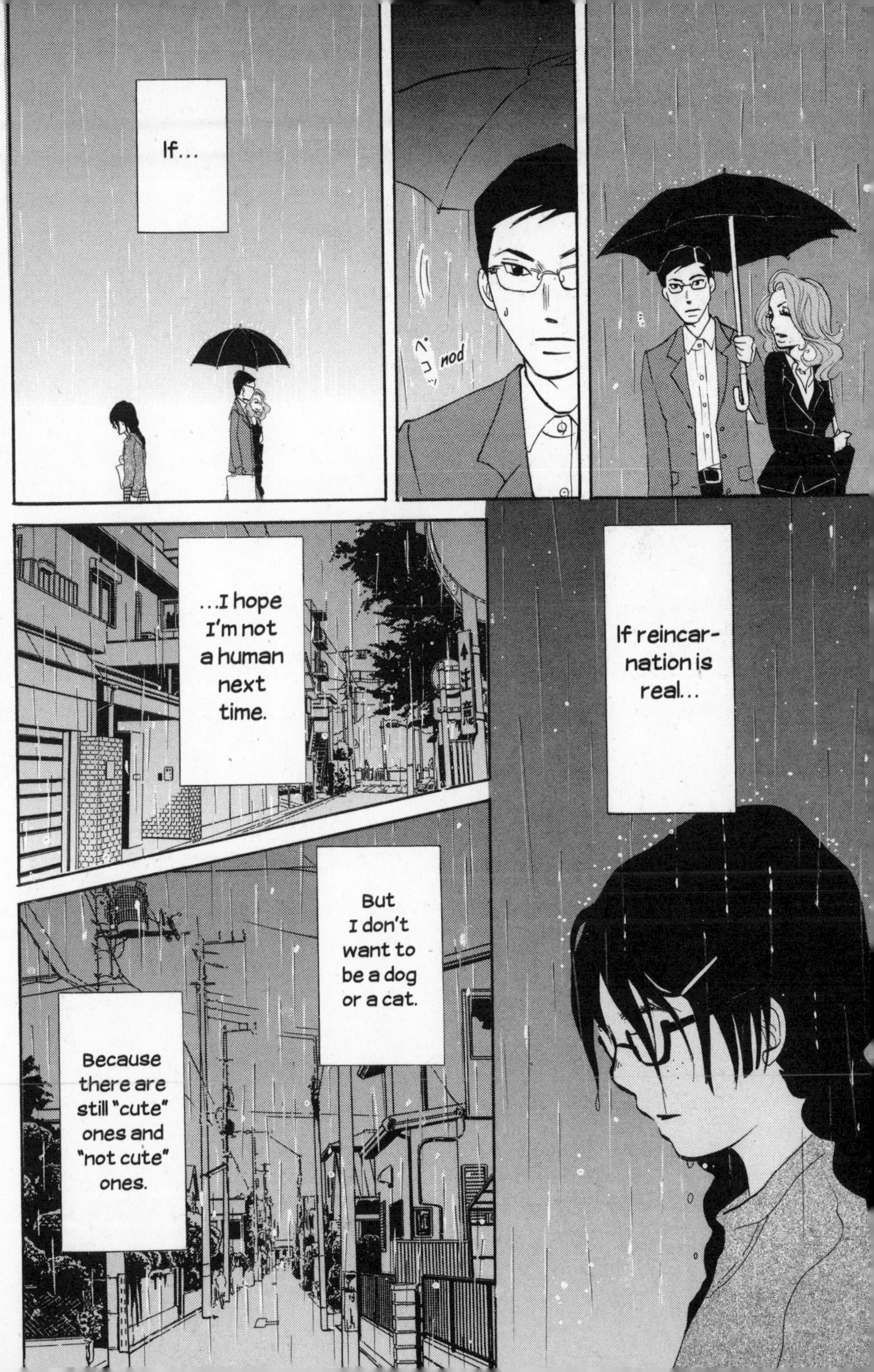
ペコ
nod
If...
If reincar-nation is real...
...I hope I'm not a human next time.
But I don't want to be a dog or a cat.
Because there are still "cute" ones and "not cute" ones.

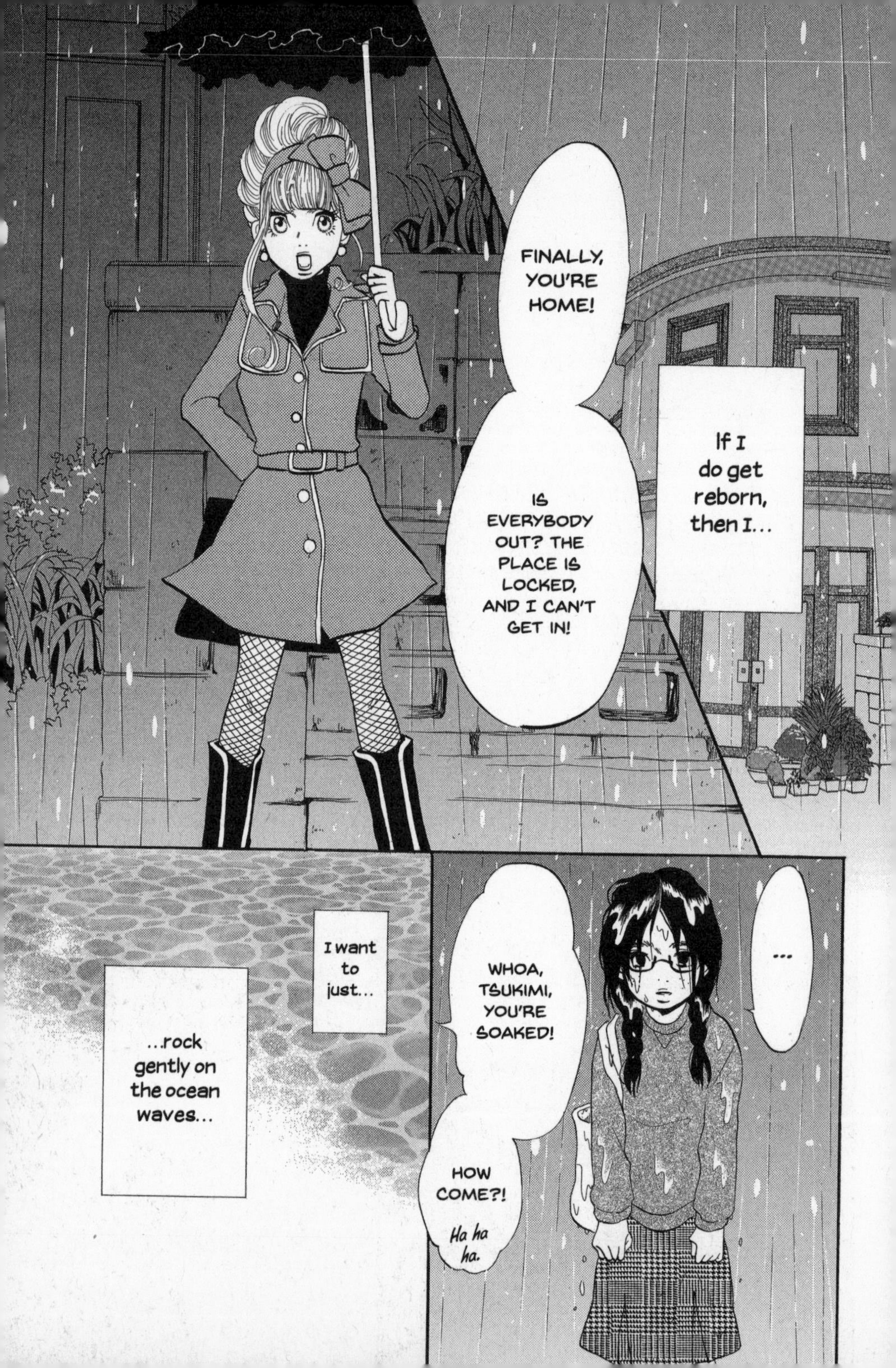

If I do get reborn, then I...
FINALLY, YOU'RE HOME!
IS EVERYBODY OUT? THE PLACE IS LOCKED, AND I CAN'T GET IN!
...
WHOA, TSUKIMI, YOU'RE SOAKED!
HOW COME?!
Ha ha ha.
I want to just...
...rock gently on the ocean waves...

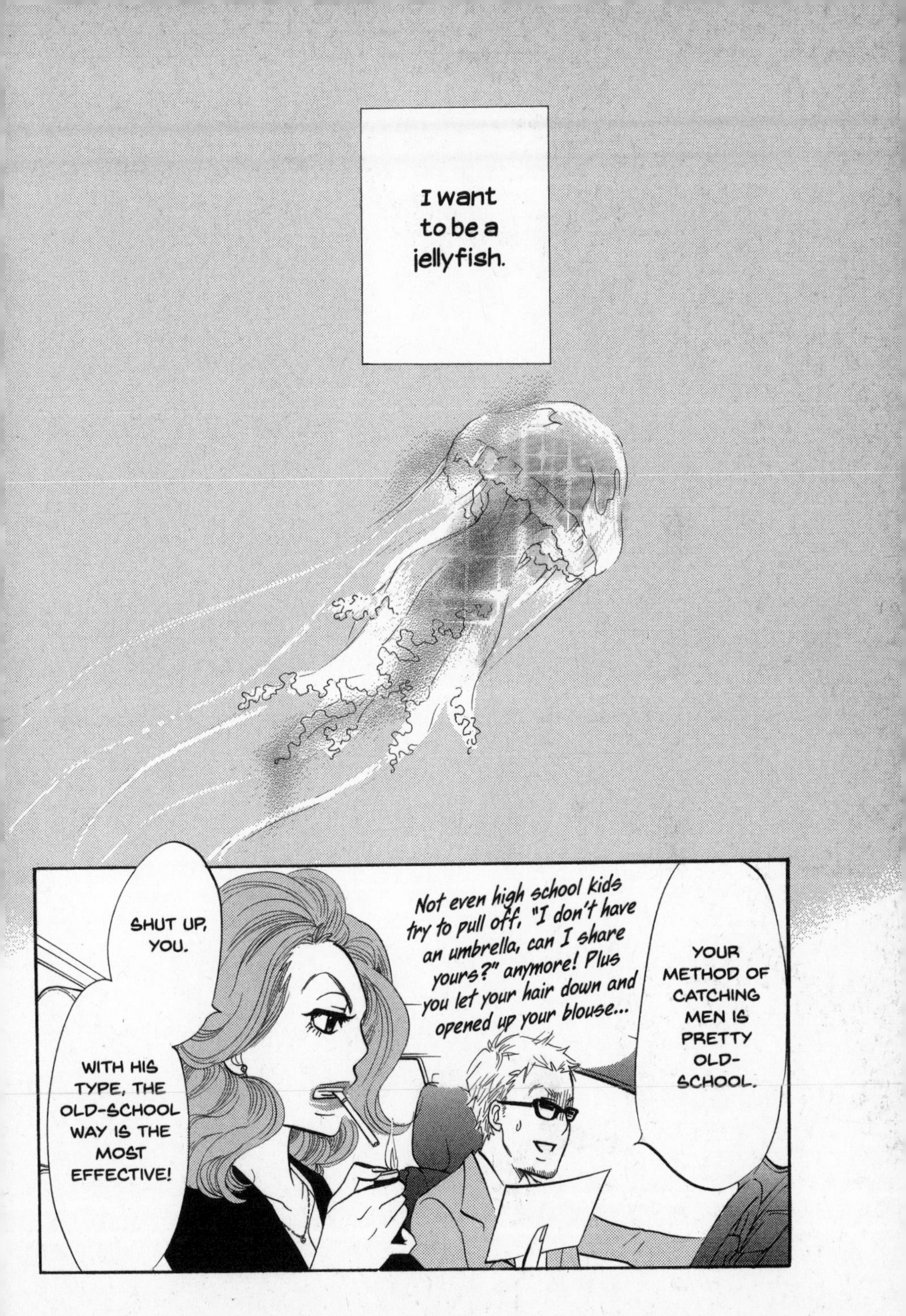
I want to be a jellyfish.
YOUR METHOD OF CATCHING MEN IS PRETTY OLD-SCHOOL.
Not even high school kids try to pull off, "I don't have an umbrella, can I share yours?" anymore! Plus you let your hair down and opened up your blouse...
SHUT UP, YOU.
WITH HIS TYPE, THE OLD-SCHOOL WAY IS THE MOST EFFECTIVE!

Episode 9
Seven Sisters

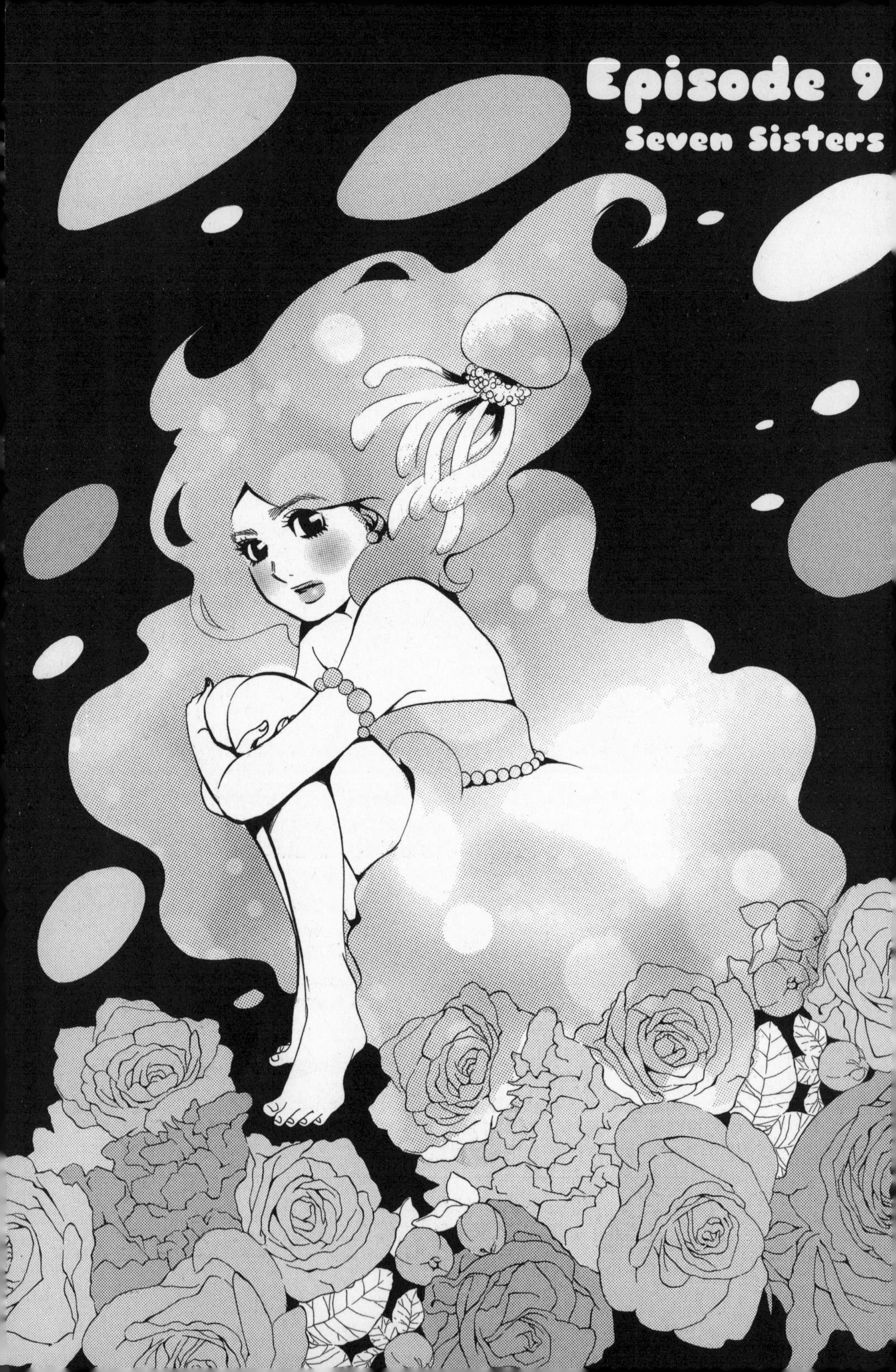

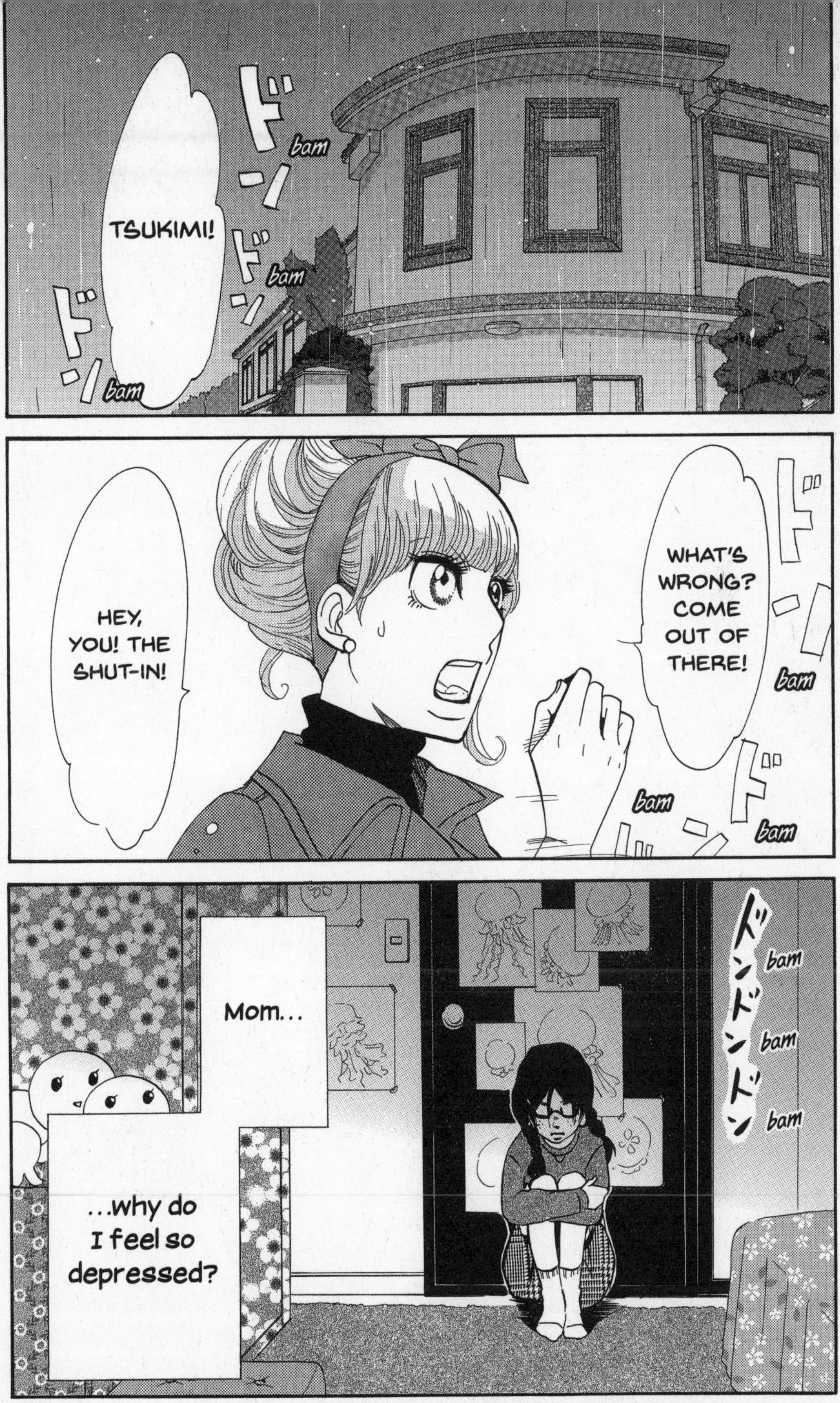
bam
bam
TSUKIMI!
bam
bam
WHAT'S WRONG? COME OUT OF THERE!
bam
bam
HEY, YOU! THE SHUT-IN!
ドンドンドンドン
bam
bam
bam
Mom...
...why do I feel so depressed?

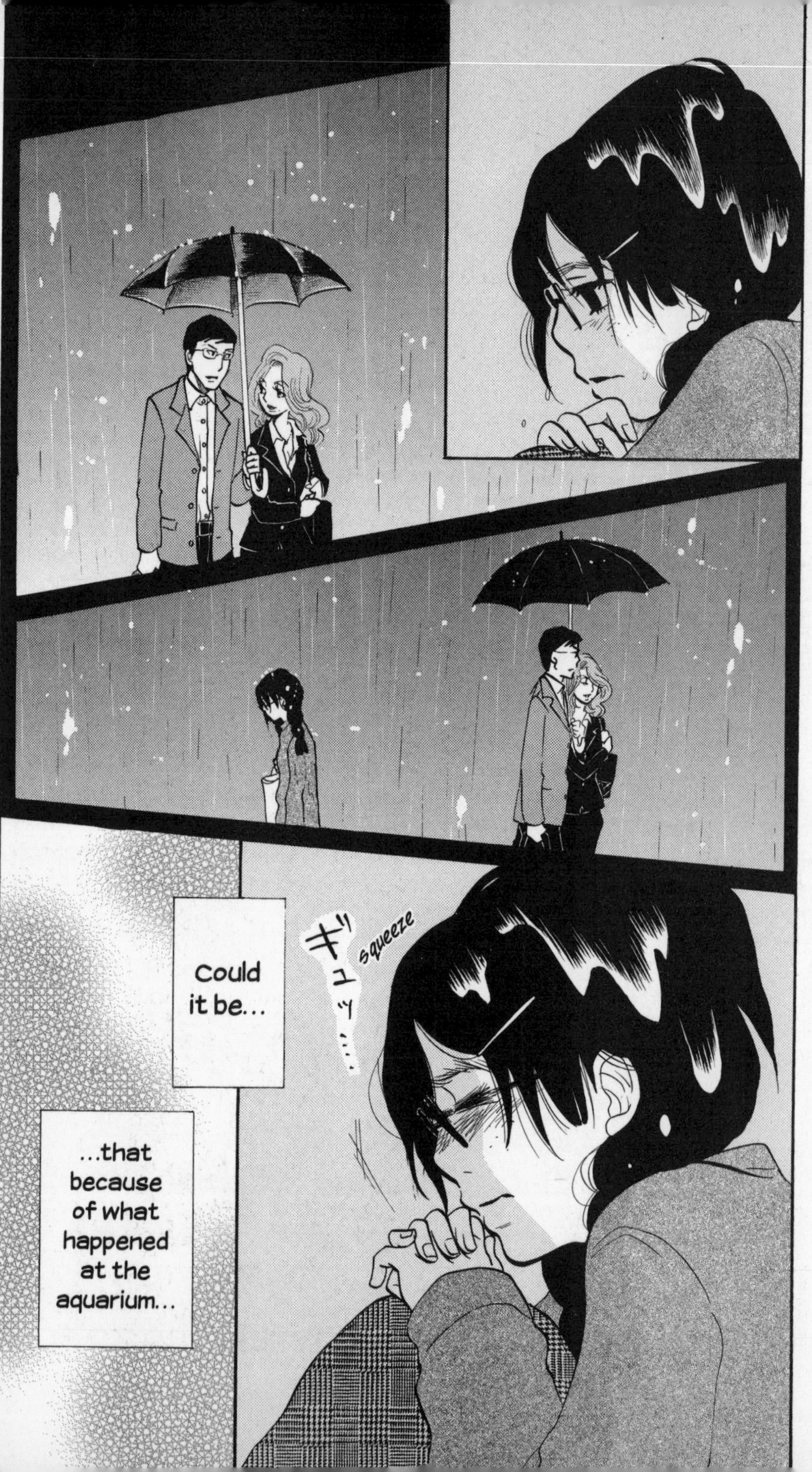
Could it be...
ギュッ...
squeeze
...that because of what happened at the aquarium...

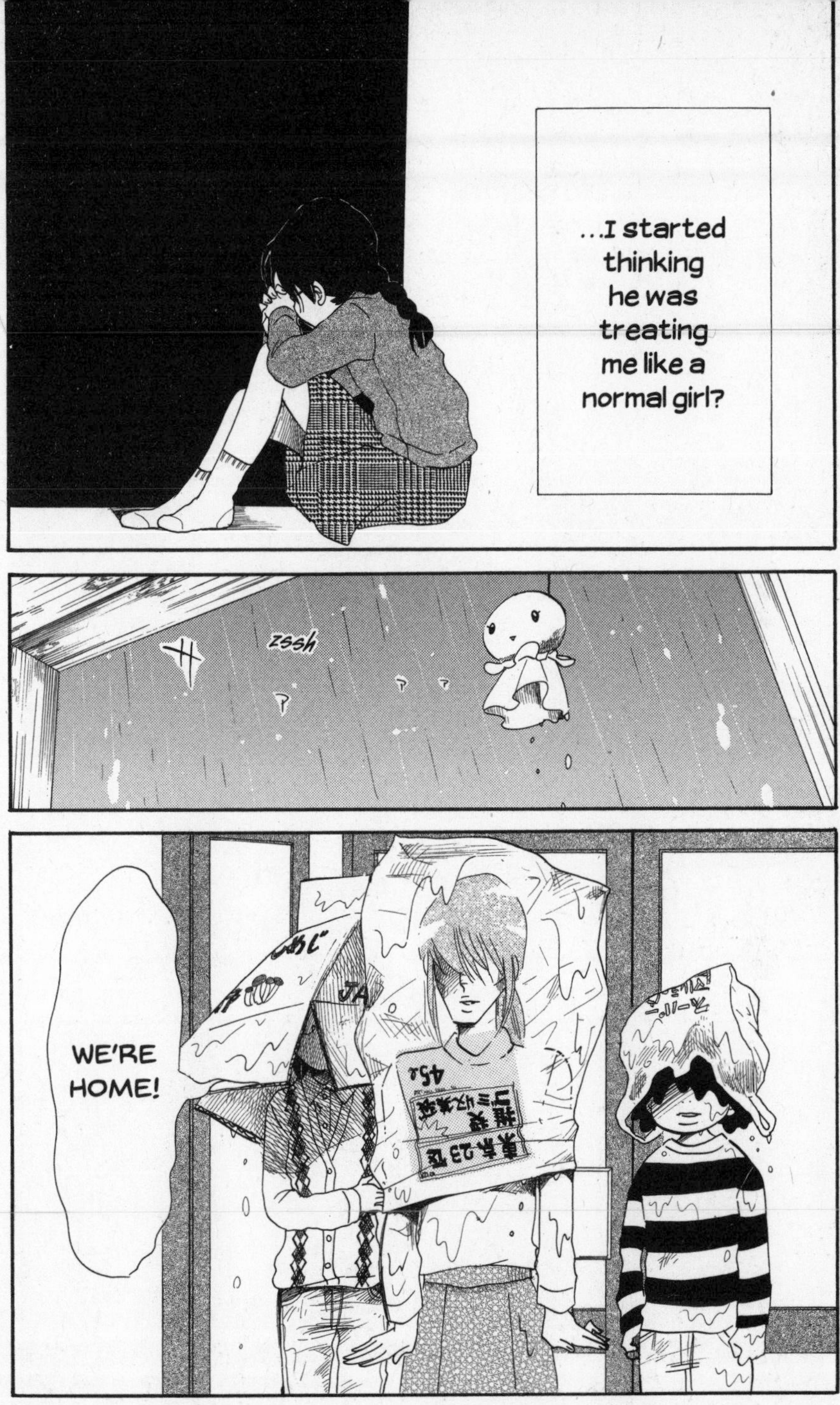
...I started thinking he was treating me like a normal girl?
zssh
WE'RE HOME!

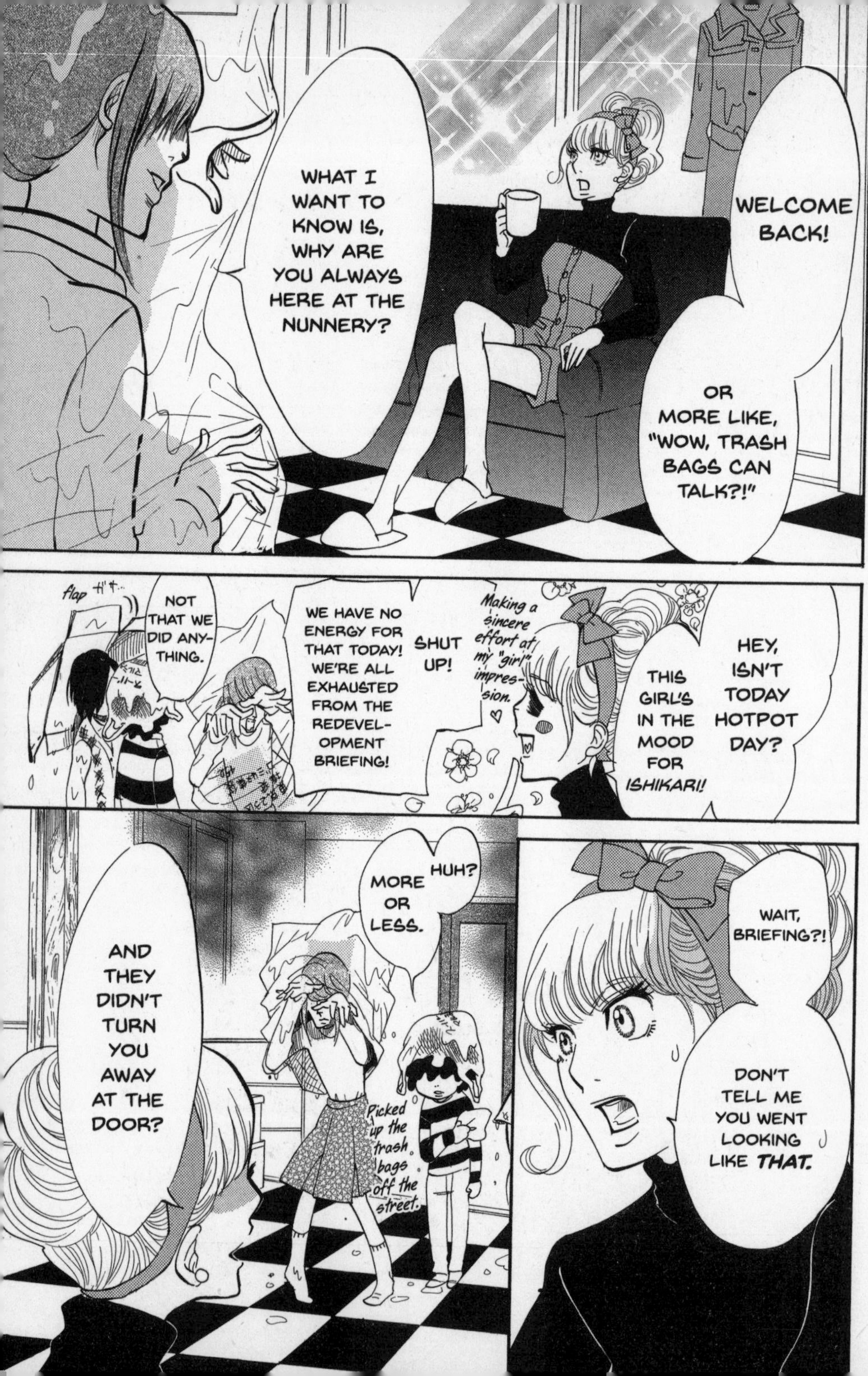
WELCOME BACK!
OR MORE LIKE, "WOW, TRASH BAGS CAN TALK?!"
WHAT I WANT TO KNOW IS, WHY ARE YOU ALWAYS HERE AT THE NUNNERY?
HEY, ISN'T TODAY HOTPOT DAY?
THIS GIRL'S IN THE MOOD FOR ISHIKARI!
Making a sincere effort at my "girl" impression.
SHUT UP!
WE HAVE NO ENERGY FOR THAT TODAY! WE'RE ALL EXHAUSTED FROM THE REDEVEL-OPMENT BRIEFING!
NOT THAT WE DID ANY-THING.
flap
WAIT, BRIEFING?!
DON'T TELL ME YOU WENT LOOKING LIKE *THAT.*
HUH?
MORE OR LESS.
Picked up the trash bags off the street.
AND THEY DIDN'T TURN YOU AWAY AT THE DOOR?

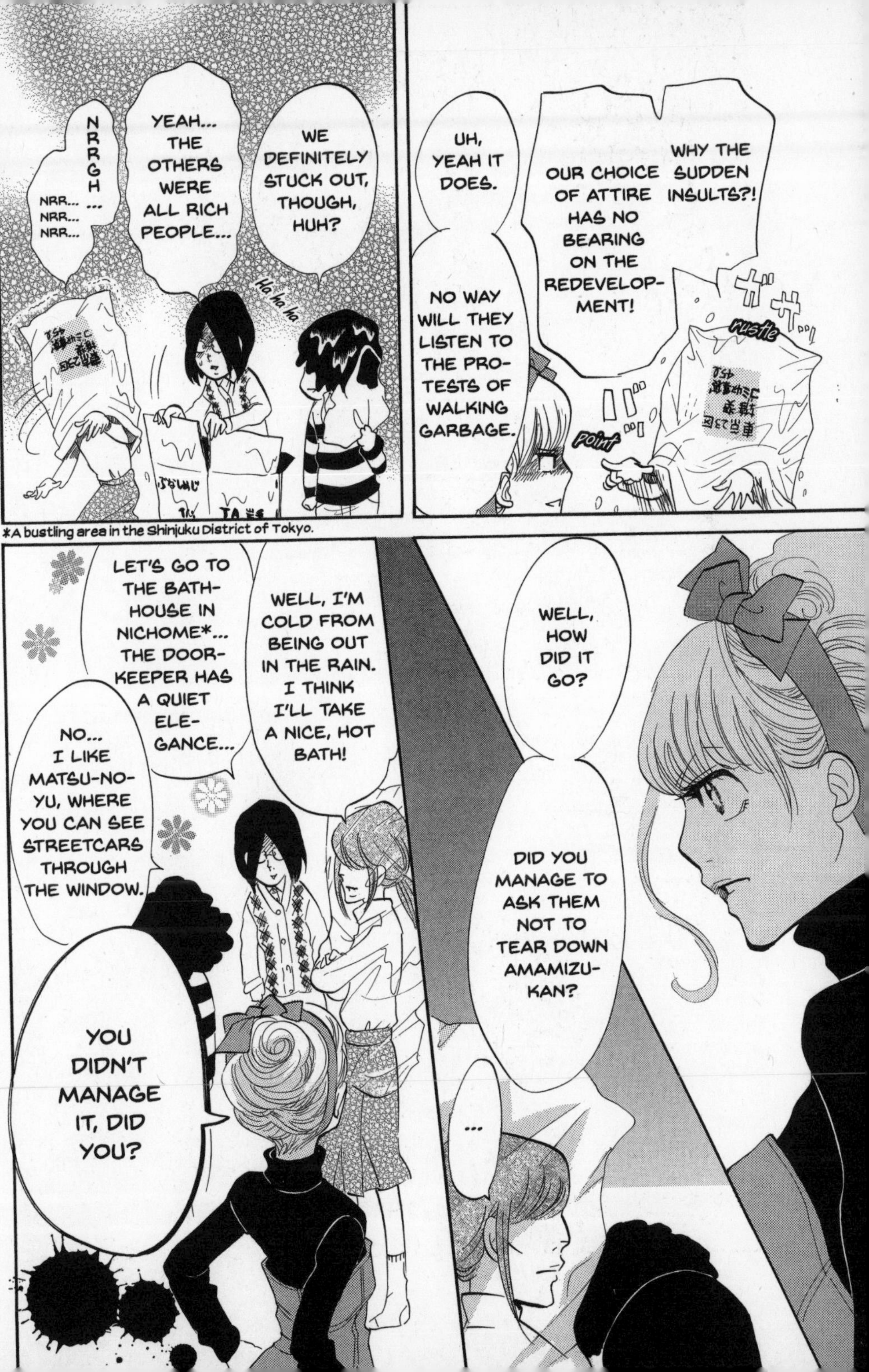
WHY THE SUDDEN INSULTS?!
OUR CHOICE OF ATTIRE HAS NO BEARING ON THE REDEVELOPMENT!
rustle
UH, YEAH IT DOES.
NO WAY WILL THEY LISTEN TO THE PROTESTS OF WALKING GARBAGE.
point
WE DEFINITELY STUCK OUT, THOUGH, HUH?
Ha ha ha
YEAH... THE OTHERS WERE ALL RICH PEOPLE...
NRRGH...
NRR... NRR... NRR...
WELL, HOW DID IT GO?
DID YOU MANAGE TO ASK THEM NOT TO TEAR DOWN AMAMIZU-KAN?
...
WELL, I'M COLD FROM BEING OUT IN THE RAIN. I THINK I'LL TAKE A NICE, HOT BATH!
LET'S GO TO THE BATH-HOUSE IN NICHOME*... THE DOOR-KEEPER HAS A QUIET ELE-GANCE...
NO... I LIKE MATSU-NO-YU, WHERE YOU CAN SEE STREETCARS THROUGH THE WINDOW.
YOU DIDN'T MANAGE IT, DID YOU?

*A bustling area in the Shinjuku District of Tokyo.

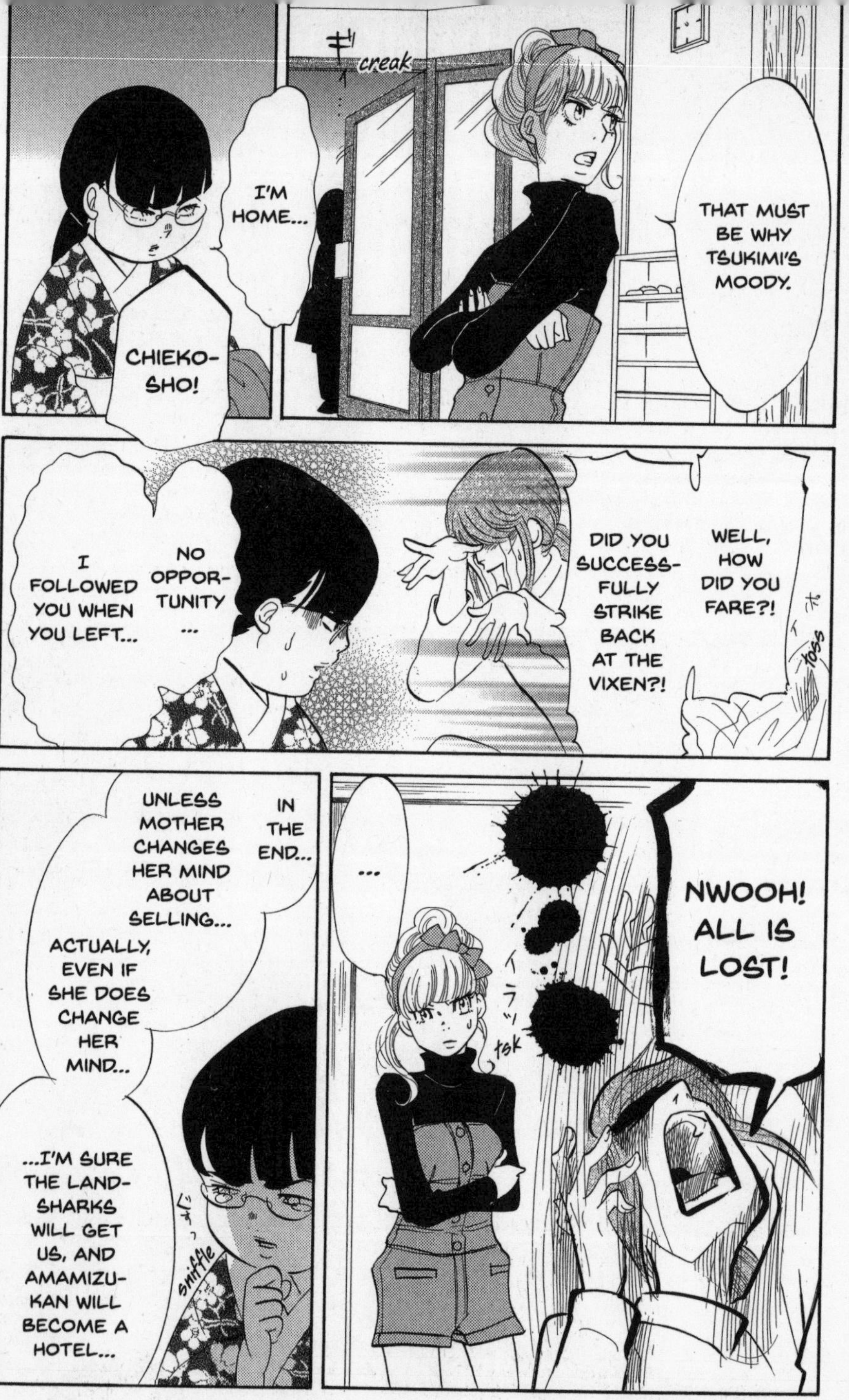
creak
THAT MUST BE WHY TSUKIMI'S MOODY.
I'M HOME...
CHIEKO-SHO!
WELL, HOW DID YOU FARE?!
DID YOU SUCCESSFULLY STRIKE BACK AT THE VIXEN?!
toss
NO OPPORTUNITY...
I FOLLOWED YOU WHEN YOU LEFT...
NWOOH! ALL IS LOST!
tsk
...
IN THE END...
UNLESS MOTHER CHANGES HER MIND ABOUT SELLING...
ACTUALLY, EVEN IF SHE DOES CHANGE HER MIND...
...I'M SURE THE LAND-SHARKS WILL GET US, AND AMAMIZU-KAN WILL BECOME A HOTEL...
sniffle

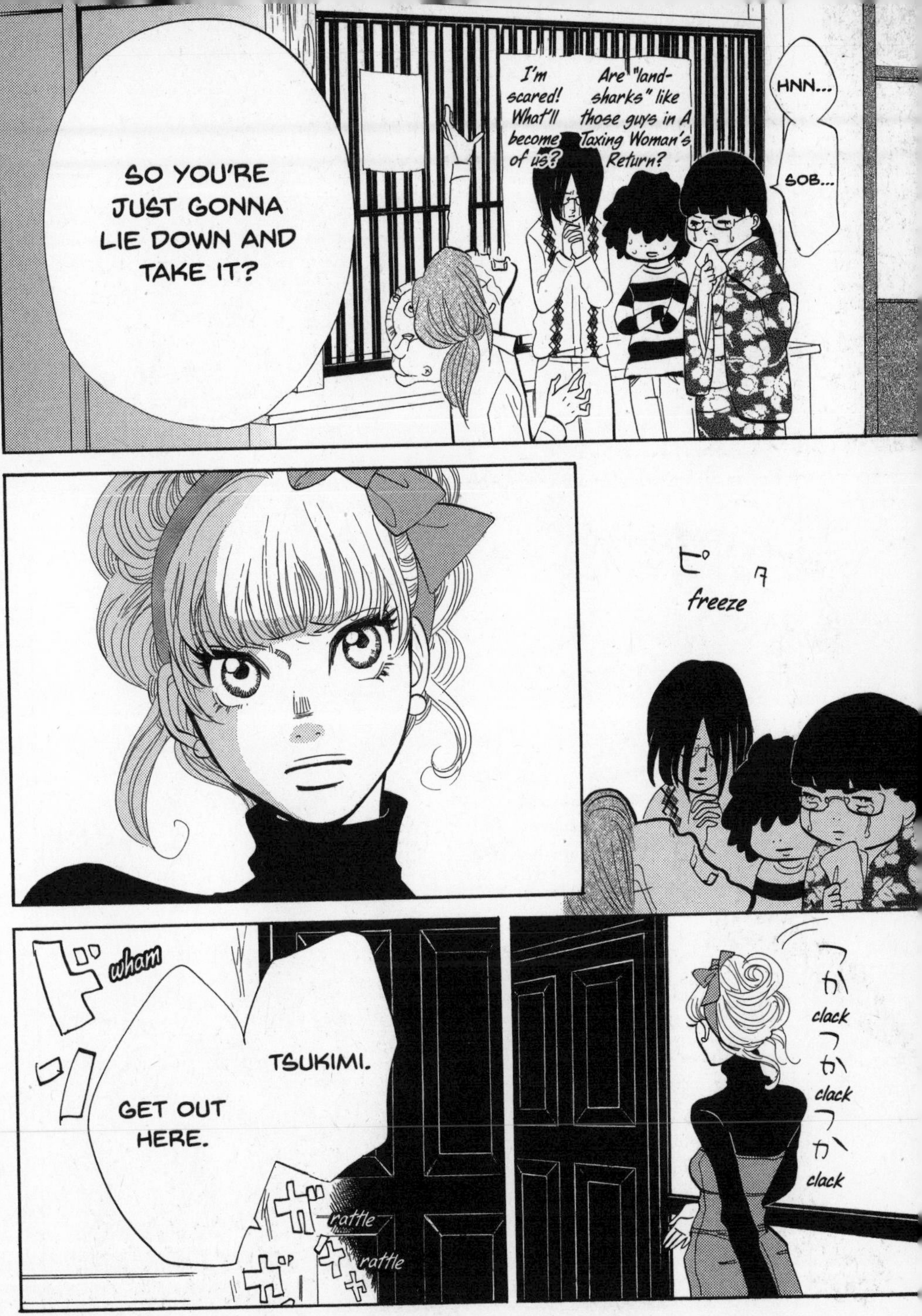
HNN...
SOB...
Are "land-sharks" like those guys in A Taxing Woman's Return?
I'm scared! What'll become of us?
SO YOU'RE JUST GONNA LIE DOWN AND TAKE IT?
freeze
つか clack
つか clack
つか clack
wham
TSUKIMI.
GET OUT HERE.
rattle
rattle

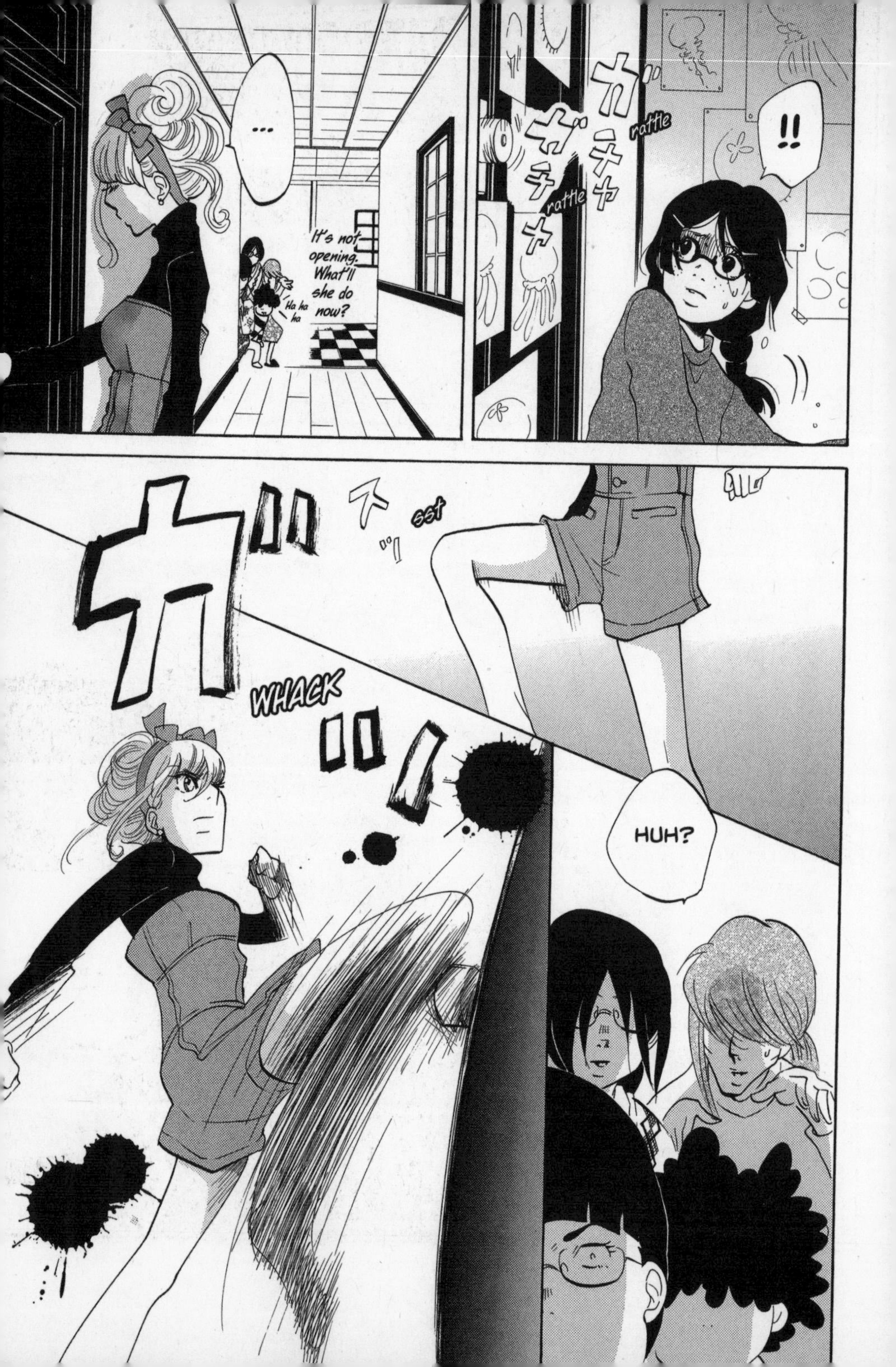
rattle
rattle
!!
...
It's not opening. What'll she do now?
Ha ha ha
sst
WHACK
HUH?

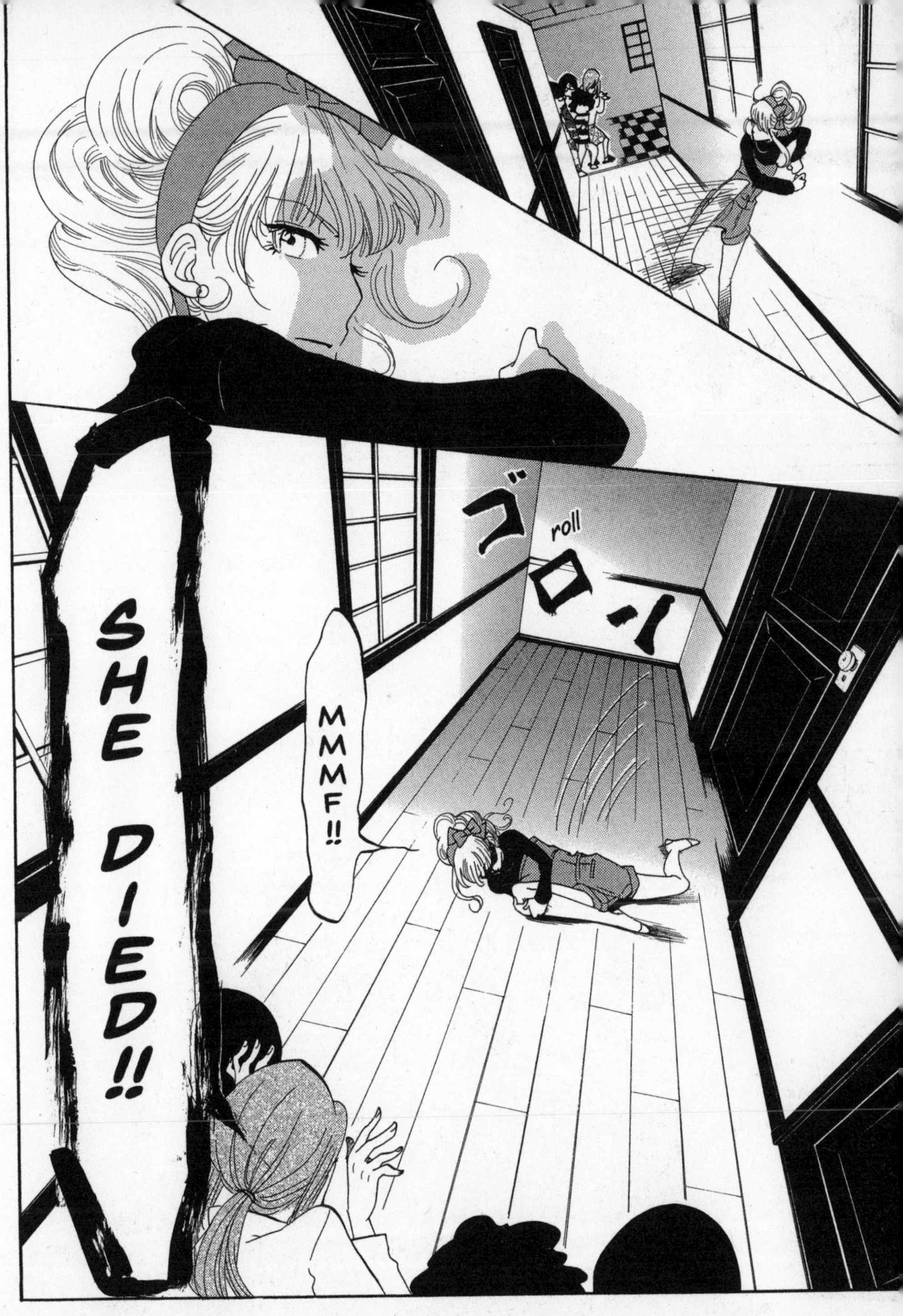
ゴロ―ン
roll
MMMF!!
SHE DIED!!

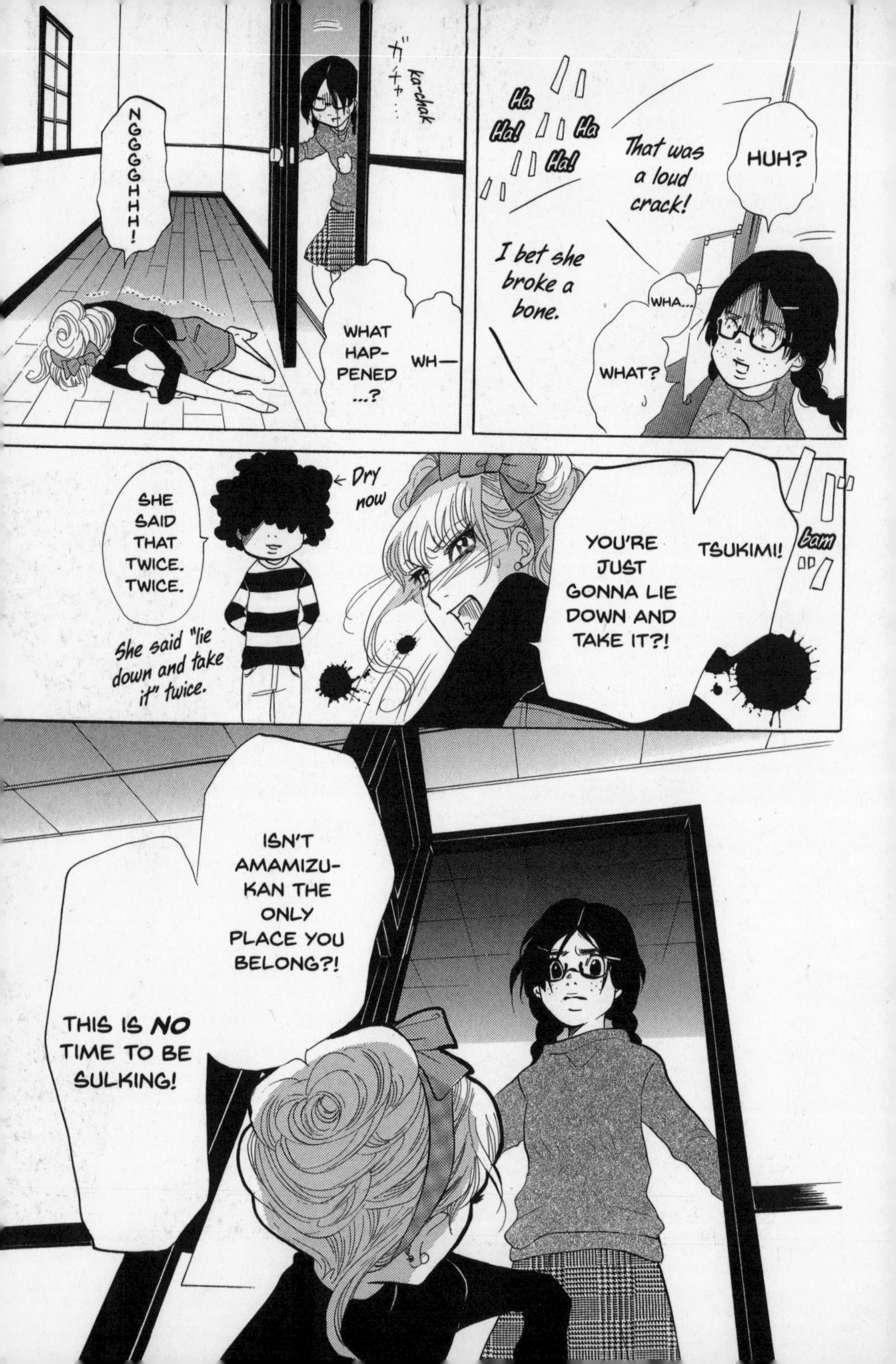

HUH?
That was a loud crack!
Ha Ha! Ha Ha!
I bet she broke a bone.
WHA...
WHAT?
ガチャ…
ka-chak
WH—
WHAT HAP-PENED ...?
NGGGGHHH!
bam
TSUKIMI!
YOU'RE JUST GONNA LIE DOWN AND TAKE IT?!
← Dry now
SHE SAID THAT TWICE. TWICE.
She said "lie down and take it" twice.
ISN'T AMAMIZU-KAN THE ONLY PLACE YOU BELONG?!
THIS IS **NO** TIME TO BE SULKING!

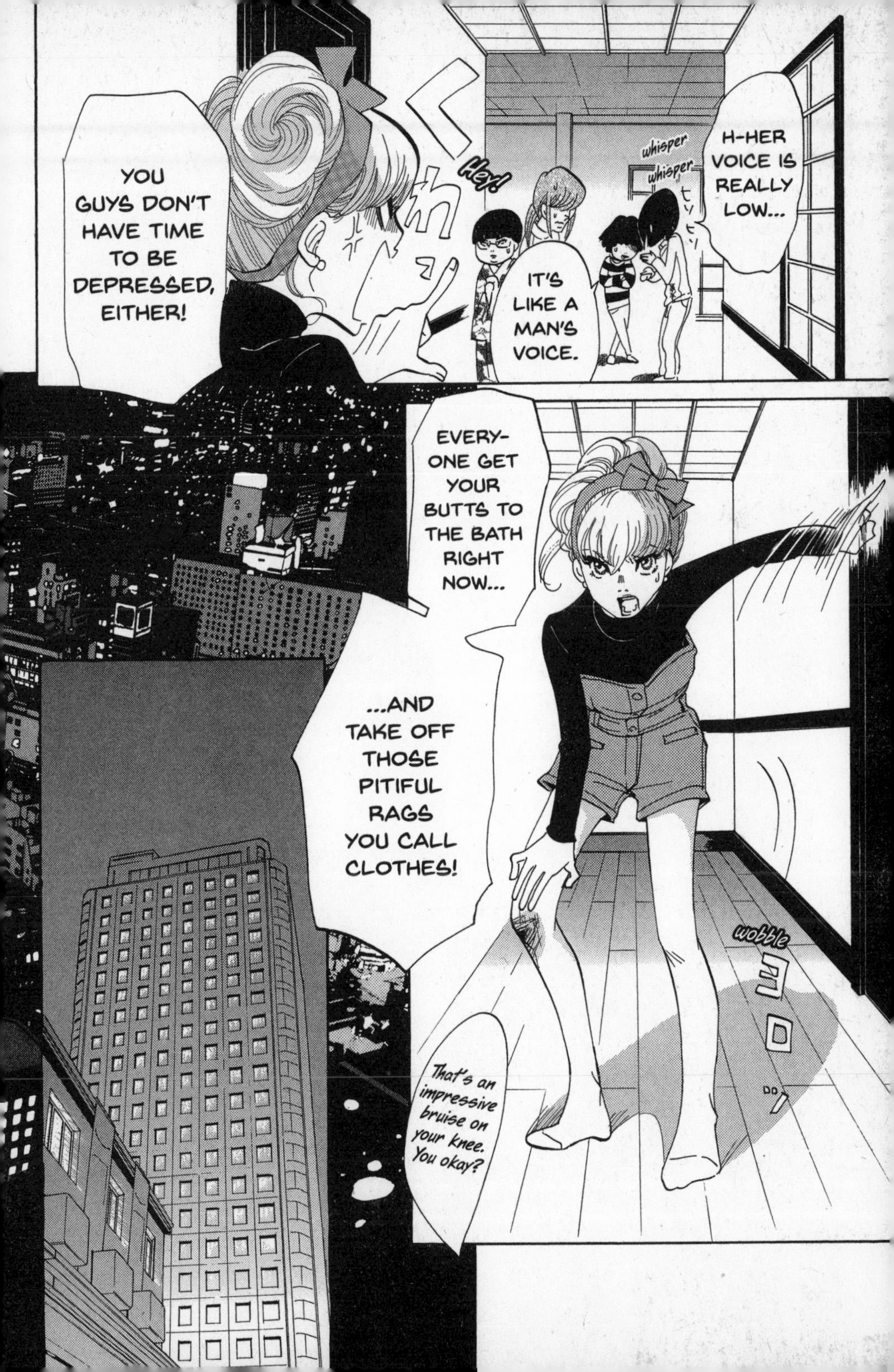
H-HER VOICE IS REALLY LOW...
whisper whisper
IT'S LIKE A MAN'S VOICE.
Hey!
YOU GUYS DON'T HAVE TIME TO BE DEPRESSED, EITHER!
EVERY-ONE GET YOUR BUTTS TO THE BATH RIGHT NOW...
...AND TAKE OFF THOSE PITIFUL RAGS YOU CALL CLOTHES!
wobble
That's an impressive bruise on your knee. You okay?

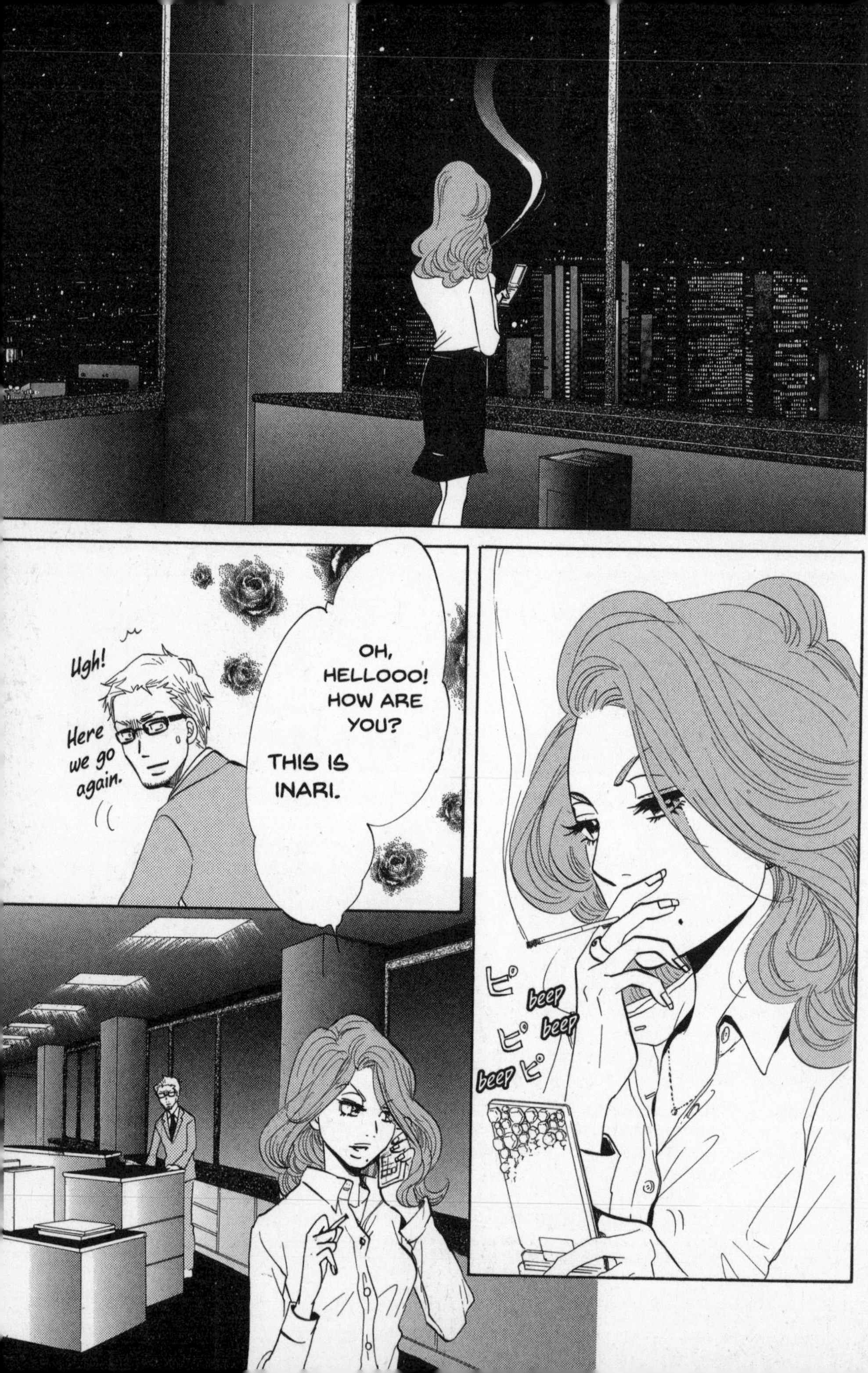
ピ
beep
ピ
beep
beep
ピ
OH, HELLOOO! HOW ARE YOU?
THIS IS INARI.
Ugh!
Here we go again.

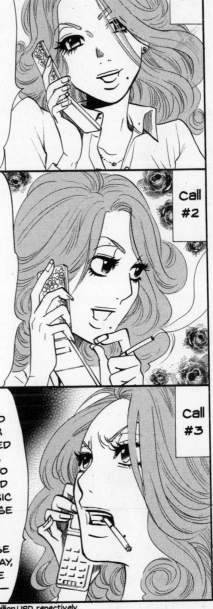

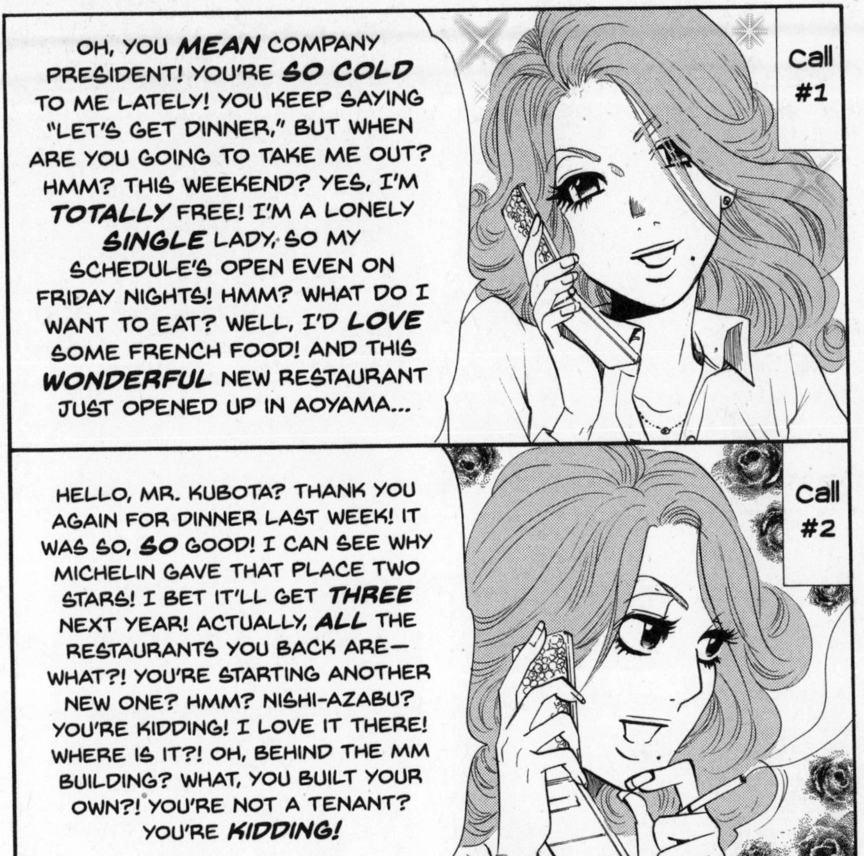

OH, YOU **MEAN** COMPANY PRESIDENT! YOU'RE **SO COLD** TO ME LATELY! YOU KEEP SAYING "LET'S GET DINNER," BUT WHEN ARE YOU GOING TO TAKE ME OUT? HMM? THIS WEEKEND? YES, I'M **TOTALLY** FREE! I'M A LONELY **SINGLE** LADY, SO MY SCHEDULE'S OPEN EVEN ON FRIDAY NIGHTS! HMM? WHAT DO I WANT TO EAT? WELL, I'D **LOVE** SOME FRENCH FOOD! AND THIS **WONDERFUL** NEW RESTAURANT JUST OPENED UP IN AOYAMA...

Call #1

HELLO, MR. KUBOTA? THANK YOU AGAIN FOR DINNER LAST WEEK! IT WAS SO, **SO** GOOD! I CAN SEE WHY MICHELIN GAVE THAT PLACE TWO STARS! I BET IT'LL GET **THREE** NEXT YEAR! ACTUALLY, **ALL** THE RESTAURANTS YOU BACK ARE— WHAT?! YOU'RE STARTING ANOTHER NEW ONE? HMM? NISHI-AZABU? YOU'RE KIDDING! I LOVE IT THERE! WHERE IS IT?! OH, BEHIND THE MM BUILDING? WHAT, YOU BUILT YOUR OWN?! YOU'RE NOT A TENANT? YOU'RE **KIDDING!**

Call #2

WHAT? TOMORROW? NO CAN DO. AND ANYWAY, WHAT'S TAKING YOU SO LONG? HAVE YOU CONVINCED YOUR WIFE YET? EXCUSE ME?! YOU BOOKED A ROOM AT THE SS HOTEL? SURE, I'LL COME IF YOU GET YOUR WIFE TO SIGN THE PAPERS, SO HURRY UP AND SELL THAT DEAD-END KIMONO FABRIC SHOP! BETTER SELL IT FAST, BECAUSE PROPERTY VALUES ARE GONNA PLUMMET NEXT YEAR. YOUR 300 MIL WILL DROP TO 100 MIL*. EXCUSE ME?! YOU BOUGHT ME CHANEL? OKAY, I'LL GET IT FROM YOU WHEN I SEE YOU, BUT WHAT YOU NEED TO DO IS—

Call #3

*She is refering to JPY. About three million USD and one million USD, repectively.

-268-

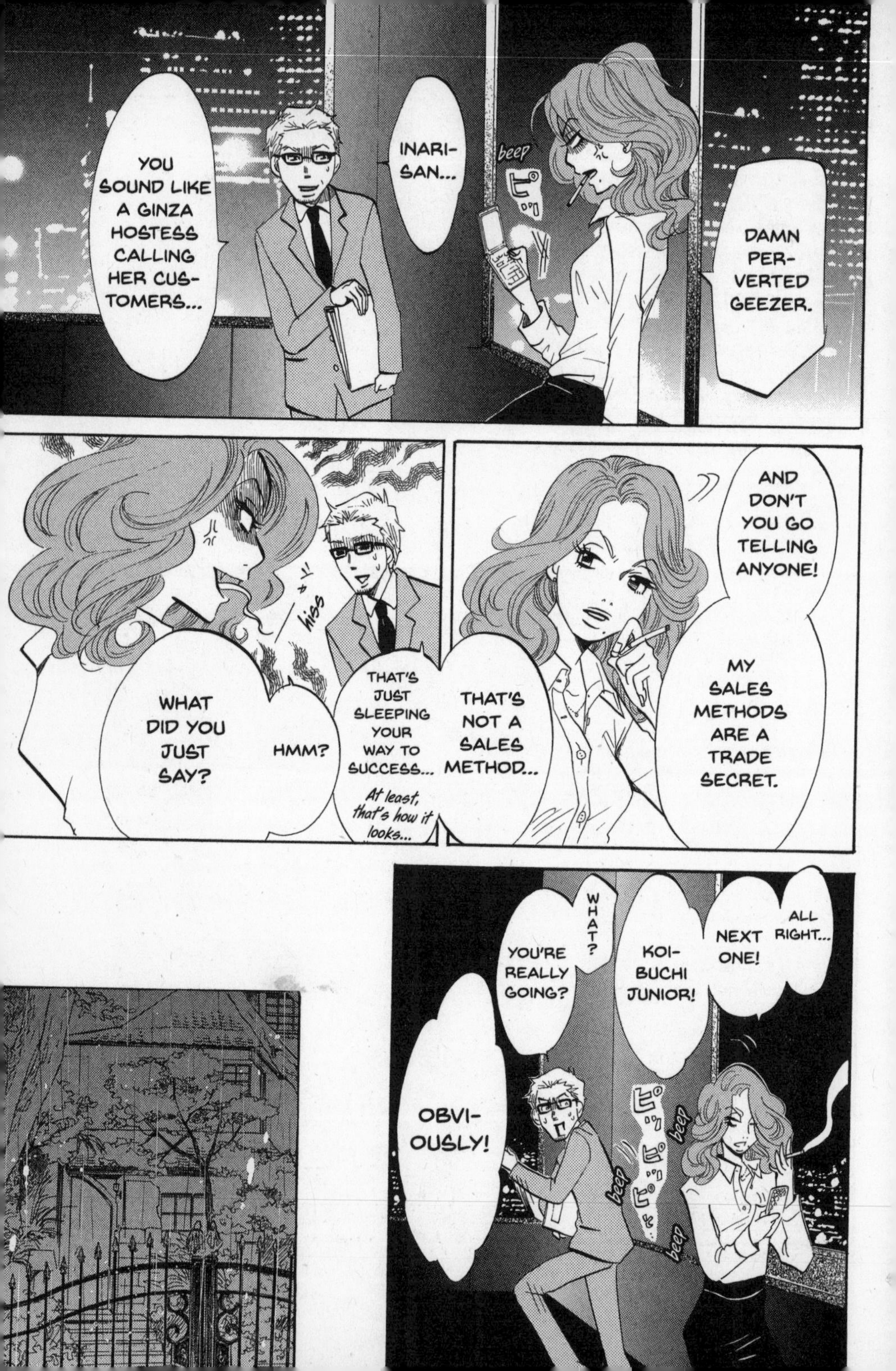
DAMN PER-VERTED GEEZER.
beep
INARI-SAN...
YOU SOUND LIKE A GINZA HOSTESS CALLING HER CUS-TOMERS...
AND DON'T YOU GO TELLING ANYONE!
MY SALES METHODS ARE A TRADE SECRET.
THAT'S NOT A SALES METHOD...
THAT'S JUST SLEEPING YOUR WAY TO SUCCESS...
At least, that's how it looks...
hiss
HMM?
WHAT DID YOU JUST SAY?
ALL RIGHT...
NEXT ONE!
KOI-BUCHI JUNIOR!
WHAT?
YOU'RE REALLY GOING?
OBVI-OUSLY!
beep
beep
beep

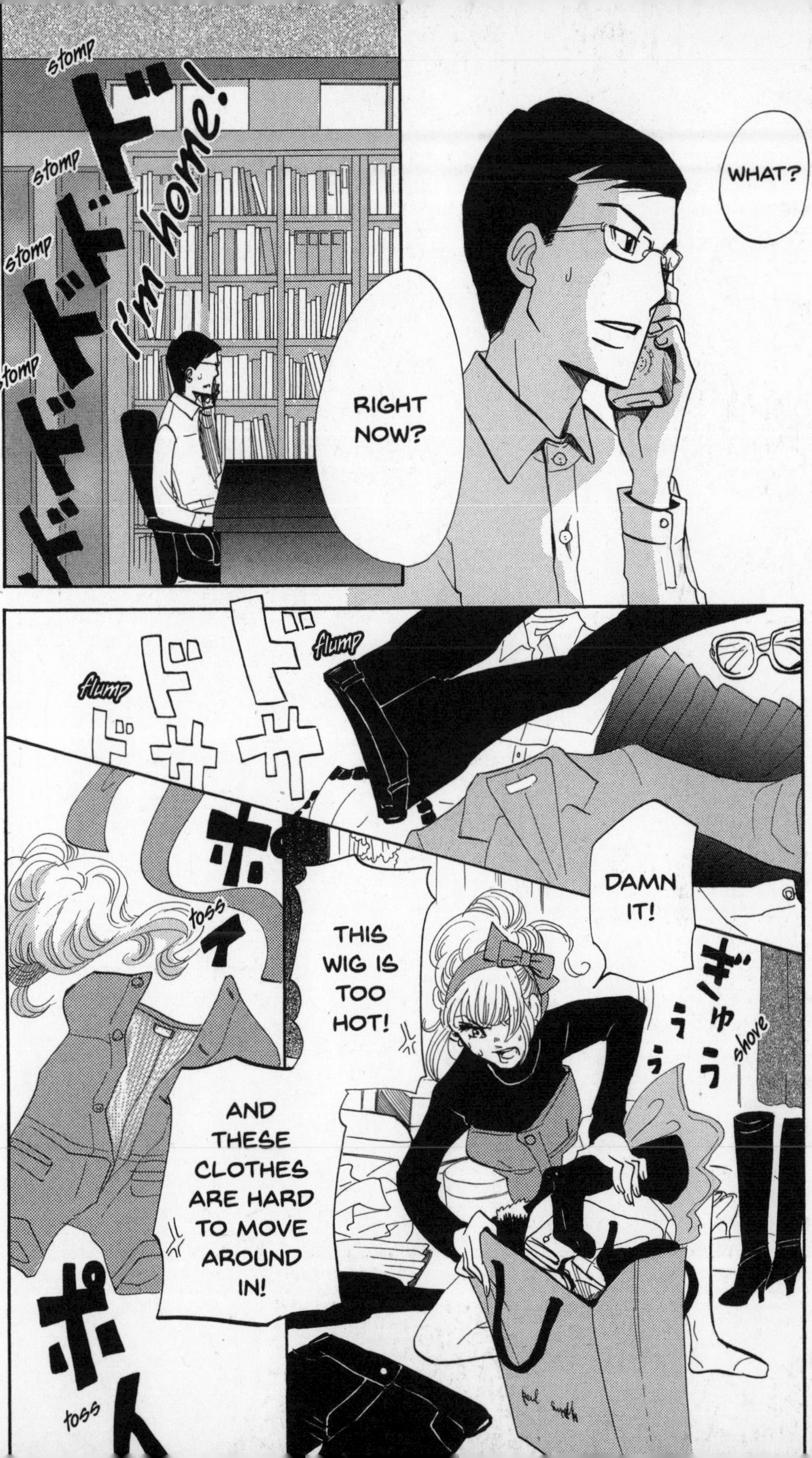
WHAT?
RIGHT NOW?
stomp
stomp
stomp
stomp
I'M HOME!
flump
flump
DAMN IT!
ぎゅううう
shove
THIS WIG IS TOO HOT!
toss
AND THESE CLOTHES ARE HARD TO MOVE AROUND IN!
toss

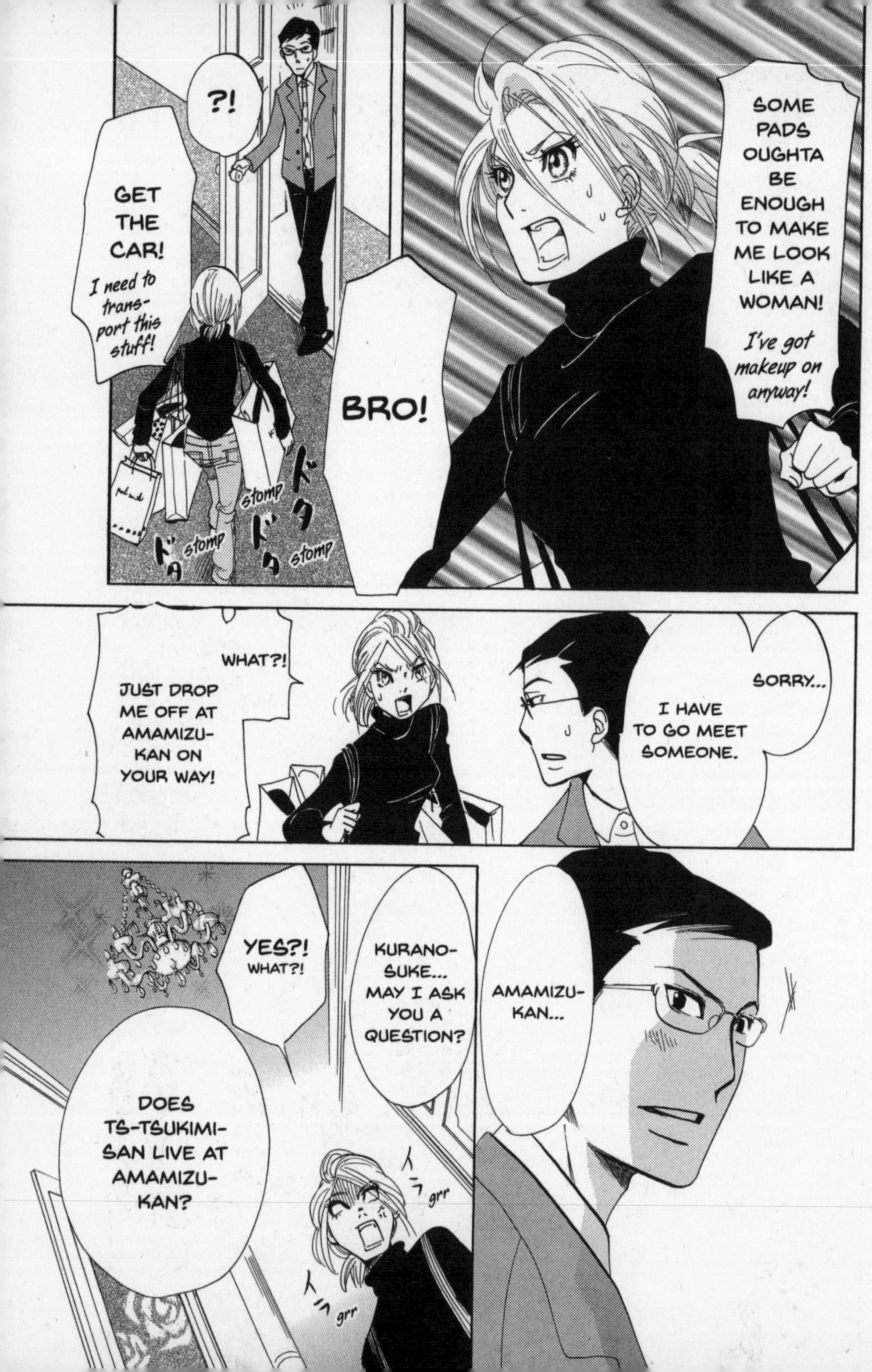
SOME PADS OUGHTA BE ENOUGH TO MAKE ME LOOK LIKE A WOMAN!
I've got makeup on anyway!
BRO!
?!
GET THE CAR!
I need to transport this stuff!
stomp
stomp
stomp
SORRY...
I HAVE TO GO MEET SOMEONE.
WHAT?!
JUST DROP ME OFF AT AMAMIZU-KAN ON YOUR WAY!
AMAMIZU-KAN...
KURANOSUKE... MAY I ASK YOU A QUESTION?
YES?! WHAT?!
DOES TS-TSUKIMI-SAN LIVE AT AMAMIZU-KAN?
grr
grr

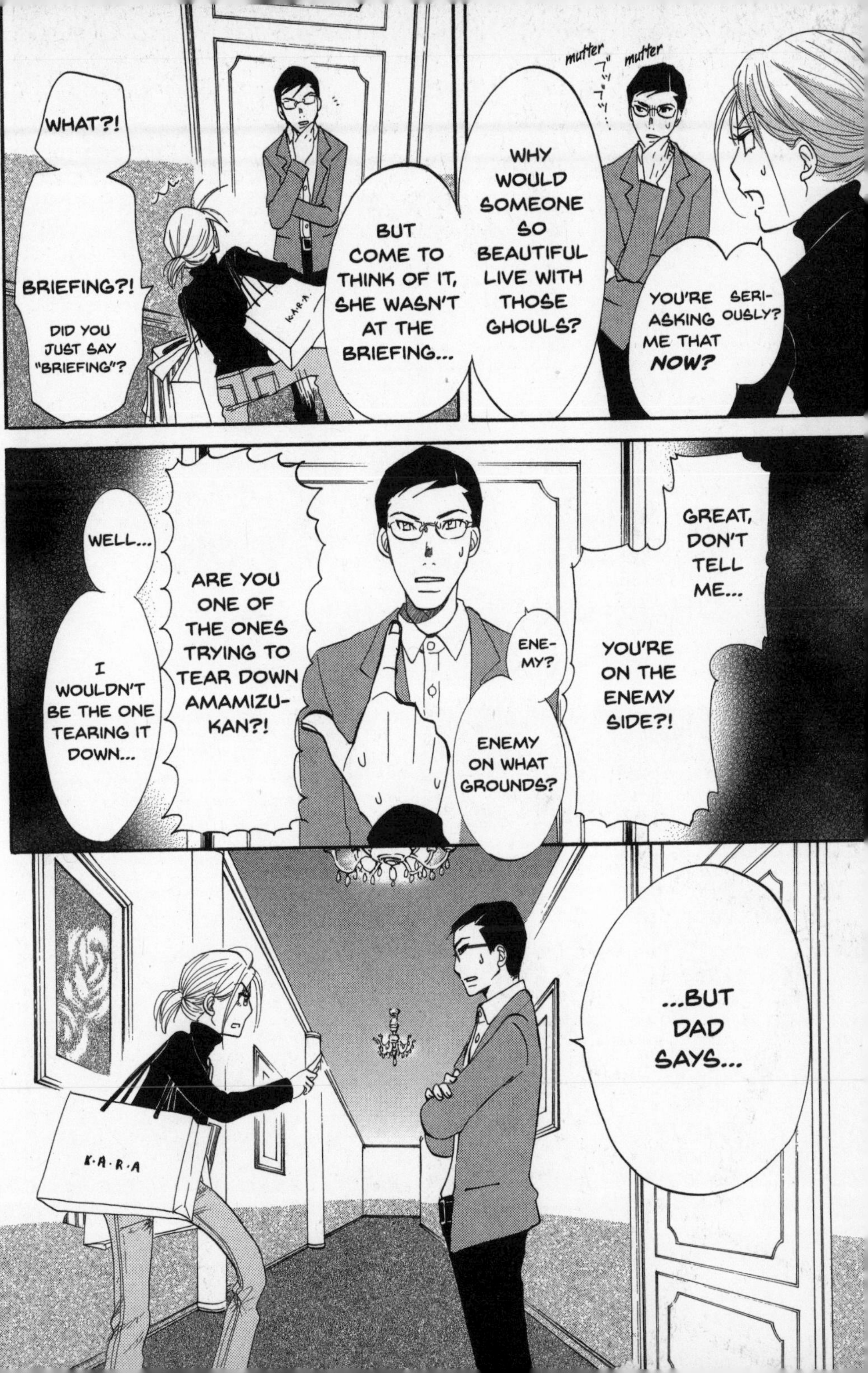
mutter mutter
ブツブツ…
WHY WOULD SOMEONE SO BEAUTIFUL LIVE WITH THOSE GHOULS?
YOU'RE SERIOUSLY ASKING ME THAT *NOW?*
BUT COME TO THINK OF IT, SHE WASN'T AT THE BRIEFING...
WHAT?!
BRIEFING?!
DID YOU JUST SAY "BRIEFING"?
GREAT, DON'T TELL ME...
YOU'RE ON THE ENEMY SIDE?!
ENEMY?
ENEMY ON WHAT GROUNDS?
ARE YOU ONE OF THE ONES TRYING TO TEAR DOWN AMAMIZU-KAN?!
WELL...
I WOULDN'T BE THE ONE TEARING IT DOWN...
...BUT DAD SAYS...

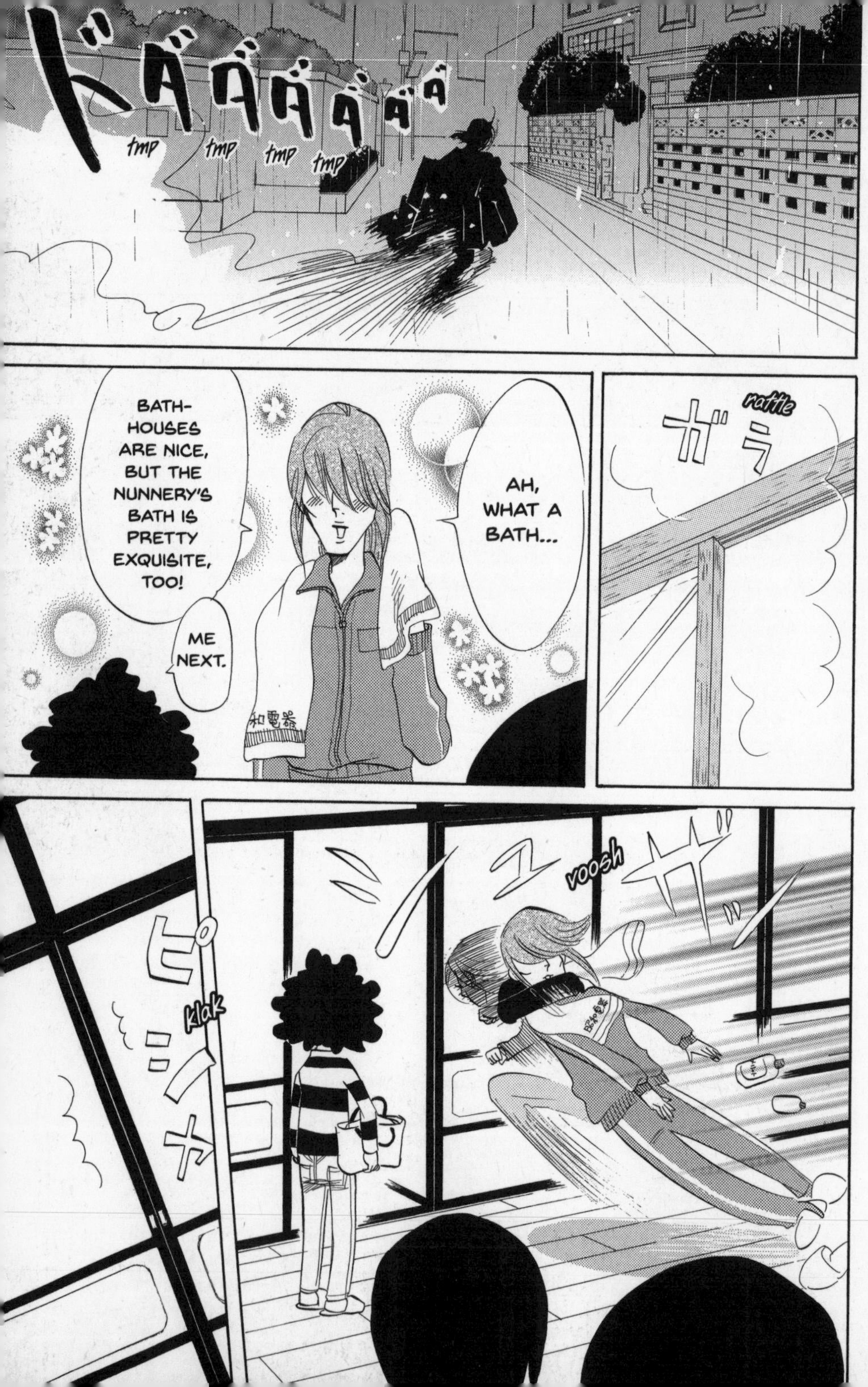

tmp tmp tmp tmp
rattle
ガラ
AH, WHAT A BATH...
BATH-HOUSES ARE NICE, BUT THE NUNNERY'S BATH IS PRETTY EXQUISITE, TOO!
ME NEXT.
voosh
klak

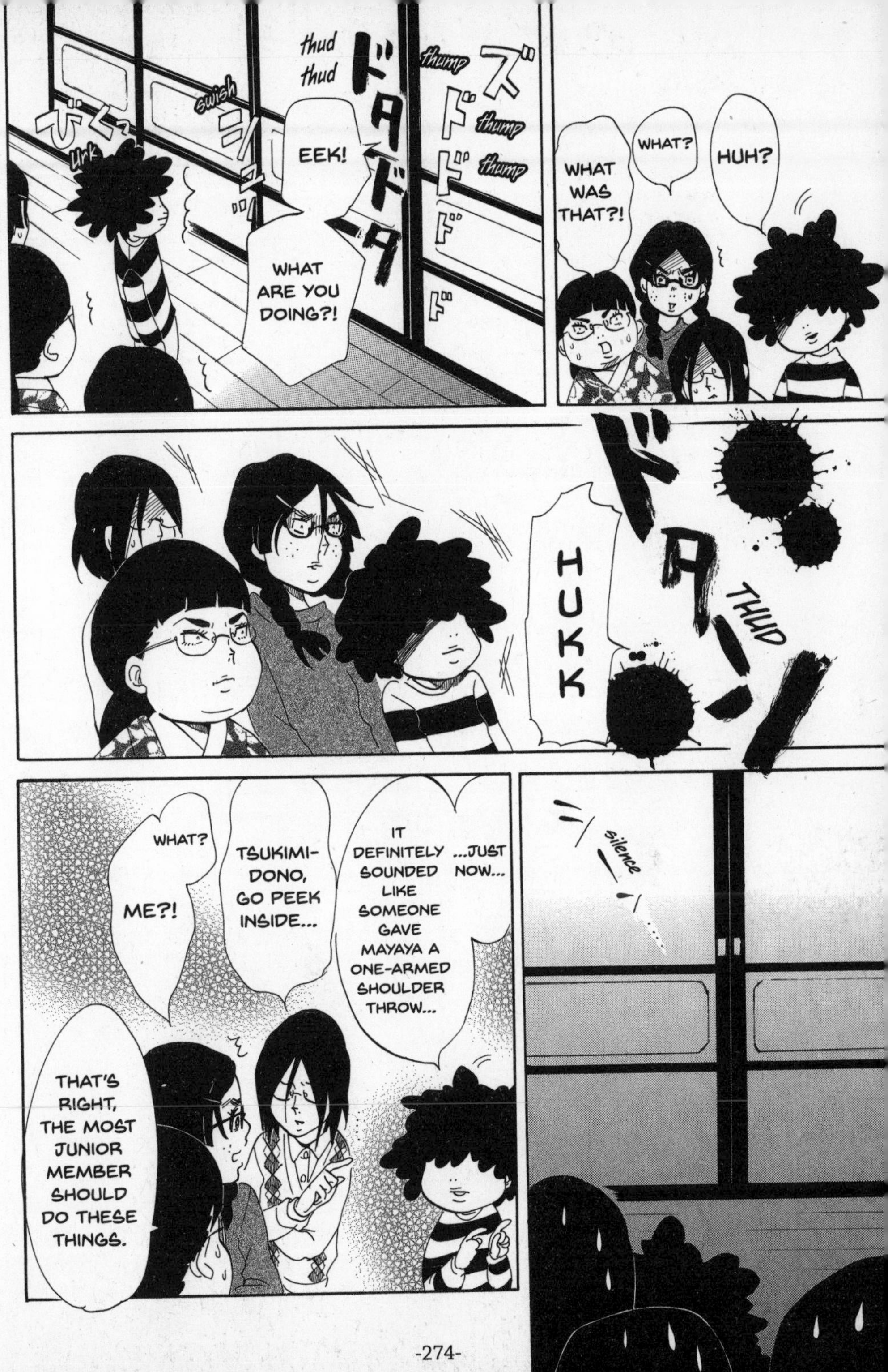
HUH?
WHAT?
WHAT WAS THAT?!
thump thump thump
thud thud
EEK!
WHAT ARE YOU DOING?!
swish
Urk
THUD
HUKK
silence
...JUST NOW...
IT DEFINITELY SOUNDED LIKE SOMEONE GAVE MAYAYA A ONE-ARMED SHOULDER THROW...
TSUKIMI-DONO, GO PEEK INSIDE...
WHAT? ME?!
THAT'S RIGHT, THE MOST JUNIOR MEMBER SHOULD DO THESE THINGS.

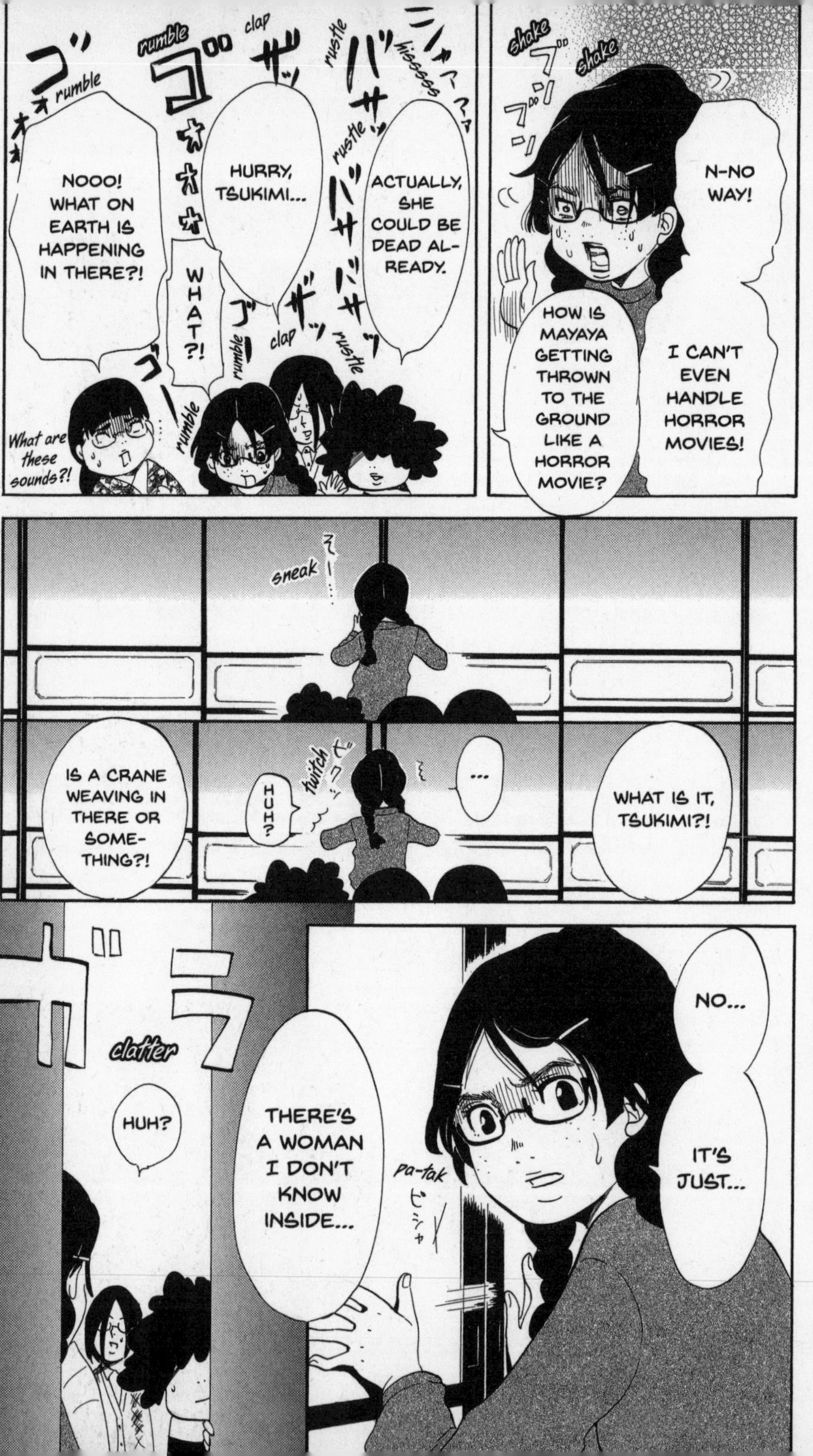
shake
shake
N-NO WAY!
I CAN'T EVEN HANDLE HORROR MOVIES!
HOW IS MAYAYA GETTING THROWN TO THE GROUND LIKE A HORROR MOVIE?
hissssss
rustle
rustle
ACTUALLY, SHE COULD BE DEAD AL-READY.
clap
HURRY, TSUKIMI...
rumble
rumble
NOOO! WHAT ON EARTH IS HAPPENING IN THERE?!
WHAT?!
rustle
clap
rumble
rumble
What are these sounds?!
sneak
WHAT IS IT, TSUKIMI?!
...
twitch
HUH?
IS A CRANE WEAVING IN THERE OR SOME-THING?!
NO...
IT'S JUST...
THERE'S A WOMAN I DON'T KNOW INSIDE...
pa-tak
clatter
HUH?

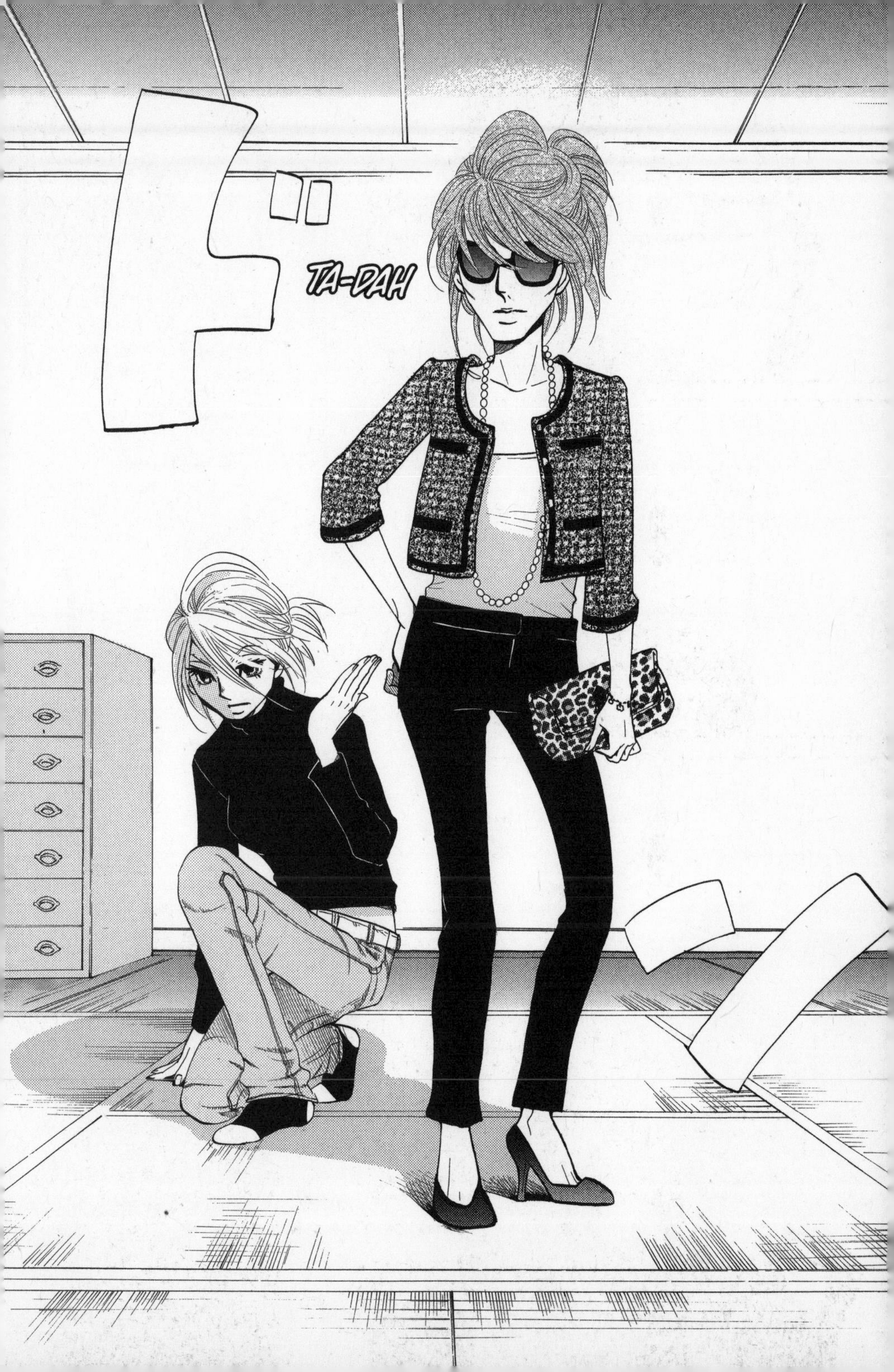
TA-DAH

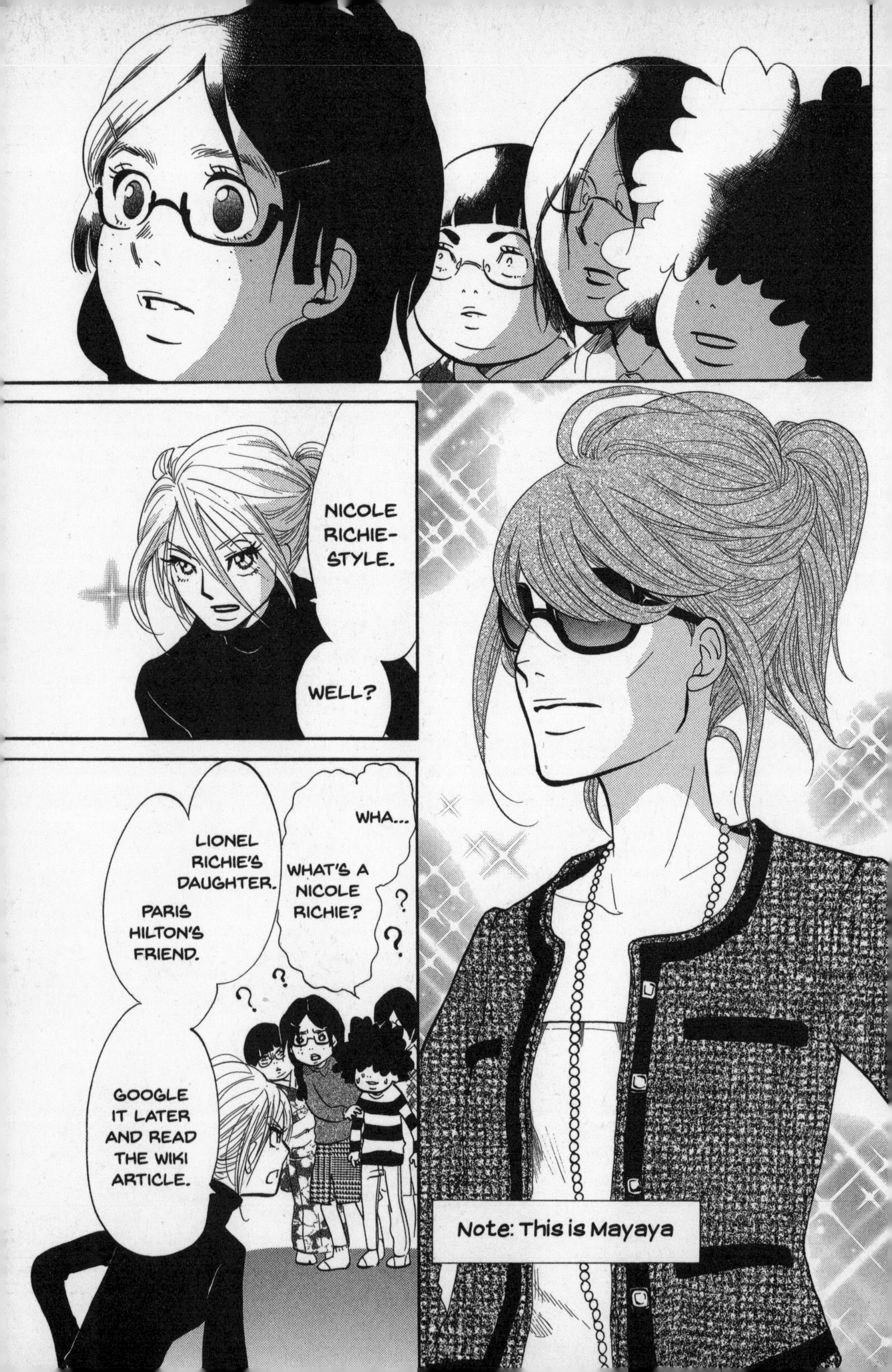
Note: This is Mayaya
NICOLE RICHIE-STYLE.
WELL?
WHA...
WHAT'S A NICOLE RICHIE?
LIONEL RICHIE'S DAUGHTER.
PARIS HILTON'S FRIEND.
GOOGLE IT LATER AND READ THE WIKI ARTICLE.

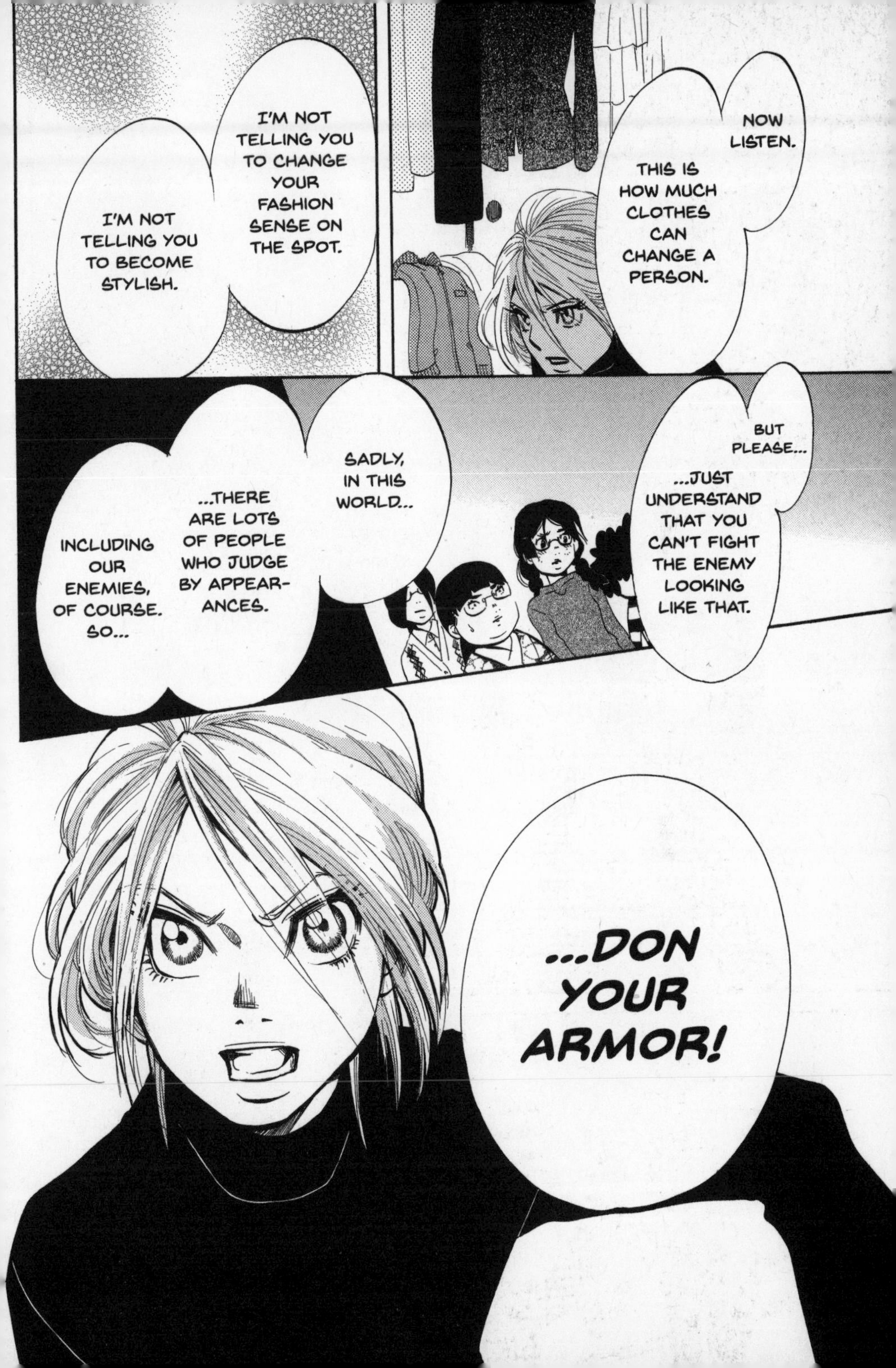
NOW LISTEN.
THIS IS HOW MUCH CLOTHES CAN CHANGE A PERSON.
I'M NOT TELLING YOU TO CHANGE YOUR FASHION SENSE ON THE SPOT.
I'M NOT TELLING YOU TO BECOME STYLISH.
BUT PLEASE...
...JUST UNDERSTAND THAT YOU CAN'T FIGHT THE ENEMY LOOKING LIKE THAT.
SADLY, IN THIS WORLD...
...THERE ARE LOTS OF PEOPLE WHO JUDGE BY APPEARANCES.
INCLUDING OUR ENEMIES, OF COURSE. SO...
...DON YOUR ARMOR!

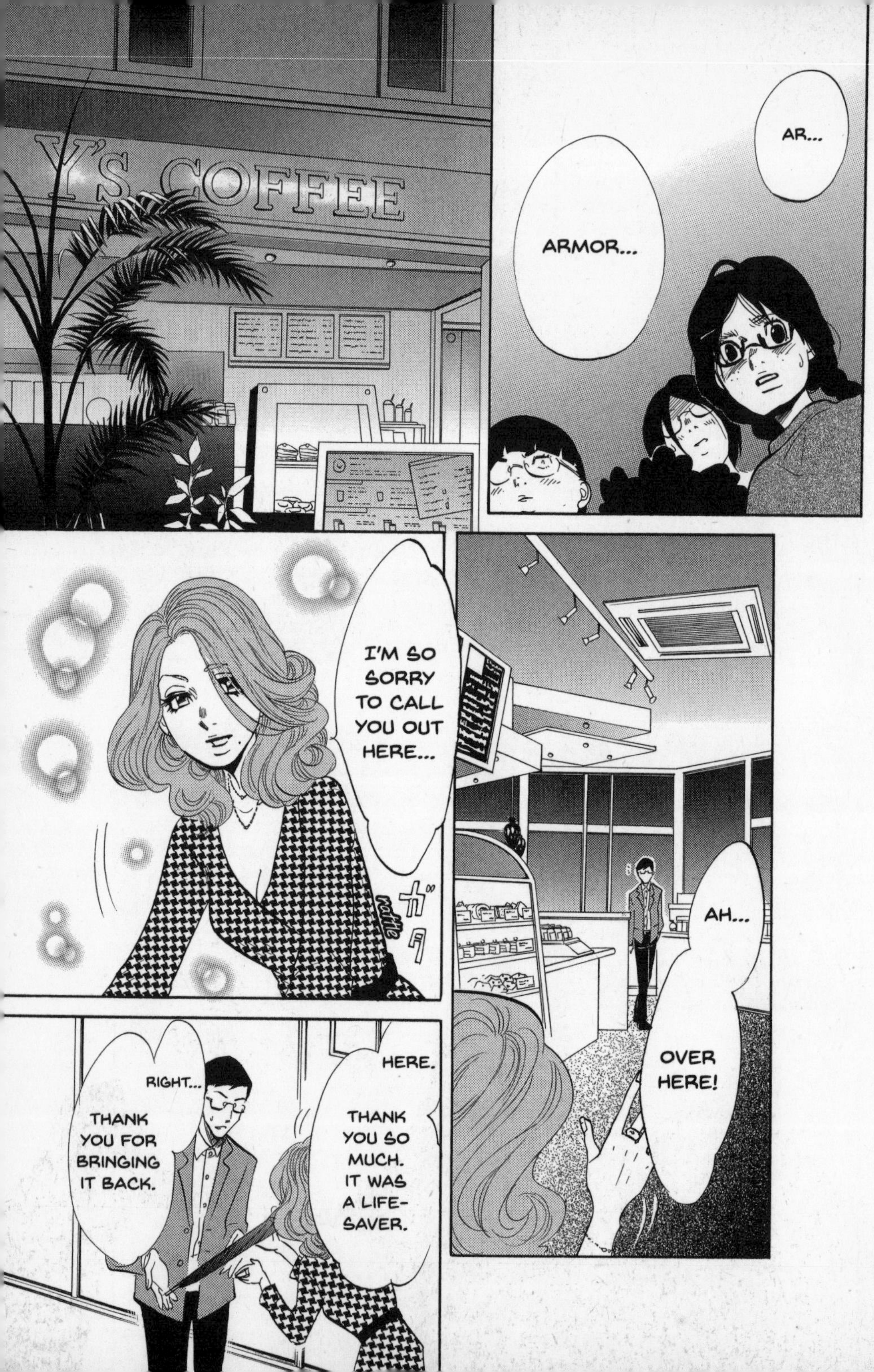
AR...
ARMOR...
Y'S COFFEE
AH...
OVER HERE!
I'M SO SORRY TO CALL YOU OUT HERE...
rattle
HERE.
THANK YOU SO MUCH. IT WAS A LIFE-SAVER.
RIGHT...
THANK YOU FOR BRINGING IT BACK.

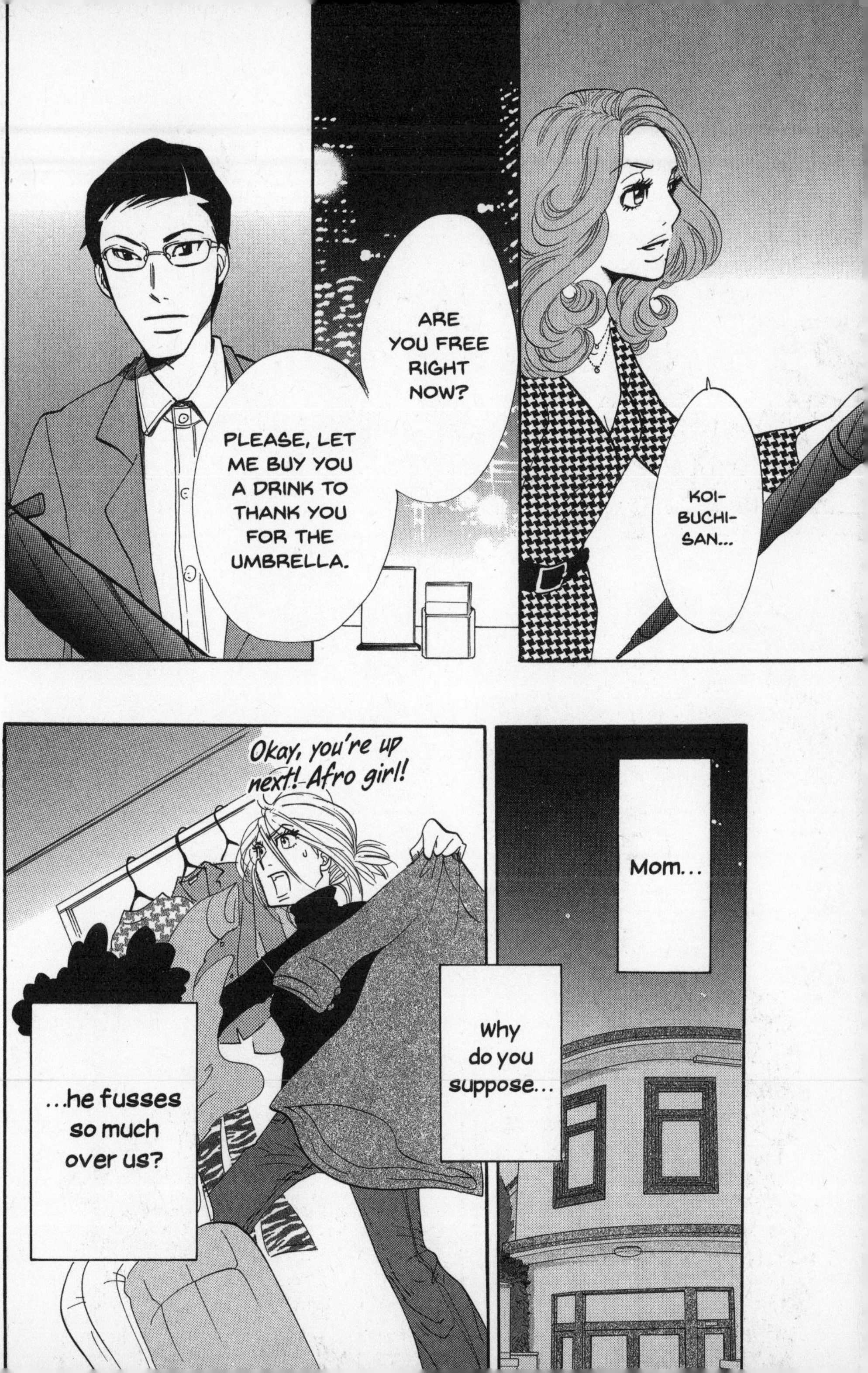
KOI-BUCHI-SAN...
ARE YOU FREE RIGHT NOW?
PLEASE, LET ME BUY YOU A DRINK TO THANK YOU FOR THE UMBRELLA.
Mom...
Why do you suppose...
Okay, you're up next! Afro girl!
...he fusses so much over us?

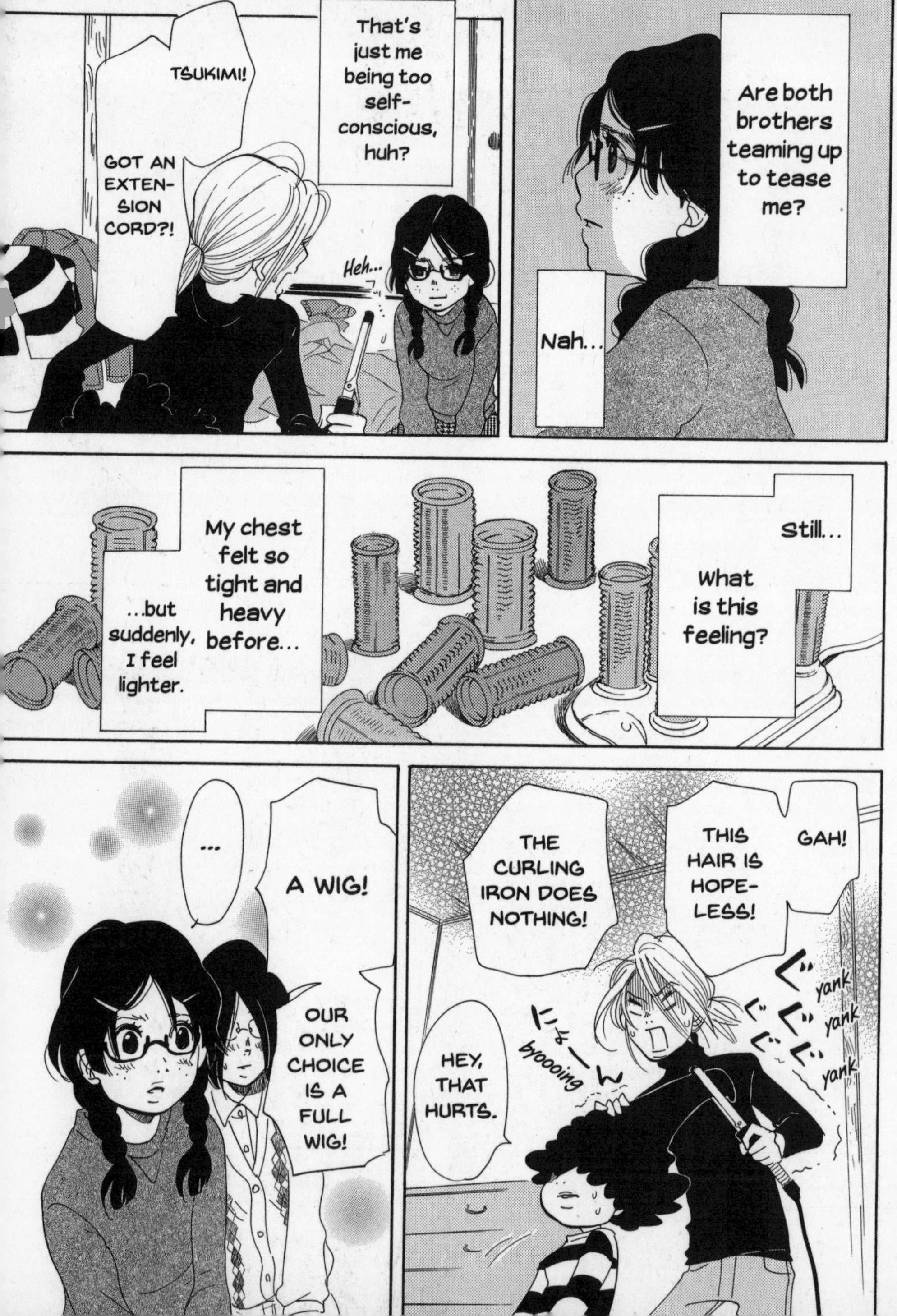
Are both brothers teaming up to tease me?
Nah...
That's just me being too self-conscious, huh?
TSUKIMI!
GOT AN EXTENSION CORD?!
Heh...
Still...
What is this feeling?
My chest felt so tight and heavy before...
...but suddenly, I feel lighter.
GAH!
THIS HAIR IS HOPELESS!
THE CURLING IRON DOES NOTHING!
yank
yank
yank
byoooing
HEY, THAT HURTS.
A WIG!
...
OUR ONLY CHOICE IS A FULL WIG!

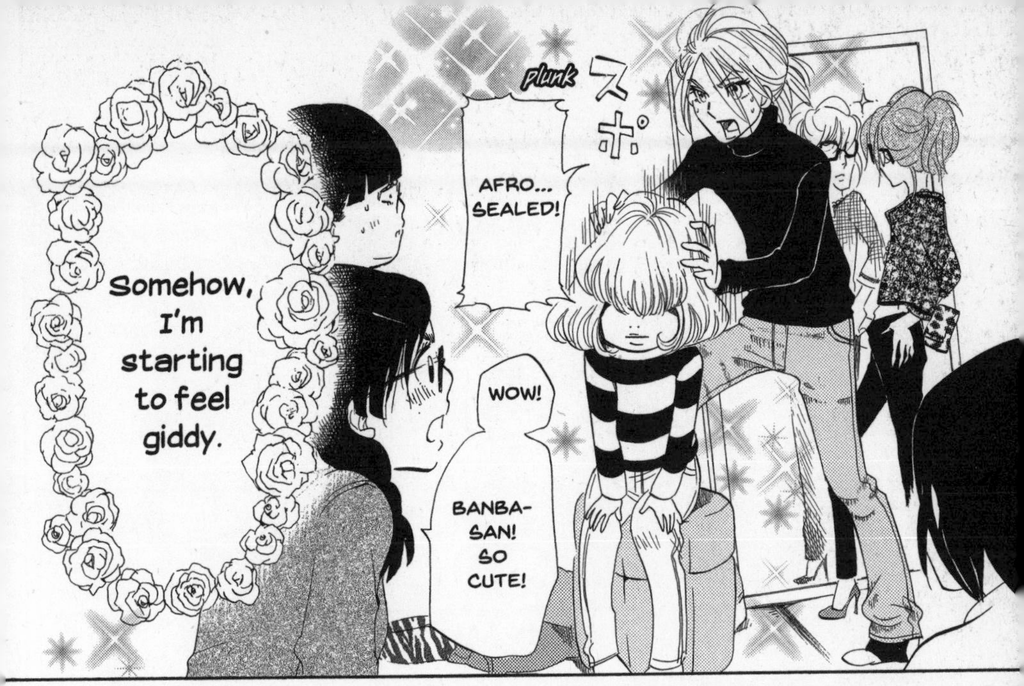
plunk
スポ
AFRO... SEALED!
WOW!
BANBA-SAN! SO CUTE!
Somehow, I'm starting to feel giddy.

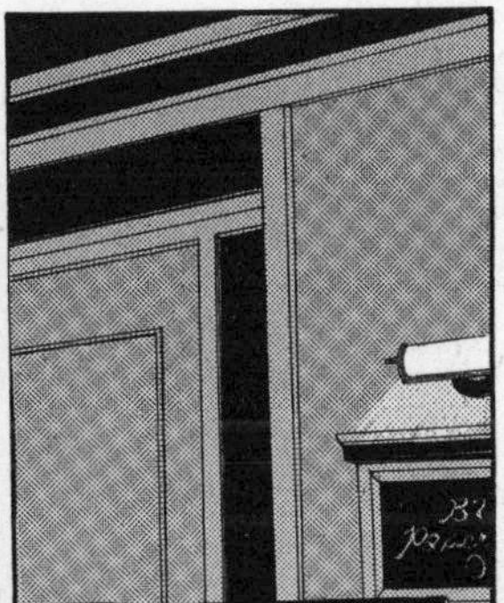

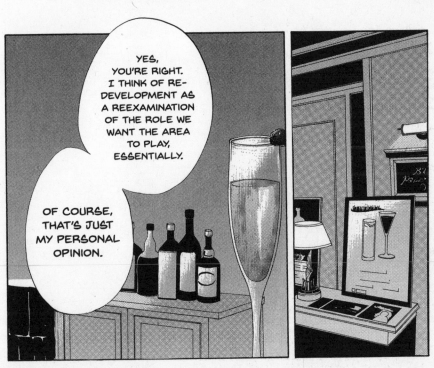

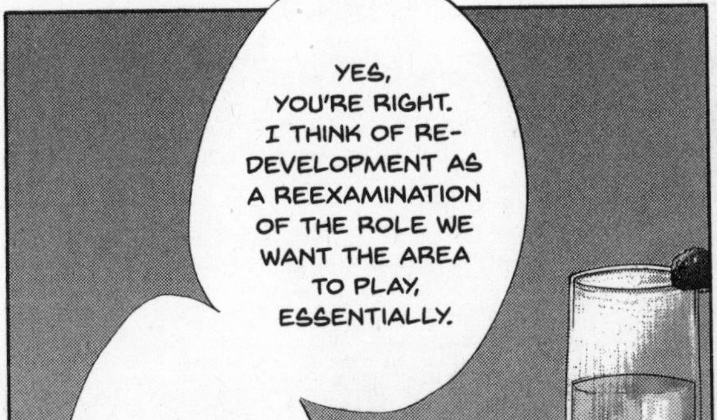
YES, YOU'RE RIGHT. I THINK OF RE-DEVELOPMENT AS A REEXAMINATION OF THE ROLE WE WANT THE AREA TO PLAY, ESSENTIALLY.
OF COURSE, THAT'S JUST MY PERSONAL OPINION.

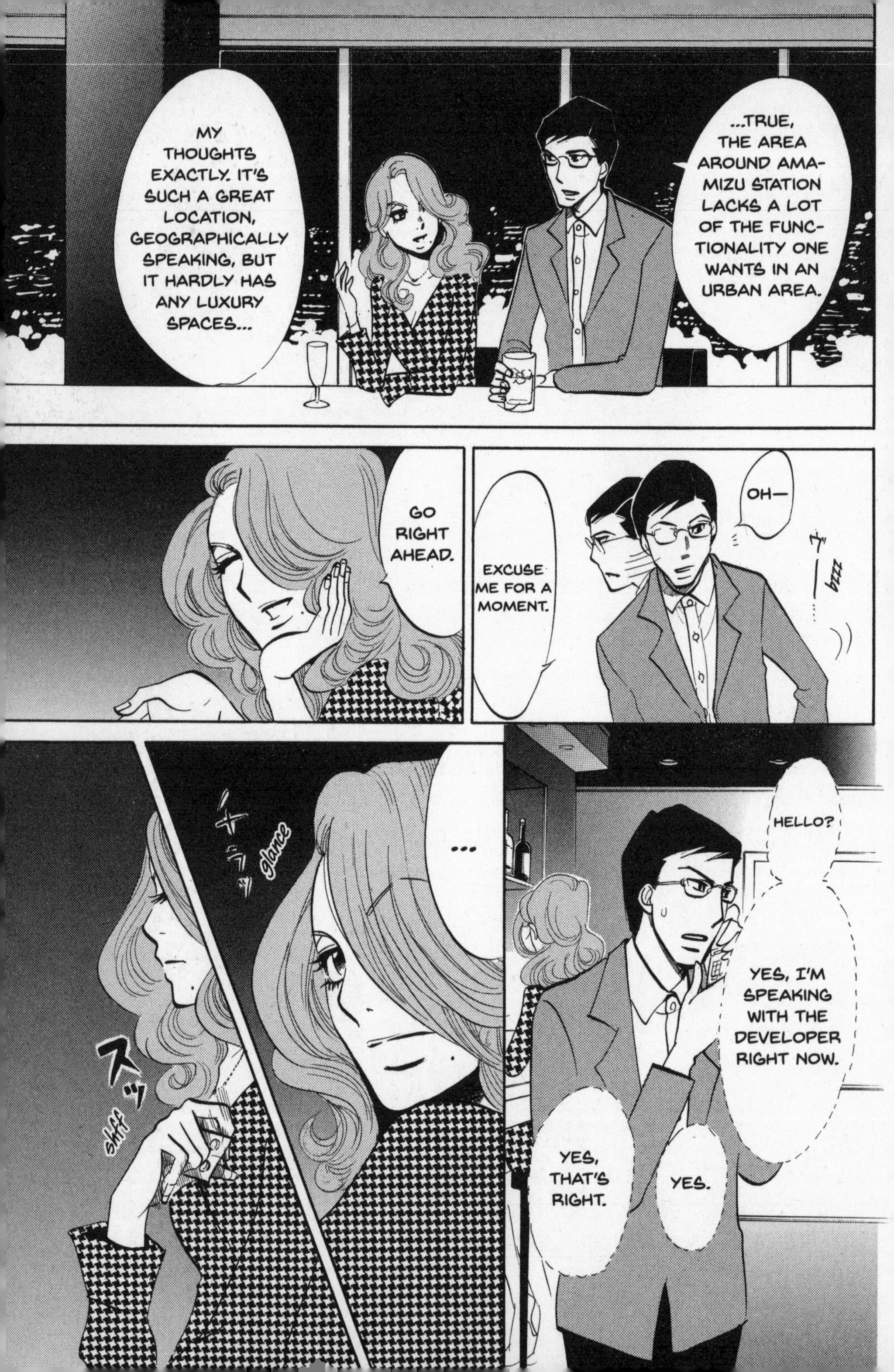
...TRUE, THE AREA AROUND AMA-MIZU STATION LACKS A LOT OF THE FUNC-TIONALITY ONE WANTS IN AN URBAN AREA.
MY THOUGHTS EXACTLY. IT'S SUCH A GREAT LOCATION, GEOGRAPHICALLY SPEAKING, BUT IT HARDLY HAS ANY LUXURY SPACES...
OH—
bzzz
EXCUSE ME FOR A MOMENT.
GO RIGHT AHEAD.
HELLO?
YES, I'M SPEAKING WITH THE DEVELOPER RIGHT NOW.
YES.
YES, THAT'S RIGHT.
...
glance
shff

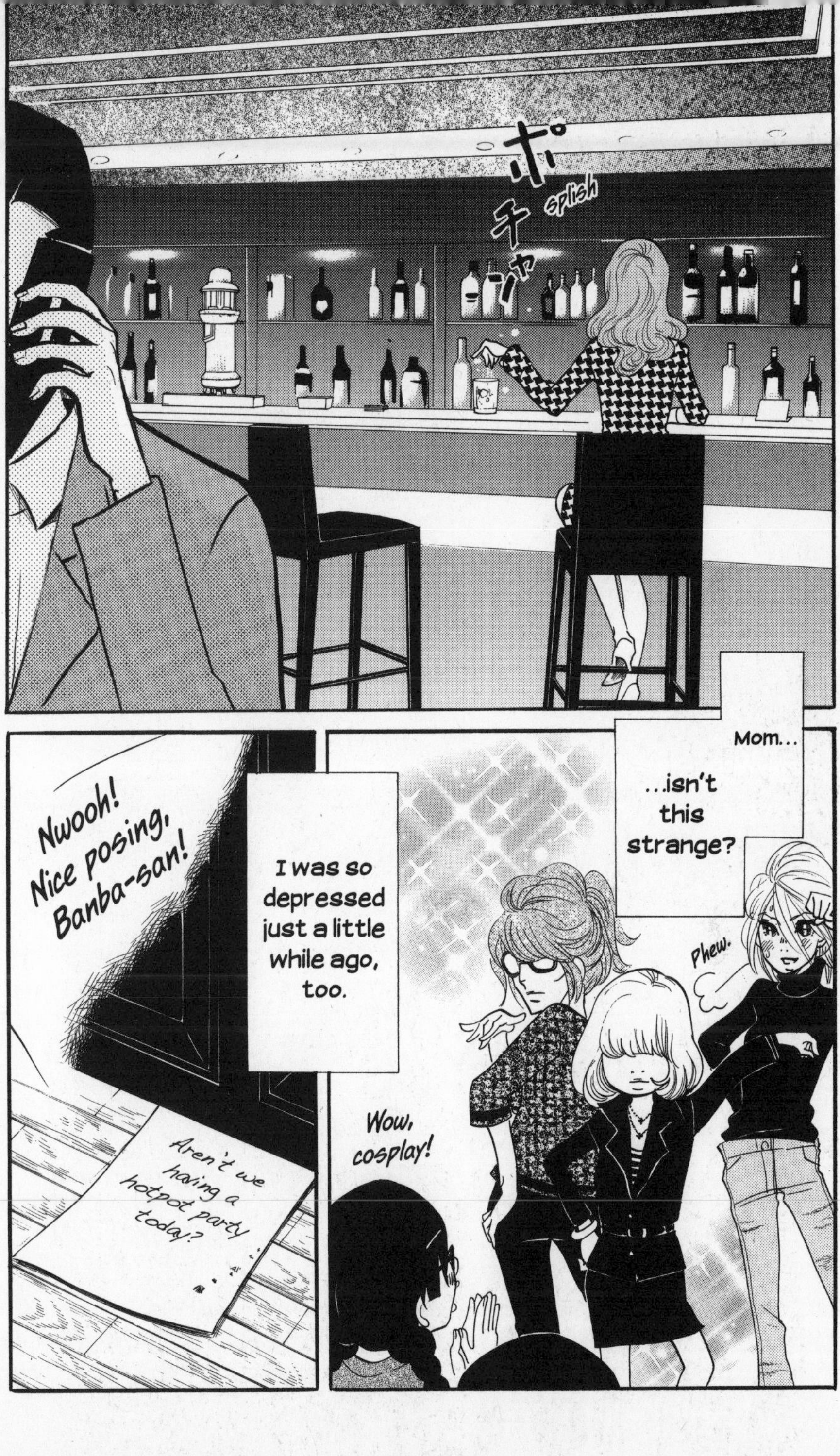

ポチャ
splish
Mom...
...isn't this strange?
Phew.
I was so depressed just a little while ago, too.
Wow, cosplay!
Nwooh! Nice posing, Banba-san!
Aren't we having a hotpot party today?

Episode 10
Fatal Attraction

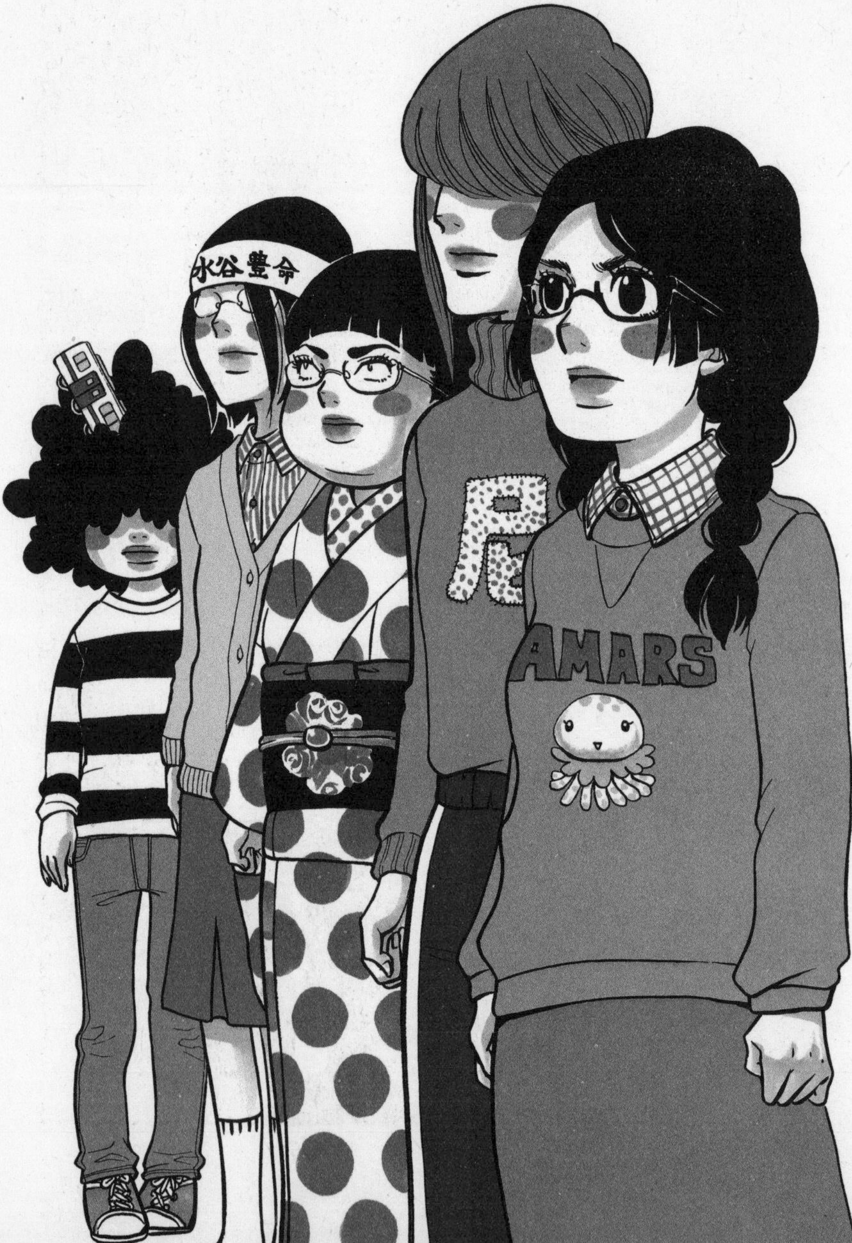
水谷豊命
AMARS

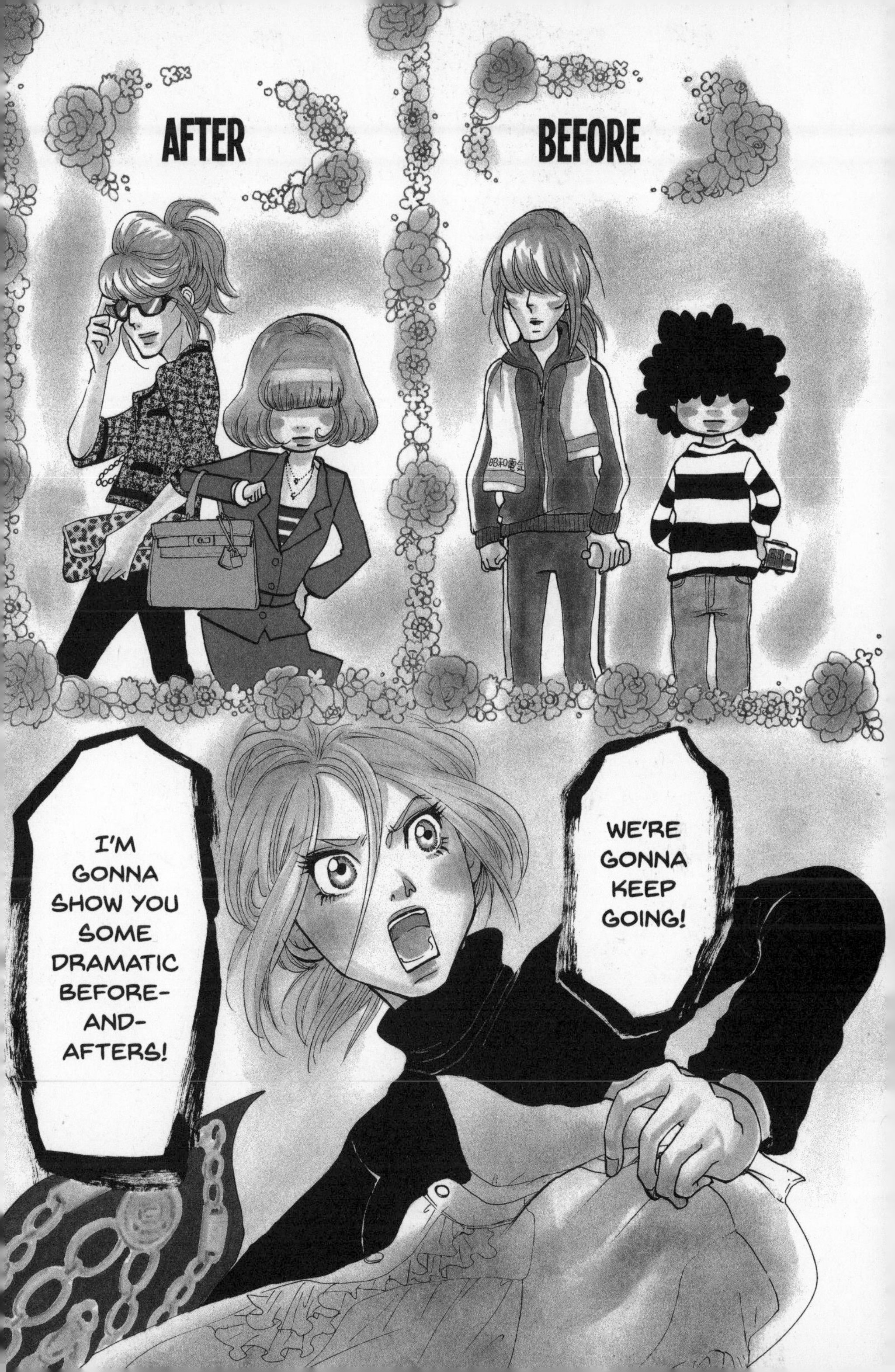
BEFORE
AFTER
WE'RE GONNA KEEP GOING!
I'M GONNA SHOW YOU SOME DRAMATIC BEFORE-AND-AFTERS!

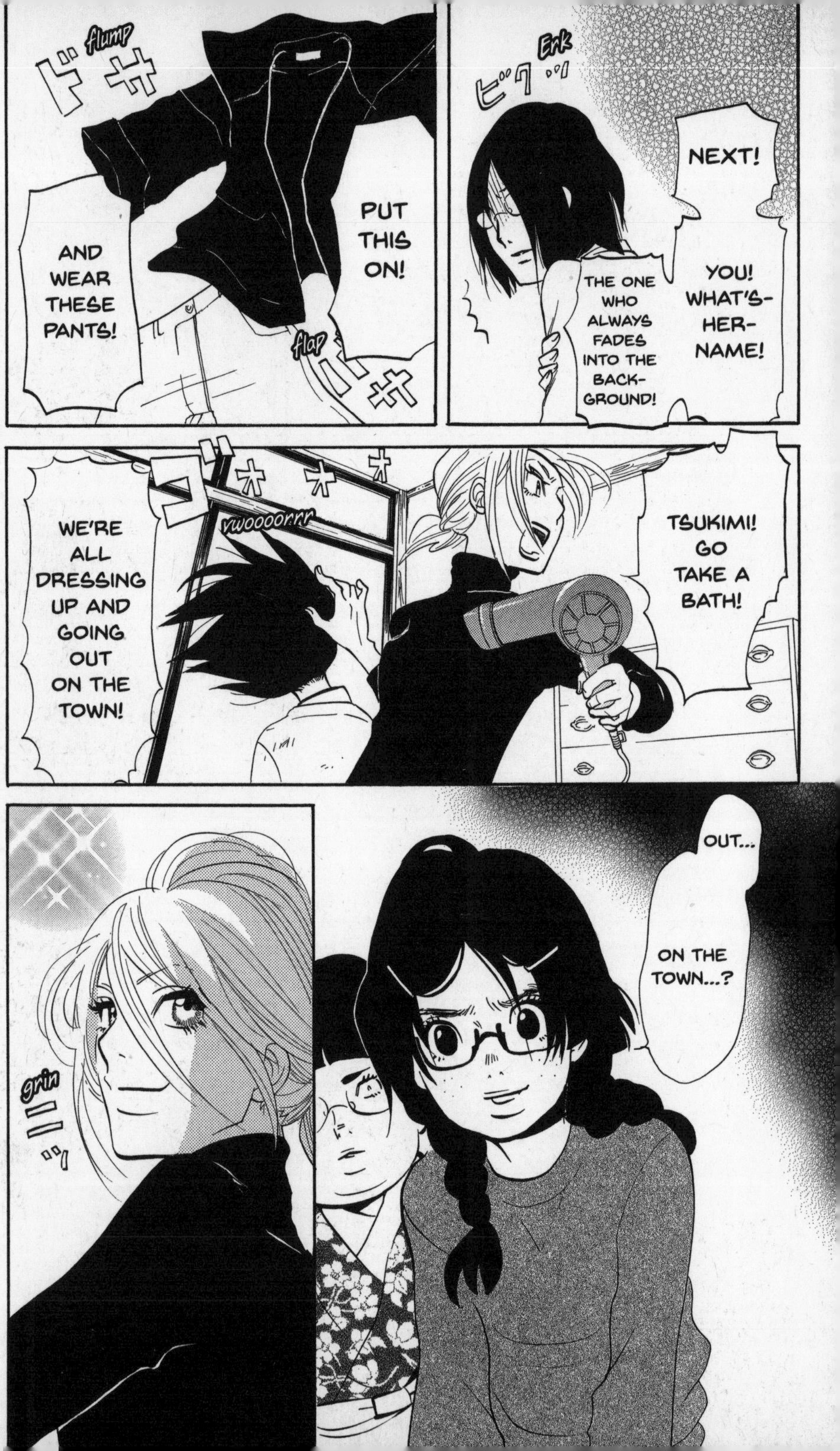
Erk
NEXT!
YOU! WHAT'S-HER-NAME!
THE ONE WHO ALWAYS FADES INTO THE BACKGROUND!
flump
PUT THIS ON!
AND WEAR THESE PANTS!
flap
TSUKIMI! GO TAKE A BATH!
vwoooorrr
WE'RE ALL DRESSING UP AND GOING OUT ON THE TOWN!
OUT...
ON THE TOWN...?
grin

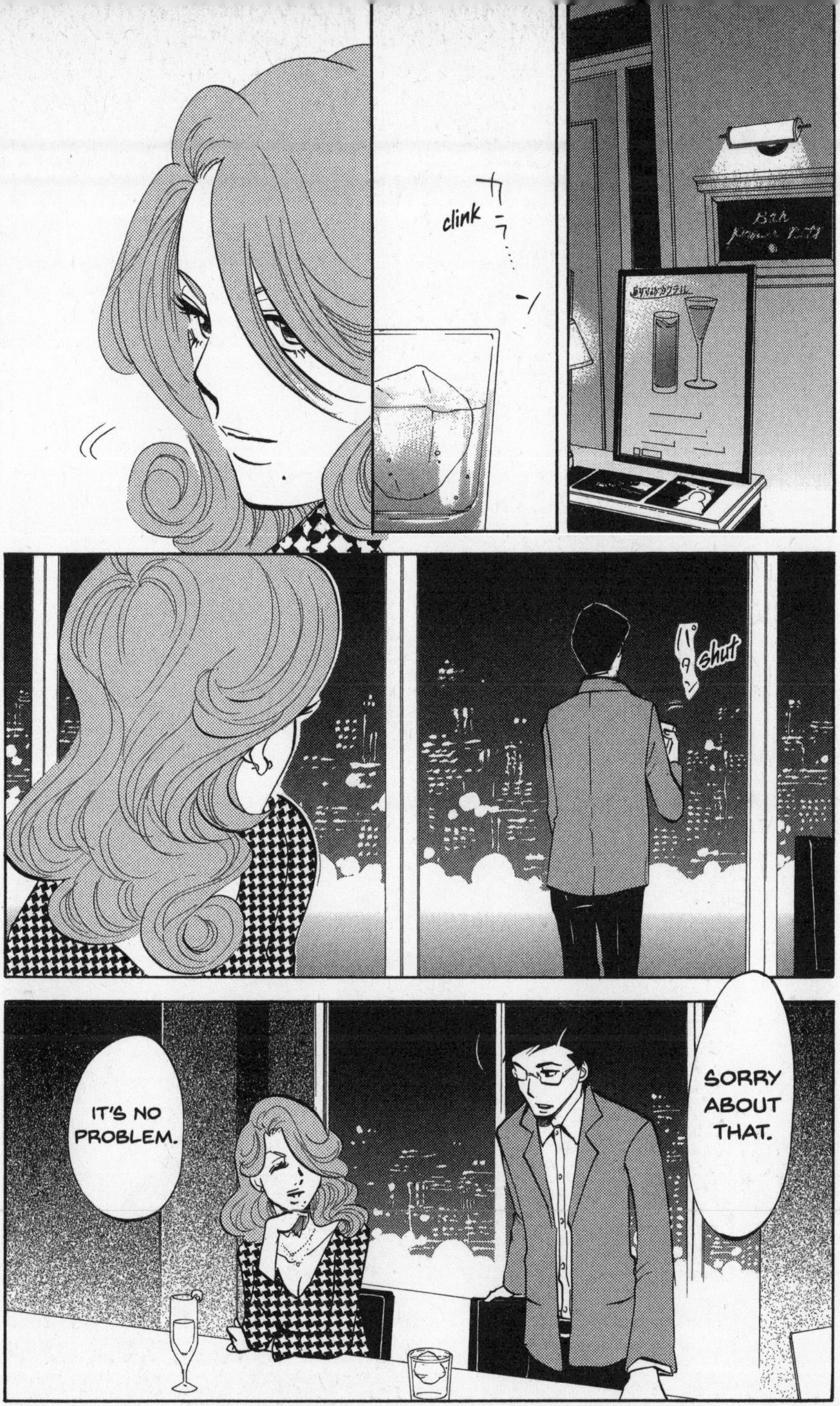
clink
shut
SORRY ABOUT THAT.
IT'S NO PROBLEM.

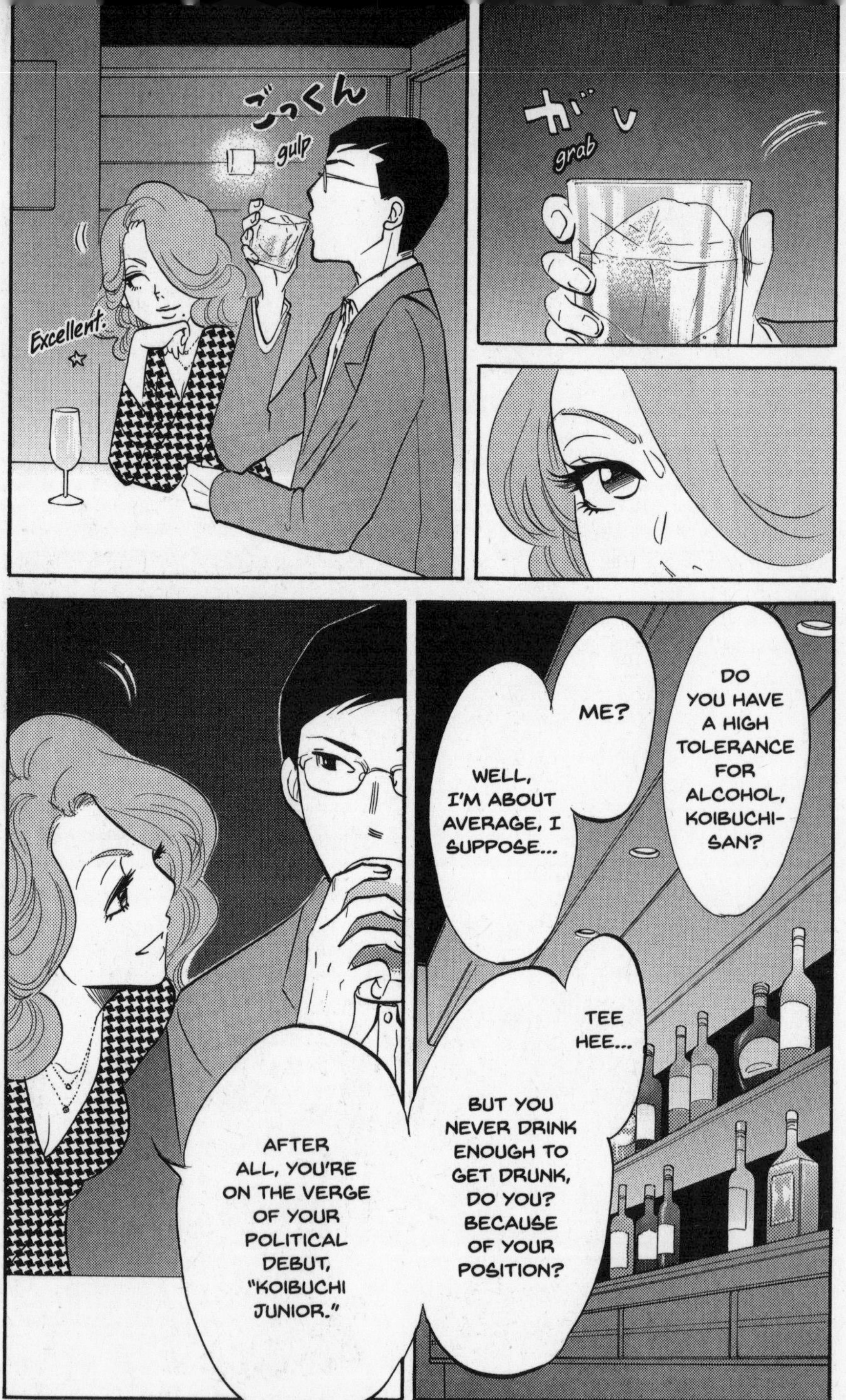

がし
grab
ごっくん
gulp
Excellent.
DO YOU HAVE A HIGH TOLERANCE FOR ALCOHOL, KOIBUCHI-SAN?
ME?
WELL, I'M ABOUT AVERAGE, I SUPPOSE...
TEE HEE...
BUT YOU NEVER DRINK ENOUGH TO GET DRUNK, DO YOU? BECAUSE OF YOUR POSITION?
AFTER ALL, YOU'RE ON THE VERGE OF YOUR POLITICAL DEBUT, "KOIBUCHI JUNIOR."

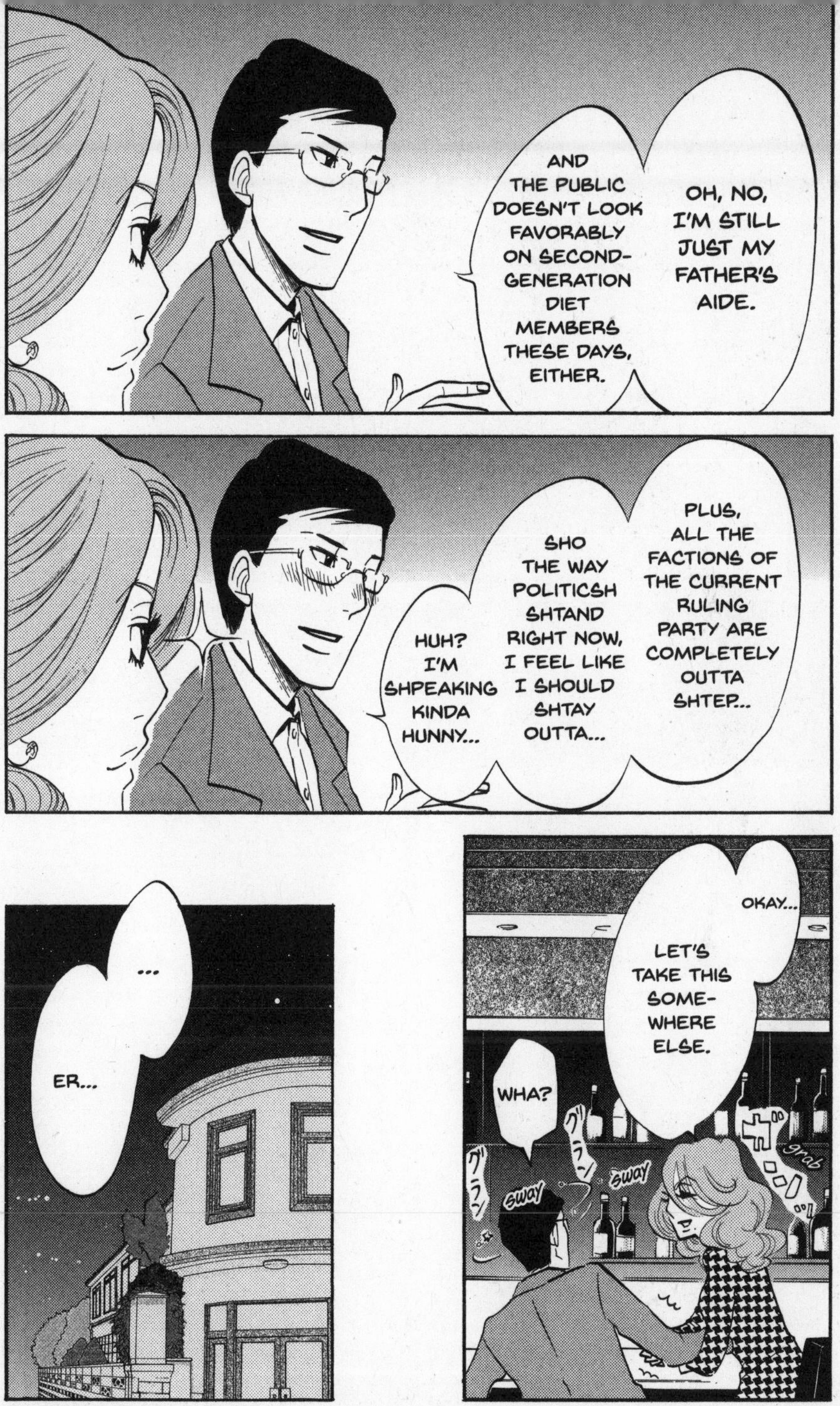
OH, NO, I'M STILL JUST MY FATHER'S AIDE.
AND THE PUBLIC DOESN'T LOOK FAVORABLY ON SECOND-GENERATION DIET MEMBERS THESE DAYS, EITHER.
PLUS, ALL THE FACTIONS OF THE CURRENT RULING PARTY ARE COMPLETELY OUTTA SHTEP...
SHO THE WAY POLITICSH SHTAND RIGHT NOW, I FEEL LIKE I SHOULD SHTAY OUTTA...
HUH? I'M SHPEAKING KINDA HUNNY...
OKAY...
LET'S TAKE THIS SOME-WHERE ELSE.
WHA?
grab
sway
sway
...
ER...

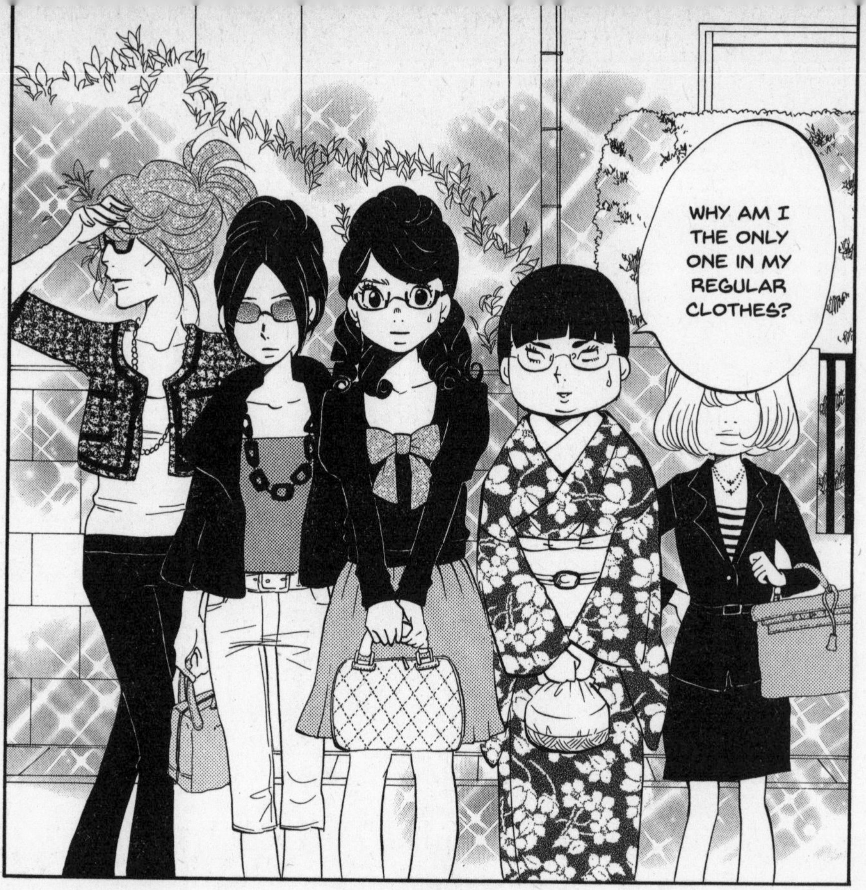
WHY AM I THE ONLY ONE IN MY REGULAR CLOTHES?

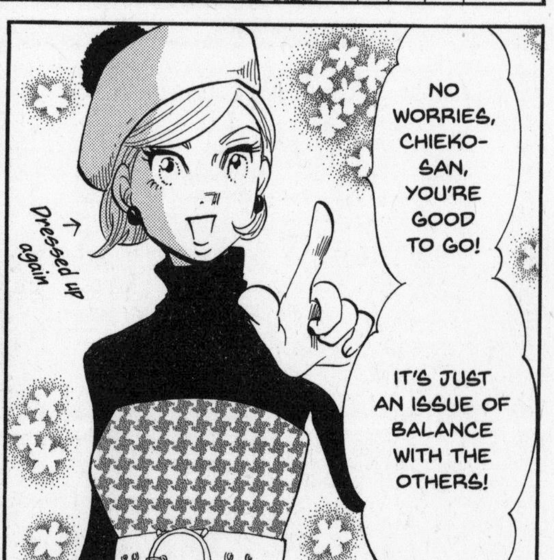
NO WORRIES, CHIEKO-SAN, YOU'RE GOOD TO GO!
IT'S JUST AN ISSUE OF BALANCE WITH THE OTHERS!
← Dressed up again

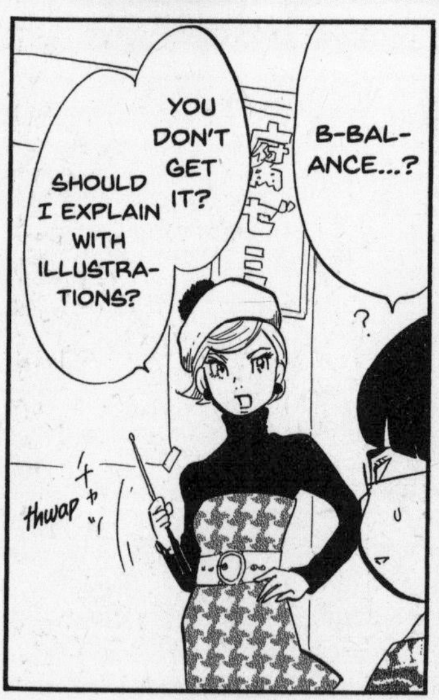
B-BALANCE...?
?
YOU DON'T GET IT?
SHOULD I EXPLAIN WITH ILLUSTRATIONS?
thwap

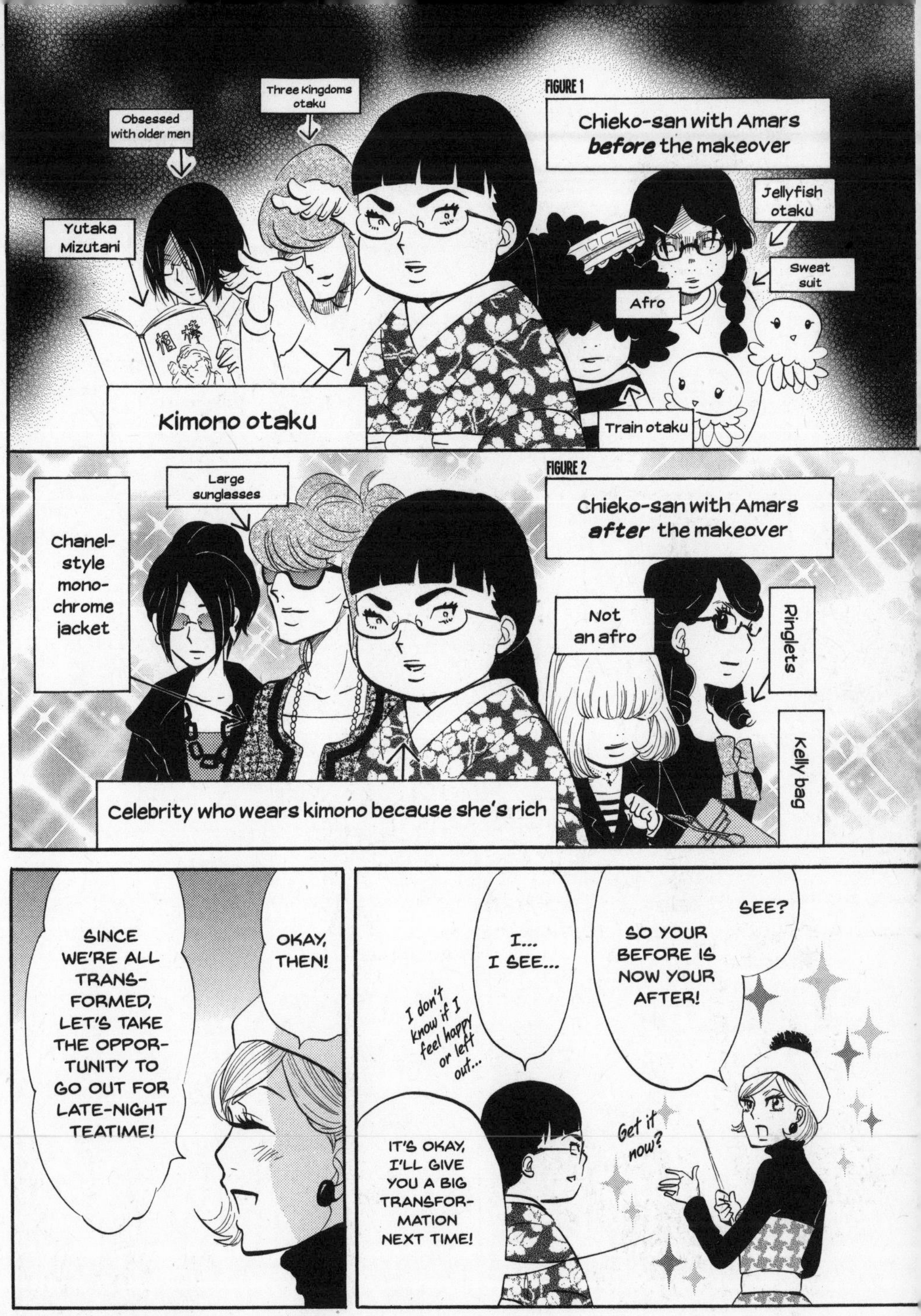
FIGURE 1
Chieko-san with Amars *before* the makeover
Jellyfish otaku
Sweat suit
Afro
Three Kingdoms otaku
Obsessed with older men
Yutaka Mizutani
Train otaku
Kimono otaku
FIGURE 2
Chieko-san with Amars *after* the makeover
Ringlets
Kelly bag
Not an afro
Large sunglasses
Chanel-style mono-chrome jacket
Celebrity who wears kimono because she's rich
SEE? SO YOUR BEFORE IS NOW YOUR AFTER!
I... I SEE...
I don't know if I feel happy or left out...
Get it now?
IT'S OKAY, I'LL GIVE YOU A BIG TRANSFORMATION NEXT TIME!
OKAY, THEN!
SINCE WE'RE ALL TRANSFORMED, LET'S TAKE THE OPPORTUNITY TO GO OUT FOR LATE-NIGHT TEATIME!

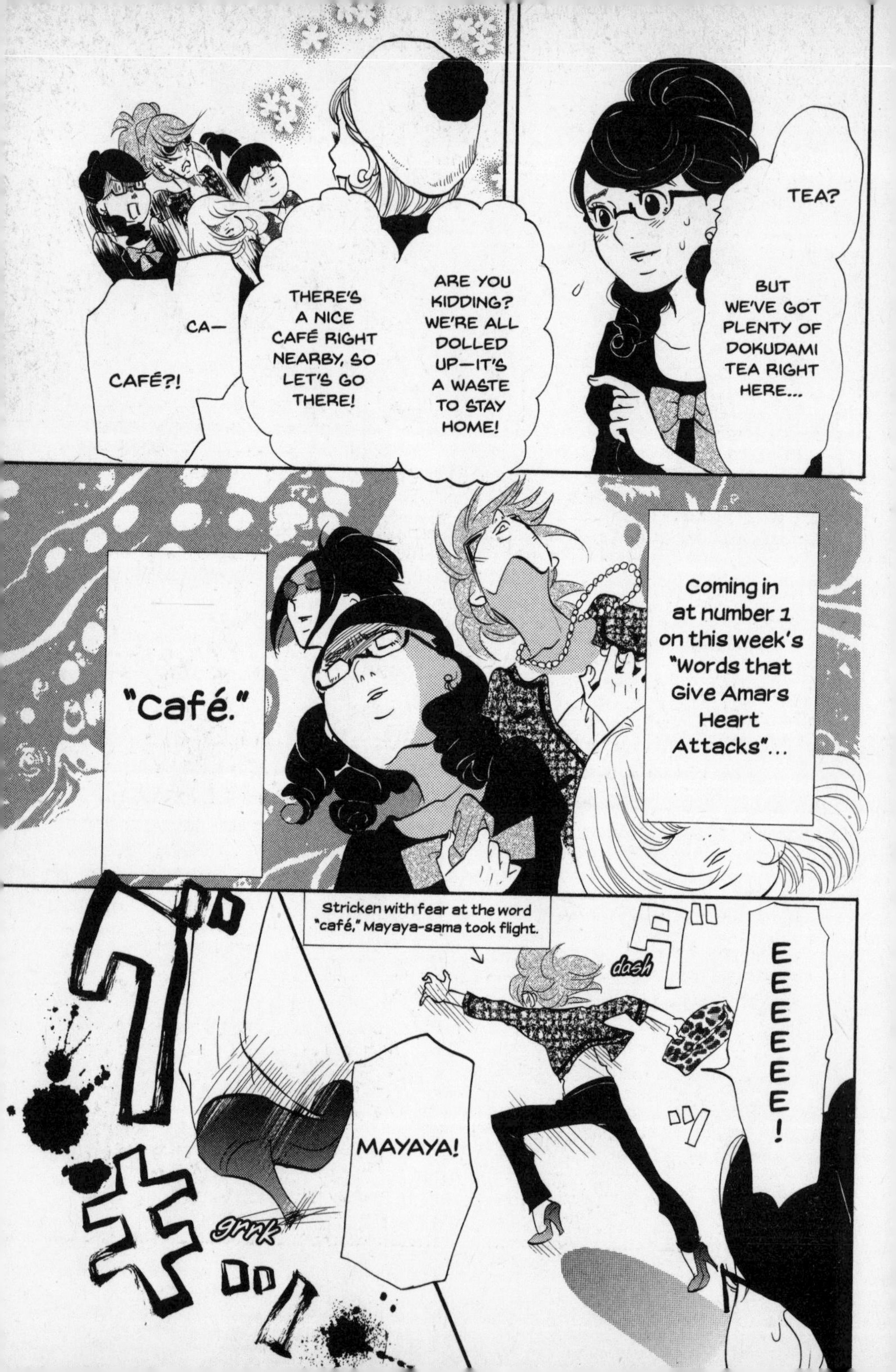
TEA?
BUT WE'VE GOT PLENTY OF DOKUDAMI TEA RIGHT HERE...
ARE YOU KIDDING? WE'RE ALL DOLLED UP—IT'S A WASTE TO STAY HOME!
THERE'S A NICE CAFÉ RIGHT NEARBY, SO LET'S GO THERE!
CA—
CAFÉ?!
Coming in at number 1 on this week's "Words that Give Amars Heart Attacks"...
"Café."
EEEEEEE!
Stricken with fear at the word "café," Mayaya-sama took flight.
dash
MAYAYA!
grrk

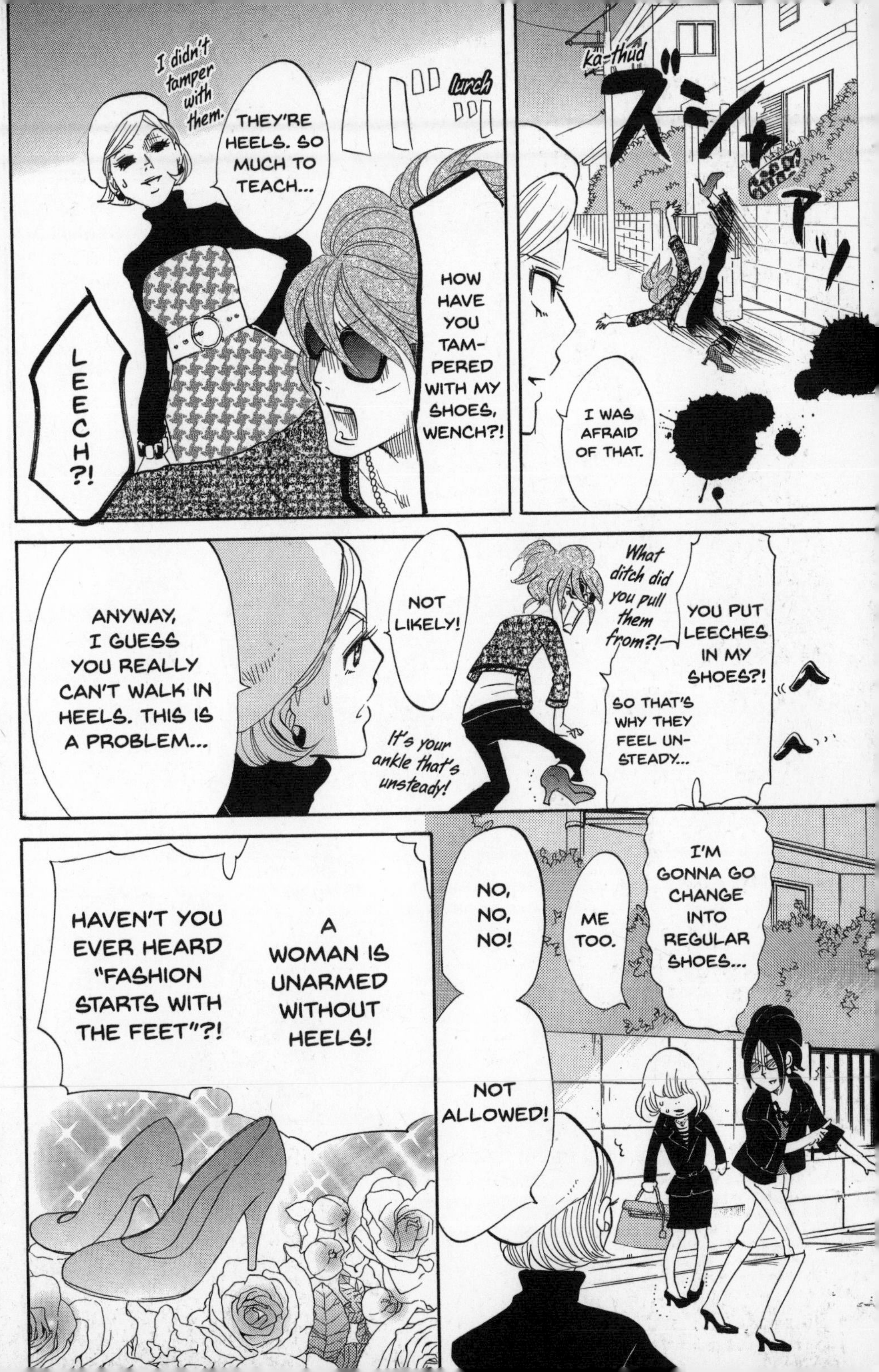

Ka-thud
I WAS AFRAID OF THAT.
lurch
HOW HAVE YOU TAMPERED WITH MY SHOES, WENCH?!
THEY'RE HEELS. SO MUCH TO TEACH...
I didn't tamper with them.
LEECH?!
YOU PUT LEECHES IN MY SHOES?!
What ditch did you pull them from?!
SO THAT'S WHY THEY FEEL UNSTEADY...
It's your ankle that's unsteady!
NOT LIKELY!
ANYWAY, I GUESS YOU REALLY CAN'T WALK IN HEELS. THIS IS A PROBLEM...
I'M GONNA GO CHANGE INTO REGULAR SHOES...
ME TOO.
NO, NO, NO!
NOT ALLOWED!
A WOMAN IS UNARMED WITHOUT HEELS!
HAVEN'T YOU EVER HEARD "FASHION STARTS WITH THE FEET"?!

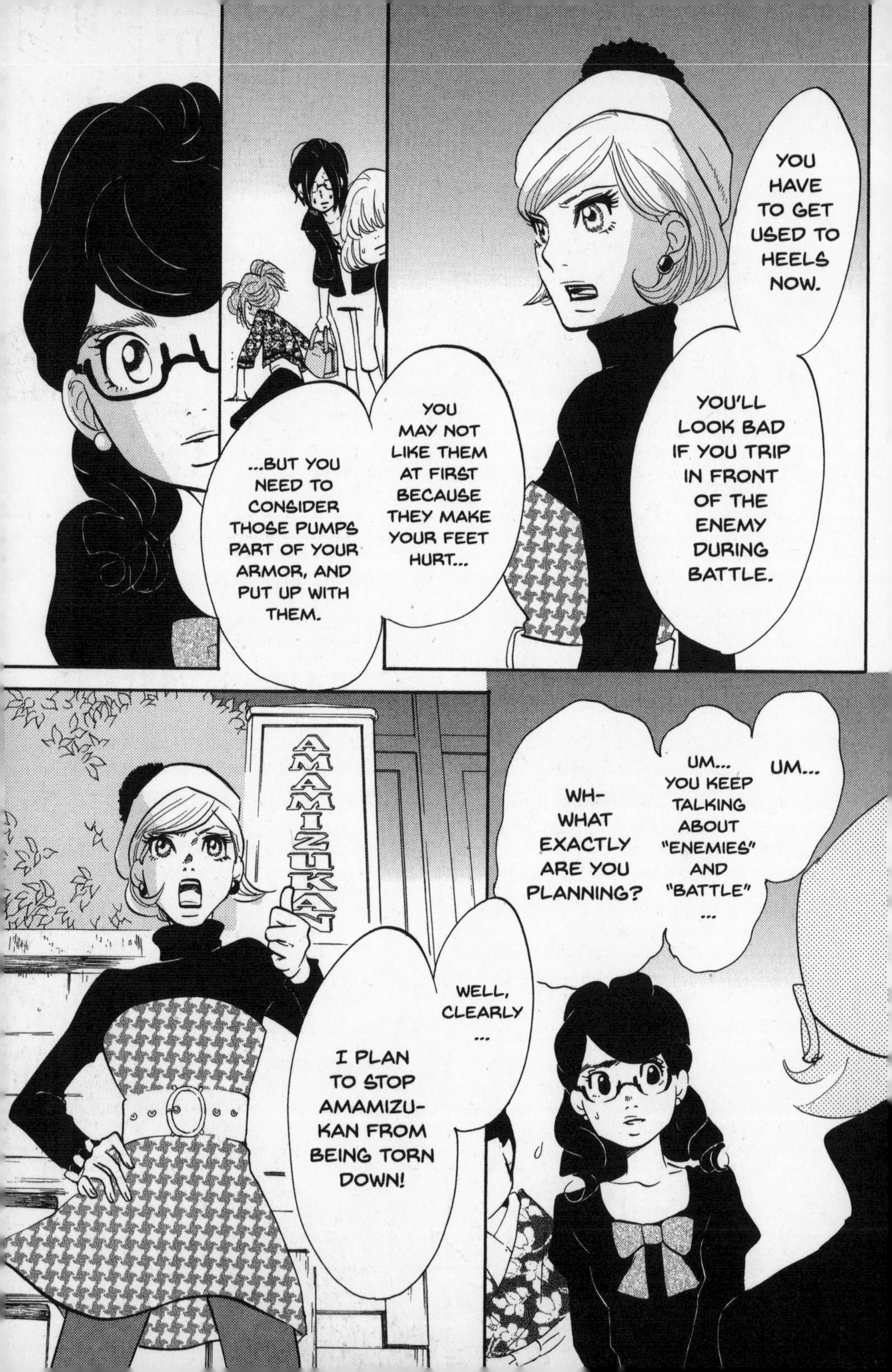
YOU HAVE TO GET USED TO HEELS NOW.
YOU'LL LOOK BAD IF YOU TRIP IN FRONT OF THE ENEMY DURING BATTLE.
YOU MAY NOT LIKE THEM AT FIRST BECAUSE THEY MAKE YOUR FEET HURT...
...BUT YOU NEED TO CONSIDER THOSE PUMPS PART OF YOUR ARMOR, AND PUT UP WITH THEM.
UM...
UM... YOU KEEP TALKING ABOUT "ENEMIES" AND "BATTLE" ...
WH- WHAT EXACTLY ARE YOU PLANNING?
AMAMIZUKAN
WELL, CLEARLY ...
I PLAN TO STOP AMAMIZU-KAN FROM BEING TORN DOWN!

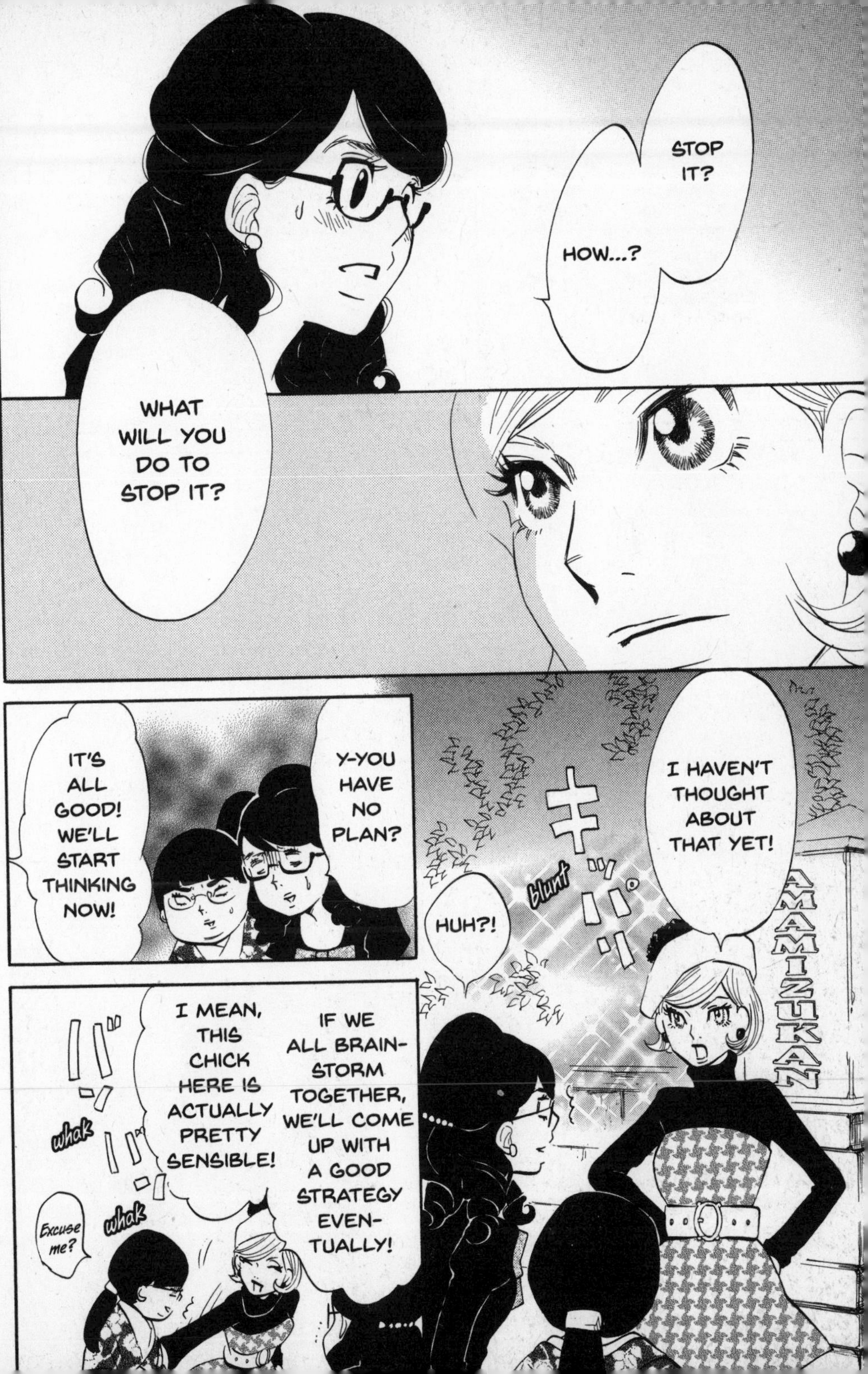
STOP IT?
HOW...?
WHAT WILL YOU DO TO STOP IT?
I HAVEN'T THOUGHT ABOUT THAT YET!
blunt
HUH?!
AMAMIZUKAN
Y-YOU HAVE NO PLAN?
IT'S ALL GOOD! WE'LL START THINKING NOW!
IF WE ALL BRAIN-STORM TOGETHER, WE'LL COME UP WITH A GOOD STRATEGY EVEN-TUALLY!
I MEAN, THIS CHICK HERE IS ACTUALLY PRETTY SENSIBLE!
whak
whak
Excuse me?

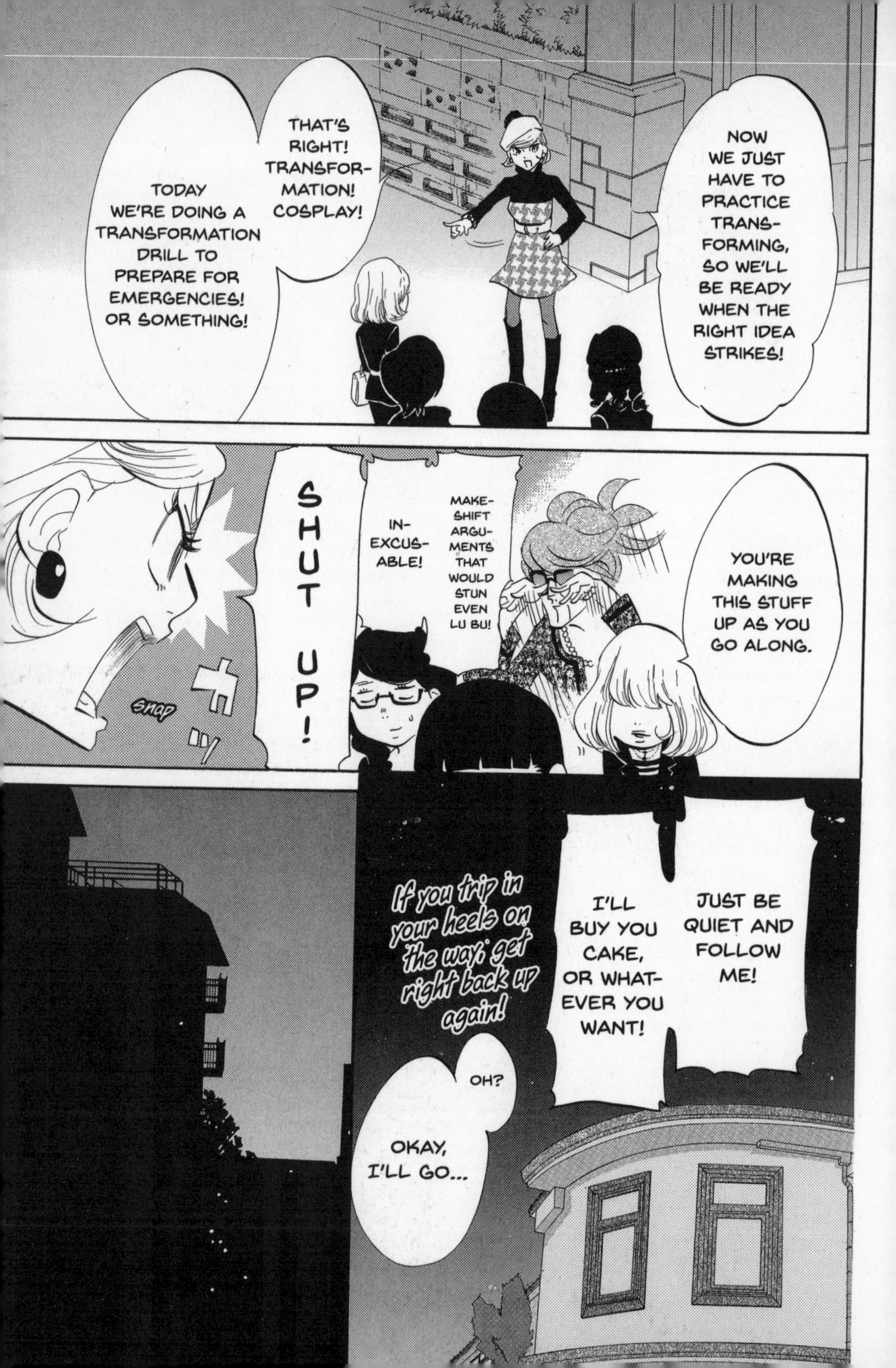
NOW WE JUST HAVE TO PRACTICE TRANS-FORMING, SO WE'LL BE READY WHEN THE RIGHT IDEA STRIKES!
THAT'S RIGHT! TRANSFOR-MATION! COSPLAY!
TODAY WE'RE DOING A TRANSFORMATION DRILL TO PREPARE FOR EMERGENCIES! OR SOMETHING!
YOU'RE MAKING THIS STUFF UP AS YOU GO ALONG.
MAKE-SHIFT ARGU-MENTS THAT WOULD STUN EVEN LU BU!
IN-EXCUS-ABLE!
SHUT UP!
Snap
JUST BE QUIET AND FOLLOW ME!
I'LL BUY YOU CAKE, OR WHAT-EVER YOU WANT!
If you trip in your heels on 'the way,' get right back up again!
OH?
OKAY, I'LL GO...

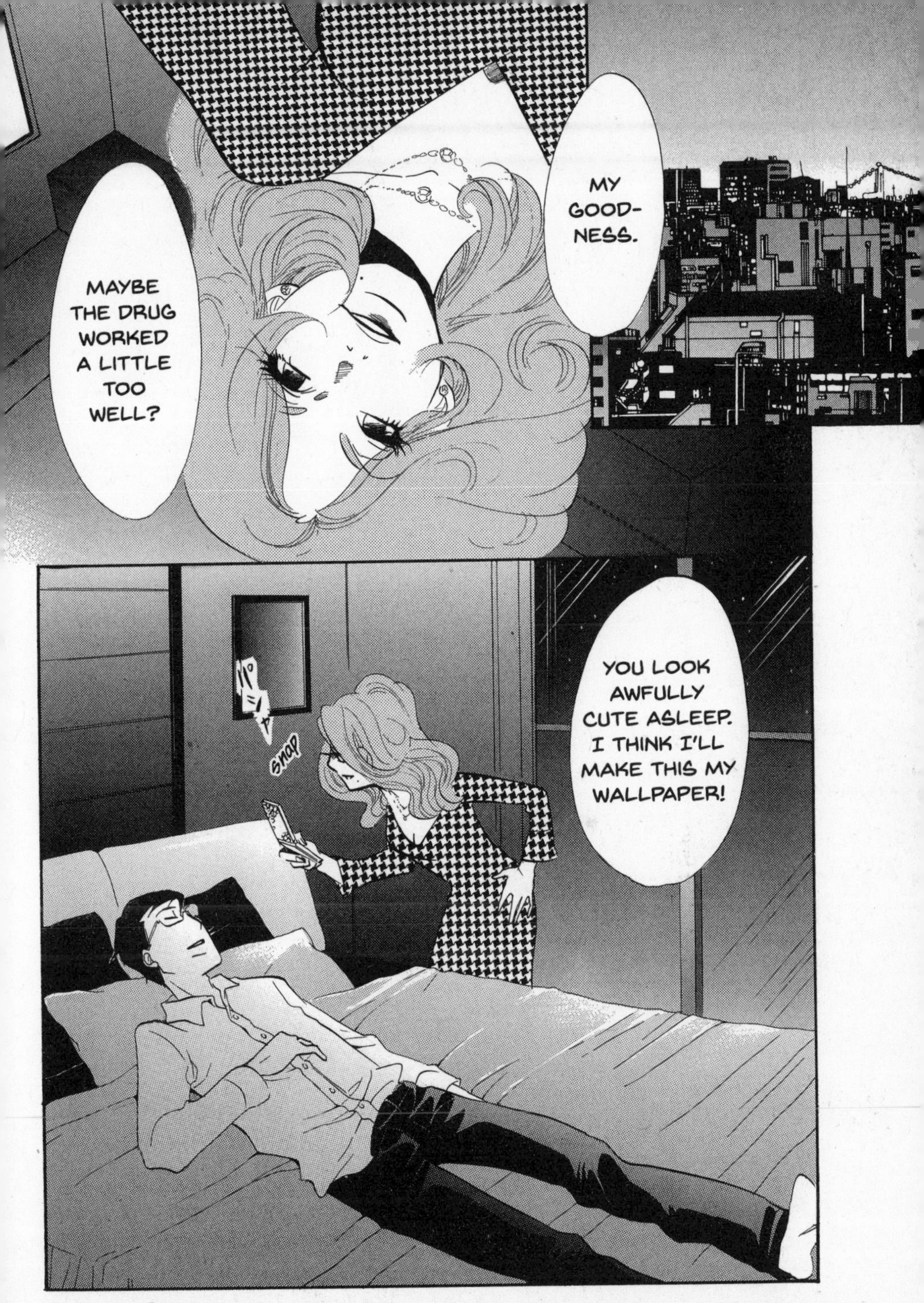
MY GOODNESS.
MAYBE THE DRUG WORKED A LITTLE TOO WELL?
YOU LOOK AWFULLY CUTE ASLEEP. I THINK I'LL MAKE THIS MY WALLPAPER!
SNAP

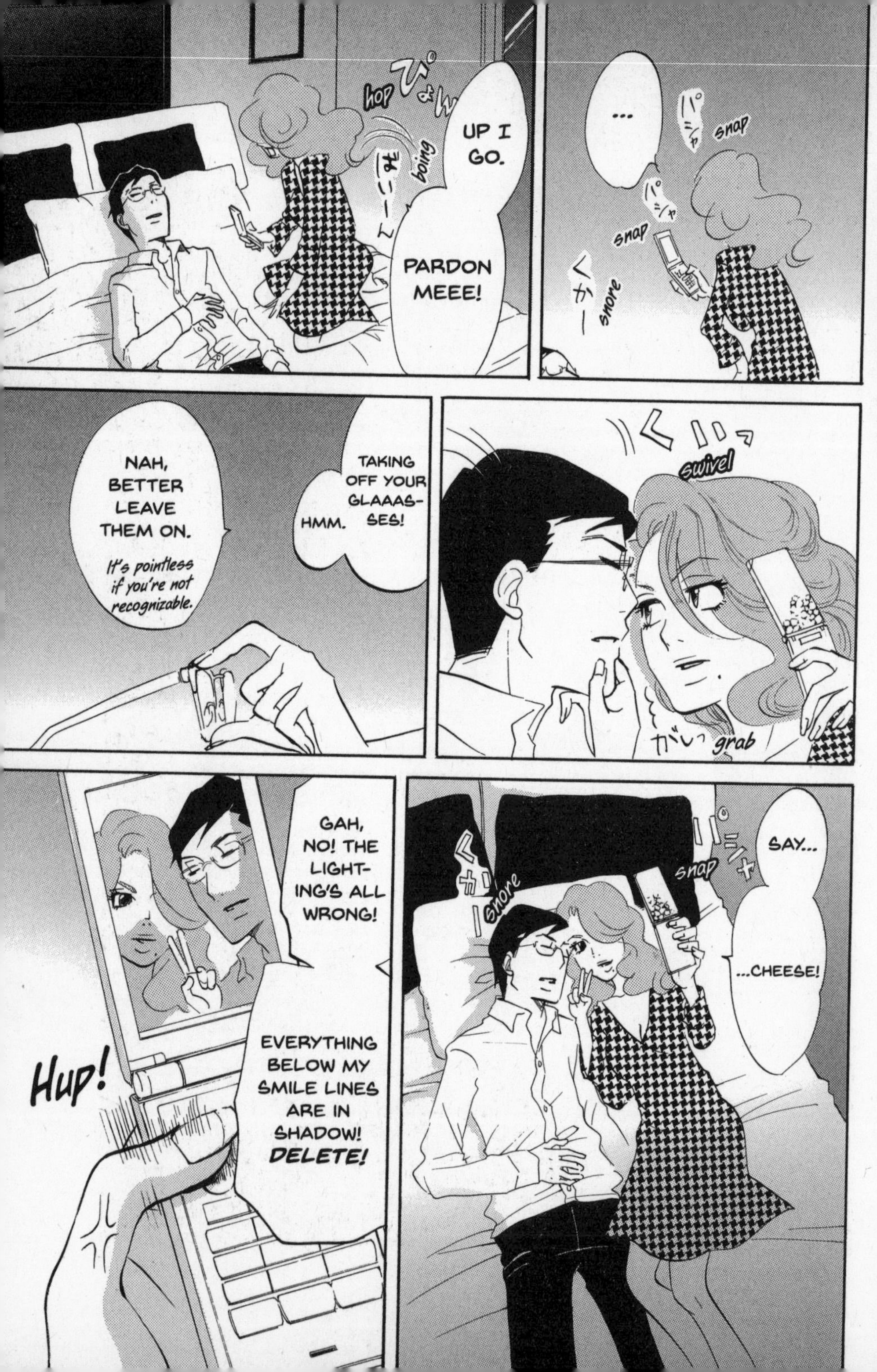
...
パシャ snap
パシャ snap
くかー snore
UP I GO.
hop ぴょん
むにーん boing
PARDON MEEE!
くいっ swivel
がしっ grab
TAKING OFF YOUR GLAAAS-SES!
HMM.
NAH, BETTER LEAVE THEM ON.
It's pointless if you're not recognizable.
SAY...
パシャッ snap
くかー snore
...CHEESE!
GAH, NO! THE LIGHT-ING'S ALL WRONG!
EVERYTHING BELOW MY SMILE LINES ARE IN SHADOW! ***DELETE!***
Hup!

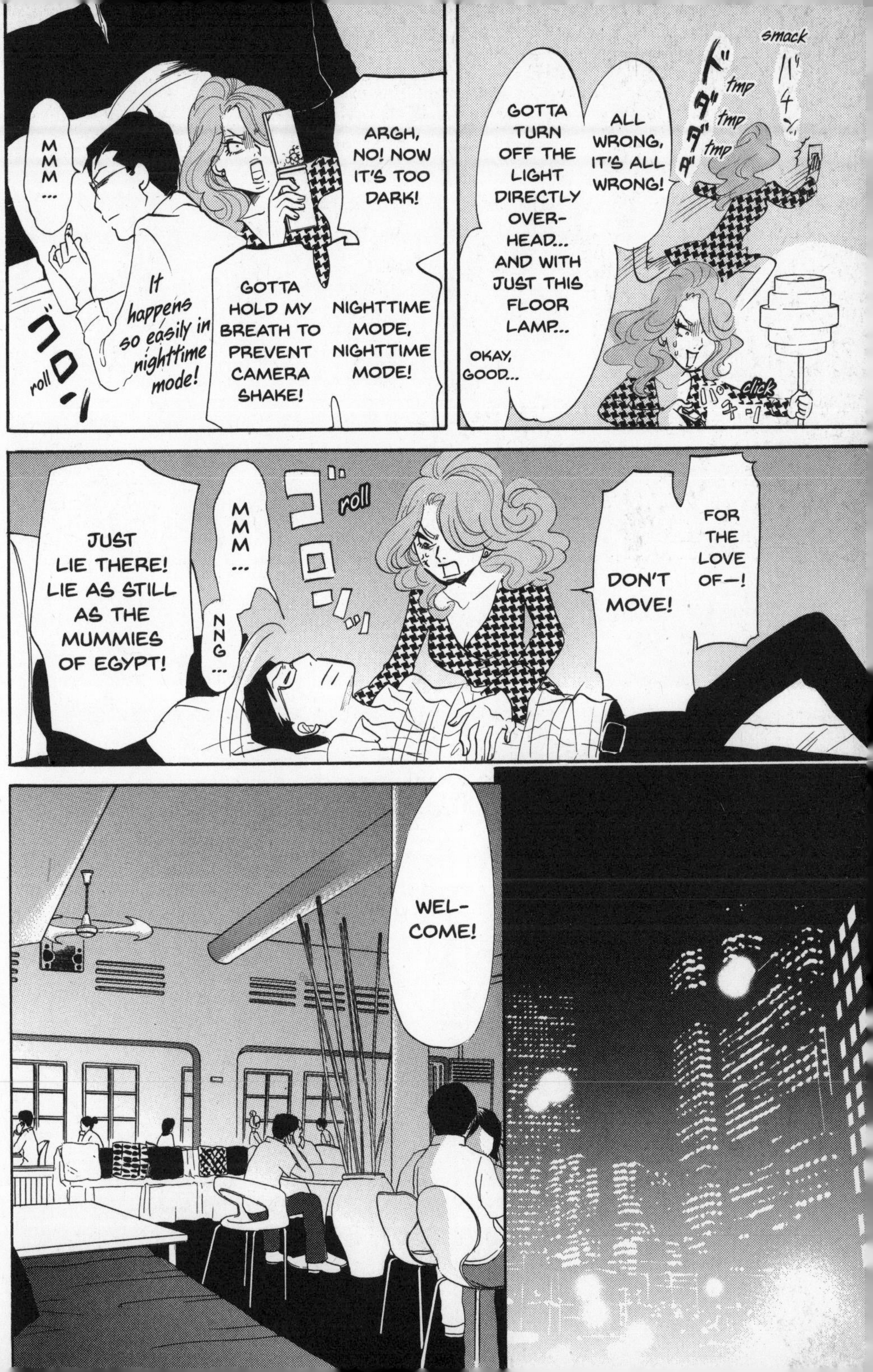
smack
tmp tmp tmp
ALL WRONG, IT'S ALL WRONG!
GOTTA TURN OFF THE LIGHT DIRECTLY OVER-HEAD... AND WITH JUST THIS FLOOR LAMP...
OKAY, GOOD...
click
ARGH, NO! NOW IT'S TOO DARK!
NIGHTTIME MODE, NIGHTTIME MODE!
GOTTA HOLD MY BREATH TO PREVENT CAMERA SHAKE!
It happens so easily in nighttime mode!
MMM...
roll
FOR THE LOVE OF—!
DON'T MOVE!
roll
MMM... NNG...
JUST LIE THERE! LIE AS STILL AS THE MUMMIES OF EGYPT!
WEL-COME!

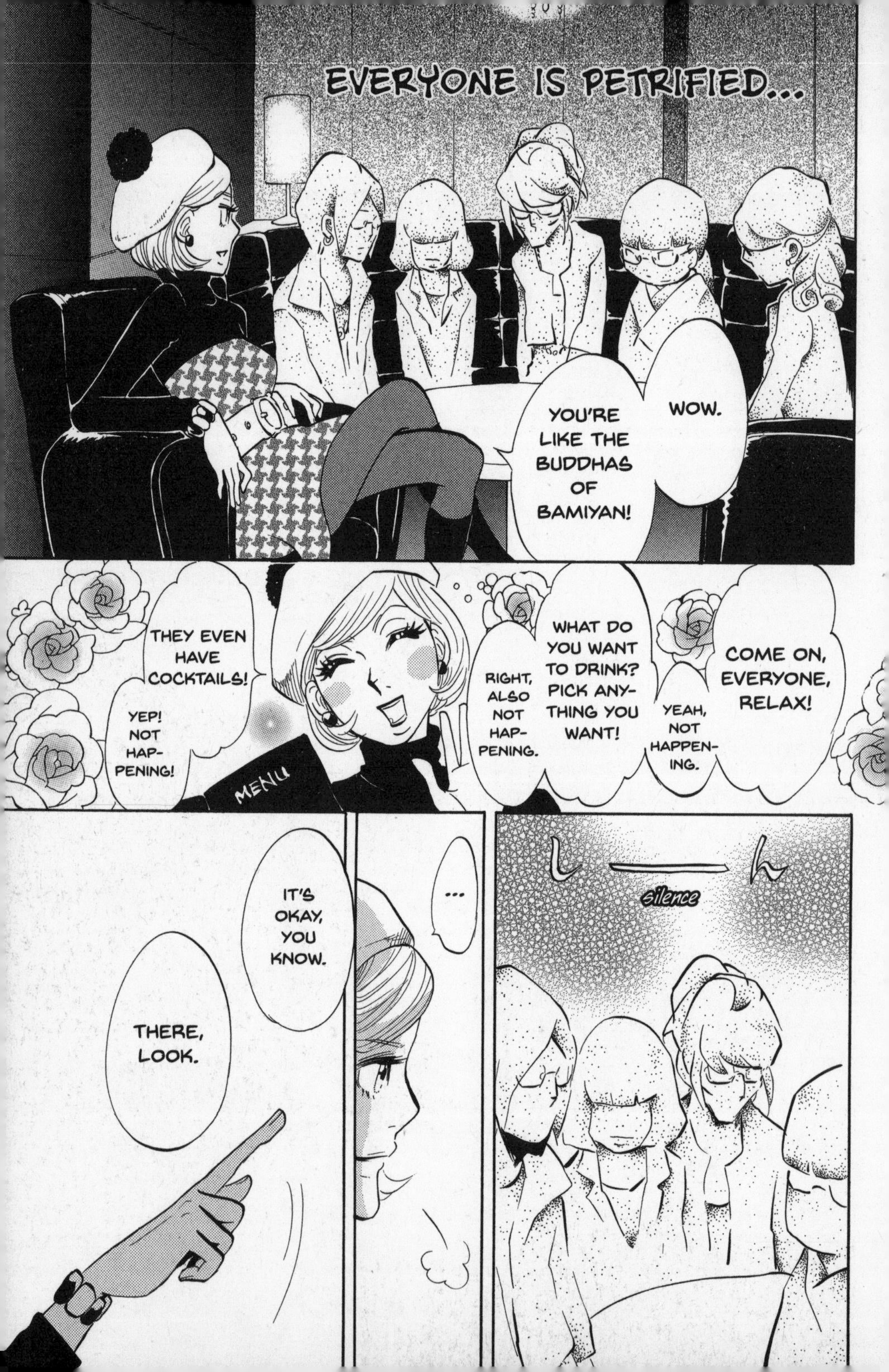
EVERYONE IS PETRIFIED...
WOW.
YOU'RE LIKE THE BUDDHAS OF BAMIYAN!
COME ON, EVERYONE, RELAX!
YEAH, NOT HAPPEN-ING.
WHAT DO YOU WANT TO DRINK? PICK ANY-THING YOU WANT!
RIGHT, ALSO NOT HAP-PENING.
THEY EVEN HAVE COCKTAILS!
YEP! NOT HAP-PENING!
MENU
しーん
silence
...
IT'S OKAY, YOU KNOW.
THERE, LOOK.

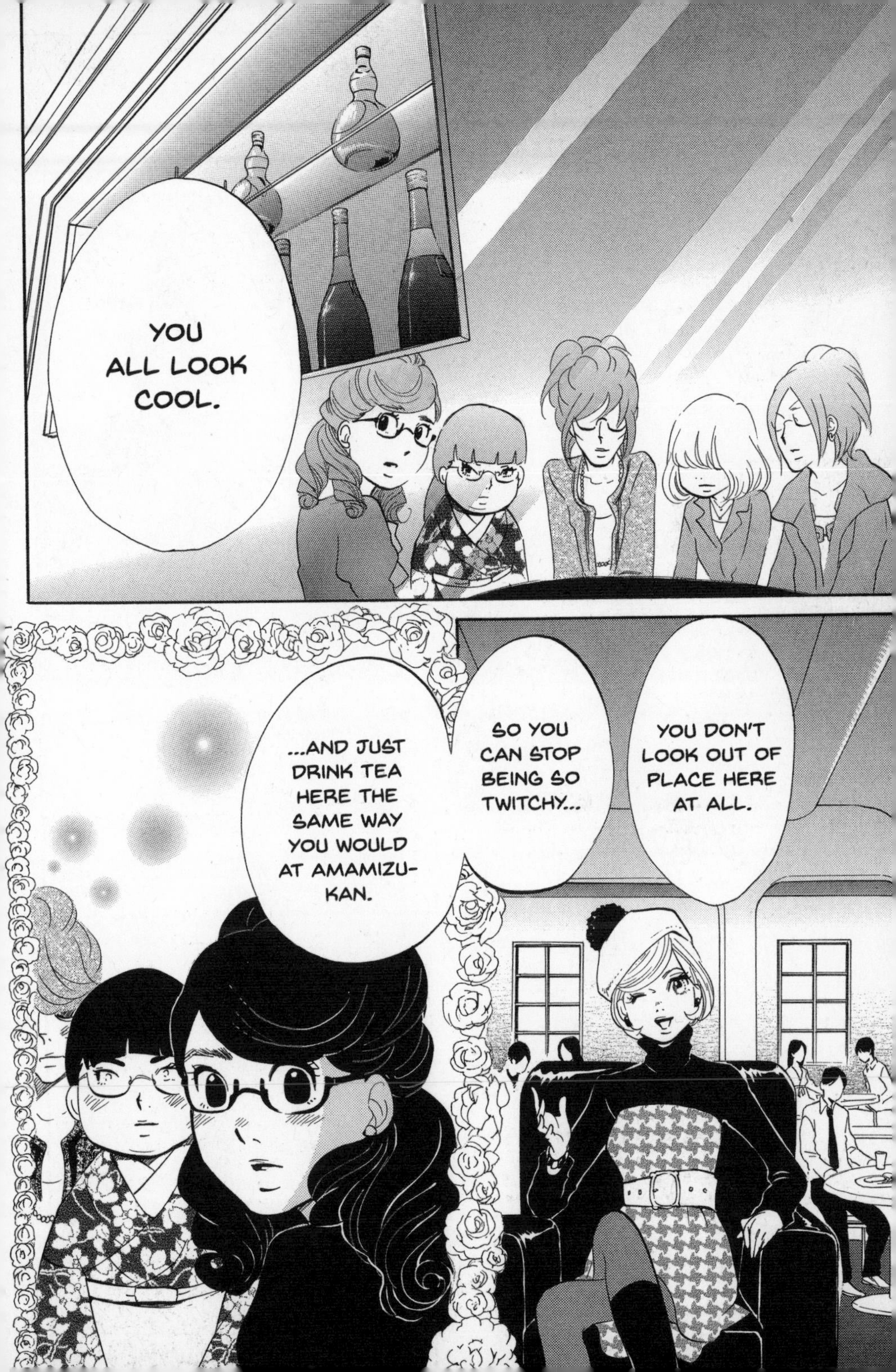
YOU ALL LOOK COOL.
YOU DON'T LOOK OUT OF PLACE HERE AT ALL.
SO YOU CAN STOP BEING SO TWITCHY...
...AND JUST DRINK TEA HERE THE SAME WAY YOU WOULD AT AMAMIZU-KAN.

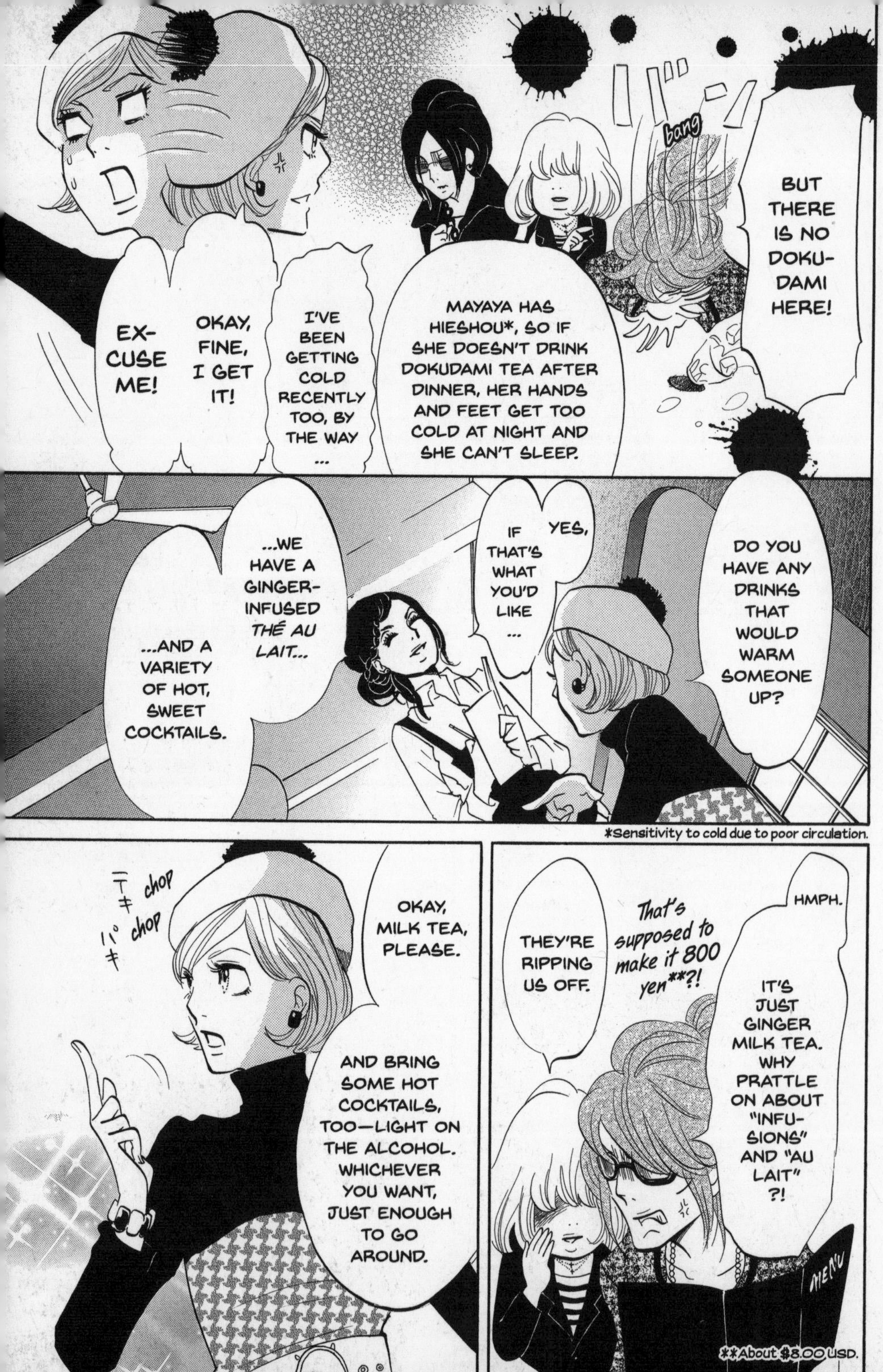
bang
BUT THERE IS NO DOKUDAMI HERE!
MAYAYA HAS HIESHOU*, SO IF SHE DOESN'T DRINK DOKUDAMI TEA AFTER DINNER, HER HANDS AND FEET GET TOO COLD AT NIGHT AND SHE CAN'T SLEEP.
I'VE BEEN GETTING COLD RECENTLY TOO, BY THE WAY ...
OKAY, FINE, I GET IT!
EX-CUSE ME!
DO YOU HAVE ANY DRINKS THAT WOULD WARM SOMEONE UP?
YES,
IF THAT'S WHAT YOU'D LIKE ...
...WE HAVE A GINGER-INFUSED *THÉ AU LAIT*...
...AND A VARIETY OF HOT, SWEET COCKTAILS.
HMPH.
IT'S JUST GINGER MILK TEA. WHY PRATTLE ON ABOUT "INFUSIONS" AND "AU LAIT"?!
That's supposed to make it 800 yen**?!
THEY'RE RIPPING US OFF.
MENU
chop chop
OKAY, MILK TEA, PLEASE.
AND BRING SOME HOT COCKTAILS, TOO—LIGHT ON THE ALCOHOL. WHICHEVER YOU WANT, JUST ENOUGH TO GO AROUND.

*Sensitivity to cold due to poor circulation.

**About $8.00 USD.

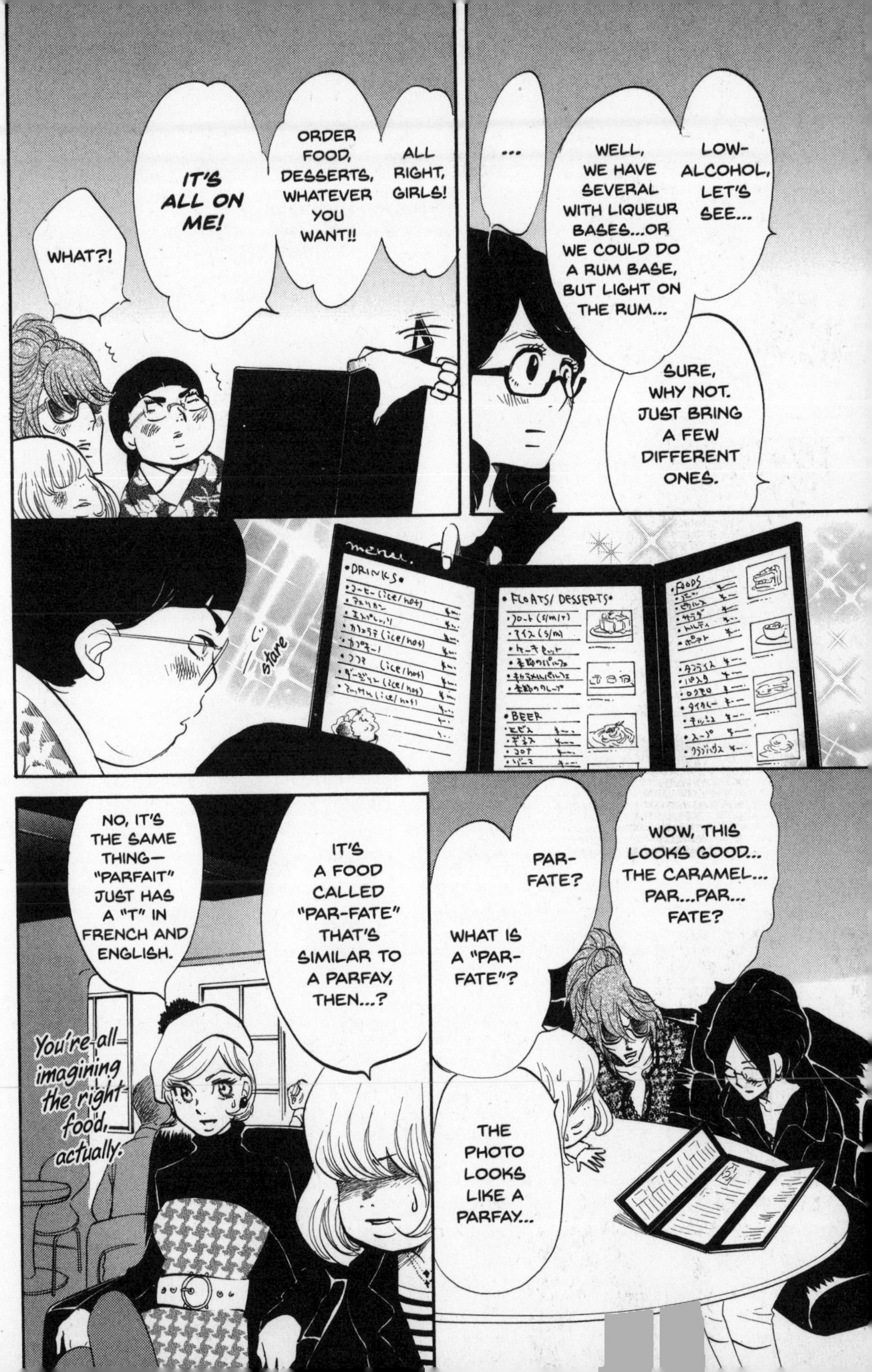
LOW-ALCOHOL, LET'S SEE...
WELL, WE HAVE SEVERAL WITH LIQUEUR BASES...OR WE COULD DO A RUM BASE, BUT LIGHT ON THE RUM...
...
SURE, WHY NOT. JUST BRING A FEW DIFFERENT ONES.
ALL RIGHT, GIRLS!
ORDER FOOD, DESSERTS, WHATEVER YOU WANT!!
IT'S ALL ON ME!
WHAT?!
menu.
DRINKS
FLOATS/ DESSERTS
BEER
FOODS
stare
WOW, THIS LOOKS GOOD... THE CARAMEL... PAR...PAR... FATE?
PAR-FATE?
WHAT IS A "PAR-FATE"?
THE PHOTO LOOKS LIKE A PARFAY...
IT'S A FOOD CALLED "PAR-FATE" THAT'S SIMILAR TO A PARFAY, THEN...?
NO, IT'S THE SAME THING— "PARFAIT" JUST HAS A "T" IN FRENCH AND ENGLISH.
You're all imagining the right food, actually.

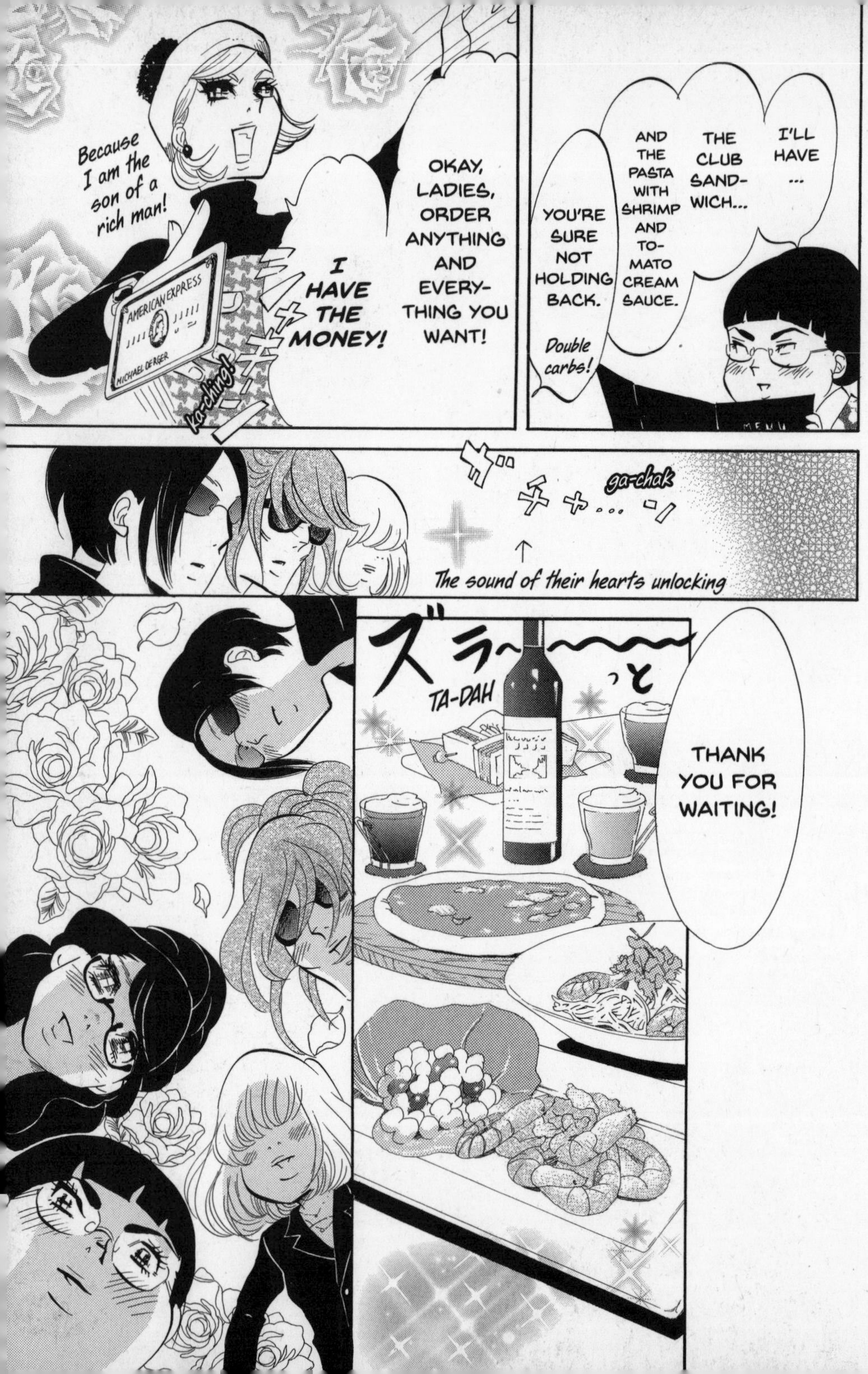
I'LL HAVE ...
THE CLUB SANDWICH...
AND THE PASTA WITH SHRIMP AND TOMATO CREAM SAUCE.
YOU'RE SURE NOT HOLDING BACK.
Double carbs!
OKAY, LADIES, ORDER ANYTHING AND EVERYTHING YOU WANT!
I HAVE THE MONEY!
Because I am the son of a rich man!
AMERICAN EXPRESS
MICHAEL DERGER
ka-ching!
ga-chak
The sound of their hearts unlocking
TA-DAH
THANK YOU FOR WAITING!

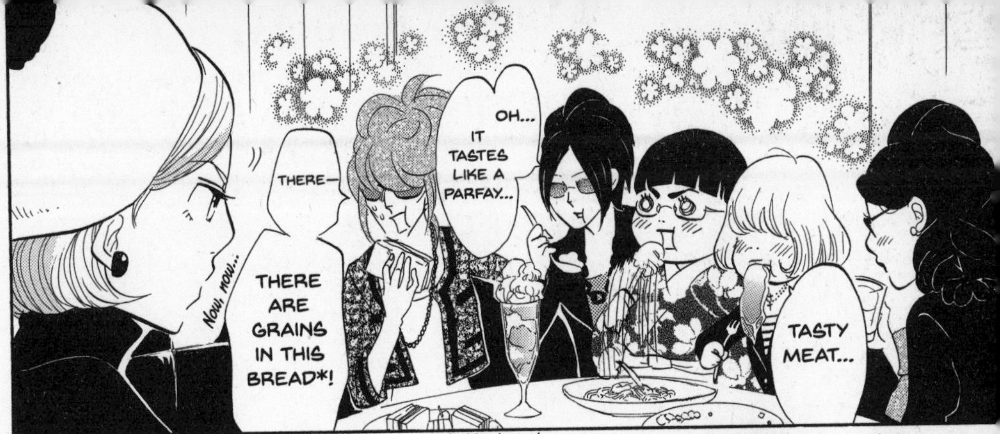
TASTY MEAT...
OH... IT TASTES LIKE A PARFAY...
THERE—
THERE ARE GRAINS IN THIS BREAD*!
Now, now...

*Most bread sold at Japanese grocery stores are processed white bread.

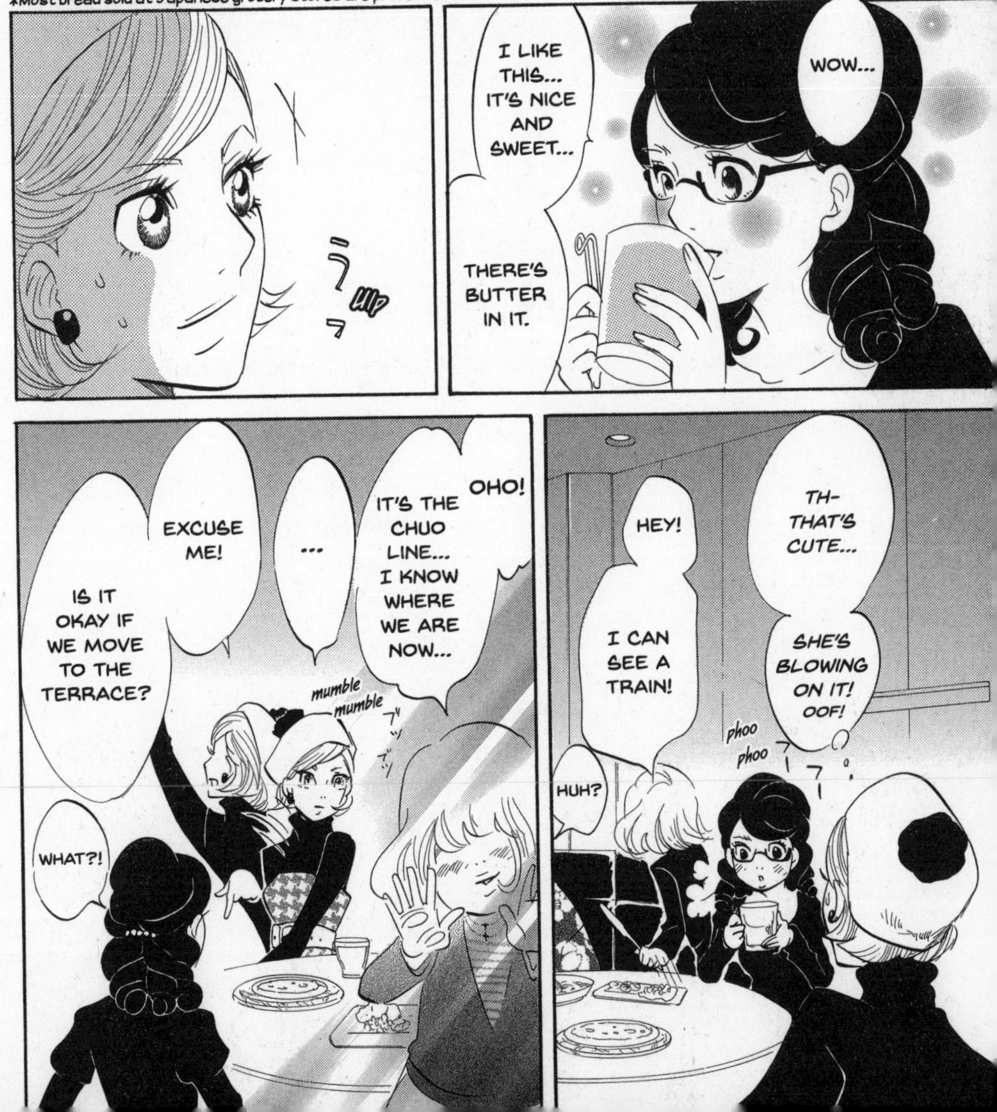
WOW...
I LIKE THIS... IT'S NICE AND SWEET...
THERE'S BUTTER IN IT.
ULP
TH-THAT'S CUTE...
HEY!
I CAN SEE A TRAIN!
SHE'S BLOWING ON IT! OOF!
phoo phoo
HUH?
OHO!
IT'S THE CHUO LINE... I KNOW WHERE WE ARE NOW...
...
EXCUSE ME!
IS IT OKAY IF WE MOVE TO THE TERRACE?
mumble mumble
WHAT?!

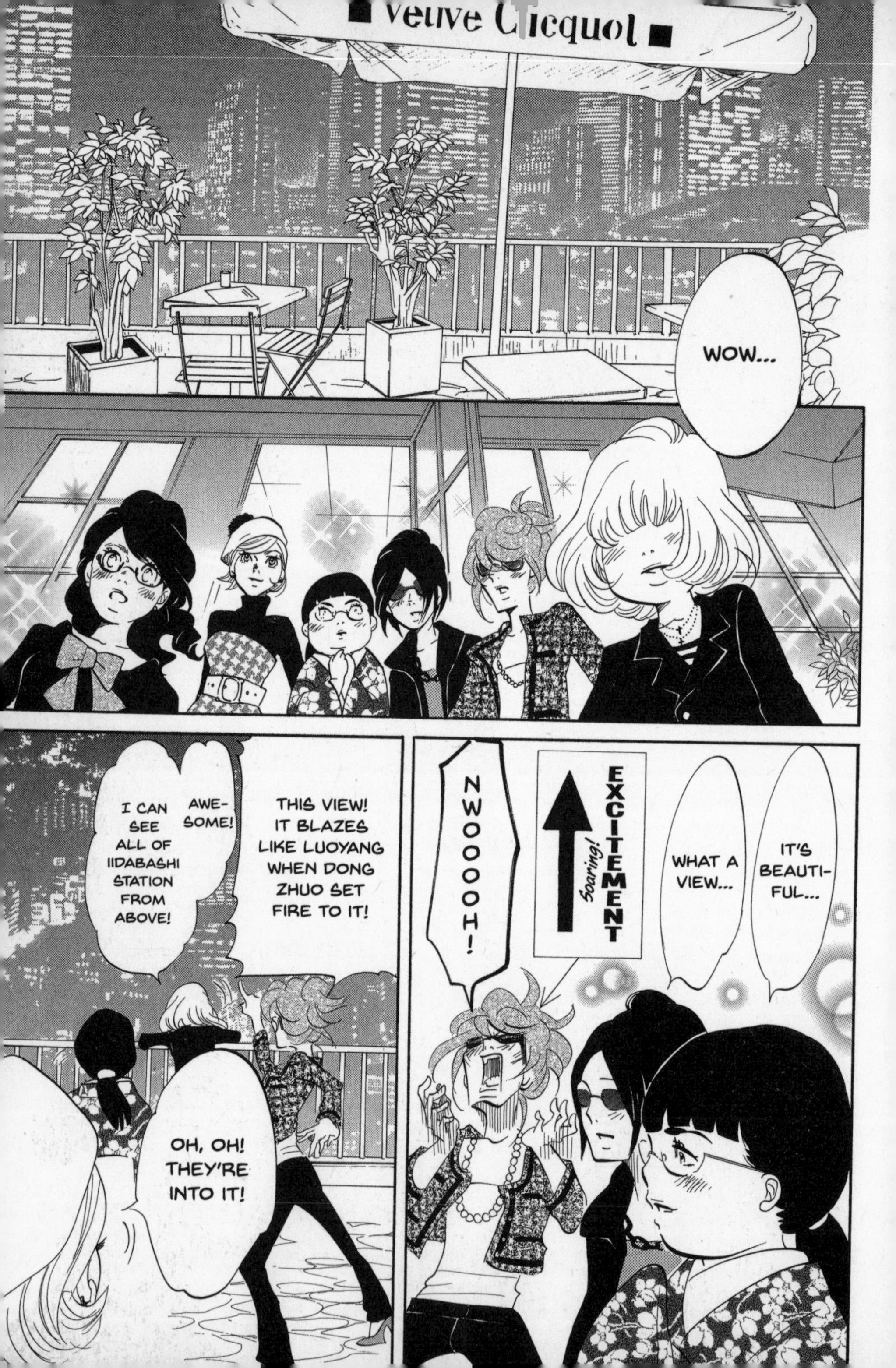
Veuve Clicquot
WOW...
IT'S BEAUTIFUL...
WHAT A VIEW...
EXCITEMENT
Soaring!
NWOOOOOH!
THIS VIEW! IT BLAZES LIKE LUOYANG WHEN DONG ZHUO SET FIRE TO IT!
AWESOME!
I CAN SEE ALL OF IIDABASHI STATION FROM ABOVE!
OH, OH! THEY'RE INTO IT!

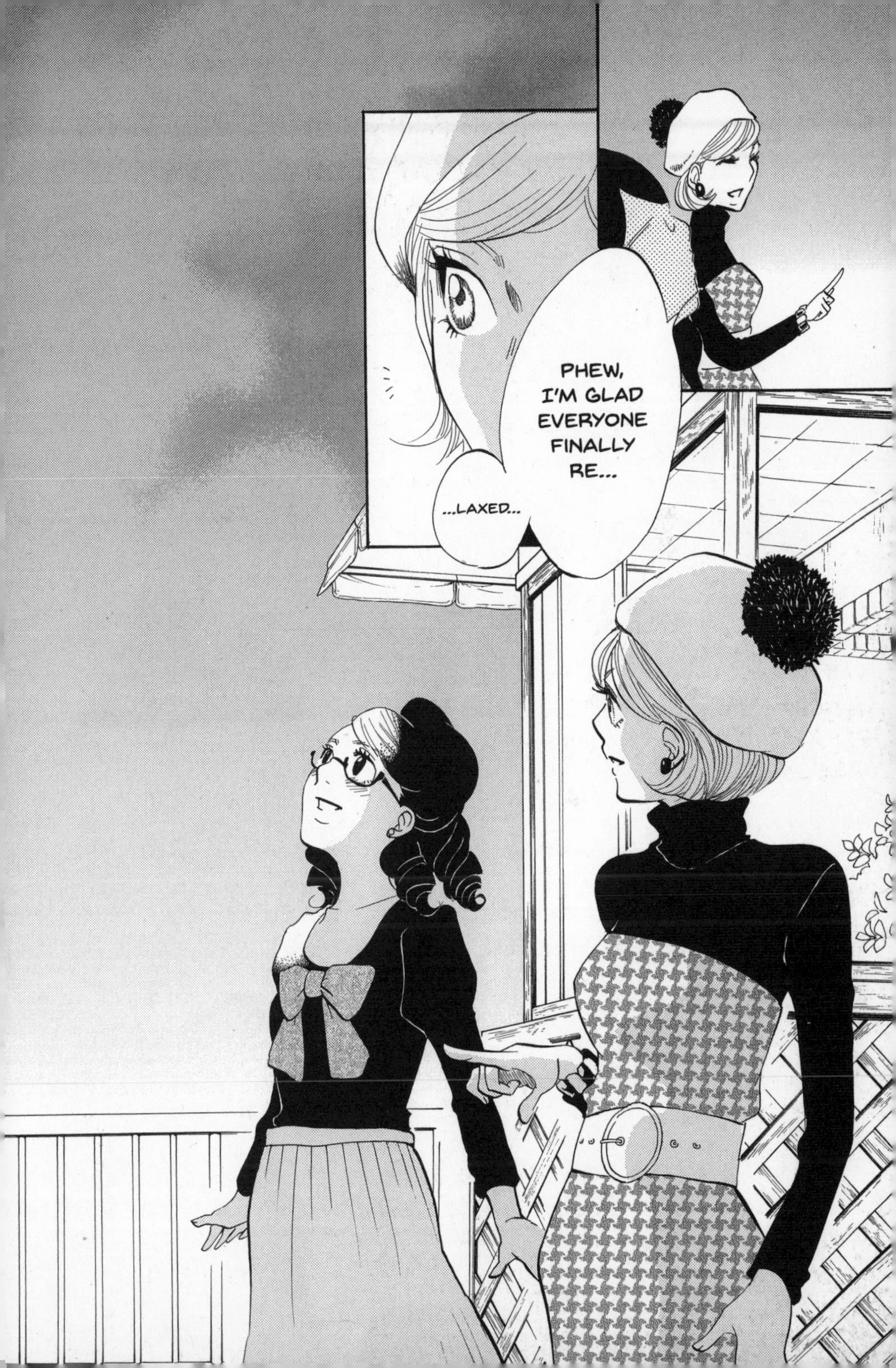
PHEW, I'M GLAD EVERYONE FINALLY RE...
...LAXED...

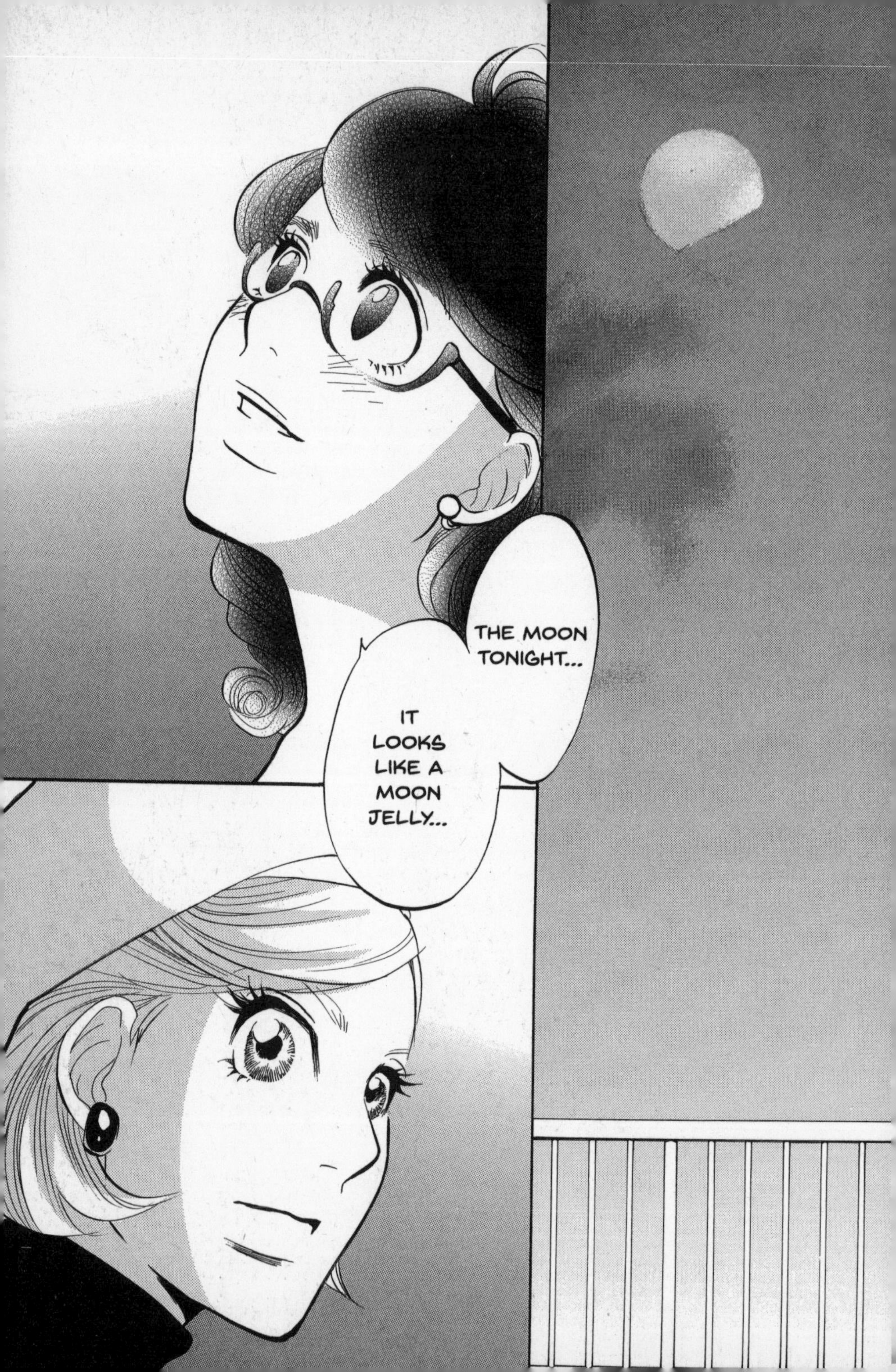
THE MOON TONIGHT...
IT LOOKS LIKE A MOON JELLY...

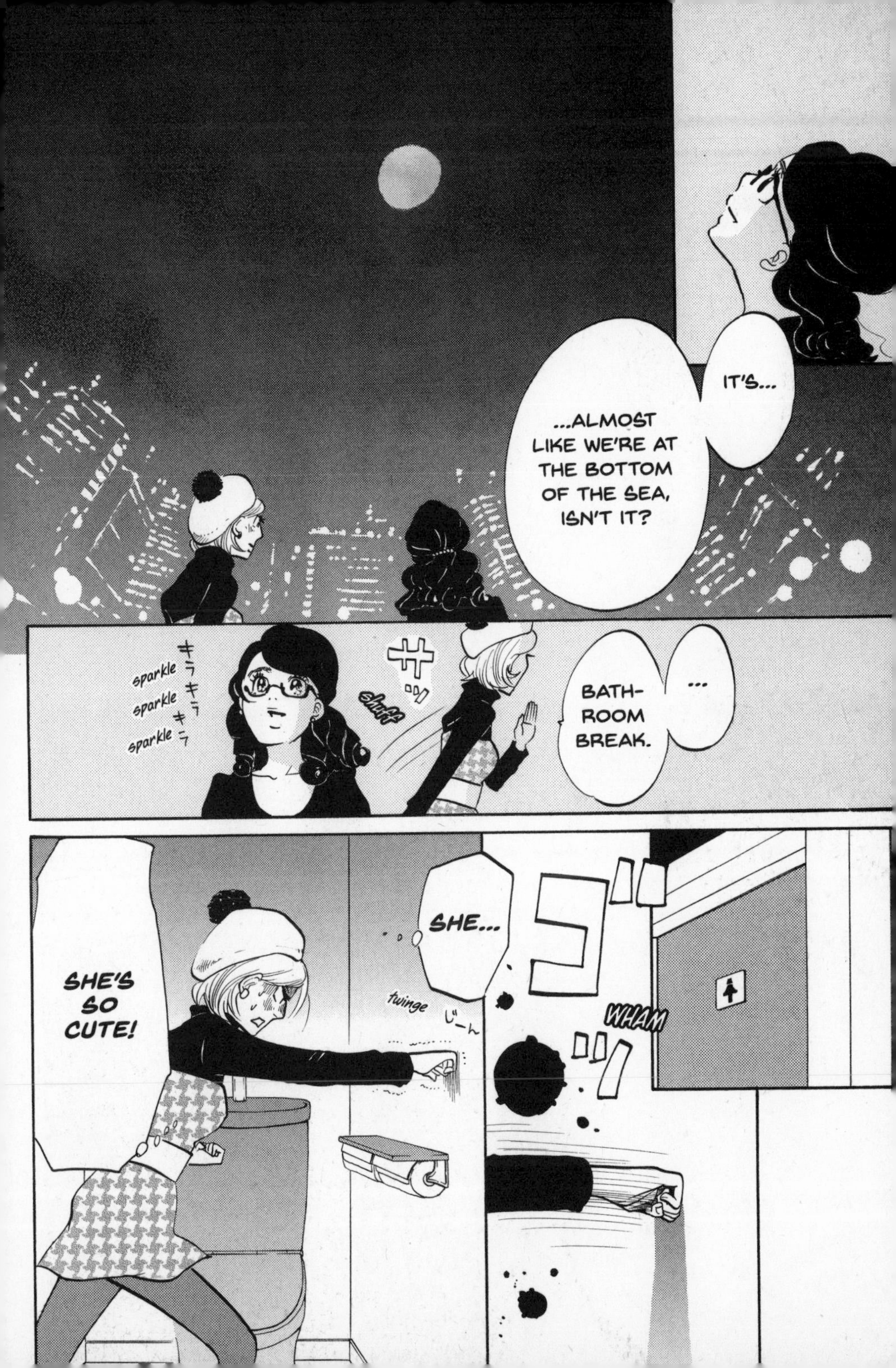
IT'S...
...ALMOST LIKE WE'RE AT THE BOTTOM OF THE SEA, ISN'T IT?
...
BATH-ROOM BREAK.
サッ
shuff
キラキラキラ
sparkle sparkle sparkle
WHAM
SHE...
じーん
twinge
SHE'S SO CUTE!

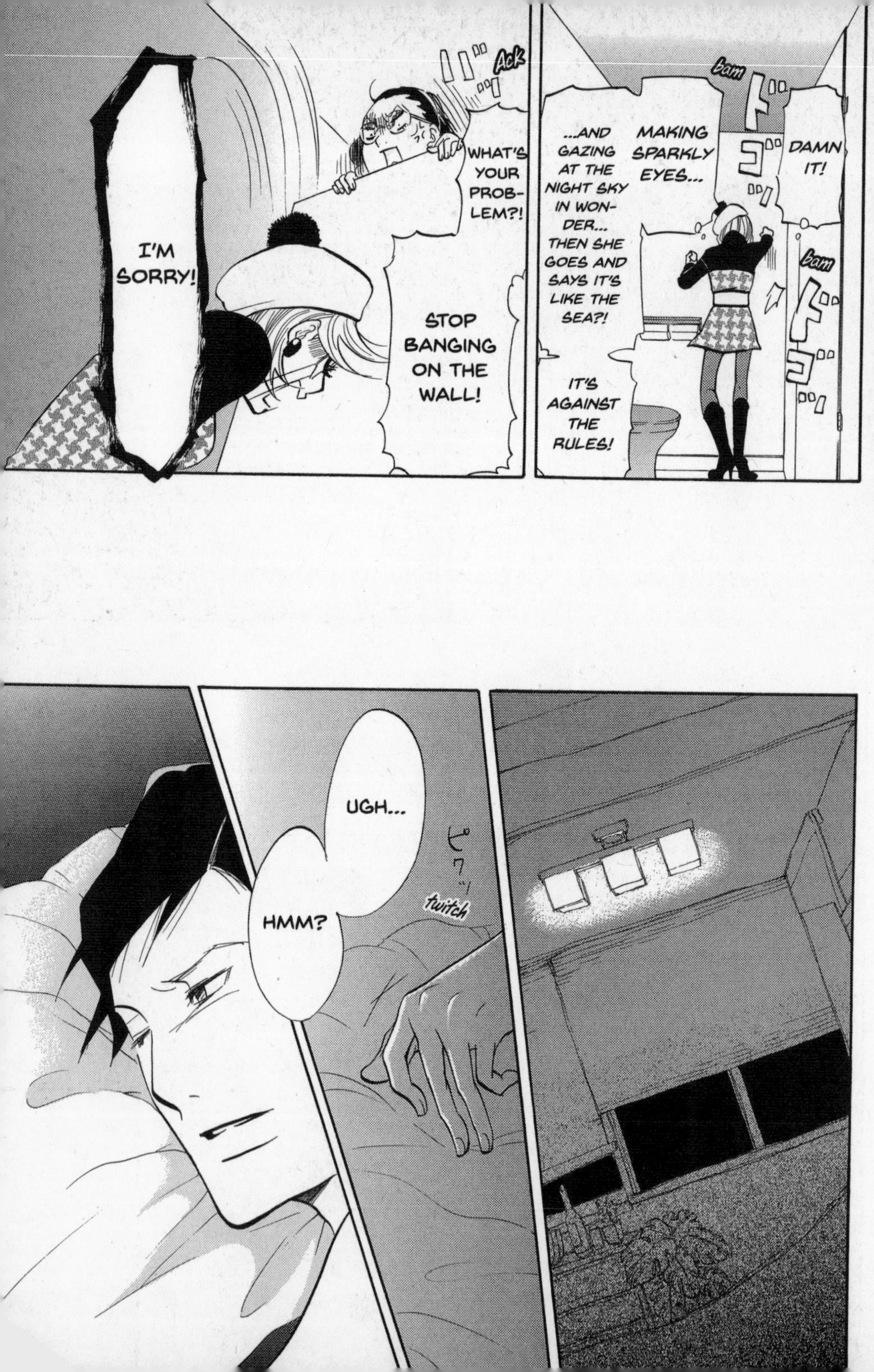
bam
DAMN IT!
MAKING SPARKLY EYES...
...AND GAZING AT THE NIGHT SKY IN WON-DER... THEN SHE GOES AND SAYS IT'S LIKE THE SEA?!
IT'S AGAINST THE RULES!
bam
Ack
WHAT'S YOUR PROB-LEM?!
STOP BANGING ON THE WALL!
I'M SORRY!
UGH...
twitch
HMM?

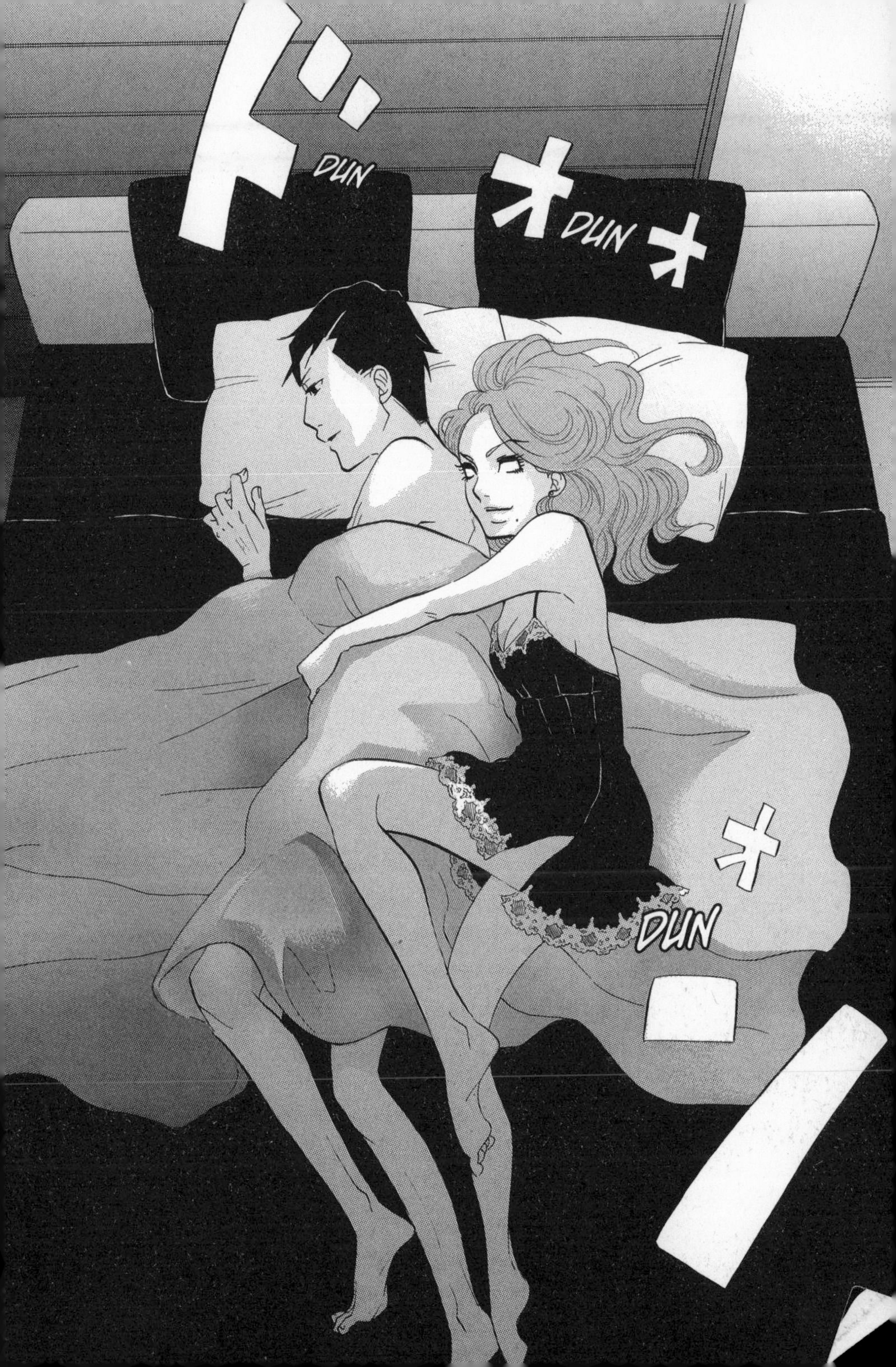
ド
DUN
オ
DUN
オ
DUN
オ
DUN
ー

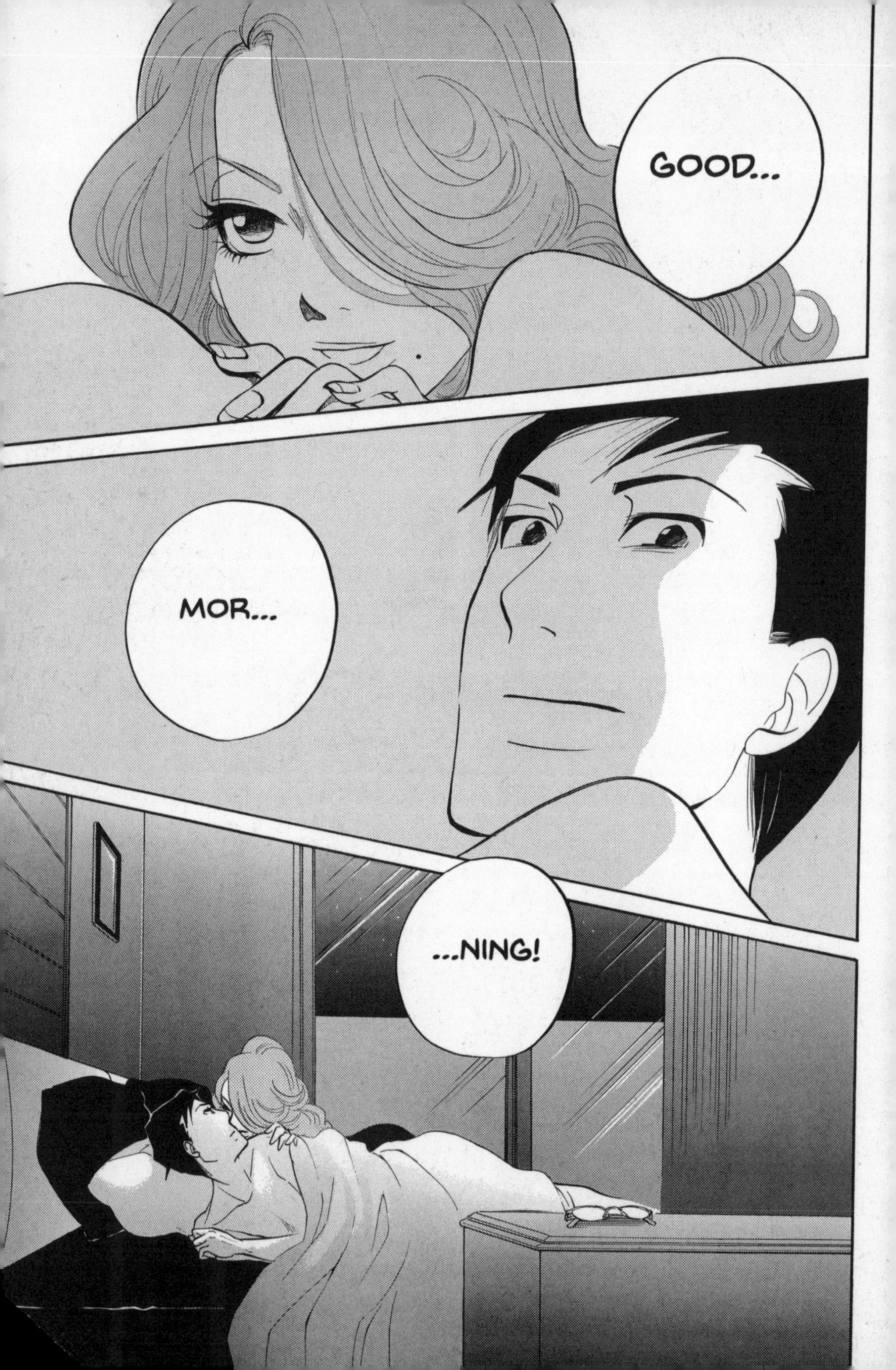
GOOD...
MOR...
...NING!

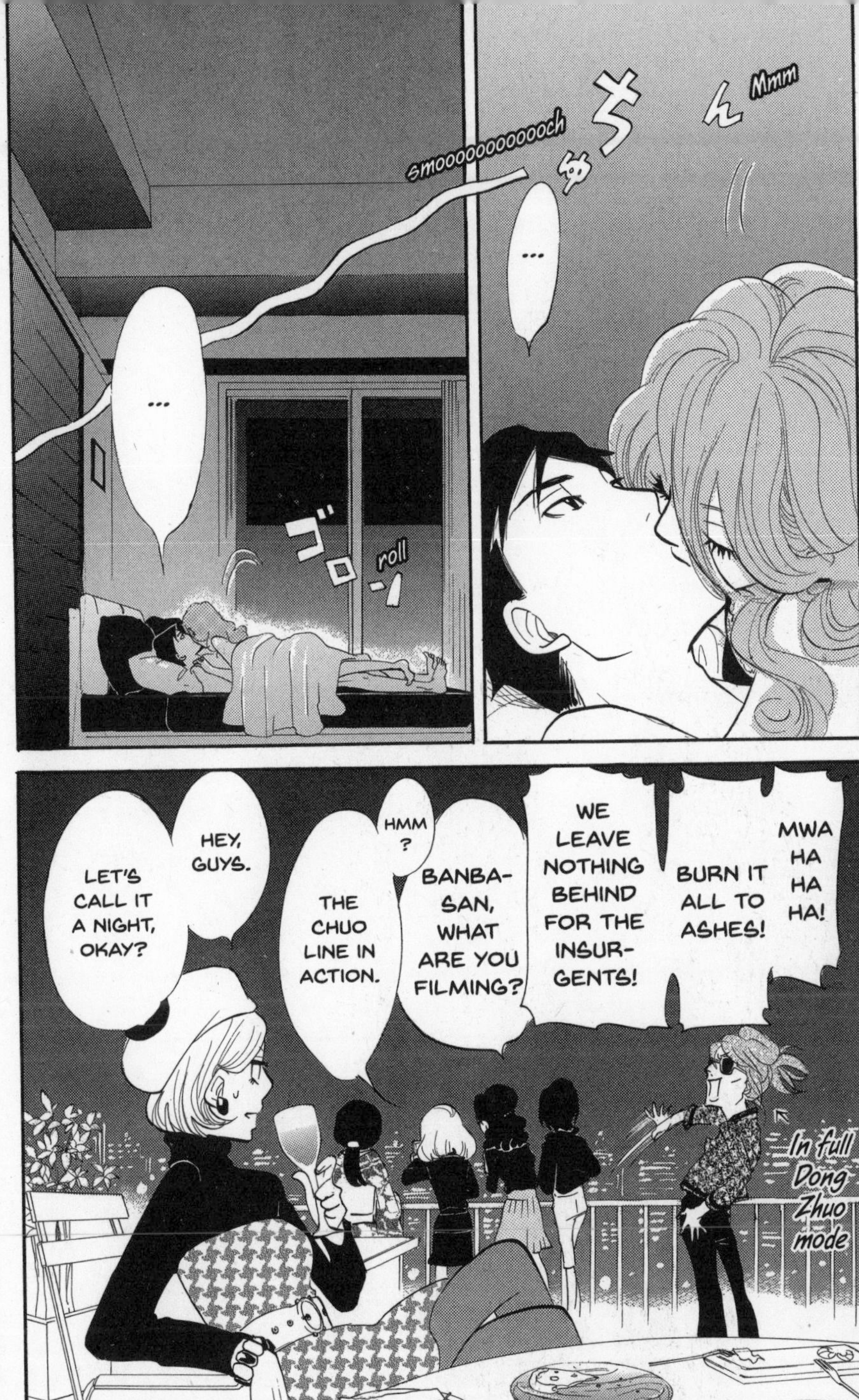

ちゅ
ん
Mmm
smoooooooooooooch
...
...
ゴロー
roll
MWA HA HA HA!
BURN IT ALL TO ASHES!
WE LEAVE NOTHING BEHIND FOR THE INSURGENTS!
In full Dong Zhuo mode
HMM?
BANBA-SAN, WHAT ARE YOU FILMING?
THE CHUO LINE IN ACTION.
HEY, GUYS.
LET'S CALL IT A NIGHT, OKAY?

Episode 11

Driving Mr. Hanamori

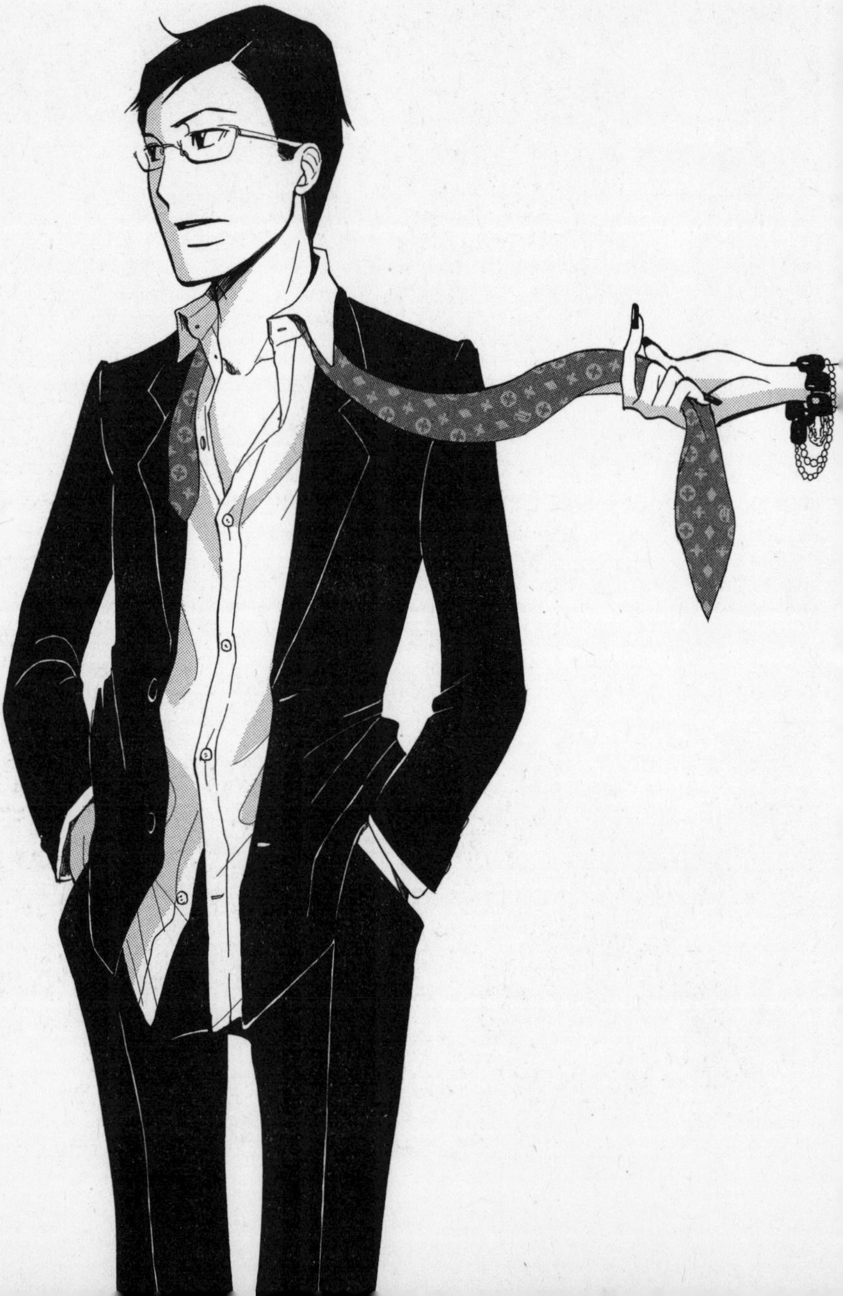

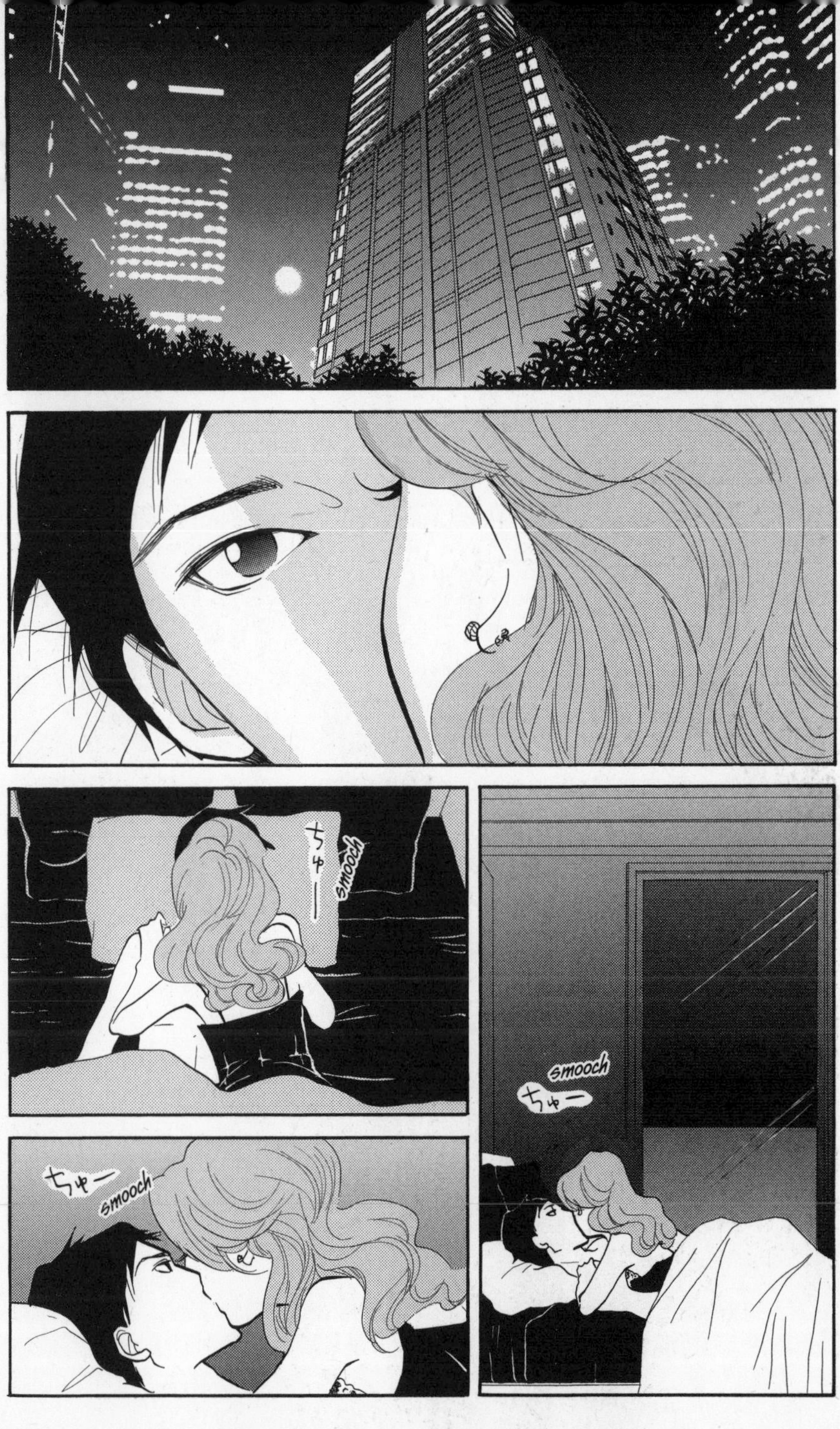
smooch
ちゅー
ちゅーー
smooch
ちゅー
smooch

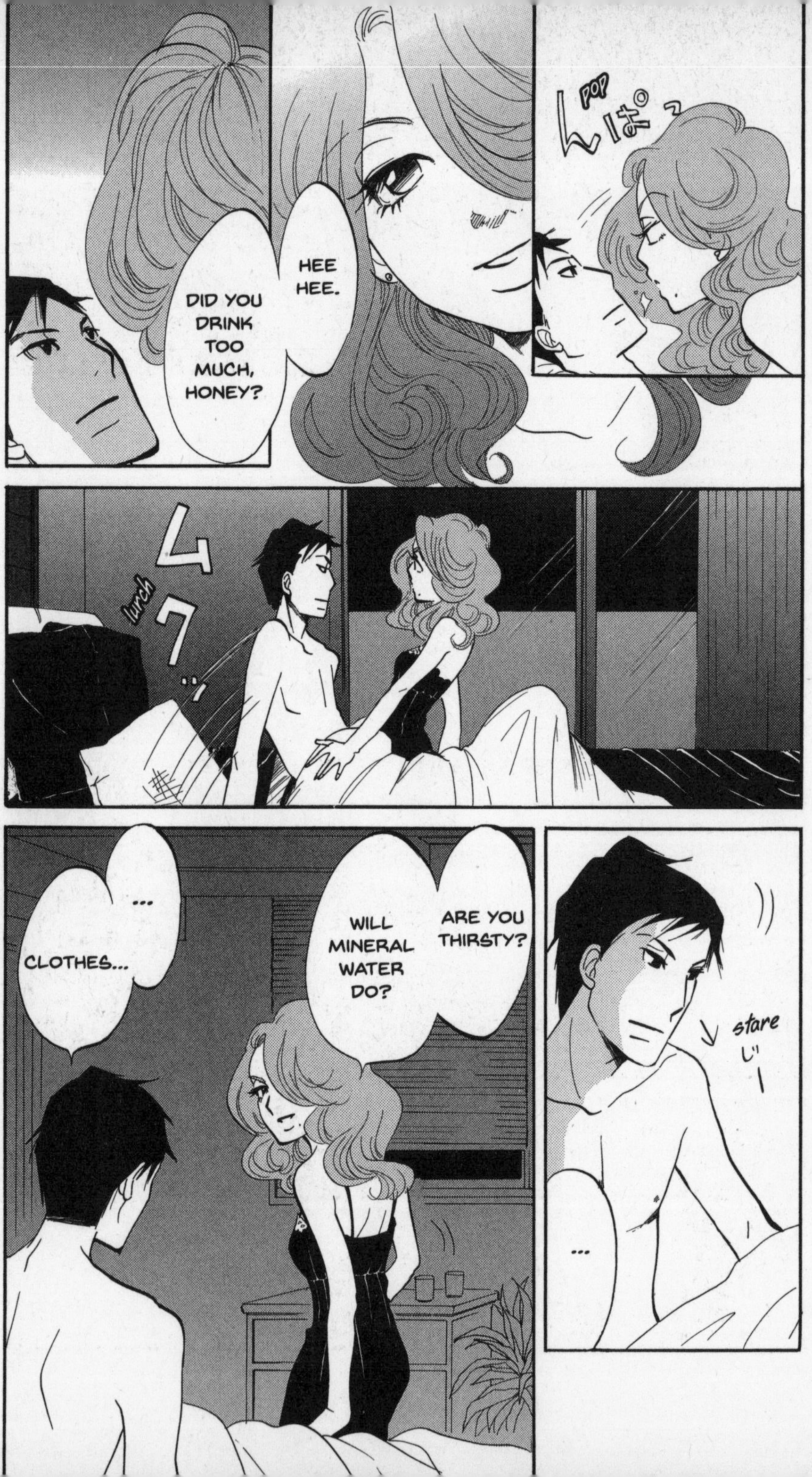

pop
んぽっ
HEE HEE.
DID YOU DRINK TOO MUCH, HONEY?
lurch
ムク
stare
じー
...
ARE YOU THIRSTY?
WILL MINERAL WATER DO?
... CLOTHES...

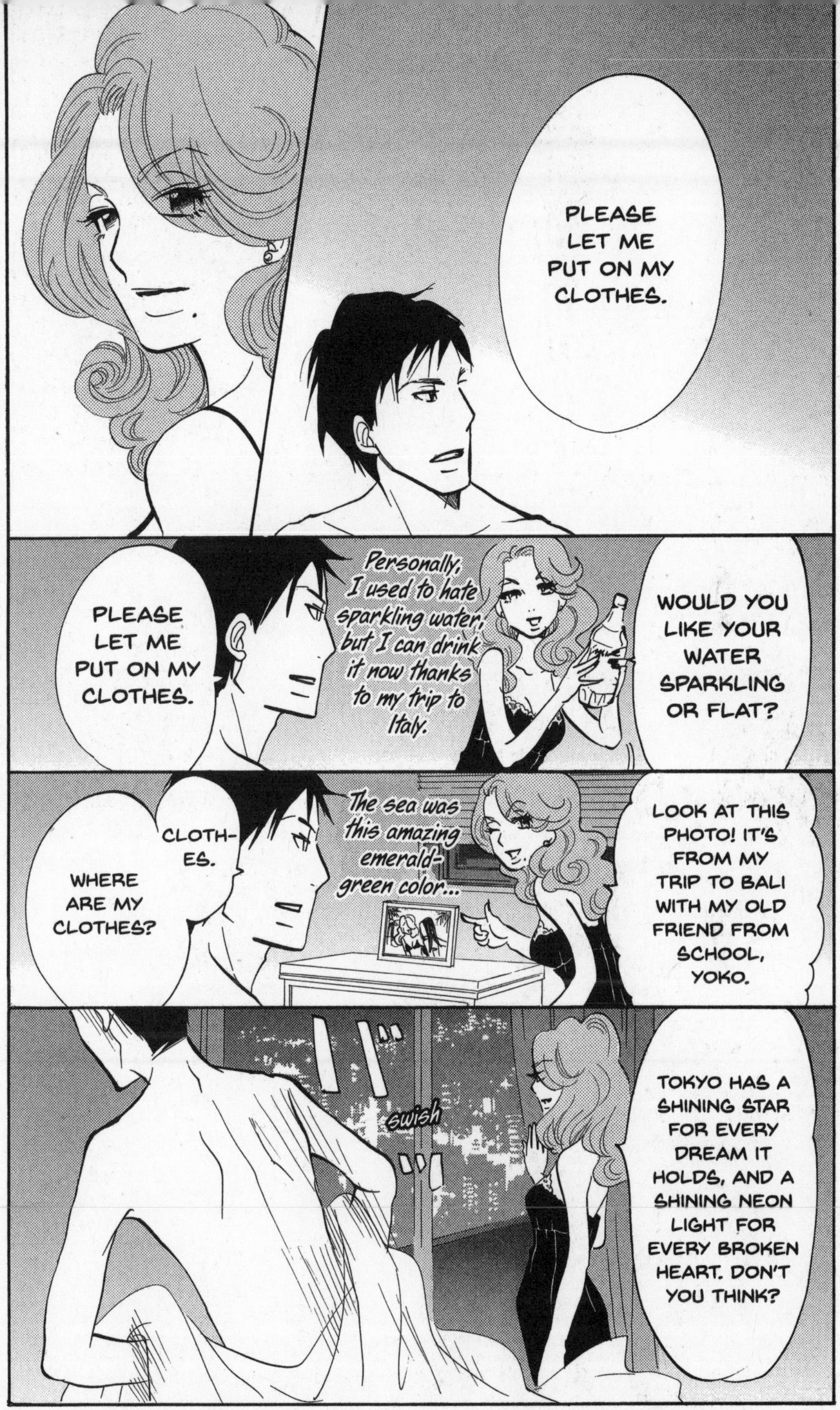
PLEASE LET ME PUT ON MY CLOTHES.
WOULD YOU LIKE YOUR WATER SPARKLING OR FLAT?
Personally, I used to hate sparkling water, but I can drink it now thanks to my trip to Italy.
PLEASE LET ME PUT ON MY CLOTHES.
LOOK AT THIS PHOTO! IT'S FROM MY TRIP TO BALI WITH MY OLD FRIEND FROM SCHOOL, YOKO.
The sea was this amazing emerald-green color...
CLOTH-ES.
WHERE ARE MY CLOTHES?
TOKYO HAS A SHINING STAR FOR EVERY DREAM IT HOLDS, AND A SHINING NEON LIGHT FOR EVERY BROKEN HEART. DON'T YOU THINK?
swish

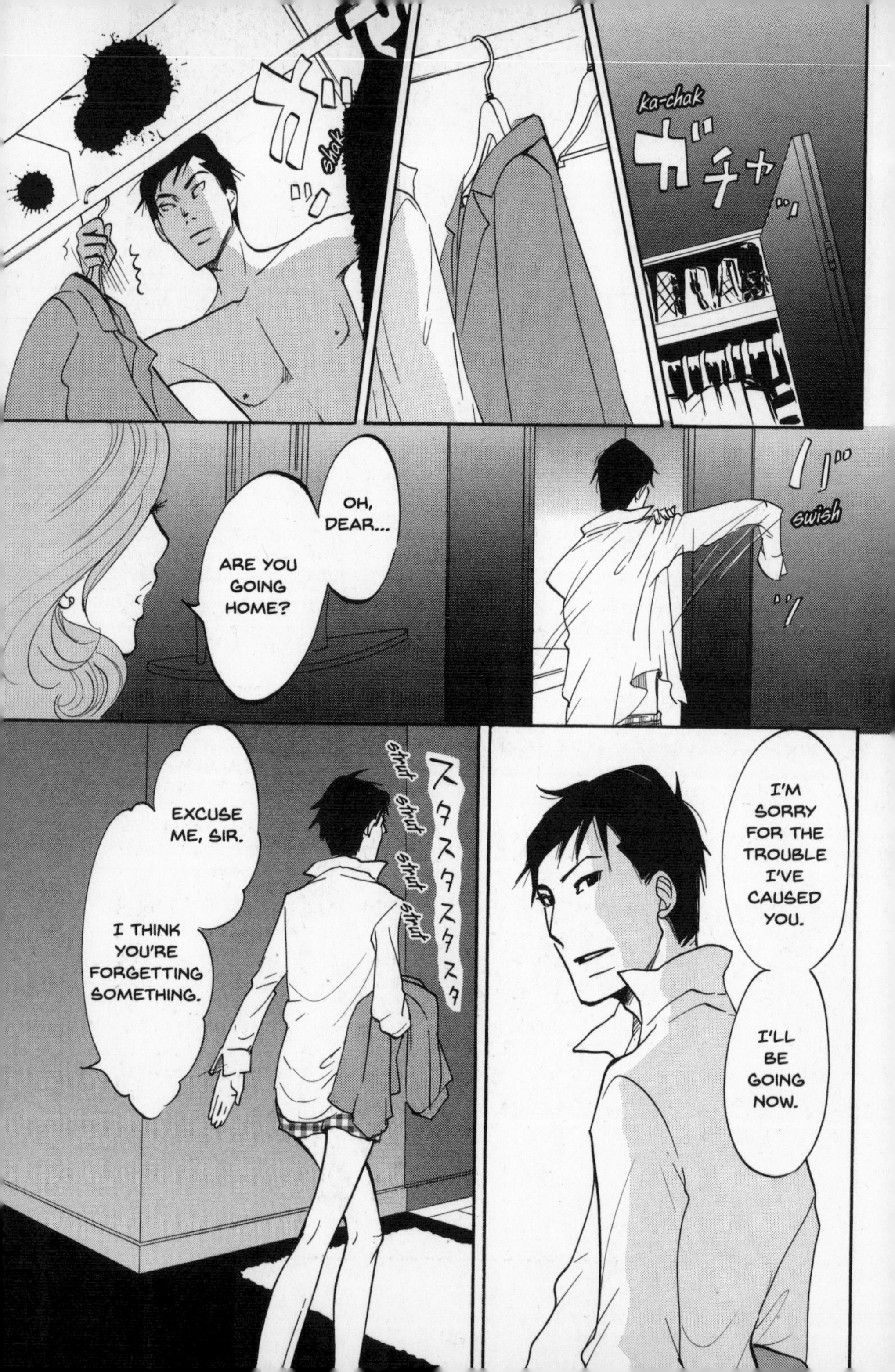
ka-chak
ガチャッ
shak
ガッ
ノバッ
swish
OH, DEAR...
ARE YOU GOING HOME?
I'M SORRY FOR THE TROUBLE I'VE CAUSED YOU.
I'LL BE GOING NOW.
スタスタスタスタ
strut strut strut strut
EXCUSE ME, SIR.
I THINK YOU'RE FORGETTING SOMETHING.

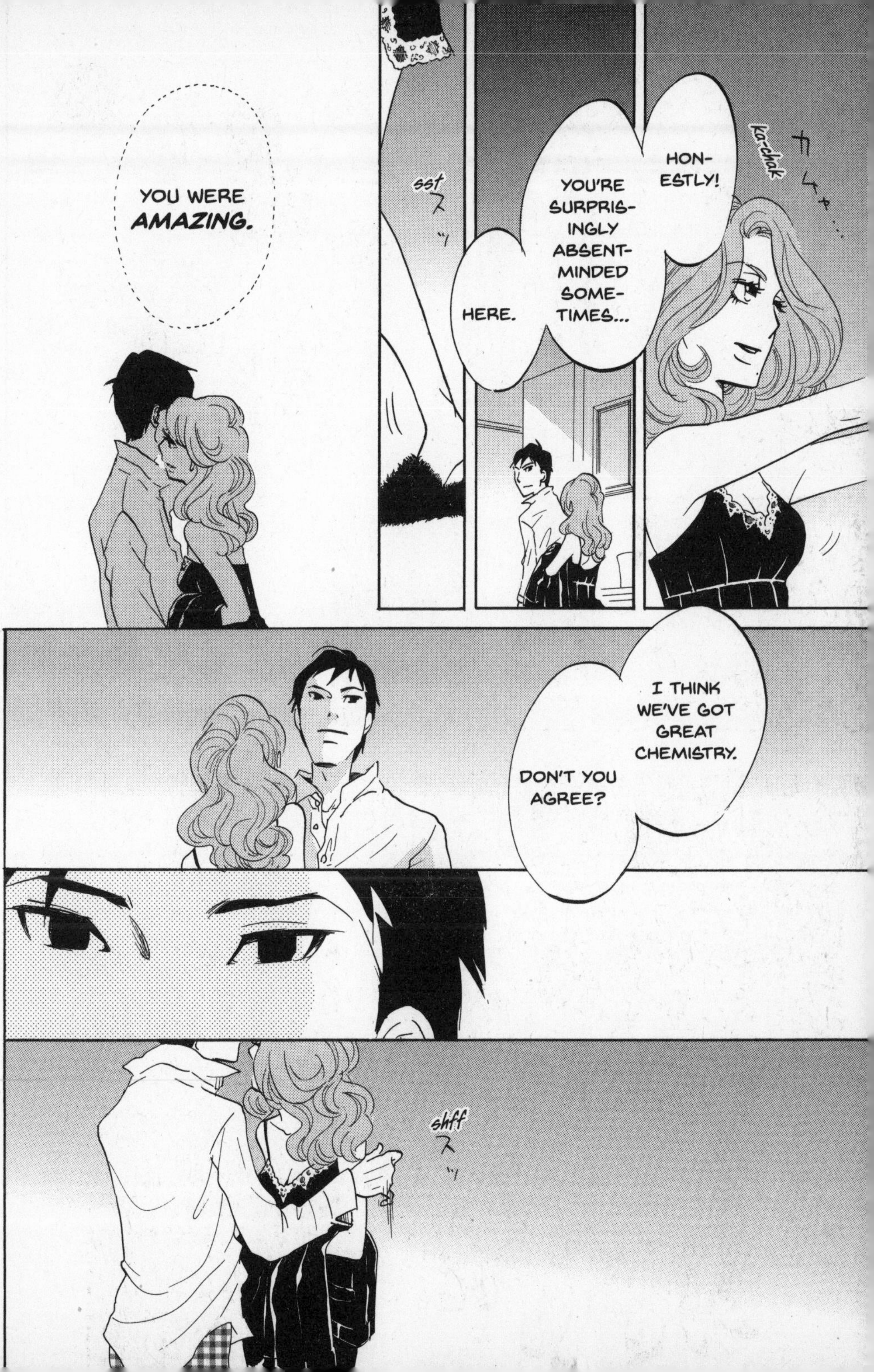
ka-chak
HON-ESTLY!
YOU'RE SURPRIS-INGLY ABSENT-MINDED SOME-TIMES...
HERE.
sst
YOU WERE AMAZING.
I THINK WE'VE GOT GREAT CHEMISTRY.
DON'T YOU AGREE?
shff

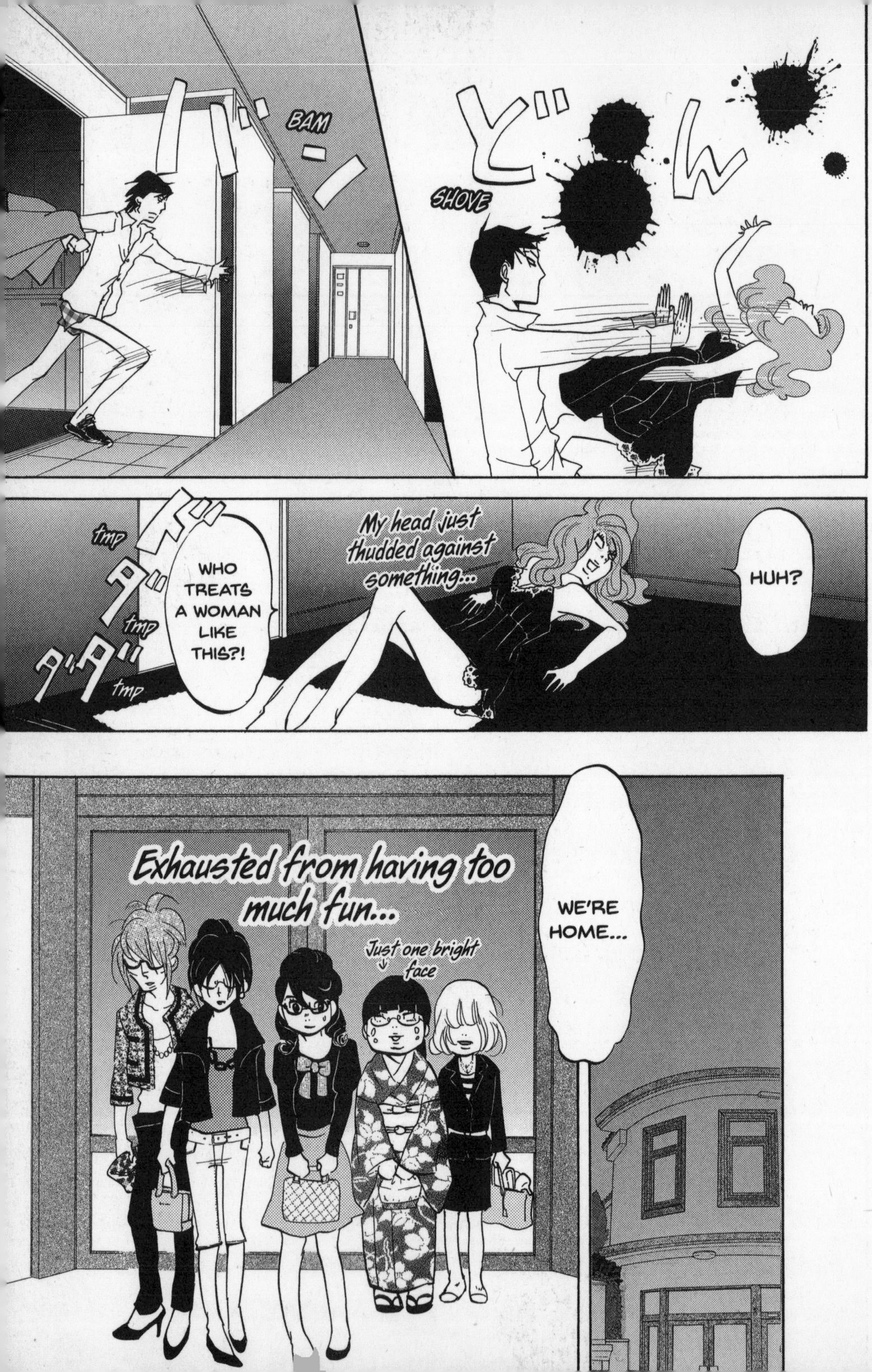
どん
SHOVE
BAM
HUH?
My head just thudded against something...
WHO TREATS A WOMAN LIKE THIS?!
tmp
tmp
tmp
WE'RE HOME...
Exhausted from having too much fun...
Just one bright face

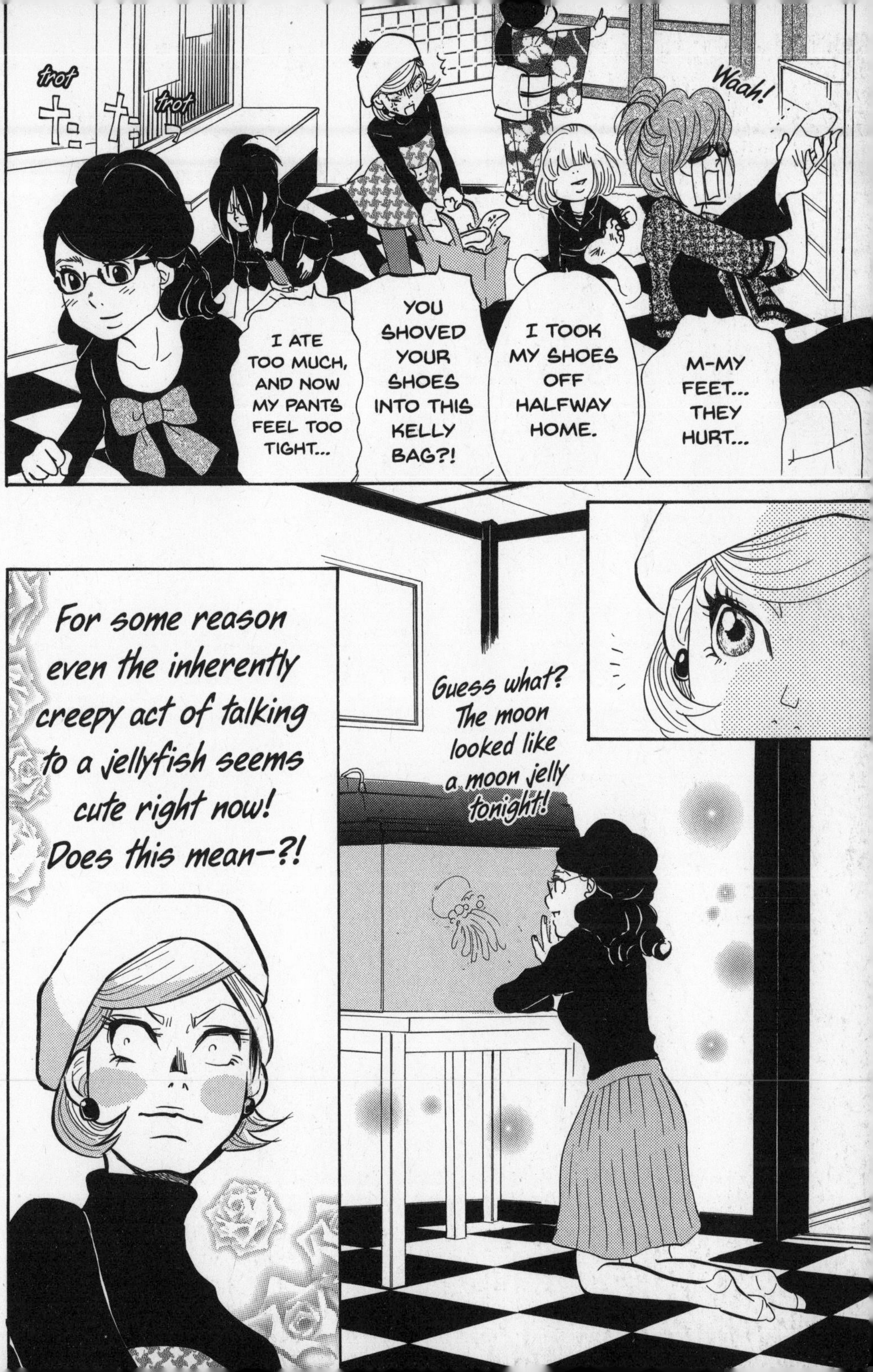
Waah!
M-MY FEET... THEY HURT...
I TOOK MY SHOES OFF HALFWAY HOME.
YOU SHOVED YOUR SHOES INTO THIS KELLY BAG?!
I ATE TOO MUCH, AND NOW MY PANTS FEEL TOO TIGHT...
trot
trot
Guess what? The moon looked like a moon jelly tonight!
For some reason even the inherently creepy act of talking to a jellyfish seems cute right now! Does this mean-?!

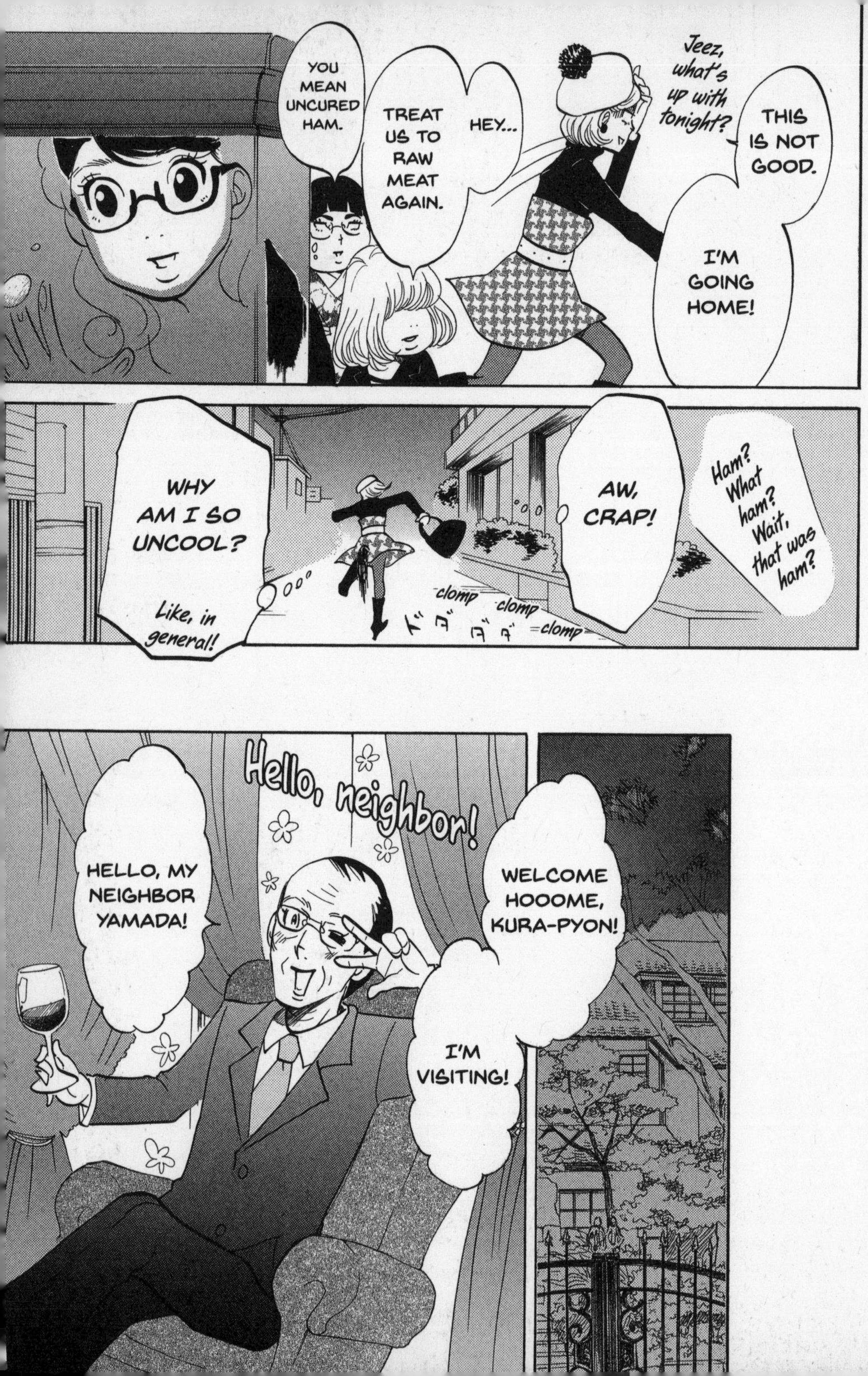
Jeez, what's up with tonight?
THIS IS NOT GOOD.
I'M GOING HOME!
HEY...
TREAT US TO RAW MEAT AGAIN.
YOU MEAN UNCURED HAM.
Ham? What ham? Wait, that was ham?
AW, CRAP!
clomp
clomp
clomp
WHY AM I SO UNCOOL?
Like, in general!
Hello, neighbor!
WELCOME HOOOME, KURA-PYON!
I'M VISITING!
HELLO, MY NEIGHBOR YAMADA!

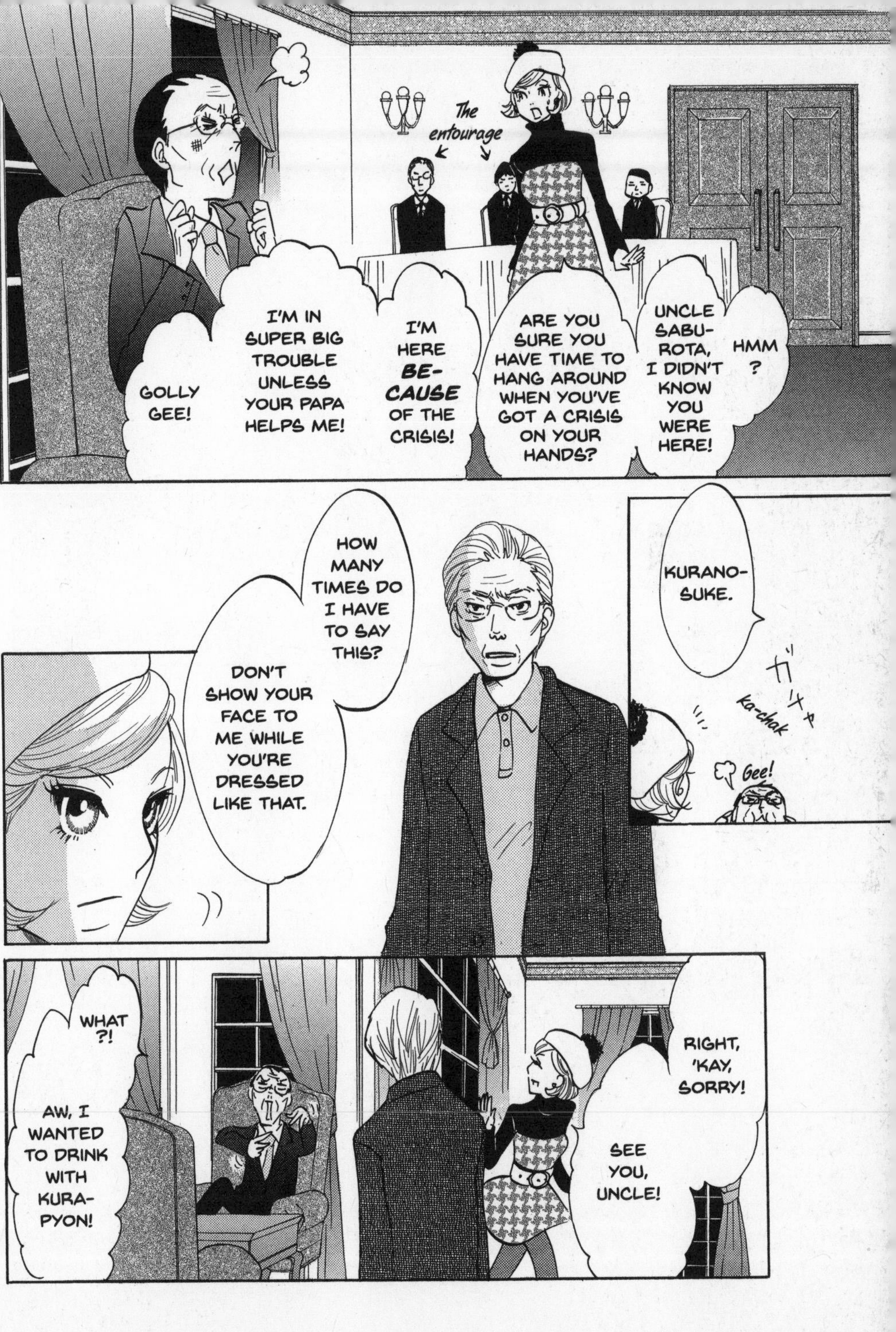
The entourage
HMM ?
UNCLE SABURO-TA, I DIDN'T KNOW YOU WERE HERE!
ARE YOU SURE YOU HAVE TIME TO HANG AROUND WHEN YOU'VE GOT A CRISIS ON YOUR HANDS?
I'M HERE **BE-CAUSE** OF THE CRISIS!
I'M IN SUPER BIG TROUBLE UNLESS YOUR PAPA HELPS ME!
GOLLY GEE!
KURANO-SUKE.
ガチャ
ka-chak
Gee!
HOW MANY TIMES DO I HAVE TO SAY THIS?
DON'T SHOW YOUR FACE TO ME WHILE YOU'RE DRESSED LIKE THAT.
RIGHT, 'KAY, SORRY!
SEE YOU, UNCLE!
WHAT ?!
AW, I WANTED TO DRINK WITH KURA-PYON!

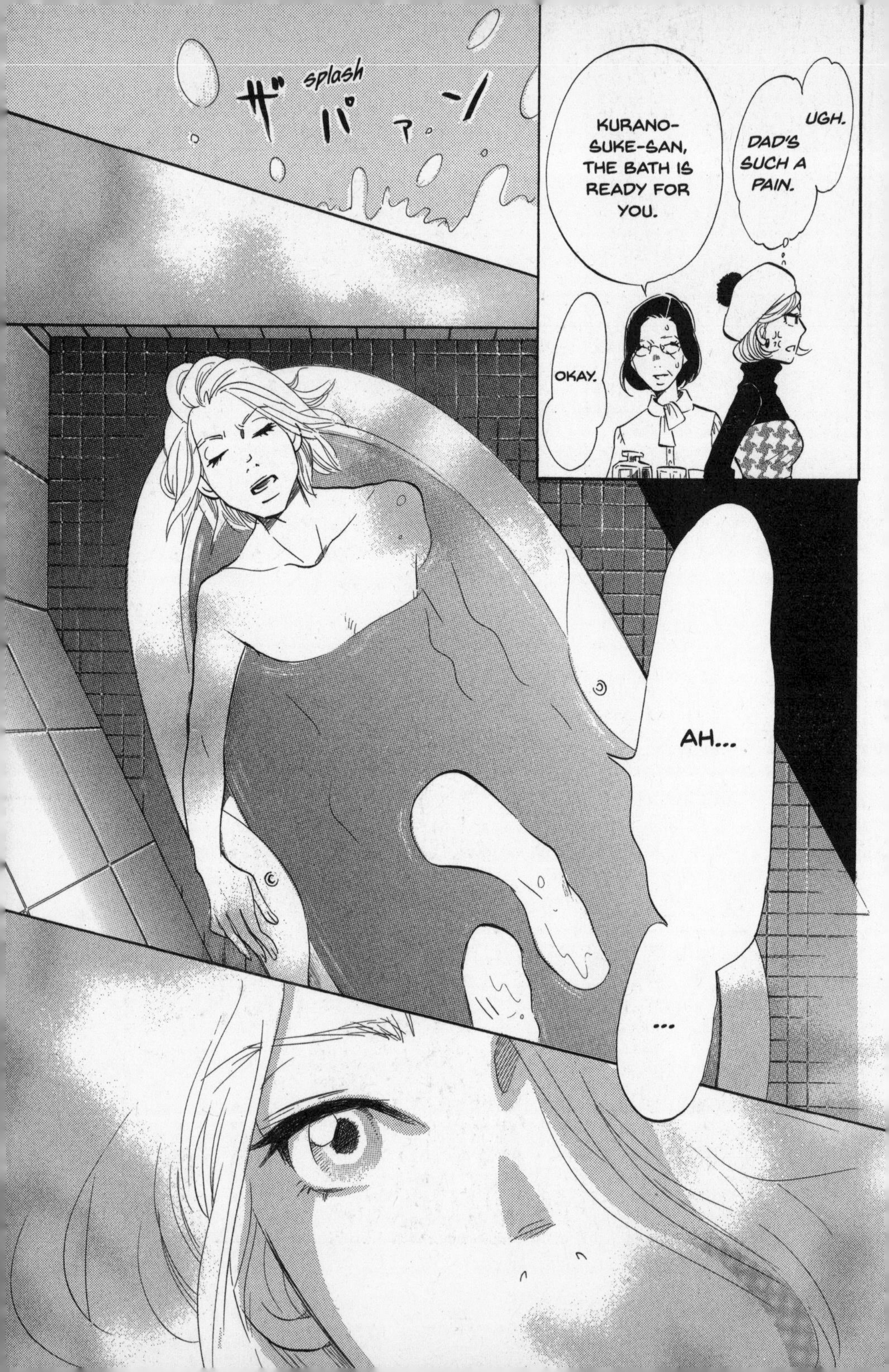
UGH. DAD'S SUCH A PAIN.
KURANOSUKE-SAN, THE BATH IS READY FOR YOU.
OKAY.
splash
AH...
...

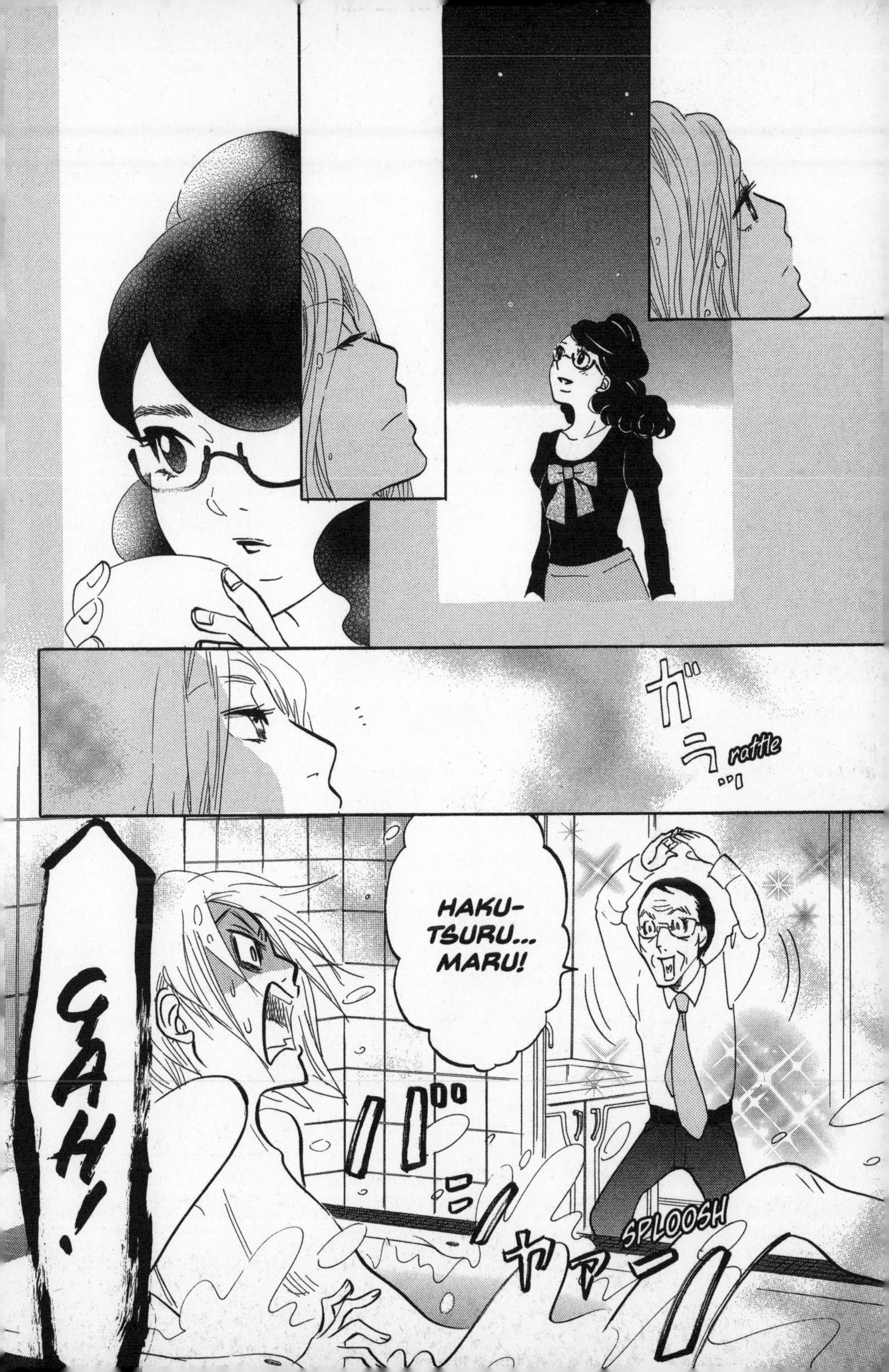
ガラッ
rattle
HAKU-
TSURU...
MARU!
GAH!
ザバー
SPLOOSH
ヤァー

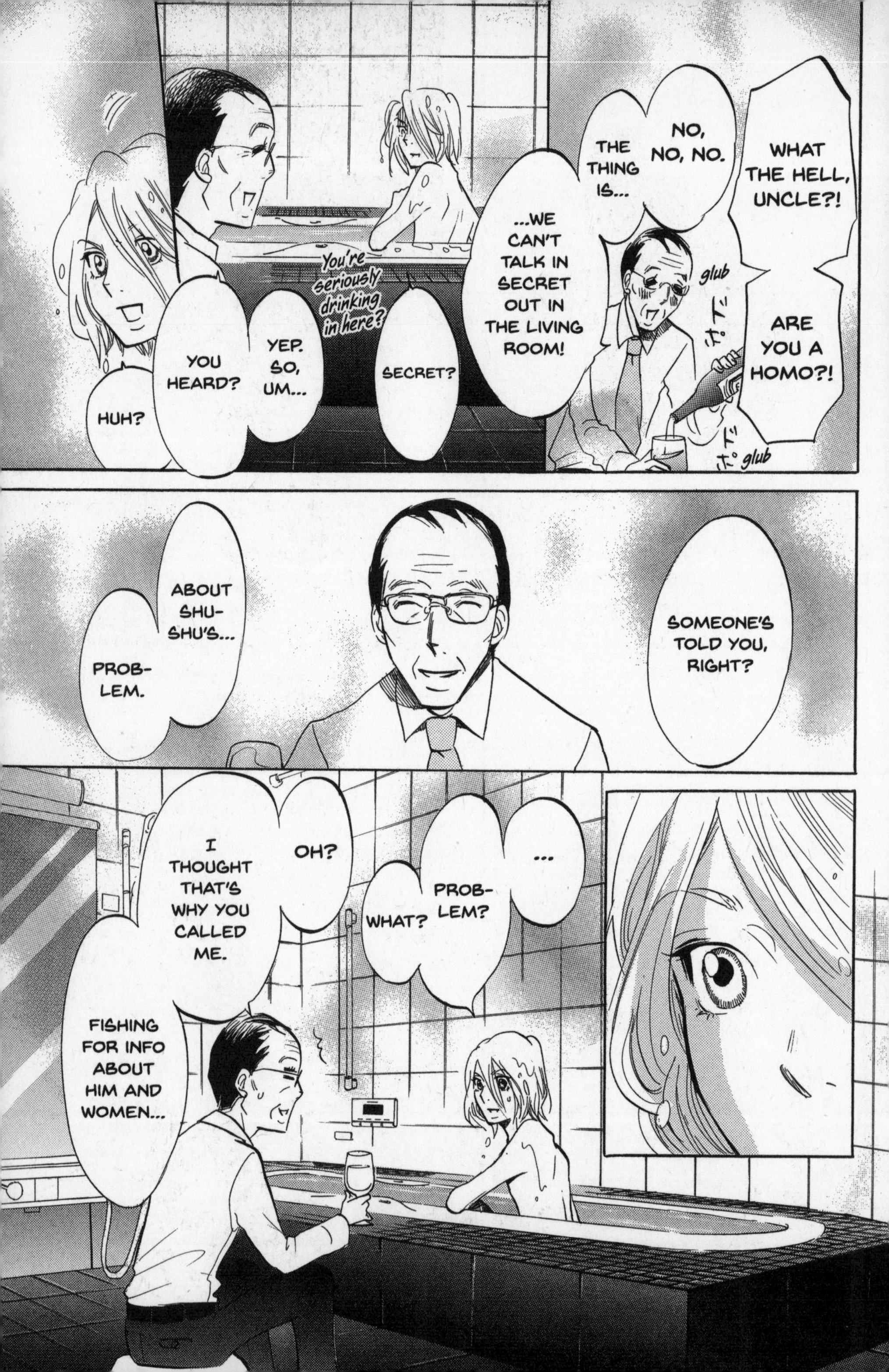
WHAT THE HELL, UNCLE?!
ARE YOU A HOMO?!
NO, NO, NO.
THE THING IS...
...WE CAN'T TALK IN SECRET OUT IN THE LIVING ROOM!
glub
glub
SECRET?
You're seriously drinking in here?
YEP. SO, UM...
YOU HEARD?
HUH?
SOMEONE'S TOLD YOU, RIGHT?
ABOUT SHU-SHU'S...
PROB-LEM.
...
PROB-LEM?
WHAT?
OH?
I THOUGHT THAT'S WHY YOU CALLED ME.
FISHING FOR INFO ABOUT HIM AND WOMEN...

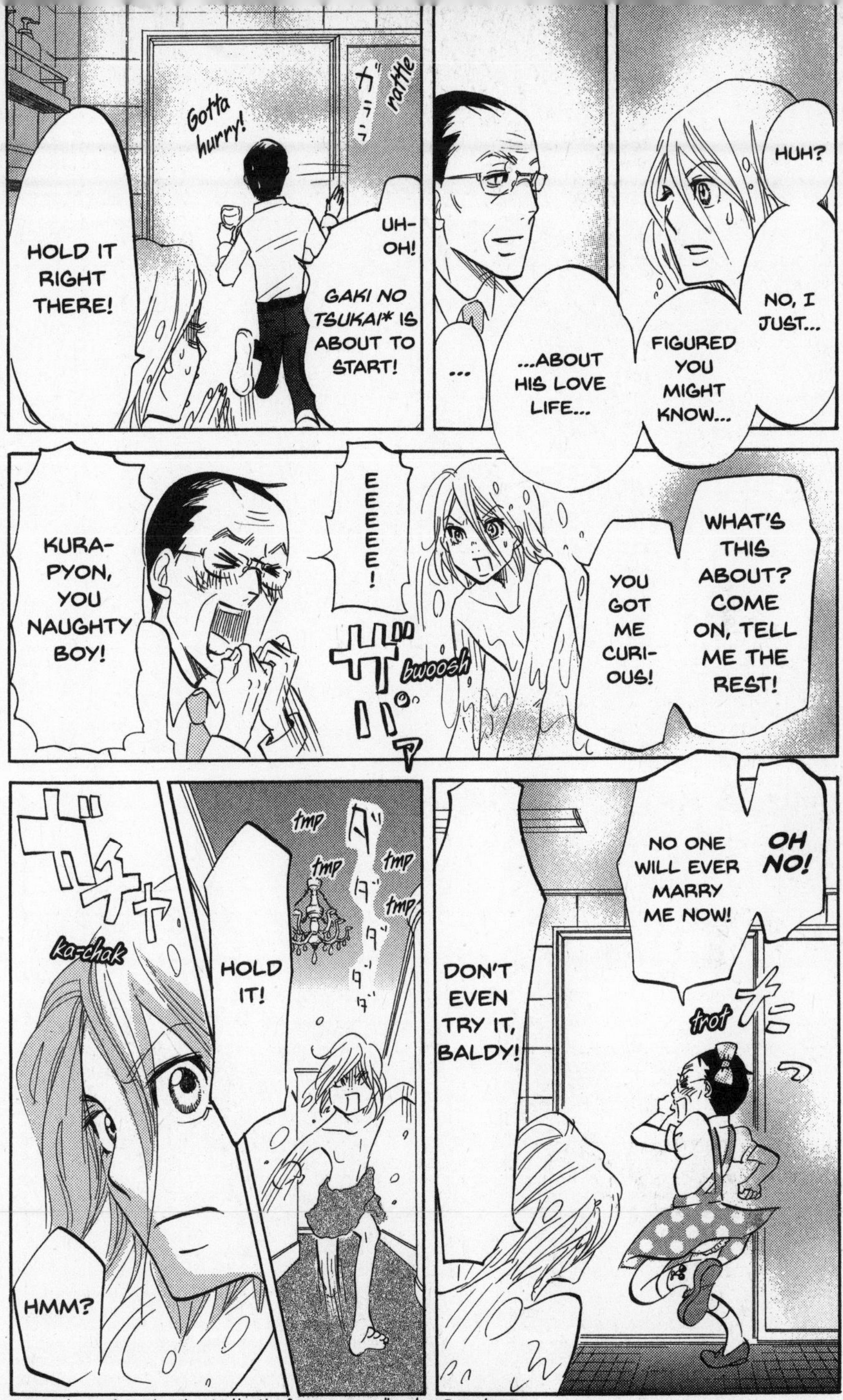
HUH?
NO, I JUST...
FIGURED YOU MIGHT KNOW...
...ABOUT HIS LOVE LIFE...
...
rattle
UH-OH!
GAKI NO TSUKAI* IS ABOUT TO START!
Gotta hurry!
HOLD IT RIGHT THERE!
WHAT'S THIS ABOUT? COME ON, TELL ME THE REST!
YOU GOT ME CURIOUS!
bwoosh
EEEEEE!
KURA-PYON, YOU NAUGHTY BOY!
OH NO!
NO ONE WILL EVER MARRY ME NOW!
trot
DON'T EVEN TRY IT, BALDY!
tmp
tmp
tmp
tmp
HOLD IT!
ka-chak
HMM?

*A popular variety show hosted by the famous comedian duo, *Downtown*.

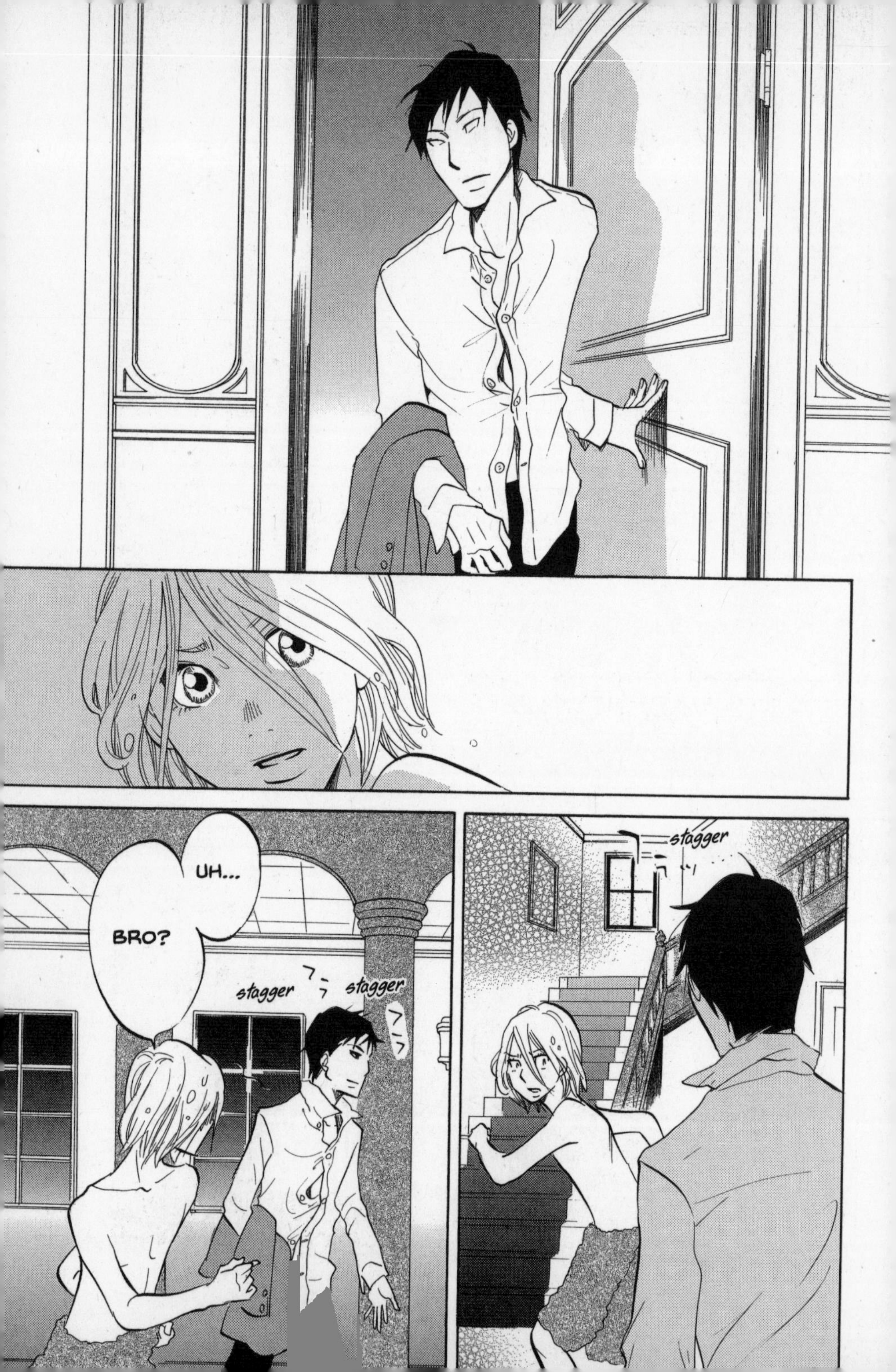
stagger
UH...
BRO?
stagger
stagger

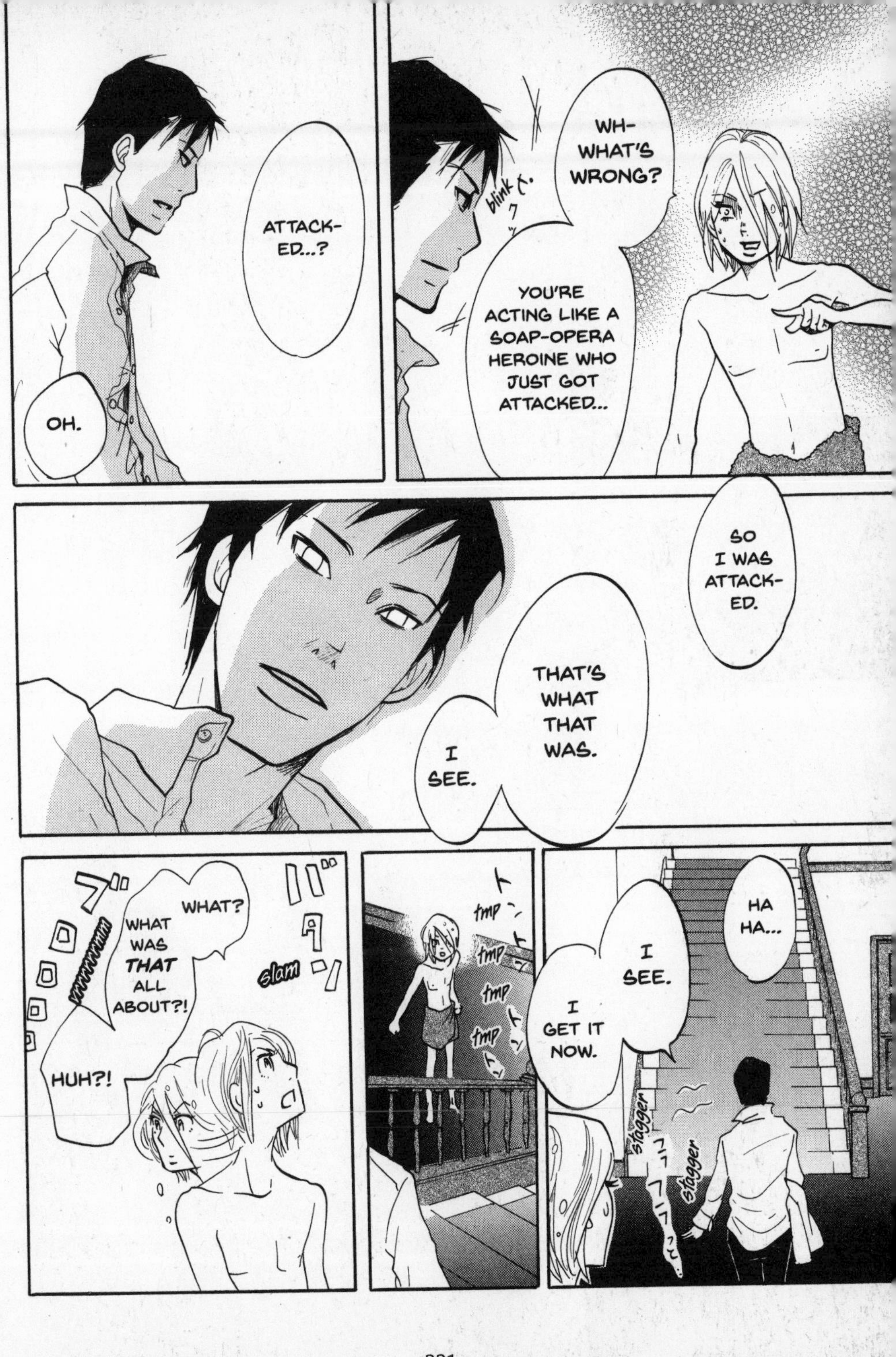
WH- WHAT'S WRONG?
blink
YOU'RE ACTING LIKE A SOAP-OPERA HEROINE WHO JUST GOT ATTACKED...
ATTACK-ED...?
OH.
SO I WAS ATTACK-ED.
THAT'S WHAT THAT WAS.
I SEE.
HA HA...
I SEE.
I GET IT NOW.
stagger
stagger
tmp
tmp
tmp
tmp
slam
WHAT?
WHAT WAS **THAT** ALL ABOUT?!
HUH?!

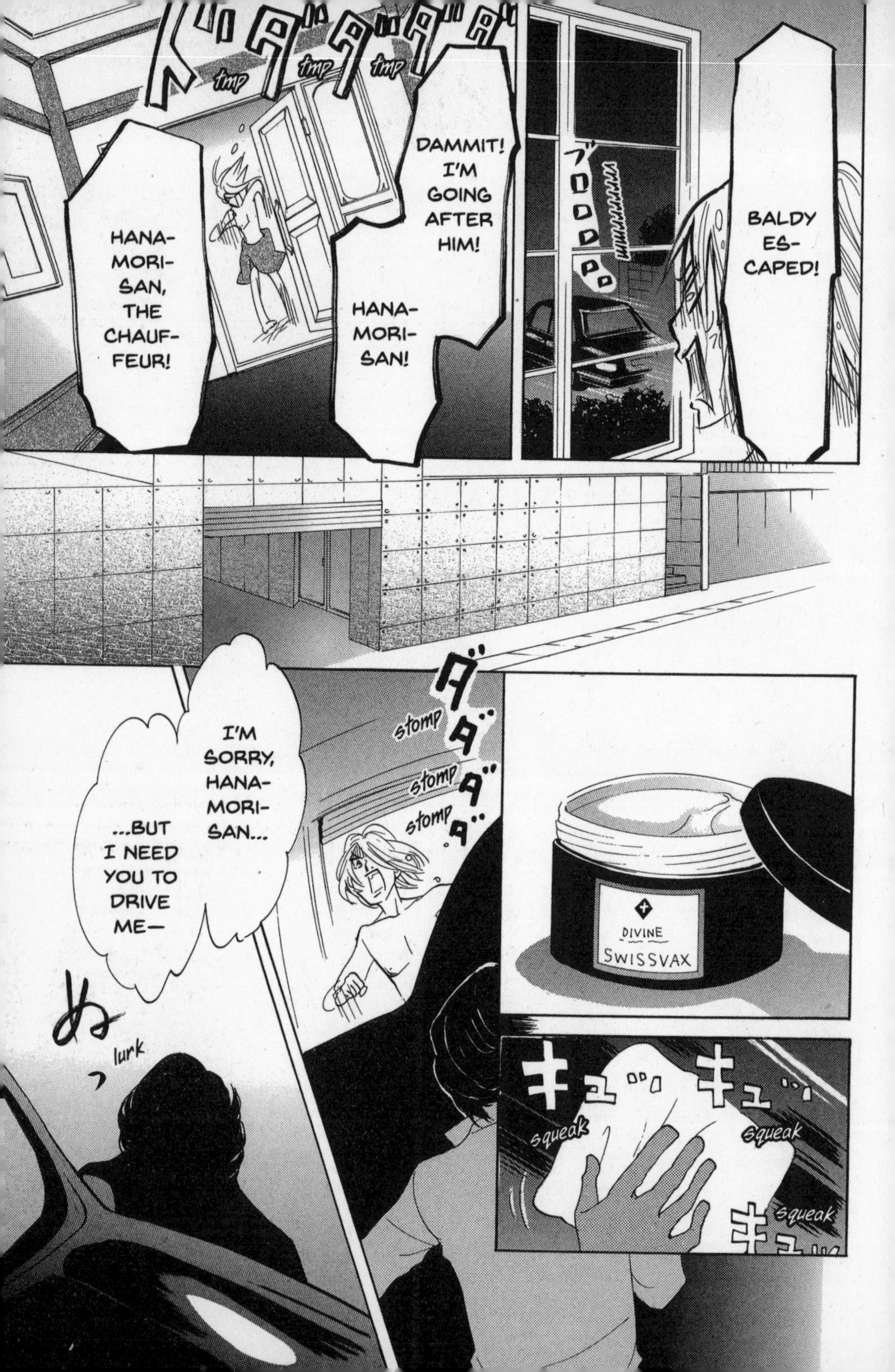
BALDY ES-CAPED!
ブロロロロロ
vrrrrrmm
DAMMIT! I'M GOING AFTER HIM!
HANA-MORI-SAN!
ドダダダダ
tmp tmp tmp
HANA-MORI-SAN, THE CHAUF-FEUR!
DIVINE SWISSVAX
キュッキュッキュッ
squeak squeak squeak
ダダダダ
stomp stomp stomp
I'M SORRY, HANA-MORI-SAN...
...BUT I NEED YOU TO DRIVE ME—
ぬっ
lurk

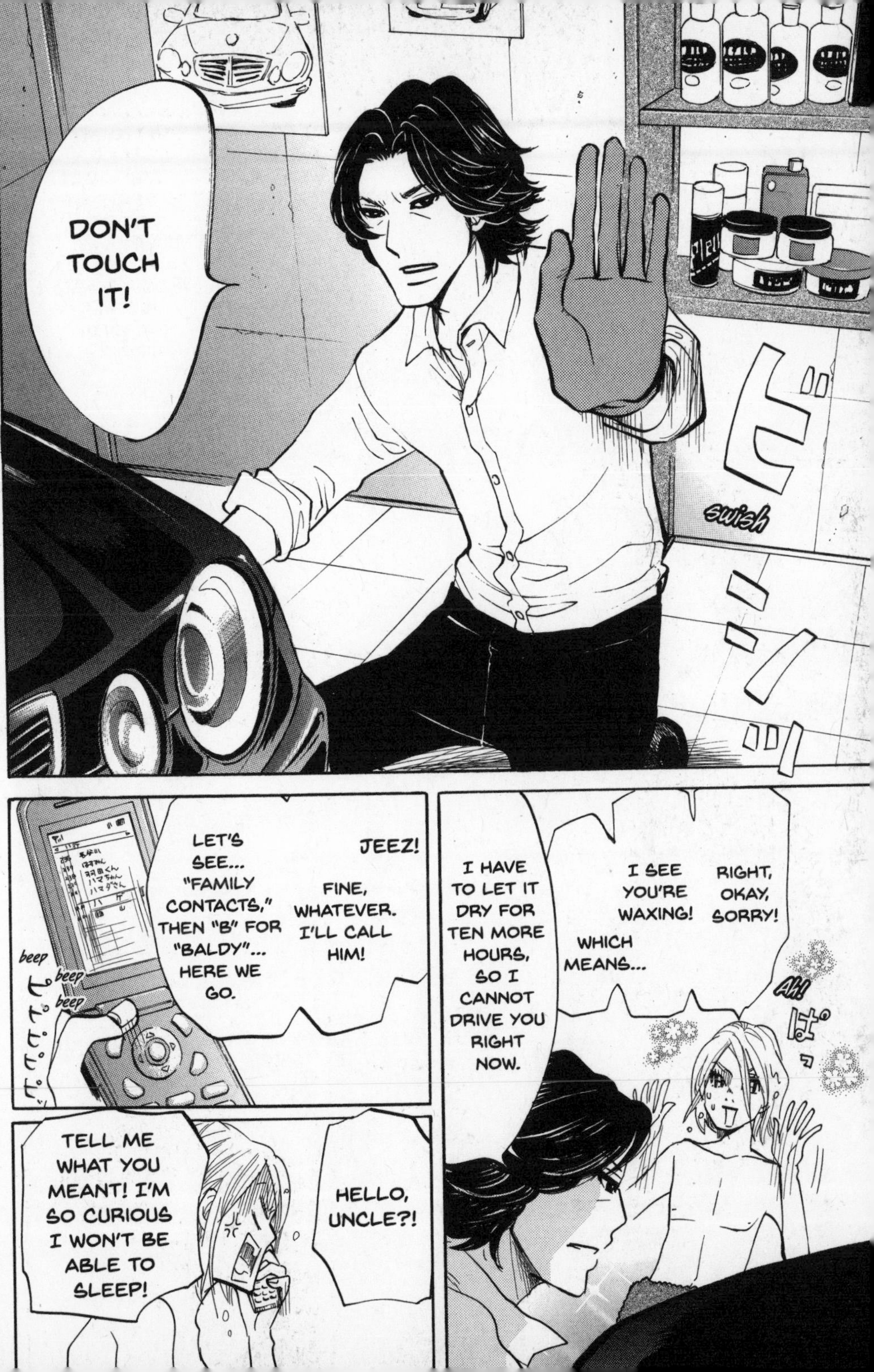
DON'T TOUCH IT!
swish
RIGHT, OKAY, SORRY!
I SEE YOU'RE WAXING!
WHICH MEANS...
I HAVE TO LET IT DRY FOR TEN MORE HOURS, SO I CANNOT DRIVE YOU RIGHT NOW.
Ah!
JEEZ!
FINE, WHATEVER. I'LL CALL HIM!
LET'S SEE... "FAMILY CONTACTS," THEN "B" FOR "BALDY"... HERE WE GO.
beep
beep
beep
HELLO, UNCLE?!
TELL ME WHAT YOU MEANT! I'M SO CURIOUS I WON'T BE ABLE TO SLEEP!

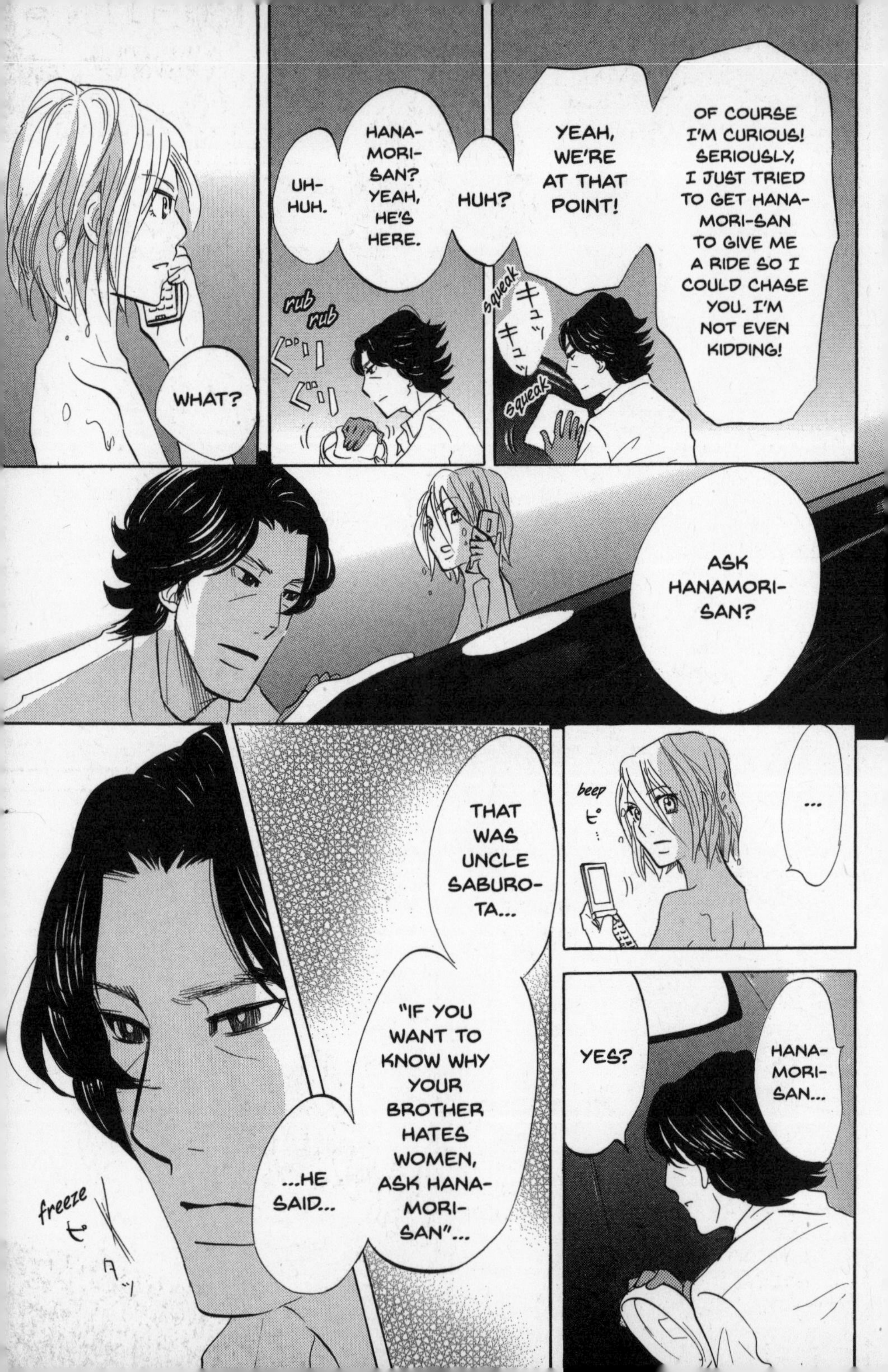
OF COURSE I'M CURIOUS! SERIOUSLY, I JUST TRIED TO GET HANA-MORI-SAN TO GIVE ME A RIDE SO I COULD CHASE YOU. I'M NOT EVEN KIDDING!
YEAH, WE'RE AT THAT POINT!
squeak
squeak
HUH?
HANA-MORI-SAN? YEAH, HE'S HERE.
UH-HUH.
rub rub
WHAT?
ASK HANAMORI-SAN?
...
beep
HANA-MORI-SAN...
YES?
THAT WAS UNCLE SABURO-TA...
"IF YOU WANT TO KNOW WHY YOUR BROTHER HATES WOMEN, ASK HANA-MORI-SAN"...
...HE SAID...
freeze

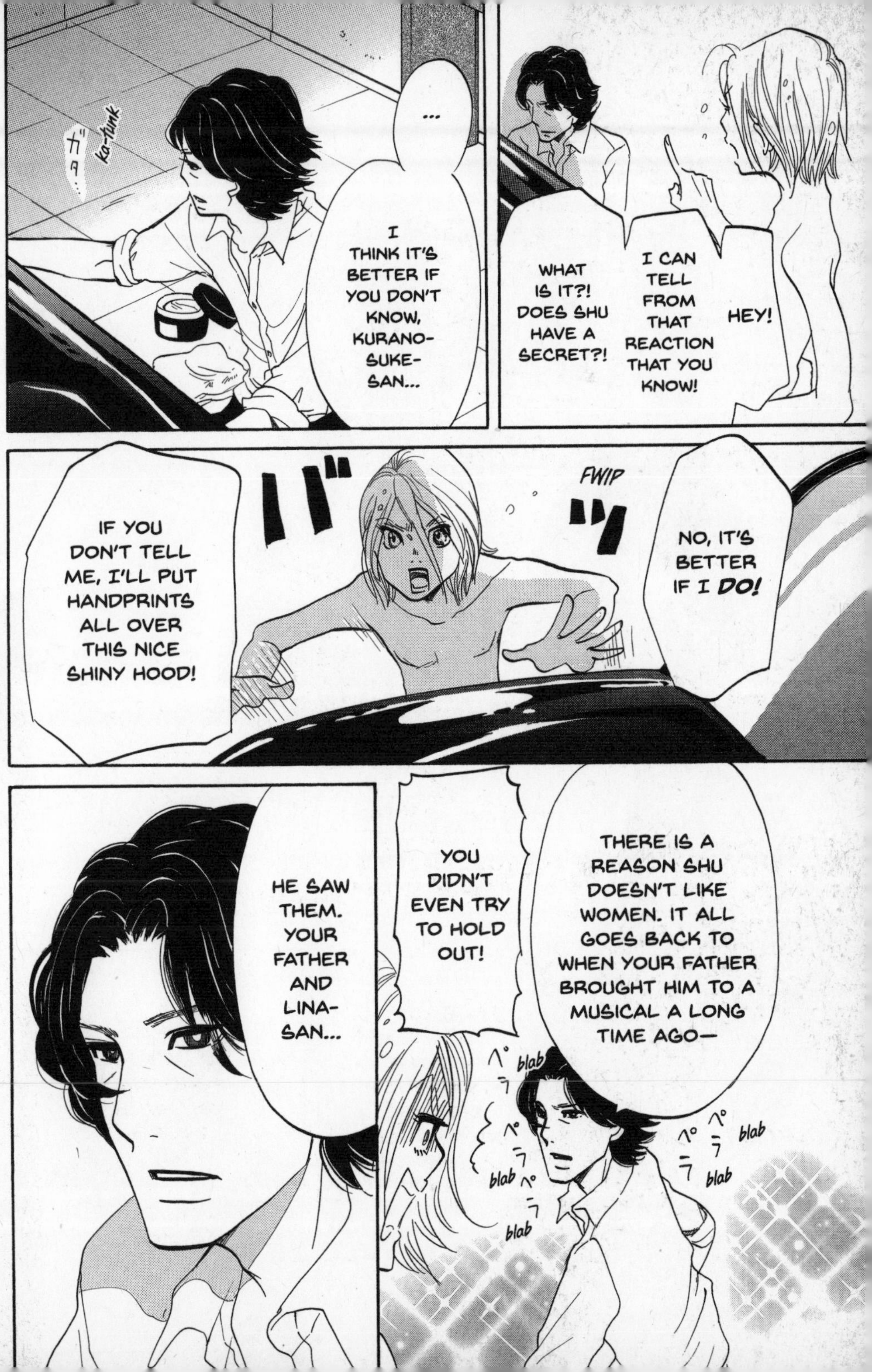
HEY!
I CAN TELL FROM THAT REACTION THAT YOU KNOW!
WHAT IS IT?! DOES SHU HAVE A SECRET?!
...
I THINK IT'S BETTER IF YOU DON'T KNOW, KURANOSUKE-SAN...
ガタ…
ka-tunk
NO, IT'S BETTER IF I DO!
FWIP
IF YOU DON'T TELL ME, I'LL PUT HANDPRINTS ALL OVER THIS NICE SHINY HOOD!
THERE IS A REASON SHU DOESN'T LIKE WOMEN. IT ALL GOES BACK TO WHEN YOUR FATHER BROUGHT HIM TO A MUSICAL A LONG TIME AGO—
ペラ blab
ペラ blab
YOU DIDN'T EVEN TRY TO HOLD OUT!
ペラ blab
ペラ blab
ペラ blab
HE SAW THEM. YOUR FATHER AND LINA-SAN...

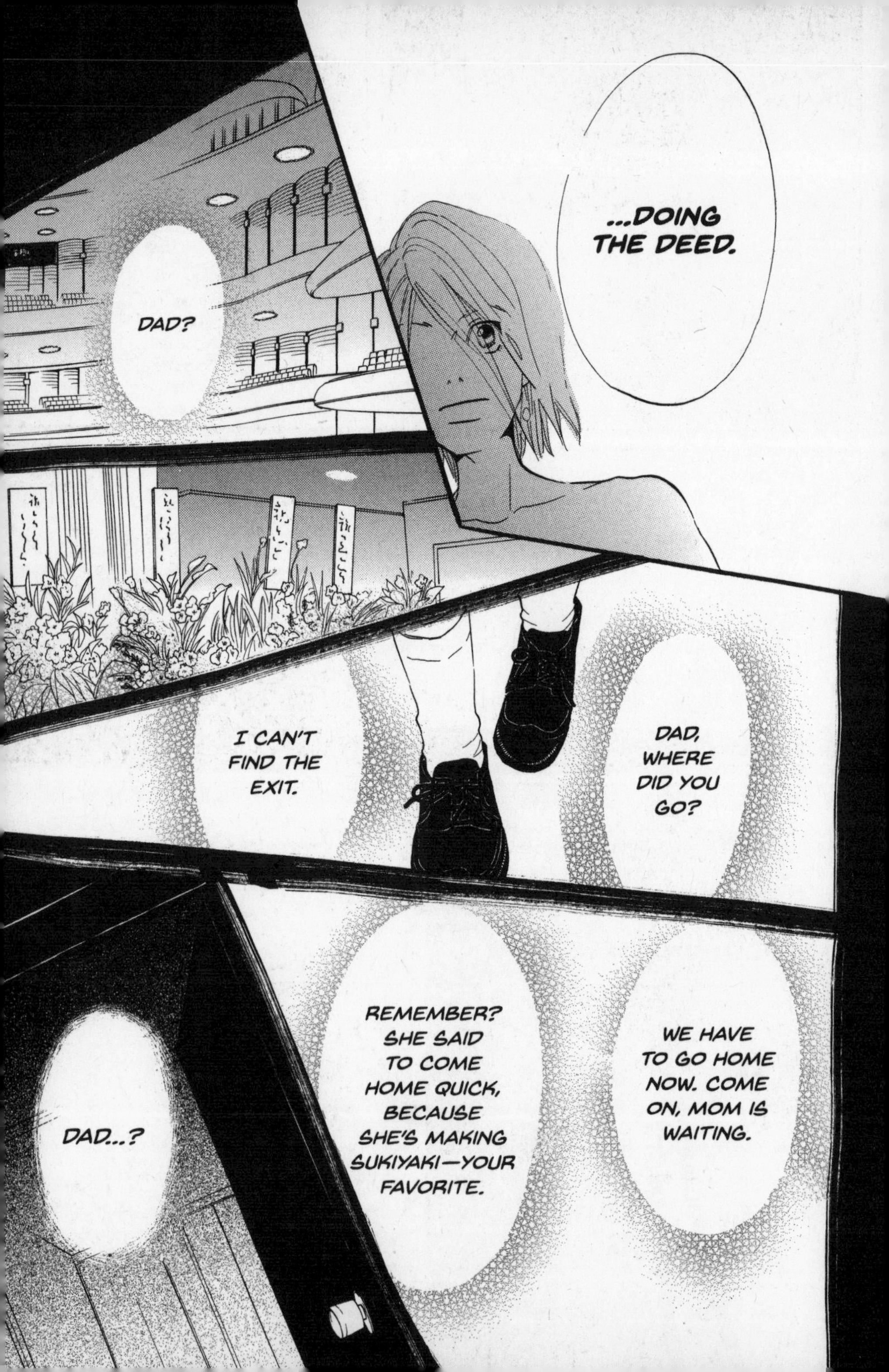
...DOING THE DEED.
DAD?
DAD, WHERE DID YOU GO?
I CAN'T FIND THE EXIT.
WE HAVE TO GO HOME NOW. COME ON, MOM IS WAITING.
REMEMBER? SHE SAID TO COME HOME QUICK, BECAUSE SHE'S MAKING SUKIYAKI—YOUR FAVORITE.
DAD...?

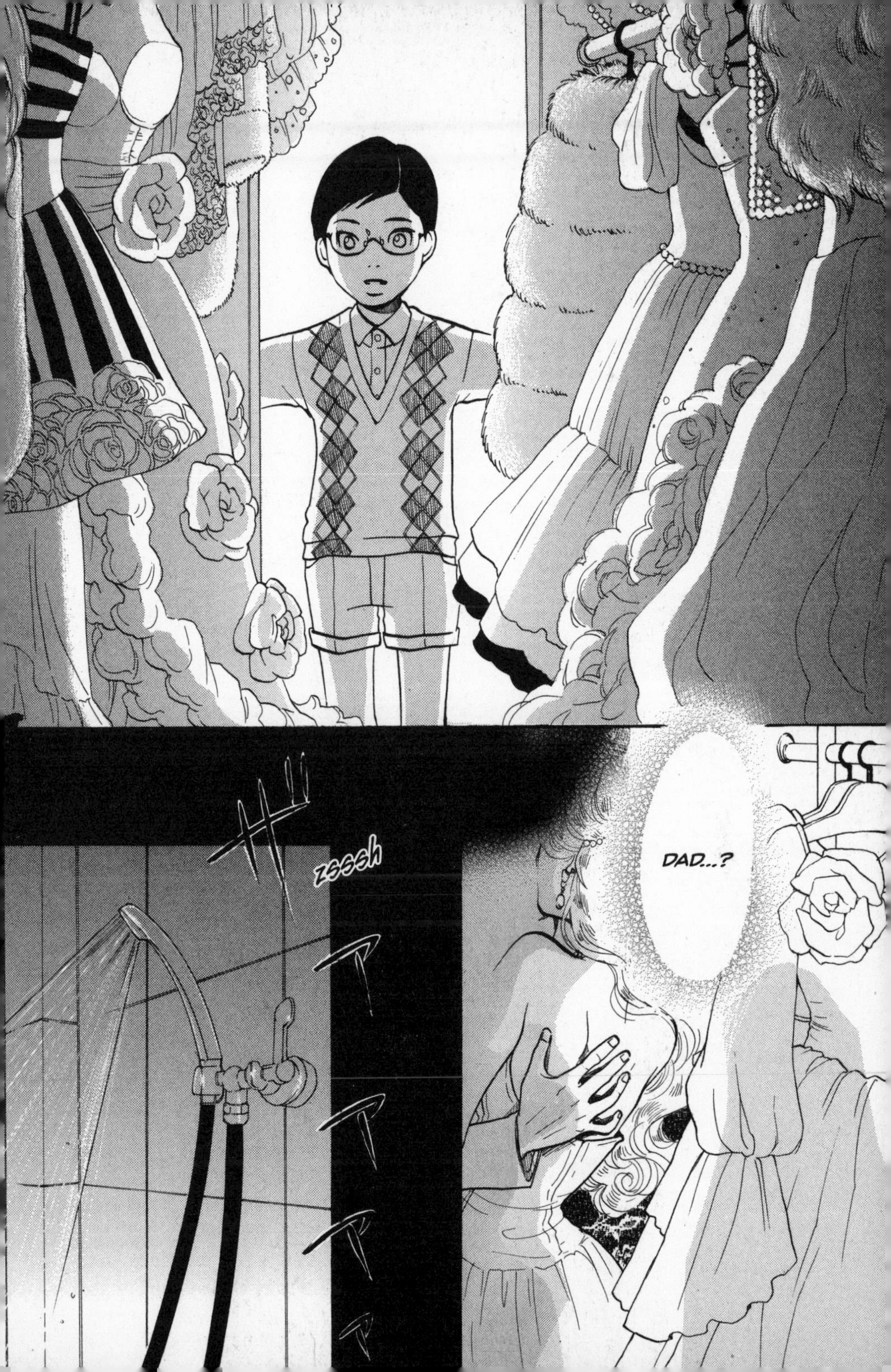
DAD...?
zsssh

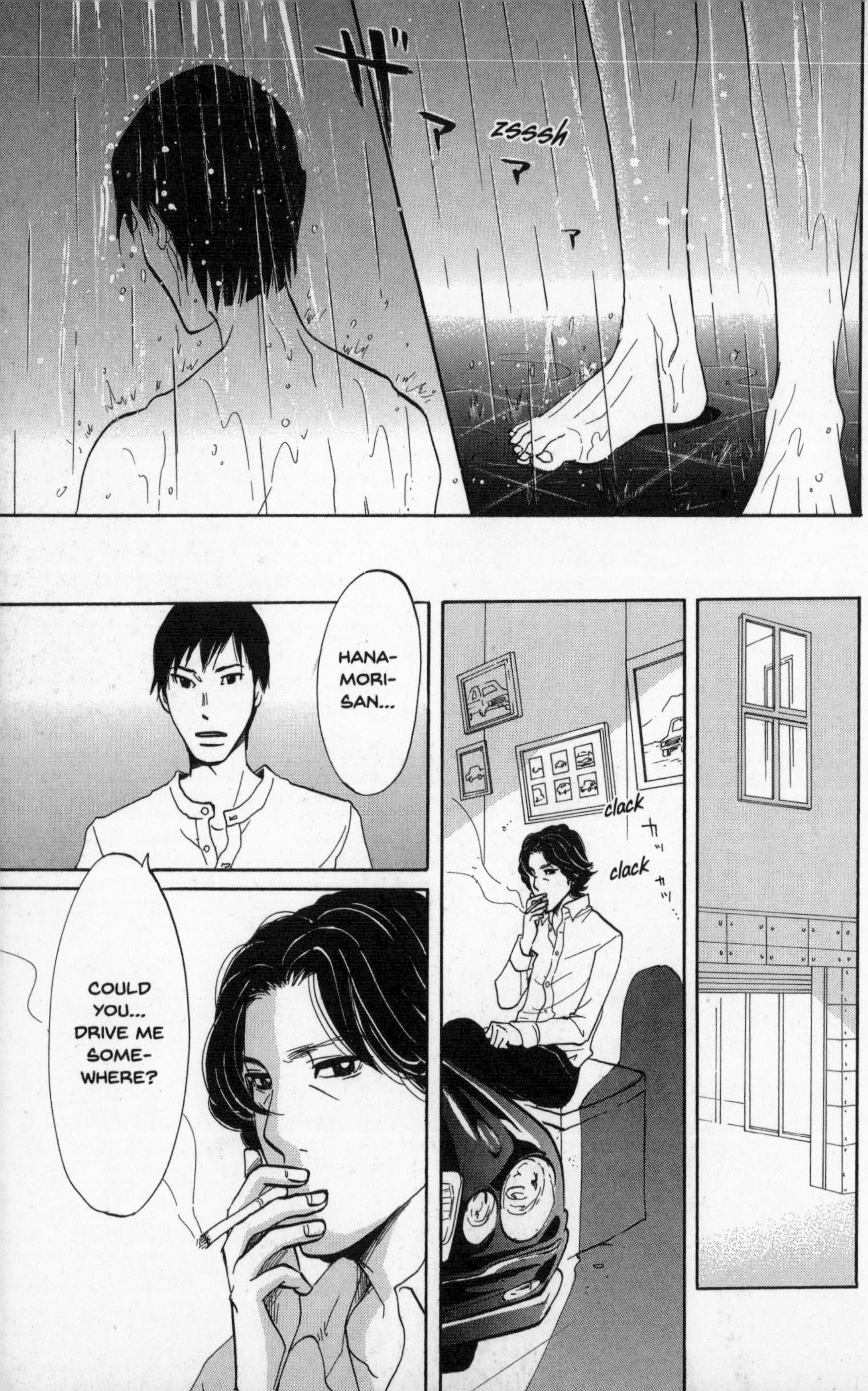
ザァァァ
zsssh
clack
カッ
clack
カッ…
HANAMORI-SAN...
COULD YOU... DRIVE ME SOMEWHERE?

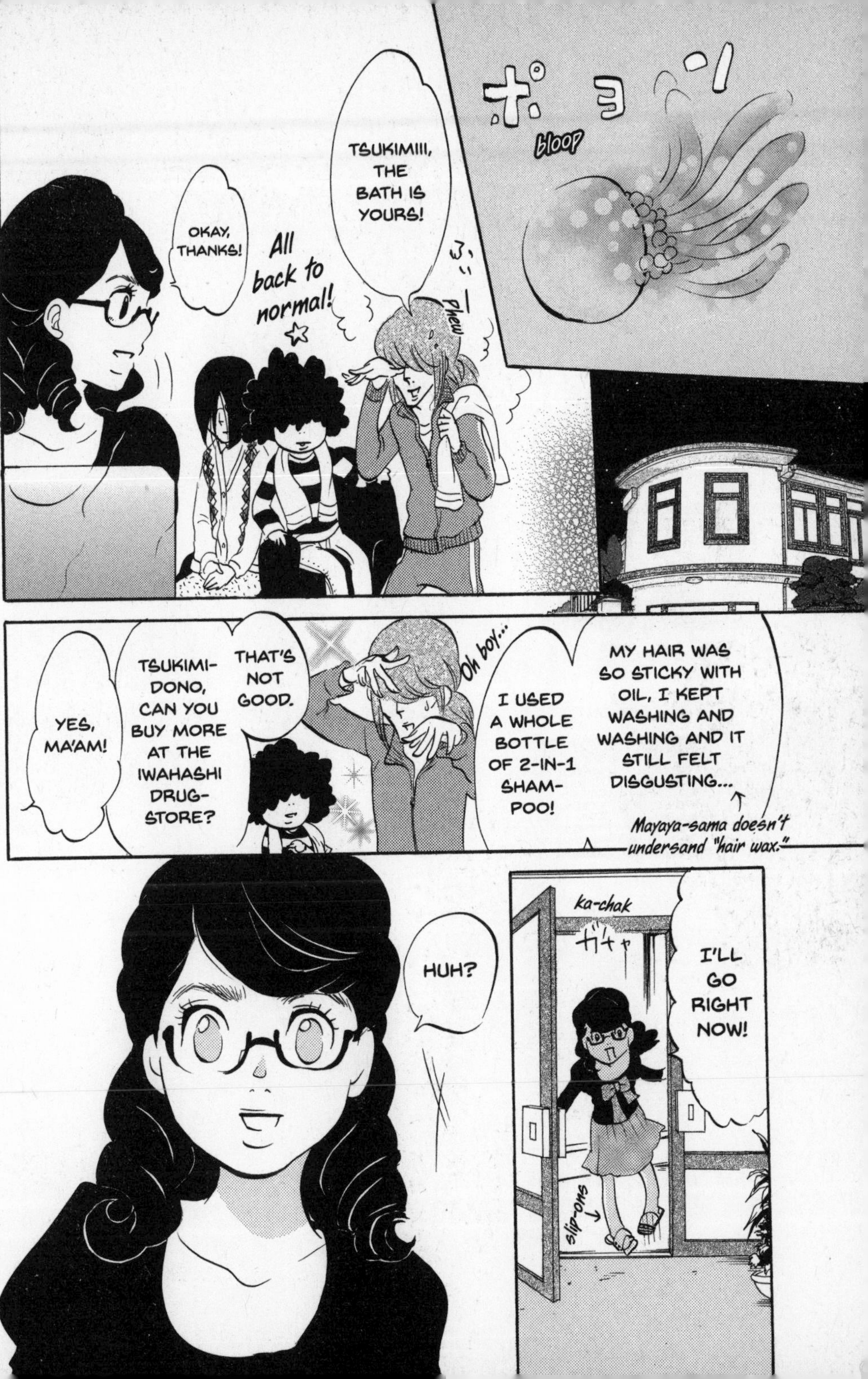
ポヨン
bloop
TSUKIMIII, THE BATH IS YOURS!
Phew
All back to normal!
OKAY, THANKS!
MY HAIR WAS SO STICKY WITH OIL, I KEPT WASHING AND WASHING AND IT STILL FELT DISGUSTING...
Mayaya-sama doesn't undersand "hair wax."
I USED A WHOLE BOTTLE OF 2-IN-1 SHAMPOO!
Oh boy...
THAT'S NOT GOOD.
TSUKIMI-DONO, CAN YOU BUY MORE AT THE IWAHASHI DRUG-STORE?
YES, MA'AM!
ka-chak
ガチャ
I'LL GO RIGHT NOW!
slip-ons
HUH?

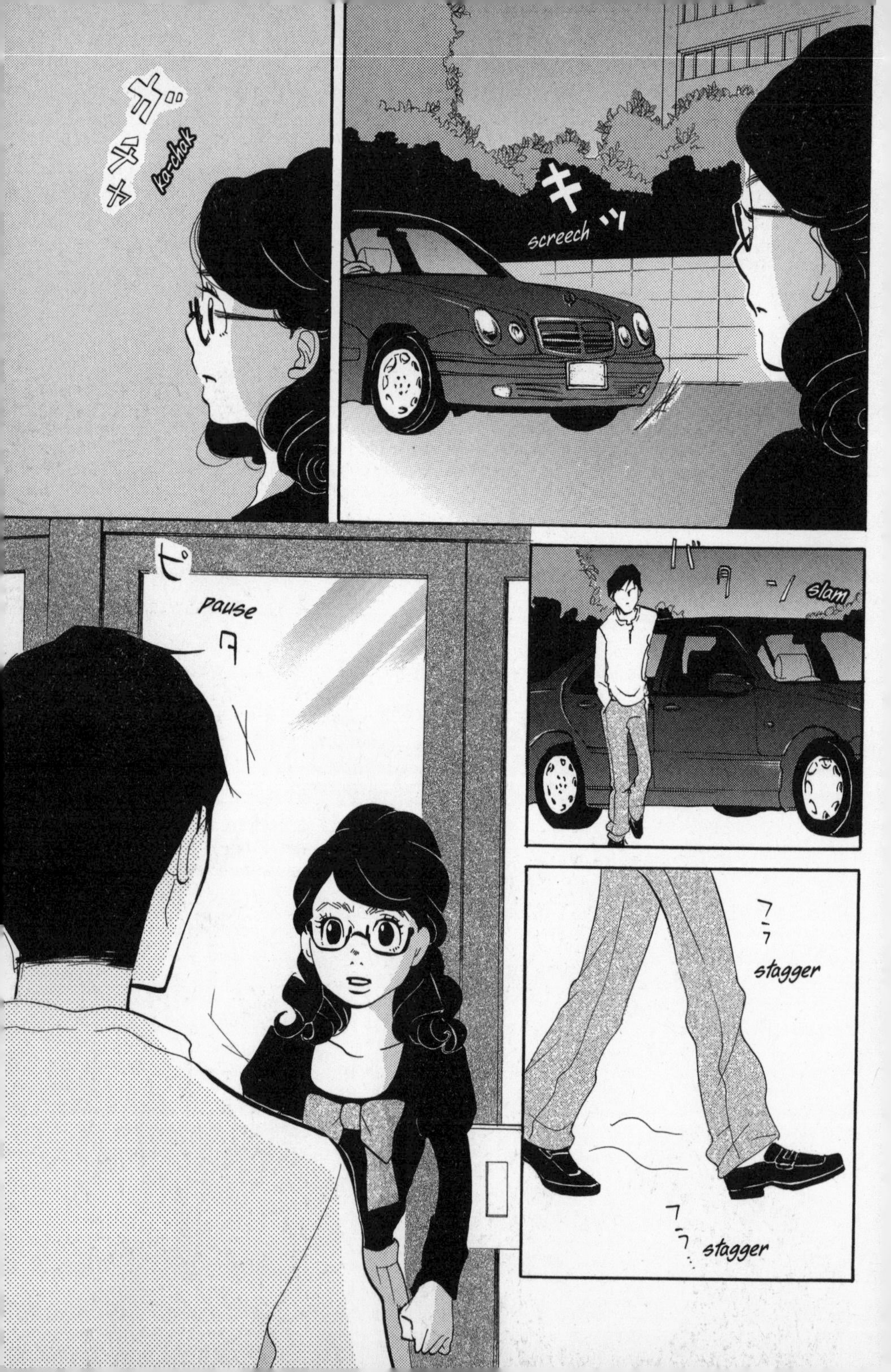
キッ
screech
ガチャ
ka-chak
バタ―ン
slam
フラ
stagger
フラ…
stagger
ピタ
pause

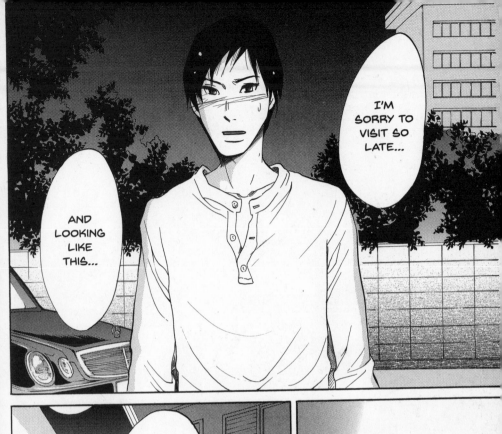

I'M SORRY TO VISIT SO LATE...

AND LOOKING LIKE THIS...

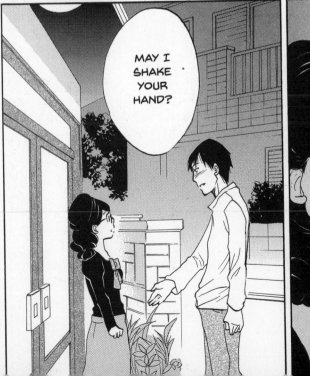

MAY I SHAKE YOUR HAND?

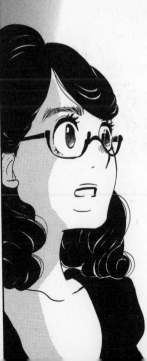

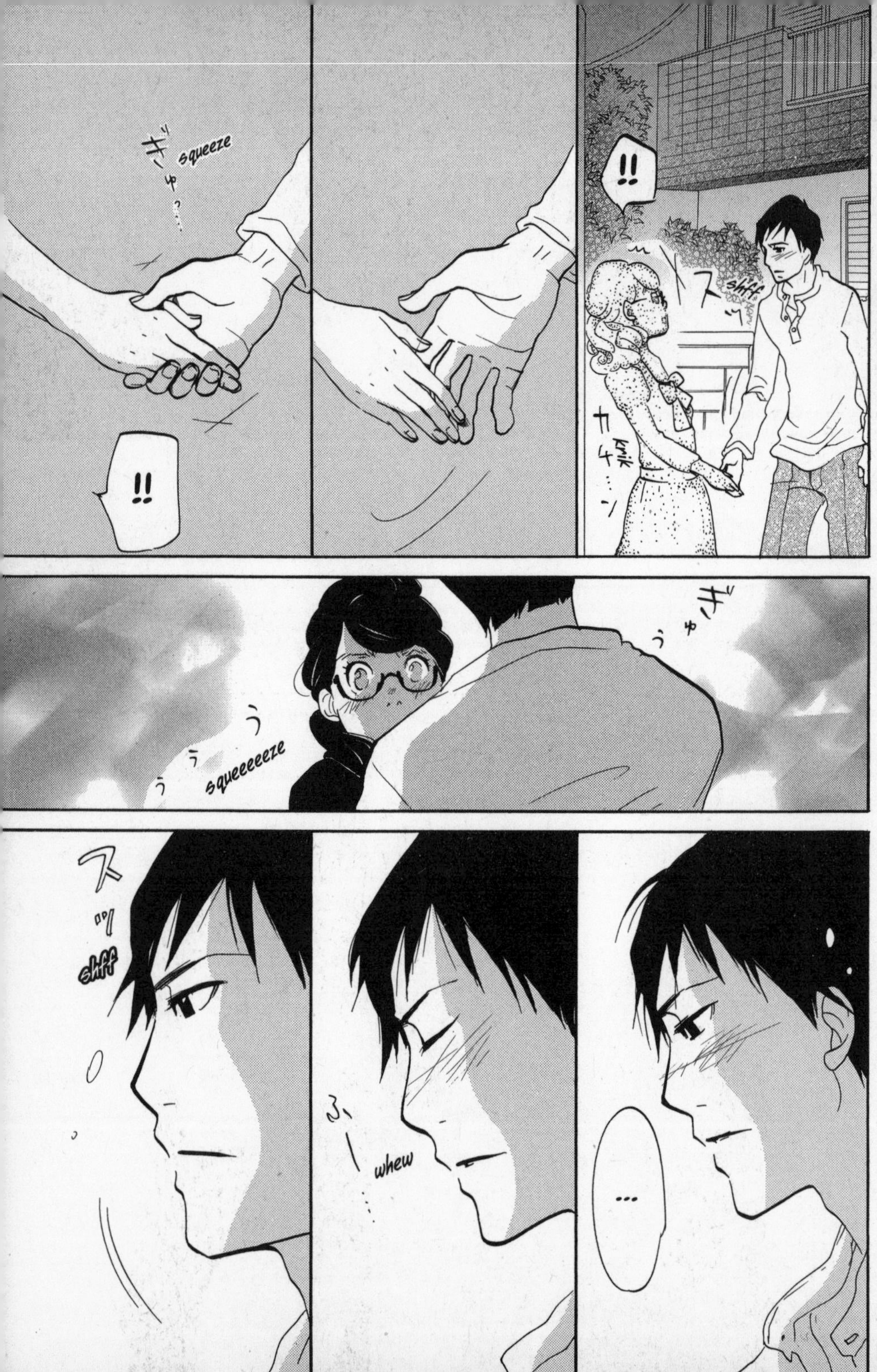

!!
スッ
shff
カチ…ン
krik
ぎゅっ…
squeeze
!!
ぎゅうううう
squeeeeeze
…
ふー…
whew
スッ
shff

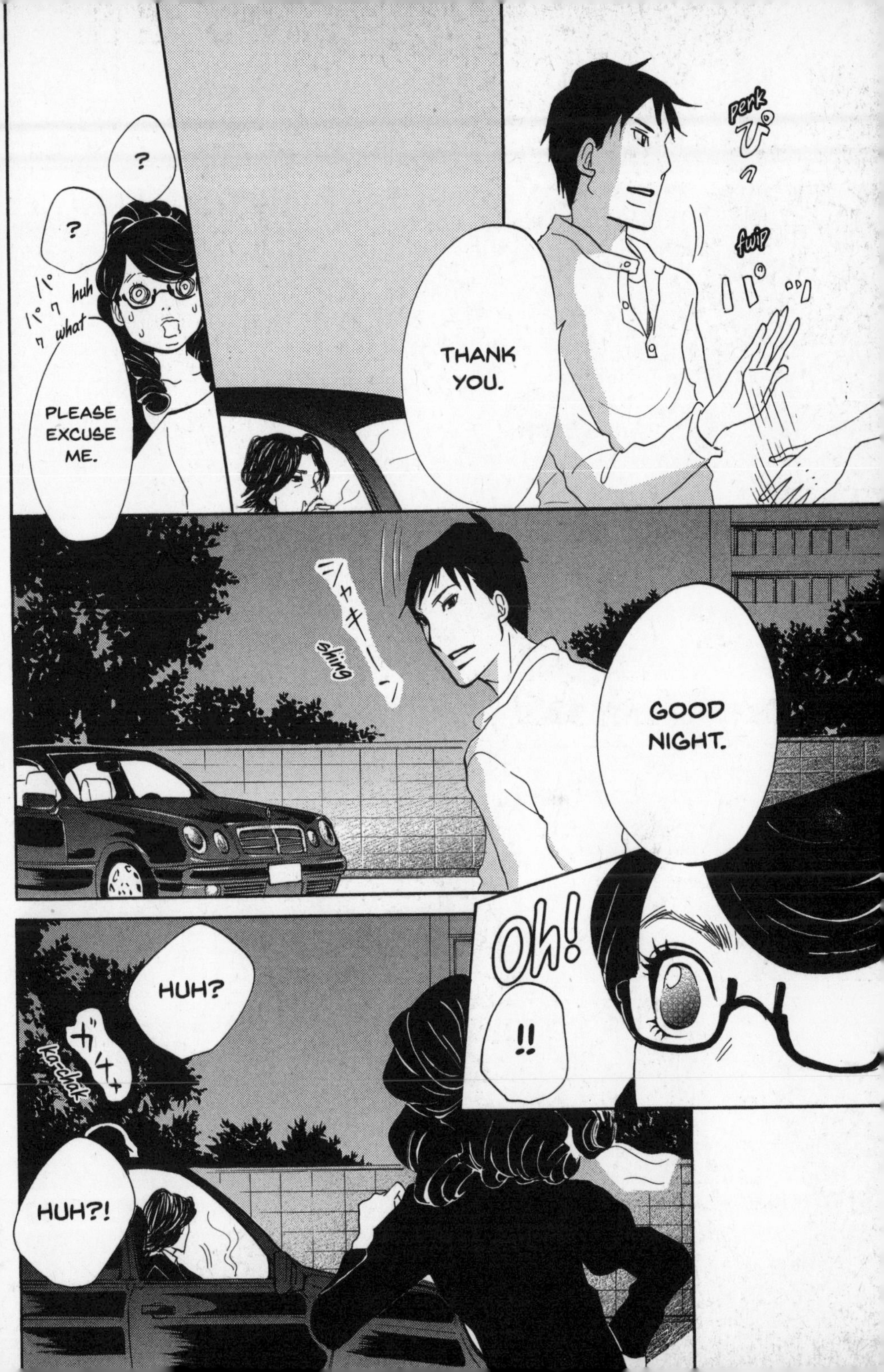
perk
THANK YOU.
fwip
?
?
huh
what
PLEASE EXCUSE ME.
shing
GOOD NIGHT.
Oh!
!!
HUH?
ka-chak
HUH?!

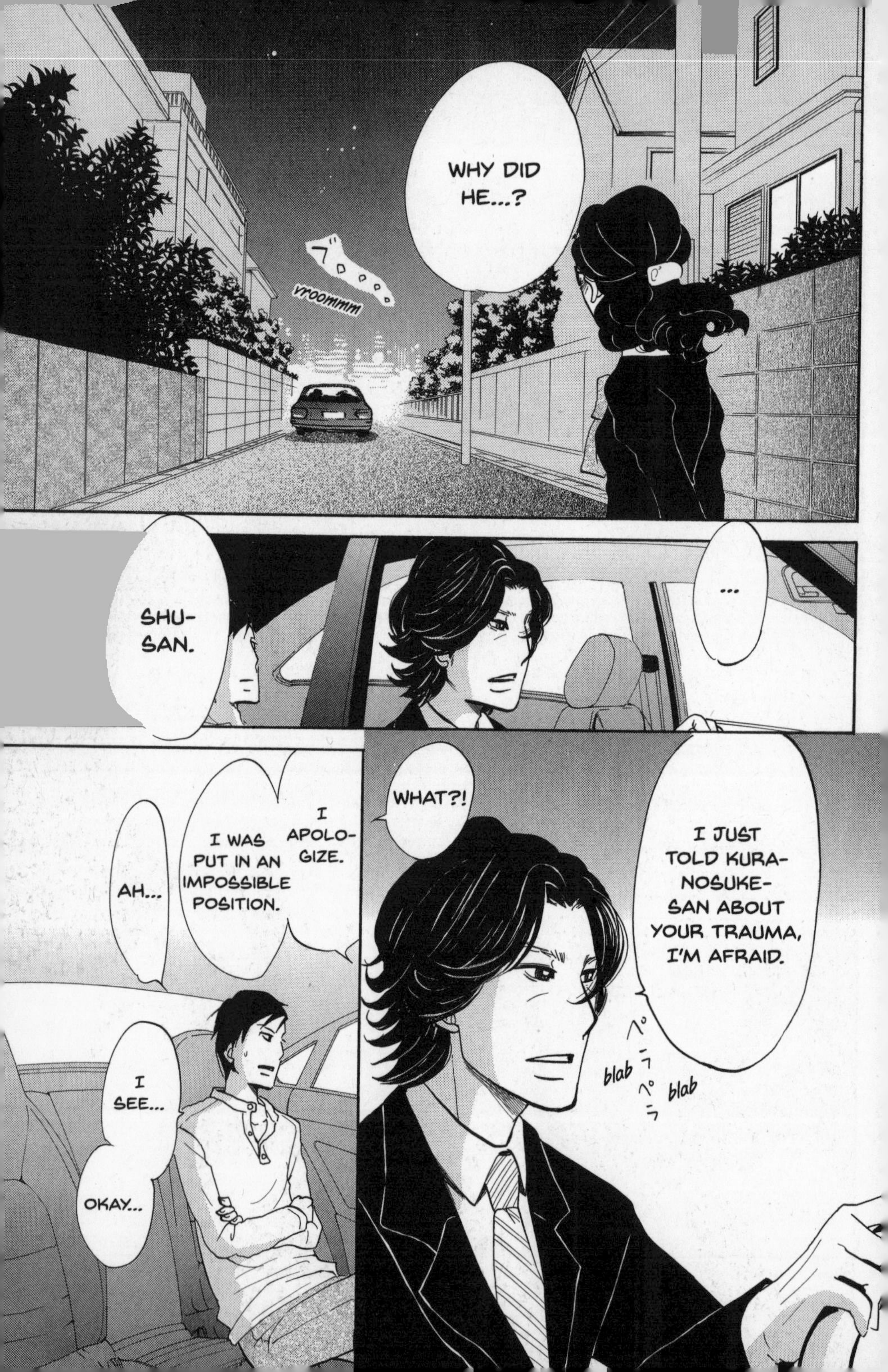
WHY DID HE...?
vroommm
...
SHU-SAN.
I JUST TOLD KURANOSUKE-SAN ABOUT YOUR TRAUMA, I'M AFRAID.
WHAT?!
blab blab
I APOLOGIZE.
I WAS PUT IN AN IMPOSSIBLE POSITION.
AH...
I SEE...
OKAY...

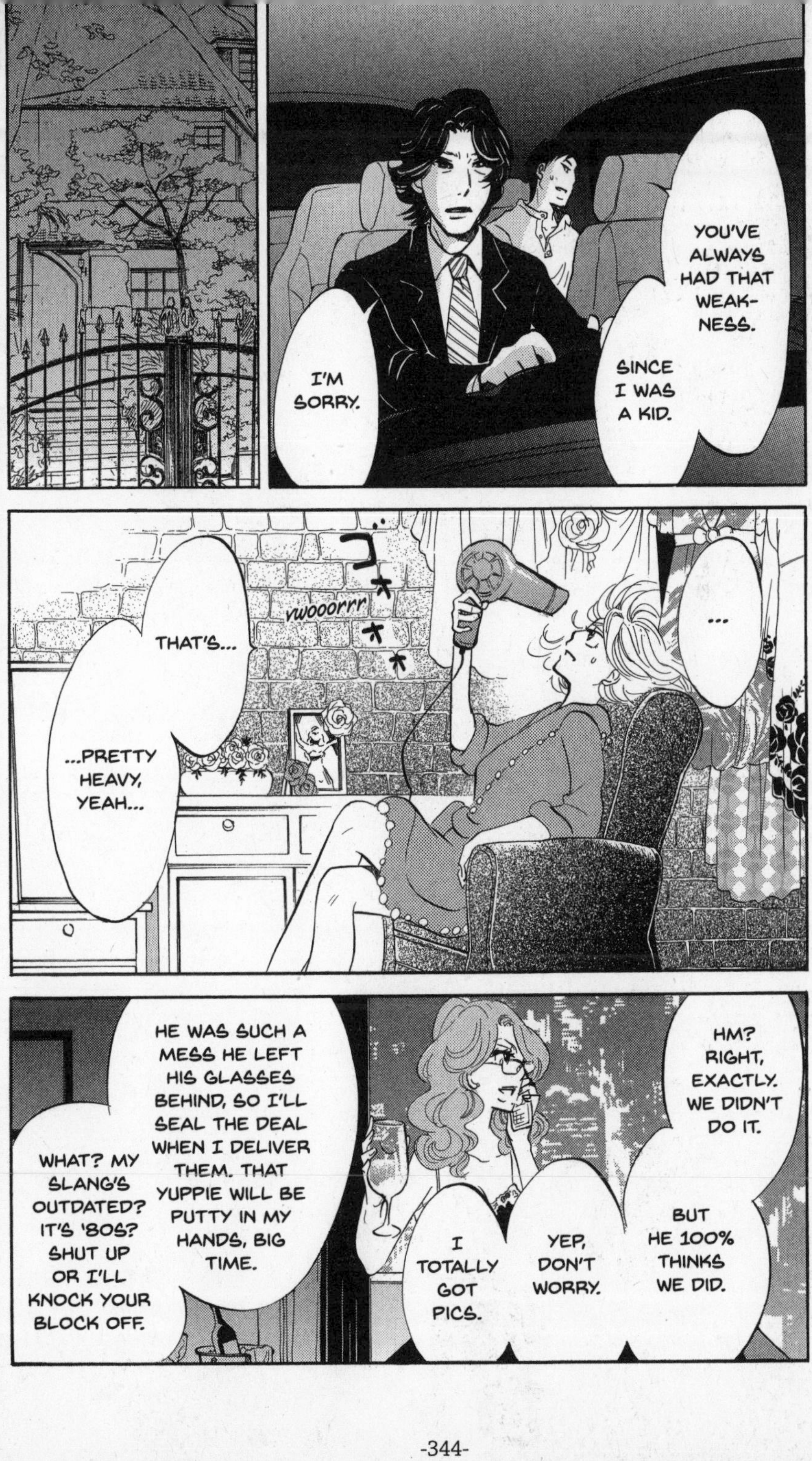
YOU'VE ALWAYS HAD THAT WEAK-NESS.
SINCE I WAS A KID.
I'M SORRY.
...
vwooorrr
THAT'S...
...PRETTY HEAVY, YEAH...
HM? RIGHT, EXACTLY. WE DIDN'T DO IT.
BUT HE 100% THINKS WE DID.
YEP, DON'T WORRY.
I TOTALLY GOT PICS.
HE WAS SUCH A MESS HE LEFT HIS GLASSES BEHIND, SO I'LL SEAL THE DEAL WHEN I DELIVER THEM. THAT YUPPIE WILL BE PUTTY IN MY HANDS, BIG TIME.
WHAT? MY SLANG'S OUTDATED? IT'S '80S? SHUT UP OR I'LL KNOCK YOUR BLOCK OFF.

Episode 12
In the Closet

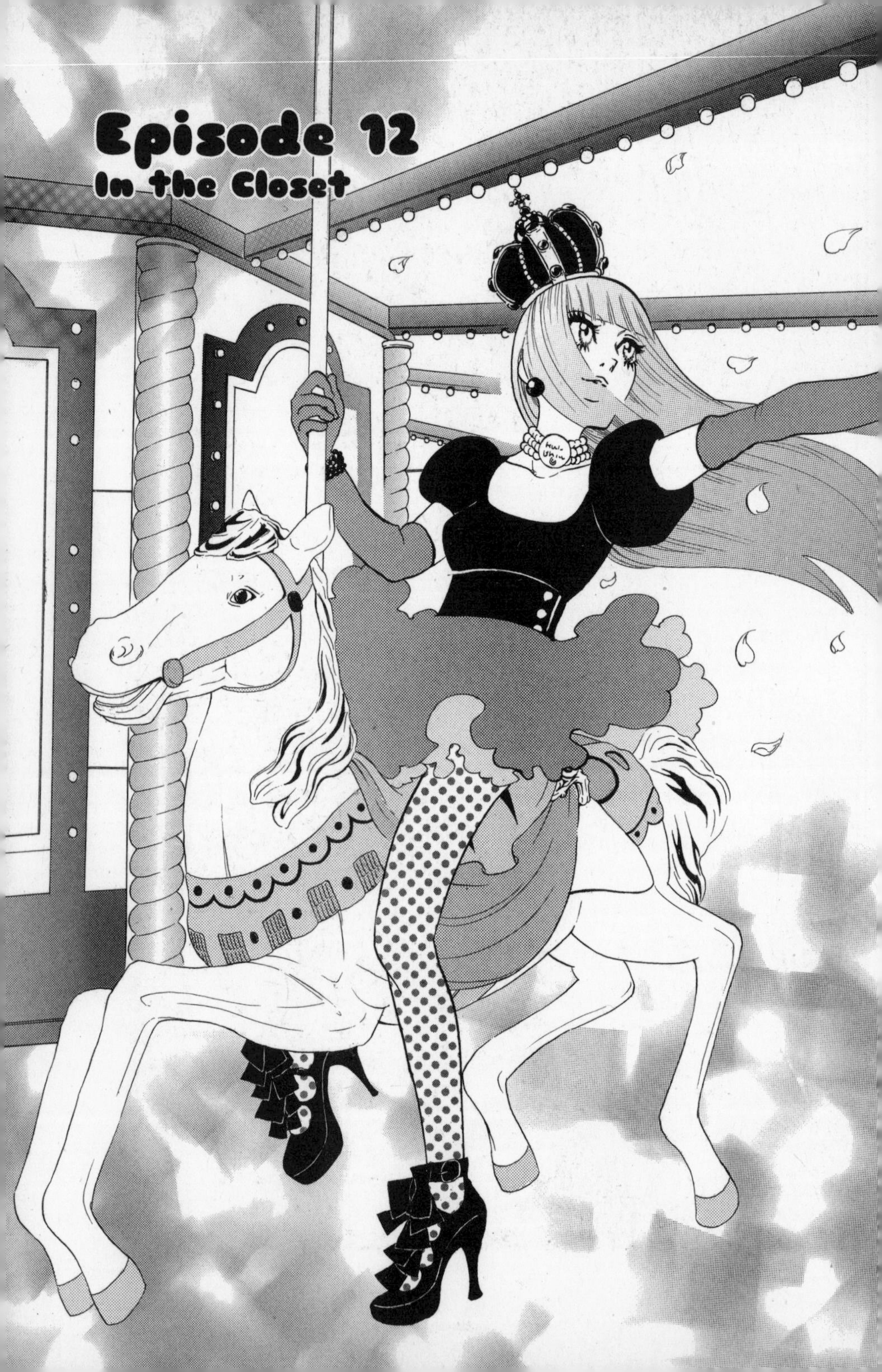

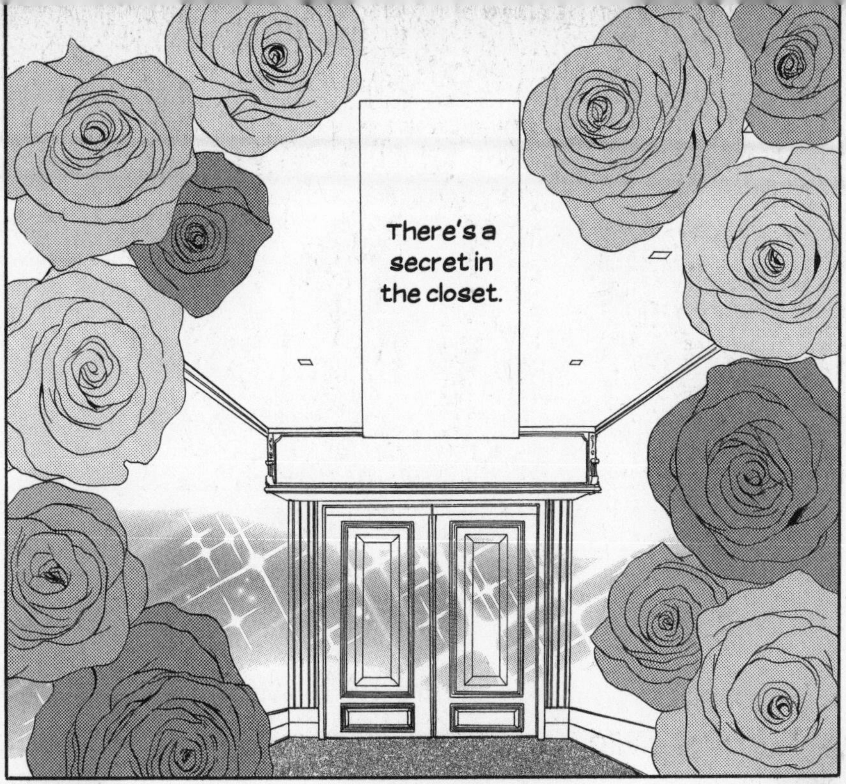
There's a secret in the closet.
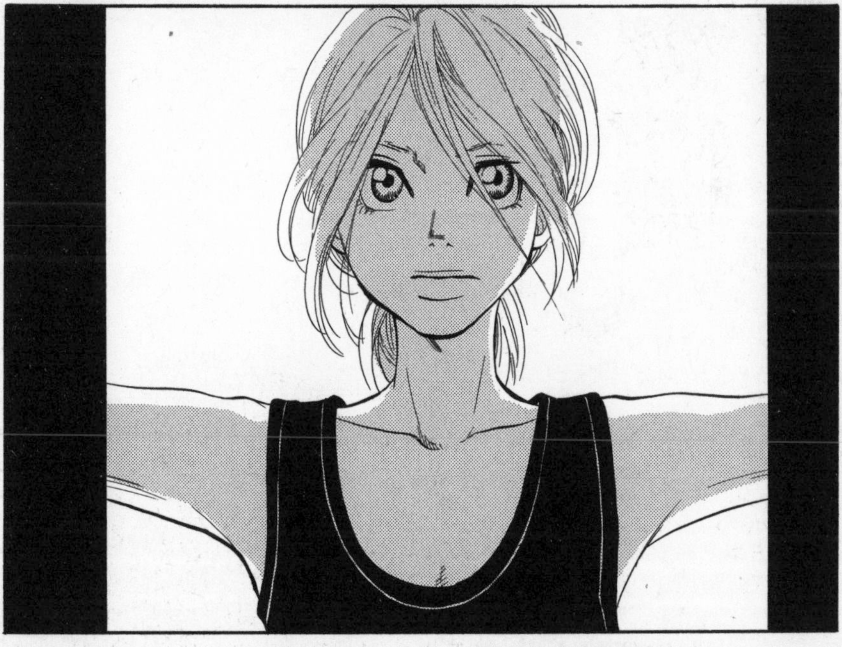

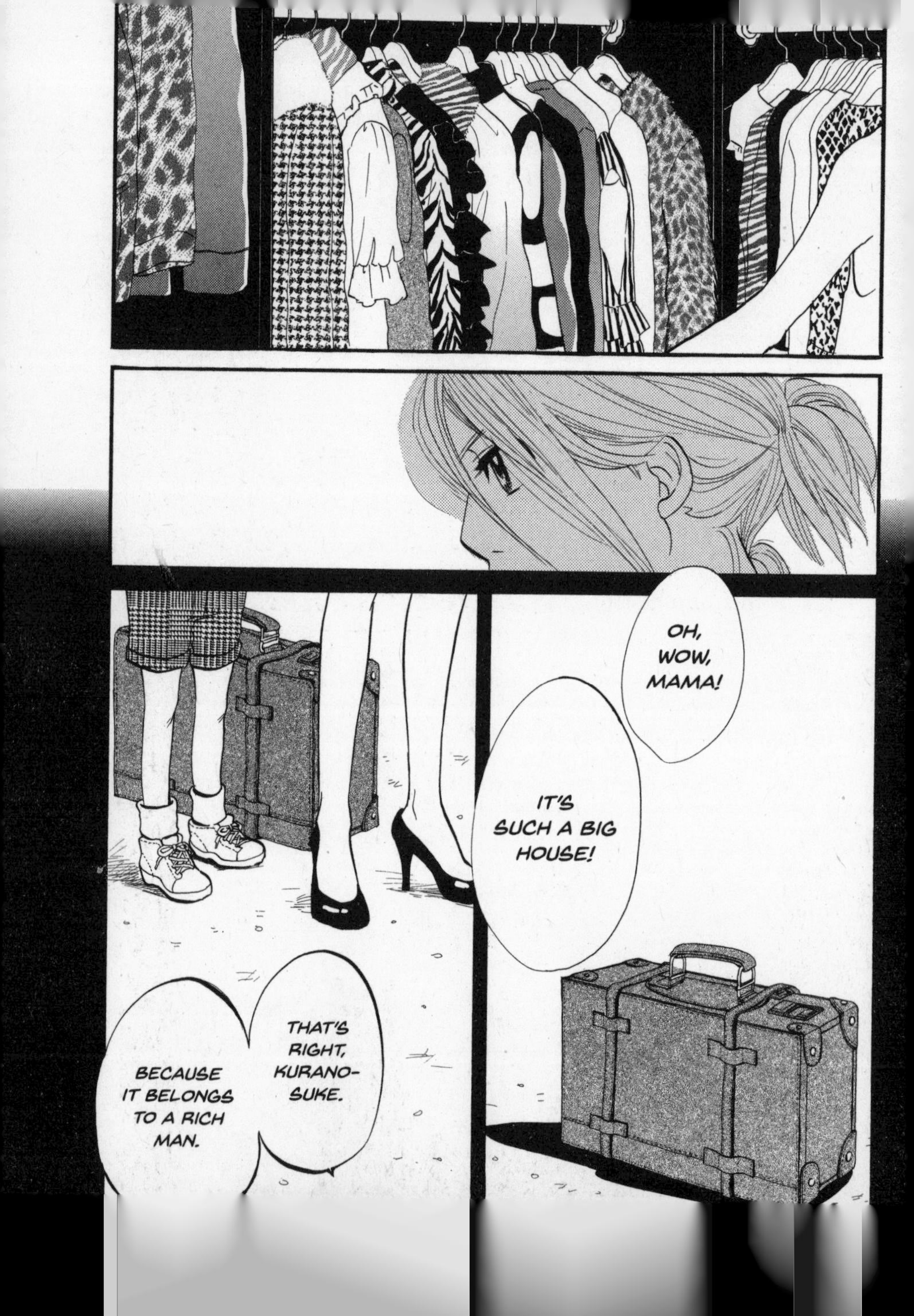
OH, WOW, MAMA!
IT'S SUCH A BIG HOUSE!
THAT'S RIGHT, KURANOSUKE.
BECAUSE IT BELONGS TO A RICH MAN.

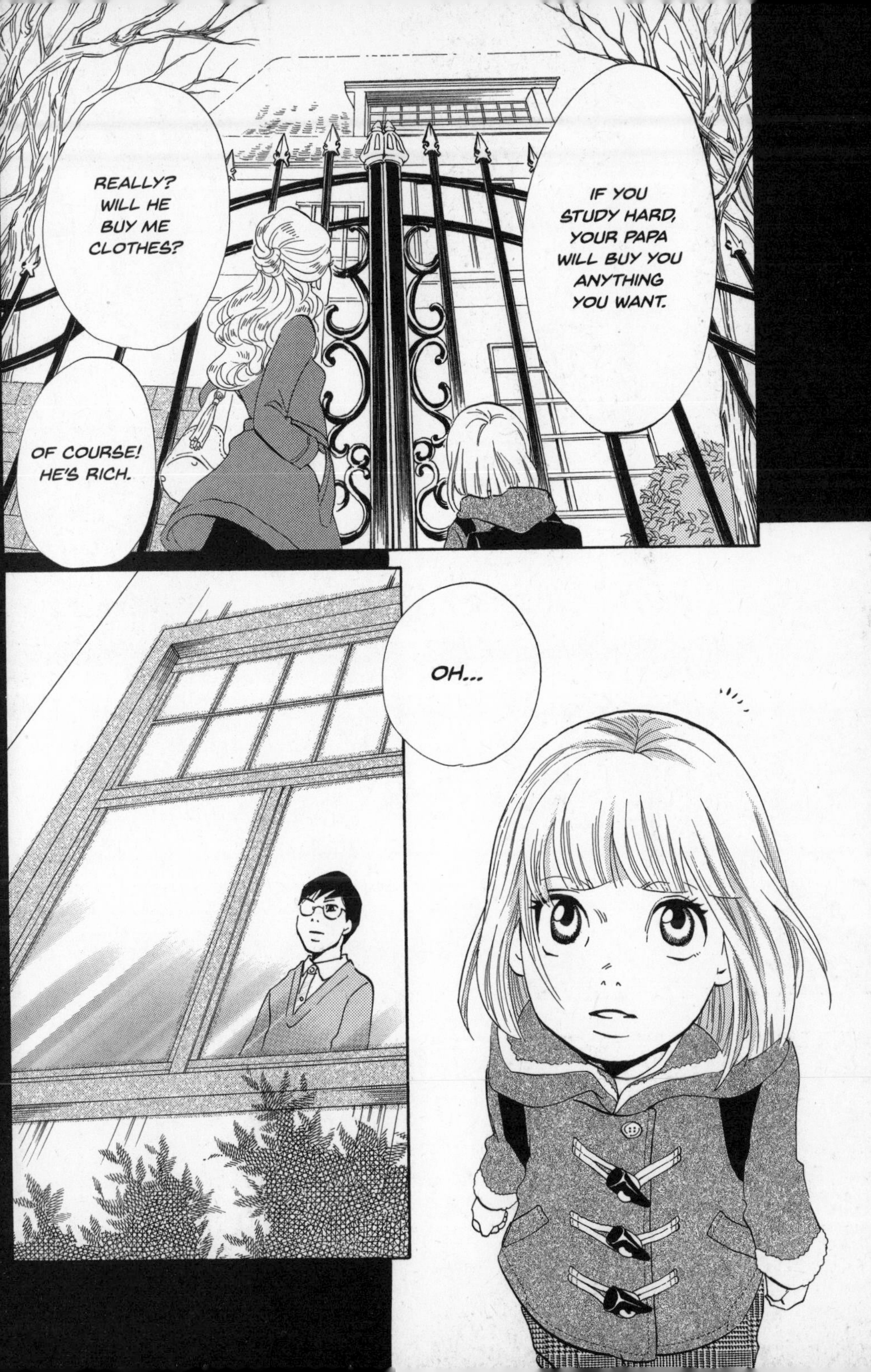
IF YOU STUDY HARD, YOUR PAPA WILL BUY YOU ANYTHING YOU WANT.
REALLY? WILL HE BUY ME CLOTHES?
OF COURSE! HE'S RICH.
OH...

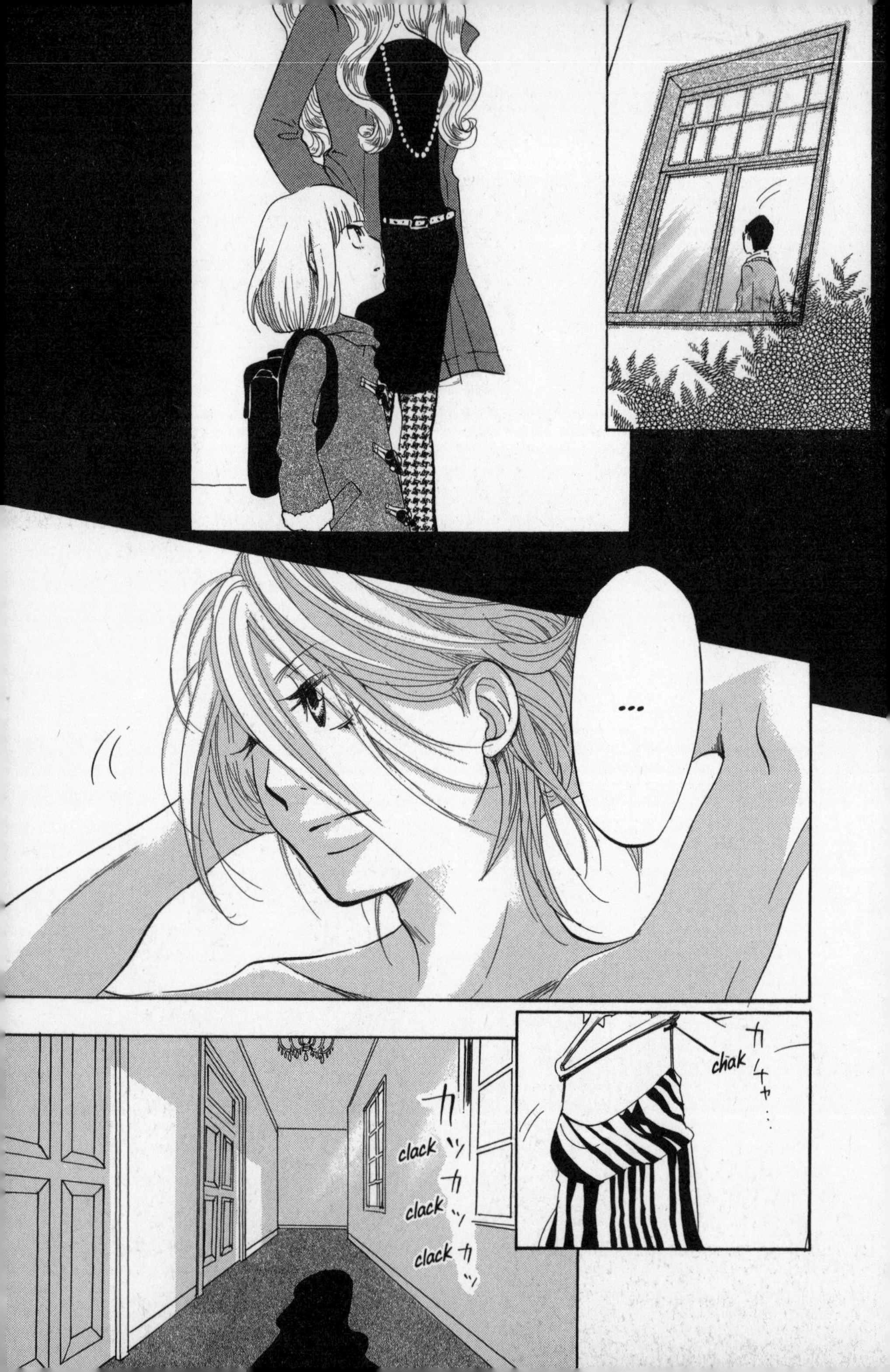
...
chak
カチャ...
clack
カッ
clack
カッ
clack
カッ

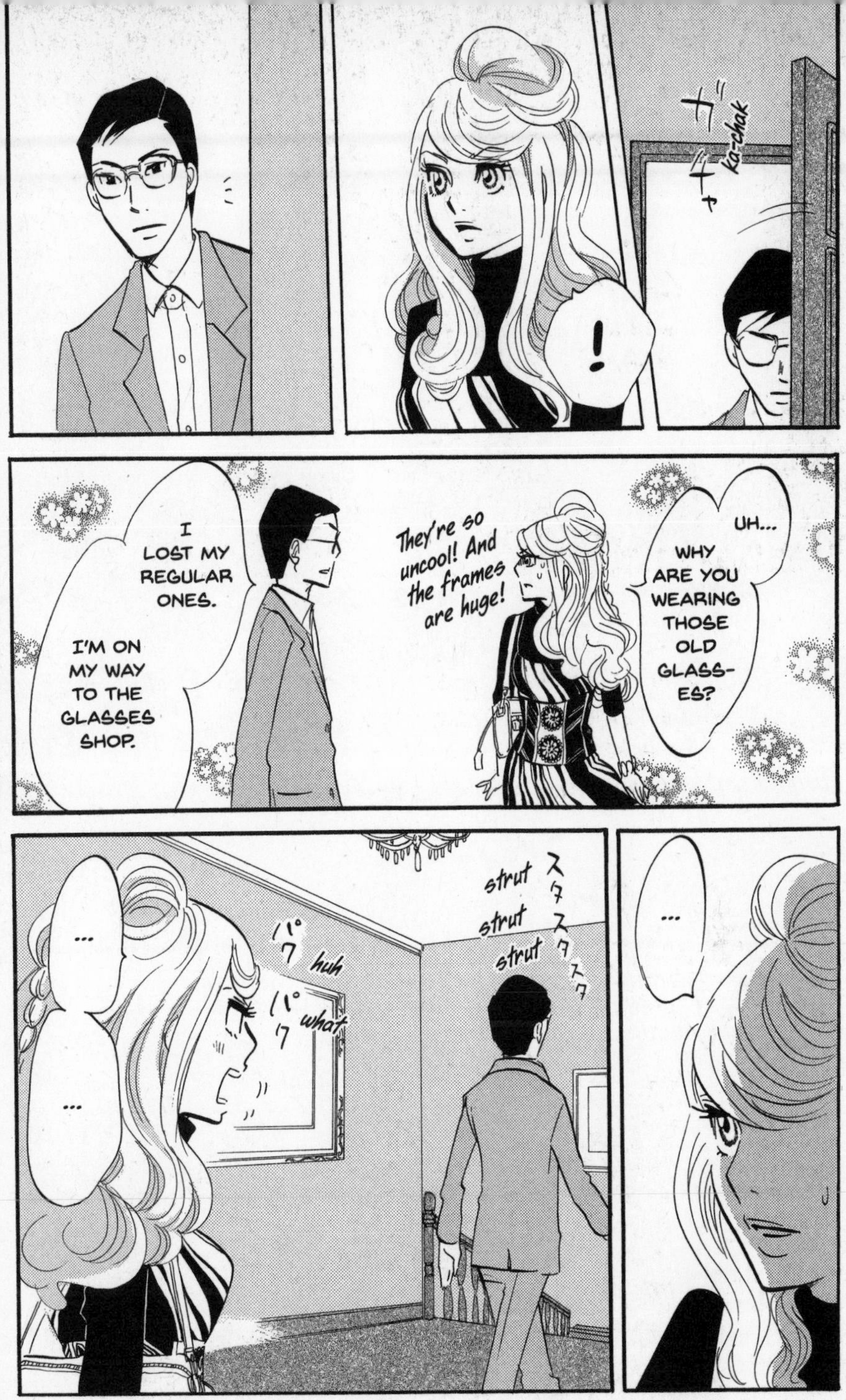
ガチャ
ka-chak
!
UH...
WHY ARE YOU WEARING THOSE OLD GLASSES?
They're so uncool! And the frames are huge!
I LOST MY REGULAR ONES.
I'M ON MY WAY TO THE GLASSES SHOP.
...
スタスタスタ
strut
strut
strut
パクパク
huh
what
...
...

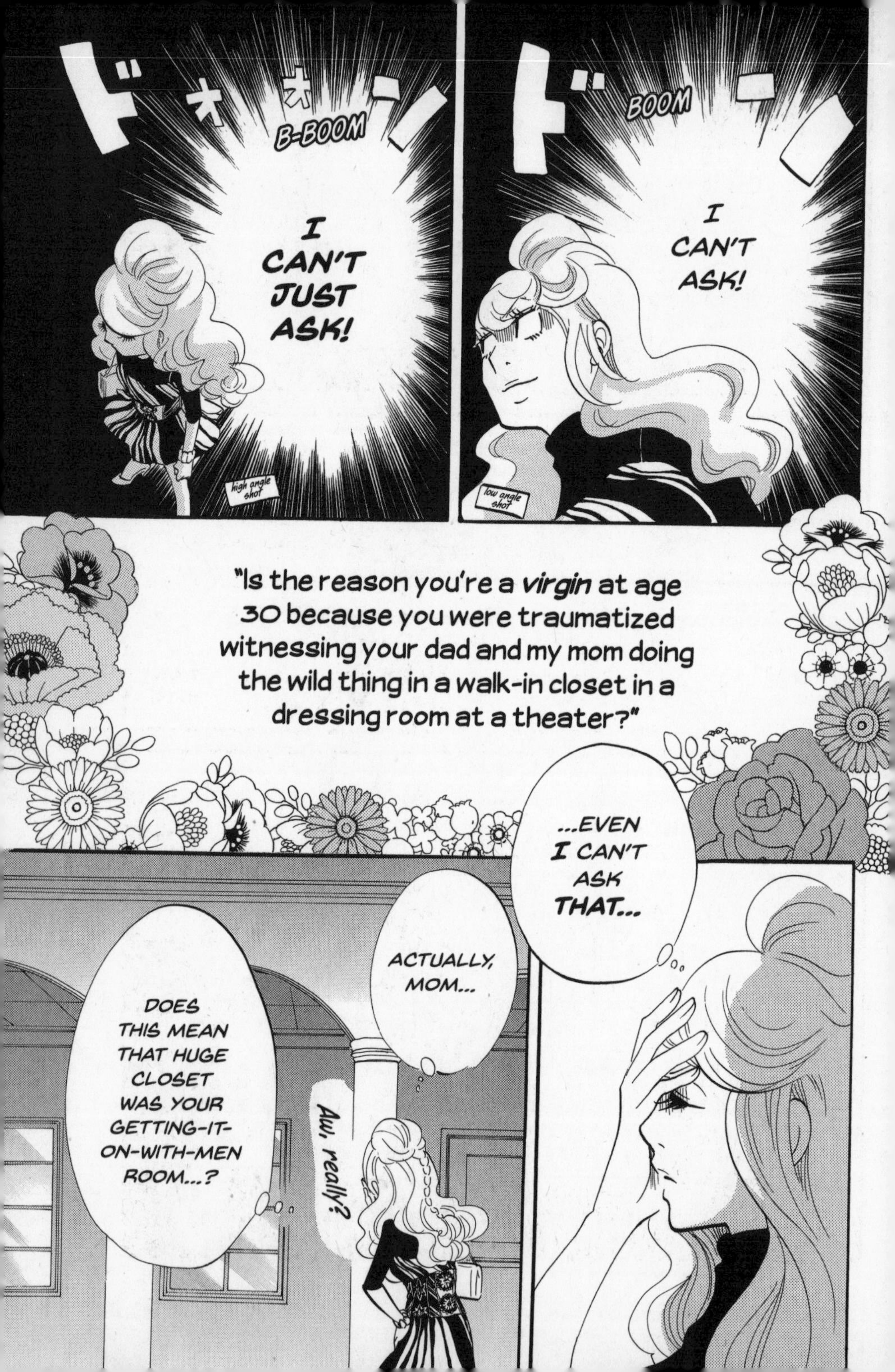
ドーン
BOOM
I CAN'T ASK!
low angle shot
ドォオーン
B-BOOM
I CAN'T JUST ASK!
high angle shot
"Is the reason you're a *virgin* at age 30 because you were traumatized witnessing your dad and my mom doing the wild thing in a walk-in closet in a dressing room at a theater?"
...EVEN I CAN'T ASK THAT...
ACTUALLY, MOM...
DOES THIS MEAN THAT HUGE CLOSET WAS YOUR GETTING-IT-ON-WITH-MEN ROOM...?
Aw, really?

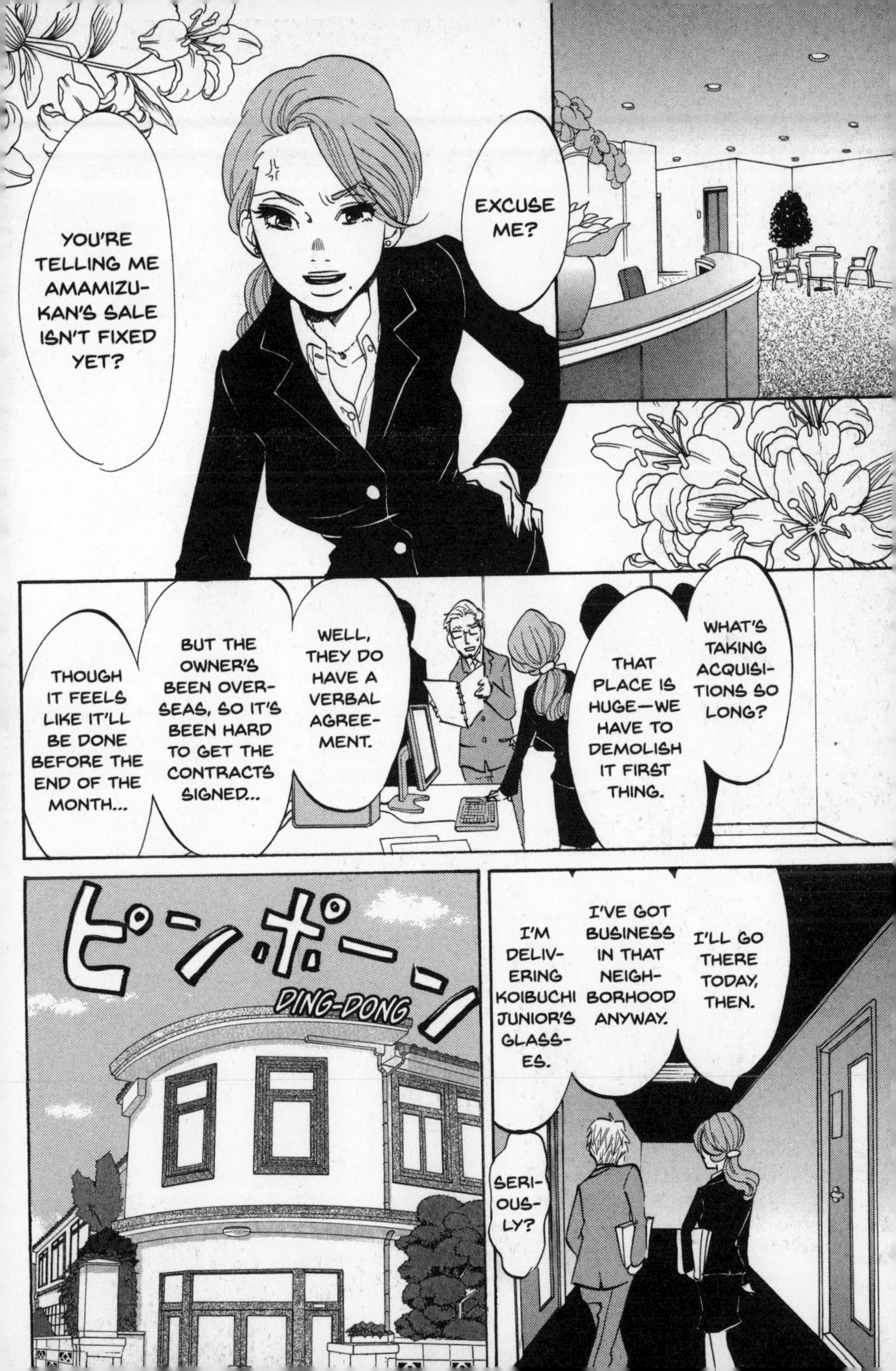
EXCUSE ME?
YOU'RE TELLING ME AMAMIZUKAN'S SALE ISN'T FIXED YET?
WHAT'S TAKING ACQUISITIONS SO LONG?
THAT PLACE IS HUGE—WE HAVE TO DEMOLISH IT FIRST THING.
WELL, THEY DO HAVE A VERBAL AGREEMENT.
BUT THE OWNER'S BEEN OVERSEAS, SO IT'S BEEN HARD TO GET THE CONTRACTS SIGNED...
THOUGH IT FEELS LIKE IT'LL BE DONE BEFORE THE END OF THE MONTH...
I'LL GO THERE TODAY, THEN.
I'VE GOT BUSINESS IN THAT NEIGHBORHOOD ANYWAY.
I'M DELIVERING KOIBUCHI JUNIOR'S GLASSES.
SERIOUSLY?
ピンポーン
DING-DONG

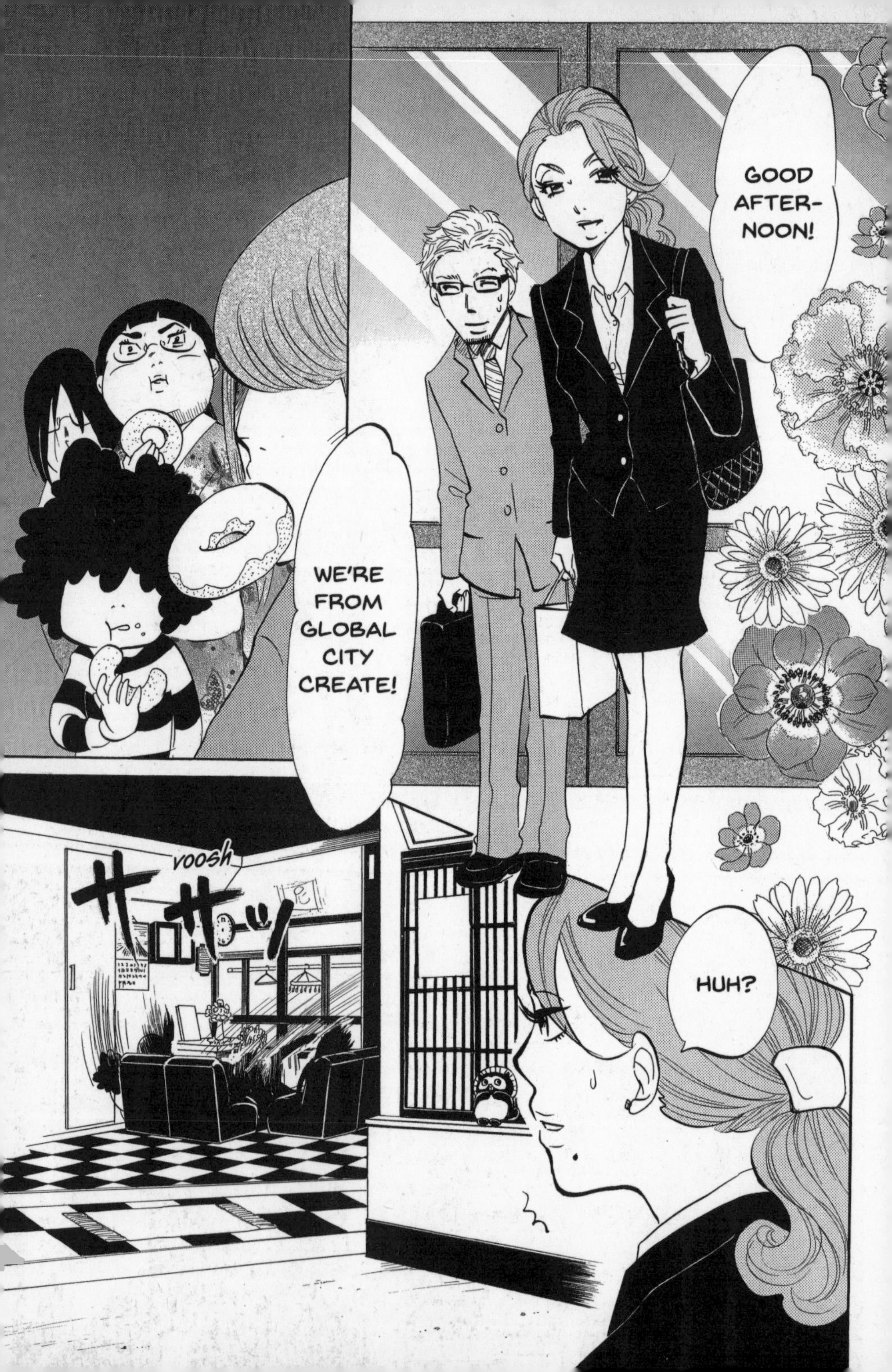
GOOD AFTER-NOON!
WE'RE FROM GLOBAL CITY CREATE!
HUH?
voosh

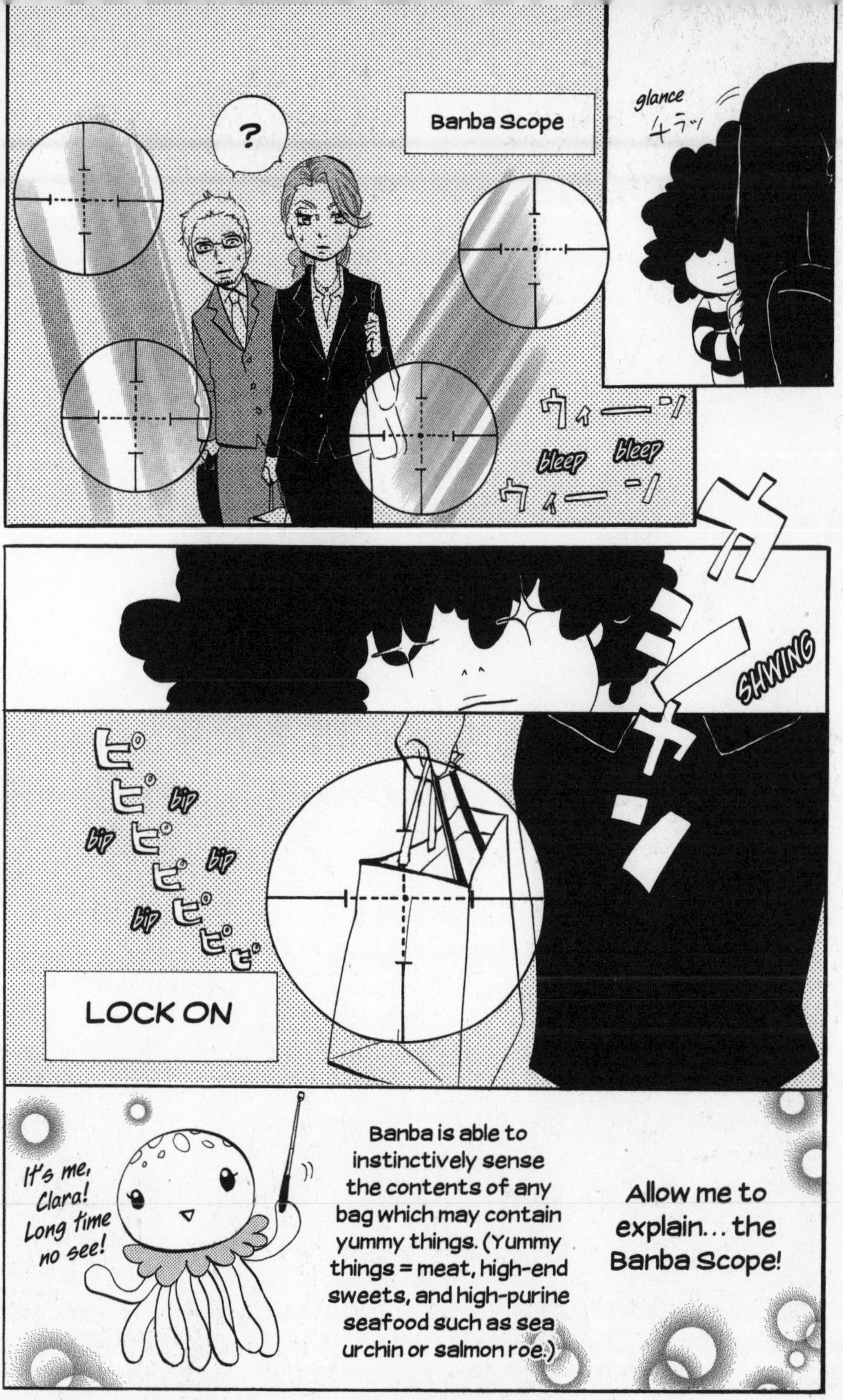
glance
Banba Scope
?
bleep
bleep
SHWING
bip
bip
bip
bip
LOCK ON
Allow me to explain… the Banba Scope!
Banba is able to instinctively sense the contents of any bag which may contain yummy things. (Yummy things = meat, high-end sweets, and high-purine seafood such as sea urchin or salmon roe.)
It's me, Clara! Long time no see!

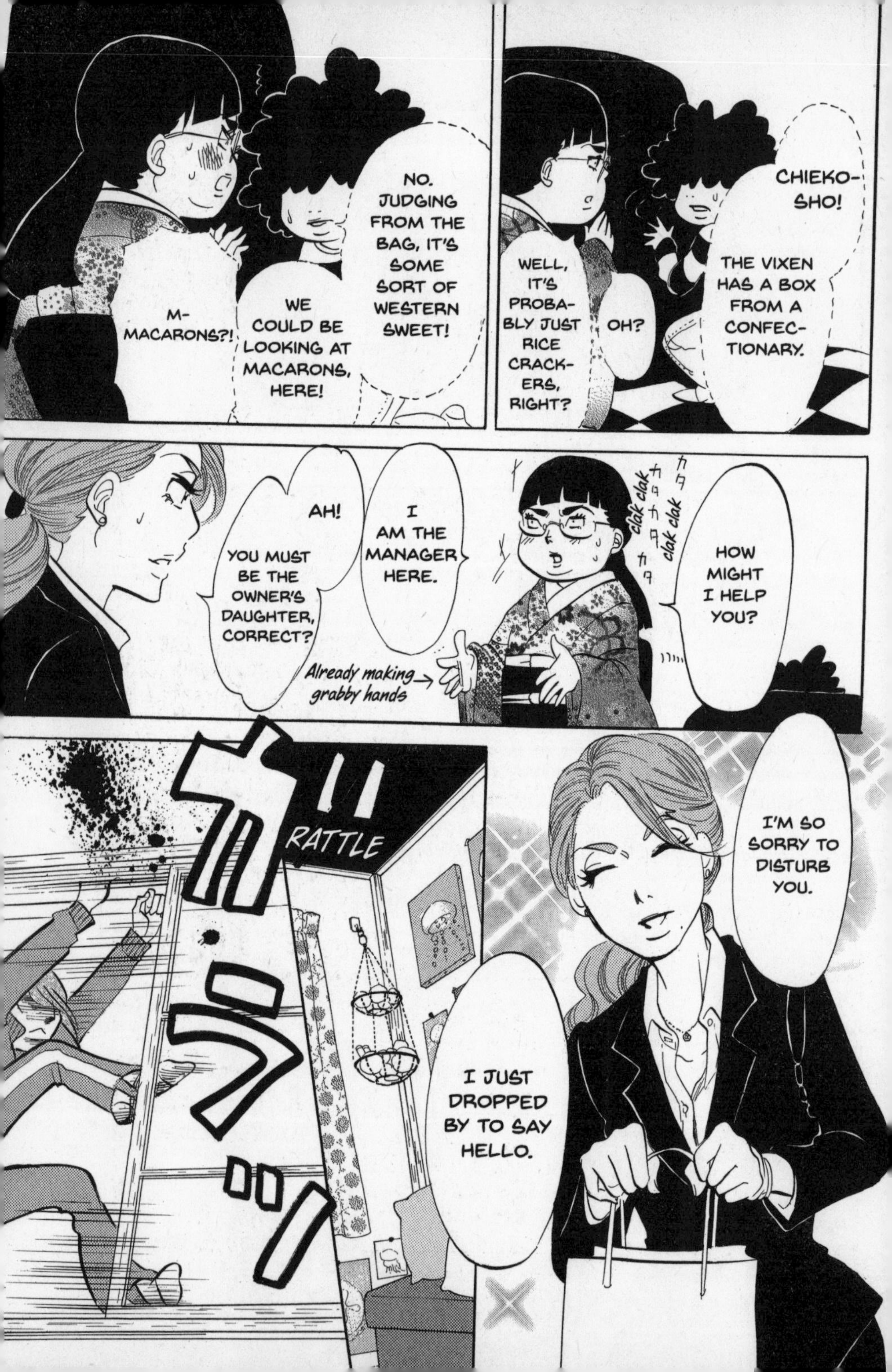
CHIEKO-SHO!
THE VIXEN HAS A BOX FROM A CONFECTIONARY.
OH?
WELL, IT'S PROBABLY JUST RICE CRACKERS, RIGHT?
NO. JUDGING FROM THE BAG, IT'S SOME SORT OF WESTERN SWEET!
WE COULD BE LOOKING AT MACARONS, HERE!
M-MACARONS?!
HOW MIGHT I HELP YOU?
clak clak clak clak
I AM THE MANAGER HERE.
AH!
YOU MUST BE THE OWNER'S DAUGHTER, CORRECT?
Already making grabby hands
I'M SO SORRY TO DISTURB YOU.
I JUST DROPPED BY TO SAY HELLO.
RATTLE

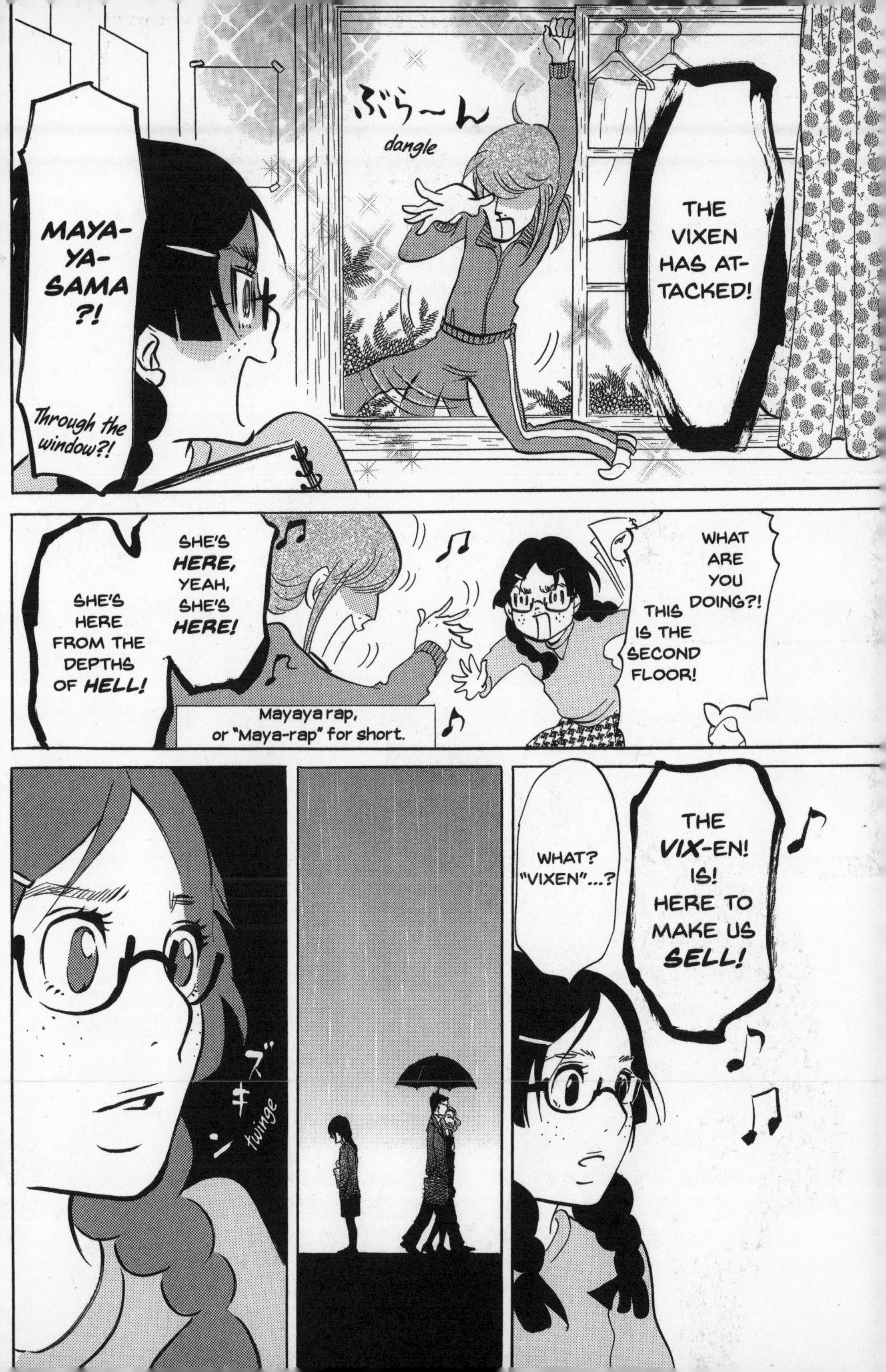
THE VIXEN HAS AT-TACKED!
ぶら～ん
dangle
MAYA-YA-SAMA?!
Through the window?!
WHAT ARE YOU DOING?!
THIS IS THE SECOND FLOOR!
SHE'S HERE, YEAH, SHE'S HERE!
SHE'S HERE FROM THE DEPTHS OF HELL!
Mayaya rap, or "Maya-rap" for short.
THE VIX-EN! IS! HERE TO MAKE US SELL!
WHAT? "VIXEN"...?
ズキン
twinge

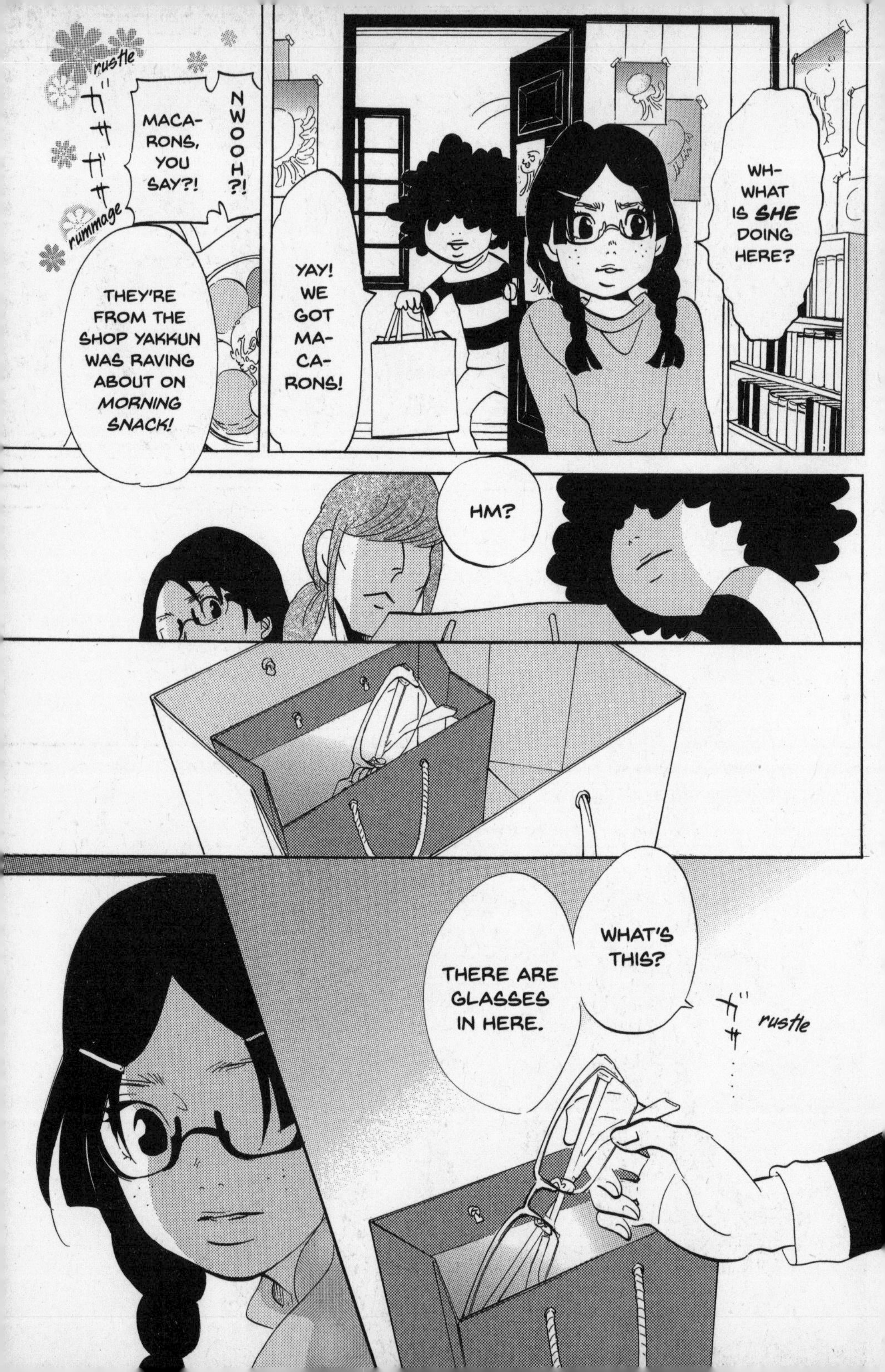
WH- WHAT IS SHE DOING HERE?
YAY! WE GOT MACA-RONS!
NWOOOH?!
MACA-RONS, YOU SAY?!
ガサガサ
rustle rummage
THEY'RE FROM THE SHOP YAKKUN WAS RAVING ABOUT ON MORNING SNACK!
HM?
WHAT'S THIS?
THERE ARE GLASSES IN HERE.
ガサ
rustle

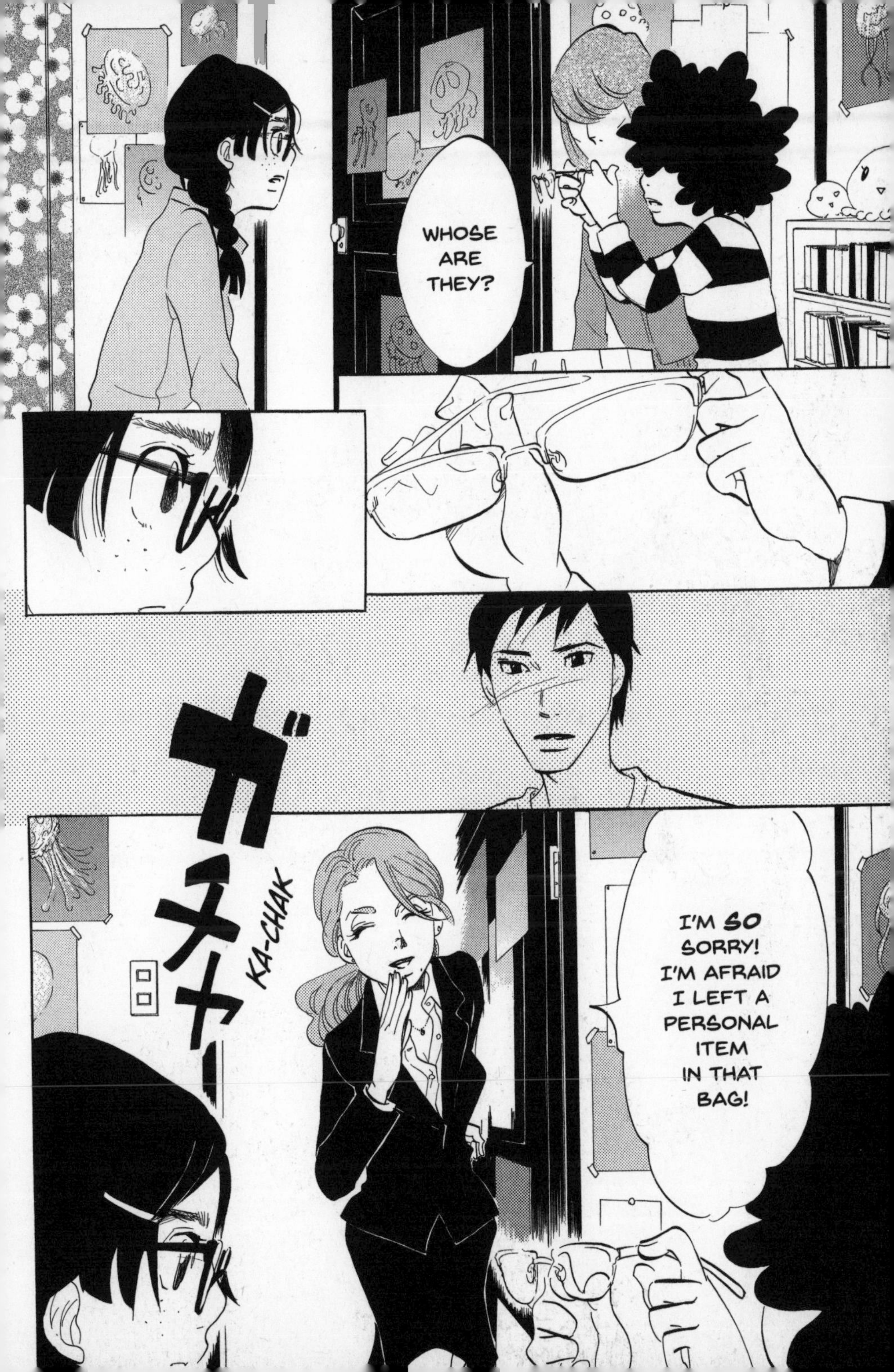
WHOSE ARE THEY?
ガチャ
KA-CHAK
I'M **SO** SORRY! I'M AFRAID I LEFT A PERSONAL ITEM IN THAT BAG!

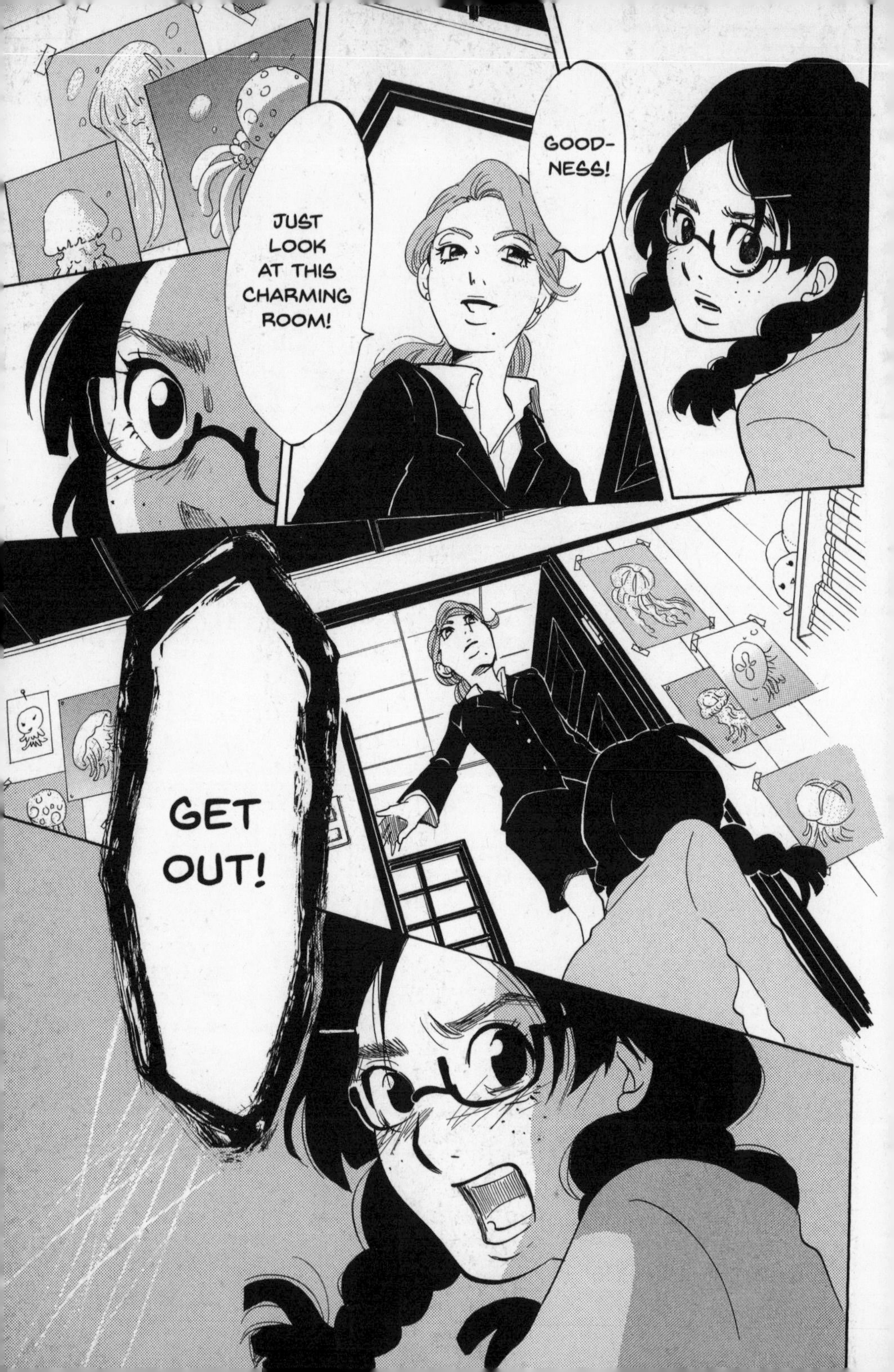
GOOD-NESS!
JUST LOOK AT THIS CHARMING ROOM!
GET OUT!

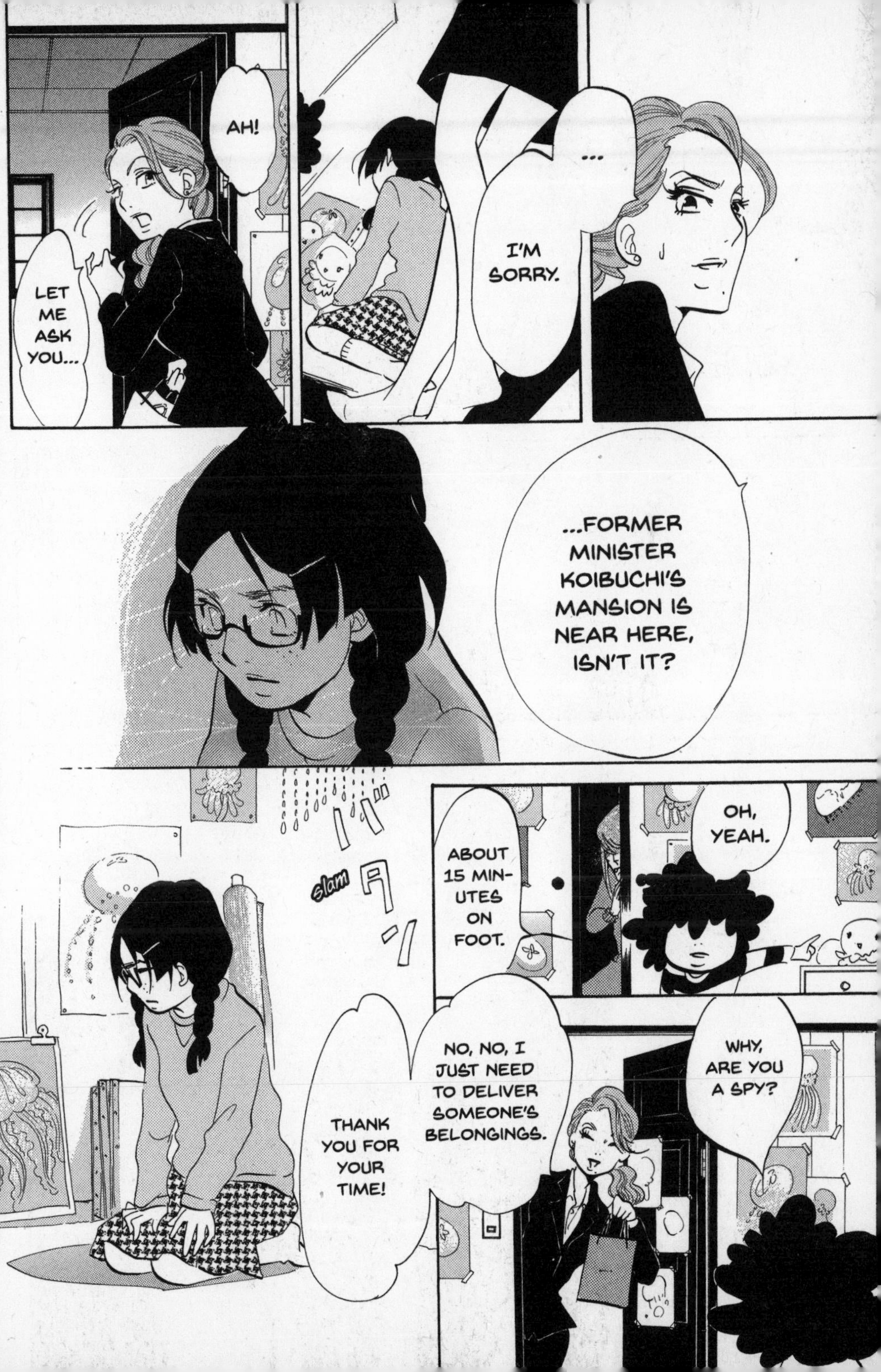
...
I'M SORRY.
AH!
LET ME ASK YOU...
...FORMER MINISTER KOIBUCHI'S MANSION IS NEAR HERE, ISN'T IT?
OH, YEAH.
ABOUT 15 MIN-UTES ON FOOT.
WHY, ARE YOU A SPY?
NO, NO, I JUST NEED TO DELIVER SOMEONE'S BELONGINGS.
THANK YOU FOR YOUR TIME!
slam

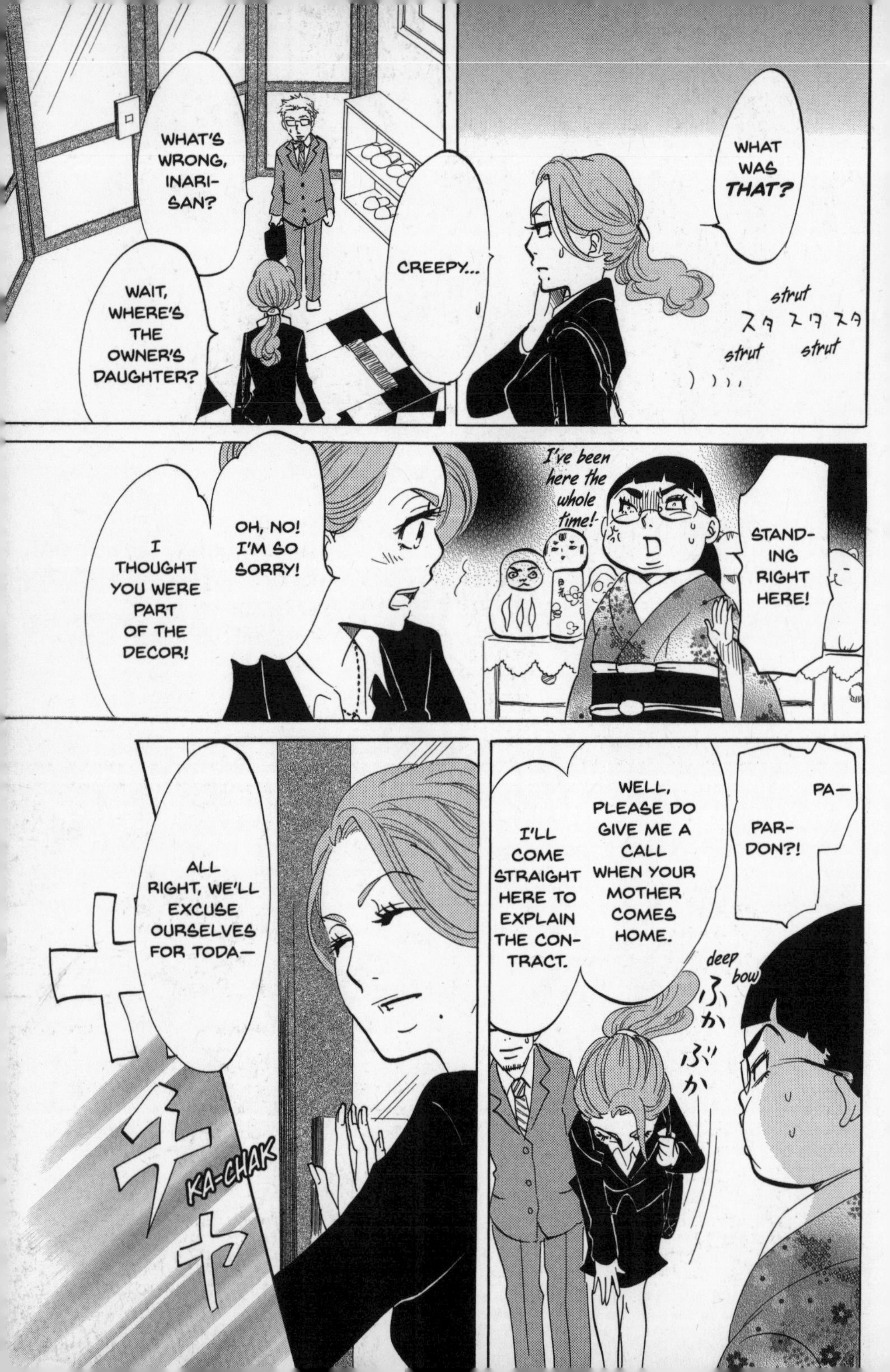
WHAT WAS THAT?
strut スタスタスタ strut strut
CREEPY...
WHAT'S WRONG, INARI-SAN?
WAIT, WHERE'S THE OWNER'S DAUGHTER?
STANDING-ING RIGHT HERE!
I've been here the whole time!
OH, NO! I'M SO SORRY!
I THOUGHT YOU WERE PART OF THE DECOR!
PA— PAR-DON?!
WELL, PLEASE DO GIVE ME A CALL WHEN YOUR MOTHER COMES HOME.
I'LL COME STRAIGHT HERE TO EXPLAIN THE CON-TRACT.
deep bow ふかぶか
ALL RIGHT, WE'LL EXCUSE OURSELVES FOR TODA—
KA-CHAK

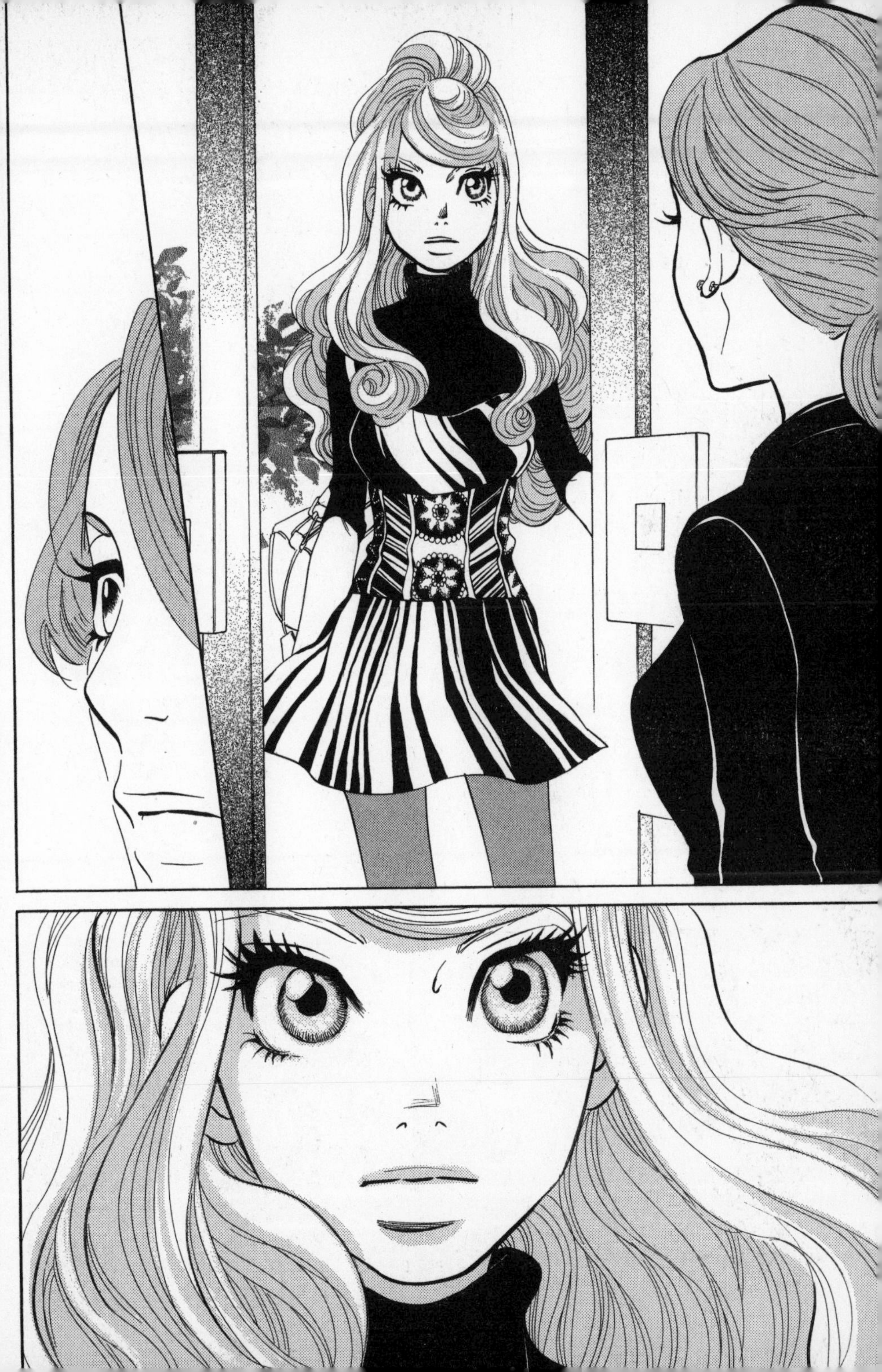

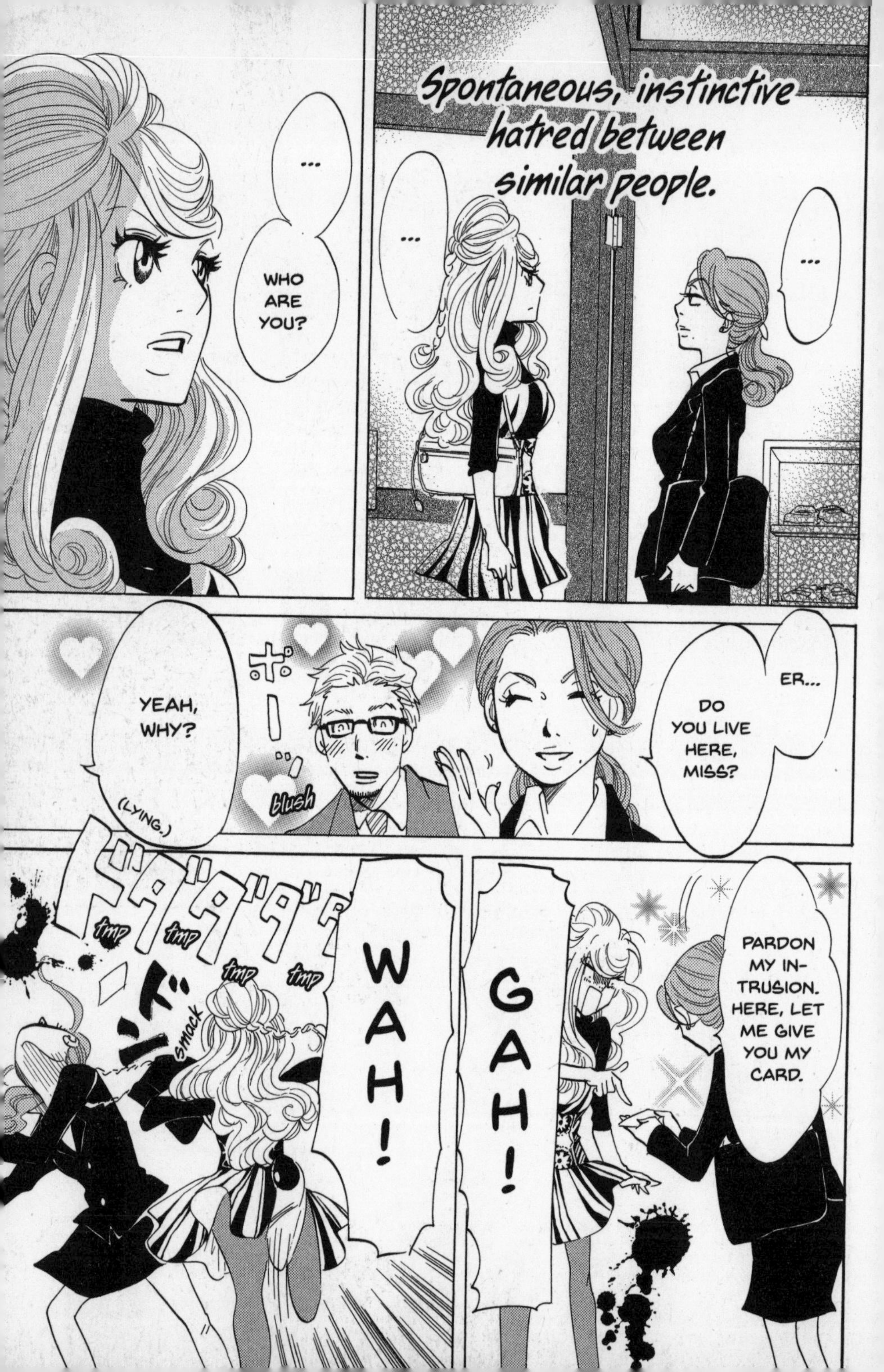

Spontaneous, instinctive hatred between similar people.
...
...
...
WHO ARE YOU?
ER... DO YOU LIVE HERE, MISS?
blush
YEAH, WHY?
(LYING.)
PARDON MY IN-TRUSION. HERE, LET ME GIVE YOU MY CARD.
GAH!
WAH!
tmp
tmp
tmp
tmp
smack

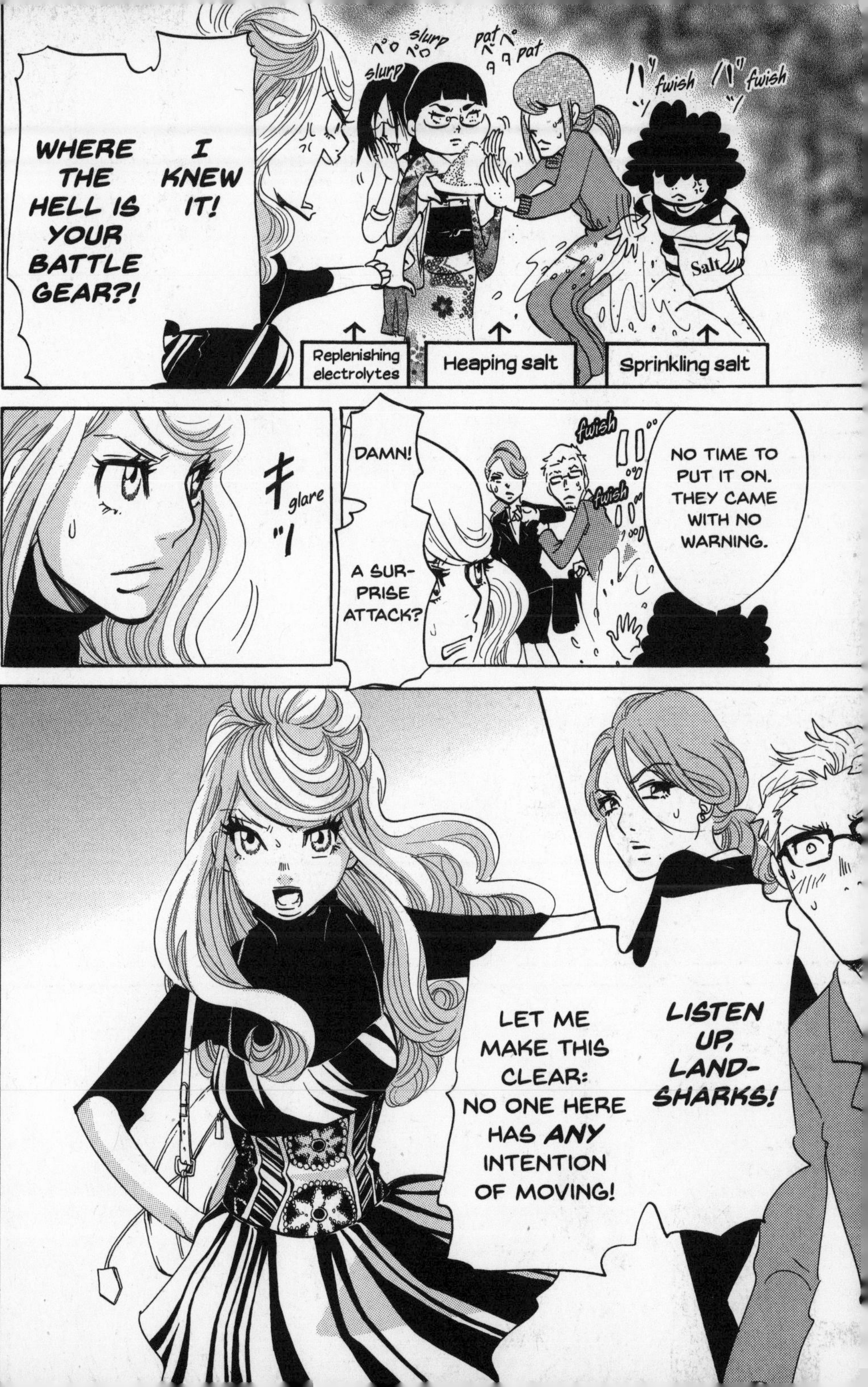
fwish fwish
pat pat
slurp slurp
I KNEW IT!
WHERE THE HELL IS YOUR BATTLE GEAR?!
Sprinkling salt
Heaping salt
Replenishing electrolytes
NO TIME TO PUT IT ON. THEY CAME WITH NO WARNING.
fwish
fwish
DAMN!
A SUR-PRISE ATTACK?
glare
LISTEN UP, LAND-SHARKS!
LET ME MAKE THIS CLEAR: NO ONE HERE HAS ANY INTENTION OF MOVING!

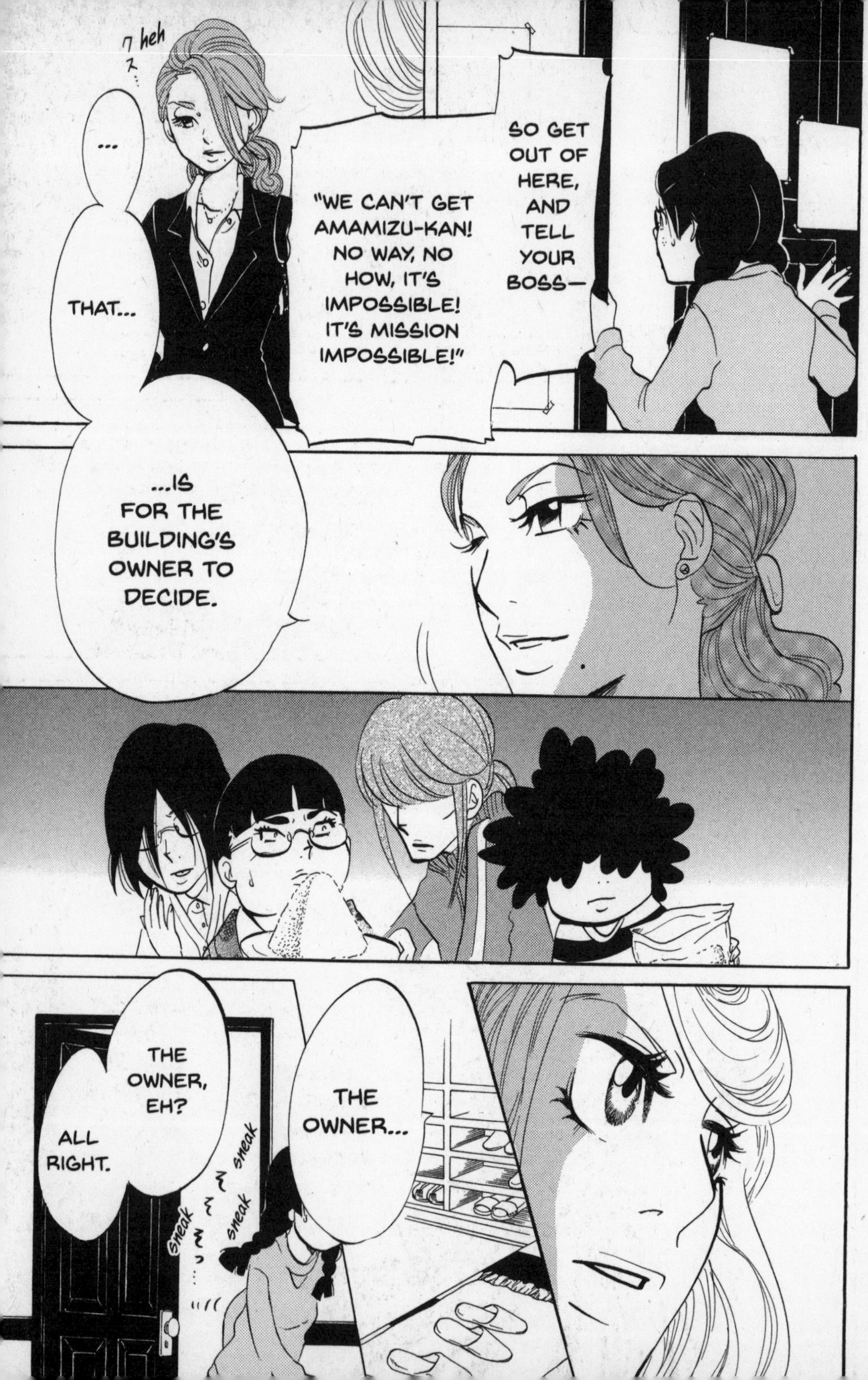
SO GET OUT OF HERE, AND TELL YOUR BOSS—
"WE CAN'T GET AMAMIZU-KAN! NO WAY, NO HOW, IT'S IMPOSSIBLE! IT'S MISSION IMPOSSIBLE!"
heh
...
THAT...
...IS FOR THE BUILDING'S OWNER TO DECIDE.
THE OWNER...
THE OWNER, EH?
ALL RIGHT.
sneak
sneak
sneak

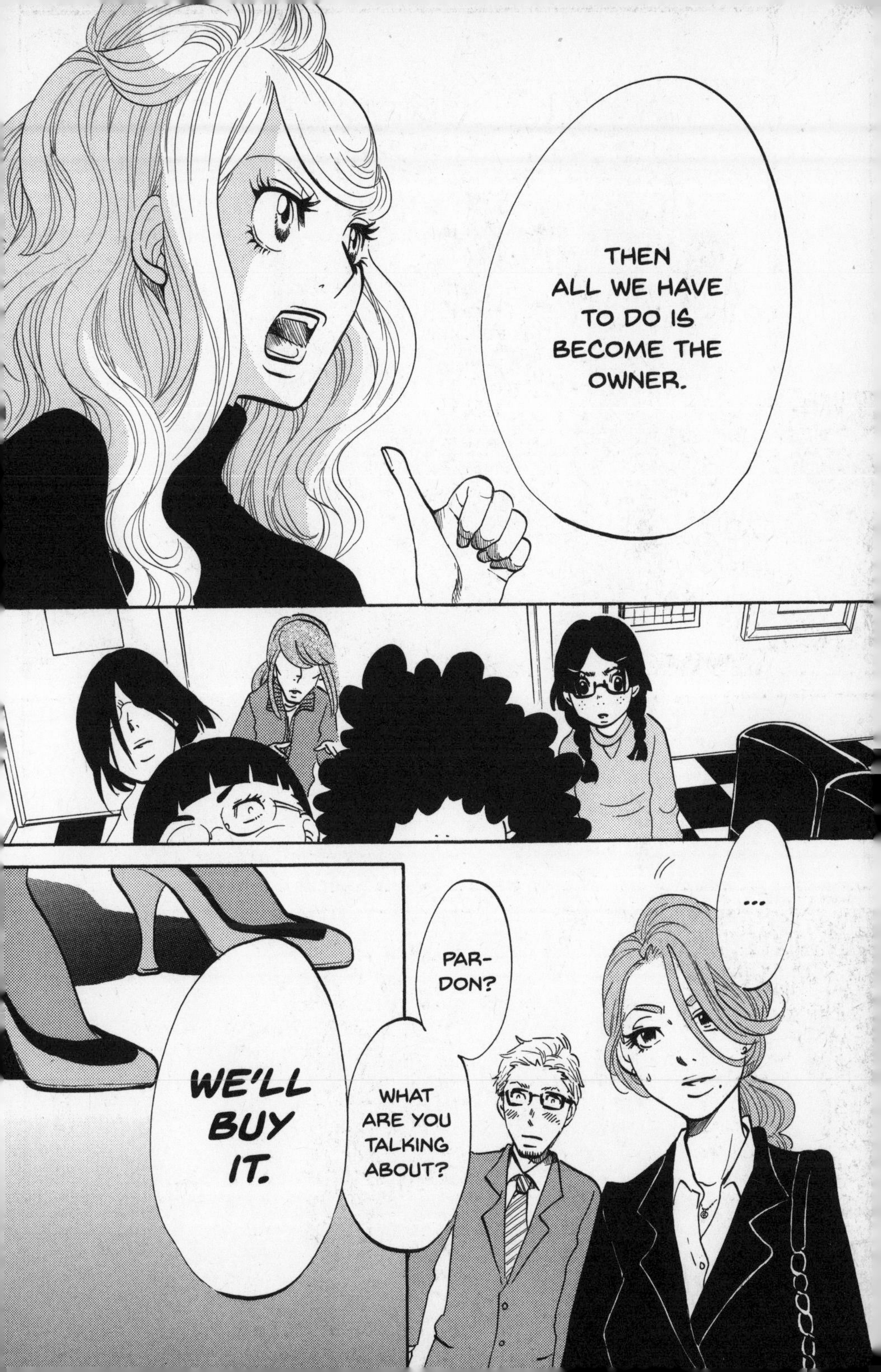
THEN ALL WE HAVE TO DO IS BECOME THE OWNER.
...
PAR-DON?
WHAT ARE YOU TALKING ABOUT?
WE'LL BUY IT.

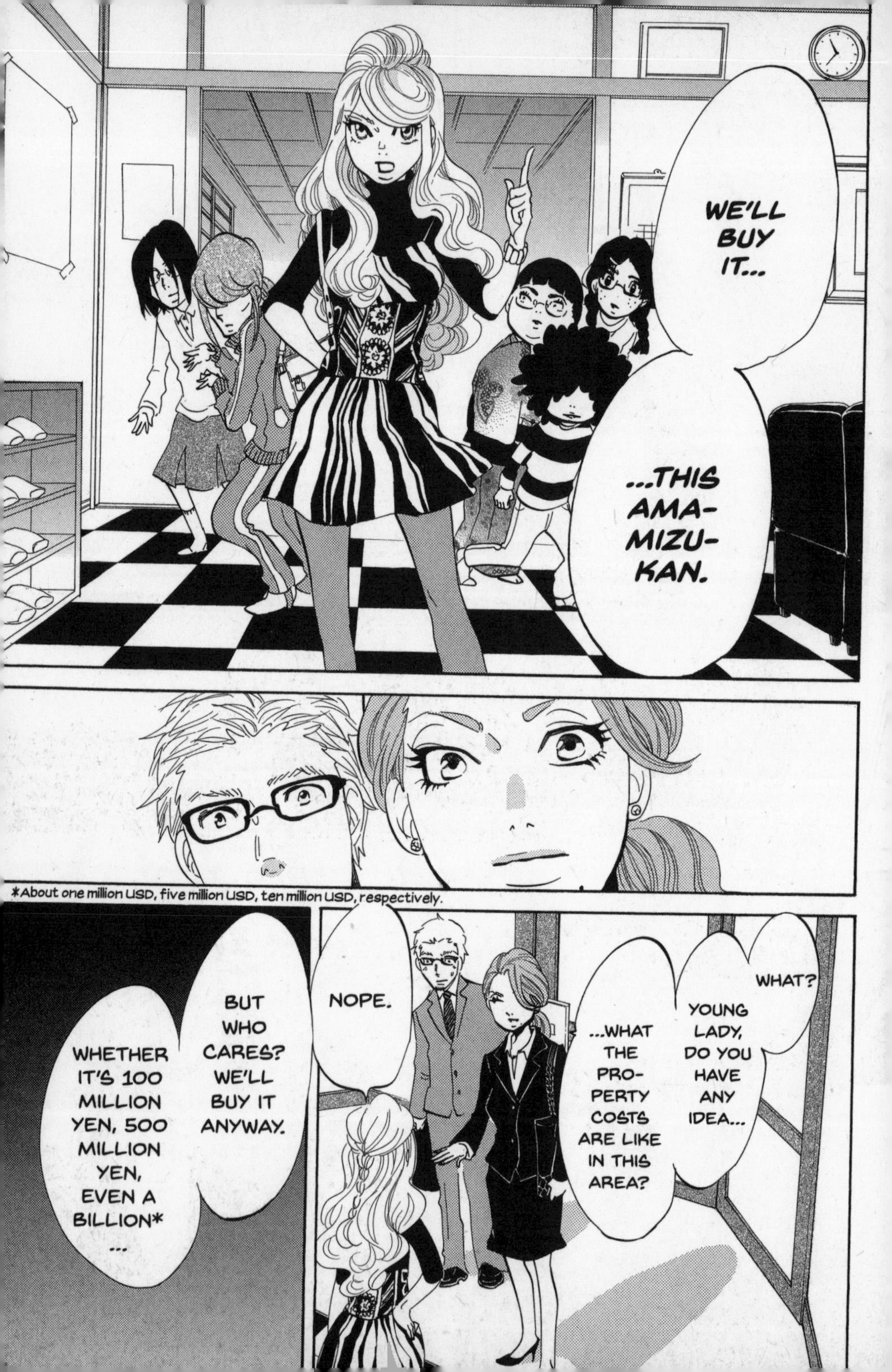
WE'LL BUY IT...
...THIS AMA-MIZU-KAN.
WHAT?
YOUNG LADY, DO YOU HAVE ANY IDEA...
...WHAT THE PROPERTY COSTS ARE LIKE IN THIS AREA?
NOPE.
BUT WHO CARES? WE'LL BUY IT ANYWAY.
WHETHER IT'S 100 MILLION YEN, 500 MILLION YEN, EVEN A BILLION* ...

*About one million USD, five million USD, ten million USD, respectively.

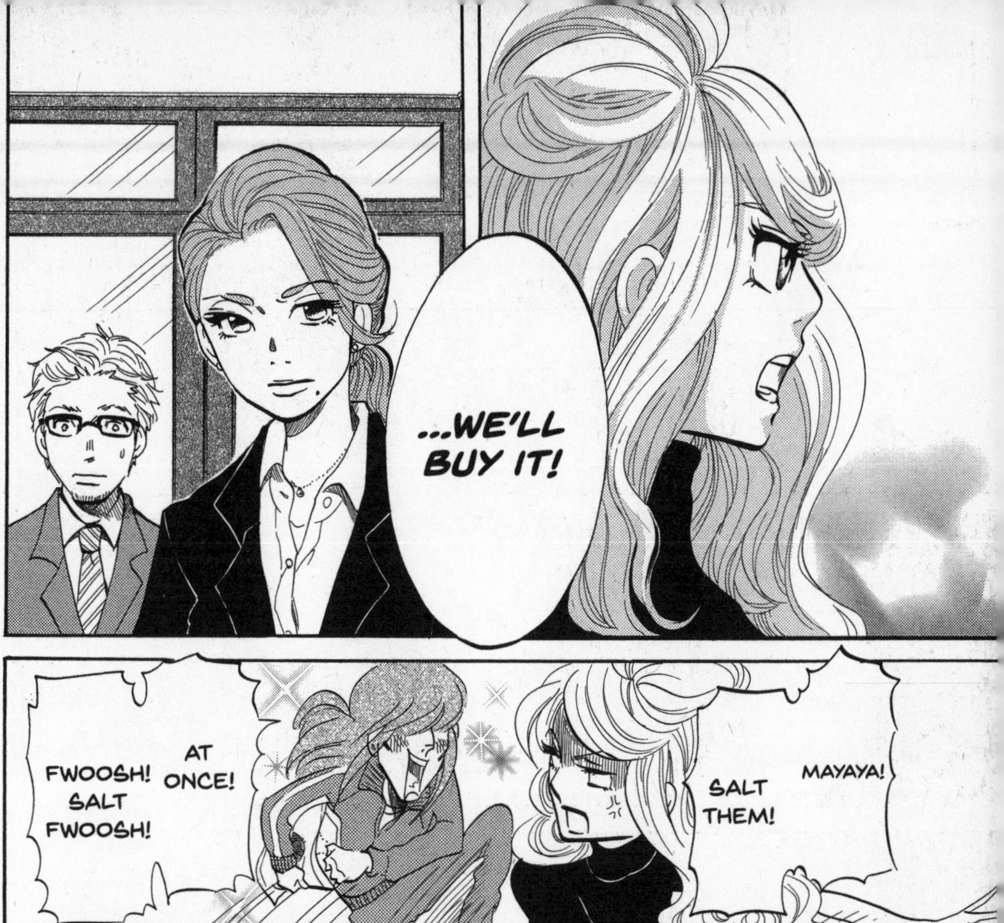
...WE'LL BUY IT!
MAYAYA!
SALT THEM!
AT ONCE!
FWOOSH! SALT FWOOSH!

*"Hakata no shio" means "Hakata salt" and was a popular commercial jingle for the Hakata Salt Company.

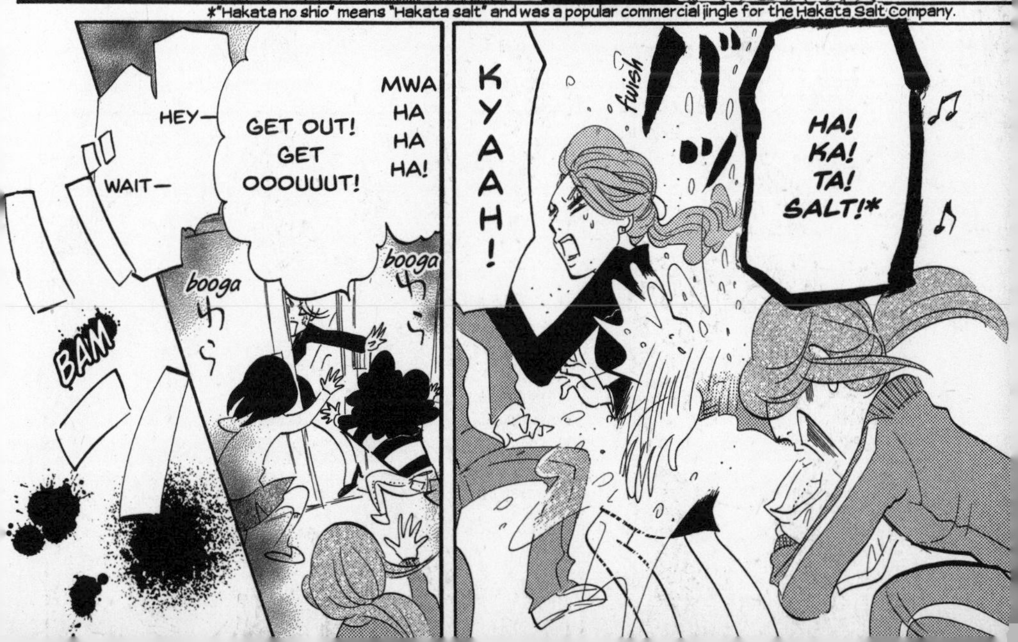
HA! KA! TA! SALT!*
fwish
KYAAH!
MWA HA HA HA!
GET OUT! GET OOOUUUT!
HEY—
WAIT—
booga
booga
BAM

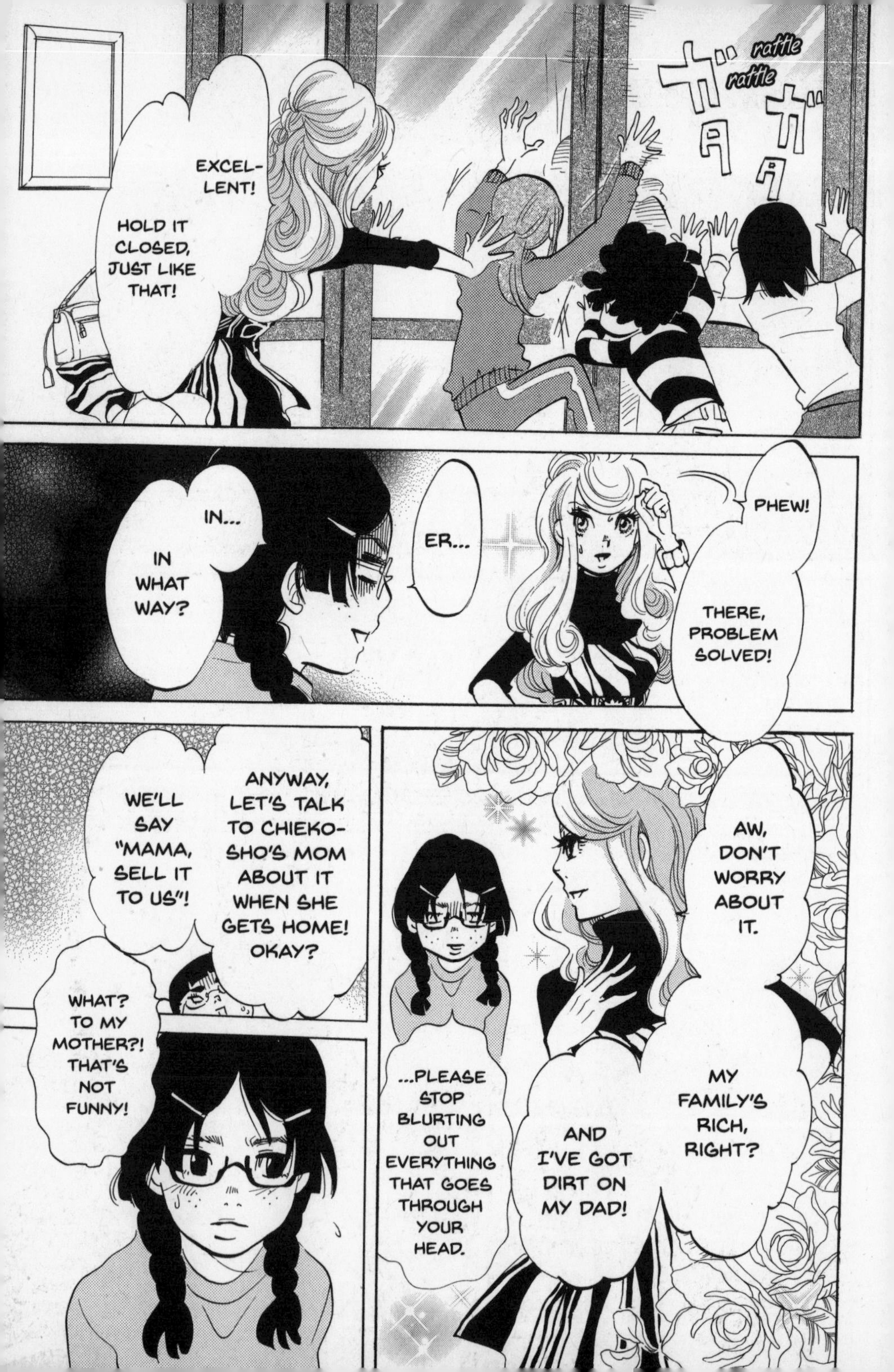
ガタガタ
rattle rattle
EXCEL-LENT!
HOLD IT CLOSED, JUST LIKE THAT!
PHEW!
THERE, PROBLEM SOLVED!
ER...
IN...
IN WHAT WAY?
AW, DON'T WORRY ABOUT IT.
MY FAMILY'S RICH, RIGHT?
AND I'VE GOT DIRT ON MY DAD!
...PLEASE STOP BLURTING OUT EVERYTHING THAT GOES THROUGH YOUR HEAD.
ANYWAY, LET'S TALK TO CHIEKO-SHO'S MOM ABOUT IT WHEN SHE GETS HOME! OKAY?
WE'LL SAY "MAMA, SELL IT TO US"!
WHAT? TO MY MOTHER?! THAT'S NOT FUNNY!

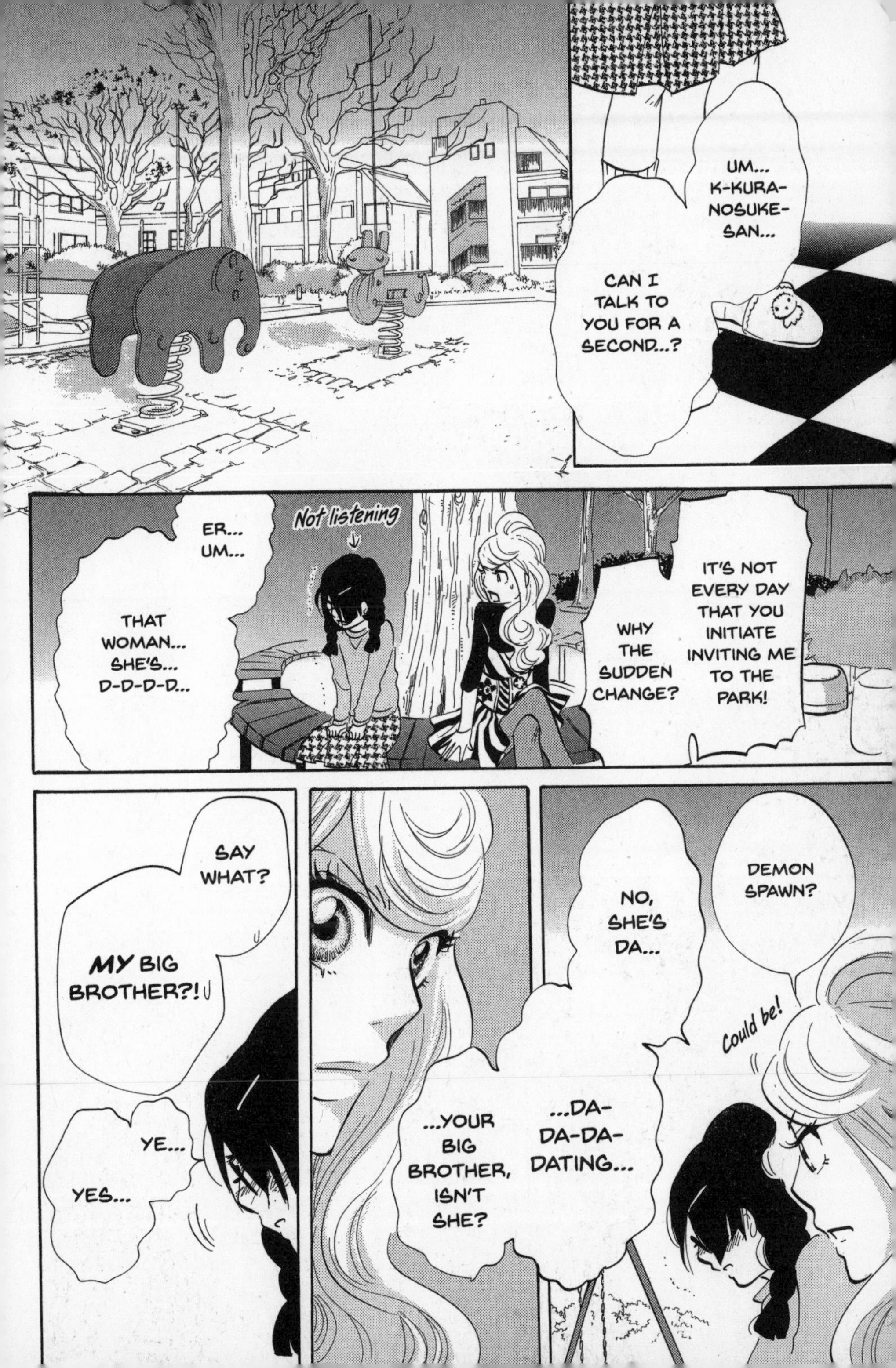
UM... K-KURA-NOSUKE-SAN...
CAN I TALK TO YOU FOR A SECOND...?
IT'S NOT EVERY DAY THAT YOU INITIATE INVITING ME TO THE PARK!
WHY THE SUDDEN CHANGE?
Not listening
ER... UM...
THAT WOMAN... SHE'S... D-D-D-D...
DEMON SPAWN?
NO, SHE'S DA...
Could be!
...DA-DA-DA-DATING...
...YOUR BIG BROTHER, ISN'T SHE?
SAY WHAT?
MY BIG BROTHER?!
YE...
YES...

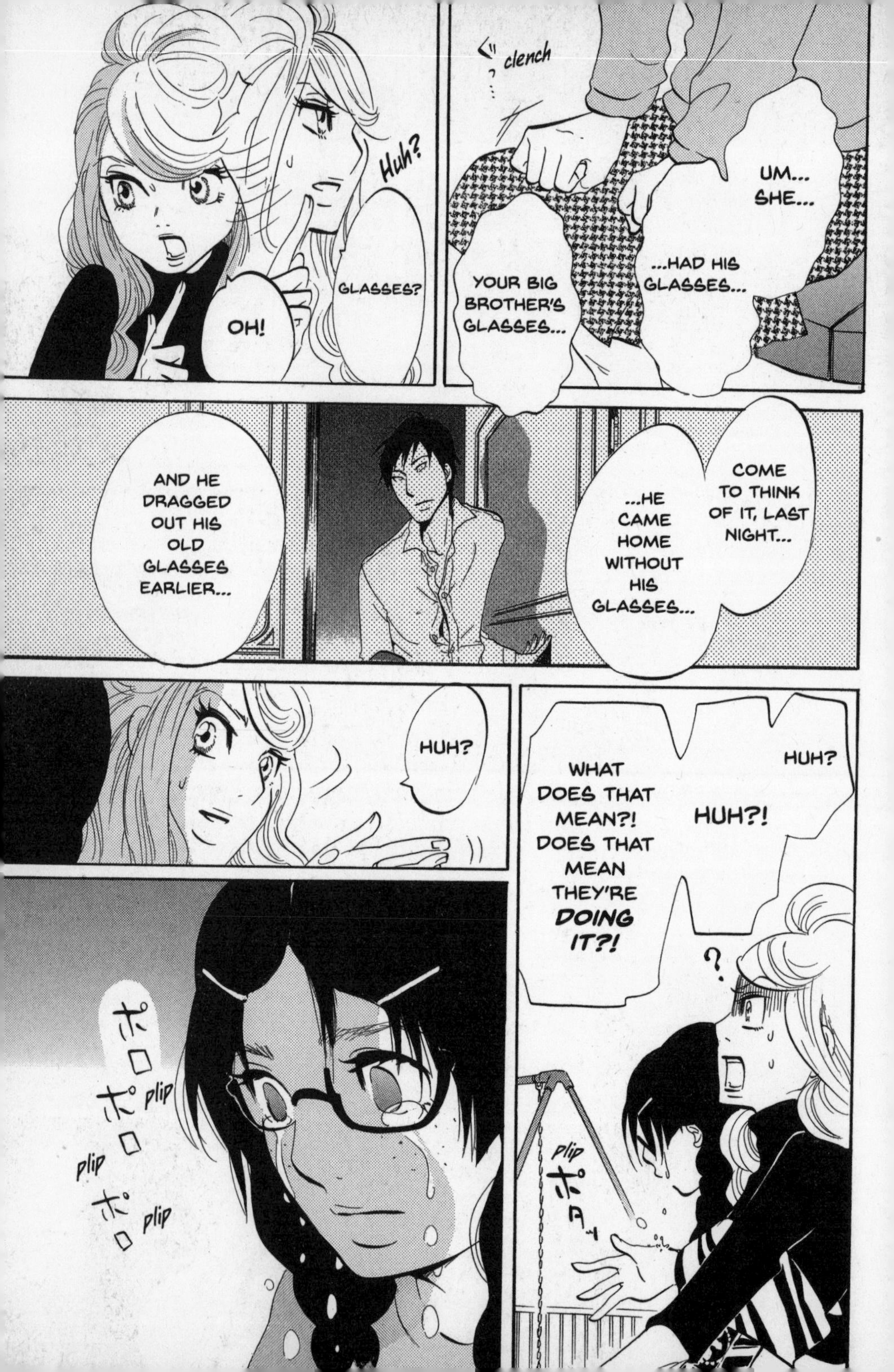
ぐっ
clench
UM... SHE...
...HAD HIS GLASSES...
YOUR BIG BROTHER'S GLASSES...
Huh?
GLASSES?
OH!
COME TO THINK OF IT, LAST NIGHT...
...HE CAME HOME WITHOUT HIS GLASSES...
AND HE DRAGGED OUT HIS OLD GLASSES EARLIER...
HUH?
HUH?!
WHAT DOES THAT MEAN?! DOES THAT MEAN THEY'RE **DOING IT?!**
?
ポ
plip
HUH?
ポロ
plip
ポロ
plip
ポロ
plip

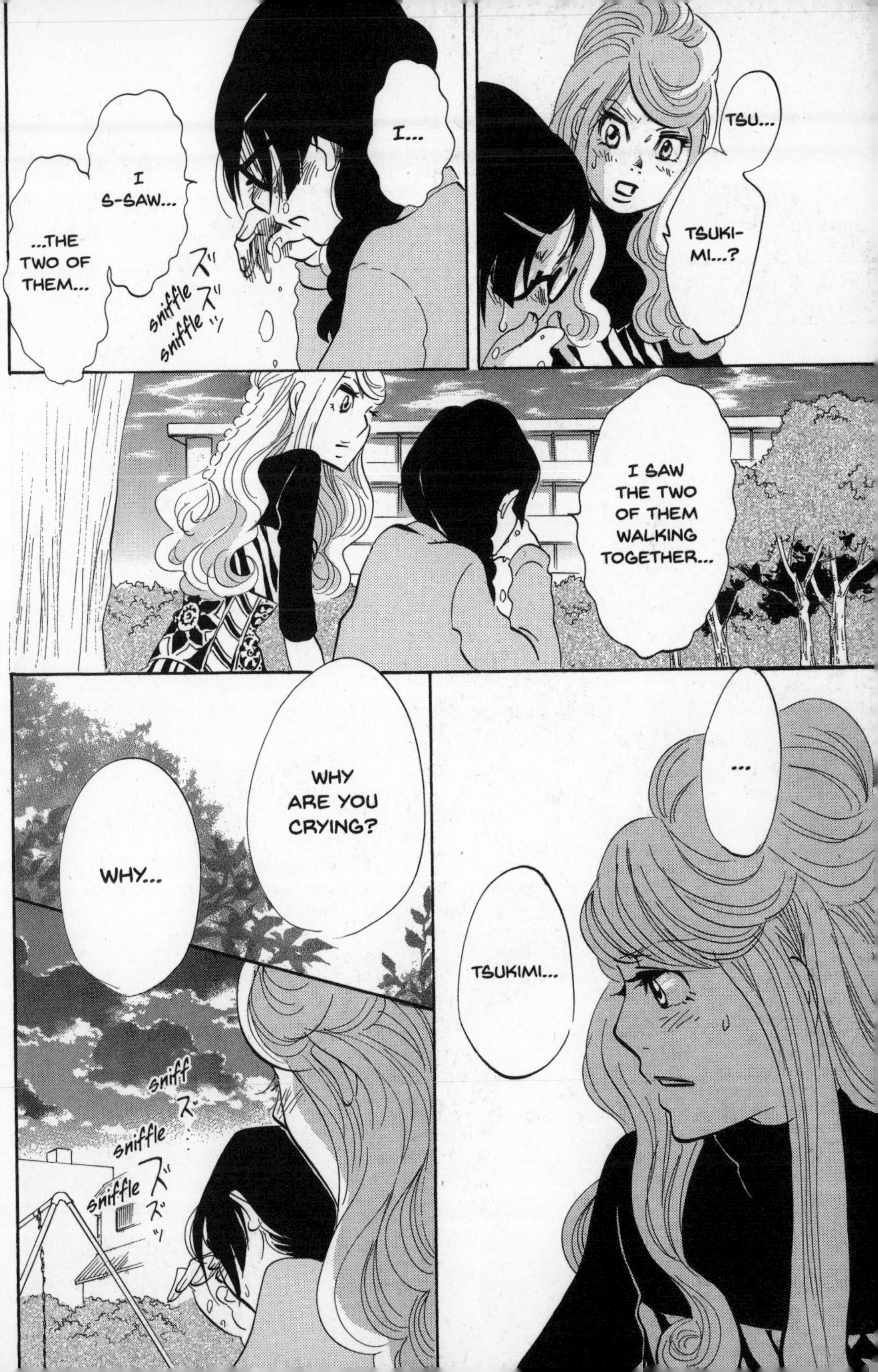
TSU...
TSUKI-MI...?
I...
I S-SAW...
...THE TWO OF THEM...
sniffle ズ
sniffle ズッ
I SAW THE TWO OF THEM WALKING TOGETHER...
...
TSUKIMI...
WHY ARE YOU CRYING?
WHY...
sniff ズ
sniffle ズ
sniffle ズッ

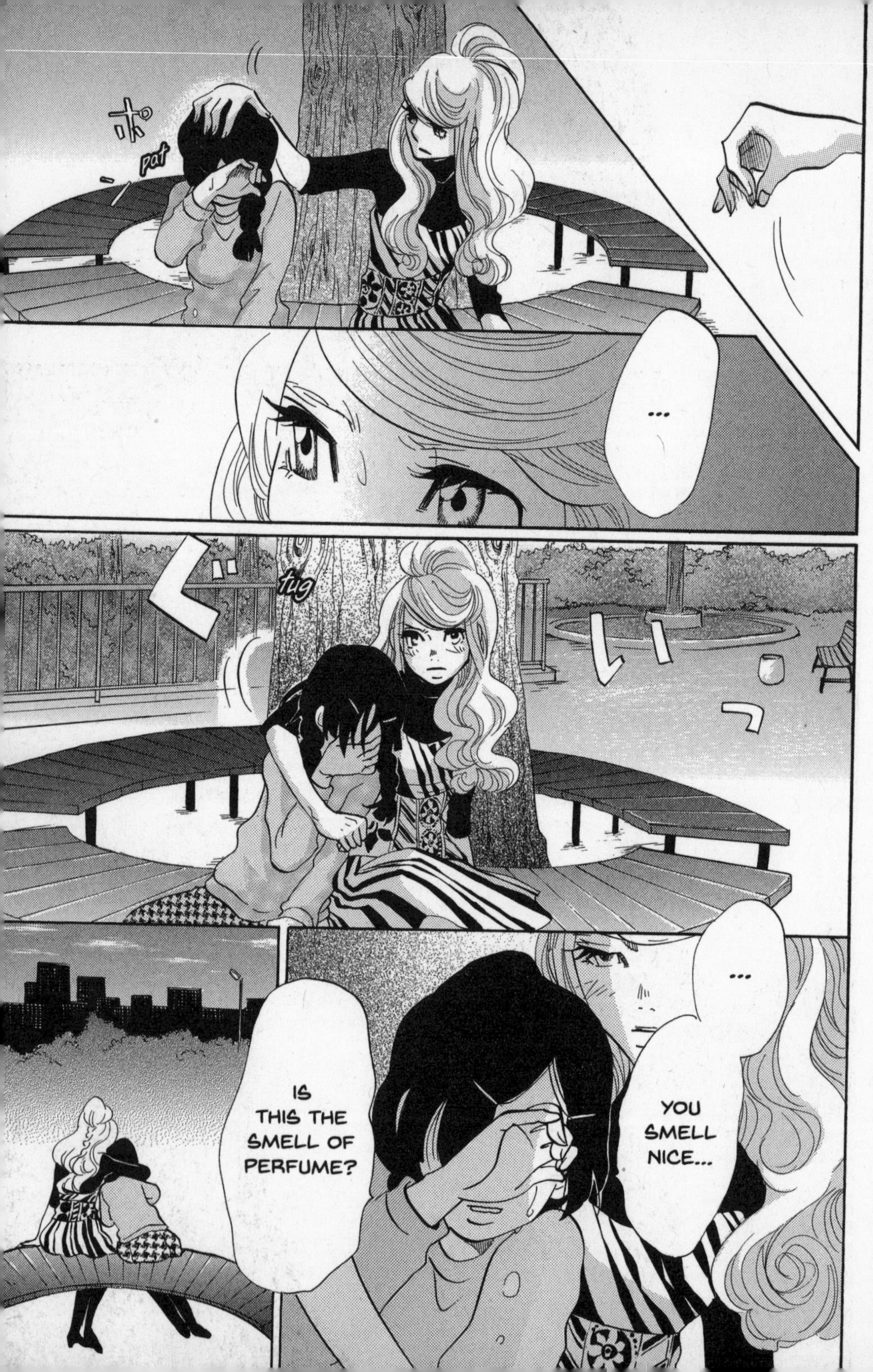
pat
...
tug
...
YOU SMELL NICE...
IS THIS THE SMELL OF PERFUME?

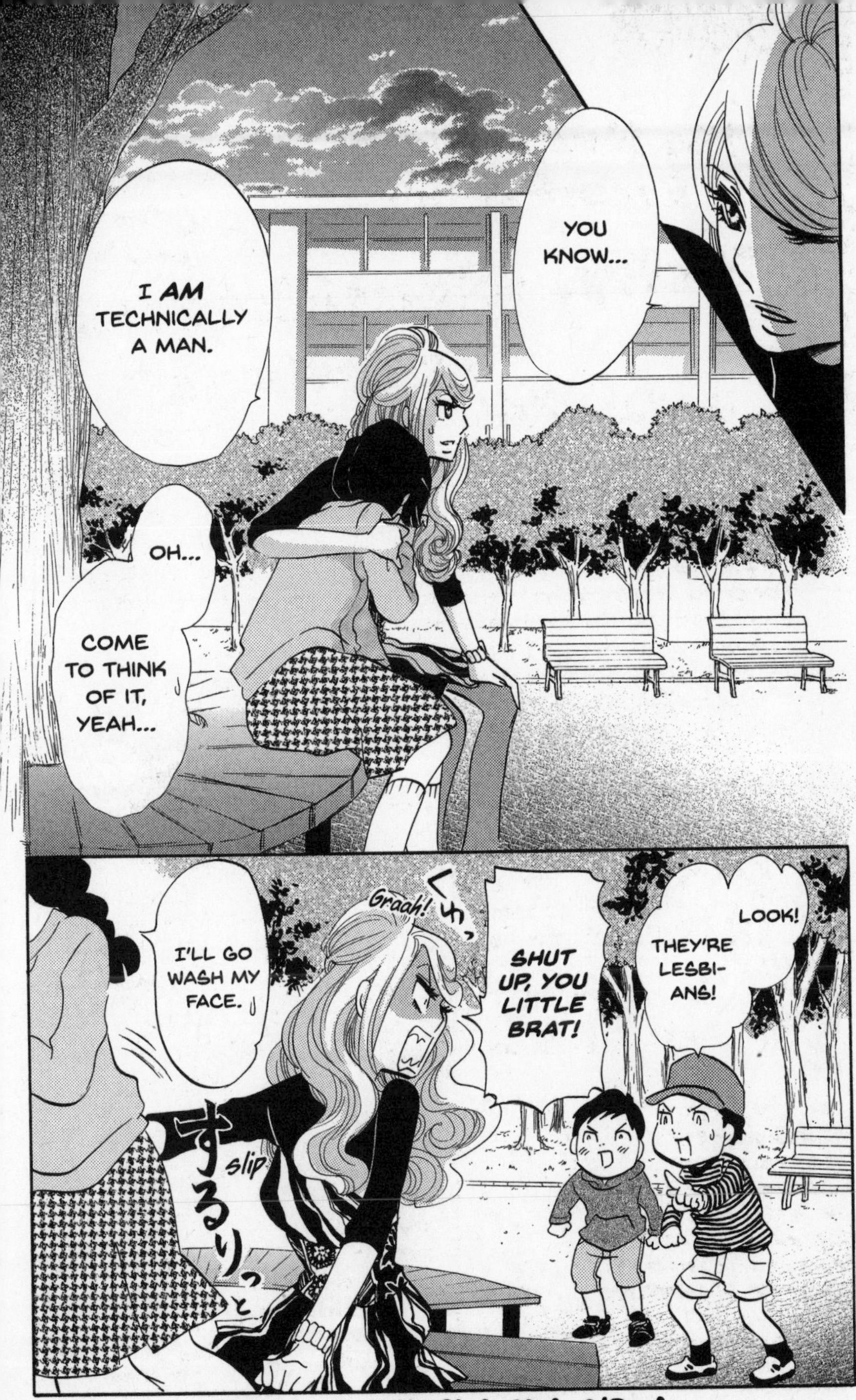
YOU KNOW...
I AM TECHNICALLY A MAN.
OH...
COME TO THINK OF IT, YEAH...
LOOK! THEY'RE LESBI-ANS!
Graah!
SHUT UP, YOU LITTLE BRAT!
I'LL GO WASH MY FACE.
するりっと
slip

Princess Jellyfish Vol. 1/End

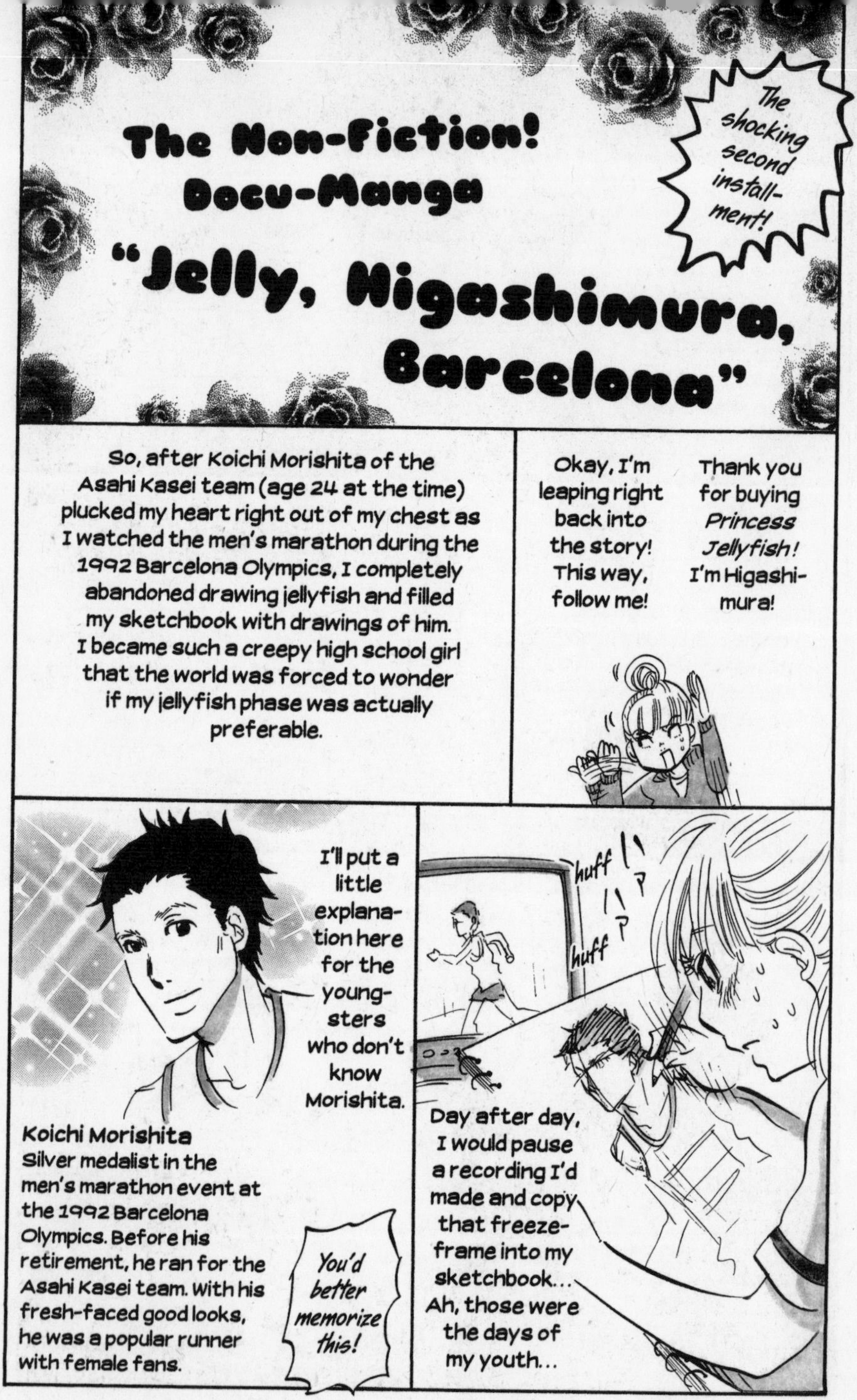
The shocking second install-ment!
The Non-Fiction! Docu-Manga "Jelly, Higashimura, Barcelona"
Thank you for buying *Princess Jellyfish*! I'm Higashi-mura!
Okay, I'm leaping right back into the story! This way, follow me!
So, after Koichi Morishita of the Asahi Kasei team (age 24 at the time) plucked my heart right out of my chest as I watched the men's marathon during the 1992 Barcelona Olympics, I completely abandoned drawing jellyfish and filled my sketchbook with drawings of him. I became such a creepy high school girl that the world was forced to wonder if my jellyfish phase was actually preferable.
huff
huff
Day after day, I would pause a recording I'd made and copy that freeze-frame into my sketchbook... Ah, those were the days of my youth...
I'll put a little explana-tion here for the young-sters who don't know Morishita.
Koichi Morishita
Silver medalist in the men's marathon event at the 1992 Barcelona Olympics. Before his retirement, he ran for the Asahi Kasei team. With his fresh-faced good looks, he was a popular runner with female fans.
You'd better memorize this!

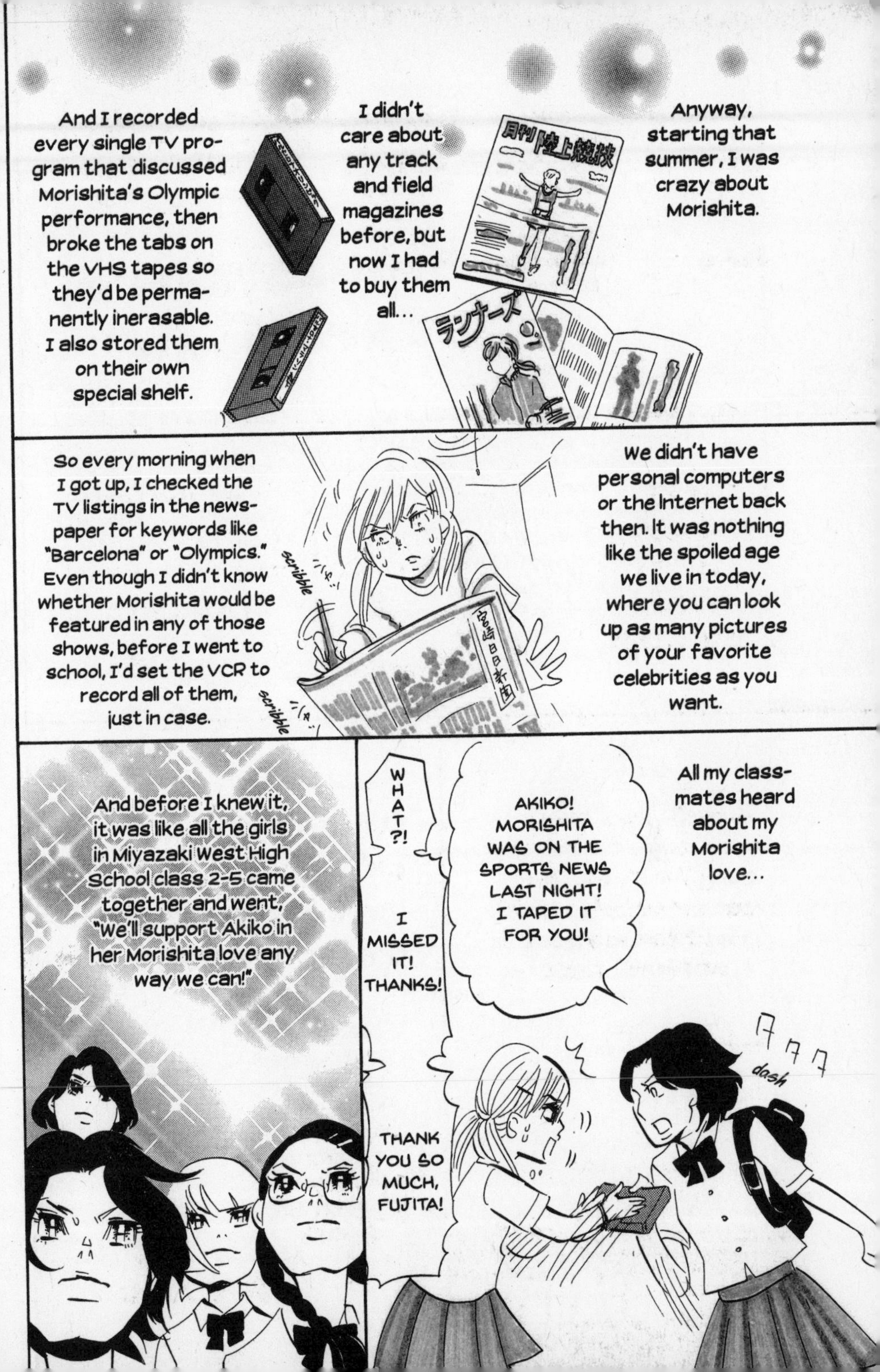
Anyway, starting that summer, I was crazy about Morishita.
I didn't care about any track and field magazines before, but now I had to buy them all...
月刊陸上競技
ランナーズ
And I recorded every single TV program that discussed Morishita's Olympic performance, then broke the tabs on the VHS tapes so they'd be permanently inerasable. I also stored them on their own special shelf.
We didn't have personal computers or the Internet back then. It was nothing like the spoiled age we live in today, where you can look up as many pictures of your favorite celebrities as you want.
So every morning when I got up, I checked the TV listings in the newspaper for keywords like "Barcelona" or "Olympics." Even though I didn't know whether Morishita would be featured in any of those shows, before I went to school, I'd set the VCR to record all of them, just in case.
scribble
宮崎日日新聞
scribble
All my classmates heard about my Morishita love...
AKIKO! MORISHITA WAS ON THE SPORTS NEWS LAST NIGHT! I TAPED IT FOR YOU!
WHAT?!
I MISSED IT! THANKS!
dash
THANK YOU SO MUCH, FUJITA!
And before I knew it, it was like all the girls in Miyazaki West High School class 2-5 came together and went, "We'll support Akiko in her Morishita love any way we can!"

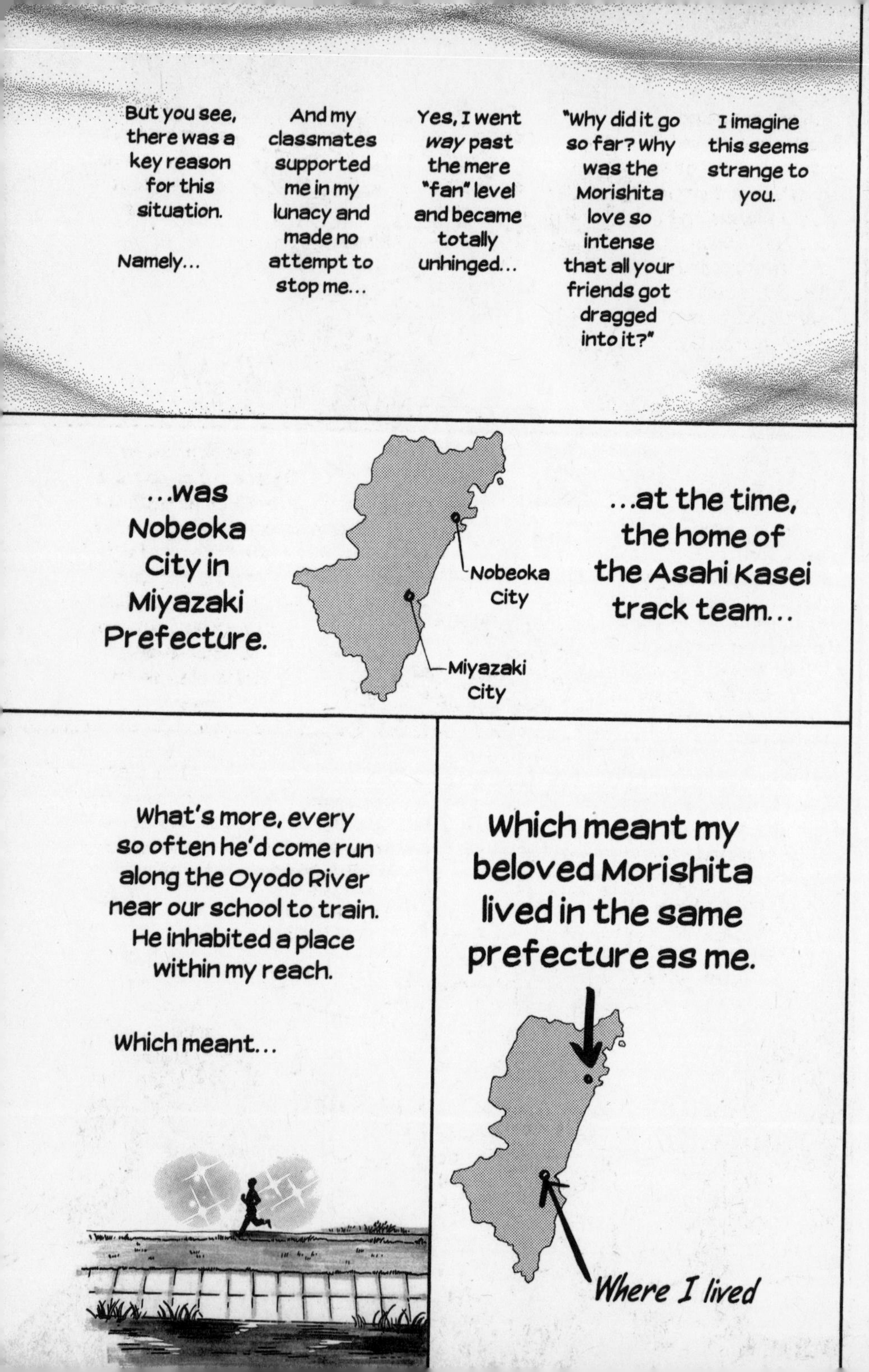

I imagine this seems strange to you.
"Why did it go so far? Why was the Morishita love so intense that all your friends got dragged into it?"
Yes, I went *way* past the mere "fan" level and became totally unhinged...
And my classmates supported me in my lunacy and made no attempt to stop me...
But you see, there was a key reason for this situation.
Namely...
...at the time, the home of the Asahi Kasei track team...
...was Nobeoka City in Miyazaki Prefecture.
Nobeoka City
Miyazaki City
Which meant my beloved Morishita lived in the same prefecture as me.
Where I lived
What's more, every so often he'd come run along the Oyodo River near our school to train. He inhabited a place within my reach.
Which meant...

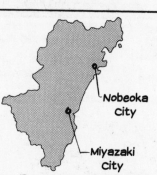

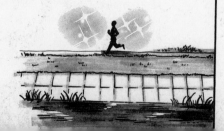

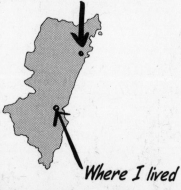

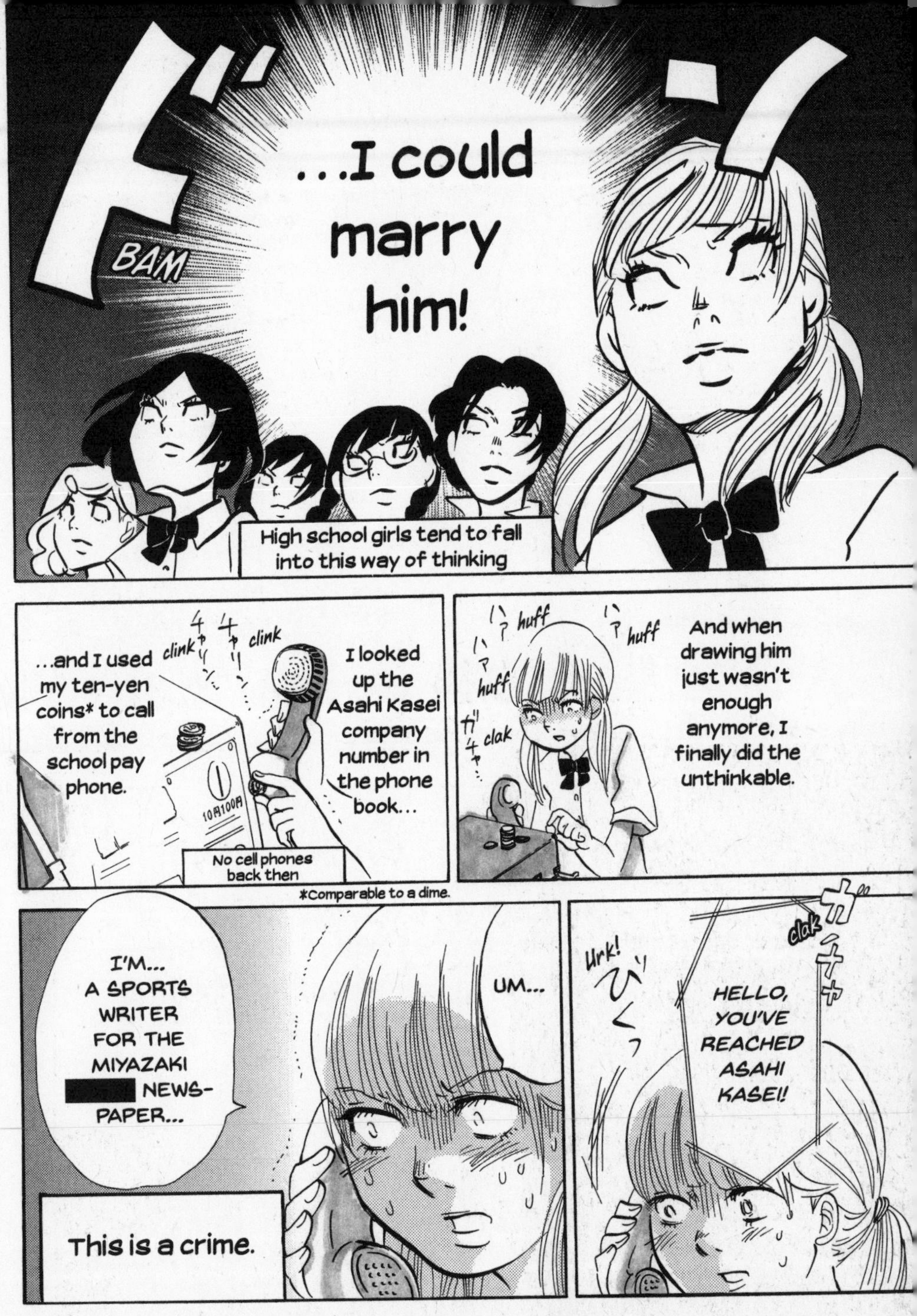
BAM
...I could marry him!
High school girls tend to fall into this way of thinking
huff
huff
huff
clak
And when drawing him just wasn't enough anymore, I finally did the unthinkable.
I looked up the Asahi Kasei company number in the phone book...
clink
clink
...and I used my ten-yen coins* to call from the school pay phone.
10円100円
No cell phones back then
clak
Urk!
HELLO, YOU'VE REACHED ASAHI KASEI!
UM...
I'M... A SPORTS WRITER FOR THE MIYAZAKI [redacted] NEWS-PAPER...
This is a crime.

*Comparable to a dime.

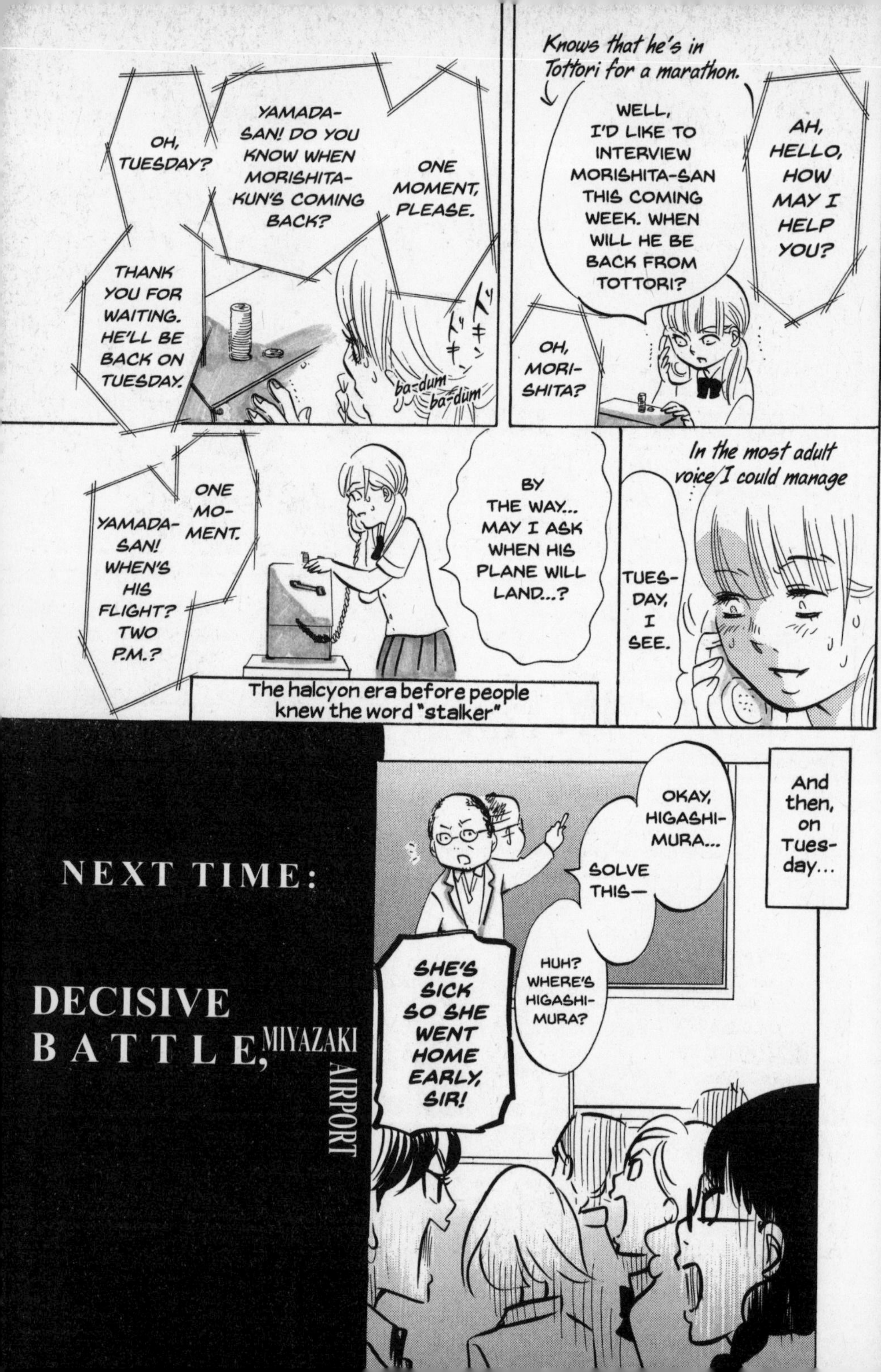
Knows that he's in Tottori for a marathon.
AH, HELLO, HOW MAY I HELP YOU?
WELL, I'D LIKE TO INTERVIEW MORISHITA-SAN THIS COMING WEEK. WHEN WILL HE BE BACK FROM TOTTORI?
OH, MORI-SHITA?
ONE MOMENT, PLEASE.
YAMADA-SAN! DO YOU KNOW WHEN MORISHITA-KUN'S COMING BACK?
OH, TUESDAY?
ドキン ドキン
ba-dum ba-dum
THANK YOU FOR WAITING. HE'LL BE BACK ON TUESDAY.
In the most adult voice I could manage
TUES-DAY, I SEE.
BY THE WAY... MAY I ASK WHEN HIS PLANE WILL LAND...?
ONE MO-MENT.
YAMADA-SAN! WHEN'S HIS FLIGHT? TWO P.M.?
The halcyon era before people knew the word "stalker"
And then, on Tues-day...
OKAY, HIGASHI-MURA...
SOLVE THIS—
HUH? WHERE'S HIGASHI-MURA?
SHE'S SICK SO SHE WENT HOME EARLY, SIR!
NEXT TIME:
DECISIVE BATTLE, MIYAZAKI AIRPORT

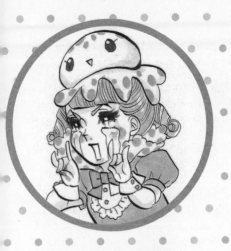

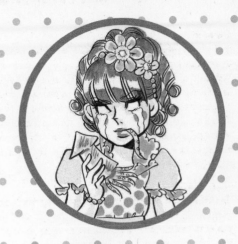

DEAREST READERS!

WHAT KIND OF INSECURITIES
DO *YOU* HAVE?!
YOUR WEIGHT?
YOUR SPLIT-ENDS?
IN *PRINCESS JELLYFISH*,
YOU'LL MEET 4 ~ 5 GIRLS
WHO ARE LIKE A BUNDLE
OF INSECURITIES!
YES, IT'S THAT ROTTEN
SOCIETY, "AMARS!"
EVEN SO, THE GIRLS LIVE
HAPPILY EVERY DAY!
ABOVE ALL ELSE,
PLEASE CHEER ON AMARS!

DEAREST READERS!

WHAT DO *YOU* LOVE THE MOST?!
YOUR BOYFRIEND?
YOUR HUSBAND?
THAT SPECIAL SOMEONE
FOR WHOM YOU HAVE AN
UNREQUITED LOVE?!
THIS MANGA IS OVER-
FLOWING WITH LOVE!
BUT...UNFORTUNATELY,
IT'S NO *ORDINARY* LOVE!
PREPARE YOURSELF
WHENEVER YOU TURN
THE PAGE!

- AKIKO HIGASHIMURA

Translation Notes

Fujoshi, page 10

Fujoshi in Japanese translates to "rotten woman," referencing how these women self-identify as individuals opposite from Japan's patriarchal definition of what a "good woman" is—a helpful wife and a wise mother. Fujoshi indulge their desires, regardless of the purity and innocence that is expected of them. For Amars, the characters cannot help but put their love of jellyfish, kimono, *Romance of the Three Kingdoms*, etc. before their social obligations as "good women" in society. Thus, it is considered unladylike, unattractive, and even shameful to be a fujoshi. Many women attempt to keep their fujoshi identity a secret outside of their fujoshi circle. More commonly, fujoshi can refer to a passionate fangirl of anime and manga that objectifies male characters and male-to-male sexuality.

Otaku, page 15

The term used here is actually *ota-joshi*, which is the combination of otaku and *joshi*, the Japanese word for "girl." Often mistakenly appropriated in English as "nerd/geek," an otaku is an obsessive fan who hoards information and merchandise of their favorite things—there are train otaku, jellyfish otaku, and most famously, anime and manga otaku. The word "otaku" in Japanese is a formal and honorific pronoun that the speaker uses to address "you" or "your family," reflecting an insider culture that respects each individual as an expert in their own obsession. In general, otaku connotes an inability to function "normally" in society, so Japanese otaku are shamed for it and might try to hide it in their public lives.

Amars, page 15

There's a reason why you see the nun and the temple bell in the background of this panel. Amars takes its name—the made-up word *Amaazu*—from the Japanese word *ama*. *Ama* means "nun" and is sometimes used as a gendered insult.

Kagoshima dialect, page 19

Tsukimi's home prefecture of Kagoshima is in the far south of Japan on the island of Kyushu. Tsukimi's mother spoke in a Kagoshima dialect, and even though present-day Tsukimi does not have a particular accent, her younger self in scenes like this speaks completely in Kagoshima dialect, too. At some point between then and now, she purged the country roots from her speech. However, they still come through at certain times, like when she talks to her father on the phone.

Heidi, page 28

This fantasy is an allusion to the classic Swiss children's novel, Heidi by Johanna Spyri, which received a popular anime adaptation in the 1970s. After a girl named Clara, a wheelchair user, comes to live with Heidi and her grandfather, the fresh mountain air and steady diet of wholesome goat's milk helps her recover and walk again.

Okama, page 52

Japanese non-heterosexual identities, culture, and terminology differ from Western-European concepts of LGBTQ identities, despite many borrowed English terms. These definitions are fluid and have even changed since this manga was first published in 2009. Of course, these words will continue to change and mean different things to different people. To put it simply, in the context of this fictional story and most commonly in Japanese society, *okama* are physically male, but effeminate in personality, character, mannerisms, and speech. In the early 2000s, the term connoted more of a gendered performance, not just a specific sexuality or romantic interest. Since then, and today, *okama* has come to refer to people in male-to-male relationships more broadly.

Dressing like a woman, page 52

The literal translation of the term *josou* that is used here is "dressing up like a woman." It is similar to, but not synonymous with the English term "cross-dressing," because *josou* refers specifically to women's clothes. Here, Kuranosuke distinguishes this as a "hobby" of his, not a lifestyle.

Jellyfish maniac, page 53

In Japan, the term "mania" can mean a fervent obsession; it is often paired with being an otaku of some sort. Here, Kuranosuke asks Tsukimi if she has jellyfish mania, and then asks if she's a jellyfish otaku.

Shichi-Go-San Festival, page 53

This is a November festival day for children seven (*shichi*), five (*go*), and three (*san*) years of age. Traditionally, all three-year-olds participate, five-year-old boys participate, and seven-year-old girls participate. Three was historically the age when noble children's hair was first allowed to grow naturally, five was the age when male nobles first wore *hakama* pants, and seven was the age when female nobles first wore adult *obi* sashes. Since the significance of these ages is rooted in now-obsolete fashion practices, the celebration is now more ritual than practical. Children are dressed up in nice clothes for a trip to the shrine, and then given a special candy.

Oni shorts, page 56

The original Japanese here is "*oni* undies" or "ogre undies." An *oni* is a type of ogre or demon which has fangs, horns on its head, and a short temper. *Oni* are stereotypically depicted wearing underwear made of tiger hide. The animal print on Kuranosuke's shorts here reminds Tsukimi of *oni*.

Ichimatsu dolls, page 60

An Ichimatsu doll is a specific type of traditional Japanese doll. Its clothes can be taken on and off, so it's not only a toy, but an excuse to practice your needlework! However, it's common in Japan to hear spooky tales of Ichimatsu dolls growing longer hair, roaming through houses at night, or even being possessed by evil spirits.

Zhou Yu of Wu, page 60

Based on a real historical figure, Zhou Yu was a keen military strategist and general for the Sun family. In *Romance of the Three Kingdoms*, he is the rival of Kongming (mentioned on page 334). His earlier victories in battle helped to create the state of Eastern Wu during the Three Kingdoms period.

Zhao Yun of Shu, page 60

Based on a real historical figure, Zhao Yun was a military general for the Shu Han state. In *Romance of the Three Kingdoms*, he is depicted as the ideal warrior who is loyal, smart, calm, and powerful in combat.

Gay, page 65

Most commonly in Japanese, and within the context of this story, the borrowed English term "gay" refers to someone who is physically male with a masculine personality, character, mannerisms, etc. Generally, this term refers to men who love men, as a masculine man themselves. This definition is quite different from *okama*, though both terms are used interchangeably at times, and both identities can intersect.

Being too much of a boy, pages 72-73

There are a variety of pronouns in Japanese that equate to "I" or "me," some of which are traditionally masculine or feminine forms of speech. Kuranosuke will accidentally use the informal and

masculine pronoun *ore* for himself, even when he's hiding his identity from Amars. That's what's happening here. Tsukimi quickly covers for him and cries, "*Olè!*" and starts singing a song about a matador (see below). Luckily, this type of distraction actually works on Amars.

Torero Camomillo and NHK Minna no Uta, page 73
The NHK (*Nippon Housou Kyokai*) is Japan's public broadcasting organization. "*Torero Camomillo*" is an Italian children's song about a matador who loves his sleep, and one of the many songs to have been featured on the NHK's long-running musical segment NHK *Minna no Uta*, or "Songs for Everyone."

Kihachiro Kawamoto, page 73
Kihachiro Kawamoto was a famous Japanese puppet designer who created the puppets for the *Romance of the Three Kingdoms* puppet show on the NHK.

Uke, page 94
Roughly equivalent to the slang term "bottom" in English, *Uke* is a term often used in BL (Boys' Love) which refers to the submissive partner in a relationship. *Uke* is short for *ukeru*, which means "to receive" in Japanese.

Flapper, page 108
Localized as flapper, in the original Japanese, Kuranosuke says his outfit's theme is partly inspired by *showa hito keta onna*. This phrase refers to a woman during an eight-year period (1926-1934) within the Shōwa period.

No, Not "Fanatics"…I meant your…Family…, page 108
Tsukimi used the formal word *otaku* here to refer to Kuranosuke's family (see previous translation note for otaku), but Kuranosuke thought she was talking about *being* an otaku.

Kinozen, page 109
As with almost every traditional sweet shop mentioned in *Princess Jellyfish*, Kinozen is a real place. Everyone in Amars, especially Banba, has an almost encyclopedic knowledge of traditional Japanese sweets and where to get them.

The bubble, the "Lost Decade," and the hiring ice age, page 112
In the 1980s, an asset price bubble of inflation fueled Japan's booming economy–but then the bubble burst. The 1990s were known as the "Lost Decade" as the economy struggled to recover from the crash, and a "hiring ice age" ensued as companies stopped hiring new workers. The years from 2000 to 2010 are sometimes considered a second Lost Decade, causing people to refer to the two collectively as the "Lost Twenty Years."

Otome Road, page 124
The "Otome Road" is a road in Ikebukuro, Tokyo famous for shops, bookstores, and themed cafès catering to female manga or anime otaku, as well as fujoshi.

Vampires from Amars, page 127
Readers may have noticed that the title of each *Princess Jellyfish* chapter is a reference to a TV show or movie. In Japanese, this chapter was titled *RaiRai! Amaazu*, referencing a TV series that was produced in Taiwan, but was only aired in Japan, *RaiRai! Jiangshis*. It was a spinoff of the movie, *Hello Dracula* or *Son of Chinese Vampire*.

Chinese hopping vampire, page 132
The Chinese vampire, or *jiangshi*, is notable for the distinctive "hopping" movement it employs to get from place to place; it is a reanimated corpse.

Collector for the NHK, page 147
Everyone in Japan with a TV is supposed to pay a fee to support the NHK, because it is a national public broadcasting organization. In the past, the NHK used to send someone to your house to collect the fee.

Take Me Out to the Aquarium, page 157
This title is based on the 1987 movie *Watashi wo Ski ni Tsuretette*, known in English as *Take Me Out to the Snowland.*

Better to wrong the world than have it wrong me!, page 166
Here Mayaya is quoting her favorite novel, *Romance of the Three Kingdoms*. The source of this English translation is Volume 1 of Luo Guanzhong's *Three Kingdoms*, translated by Moss Roberts.

Kyu! Kyu! Baldy dance!, page 220
Prime Minister Negishi is doing the cat dance from the Data Install screen of *Monster Hunter Freedom Unite.*

Dissolution and snap election, page 245
Similar to the two houses of the U.S. Congress, Japan's Diet has two houses, the Upper House (also called the House of Councillors) and the Lower House (also called the House of Representatives). The Prime Minister and his Cabinet have the power to call on the Emperor to dissolve the Lower House, and assuming the correct protocol has been followed, the Emperor must issue a proclamation of dissolution. When the Lower House is dissolved, an early election–also known as a "snap" election– must be held within forty days to replace the dissolved House.

Seven Sisters, page 255
This chapter title is riffing on Akira Kurosawa's famous movie, *Seven Samurai.*

In the mood for ishikari, page 259
Ishikari hotpot is a type of hotpot dish that features salmon instead of meat. It's associated with the northern island of Hokkaido.

A Taxing Woman's Return, page 262
In this 1988 movie, also known as *Marusa no Onna 2* in Japanese, tax investigator Ryoko Itakura has adversaries who forcefully take land involving substantially more yakuza violence than the situation depicted here.

Is a crane weaving in there or something?!, page 275
This is a reference to "The Crane Wife," a Japanese folk tale in which a man discovers that his beautiful spouse is a bird in disguise when he breaks his promise not to peek in on her while she's at work weaving. It turns out that she is weaving her own feathers into the cloth to give it its beauty. Of course, with the promise broken, she must leave him forever.

Obsessed with older men, page 292
Jiji is obsessed with older men, but the term for her obsession is *karesen*, which is also a type of otaku in Japan. *Kare* comes from the Japanese word *kareru*, or "to wither," referring to older men. The *-sen* is short for *senmon*, which translates to "expert" or "specialty" in a certain field.

Yutaka Mizutani, page 292
Born in 1952, Yutaka Mizutani is a famous Japanese actor who has so thoroughly captured Jiji's heart that you can see her wearing a "Yutaka Mizutani Life" headband on page 285. He's most well-known for playing the lead in the long-running crime series *Aibou*. His character Ukyo Sugishita is often described as a Japanese Sherlock Holmes.

Hello, my neighbor Yamada!, page 323
The original Japanese reference was almost exactly the same joke, just featuring a different anime with "Yamada" in it. The Prime Minister begins by saying *o-jama shimasu*, a common greeting when entering someone's home, and then tosses in a reference to the 1980s anime *Ojamanga Yamada-kun* just to be silly. Here, it is localized with a "Hello, neighbor–" followed by a reference to the 1999 Studio Ghibli film *My Neighbors the Yamadas*.

Hakutsuru... Maru!, page 326
The Hakutsuru Sake Brewing Company's "Maru" drink is one example of what's known as cup *sake*: a single-serving bottle, can, or even box of *sake* that you can buy individually (the "cup" refers to fact that you can drink it directly from the container, which serves as your cup). The Prime Minister seems to be rolling with the "water" theme of the bathtub by performing a Maru commercial—all Maru commercials feature a fishing boat, fresh-caught seafood, and in the end, a group of men putting their hands above their head like this and shouting, "Maru!" In Japanese, *maru* means circle and also indicates approval, like an "okay!"

Are you a homo?!, page 327
In the original Japanese, Kuranosuke uses the borrowed English term, "homo." In nuance, the Japanese usage of "homo" is not as aggressive as the English, and is more casual. In Japanese, it is the general term for people in same-sex relationships.

They're from the shop Yakkun was raving about on Morning Snack!, page 357
Omeza or *Morning Snack* was a segment on a morning variety show called *Hanamaru Market*, which aired between 1996 and 2014. As its name suggests, the segment mainly involved sampling guests' favorite snack foods. *Hanamaru Market* co-emcee Hirohide Yakumaru, affectionately known as "Yakkun" to his fans, was deeply moved by the maker of these macarons.

Mayaya's pile of salt, page 364
People of various cultures throw salt to drive away bad luck or evil spirits, so it's easy to understand what Banba is doing here. Mayaya and Chieko are building a pile of salt because in Japan, putting a heap of salt by the door of a restaurant or bar is supposed to bring good luck.

Lesbian, page 374
In the original Japanese, the kid shouts, "*rezu!*" *Rezu* is the shortened form of *rezubian*, first introduced from the English term "lesbian" in the 1960s. In Japanese, *rezubian* initially referred to masculine women and women who had sexual interactions with women. In the context of this story, and more recently, the term no longer signifies masculinity. There is a more commonly used term *onabe*, which is used to identify masculine women who are interested in other women.

"Decisive Battle, Miyazaki Airport", page 379
This preview features the iconic white-on-black coloring and horizontal to vertical layout of the title cards in the original *Neon Genesis Evangelion* anime series. As for the text itself, fans may notice a certain similarity to the title card in the sixth episode, "Rei II."

A Kodansha Comics Trade Paperback Original.

Princess Jellyfish volume 1 copyright © 2009 Akiko Higashimura
English translation copyright © 2016 Akiko Higashimura

Published in the United States by Kodansha Comics,
an imprint of Kodansha USA Publishing, LLC, New York.

Publication rights for this English edition arranged through Kodansha Ltd., Tokyo.

First published in Japan in 2009 by Kodansha Ltd., Tokyo, as *Kuragehime* volumes 1 & 2.

ISBN 978-1-63236-228-5

Printed in the United States of America.

www.kodanshacomics.com

9 8 7 6 5 4 3

Translation: Sarah Alys Lindholm
Lettering: Carl Vanstiphout
Editing: Haruko Hashimoto
Kodansha Comics Edition Cover Design: Phil Balsman